TRANSLATOR AND EDITOR:
Rabbi David Strauss

MANAGING EDITOR:
Baruch Goldberg

EDITOR:
Dr. Edward L. Tepper

ASSOCIATE EDITOR:
Dr. Jeffrey M. Green

COPY EDITOR:
Alec Israel

BOOK DESIGNER:
Ben Gasner

GRAPHIC ARTIST:
Michael Etkin

TECHNICAL STAFF:
Muriel Stein

Random House Staff

PRODUCTION MANAGER:
Richard Elman

ART DIRECTOR:
Bernard Klein

CHIEF COPY EDITOR:
Amy Edelman

The Talmud
The Steinsaltz Edition

Volume XXI
Tractate Sanhedrin
Part VII

VOLUME XXI

TRACTATE SANHEDRIN

PART VII

RANDOM HOUSE
NEW YORK

THE TALMUD

תלמוד בבלי

THE STEINSALTZ EDITION

Commentary by Rabbi Adin Steinsaltz (Even Yisrael)

 Published in the United States by
Random House, Inc., New York, and simultaneously in Canada by
Random House of Canada Limited, Toronto.

This is an English translation of a work originally published
in Hebrew by The Israel Institute for Talmudic Publications,
Jerusalem, Israel.

Library of Congress Cataloging-in-Publication Data
(Revised for volume XXI)
The Talmud
English, Hebrew, Aramaic.
Includes bibliographical references.
Contents: v. 1. Tractate Bava metzia—
v. 21. Tractate Sanhedrin, pt. 7
Accompanied by a reference guide.
I. Title.
BM499.5.E4 1989 89-842911
ISBN 0-394-57665-9 (guide)
ISBN 0-394-57666-7 (v. 1)
ISBN 0-375-50350-1 (v. 21)

Random House website address: www.atrandom.com
Printed in the United States of America on acid-free paper

2 4 6 8 9 7 5 3

First Edition

Ann and Marcus Rosenberg
dedicate this book
in honor of our grandchildren

Jacob Greif
יעקב מאיר גרייץ
Gabriella Greif
גבריאלה שפרה גרייץ

Jessica Pulitzer
חנה פוליצר
Samuel Charles Pulitzer
שמואל חיים פוליצר
Miles Louis Pulitzer
מאיר אריה פוליצר
Mina Rachel Pulitzer
מינה רחל פוליצר

Eliezer Michael Rosenberg
אליעזר רוזנברג
Ariela Rosenberg
אריאלה שרה רוזנברג
Dana Suzanne Rosenberg
ירדנה שושנה רוזנברג

David Meir Waks
דוד מאיר וקס
Daniel Aaron Waks
דניאל אהרון וקס
Noa Chantal Waks
נועה שנטל וקס

The Steinsaltz Talmud in English

The English edition of the Steinsaltz Talmud is a translation and adaptation of the Hebrew edition. It includes most of the additions and improvements that characterize the Hebrew version, but it has been adapted and expanded especially for the English reader. This edition has been designed to meet the needs of advanced students capable of studying from standard Talmud editions, as well as of beginners, who know little or no Hebrew and have had no prior training in studying the Talmud.

The overall structure of the page is similar to that of the traditional pages in the standard printed editions. The text is placed in the center of the page, and alongside it are the main auxiliary commentaries. At the bottom of the page and in the margins are additions and supplements.

The original Hebrew-Aramaic text, which is framed in the center of each page, is exactly the same as that in the traditional Talmud (although material that was removed by non-Jewish censors has been restored on the basis of manuscripts and old printed editions). The main innovation is that this Hebrew-Aramaic text has been completely vocalized and punctuated, and all the terms usually abbreviated have been fully spelled out. In order to retain the connection with the page numbers of the standard editions, these are indicated at the head of every page.

We have placed a *Literal Translation* on the right-hand side of the page, and its punctuation has been introduced into the Talmud text, further helping the student to orientate himself. The *Literal Translation* is intended to help the student to learn the meaning of specific Hebrew and Aramaic words. By comparing the original text with this translation, the reader develops an understanding of the Talmudic text and can follow the words and sentences in the original. Occasionally, however, it has not been possible

to present an exact literal translation of the original text, because it is so different in structure from English. Therefore we have added certain auxiliary words, which are indicated in square brackets. In other cases it would make no sense to offer a literal translation of a Talmudic idiom, so we have provided a close English equivalent of the original meaning, while a note, marked "lit.," explaining the literal meaning of the words, appears in parentheses. Our purpose in presenting this literal translation was to give the student an appreciation of the terse and enigmatic nature of the Talmud itself, before the arguments are opened up by interpretation.

Nevertheless, no one can study the Talmud without the assistance of commentaries. The main aid to understanding the Talmud provided by this edition is the *Translation and Commentary,* appearing on the left side of the page. This is Rabbi Adin Steinsaltz's highly regarded Hebrew interpretation of the Talmud, translated into English, adapted and expanded.

This commentary is not merely an explanation of difficult passages. It is an integrated exposition of the entire text. It includes a full translation of the Talmud text, combined with explanatory remarks. Where the translation in the commentary reflects the literal translation, it has been set off in bold type. It has also been given the same reference numbers that are found both in the original text and in the literal translation. Moreover, each section of the commentary begins with a few words of the Hebrew-Aramaic text. These reference numbers and paragraph headings allow the reader to move from one part of the page to another with ease.

There are some slight variations between the literal translation and the words in bold face appearing in the *Translation and Commentary.* These variations are meant to enhance understanding, for a juxtaposition of the literal translation and the sometimes freer translation in the commentary will give the reader a firmer grasp of the meaning.

The expanded *Translation and Commentary* in the left-hand column is intended to provide a conceptual understanding of the arguments of the Talmud, their form, content, context, and significance. The commentary also brings out the logic of the questions asked by the Sages and the assumptions they made.

Rashi's traditional commentary has been included in the right-hand column, under the *Literal Translation.* We have left this commentary in the traditional "Rashi script," but all quotations of the Talmud text appear in standard square type, the abbreviated expressions have all been printed in full, and Rashi's commentary is fully punctuated.

Since the *Translation and Commentary* cannot remain cogent and still encompass all the complex issues that arise in the Talmudic discussion, we have included a number of other features, which are also found in Rabbi Steinsaltz's Hebrew edition.

At the bottom of the page, under the *Translation and Commentary,* is the *Notes* section, containing additional material on issues raised in the text. These notes deepen understanding of the Talmud in various ways. Some provide a deeper and more profound analysis of the issues discussed in the text, with regard to individual points and to the development of the entire discussion. Others explain Halakhic concepts and the terms of Talmudic discourse.

The *Notes* contain brief summaries of the opinions of many of the major commentators on the Talmud, from the period after the completion of the Talmud to the present. Frequently the *Notes* offer interpretations different from that presented in the commentary, illustrating the richness and depth of Rabbinic thought.

The *Halakhah* section appears below the *Notes.* This provides references to the authoritative legal decisions reached over the centuries by the Rabbis in their discussions of the matters dealt with in the Talmud. It explains what reasons led to these Halakhic decisions and the close connection between the Halakhah today and the Talmud and its various interpreters. It should be noted that the summary of the Halakhah presented here is not meant to serve as a reference source for actual religious practice but to introduce the reader to Halakhic conclusions drawn from the Talmudic text.

English commentary and expanded translation of the text, making it readable and comprehensible

Hebrew/Aramaic text of the Talmud, fully vocalized, and punctuated

Literal translation of the Talmud text into English

9B BAVA METZIA ט ע״ב

REALIA

קַלְתָּהּ **Her basket**. The source of this word is the Greek κάλαθος, kalathos, and it means a basket with a narrow base.

Illustration from a Greek drawing depicting such a basket of fruit.

CONCEPTS

פֵּאָה *Pe'ah*. **One of the presents left for the poor** (מַתְּנוֹת עֲנִיִּים). The Torah forbids harvesting "the corners of your field," so that the produce left standing may be harvested and kept by the poor (Leviticus 19:9).

The Torah did not specify a minimum amount of produce to be left as *pe'ah*. But the Sages stipulated that it must be at least one-sixtieth of the crop.

Pe'ah is set aside only from crops that ripen at one time and are harvested at one time. The poor are allowed to use their own initiative to reap the *pe'ah* left in the fields. But the owner of an orchard must see to it that each of the poor gets a fixed share of the *pe'ah* from places that are difficult to reach. The poor come to collect *pe'ah* three times a day. The laws of *pe'ah* are discussed in detail in tractate *Pe'ah*.

Marginal notes provide essential background information

TRANSLATION AND COMMENTARY

[1]**and her husband threw her a bill of divorce into her lap or into her basket**, which she was carrying on her head, [2]would you say **here, too, that she would not be divorced**? Surely we know that the law is that she *is* divorced in such a case, as the Mishnah (*Gittin* 77a) states explicitly!

אֲמַר לֵיהּ [3]Rav Ashi **said** in reply **to** Ravina: The woman's **basket is** considered to be **at rest, and it is she who walks beneath it.** Thus the basket is considered to be a "stationary courtyard," and the woman acquires whatever is thrown into it.

MISHNAH הָיָה רוֹכֵב [4]**If a person was riding on an animal and he saw an ownerless object** lying on the ground, **and he said to another person** standing nearby, **"Give** that object **to me,"** [5]**if the other person took** the ownerless object **and said, "I have acquired it for myself,"** [6]he **has acquired it** by lifting it up, even though he was not the first to see it, and the rider has no claim to it. [7]But **if, after he gave** the object **to** the rider, the person who picked it up **said, "I acquired** the object **first,"** [8]**he** in fact **said nothing**. His words are of no effect, and the rider may keep it. Since the person walking showed no intention of acquiring the object when he originally picked it up, he is not now believed when he claims that he acquired it first. Indeed, even if we maintain that when a person picks up an ownerless object on behalf of someone else, the latter does *not* acquire it automatically, here, by *giving* the object to the rider, he makes a gift of it to the rider.

GEMARA תְּנַן הָתָם [9]**We have learned elsewhere** in a Mishnah in tractate *Pe'ah* (4:9): **"Someone who gathered *pe'ah*** — produce which by Torah law [Leviticus 23:22] is left unharvested in the corner of a field by the owner of the field, to be gleaned by the poor — **and said, 'Behold, this** *pe'ah* which I have gleaned **is** intended **for so-and-so the poor man,'** [10]**Rabbi Eliezer says:** The person who gathered the *pe'ah* **has acquired it**

בִּרְשׁוּת הָרַבִּים [1]וְזָרַק לָהּ גֵּט לְתוֹךְ חֵיקָהּ אוֹ לְתוֹךְ קַלְתָּהּ — [2]הָכָא נַמִי דְּלָא מִגָּרְשָׁה? [3]אֲמַר לֵיהּ: קַלְתָּהּ מֵינָח נַיְיחָא, וְאִיהִי דְּקָא מְסַגְּיָא מְתּוּתָהּ.

משנה [4]הָיָה רוֹכֵב עַל גַּבֵּי בְהֵמָה וְרָאָה אֶת הַמְּצִיאָה, וְאָמַר לַחֲבֵירוֹ "תְּנָה לִי", [5]נְטָלָהּ וְאָמַר, "אֲנִי זָכִיתִי בָּהּ", [6]זָכָה בָּהּ. [7]אִם, מִשֶּׁנְּתָנָהּ לוֹ, אָמַר, "אֲנִי זָכִיתִי בָּהּ תְּחִלָּה", [8]לֹא אָמַר כְּלוּם.

גמרא [9]תְּנַן הָתָם: "מִי שֶׁלִּיקֵּט אֶת הַפֵּאָה וְאָמַר, 'הֲרֵי זוֹ לִפְלוֹנִי עָנִי', [10]רַבִּי אֱלִיעֶזֶר

LITERAL TRANSLATION

in a public thoroughfare [1]and [her husband] threw her a bill of divorce into her lap or into her basket, [2]here, too, would she not be divorced?

[3]He said to him: Her basket is at rest, and it is she who walks beneath it.

MISHNAH [4][If a person] was riding on an animal and he saw a found object, and he said to another person, "Give it to me," [5][and the other person] took it and said, "I have acquired it," [6]he has acquired it. [7]If, after he gave it to him, he said, "I acquired it first," [8]he said nothing.

GEMARA [9]We have learned there: "Someone who gathered *pe'ah* and said, 'Behold this is for so-and-so the poor man,' [10]Rabbi Eliezer says:

RASHI

קלתה — סל שעל ראשה, שנותנת בה כלי מלאכתה וטווי שלה. הכי נמי דלא הוי גיטא — והאנן תנן במסכת גיטין (עז,א): זרק לה גיטה לתוך חיקה או לתוך קלתה — הרי זו מגורשת!

משנה לא אמר כלום — דאפילו אמרינן המגביה מציאה לחבירו לא קנה חבירו, כיון דיהבה ליה — קנייה ממה נפשך. אי קנייה קמא דלא מתכוין להקנות לחבירו — הא יהבה ניהליה במתנה. ואי לא קנייה קמא משום דלא היה מתכוין לקנות — הויא ליה הפקר עד דמטא לידיה דהאי, וקנייה האי במאי דעקרה מידיה דקמא לשם קנייה.

גמרא מי שליקט את הפאה — אדם בעלמא שאינו בעל שדה. דאי בבעל שדה — לא אמר רבי אליעזר זכה. דליכא למימר "מגו דזכי לנפשיה", דאפילו הוא עני מוזהר הוא שלא ללקט פאה משדה שלו, כדאמר בשחיטת חולין (קלא,ב): "לא תלקט לעני" — להזהיר עני על שלו.

Hebrew commentary of Rashi, the classic explanation that accompanies all editions of the Talmud

NOTES

מִי שֶׁלִּיקֵּט אֶת הַפֵּאָה **If a person gathered *pe'ah***. According to *Rashi*, the Mishnah must be referring to someone other than the owner of the field. By Torah law the owner of a field is required to separate part of his field as *pe'ah*, even if he himself is poor, and he may not take the *pe'ah* for himself. Therefore the "since" (מִגּוֹ) argument

HALAKHAH

קַלְתָּהּ **A woman's basket**. "If a man throws a bill of divorce into a container that his wife is holding, she thereby acquires the bill of divorce and the divorce takes effect." (*Shulḥan Arukh, Even HaEzer* 139:10.)

הַמְלַקֵּט פֵּאָה עֲבוּר אַחֵר **A person who gathered *pe'ah* for someone else**. "If a poor person, who is himself entitled to collect *pe'ah*, gathered *pe'ah* for another poor person, and said, 'This *pe'ah* is for X, the poor person,' he acquires the *pe'ah* on behalf of that other poor person. But if the person who collected the *peah* was wealthy, he does not acquire the *pe'ah* on behalf of the poor person. He must give it instead to the first poor person who appears in the field," following the opinion of the Sages, as explained by Rabbi Yehoshua ben Levi. (*Rambam, Sefer Zeraim, Hilkhot Mattenot Aniyyim* 2:19.)

106

Numbers link the three main sections of the page and allow readers to refer rapidly from one to the other

Notes highlight points of interest in the text and expand the discussion by quoting other classical commentaries

On the outer margin of the page, factual information clarifying the meaning of the Talmudic discussion is presented. Entries under the heading *Language* explain unusual terms, often borrowed from Greek, Latin, or Persian. *Sages* gives brief biographies of the major figures whose opinions are presented in the Talmud. *Terminology* explains the terms used in the Talmudic discussion. *Concepts* gives information about fundamental Halakhic principles. *Background* provides historical, geographical, and other information needed to understand the text. *Realia* explains the artifacts mentioned in the text. These notes are sometimes accompanied by illustrations.

The best way of studying the Talmud is the way in which the Talmud itself evolved - a combination of frontal teaching and continuous interaction between teacher and pupil, and between pupils themselves.

This edition is meant for a broad spectrum of users, from those who have considerable prior background and who know how to study the Talmud from any standard edition to those who have never studied the Talmud and do not even know Hebrew.

The division of the page into various sections is designed to enable students of every kind to derive the greatest possible benefit from it.

For those who know how to study the Talmud, the book is intended to be a written Gemara lesson, so that, either alone, with partners, or in groups, they can have the sense of studying with a teacher who explains the difficult passages and deepens their understanding both of the development of the dialectic and also of the various approaches that have been taken by the Rabbis over the centuries in interpreting the material. A student of this kind can start with the Hebrew-Aramaic text, examine Rashi's commentary, and pass on from there to the expanded commentary. Afterwards the student can turn to the Notes section. Study of the *Halakhah* section will clarify the conclusions reached in the course of establishing the Halakhah, and the other items in the margins will be helpful whenever the need arises to clarify a concept or a word or to understand the background of the discussion.

For those who do not possess sufficient knowledge to be able to use a standard edition of the Talmud, but who know how to read Hebrew, a different method is proposed. Such students can begin by reading the Hebrew-Aramaic text and comparing it immediately to the *Literal Translation*. They can then move over to the *Translation and Commentary*, which refers both to the original text and to the *Literal Translation*. Such students would also do well to read through the *Notes* and choose those that explain matters at greater length. They will benefit, too, from the terms explained in the side margins.

The beginner who does not know Hebrew well enough to grapple with the original can start with the *Translation and Commentary*. The inclusion of a translation within the commentary permits the student to ignore the *Literal Translation*, since the commentary includes both the Talmudic text and an interpretation of it. The beginner can also benefit from the *Notes*, and it is important for him to go over the marginal notes on the concepts to improve his awareness of the juridical background and the methods of study characteristic of this text.

Apart from its use as study material, this book can also be useful to those well versed in the Talmud, as a source of additional knowledge in various areas, both for understanding the historical and archeological background and also for an explanation of words and concepts. The general reader, too, who might not plan to study the book from beginning to end, can find a great deal of interesting material in it regarding both the spiritual world of Judaism, practical Jewish law, and the life and customs of the Jewish people during the thousand years (500 B.C.E.-500 C.E.) of the Talmudic period.

Contents

THE TALMUD
THE STEINSALTZ EDITION

VOLUME XXI
TRACTATE SANHEDRIN
PART VII

Chapter Eleven — Part II

(Pages 96B–113B)

TRANSLATION AND COMMENTARY

אֲמַר לֵיהּ [1] **Rav Nahman asked Rabbi Yitzhak: "Have you heard** anything about **when 'the son of the giants' will come?"** [2] Rabbi Yitzhak **asked** Rav Nahman: **"Who is 'the son of the giants'?"** [3] Rav Nahman **explained: "The Messiah."** [4] Rabbi Yitzhak asked in astonishment: **"Is the Messiah** really **called 'the son of the giants'?"** [5] Rav Nahman **answered: "Indeed, as the verse states** (Amos 9:11): **'On that day I will raise up** [97A] **the tabernacle of David that is fallen** [הַנֹּפֶלֶת]' — this refers to the Davidic kingdom that will be reinstated by the Messianic king. Since the Messiah will restore the Davidic kingdom that has fallen [*hanofelet*], he is therefore called *bar niflei*, 'the son of the giants.'"

אֲמַר לֵיהּ [6] Rabbi Yitzhak **said to** Rav Nahman: **Rabbi Yohanan said the following:** [7] **In the generation when the son of David** — the Messiah — **comes, Torah scholars will diminish** in number, [8] **and as for the rest** of the people, **their eyes will fail with pain and grief, and troubles will increase, and harsh decrees will** constantly **be renewed,** [9] **so that as soon as the first** evil decree **has passed, the second** evil decree **will speedily come** in its place.

תָּנוּ רַבָּנַן [10] **Our Rabbis taught** a related Baraita: "In the **Sabbatical cycle when the son of David will come,** the following will occur: [11] **During the first year** of the cycle, **this verse** (Amos 4:7) **will be fulfilled: 'And I caused it to rain upon one city, and caused it not to rain upon another city,'** bringing famine in one place and plenty in another; [12] **during the second year, arrows of a famine will be shot** everywhere, and nowhere will there be plenty; [13] **during the third year,** there will be **a great famine** in all places, **and men, women, and children, pious people, and men of** good **deeds will die, and** as

[1] אֲמַר לֵיהּ רַב נַחְמָן לְרַבִּי יִצְחָק: ״מִי שְׁמִיעַ לָךְ אֵימַת אָתֵי ׳בַּר נִפְלֵי׳״? [2] אֲמַר לֵיהּ: ״מַאן ׳בַּר נִפְלֵי׳?״ [3] אֲמַר לֵיהּ: ״מָשִׁיחַ״. [4] ״מָשִׁיחַ ׳בַּר נִפְלֵי׳ קָרֵית לֵיהּ״? [5] אֲמַר לֵיהּ: ״אִין, דִּכְתִיב: ׳בַּיּוֹם הַהוּא אָקִים [97A] אֶת סֻכַּת דָּוִיד הַנֹּפֶלֶת׳״. [6] אֲמַר לֵיהּ: הָכִי אָמַר רַבִּי יוֹחָנָן: [7] דּוֹר שֶׁבֶּן דָּוִד בָּא בּוֹ תַּלְמִידֵי חֲכָמִים מִתְמַעֲטִים, [8] וְהַשְּׁאָר עֵינֵיהֶם כָּלוֹת בְּיָגוֹן וַאֲנָחָה, וְצָרוֹת רַבּוֹת וּגְזֵרוֹת קָשׁוֹת מִתְחַדְּשׁוֹת, [9] עַד שֶׁהָרִאשׁוֹנָה פְּקוּדָה שְׁנִיָּה מְמַהֶרֶת לָבֹא.

[10] תָּנוּ רַבָּנַן: ״שָׁבוּעַ שֶׁבֶּן דָּוִד בָּא בּוֹ — [11] שָׁנָה רִאשׁוֹנָה מִתְקַיֵּים מִקְרָא זֶה: ׳וְהִמְטַרְתִּי עַל עִיר אֶחָת וְעַל עִיר אַחַת לֹא אַמְטִיר׳; [12] שְׁנִיָּה חִיצֵּי רָעָב מִשְׁתַּלְּחִים; [13] שְׁלִישִׁית רָעָב גָּדוֹל, וּמֵתִים אֲנָשִׁים וְנָשִׁים וְטַף חֲסִידִים וְאַנְשֵׁי מַעֲשֶׂה,

LITERAL TRANSLATION

[1] Rav Nahman said to Rabbi Yitzhak: "Have you heard when 'the son of the giants' will come?" [2] He said to him: "Who is 'the son of the giants'?" [3] He said to him: "The Messiah." [4] "Is the Messiah called 'the son of the giants'?" [5] He said to him: "Yes, as it is written: 'On that day I will raise up [97A] the tabernacle of David that is fallen.'"

[6] He said to him: Thus said Rabbi Yohanan: [7] In the generation when the son of David comes, Torah scholars will diminish, [8] and as for the rest, their eyes will fail with pain and grief, and troubles will increase, and harsh decrees will be renewed, [9] so that when the first one will pass, the second will speedily come.

[10] Our Rabbis taught: "The Sabbatical cycle when the son of David comes — [11] [during] the first year, this verse will be fulfilled: 'And I caused it to rain upon one city, and caused it not to rain upon another city'; [12] [during] the second [year], arrows of a famine will be shot; [13] [during] the third [year], a great famine, and men, women, and children, pious people, and men of deeds will die,

RASHI

אימת אתי בר נפלי — איידי דאמרינן ״צרור הכסף לקח בידו״ שנתמעטו הצדיקים, קא מיירי הא נמי במשיח, וקאמר תלמידים מתמעטין ואיידי דאמרינן ״ותהי האמת נעדרת״ אייתי הא דההוא אתרא דשמיה קושטא. **את סוכת דוד הנופלת** — מלכות דוד שנפלה, להכי קרי משיח בר נפלי. **עד שהראשונה פקודה** — עד שלא כלתה צרה ראשונה שניה ממהרת לבא; פקודה כמו ״לא נפקד״ (במדבר לא). **שבוע** — שמיטה. **והמטרתי על עיר אחת** — שיהא מעט מטר, ויהא רעב במקום זה ושובע במקום זה. **חיצי רעב** — רעב מעט, שלא יהא שובע בשום מקום.

NOTES

אֵימַת אָתֵי **When will he come.** It is not clear how this discussion between Rav Nahman and Rabbi Yitzhak is connected to the previous passage. *Ramah* explains that, since it was stated above that the time of redemption following the destruction of the First Temple had already been set before the Temple was destroyed, the Gemara now asks whether a time has also been set for the arrival of the Messiah, who will bring redemption following the destruction of the Second Temple.

בַּר נִפְלֵי **The son of the giants.** The Rishonim have already noted that the Gemara's explanation of the designation "the son of the giants" is inadequate. The expression *bar niflei* might be derived from the Greek, according to which the words mean "the son of the cloud," and allude to what is stated regarding the Messiah (Daniel 7:13): "One like a son of man came with the clouds of Heaven."

רִאשׁוֹנָה פְּקוּדָה **The first one will pass.** *Ramah* explains: Before it is even decreed that the first decree will be canceled, a second decree speedily comes in its place.

BACKGROUND

הַגַּבְלָן **Gavlan.** This appears to be the Aramaic term for the Golan, where a considerable Jewish community still lived at that time.

TRANSLATION AND COMMENTARY

a result of the hunger **the Torah will be forgotten by its students;** [1] **during the fourth year,** the situation will begin to improve, and there will be **plenty** in some places **but** still **a lack of plenty** in other places; [2] **during the fifth year,** there will be **great plenty** in all places, **and** people **will eat, and drink, and be happy, and the Torah will be restored to its students;** [3] **during the sixth year, rumors** will begin to circulate that the Messiah is on his way; [4] **during the seventh year,** great **wars** will be fought between Israel and the nations, the war of Gog and Magog; [5] in the year **following the seventh year, the son of David will come."**

אָמַר [6] **Rav Yosef said:** But **surely many Sabbatical cycles** have already passed that **were like that** — a year of famine followed by a year of plenty — [7] **and** still the Messiah **has not come!**

אָמַר [8] **Abaye said: Did rumors** regarding the Messiah's impending arrival spread **during the sixth year** of the cycle, **and did wars** break out between Israel and the nations **during the seventh year?** [9] **And furthermore,** did the years of famine and plenty occur **in the** precise **order** that is found in the Baraita?

אֲשֶׁר חֵרְפוּ [10] The verse states (Psalms 89:52): **"How Your enemies have insulted, O Lord; how they have insulted the footsteps of Your anointed."**

תַּנְיָא [11] **It was taught** in a Baraita: **"Rabbi Yehudah says: In the generation when the son of David will come, the Academy** where the Sages once gathered for the study of Torah **will be used for prostitution, Galilee will be destroyed,** [12] **the Gavlan** (the Bashan) **will lie desolate, people living along the border** of

וְתוֹרָה מִשְׁתַּכַּחַת מִלּוֹמְדֶיהָ; [1] בָּרְבִיעִית, שׂוֹבַע וְאֵינוֹ שׂוֹבַע; [2] בַּחֲמִישִׁית, שׂוֹבַע גָּדוֹל, וְאוֹכְלִין וְשׁוֹתִין וּשְׂמֵחִין, וְתוֹרָה חוֹזֶרֶת לְלוֹמְדֶיהָ; [3] בַּשִּׁשִּׁית, קוֹלוֹת, [4] בַּשְּׁבִיעִית, מִלְחָמוֹת; [5] בְּמוֹצָאֵי שְׁבִיעִית, בֶּן דָּוִד בָּא״.

[6] אָמַר רַב יוֹסֵף: הָא כַּמָּה שְׁבִיעִית דַּהֲוָה כֵּן, [7] וְלָא אֲתָא! [8] אָמַר אַבַּיֵי: בַּשִּׁשִּׁית קוֹלוֹת, בַּשְּׁבִיעִית מִלְחָמוֹת מִי הֲוָה? [9] וְעוֹד: כְּסִדְרָן מִי הֲוָה?

[10] ״אֲשֶׁר חֵרְפוּ אוֹיְבֶיךָ ה׳ אֲשֶׁר חֵרְפוּ עִקְּבוֹת מְשִׁיחֶךָ״.

[11] תַּנְיָא: ״רַבִּי יְהוּדָה אוֹמֵר: דּוֹר שֶׁבֶּן דָּוִד בָּא בּוֹ בֵּית הַוַּעַד יִהְיֶה לִזְנוּת, וְהַגָּלִיל יֶחֱרַב, וְהַגַּבְלָן יֵאָשֵׁם, [12] וְאַנְשֵׁי גְּבוּל

LITERAL TRANSLATION

and the Torah will be forgotten by its students; [1] during the fourth [year], plenty and no plenty; [2] during the fifth [year], great plenty, and they will eat, and drink, and be happy, and the Torah will return to its students; [3] during the sixth [year], rumors; [4] during the seventh [year], wars; [5] following the seventh [year], the son of David will come."

[6] Rav Yosef said: Surely many Sabbatical cycles were like that, [7] and he did not come!

[8] Abaye said: Were there rumors during the sixth [year, and] wars during the seventh [year]? [9] And furthermore, were they in that order?

[10] "How Your enemies have insulted, O Lord; how they have insulted the footsteps of Your anointed."

[11] It was taught: "Rabbi Yehudah says: In the generation when the son of David comes, the Academy will be used for prostitution, and Galilee will be destroyed, and the Gavlan will lie desolate, [12] and people living along the border

RASHI

משתכחת — מלומדיה — מתוך שאין להם מה לאכול. **בששית קולות** — יצאו קולות שבן דוד בא, לישנא אחרינא: קולות מתקיעת שופר שנאמר "יתקע בשופר גדול" (ישעיה כז). **מלחמות** — בין עובדי כוכבים לישראל. **דהוה הכי** — שנה אחת רעב שנה אחת שובע ואף על פי כן לא בא בן דוד. **בששית קולות מי הוה** — כלום יצאו קולות שבן דוד בא. **ועוד בסדרן מי הוה** — כלומר, אלו הצרות דקתני הכא, כסדרן לא אתרמו בשבוע אחד, אבל כי אתרמו אתי משיח. **אשר חרפו אויביך ה׳ אשר חרפו עקבות משיחך** — לא אתפרש האי קרא למאי איכתיב הכא, דהא לא קא דריש ביה מידי, ונראה למורי שכן נכתב בספרים תחלה כמו ששנינו בפרק אחרון דסוטה (מט,ב): בעקבות המשיח חוצפא יסגא, וכתבו פירוש זה על "בעקבות" שהוא לשון סוף, כמו אשר חרפו עקבות משיחך. **בית הועד** — מקום שתלמידי חכמים מתוועדין שם ללמוד תורה. הכי גרסינן: **והגבלן** — מקום ששמו כך, ישתומם. **ואנשי הגבול** — אנשי גבול ארץ ישראל, לישנא אחרינא: אנשי גזית — סנהדרין.

NOTES

קוֹלוֹת **Rumors.** *Ramah* understands that during the sixth year of the Sabbatical cycle, when the Messiah comes, there will be great heavenly noises, similar to thunder, but unconnected to clouds or rain.

אֲשֶׁר חֵרְפוּ אוֹיְבֶיךָ **Wherewith Your enemies have insulted.** Already *Rashi* noted that it is not at all clear why this verse is cited here, for no Midrashic interpretation of the verse is offered. *Maharshal* omits the verse from the text. *Maharsha* suggests that this verse introduces the Gemara's discussion about the length of the exile and the delay in the arrival of the Messiah, for the enemies of the people of Israel insult and mock them when they see that their exile continues with no end in sight.

בֵּית הַוַּעַד יִהְיֶה לִזְנוּת **The Academy will be used for prostitution.** Alternatively: The Messiah will not come until promiscuity increases so much that a public gathering-place will be set aside and designated for prostitution (*Ramah*).

וְהַגַּבְלָן יֵאָשֵׁם **And the Gavlan will lie desolate.** According to another reading, the text reads: וְהַגְּוִיל יֵאָשֵׁם — "the parchment will be punished." The parchment of the Torah

TRANSLATION AND COMMENTARY

Eretz Israel who flee from the invading armies **will go from town to town and not be shown mercy, the wisdom of the scholars will become dull, those who fear sin will be despised** by the rest of the nation, **the face of the generation will be like the face of a dog, and the truth will be absent,** [1]**as the** verse **states** (Isaiah 59:15): **'And the truth is absent, and he who departs from evil is despoiled.'"**

מַאי [2]The Gemara asks: **What is** the meaning of the words: **"And the truth is absent** [נֶעְדֶּרֶת]"? [3]**The Sages of the School of Rav said: This teaches that** the truth **will be like flock** [עֵדֶר] **after flock that go** to the wilderness to pasture. So, too, the people of truth will hide in the desert from the rest of the wicked generation.

מַאי [4]The Gemara asks: **What is** the meaning of the words: **"And he that departs from evil is despoiled"?** [5]**Whoever departs from evil is despoiled by people.**

אֲמַר רָבָא [6]Having mentioned that after the Messiah's arrival truth will be absent, the Gemara presents the following anecdote: **Rava said: At first I said** that **there is no** place **in the world** where everybody always speaks the **truth.** [7]But then **a certain Sage named Rav Tevut (and some say** that **his name was Rav Tavyume), who** was so honest that **even if he were offered all the space in the world, he would not lie,** [8]**said to me: "I once came to a certain place named Truth,** where the people never **lied, and nobody** ever **died prematurely.** I myself **married a woman from among** those people, **and I had two sons from her."** [9]**One day his wife sat down and washed her hair.** [10]**Her neighbor came and knocked on the door,** hoping to pay her a visit.

יְסוֹבְבוּ מֵעִיר לְעִיר וְלֹא יְחוּנְּנוּ, וְחָכְמַת הַסּוֹפְרִים תִּסְרַח, וְיִרְאֵי חֵטְא יִמָּאֲסוּ, וּפְנֵי הַדּוֹר כִּפְנֵי כֶלֶב, וְהָאֱמֶת נֶעֱדֶרֶת, [1]שֶׁנֶּאֱמַר: 'וַתְּהִי הָאֱמֶת נֶעְדֶּרֶת וְסָר מֵרָע מִשְׁתּוֹלֵל'״.

[2]מַאי ״וַתְּהִי הָאֱמֶת נֶעְדֶּרֶת״? [3]אָמְרִי דְּבֵי רַב: מְלַמֵּד שֶׁנַּעֲשֵׂית עֲדָרִים עֲדָרִים וְהוֹלֶכֶת לָהּ.

[4]מַאי ״וְסָר מֵרָע מִשְׁתּוֹלֵל״? [5]אָמְרִי דְּבֵי רַבִּי שֵׁילָא: כָּל מִי שֶׁסָּר מֵרַע מִשְׁתּוֹלֵל עַל הַבְּרִיּוֹת.

[6]אֲמַר רָבָא: מֵרֵישׁ הֲוָה אָמִינָא לֵיכָּא קוּשְׁטָא בְּעָלְמָא. [7]אֲמַר לִי הַהוּא מֵרַבָּנַן וְרַב טָבוּת שְׁמֵיהּ, וְאָמְרִי לָהּ רַב טַבְיוֹמֵי שְׁמֵיהּ, דְּאִי הָווּ יָהֲבִי לֵיהּ כָּל חֲלָלֵי דְעָלְמָא לָא הֲוָה מְשַׁנֵּי בְּדִיבּוּרֵיהּ: [8]״זִימְנָא חֲדָא אִיקְלַעִי לְהַהוּא אַתְרָא, וְקוּשְׁטָא שְׁמֵיהּ, וְלָא הֲווּ מְשַׁנּוּ בְּדִיבּוּרַיְיהוּ, וְלָא הֲוָה מָיֵית אִינִישׁ מֵהָתָם בְּלָא זִימְנֵיהּ. נְסִיבִי אִיתְּתָא מִינַּהוֹן, וַהֲווּ לִי תַּרְתֵּין בְּנִין מִינָּהּ״. [9]יוֹמָא חַד הֲוָה יָתְבָא דְּבֵיתְהוּ וְקָא חָיְיפָא רֵישָׁא. [10]אֲתַאי שִׁיבַבְתָּה טַרְפָּא

LITERAL TRANSLATION

will go from town to town and not be shown mercy, and the wisdom of the scholars will become dull, and those who fear sin will be despised, and the face of the generation will be like the face of a dog, and the truth will be absent, [1]as it is stated: 'And the truth is absent, and he who departs from evil is despoiled.'"

[2]What is: "And the truth is absent"? [3][The Sages] of the School of Rav say: This teaches that it will become like flock after flock and go off.

[4]What is: "And he that departs from evil is despoiled"? [5][Sages] of the School of Rabbi Shela say: Whoever departs from evil is despoiled by people.

[6]Rava said: At first I said there is no truth in the world. [7]A certain Sage named Rav Tevut (and some say his name was Rav Tavyume), who [even] if they gave him all the space in the world would not change his word, [8]said to me: "One time I came to a certain place named Truth, and they did not change their words. And nobody would die there before his time. I married a woman from among them, and I had two sons from her." [9]One day his wife sat down and washed her hair. [10]Her neighbor came and knocked on

RASHI

כפני כלב — דדמיין ממש לכלב, מפי רבי, לישנא אחרינא: כפני הכלב — שלא יתביישו זה מזה. **משתולל על הבריות** — כל העולם אומרין עליו שוטה הוא, היינו משתולל, לשון שטות, כמו ״מוליך יועצים שולל״ (איוב יב). **ליכא קושטא בעלמא** — אין אדם בעולם שידבר אמת תמיד. **אמר לי ההוא מרבנן דאי הוו יהבי ליה כל חללי דעלמא לא משני בדבוריה** — לשקר, ואישתעי לי הכי: זימנא חדא אקלעי לההוא אתרא וקושטא שמיה. **טרפא אבבא** — שהיתה שואלת אותה.

NOTES

scrolls will be punished and consumed because so few people are engaged in Torah study. Similarly below, some have the reading: וְאַנְשֵׁי גְוִיל יְסוֹבְבוּ — "the people of parchment will go from town to town." Those who write or deal in Torah scrolls will go from town to town trying to earn a living, but nobody will be interested in what they have to offer (see *Ramah, Geonim*).

מְלַמֵּד שֶׁנַּעֲשֵׂית עֲדָרִים **It will become like a flock.** Some understand that this alludes to the proliferation of ideas and factions in the pre-Messianic period, with each group claiming exclusive possession of the truth.

TRANSLATION AND COMMENTARY

When Rav Tevut answered the door, [1]**he thought** to himself: **It is not becoming** to tell her that my wife is washing her hair, [2]and so **he said to her** instead: **"She is not here** now." Shortly after he told this lie, [3]**his two sons died.** [4]**The local people came to him, and asked: "What is this?"** [5]Rav Tevut **said to them: "This is what happened."** He explained that he had told a trivial lie out of respect for his wife. [6]They did not accept this explanation and so **they said to him: "Please, leave our place** at once, **and do not set** premature **death against our people."**

תַּנְיָא [7]**It was taught** in a related Baraita: **"Rabbi Nehorai said: In the generation when the son of David comes, youths will put the elders to shame, elders will stand up before youths** to honor them, **daughters will rise up against their mothers** to insult and humiliate them, [8]**and** likewise **daughters-in-law** will rise up **against their mothers-in-law, the face of the generation will be like the face of a dog,** the people being filled with arrogance, and lacking all shame, **and sons will have no shame** even **before their fathers."**

תַּנְיָא [9]**It was taught** in another Baraita: **"Rabbi Neḥemyah says: In the generation** when **the son of David comes, arrogance will increase, high prices will corrupt** people and turn them into swindlers, **the vine will yield** an adequate supply of **fruit, but wine will** nevertheless **be** expensive, because so many people will turn to drink, [10]**the entire kingdom will turn to heresy, and nobody will** accept **rebuke."**

מְסַיַּיע לֵיהּ [11]The Gemara notes that **this** Baraita **supports** what **Rabbi Yitzḥak** said, **for Rabbi Yitzḥak said: The son of David will not come until the entire kingdom turns to heresy.**

אַדִּשָׁא. [1]סְבַר: לָאו אוֹרַח אַרְעָא. [2]אֲמַר לָהּ: ״לֵיתָא הָכָא״. [3]שְׁכִיבוּ לֵיהּ תַּרְתֵּין בְּנִין. [4]אָתוּ אֱינָשֵׁי דְּאַתְרָא לְקַמֵּיהּ, אֲמַרוּ לֵיהּ: ״מַאי הַאי״? [5]אֲמַר לְהוּ: ״הָכִי הֲוָה מַעֲשֶׂה״. [6]אֲמַרוּ לֵיהּ: בְּמָטוּתָא מִינָּךְ, פּוֹק מֵאַתְרִין, וְלָא תְּגָרֵי בְּהוּ מוֹתָנָא בְּהָנָךְ אֱינָשֵׁי״.

[7]תַּנְיָא: ״רַבִּי נְהוֹרַאי אוֹמֵר: דּוֹר שֶׁבֶּן דָּוִד בָּא בּוֹ נְעָרִים יַלְבִּינוּ פְּנֵי זְקֵנִים, וּזְקֵנִים יַעַמְדוּ לִפְנֵי נְעָרִים, וּבַת קָמָה בְּאִמָּהּ, [8]וְכַלָּה בַּחֲמוֹתָהּ, וּפְנֵי הַדּוֹר כִּפְנֵי כֶלֶב, וְאֵין הַבֵּן מִתְבַּיֵּישׁ מֵאָבִיו״.

[9]תַּנְיָא: ״רַבִּי נְחֶמְיָה אוֹמֵר: דּוֹר שֶׁבֶּן דָּוִד בָּא בּוֹ הָעַזּוּת תִּרְבֶּה, וְהַיּוֹקֶר יְעַוֵּת, וְהַגֶּפֶן יִתֵּן פִּרְיוֹ וְהַיַּיִן בְּיוֹקֶר, [10]וְנֶהְפְּכָה כָּל הַמַּלְכוּת לְמִינוּת, וְאֵין תּוֹכָחָה״.

[11]מְסַיַּיע לֵיהּ לְרַבִּי יִצְחָק, דְּאָמַר רַבִּי יִצְחָק: אֵין בֶּן דָּוִד בָּא עַד שֶׁתִּתְהַפֵּךְ כָּל הַמַּלְכוּת לְמִינוּת.

LITERAL TRANSLATION

the door. [1]He thought: It is not the way of the world. [2]He said to her: "She is not here." [3]His two sons died. [4]The people of the place came to him, and said: "What is this?" [5]He said to them: "This is what happened." [6]They said to him: "Please, leave our place, and do not set death against those people."

[7]It was taught: "Rabbi Nehorai says: In the generation when the son of David comes, youths will whiten the faces of elders, and elders will stand up before youths, and a daughter will rise against her mother, [8]and a daughter-in-law against her mother-in-law, and the face of the generation will be like the face of a dog, and a son will have no shame before his father."

[9]It was taught: "Rabbi Neḥemyah says: In the generation when the son of David comes, arrogance will increase, and high prices will corrupt, and the vine will yield its fruit, but wine will be expensive, [10]and the entire kingdom will turn to heresy, and there will be no rebuke."

[11]This supports Rabbi Yitzḥak, for Rabbi Yitzḥak said: The son of David will not come until the entire kingdom turns to heresy.

RASHI

לאו אורח ארעא — לומר היכן היא, הואיל וחייפא רישה. הכי גרסינן: **נערים ילבינו פני זקנים** — כלומר: יחפרו ויביישו אותם. **וזקנים יעמדו בפני הנערים** — לכבדם, והיינו דאמרינן (בסוטה מט,ב): בעקבות המשיח חוצפא יסגא. **בת קמה באמה** — לחרפה ולביישה. **היוקר יעות** — שלא יכבדו זה את זה **יקר** — כבוד, לישנא אחרינא: **היוקר יעות** — מכובד שבהן יהא עוותן ורמאי, מפי רבי. **והגפן יתן פריו** — ואף על פי כן יהיה היין ביוקר, שלא יהיה ברכה בפרי עצמו, לישנא אחרינא: שיהיו כולן רודפין אחר היין ומשתכרין, ומתייקר היין, אף על פי שרוב יין בעולם.

NOTES

שְׁכִיבוּ לֵיהּ תַּרְתֵּין בְּנִין **His two sons died.** Even though one is permitted (and sometimes obligated) to tell a lie in order to promote goodwill and peaceful relations between people, that only applies when there is no other way to achieve those results. Here Rav Tevut could have told the truth, and nobody would have been adversely affected or insulted (*Rabbi Ya'akov Emden*).

פְּנֵי הַדּוֹר כִּפְנֵי כֶלֶב **The face of the generation will be like the face of a dog.** Some understand that the expression "the face of the generation" refers to the leaders of the generation. In the generation when the Messiah comes, even the leaders of the generation will have the audacity and lack of shame associated with dogs (see *Etz Yosef*, *Maharsha*).

[1]אָמַר רָבָא: מַאי קְרָא? [2]״כֻּלּוֹ הָפַךְ לָבָן טָהוֹר הוּא״.
[3]תָּנוּ רַבָּנַן: ״ ׳כִּי יָדִין ה׳ עַמּוֹ [וגו׳] כִּי יִרְאֶה כִּי אָזְלַת יָד וְאֶפֶס עָצוּר וְעָזוּב׳. [4]אֵין בֶּן דָּוִד בָּא עַד שֶׁיִּרְבּוּ הַמָּסוֹרוֹת. [5]דָּבָר אַחֵר: עַד שֶׁיִּתְמַעֲטוּ הַתַּלְמִידִים. [6]דָּבָר אַחֵר: עַד שֶׁתִּכְלֶה פְּרוּטָה מִן הַכִּיס. [7]דָּבָר אַחֵר: עַד שֶׁיִּתְיָיאֲשׁוּ מִן הַגְּאוּלָּה. [8]שֶׁנֶּאֱמַר: ׳וְאֶפֶס עָצוּר וְעָזוּב׳ — [9]כִּבְיָכוֹל אֵין סוֹמֵךְ וְעוֹזֵר לְיִשְׂרָאֵל.
[10]כִּי הָא דְּרַבִּי זֵירָא, כִּי הֲוָה מַשְׁכַּח רַבָּנַן דִּמְעַסְקִי בֵּיהּ, [11]אֲמַר לְהוּ: ״בְּמָטוּתָא, בָּעֵינָא מִנַּיְיכוּ לָא תְרַחֲקוּהּ, [12]דִּתְנֵינָא: ׳שְׁלֹשָׁה בָּאִין בְּהֶיסַּח הַדַּעַת, [13]אֵלּוּ הֵן: מָשִׁיחַ, מְצִיאָה, וְעַקְרָב׳״.
[14]אָמַר רַב קְטִינָא: שִׁית אַלְפֵי שְׁנֵי הָווּ עָלְמָא וְחַד חָרוּב, [15]שֶׁנֶּאֱמַר: ״וְנִשְׂגַּב ה׳ לְבַדּוֹ בַּיּוֹם הַהוּא״.
[16]אַבַּיֵי אָמַר: תְּרֵי חָרוּב, [17]שֶׁנֶּאֱמַר: ״יְחַיֵּינוּ מִיֹּמָיִם בַּיּוֹם

LITERAL TRANSLATION

[1]Rava said: What is the verse? [2]"It is all turned white; he is clean."
[3]Our Rabbis taught: "'For the Lord shall judge His people [and repent for His servants] when He sees that their power is gone, and there is none shut up, or left.' [4]The son of David will not come until the informers increase. [5]Another explanation: Until the students dwindle. [6]Another explanation: Until coin is gone from the pocket. [7]Another explanation: Until they despair of redemption, [8]as it is stated: 'And there is none shut up, or left' — [9]as if there were no upholder or helper in Israel."
[10]Like that of Rabbi Zera, when he found Rabbis engaged in it, [11]he would say to them: "Please, I ask you not to push it off, [12]as it was taught: 'Three [things] come unawares, [13]and they are: The Messiah, a found object, and a scorpion.'"
[14]Rav Katina said: The world will exist for six thousand years, and lie fallow for a thousand years, [15]as it is stated: "And the Lord alone shall be exalted on that day."
[16]Abaye said: It will lie fallow for two thousand years, [17]as it is stated: "After two days He will revive us; on the

TRANSLATION AND COMMENTARY

אָמַר רָבָא [1]**Rava said: Which verse** alludes to this? This is alluded to by the verse regarding leprous spots that states (Leviticus 13:13): [2]**"It is all turned white; he is clean."** Once the leprous spots cover all of the leper's skin, he is declared ritually pure. So, too, once the entire kingdom turns to heresy, the redemption will soon follow.

תָּנוּ רַבָּנַן [3]**Our Rabbis taught:** "The verse states (Deuteronomy 32:36): **'For the Lord shall judge His people, and repent for His servants, when He sees that their power is gone, and there is none shut up, or left.'** The verse speaks of the time when the Lord shall judge His people and bring them redemption. The words כִּי יִרְאֶה כִּי אָזְלַת יָד, translated here as 'when He sees that their power is gone,' can be explained in several ways. [4]According to one explanation, the verse teaches that **the son of David will not come until the informers increase** in number, and 'their power is gone' and grown in strength. [5]According to **another explanation,** the verse teaches that the Messiah will not come **until the** Rabbinic **students dwindle** in number, and their power to lead the people along the straight path is gone. [6]According to yet **another explanation,** the verse teaches that the Messiah will not come **until** the last **coin is gone from the pocket.** [7]According to still **another explanation,** the verse teaches that the Messiah will not come **until** people utterly **despair** of **redemption,** [8]**as the verse states: 'And there is none shut up, or left.'** [9]They will be so cast down that they feel **as if the people of Israel** no longer **have anyone to support or help them."**

כִּי [10]The Gemara adds that this is **like what Rabbi Zera** said, for **when** Rabbi Zera found other **Rabbis engaged in** speculation about the advent of the Messiah, [11]**he would say to them: "Please, I ask you not to** engage in such speculations, for they will only **push off** the Messiah's arrival, [12]**as it was taught** in a Baraita: **'Three things come unawares** when nobody is thinking about them, [13]**namely: The Messiah, a found object, and a scorpion.'"**

אָמַר רַב קְטִינָא [14]**Rav Katina said: The world will exist for six thousand years, and** then **lie fallow for the** next **thousand years,** [15]**as the verse states** (Isaiah 2:11): **"And the Lord alone shall be exalted on that day,"** and God's day is a thousand years.

אַבַּיֵי אָמַר [16]**Abaye said:** The world **will lie fallow for two thousand years,** [17]**as the verse states** (Hosea

RASHI

כלו הפך לבן טהור הוא — כשפשט הנגע בכל העור כך כשנהפכה כל המלכות למינות — תבא גאולה. **כי ידין ה׳ עמו** — להביא להם גאולה. **כי יראה כי אזלת יד** — שתלך ותחזק ידן של מסורות ומלשינין במלשינותן. **שיתמעטו התלמידים** — שמחזיקין ידי ישראל להחזירן למוטב. **שתכלה פרוטה** — והיינו אזלת יד, שיהיו בידים ריקניות. **כביכול** — כאלו יכולין לומר דבר זה כלפי מעלה. **אין עוזר ואין סומך לישראל** — שיהיו שפלים למאד, ואומר: ״אין עוזר וסומך״ — שיהיו מתייאשין מן הגאולה. **דמעסקי ביה** — לידע מתי יבא. **ועקרב** — נושך האדם פתאום. **וחד חרוב** — שאלף שנה יהיה חרוב חוץ מששת אלפים אלו, דהיינו אלף שביעי. **תרי** — אלפים הוא חרב, אלף שביעי ואלף

TRANSLATION AND COMMENTARY

6:2): **"After two days** [= two millennia] **He will revive us; in the third day He will raise us up, and we shall live in His presence."**

תַּנְיָא [1]The following Baraita **was taught in accordance with** the position of **Rav Katina: "Just as the Sabbatical Year** suspends **field work once in seven years, so, too, the world shall lie fallow for a millennium in seven millennia,** [2]**as the verse states** (Isaiah 2:11): **'And the Lord alone shall be exalted on that day.'** [3]**And** another verse **states** (Psalms 92:1): **'A psalm, a poem for the Sabbath day' — a day that is entirely a Sabbath,** when the whole world lies fallow. [4]**And** another verse **states** (Psalms 90:4): **'For a thousand years in Your sight are but like yesterday when it is past,** and like a watch in the night.'"

תָּנָא דְבֵי אֵלִיָּהוּ [5]**A Sage of the School of Eliyahu taught** a Baraita: **"The world will exist for six thousand years:** [6]The first **two thousand years** — from the days of Adam to the days of the Patriarch Abraham — the world was still in **chaos,** for the Torah had not yet been given. [7]The next **two thousand years** — from the Patriarchs to the end of the Mishnaic period — was to be the period **of the Torah.** [8]And the next **two thousand years** was to be **the period of the Messiah.** [97B] [9]**But because of our transgressions which were** so very **many,** the Messiah did not come at the end of the fourth millennium, [10]and **those** years **which have** already **passed have** already **passed."**

אֲמַר לֵיהּ [11]The Prophet **Elijah said to Rav Yehudah the brother of Rav Sila the pious: "The world will endure for not less than eighty-five Jubilee cycles** (fifty-year periods), which is four thousand two hundred and fifty years, **and in the last Jubilee cycle**

הַשְּׁלִישִׁי יְקִמֵנוּ וְנִחְיֶה לְפָנָיו״. [1]תַּנְיָא כְּוָתֵיהּ דְּרַב קְטִינָא: ״כְּשֵׁם שֶׁהַשְּׁבִיעִית מְשַׁמֶּטֶת שָׁנָה אַחַת לְשֶׁבַע שָׁנִים, כָּךְ הָעוֹלָם מְשַׁמֵּט אֶלֶף שָׁנִים לְשִׁבְעַת אֲלָפִים שָׁנָה, [2]שֶׁנֶּאֱמַר: ׳וְנִשְׂגַּב ה׳ לְבַדּוֹ בַּיּוֹם הַהוּא׳. [3]וְאוֹמֵר: ׳מִזְמוֹר שִׁיר לְיוֹם הַשַּׁבָּת׳ — יוֹם שֶׁכּוּלּוֹ שַׁבָּת. [4]וְאוֹמֵר: ׳כִּי אֶלֶף שָׁנִים בְּעֵינֶיךָ כְּיוֹם אֶתְמוֹל כִּי יַעֲבֹר׳״. [5]תָּנָא דְּבֵי אֵלִיָּהוּ: ״שֵׁשֶׁת אֲלָפִים שָׁנָה הָוֵי עָלְמָא: [6]שְׁנֵי אֲלָפִים תּוֹהוּ; [7]שְׁנֵי אֲלָפִים תּוֹרָה, [8]שְׁנֵי אֲלָפִים יְמוֹת הַמָּשִׁיחַ. [97B] [9]וּבַעֲוֹנוֹתֵינוּ שֶׁרַבּוּ, [10]יָצְאוּ מֵהֶם מַה שֶּׁיָּצְאוּ. [11]אֲמַר לֵיהּ אֵלִיָּהוּ לְרַב יְהוּדָה אֲחוּהּ דְּרַב סָלָא חֲסִידָא: ״אֵין הָעוֹלָם פָּחוּת מִשְּׁמוֹנִים וַחֲמִשָּׁה יוֹבְלוֹת, וּבַיּוֹבֵל הָאַחֲרוֹן בֶּן

LITERAL TRANSLATION

third day He will raise us up, and we shall live in His presence."

[1]It was taught in accordance with Rav Katina: "Just as the Sabbatical Year suspends field work once in seven years, so, too, the world shall lie fallow for a millennium in seven millennia, [2]as it is stated: 'And the Lord alone shall be exalted on that day.' [3]And it states: 'A psalm, a poem for the Sabbath day' — a day that is entirely Sabbath. [4]And it states: 'For a thousand years in Your sight are but like yesterday when it is past.'"

[5][A Sage] of the School of Eliyahu taught: "The world will exist for six thousand years: [6]Two thousand years of chaos, [7]two thousand years of Torah, [8]two thousand years of the days of the Messiah. [97B] [9]But because of our transgressions which were many, [10]what came out came out.

[11]Elijah said to Rav Yehudah the brother of Rav Sila the pious: "The world will not be less than eighty-five Jubilee cycles, and in the last Jubilee cycle, the son

RASHI

שמיני, יומו של הקדוש ברוך הוא אלף שנה שנאמר ״כי אלף שנים בעיניך כיום אתמול כי יעבור״. **משמט** — ונעשה חרב. **שכולו שבת** — שהעולם משמט. **הוי עלמא** — העולם כך מתקיים. **שתי אלפים היה תהו** — מתוך שלא ניתנה עדיין תורה והיה העולם כתוהו, ומאדם הראשון עד שהיה אברהם בן חמשים ושתים שנה איכא אלפים שנה כדמוכחי קראי, דכשנשלמו אלפים שנה עסק אברהם בתורה שנאמר (בראשית יב) ״ואת הנפש אשר עשו בחרן״ ומתרגמינן: דשעבידו לאורייתא בחרן, ואמרינן במסכת עבודה זרה (ט,א): גמירי, דההוא שעתא הוה אברהם בר חמשין ותרתי שנין. **ושני אלפים תורה** — מן ״הנפש אשר עשו בחרן״ עד [אלפים] שנות המשיח, ארבעים (ושמנים) [ושמנה] שנה עד שנולד יצחק, וששים שנה משנולד יצחק עד שנולד יעקב הרי מאה ושמונה, ומאה ושלשים שהיו ליעקב כשבא למצרים, הרי מאתים שלשים ושמנה, ומאתים ועשר שעמדו במצרים הרי ארבע מאות ארבעים ושמנה, ומשיצאו ממצרים עד שנבנה בית ראשון ארבע מאות ושמנים דכתיב (מלכים א, ו) ״ויהי בשמנים שנה וארבע מאות שנה לצאת בני ישראל מארץ מצרים וגו׳״ הרי תשע מאות עשרים ושמונה, וארבע מאות ועשר שעמד בית ראשון כדמוכחי קראי על פי חשבון שנות המלכים, ושבעים דגלות בבל, וארבע מאות ועשרים שעמד בית שני הרי תשע מאות ותשע מאות עשרים ושמונה, הרי אלפים פחות מאה שבעים ושתים, ומאה שבעים ושתים קודם השלמת ארבעת אלפים נחרב הבית, ולסוף אותן מאה שבעים ושתים נשלמו שני אלפים תורה, ואיידי דאמר שני אלפים תוהו — קאמר שני אלפים תורה, ולא שתכלה תורה אחר שני אלפים — מפי רבי. **ושני אלפים שנות המשיח** — שלאחר שני אלפים תורה הוה דינו שיבא משיח, ותכלה מלכות הרשעה, ויבטל השיעבוד מישראל. **אבל בשביל עונותינו שרבו** — לא בא משיח לסוף ארבעת אלפים, ויצאו מה שיצאו, שעדיין הוא מעוכב לבא. **שמנים וחמשה יובלין** — היינו ארבעת אלפים מאתים וחמשים [שנה].

NOTES

שְׁנֵי אֲלָפִים תּוֹרָה **Two thousand years of Torah.** Some understand that the two thousand years of Torah ended at the close of the Mishnaic period, because after that time Eretz Israel was no longer the center of Torah study (see *Maharsha, Rabbi Ya'akov Emden*).

TRANSLATION AND COMMENTARY

the Messiah, **the son of David, will come.**" [1]Rav Yehudah **said to** Elijah: "Will the Messiah come **at the beginning** of that last Jubilee cycle **or at the end** of that cycle?" [2]Elijah **said to him: "I do not know."** [3]Rav Yehudah posed a second question: **"Will** the last Jubilee cycle **be completed** before the Messiah comes; **or will it not** yet **be completed** when the Messiah comes?" [4]Again, Elijah **said to him: "I do not know."** [5]**Rav Ashi said:** When the Prophet Elijah set a time for the Messiah's arrival, he meant to **say as follows: "Until that time,** the eighty-fifth Jubilee cycle, **do not** even **hope for him,** for he will surely not come before then. [6]But **from then on,** you may indeed **hope for his** arrival."

שְׁלַח [7]It was related that **Rav Ḥanan bar Taḥlifa sent Rav Yosef** the following message: **"I met a certain person,** who had **in his hand a scroll written in square Hebrew letters and in the Hebrew language.** [8]**I said to him: 'Where did you get this** scroll?' [9]**He said to me: 'I** once **hired myself out to the Roman army,** and **I found** this scroll **in a Roman storehouse.'** [10]The Hebrew document **read: 'After four-thousand-two-hundred-and-ninety-one years from the creation of the world, the world will come to an end.** [11]Those years will include **wars between the sea monsters,** and **the wars of Gog and Magog, and the remaining** years will be **the Messianic age.** [12]Following the Messianic age, **the Holy One, blessed be He,** will destroy the world, and He **will not renew His world until after seven thousand years** from the creation.'" [13]**Rav Aḥa the son of Rava said:** That document discovered in a Roman storehouse **read:** [14]"God will not renew His word until **after five thousand years** from the creation."

דָּוִד בָּא". [1]אֲמַר לֵיהּ: "בְּתְחִילָּתוֹ אוֹ בְּסוֹפוֹ"? [2]אֲמַר לֵיהּ: "אֵינִי יוֹדֵעַ". [3]"כָּלֶה, אוֹ אֵינוֹ כָּלֶה"? [4]אָמַר לֵיהּ: "אֵינִי יוֹדֵעַ". [5]רַב אַשִׁי אָמַר: הָכִי אֲמַר לֵיהּ: [6]"עַד הָכָא לָא תִּיסְתְּכֵי לֵיהּ; מִכָּאן וְאֵילָךְ, אִיסְתְּכֵי לֵיהּ".

[7]שְׁלַח לֵיהּ רַב חָנָן בַּר תַּחְלִיפָא לְרַב יוֹסֵף: "מָצָאתִי אָדָם אֶחָד וּבְיָדוֹ מְגִילָּה אַחַת כְּתוּבָה אַשּׁוּרִית וּלְשׁוֹן קֹדֶשׁ. [8]אָמַרְתִּי לוֹ: 'זוֹ מִנַּיִין לְךָ'? [9]אָמַר לִי: 'לְחַיָּילוֹת שֶׁל רוֹמִי נִשְׂכַּרְתִּי, וּבֵין גִּינְזֵי רוֹמִי מְצָאתִיהָ'. [10]וְכָתוּב בָּהּ: 'לְאַחַר אַרְבַּעַת אֲלָפִים וּמָאתַיִם וְתִשְׁעִים וְאֶחָד שָׁנָה לִבְרִיאָתוֹ שֶׁל עוֹלָם, הָעוֹלָם יִתּוֹם'. [11]מֵהֶן מִלְחָמוֹת תַּנִּינִים, מֵהֶן מִלְחָמוֹת גּוֹג וּמָגוֹג, וּשְׁאָר יְמוֹת הַמָּשִׁיחַ. [12]וְאֵין הַקָּדוֹשׁ בָּרוּךְ הוּא מְחַדֵּשׁ אֶת עוֹלָמוֹ אֶלָּא לְאַחַר שִׁבְעַת אֲלָפִים שָׁנָה'". [13]רַב אַחָא בְּרֵיהּ דְּרָבָא אָמַר: [14]"לְאַחַר חֲמֵשֶׁת אֲלָפִים שָׁנָה" אִיתְּמַר.

LITERAL TRANSLATION

of David will come." [1]He said to him: "At its beginning or at its end?" [2]He said to him: "I do not know." [3]"Will it be finished, or will it not be finished?" [4]He said to him: "I do not know." [5]Rav Ashi said: Thus he said to him: [6]"Until then, do not hope for him; from then on, hope for him."

[7]Rav Ḥanan bar Taḥlifa sent to Rav Yosef: "I found a certain person, and in his hand was a scroll written in Assyrian [square Hebrew] letters and in the holy tongue. [8]I said to him: 'From where do you have this?' [9]He said to me: 'I hired myself out to the Roman army, and I found it among the Roman storehouses.' [10]And in it was written: 'After four-thousand-two-hundred-and-ninety-one years from the creation of the world, the world will come to an end. [11]Among them wars of the sea monsters, among them the wars of Gog and Magog, and the rest the days of the Messiah. [12]And the Holy One, blessed be He, will not renew His world until after seven thousand years.'" [13]Rav Aḥa the son of Rava said: It was stated: [14]"After five thousand years."

RASHI

בתחלת – היובל האחרון הוא בא או בסופו. כלה – זמן הזה קודם שיבא משיח או אינו כלה, דבתוך היובל בסופו הוא בא. עד הבא לא תיסתכבי ליה – עד יובל האחרון לא תצפה לו, דודאי לא יבא קודם הזמן הזה. איסתכבי ליה – חכה לו שיבא. אשורית – כתב שלנו אשורית, שבא מאשור, כדאמר באידך פירקין (סנהדרין כב,א). לחיילות של רומי נשכרתי – שהייתי גולייר לאחד מהם. תנינים – דגים. והשאר ימות המשיח – שכלה השעבוד ומשיח בא. מחדש עולמו – לברוא עולם חדש.

NOTES

כְּתוּבָה אַשּׁוּרִית **In square Hebrew letters.** This detail is added in order to emphasize the significance of the discovery, for in antiquity it was not customary to commit oral traditions to writing — and especially not in square Hebrew letters and in the Hebrew language — unless they were of unusual importance.

הָעוֹלָם יִתּוֹם **The world will come to an end.** *Ramah* understands the word יִתּוֹם in the sense of "orphan." In that time, the world will be like an orphan without a father, and people will do whatever they like, as if there were no law and no judgment.

מִלְחָמוֹת תַּנִּינִים **The wars of the sea monsters.** The Gemara appears to be alluding to wars that will be waged between the great powers, some of which are compared in the Bible to sea monsters (*Maharsha*). It might be referring specifically to the wars between the great naval powers that will be fought out at sea (*Ramah*). The description found here is based on the verse (Isaiah 27:1): "On that day, the

[1]תַּנְיָא: "רַבִּי נָתָן אוֹמֵר: מִקְרָא זֶה נוֹקֵב וְיוֹרֵד עַד תְּהוֹם: [2]'כִּי עוֹד חָזוֹן לַמּוֹעֵד וְיָפֵחַ לַקֵּץ וְלֹא יְכַזֵּב אִם יִתְמַהְמַהּ חַכֵּה לוֹ כִּי בֹא יָבֹא לֹא יְאַחֵר'. [3]לֹא כְּרַבּוֹתֵינוּ שֶׁהָיוּ דּוֹרְשִׁין: [4]'עַד עִדָּן עִדָּנִין וּפְלַג עִדָּן'; [5]וְלֹא כְּרַבִּי שִׂמְלַאי שֶׁהָיָה דּוֹרֵשׁ: 'הֶאֱכַלְתָּם לֶחֶם דִּמְעָה וַתַּשְׁקֵמוֹ בִּדְמָעוֹת שָׁלִישׁ'; [6]וְלֹא כְּרַבִּי עֲקִיבָא שֶׁהָיָה דּוֹרֵשׁ: 'עוֹד אַחַת מְעַט הִיא וַאֲנִי מַרְעִישׁ אֶת הַשָּׁמַיִם וְאֶת הָאָרֶץ'.

TRANSLATION AND COMMENTARY

תַּנְיָא [1]**It was taught** in a Baraita: **"Rabbi Natan says: This verse bores and descends to the depths,** that is to say, no one can fully understand it before it is fulfilled (Habakkuk 2:3): [2]**'For there is still a vision for the appointed time; and it speaks concerning the end, and does not lie; though it tarry, wait for it, because it will surely come.'** [3]It is **not like our Rabbis, who expounded** the verse (Daniel 7:25): [4]**'For a season** [עִדָּן] **and a season** [עִדָּנִין] **and half a season** [פְּלַג עִדָּן],' arguing that the present exile will be three-and-a-half times (one time [עִדָּן], two times [עִדָּנִין], and half a time [פְּלַג עִדָּן]) as long as the exile in Egypt, that is to say, one-thousand-four-hundred years. [5]**And** it is **not like Rabbi Simlai, who expounded** the verse (Psalms 80:6): **'You have fed them with the bread of tears; and have given them tears to drink in great measure** [שָׁלִישׁ],' suggesting that the present exile will be three times [שָׁלִישׁ] as long as the exiles in Egypt and in Babylonia, that is to say, one-thousand-four-hundred-and-ten years. [6]**And** it is **not like Rabbi Akiva, who expounded** the verse (Ḥaggai 2:6): **'Yet again, in just a little while, I will shake the heavens, and the earth,'** interpreting the verse as implying that the final redemption will

LITERAL TRANSLATION

[1]It was taught: "Rabbi Natan says: This verse bores and descends to the depths: [2]'For there is still a vision for the appointed time; and it speaks concerning the end, and does not lie; though it tarry, wait for it, because it will surely come.' [3]Not like our Rabbis, who expounded: [4]'For a season and a season and half a season'; [5]and not like Rabbi Simlai, who expounded: 'You have fed them with the bread of tears; and have given them tears to drink in great measure'; [6]and not like Rabbi Akiva, who expounded: 'Yet again, in just a little while, I will shake the heavens, and the earth.'

RASHI

נוקב ויורד עד התהום — מה תהום אין לו קץ וסוף — כך אין אדם יכול לעמוד על סוף פסוק זה, (וכי קא מפרש אימת קאמר, אם) **יתמהמה** — חכה לו, דאין לו סוף. **לא כרבותינו** — אל תצפו לאותו קץ שהיו רבותינו דורשין. **עד עידן עידנין ופלג עידן** — עידן כעידן הגלות של מצרים, והיינו ארבע מאות, שני עידנין — שמונה מאות, היינו שתים עשרה מאות, ופלג עידן — שתי מאות — סך הכל אלף וארבע מאות. **ותשקמו בדמעות שליש** — כלומר השקה אותם הקדוש ברוך הוא בין גלות מצרים לגלות בבל שליש גלות אדום, כי קץ גלות אדום זה יהיה לסוף שלש פעמים ארבע מאות שנים, ושלש פעמים שבעים שנה כנגד גלות בבל, דהיינו לסוף אלף וארבע מאות ועשר שנים, כבר עברו ולא היה כך, מצאתי כתוב בשם הרב רבי שמואל בר דוד זכרונו לברכה. **עוד אחת מעט היא** — בנבואת חגי כתיב, שהיה מתנבא כשיצאו ישראל מגלות בבל ויבנה בית המקדש, והיינו "עוד אחת מעט היא" מעט כבוד אתן להם לישראל, "ואני מרעיש את השמים ואת הארץ" והבאתי כל חמדת גוים לירושלים, ור׳ עקיבא דריש ליה לימות המשיח ולאחר חורבן, והכי דריש ליה: [עוד אחת מעט היא מעט כבוד אתן לישראל ואחר כך יבא המשיח ודרשה זו אינה אלא קרא אלפני הבית קאי והכי קאמר]: עוד אחת מעט היא — מעט כבוד אתן להם לישראל ושוב לא אתן להם כל ימות בית אחרון, וכן היה, דמלכות ראשונה של מלכות חשמונאי נתקיימה שבעים שנה, ואף על גב דאמרינן בסדר עולם דמלכות בית חשמונאי מאה ושלש, ומלכות הורדוס מאה ושלש, עיקר כבודם ופארם שלא שלטה בהם אומה לא נתקיים כל כך, ומלכות שניה של הורדוס חמישים ושתים שנה, ומלכות בן כוזיבא שתי שנים ומחצה ושוב לא היה להם מלך, מפי רבי, וכל הנך דרשות לאו משנה ולאו ברייתא, — לישנא אחרינא: עוד אחת מעט היא — מעט מלכות אתן להם לישראל לאחר חורבן, ולאחר אותו מלכות הנני מרעיש שמים וארץ — ויבא משיח, ואין דרשה זו כלום, שהרי ראינו כמה מלכיות לישראל לאחר חורבן ואף על פי כן לא בא משיח, שהמלכות הראשונה שהיתה להם לישראל לאחר חורבן שבעים שנה הורדוס חמישים ושתים, בן כוזיבא שתים ומחצה, ומצינו בסדר עולם: מפולמוס של אספסיאנוס עד פולמוס של טיטוס — שתים עשרה שנה, ומפולמוס של טיטוס עד מלכות בן כוזיבא — שבע עשרה שנים, ומלכות בן כוזיבא שתי שנים ומחצה, [בן כוזיבא מלך בביתר].

NOTES

Lord with sore and great and strong sword shall punish the Leviathan the flying serpent, and Leviathan that crooked serpent; and He shall slay the crocodile that is in the sea."

נוֹקֵב וְיוֹרֵד עַד תְּהוֹם **It bores and descends to the depths.** Some explain this clause to mean: Even if the exile lasts for many years ("to the depths"), the verse will ultimately be fulfilled (*Ramah*).

עַד עִדָּן עִדָּנִין **For a season and a season and half a season.** Our commentary follows *Rashi,* who understands the words "for a season" to mean for the length of the Egyptian exile, for four hundred years. *Ramah* understands that our Gemara's calculations are based on the number of years that the people of Israel actually spent in Egypt, two-hundred-and-ten years.

לֹא כְּרַבִּי עֲקִיבָא **Not like Rabbi Akiva.** The commentators disagree about how to understand Rabbi Akiva's position, but they generally agree that, according to him, the designated time for the final redemption was shortly after the destruction of the Temple. *Ramah* suggests that his calculation was based on the word מְעַט, "a little," whose

TRANSLATION AND COMMENTARY

occur soon after the destruction. [1]**Rather,** this is the order of events: **The first kingdom** — that of the Hasmoneans — lasted for **seventy years;** [2]**the second kingdom** — that of the house of Herod — lasted **fifty-two years; and the kingdom of Ben Koziba** (Bar Kochva) lasted **two-and-a-half years.** No one knows how much more time will pass before the final redemption."

מַאי [3]The Gemara asks: **What is** the meaning of the words (Habakkuk 2:3): **"And it speaks concerning the end, and does not lie"?** [4]**Rabbi Shmuel bar Naḥmani said in the name of Rabbi Yoḥanan:** [5]**May those who calculate the end** and offer a date for the Messiah's arrival **be cursed, for they say:** [6]**Since the time that** we thought **had been designated** for the Messiah's arrival has already **passed, and** still **he has not come, he will not come** at all. [7]**Rather,** the proper approach is to **wait for him** patiently, **as** the end of **the** aforementioned **verse states:** [8]**"Though it tarry, wait for it."** [9]**Because you might say: We are** longingly **waiting** for the Messiah to arrive, **but** God **is not waiting** for him with the same yearning — [10]**the verse therefore states** (Isaiah 30:18): **"And therefore will the Lord wait, to be gracious to you, and therefore will He be exalted, to have mercy upon you;** for the Lord is a God of judgment; happy are all they who wait for Him." [11]The Gemara asks: **Now, if we are waiting** for the Messiah to arrive, **and** God Himself **awaits** his arrival, **who,** then, **is preventing him** from coming? [12]The Gemara explains: **The divine quality of justice is preventing him** from coming, as the verse cited above states: "For the Lord is a God of judgment." According to divine justice, we are not yet fit for the final redemption. [13]The Gemara asks: **Now, if the divine quality of justice is preventing** the Messiah from coming, **why are we** longingly **waiting** each day for him to come? [14]In order **to receive reward** for our expectation, **as it is stated: "Happy are all they who wait for Him."**

אָמַר אַבַּיֵי [15]The Gemara now cites another Aggadic statement connected to the verse that was just cited. **Abaye said: In every generation** there are **at least thirty-six righteous people in the world who receive**

[1]אֶלָּא, מַלְכוּת רִאשׁוֹן שִׁבְעִים שָׁנָה; [2]מַלְכוּת שְׁנִיָּה חֲמִשִּׁים וּשְׁתַּיִם, וּמַלְכוּת בֶּן כּוֹזִיבָא שְׁתֵּי שָׁנִים וּמֶחֱצָה״.

[3]מַאי ״וְיָפֵחַ לַקֵּץ וְלֹא יְכַזֵּב״? [4]אָמַר רַבִּי שְׁמוּאֵל בַּר נַחְמָנִי אָמַר רַבִּי יוֹנָתָן: [5]תִּיפַּח עַצְמָן שֶׁל מְחַשְּׁבֵי קִיצִּין, שֶׁהָיוּ אוֹמְרִים: [6]כֵּיוָן שֶׁהִגִּיעַ אֶת הַקֵּץ וְלֹא בָּא, שׁוּב אֵינוֹ בָּא. [7]אֶלָּא חַכֵּה לוֹ, שֶׁנֶּאֱמַר: [8]״אִם יִתְמַהְמַהּ חַכֵּה לוֹ״. [9]שֶׁמָּא תֹּאמַר: אָנוּ מְחַכִּין, וְהוּא אֵינוֹ מְחַכֶּה — [10]תַּלְמוּד לוֹמַר: ״וְלָכֵן יְחַכֶּה ה׳ לַחֲנַנְכֶם וְלָכֵן יָרוּם לְרַחֶמְכֶם״. [11]וְכִי מֵאַחַר שֶׁאָנוּ מְחַכִּים וְהוּא מְחַכֶּה, מִי מְעַכֵּב? [12]מִדַּת הַדִּין מְעַכֶּבֶת. [13]וְכִי מֵאַחַר שֶׁמִּדַּת הַדִּין מְעַכֶּבֶת, אָנוּ לָמָּה מְחַכִּין? [14]לְקַבֵּל שָׂכָר, שֶׁנֶּאֱמַר: ״אַשְׁרֵי כָּל חוֹכֵי לוֹ״.

[15]אָמַר אַבַּיֵי: לֹא פָּחוּת עָלְמָא מִתְּלָתִין וְשִׁיתָּא צַדִּיקֵי דִּמְקַבְּלֵי

LITERAL TRANSLATION

[1]Rather, the first kingdom, seventy years; [2]the second kingdom fifty-two [years]; and the kingdom of Ben Koziba two-and-a-half years."

[3]What is: "And it speaks concerning the end, and does not lie"? [4]Rabbi Shmuel bar Naḥmani said in the name of Rabbi Yoḥanan: [5]May those who calculate the end swell up, for they said: [6]Since the designated time came, and he did not come, he will no longer come. [7]Rather, wait for him, as it is stated: [8]"Though it tarry, wait for it." [9]Lest you say: We are waiting, but He is not waiting — [10][therefore] the verse states: "And therefore will the Lord wait, to be gracious to you, and therefore will He be exalted, to have mercy upon you." [11]And since we are waiting, and He waits, who is preventing [him]? [12]The [divine] quality of justice is preventing [him]. [13]And since the [divine] quality of justice is preventing [him], why are we waiting? [14]To receive reward, as it is stated: "Happy are all they that wait for Him."

[15]Abaye said: The world does not have fewer than thirty-six righteous people who receive

RASHI

ויפח לקץ — תיפח נפשו של מחשב הקץ, שלא היה לו לכזב ולומר כיון שהגיע וכו׳. **יחכה ה׳** — הוא עצמו מחכה ומתאוה שיבא משיח.

NOTES

numerical value is one-hundred-and-nineteen. *Maharsha* argues that this calculation accounts for the support that Rabbi Akiva gave to the Bar Kochva uprising.

תְּלָתִין וְשִׁיתָּא צַדִּיקֵי **Thirty-six righteous people.** It has been suggested that the thirty-six righteous people in every generation correspond to the majority of the Sanhedrin (which is composed of seventy-one judges), or to half the Sanhedrin, if we count the High Priest or the head of the Sanhedrin.

HALAKHAH

תִּיפַּח עַצְמָן שֶׁל מְחַשְּׁבֵי קִיצִּין **May those who calculate the end swell up.** "One should not try to calculate the end, for the Rabbis already cursed those who tried to offer a date for the Messiah's arrival." (*Rambam, Sefer Shofetim, Hilkhot Melakhim* 12:2.)

BACKGROUND

אִיסְפַּקְלַרְיָא Mirror.

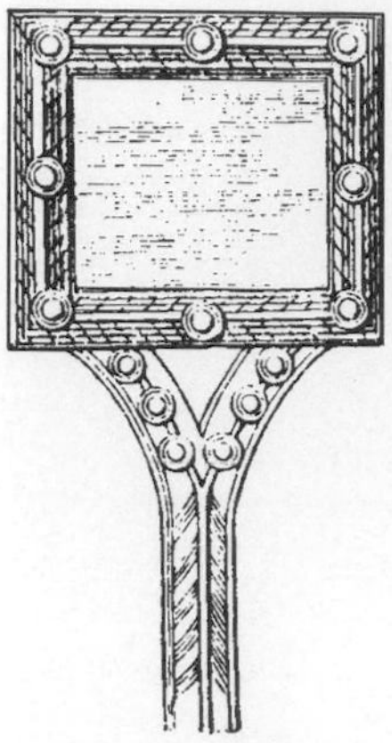

A Roman metal mirror from Mishnaic times.

LANGUAGE

אִיסְפַּקְלַרְיָא Mirror. The word derives from the Latin *specularia*, "a mirror," or "sometimes glass or some other transparent thing that can be looked through."

בַּר Permission. The word derives from the Persian *bar*, meaning "authority," "permission to enter."

אַפֵּי שְׁכִינָה בְּכָל דָּרָא, [1]שֶׁנֶּאֱמַר: "אַשְׁרֵי כָּל חוֹכֵי לוֹ". [2]לוֹ בְּגִימַטְרִיָּא תְּלָתִין וְשִׁיתָּא הָווּ.
[3]אִינִי? [4]וְהָאָמַר רָבָא: דָּרָא דְּקַמֵּי קוּדְשָׁא בְּרִיךְ הוּא תְּמָנֵי סְרֵי אַלְפֵי [פַּרְסָא] הֲוַאי, [5]שֶׁנֶּאֱמַר: "סָבִיב שְׁמֹנָה עָשָׂר אָלֶף"!
[6]לָא קַשְׁיָא. [7]הָא דְּמִסְתַּכְּלִי בְּאִיסְפַּקְלַרְיָא הַמְּאִירָה. [8]הָא דְּמִסְתַּכְּלִי בְּאִיסְפַּקְלַרְיָא שֶׁאֵינָהּ מְאִירָה.
[9]וּמִי נְפִישִׁי כּוּלֵּי הַאי? [10]וְהָאָמַר חִזְקִיָּה אָמַר רַבִּי יִרְמְיָה מִשּׁוּם רַבִּי שִׁמְעוֹן בֶּן יוֹחַי: רָאִיתִי בְּנֵי עֲלִיָּיה וְהֵן מוּעָטִין. [11]אִם אֶלֶף הֵם, אֲנִי וּבְנִי מֵהֶם. [12]אִם מֵאָה הֵם, אֲנִי וּבְנִי מֵהֶם. [13]אִם שְׁנַיִם הֵם — אֲנִי וּבְנִי הֵם!
[14]לָא קַשְׁיָא. [15]הָא דְּעָיְילִי בְּבָר. [16]הָא דְּעָיְילִי בְּלָא בָּר.

TRANSLATION AND COMMENTARY

the countenance of the Divine Presence, [1]**as the verse states** (Isaiah 30:18): **"Happy are all they who wait for Him [*lo*]."** [2]**The numerical value of the word *lo* is thirty-six** [ל = 30, ו = 6], alluding to the thirty-six righteous people who are always waiting for him.

אִינִי [3]The Gemara asks: **Is it** really **so?** [4]**But surely Rava said: The row** of righteous people standing **before the Holy One, blessed be He, is eighteen thousand Persian miles** long, [5]**as the verse** regarding the future city of God **states** (Ezekiel 48:35): **"It shall be round about eighteen thousand measures;** and the name of the city from that day shall be, the Lord is there"!

לָא קַשְׁיָא [6]The Gemara answers: **There is no difficulty.** [7]The small number refers to **those** righteous people **who behold** the divine countenance, as it were, **in a clear mirror,** directly and with full force. [8]The much larger number **refers to those** righteous people **who behold** the divine countenance **in an unclear mirror,** indirectly and from the side.

וּמִי נְפִישִׁי [9]The Gemara asks: **But** is it so clear that those who behold God with full force **are** really **that many,** at least thirty-six in every generation? [10]**Surely Ḥizkiyah said in the name of Rabbi Yirmeyah who said in the name of Rabbi Shimon ben Yoḥai: I saw the people of elevation** — the very righteous people who will reach the highest elevation — **and they are** very **few.** [11]**If they are a thousand, I and my son are among them.** [12]**If they are a hundred, I and my son are among them.** [13]**If they are** only **two — I and my son are them.** Not even Rabbi Shimon ben Yoḥai believed that there are more than two such righteous people, let alone thirty-six.

לָא קַשְׁיָא [14]The Gemara answers: **There is no difficulty.** [15]The larger number — thirty-six — **refers to those** righteous people **who** may only **enter** to behold God in a clear mirror **with the permission** of the angels. There are not fewer than thirty-six such people in every generation. [16]The smaller number — only two in a generation — **refers to those** righteous people **who** may **enter** to behold God in a clear mirror **without the permission** of any heavenly beings, for nothing is denied to people who have reached such a high spiritual level.

LITERAL TRANSLATION

the countenance of the Divine Presence in every generation, [1]as it is stated: "Happy are all they who wait for Him [*lo*]." [2]The numerical value of the word *lo* is thirty-six.

[3]Is it so? [4]But surely Rava said: The row before the Holy One, blessed be He, is eighteen thousand Persian miles, [5]as it is stated: "It shall be round about eighteen thousand measures"!

[6]It is not difficult. [7]This [refers to] those who see with a clear mirror. [8]This [refers to] those who see with an unclear mirror.

[9]But are they that many? [10]But surely Ḥizkiyah said in the name of Rabbi Yirmeyah who said in the name of Rabbi Shimon ben Yoḥai: I saw the people of elevation, and they are few. [11]If they are a thousand, I and my son are among them. [12]If they are a hundred, I and my son are among them. [13]If they are two — I and my son are them.

[14]It is not difficult. [15]This [refers to] those who enter with permission. [16]This [refers to] those who enter without permission.

RASHI

סביב שמונה עשרה אלף — בירושלים של מעלה משתעי קרא בסוף יחזקאל. **באספקלריא המאירה** — בחוזק נגהו של הקדוש ברוך הוא אין מסתכלין אלא תלתין ושית, אבל בקלישות הנוגה לצדדין מרחוק מסתכלין כמות הרבה. **ומי נפישי כולי האי** — דלהוי בריר לן תלתין ושיתא הוו ולא פחות. **והא רבי שמעון בן יוחאי** — לא הוה ידע אם אלף הם, אם מאה הם, אם שנים הם. **הא דעיילי בבר** — שצריכין ליטול רשות כשנכנסין להסתכל באספקלריא המאירה, בהנהו לא פחיתי מתלתין ושית, אבל אותן הנכנסין בלא רשות ברוב צדקם — הנהו מספקא לן כמה הוו.

NOTES

אֲנִי וּבְנִי הֵם I and my son are them. Rabbi Shimon ben Yoḥai did not mean to say that he viewed himself as being greater than all the Prophets and all the other Sages. Rather, he meant to say that while he was hiding in the cave with his son, God revealed to him that a select group of righteous people would reach the highest elevation, but He did not tell him how many righteous people were in that group, nor who they were. But because of the way God took care of them while they were in the cave, Rabbi Shimon bar Yoḥai was confident that he and his son were included in that select group (*Ramah*).

דְּעָיְילִי בְּבָר Who enter with permission. Some understand these words to mean "who enter with their son." Even though there are many great righteous people, only a few

TRANSLATION AND COMMENTARY

אָמַר רַב [1]**Rav said: All the times that have been designated** for the arrival of the Messiah **have** already **passed, and** now **the matter depends only upon repentance and good deeds.** As soon as the people of Israel repent, they will be redeemed.

וּשְׁמוּאֵל [2]**Shmuel** disagreed and **said: It is enough for the mourner that he withstand his mourning.** Even if the people of Israel do not repent, they will nevertheless be redeemed, for the sorrow and distress of the exile that they suffer will make them fit for redemption.

כְּתַנָּאֵי [3]This Amoraic disagreement parallels an earlier controversy between **the Tannaim,** for it was taught in a Baraita: **"Rabbi Eliezer says: If** the people of **Israel repent, they will be redeemed, and if not, they will not be redeemed.** [4]**Rabbi Yehoshua said to him:** Is it really true that **if they do not repent, they will not be redeemed?** [5]**Rather,** if the people of Israel fail to repent on their own, **the Holy One, blessed be He, will set a king over them whose decrees are as harsh as those of Haman, and** the people of **Israel will repent** against their will, **and He will restore them to good."**

תַּנְיָא אִידָךְ [6]The same controversy **was taught in another Baraita:** [7]**"Rabbi Eliezer says: If** the people of **Israel repent, they will be redeemed, as the verse states** (Jeremiah 3:22): **'Return, faithless children, and I will heal your backslidings,'** implying that God's healing depends upon the faithless children's return. [8]**Rabbi Yehoshua said to them: But surely the verse already states** (Isaiah 52:3): 'Thus says the Lord, **You were sold for nought; and without money you shall be redeemed.'** [9]**'You were sold for nought' — for the worship of idols,** which are all nought. [10]**'And without money you shall be redeemed' — without repentance and good deeds,** but only with the will and mercy of God. [11]**Rabbi Eliezer said to Rabbi Yehoshua: But surely the**

[1]אָמַר רַב: כָּלוּ כָּל הַקִּיצִין, וְאֵין הַדָּבָר תָּלוּי אֶלָּא בִּתְשׁוּבָה וּמַעֲשִׂים טוֹבִים.
[2]וּשְׁמוּאֵל אָמַר: דַּיּוֹ לְאָבֵל שֶׁיַּעֲמוֹד בְּאֶבְלוֹ.
[3]כְּתַנָּאֵי: "רַבִּי אֱלִיעֶזֶר אוֹמֵר: אִם יִשְׂרָאֵל עוֹשִׂין תְּשׁוּבָה נִגְאָלִין, וְאִם לָאו, אֵין נִגְאָלִין. [4]אָמַר לֵיהּ רַבִּי יְהוֹשֻׁעַ: אִם אֵין עוֹשִׂין תְּשׁוּבָה אֵין נִגְאָלִין? [5]אֶלָּא, הַקָּדוֹשׁ בָּרוּךְ הוּא מַעֲמִיד לָהֶן מֶלֶךְ שֶׁגְּזֵרוֹתָיו קָשׁוֹת כְּהָמָן, וְיִשְׂרָאֵל עוֹשִׂין תְּשׁוּבָה וּמַחֲזִירָן לְמוּטָב".
[6]תַּנְיָא אִידָךְ: [7]"רַבִּי אֱלִיעֶזֶר אוֹמֵר: אִם יִשְׂרָאֵל עוֹשִׂין תְּשׁוּבָה, נִגְאָלִין, שֶׁנֶּאֱמַר: 'שׁוּבוּ בָּנִים שׁוֹבָבִים אֶרְפָּא מְשׁוּבֹתֵיכֶם'. [8]אָמַר לוֹ רַבִּי יְהוֹשֻׁעַ: וַהֲלֹא כְּבָר נֶאֱמַר: 'חִנָּם נִמְכַּרְתֶּם וְלֹא בְכֶסֶף תִּגָּאֵלוּ'. [9]'חִנָּם נִמְכַּרְתֶּם' — בַּעֲבוֹדָה זָרָה. [10]'וְלֹא בְכֶסֶף תִּגָּאֵלוּ' — לֹא בִּתְשׁוּבָה וּמַעֲשִׂים טוֹבִים. [11]אָמַר לוֹ רַבִּי אֱלִיעֶזֶר לְרַבִּי יְהוֹשֻׁעַ: וַהֲלֹא כְּבָר

LITERAL TRANSLATION

[1]Rav said: All the ends have passed, and the matter depends only upon repentance and good deeds.

[2]And Shmuel said: It is enough for the mourner that he withstand his mourning.

[3]Like the Tannaim: "Rabbi Eliezer says: If [the people of] Israel repent, they will be redeemed, and if not, they will not be redeemed. [4]Rabbi Yehoshua said to him: If they do not repent, they will not be redeemed? [5]Rather, the Holy One, blessed be He, will set a king over them whose decrees are harsh like [those of] Haman, and Israel will repent, and He will restore them to good."

[6]It was taught in another [Baraita]: [7]"Rabbi Eliezer says: If [the people of] Israel repent, they will be redeemed, as it is stated: 'Return, faithless children, and I will heal your backslidings.' [8]Rabbi Yehoshua said to him: But surely it was already stated: 'You were sold for nought; and not with money shall you be redeemed.' [9]'You were sold for nought' — for idol worship. [10]'And not with money shall you be redeemed' — without repentance and good deeds. [11]Rabbi Eliezer said to Rabbi Yehoshua: But surely

RASHI

בתשובה — אם כל ישראל חוזרין בתשובה יבא, ואם לאו לא יבא. דיו לאבל שעומד באבלו — דיו להקדוש ברוך הוא שעומד כמה ימים וימינו אחור, כלומר, אם לא יעשו תשובה אינו עומד באבלו כל הימים אלא ודאי קץ לדבר, לישנא אחרינא: דיו לאבל — דיין לישראל צער גלות, אפילו בלא תשובה נגאלין. לא בכסף — לא בתשובה ומעשים טובים, דאפילו אין עושין תשובה — נגאלין, משום דאמר חנם נמכרתם קרי כסף בלשון תשובה.

NOTES

of them are like Rabbi Shimon bar Yoḥai, whose son merited entry to the inner spiritual sanctum at the same spiritual level as his father (*Geonim, Arukh*).

HALAKHAH

עוֹשִׂין תְּשׁוּבָה נִגְאָלִין **If they repent, they will be redeemed.** "The people of Israel will not be redeemed unless they repent. The Torah promises that in the end the people of Israel will repent, and then immediately they will be redeemed from their exile," following Rabbi Yehoshua. (*Rambam, Sefer Mada, Hilkhot Teshuvah* 7:5.)

TRANSLATION AND COMMENTARY

verse already states (Malachi 3:7): **'Return to me, and I will return to you,'** implying that God will not return to Israel until Israel has already returned to God. [1]**Rabbi Yehoshua said to him: But surely it has been stated** (Jeremiah 3:14): **"For I have taken you to myself; and I will take you one of a city, and two of a family, and I will bring you to Zion,'** implying that God will take the people of Israel to Himself even against their will.' [2]**Rabbi Eliezer said to him: But surely it has been stated** (Isaiah 30:15): **'In ease** [בְּשׁוּבָה] **and rest shall you be saved.'** The word בְּשׁוּבָה, translated here as 'in ease,' may also be understood in the sense of 'repentance,' so that the verse means to say that if the people of Israel repent, they will be saved. [3]**Rabbi Yehoshua said to Rabbi Eliezer: But surely it has been stated** (Isaiah 49:7): [4]**'Thus says the Lord, the redeemer of Israel, his holy one, to him whom man despises, to him whom the nation abhors, to a servant of rulers,** [98A] **kings shall see and arise, princes also shall prostrate themselves,** because of the Lord who is faithful, and the Holy One of Israel, who has chosen you,' which implies that the redemption will come no matter what, even if Israel does not repent. [5]**Rabbi Eliezer said to** Rabbi Yehoshua: **But surely** another **verse states** (Jeremiah 4:1): [6]**'If you will return, O Israel, says the Lord, return to Me,'** implying that the people of Israel's redemption depends upon their repentance. [7]**Rabbi Yehoshua said to** Rabbi Eliezer: **But surely** another **verse states** (Daniel 12:7): [8]**'And I heard the man clothed in linen, who was above the waters of the river, when he lifted up his right hand and his left hand to heaven and swore by that One who lives for ever that it shall be for a time, times, and a half; and when the crushing of the power of the holy people shall have been completed, all these things,'** implying that a time has already been set for the people of Israel's redemption, even without their repentance. After hearing this last proof text, [9]**Rabbi Eliezer remained silent."**

וְאָמַר רַבִּי אַבָּא [10]**Rabbi Abba said: There is no sign** of the imminence of the final redemption **more clear**

נֶאֱמַר: ׳שׁוּבוּ אֵלַי וְאָשׁוּבָה אֲלֵיכֶם׳. [1]אָמַר לֵיהּ רַבִּי יְהוֹשֻׁעַ: וַהֲלֹא כְּבָר נֶאֱמַר: ׳כִּי אָנֹכִי בָּעַלְתִּי בָכֶם וְלָקַחְתִּי אֶתְכֶם אֶחָד מֵעִיר וּשְׁנַיִם מִמִּשְׁפָּחָה וְהֵבֵאתִי אֶתְכֶם צִיּוֹן׳. [2]אָמַר לוֹ רַבִּי אֱלִיעֶזֶר: וַהֲלֹא כְּבָר נֶאֱמַר: ׳בְּשׁוּבָה וָנַחַת תִּוָּשֵׁעוּן׳! [3]אָמַר לוֹ רַבִּי יְהוֹשֻׁעַ לְרַבִּי אֱלִיעֶזֶר: וַהֲלֹא כְּבָר נֶאֱמַר: [4]״כֹּה אָמַר ה׳ גֹּאֵל יִשְׂרָאֵל קְדוֹשׁוֹ לִבְזֹה נֶפֶשׁ לִמְתָעֵב גּוֹי לְעֶבֶד מֹשְׁלִים, [98A] מְלָכִים יִרְאוּ וָקָמוּ שָׂרִים וְיִשְׁתַּחֲווּ׳. [5]אָמַר לוֹ רַבִּי אֱלִיעֶזֶר: וַהֲלֹא כְּבָר נֶאֱמַר: [6]׳אִם תָּשׁוּב יִשְׂרָאֵל נְאֻם ה׳ אֵלַי תָּשׁוּב׳. [7]אָמַר לוֹ רַבִּי יְהוֹשֻׁעַ: וַהֲלֹא כְּבָר נֶאֱמַר: [8]׳וָאֶשְׁמַע אֶת הָאִישׁ לְבוּשׁ הַבַּדִּים אֲשֶׁר מִמַּעַל לְמֵימֵי הַיְאֹר וַיָּרֶם יְמִינוֹ וּשְׂמֹאלוֹ אֶל הַשָּׁמַיִם וַיִּשָּׁבַע בְּחֵי הָעוֹלָם כִּי לְמוֹעֵד מוֹעֲדִים וָחֵצִי וּכְכַלּוֹת נַפֵּץ יַד עַם קֹדֶשׁ תִּכְלֶינָה כָל אֵלֶּה וגו׳׳. [9]וְשָׁתַק רַבִּי אֱלִיעֶזֶר״.

[10]וְאָמַר רַבִּי אַבָּא: אֵין לְךָ קֵץ

LITERAL TRANSLATION

it has been stated: 'Return to me, and I will return to you.' [1]Rabbi Yehoshua said to him: But surely it has been stated: 'For I have taken you; and I will take you one of a city, and two of a family, and I will bring you to Zion.' [2]Rabbi Eliezer said to him: But surely it has been stated: 'In ease and rest shall you be saved.' [3]Rabbi Yehoshua said to Rabbi Eliezer: But surely it has been stated: [4]'Thus says the Lord, the redeemer of Israel, his holy one, to him whom a soul despises, to him whom the nation abhors, to a servant of rulers, [98A] kings shall see and arise, princes also shall prostrate themselves.' [5]Rabbi Eliezer said to him: But surely it is already stated: [6]'If you will return, O Israel, says the Lord, return to Me.' [7]Rabbi Yehoshua said to him: But surely it is already stated: [8]'And I heard the man clothed in linen, who was above the waters of the river, when he lifted up his right hand and his left hand to heaven and swore by that One who lives for ever that it shall be for a time, times, and a half; and when the crushing of the power of the holy people shall have been completed, all these things, etc.' [9]And Rabbi Eliezer was silent."

[10]And Rabbi Abba said: You have no designated time

RASHI

בעלתי אתכם — משמע: בעל כרחכם, בלא תשובה. **אחד מעיר** — אברור הצדיקים ואביאם לציון, אף על פי שאין כולם חוזרין. **כה אמר ה׳ לבזה נפש למתעב גוי** — אותן הבזויין ומתועבין בעבירות, אף על פי כן יגאלו, "מלכים יראו וקמו". **כי למועד מועדים** — אלמא יש קץ בדבר. **וככלות נפץ יד עם קדש** — כשתכלה תקומתם וחוזק ידיהם שהיתה נפולה אילך ואילך גבורה ותועלת לפשוט אנה ואנה, ואחר שתכלה גבורתם שיהיו שפלים למאד. **תכלינה** — אלו הצרות ויבא משיח, כדאמרינן "כי אזלת יד".

NOTES

אֵין לְךָ קֵץ מְגוּלֶּה מִזֶּה **You do not have a designated time more revealed than this.** Some understand Rabbi Abba's

TRANSLATION AND COMMENTARY

and explicit **than this,** [1]**for the verse states** (Ezekiel 36:8): **"But you, O mountains of Israel, you shall give your branches, and yield your fruit to My people of Israel;** for they will soon be coming." When this verse is fulfilled, and the mountains of Israel are once again green and yield fruit, you will know that the Messiah is on his way and soon to arrive.

רַבִּי אֱלִיעֶזֶר אוֹמֵר [2]**Rabbi Eliezer says:** There is **also** no sign of the imminence of the Messiah's arrival **more** clear **than this,** [3]**for the verse states** (Zechariah 8:10): **"For before these days there was no hire for man, nor any hire for beast; nor was there peace from the oppressor to him who went out or came in;** for I set all men everyone against his neighbor." When you see that nobody can hire himself out for work, nor can he even hire out his animals, you will know that the Messiah is soon to come, as it was stated above (97a), the Messiah will not arrive until the last coin is gone from the pocket, and people are left entirely empty-handed.

מַאי [4]Having cited the verse in Zechariah, the Gemara now asks: **What is** the meaning of the words: **"Nor was there any peace from the oppressor to him who went out or came in"?** [5]**Rav said:** The verse means to say that **even for Torah scholars, who were promised** that, they could come and go in peace, **as the verse states** (Psalms 119:165): **"Great peace have they who love Your Torah;** and nothing can make them stumble," [6]**there will be no peace from the oppressor** — because of the many troubles that will befall them.

וּשְׁמוּאֵל אָמַר [7]**Shmuel said:** This verse teaches that the Messiah will not come **until** nobody comes and goes in the market, and **all the prices** are **equally** low.

מְגוּלֶּה מִזֶּה, [1]שֶׁנֶּאֱמַר: "וְאַתֶּם הָרֵי יִשְׂרָאֵל עַנְפְּכֶם תִּתֵּנוּ וּפֶרְיְכֶם תִּשְׂאוּ לְעַמִּי יִשְׂרָאֵל וגו׳".
[2]רַבִּי אֱלִיעֶזֶר אוֹמֵר: אַף מִזֶּה, [3]שֶׁנֶּאֱמַר: "כִּי לִפְנֵי הַיָּמִים הָאֵלֶּה הָהֵם שְׂכַר הָאָדָם לֹא נִהְיָה וּשְׂכַר הַבְּהֵמָה אֵינֶנָּה וְלַיּוֹצֵא וְלַבָּא אֵין שָׁלוֹם מִן הַצָּר".
[4]מַאי "לַיּוֹצֵא וְלַבָּא אֵין שָׁלוֹם מִן הַצָּר"? [5]רַב אָמַר: אַף תַּלְמִידֵי חֲכָמִים, שֶׁכָּתוּב בָּהֶם שָׁלוֹם, דִּכְתִיב: "שָׁלוֹם רָב לְאֹהֲבֵי תוֹרָתֶךָ", [6]אֵין שָׁלוֹם מִפְּנֵי צָר.
[7]וּשְׁמוּאֵל אָמַר: עַד שֶׁיִּהְיוּ כָּל הַשְּׁעָרִים כּוּלָּן שְׁקוּלִין.

LITERAL TRANSLATION

more revealed than this, [1]for it is stated: "But you, O mountains of Israel, you shall give your branches, and yield your fruit to My people of Israel, etc."

[2]Rabbi Eliezer says: Also more than this, for it is stated: [3]"For before these days there was no hire for man, nor any hire for beast; nor was there peace from the oppressor to him who went out or came in."

[4]What is "nor was there peace from the oppressor to him who went out or came in"? [5]Rav said: Even for Torah scholars, regarding whom peace is written, for it is written: "Great peace have they who love Your Torah," [6]there will be no peace from the oppressor.

[7]And Shmuel said: Until all the prices are equal.

RASHI

מגולה מזה — כשתתן ארץ ישראל פריה בעין יפה אז יקרב הקץ, ואין לך קץ מגולה יותר. **רבי אליעזר אומר מזה** — הפסוק כשתראה דאין שום אדם משתכר ואף שכר הבהמה לא נהיה, והיינו כדאמרן עד שתכלה פרוטה מן הכיס, אין מעות מצויות בכיס. **שכר בהמה** — עבודת האדמה שהיא על ידי בהמה — איננה. **וליוצא ובא אין שלום** — אז יבא משיח. [**שלום רב** — והיינו וליוצא ולבא — אלו תלמידי חכמים אותם שהיה דינם לצאת ולבא בשלום, כדכתיב "שלום רב לאוהבי תורתך" — אפילו להנהו אין שלום. **מן הצר** — מרוב הצרות, לישנא אחרינא: מיצר הרע. **שקולין** — שוין שער התבואה ויין רווחיה, כדאמרן חמישית שובע גדול, לישנא אחרינא: שקולין — שוין, שכולן יקרין.

NOTES

statement as a continuation of what Rabbi Yehoshua said above, that there is a designated time for the final redemption, for the verse cited by Rabbi Abba concludes with the words, "for they will soon be coming." If there is no designated time, how can the Prophet say that the days of the Messiah "will soon be coming." Rabbi Eliezer's statement may be understood similarly, for the verse that he cites reads: "For before these days," implying that the period of redemption will have to arrive at a fixed time.

עַנְפְּכֶם תִּתֵּנוּ **You shall give your branches.** As long as the people of Israel are exiled from their land, the Land of Israel will remain desolate and barren of fruit. Thus, there is no clearer sign of the imminence of the final redemption and the people of Israel's return to its land than the land once again growing its branches and yielding its fruit (*Maharsha*).

לַיּוֹצֵא וְלַבָּא **Who went out or came in.** Torah scholars are referred to as those "who went out or came in," because they leave the synagogue and enter the study hall, rather than going in and out of their homes like the rest of the nation (*Gilyonei HaShas*).

כָּל הַשְּׁעָרִים כּוּלָּן שְׁקוּלִין **All the prices are equal.** Our commentary follows *Ramah* and others, who understand that Shmuel means to say that the Messiah will not come until the prices of all the major commodities, like wheat and wine, will be equally depressed because the market is inactive. Others suggest that Shmuel means that the Messiah will not come until the prices in all the stores are equal, because all the storekeepers are perfectly honest and they refrain from raising prices unfairly (*Arukh*).

[1]אָמַר רַבִּי חֲנִינָא: אֵין בֶּן דָּוִד בָּא עַד שֶׁיִּתְבַּקֵּשׁ דָּג לְחוֹלֶה וְלֹא יִמָּצֵא, [2]שֶׁנֶּאֱמַר: ״אָז אַשְׁקִיעַ מֵימֵיהֶם וְנַהֲרוֹתָם כַּשֶּׁמֶן אוֹלִיךְ״. [3]וּכְתַב בַּתְרֵיהּ: ״בַּיּוֹם הַהוּא אַצְמִיחַ קֶרֶן לְבֵית יִשְׂרָאֵל״.

[4]אָמַר רַבִּי חָמָא בַּר חֲנִינָא: אֵין בֶּן דָּוִד בָּא עַד שֶׁתִּכְלֶה מַלְכוּת הַזָּלָה מִיִּשְׂרָאֵל, [5]שֶׁנֶּאֱמַר: ״וְכָרַת הַזַּלְזַלִּים בַּמַּזְמֵרוֹת״. [6]וּכְתִיב בַּתְרֵיהּ: ״בָּעֵת הַהִיא יוּבַל שַׁי לַה׳ צְבָאוֹת עַם מְמֻשָּׁךְ וּמוֹרָט״.

[7]אָמַר זְעֵירִי אָמַר רַבִּי חֲנִינָא: אֵין בֶּן דָּוִד בָּא עַד שֶׁיִּכְלוּ גַּסֵּי הָרוּחַ מִיִּשְׂרָאֵל, [8]שֶׁנֶּאֱמַר: ״כִּי אָז אָסִיר מִקִּרְבֵּךְ עַלִּיזֵי גַּאֲוָתֵךְ״. [9]וּכְתִיב: ״וְהִשְׁאַרְתִּי בְקִרְבֵּךְ עַם עָנִי וָדָל וְחָסוּ בְּשֵׁם ה׳״.

[10]אָמַר רַבִּי שִׂמְלַאי מִשּׁוּם רַבִּי אֶלְעָזָר בְּרַבִּי שִׁמְעוֹן: אֵין בֶּן דָּוִד בָּא עַד שֶׁיִּכְלוּ כָּל שׁוֹפְטִים וְשׁוֹטְרִים מִיִּשְׂרָאֵל, [11]שֶׁנֶּאֱמַר:

TRANSLATION AND COMMENTARY

אָמַר רַבִּי חֲנִינָא [1]**Rabbi Ḥanina said: The son of David will not come until** people **look for a fish** to give to **a sick person, but** none **is found** to give him, [2]**for the verse** regarding the fall of Egypt **states** (Ezekiel 32:14): **"Then will I make their waters clear; and cause their rivers to run like oil,** says the Lord God." No fish will be able to survive there. [3]**And the verse** describing what will happen **after** the fall of Egypt **states** (Ezekiel 29:21): **"On that day will I cause the horn of the house of Israel to grow"** — and the Messiah will come.

אָמַר רַבִּי חָמָא בַּר חֲנִינָא [4]**Rabbi Ḥama bar Ḥanina said: The son of David will not come until the despicable** Roman **government will be** utterly **wiped out from Israel,** [5]**for the verse states** (Isaiah 18:5): "For before the harvest, when the blossom is past, and the bud is ripening into young grapes, **he shall cut off the sprigs** [הַזַּלְזַלִּים] **with pruning hooks,** and remove and cut down the branches." Rabbi Ḥama bar Ḥanina understands the word הַזַּלְזַלִּים, translated here as "sprigs," as a reference to the despicable [הַזַּל] government of Rome. Only after that government is cut off will the final redemption come, [6]**for the verse that follows states** (Isaiah 18:7): **"In that time shall a present be brought to the Lord of hosts, by a people tall and smooth."**

אָמַר זְעֵירִי [7]**Rabbi Ze'eiri said in the name of Rabbi Ḥanina: The son of David will not come until the arrogant of spirit are** utterly **wiped out from Israel,** [8]**for the verse states** (Zephaniah 3:11): "On that day you shall not be ashamed for all your doings, in which you have transgressed against Me; **for then I will take away from your midst those who rejoice in your pride,** and you shall no more be haughty in My holy mountain." [9]**And the next verse states** (Zephaniah 3:12): **"And I will leave in your midst a poor and lowly people, and they shall trust in the name of the Lord."**

אָמַר [10]**Rabbi Simlai said in the name of Rabbi Elazar the son of Rabbi Shimon: The son of David will not come until all the judges and officers are wiped out from Israel,** and the last vestiges of Jewish self-rule disappear, [11]**for**

LITERAL TRANSLATION

[1]Rabbi Ḥanina said: The son of David will not come until fish are sought for a sick person, and not be found, [2]for it is stated: "Then will I make their waters clear; and cause their rivers to run like oil." [3]And it is written after it: "On that day will I cause the horn of the house of Israel to grow." [4]Rabbi Ḥama bar Ḥanina said: The son of David will not come until the despicable kingdom is wiped out from Israel, [5]for it is stated: "He shall cut off the sprigs with pruning hooks." [6]And it is written after it: "In that time shall a present be brought to the Lord of hosts, by a people tall and smooth."

[7]Rabbi Ze'eiri said in the name of Rabbi Ḥanina: The son of David will not come until the arrogant of spirit are wiped out from Israel, [8]for it is stated: "For then I will take from your midst those who rejoice in your pride." [9]And it is written: "And I will leave in your midst a poor and lowly people, and they shall trust in the name of the Lord."

[10]Rabbi Simlai said in the name of Rabbi Elazar the son of Rabbi Shimon: The son of David will not come until all the judges and officers are wiped out from Israel, [11]for it is stated:

RASHI

בשמן אוליך – שיהיו כולן קפויין, וכיון שהם קפויין אין דגים נמצאין בהם. **עד שתכלה מלכות הזלה** – שלא תהא להם שום שולטנות לישראל אפילו שולטנות קלה ודלה. **נטישותיו** – ענפים קטנים כלומר השרים והשופטים. **וחסו בשם השם** – כלומר שתבא להם גאולה ויחסו בצל שדי.

NOTES

מַלְכוּת הַזָּלָה **The despicable government.** Our commentary follows the Geonim, who understand this expression [מַלְכוּת הַזָּלָה] as referring to the Roman government that is despicable [זוֹלָה] and despises [מְזַלְזֶלֶת] the people of Israel. *Rashi* and *Ramah* understand the expression to mean "sovereignty of little value." The Messiah will not come until the last vestiges of sovereignty and self-rule, meager as they might be, are utterly wiped out from Israel.

שֶׁיִּכְלוּ כָּל שׁוֹפְטִים וְשׁוֹטְרִים **Until the judges and officers are wiped out.** Some understand that Rabbi Simlai means to say that the Messiah will not come until the wicked judges and officers of Israel are utterly wiped out, for their sins and wicked deeds cause the exile to continue so long (see *Maharsha*).

"וְאָשִׁיבָה יָדִי עָלַיִךְ וְאֶצְרֹף כַּבֹּר סִגָּיִךְ וגו׳...וְאָשִׁיבָה שֹׁפְטַיִךְ".
1 אָמַר עוּלָּא: אֵין יְרוּשָׁלַיִם נִפְדֵּית אֶלָּא בִּצְדָקָה, 2 שֶׁנֶּאֱמַר: "צִיּוֹן בְּמִשְׁפָּט תִּפָּדֶה וְשָׁבֶיהָ בִּצְדָקָה".
3 אָמַר רַב פַּפָּא: אִי בָּטְלִי יְהִירֵי, בָּטְלִי אַמְגוּשֵׁי. 4 אִי בָּטְלִי דַּיָּינֵי, בָּטְלִי גַזִירְפַּטֵי. 5 אִי בָּטְלִי יְהִירֵי בָּטְלִי אַמְגוּשֵׁי, 6 דִּכְתִיב: "וְאֶצְרֹף כַּבֹּר סִגָּיִךְ וְאָסִירָה כָּל בְּדִילָיִךְ". 7 וְאִי בָּטְלִי דַּיָּינֵי בָּטְלִי גַזִירְפַּטֵי, 8 דִּכְתִיב: "הֵסִיר ה׳ מִשְׁפָּטַיִךְ פִּנָּה אֹיְבֵךְ".
9 אָמַר רַבִּי יוֹחָנָן: אִם רָאִיתָ דּוֹר שֶׁמִּתְמַעֵט וְהוֹלֵךְ, חַכֵּה לוֹ, 10 שֶׁנֶּאֱמַר: "וְאֶת עַם עָנִי תּוֹשִׁיעַ וגו׳".
11 אָמַר רַבִּי יוֹחָנָן: אִם רָאִיתָ דּוֹר שֶׁצָּרוֹת רַבּוֹת בָּאוֹת עָלָיו

LITERAL TRANSLATION

"And I will turn My hand against you, and purge away your dross as with lye....And I will restore your judges."

[1] Ulla said: Jerusalem will only be redeemed with righteousness, [2] for it is stated: "Zion shall be redeemed with judgment, and those who return to her with righteousness."

[3] Rav Pappa said: When the arrogant cease to exist, the sorcerers will cease to exist. [4] When the judges cease to exist, the court officers will cease to exist. [5] When the arrogant cease to exist, the sorcerers will cease to exist, [6] for it is written: "And I will purge away your dross as with lye, and take away all your base alloy." [7] And when the judges cease to exist, the court officers will cease to exist, [8] for it is written: "The Lord has taken away your judgments, He has cast out your enemy."

[9] Rabbi Yoḥanan said: When you see a generation decline, wait for him, [10] for it is stated: "And the afflicted people You will save, etc."

[11] Rabbi Yoḥanan said: When you see a generation upon whom many troubles come

TRANSLATION AND COMMENTARY

the verses state (Isaiah 1:25-26): **"And I will turn My hand against you, and purge away your dross as with lye**, and take away all your base alloy. **And I will restore your judges as at the first,** and your counselors as at the beginning; afterwards you shall be called, The city of righteousness, a faithful city," implying that only then will the judges be restored to Israel.

אָמַר עוּלָּא [1] **Ulla said: Jerusalem will only be redeemed with righteousness,** [2] **for the verse states** (Isaiah 1:27): **"Zion shall be redeemed with judgment, and those who return to her with righteousness."**

אָמַר רַב פַּפָּא [3] **Rav Pappa said: When the arrogant** in spirit in Israel **cease to exist, the** Persian **sorcerers** who vex Israel **will** also **cease to exist.** [4] **When the** wicked Persian **judges cease to exist, the court officers** who execute the judges' verdicts **will** also **cease to exist.** [5] The Gemara explains: **When the arrogant** in spirit in Israel **cease to exist, the** Persian **sorcerers will** also **cease to exist,** [6] **for the verse states** (Isaiah 1:25): **"And I will** turn My hand against you, and **purge away your dross** [סִגָּיִךְ] **as with lye"** — those who think themselves great [סַגִּיאִין] — **"and take away all your base alloy** [בְּדִילָיִךְ]" — the Persian sorcerers who separate themselves [בְּדֵלִים] from the fear of God. [7] **And when the** wicked Persian **judges cease to exist, the court officers** who execute their verdicts **will** also **cease to exist,** [8] **for the verse states** (Zephaniah 3:15): **"The Lord has taken away your judgments"** — the judges — **"He has cast out your enemy"** — the officers of the court who execute punishment.

אָמַר רַבִּי יוֹחָנָן [9] **Rabbi Yoḥanan said: When you see a generation declining** in learning and knowledge, **wait for** the Messiah, for he is soon to come, [10] **as it is stated** (II Samuel 22:28): **"And the afflicted people You will save."**

אָמַר רַבִּי יוֹחָנָן [11] **Rabbi Yoḥanan said: When you see a generation inundated with many troubles like a river,**

LANGUAGE

גַזִירְפַּטֵי **Court officer.** This word apparently derives from the Persian *gizir-pat*, meaning "the chief police officer," "the chief emissary of a court."

RASHI

סיגיך — תערובות שבך. בדיליך — המובדלים לראשי עם. יהירי — גסי רוח מישראל. אמגושי — פרסיים מכשפין שמצערין ישראל, במסכת שבת (עה,א) פלוגתא איכא למאן דאמר אמגושי חרשי, ואיכא למאן דאמר גדופי עובדי כוכבים. גזירפטי — שופטים עובדי כוכבים השוטטין את ישראל במקלות. ואצרוף כבור סיגיך — רבים וגדולים בגסותם כשאצרוף ואסלקם ממך — אזי אסירה כל בדיליך. אמגושי — הבדלים מיראת המקום. סיגיך — כמו רב דמתרגמינן: סגי. משפטיך — כמו (צפניה ג) שופטיך. פנה אויבך — גזירפטי.

NOTES

יְהִירֵי — אַמְגוּשֵׁי, דַּיָּינֵי — גַזִירְפַּטֵי **The arrogant — the sorcerers, the judges — the court officers.** *Ramah* explains that when the arrogant in Israel cease to exist, the Persian sorcerers who oppress Israel will also cease to exist, for the sorcerers only practice their arts against Jews at the bidding of the arrogant, who are too embarrassed to act on their own and therefore employ sorcerers to act for them. So, too, when the Persian judges who issue perverted decisions cease to exist, the court officers who carry out those decisions will also cease to exist.

כַּנָּהָר, חַכֵּה לוֹ, [1]שֶׁנֶּאֱמַר: ״כִּי יָבֹא כַנָּהָר צָר וְרוּחַ ה׳ נֹסְסָה בוֹ״. [2]וּסְמִיךְ לֵיהּ: ״וּבָא לְצִיּוֹן גּוֹאֵל״.

[3]וְאָמַר רַבִּי יוֹחָנָן: אֵין בֶּן דָּוִד בָּא אֶלָּא בְּדוֹר שֶׁכּוּלּוֹ זַכַּאי אוֹ כּוּלּוֹ חַיָּיב. [4]בְּדוֹר שֶׁכּוּלּוֹ זַכַּאי, דִּכְתִיב: ״וְעַמֵּךְ כֻּלָּם צַדִּיקִים לְעוֹלָם יִירְשׁוּ אָרֶץ״. [5]בְּדוֹר שֶׁכּוּלּוֹ חַיָּיב, דִּכְתִיב: ״וַיַּרְא כִּי אֵין אִישׁ וַיִּשְׁתּוֹמֵם כִּי אֵין מַפְגִּיעַ״, [6]וּכְתִיב: ״לְמַעֲנִי אֶעֱשֶׂה״.

[7]אָמַר רַבִּי אֲלֶכְּסַנְדְּרִי: רַבִּי יְהוֹשֻׁעַ בֶּן לֵוִי רָמֵי: [8]כְּתִיב: ״בְּעִתָּהּ״, [9]וּכְתִיב: ״אֲחִישֶׁנָּה״! [10]זָכוּ — ״אֲחִישֶׁנָּה״; [11]לֹא זָכוּ — ״בְּעִתָּהּ״.

[12]אָמַר רַבִּי אֲלֶכְּסַנְדְּרִי: רַבִּי יְהוֹשֻׁעַ בֶּן לֵוִי רָמֵי: [13]כְּתִיב: ״וַאֲרוּ עִם עֲנָנֵי שְׁמַיָּא כְּבַר אֱנָשׁ

LITERAL TRANSLATION

like a river, wait for him, [1]for it is stated: "When affliction comes like a river which the wind of the Lord drives forth." [2]And juxtaposed to it is: "But to Zion a redeemer shall come."

[3]And Rabbi Yoḥanan said: The son of David will only come in a generation that is entirely guiltless or entirely liable. [4]In a generation that is entirely guiltless, for it is written: "Your people shall all be righteous; they shall inherit the land." [5]In a generation that is entirely liable, for it is written: "And He saw that there was no man, and was astonished that there was no intercessor," [6]and it is written: "For My own sake, will I do it."

[7]Rabbi Alexandri said: Rabbi Yehoshua ben Levi cast [together two parts of a verse]: [8]It is written: "In its time," [9]and it is written: "I will hasten it"! [10]If they merit — "I will hasten it"; [11]if they do not merit — "in its time."

[12]Rabbi Alexandri said: Rabbi Yehoshua ben Levi cast [together two verses]: [13]It is written: "And, behold, one like a son of man came with the clouds of heaven,"

TRANSLATION AND COMMENTARY

wait for the Messiah, for the redemption is soon to come, [1]**as the verse states** (Isaiah 59:19): "So shall they fear the name of the Lord from the west, and His glory from the rising of the sun; **when affliction comes like a river which the wind of the Lord drives forth."** [2]**And juxtaposed to** that verse **is** the verse that states (Isaiah 59:20): **"But to Zion a redeemer shall come,** and to them that turn from transgression in Jacob, says the Lord."

וְאָמַר רַבִּי יוֹחָנָן [3]**Rabbi Yoḥanan said: The son of David will only come in a generation that is** either **entirely guiltless** and worthy of the Messiah, **or entirely liable** and urgently in need of redemption. [4]The Messiah can come **in a generation that is entirely guiltless, for the verse states** (Isaiah 60:21): **"Your people also shall be all righteous; they shall inherit the land for ever,"** meaning that they will enjoy the redemption. [5]The Messiah can also come **in a generation that is entirely liable, for the verse states** (Isaiah 59:16): **"And He saw that there was no man, and was astonished that there was no intercessor;** therefore His arm brought salvation to him, and His righteousness, it sustained him." [6]**And the verse states:** (Isaiah 48:11): "For My own sake, **for My own sake, will I do it**; for how should My name be profound? And I will not give My glory to another."

אָמַר רַבִּי אֲלֶכְּסַנְדְּרִי [7]**Rabbi Alexandri said: Rabbi Yehoshua ben Levi raised the** following **contradiction** between two parts of the same verse dealing with the promise of redemption (Isaiah 60:22): "I the Lord will hasten it in its time." [8]**The verse states** that redemption will come **"in its time,"** implying that redemption will only come at its predetermined time. [9]And **that** same **verse states** that **"I will hasten it,"** implying that redemption might come before that time! [10]Rabbi Yehoshua ben Levi explained: **If** Israel **merits** it through repentance and good deeds, God will fulfill the promise, **"I will hasten it,"** and bring redemption before its appointed time. [11]But **if** Israel **does not merit** it, God will only bring redemption **"in its time."**

אָמַר רַבִּי אֲלֶכְּסַנְדְּרִי [12]**Rabbi Alexandri said: Rabbi Yehoshua ben Levi raised the** following **contradiction** between two verses dealing with the Messiah's arrival: [13]In one place, **the verses state** (Daniel 7:13-14): "I saw in the night visions, and, behold, **one like a son of man came with the clouds of heaven,** and came to

RASHI

נוססה — כמו (ישעיה י) ״כמסוס נוסס״ וכמו (שם נא) ״יאכלם סס״ רוח המקום נוקבת ומחרבת אותן עם הצרות הבאות, שאף הוא מתכוין להשמידם. יירשו ארץ — היינו גאולה. עם ענני שמיא כבר אינש אתי — במהירות.

NOTES

כּוּלּוֹ זַכַּאי אוֹ כּוּלּוֹ חַיָּיב **Entirely guiltless or entirely liable.** The *Vilna Gaon* explains that in the generation preceding the Messiah's arrival there will be no hypocrisy. People will either be entirely liable (the wicked will not be embarrassed to display their wickedness in public), or they will be entirely guiltless (the righteous of that generation will have no hope of receiving any material benefit for their righteousness, and so their sole motivation will be the sake of Heaven).

אָתֵה", [1]וּכְתִיב: "עָנִי וְרֹכֵב עַל חֲמוֹר"! [2]זָכוּ — "עִם עֲנָנֵי שְׁמַיָּא", [3]לֹא זָכוּ — "עָנִי וְרוֹכֵב עַל חֲמוֹר".

[4]אֲמַר לֵיהּ שָׁבוֹר מַלְכָּא לִשְׁמוּאֵל: "אָמְרִיתוּ, מָשִׁיחַ עַל חֲמָרָא אָתֵי, [5]אִישַׁדַּר לֵיהּ סוּסְיָא בַּרְקָא דְּאִית לִי"! [6]אֲמַר לֵיהּ: "מִי אִית לָךְ בַּר חִיוַּר גַּוְּונֵי"?

[7]רַבִּי יְהוֹשֻׁעַ בֶּן לֵוִי אַשְׁכַּח לְאֵלִיָּהוּ, דַּהֲוֵי קָיְימִי אַפִּיתְחָא דִּמְעַרְתָּא דְּרַבִּי שִׁמְעוֹן בֶּן יוֹחַאי. [8]אֲמַר לֵיהּ: "אָתֵינָא לְעָלְמָא דְּאָתֵי"? [9]אֲמַר לֵיהּ: "אִם יִרְצֶה אָדוֹן הַזֶּה". [10]אֲמַר רַבִּי יְהוֹשֻׁעַ בֶּן לֵוִי: "שְׁנַיִם רָאִיתִי וְקוֹל שְׁלֹשָׁה שָׁמַעְתִּי". [11]אֲמַר לֵיהּ: "אֵימַת אָתֵי מָשִׁיחַ"? [12]אֲמַר לֵיהּ: "זִיל שַׁיְילֵיהּ לְדִידֵיהּ". [13]"וְהֵיכָא יָתֵיב"? [14]"אַפִּיתְחָא דְּרוֹמִי". [15]"וּמַאי סִימָנֵיהּ"? [16]"יָתֵיב בֵּינֵי עֲנִיֵּי סוֹבְלֵי חֳלָאִים, [17]וְכוּלָּן שָׁרוּ וַאֲסִירִי בְּחַד זִימְנָא, [18]אִיהוּ שָׁרֵי חַד וַאֲסִיר חַד. [19]אֲמַר:

LITERAL TRANSLATION

[1]and it is written: "Humble, and riding on an ass"! [2]If they merit — "with the clouds of heaven"; [3]if they do not merit — "humble, and riding on an ass."

[4]King Shavor said to Shmuel: "You say [that] the Messiah will come on an ass. [5]I will send him the fine horse that I have." [6]He said to him: "Have you a horse of a thousand colors?"

[7]Rabbi Yehoshua ben Levi found Elijah while he was standing at the entrance to the cave of Rabbi Shimon ben Yoḥai. [8]He said to him: "Will I enter the World to Come?" [9]He said to him: "If this Master wishes." [10]Rabbi Yehoshua ben Levi said: "I saw two, and I heard the voice of three." [11]He said to him: "When will the Messiah come?" [12]He said to him: "Go ask him." [13]"And where does he sit?" [14]"At the entrance to Rome." [15]"And what is his identifying mark?" [16]"He sits among the poor, those suffering with disease, [17]and all of them untie and tie [at] one time, [18][and] he unties one and ties one. [19]He says:

TRANSLATION AND COMMENTARY

the Ancient of Days, and they brought him near before Him." [1]Elsewhere **the verse states** (Zechariah 9:9): "Rejoice greatly, O daughter of Zion; shout, O daughter of Jerusalem; behold, your king comes to you; he is just, and victorious; **humble, and riding upon an ass,** and upon a colt, the foal of an ass." [2]Rabbi Yehoshua ben Levi explained: **If** Israel **merits** it through repentance and good deeds, the Messiah will come speedily **"with the clouds of heaven."** [3]But **if** Israel **does not merit** it, the Messiah will come slowly, **"humble, and riding upon an ass."**

אֲמַר לֵיהּ [4]It was related that **King Shavor,** the ruler of Persia, once **said to Shmuel** in derision: **"You say that the Messiah will come on an ass. [5]**Perhaps **I should send him the fine horse that I have,** for surely it is beneath his dignity to come riding on an ass." [6]Shmuel **said to him: "Do you have a horse of a thousand colors** like the ass of the Messiah?"

רַבִּי יְהוֹשֻׁעַ בֶּן לֵוִי [7]It was further related that **Rabbi Yehoshua ben Levi** once **met** the Prophet **Elijah while he was standing at the entrance to Rabbi Shimon ben Yoḥai's** burial **cave.** [8]Rabbi Yehoshua ben Levi **asked** Elijah: **"Will I** merit **entering the World to Come?"** [9]Elijah **said to him: "If this Master,** the Divine Presence who is standing here with us, **wishes,** you will enter." [10]**Rabbi Yehoshua ben Levi said: "I saw two** beings, the Prophet Elijah and myself, **but I heard** also **the voice of a third** being, for the Divine Presence was standing there with us." [11]Rabbi Yehoshua ben Levi **asked** Elijah another question: **"When will the Messiah come?"** [12]Elijah **said to him: "Go ask** the Messiah **himself."** [13]Rabbi Yehoshua ben Levi continued: **"And where does** the Messiah **sit?"** [14]Elijah explained: "The Messiah sits **at the entrance to** the city of **Rome."** [15]Rabbi Yehoshua ben Levi posed one final question: **"And what is** the Messiah's **identifying mark?** [16]Elijah answered: "You will find the Messiah **sitting among the poor lepers.** [17]**All** the other lepers **untie** their bandages, dress their leprous scabs, **and** then **retie** their bandages **at one time.** [18]**But** the Messiah **unties one** bandage, dresses the scab, **reties the one** bandage, and only then does he proceed to the next bandage, [19]for

RASHI

וכתיב עני ורוכב על החמור — כעני הבא על חמורו בעצלות. **סוסי ברקא** — סוס מסורק ומכוון ונאה שיש לי, דגנאי הוא שיבא על חמור, מלגלג היה. לישנא אחרינא: סוסיא בדקא — סוס בדוק לרוץ. **בר חיור גווני** — כלום יש לך סוס בר מאה גוונין — שחמור שלו כן הוא, במלתא בעלמא דחייה. חיור — מאה בלשון פרסי. **האדון הזה** — שכינה היתה עמהם. **קול שלשה** — דשכינה הוה בהדייהו. **לדידיה** — למשיח. **בפתחא** (דקרתא) — נראה למורי: לא בפתח העיר ממש, אלא גן עדן הוא כנגד כל העולם, וקאמר ליה דבאותו צד של גן עדן שכנגד פתח העיר, משיח שרוי. **סובלי חלאים** — מנוגעים, והוא נמי מנוגע דכתיב (ישעיה נג) "והוא מחולל מפשעינו" וכתיב (שם) "חליינו הוא נשא". **כולהו** — מי שיש לו ארבע וחמש נגעים. **אסרי להו ושרו בחדא זימנא** — מתירין כל נגעתן ביחד ומקנחין אותן, וחוזרין וקושרין אותן. **ואיהו** — משיח. **שרי חד** — נגע ומקנחו וקושרו, ואחר כך מתיר האחר ועושה כן ואינו מתיר שני נגעים יחד, דסבר, אי בעי לי לצאת וליגאל את ישראל לא איתעכב כדי קשירת שני נגעים.

PEOPLE

שָׁבוֹר מַלְכָּא **King Shavor.**

A coin with the portrait of Shapur I.

The "King Shavor" mentioned here was probably Shapur I (reigned 241-272 C.E.), the son of the founder of the Sassanid dynasty. He extended the boundaries of the Persian Empire as far as Syria. He fought against the Romans and won large tracts of Roman territory (he even managed to take the Roman Emperor Valerian into captivity). However, not all of his battles against the Romans were successful.
Unlike most other members of the Sassanid dynasty, Shapur I had his prisoners of war build many important cities and dams. With respect to his domestic policies, he seems to have been tolerant toward various religions and to have been interested in the Jews. He had friendly relations with the Amora Shmuel.

TRANSLATION AND COMMENTARY

he says to himself: **'Perhaps I will be needed** to bring the redemption, and so **I should not** do anything now that will **delay** me.'" [1]Rabbi Yehoshua ben Levi **went to** Rome, located the Messiah, and **said to him: "Peace be with you, my master, and my teacher."** [2]The Messiah **answered him: "Peace be with you, O son of Levi."** [3]Rabbi Yehoshua ben Levi **said to him: "When will Master come** and bring the redemption?" [4]The Messiah **said to him:** "I will be coming **today."** [5]Rabbi Yehoshua ben Levi **went** back **to** the Prophet **Elijah.** [6]Elijah **asked him: "What did** the Messiah **say to you?"** [7]Rabbi Yehoshua ben Levi **said to him: "Peace be with you, O son of Levi."** [8]Elijah **said to him:** "With those words, the Messiah **promised you and your father the World to Come."** [9]Rabbi Yehoshua ben Levi **said** to Elijah: "The Messiah **lied to me,** [10]**for he said to me: 'Today I am coming,'** and we see that **he has** still **not come."** [11]Elijah **said to him: "He** meant to **say to you as follows,** citing a verse from Psalms 95:7: 'For He is our God; and we are the people of His pasture, and the flock of His hand; [12]**today if you will only heed His voice.'"**

שָׁאֲלוּ [13]**Rabbi Yose ben Kisma was** once **asked by his disciples: "When will the son of David come?"** [14]**He said: "I am afraid** to answer you, **lest you ask me** to produce **a sign** as proof of what I say." [15]His disciples **said to him: "We will not ask you** to produce **a sign."** [16]**He said to them: "When this gate** in the city of Rome **falls, and is rebuilt, and** then **falls** once again, **and is rebuilt** once again, **and** then **falls** for a third time, **and they do not manage to rebuild it** a third time **before the son of David** has **come."** [17]His disciples **said to him: "Our master, give us a sign** to confirm what you have just told us." [18]Rabbi Yose ben Kisma **said to them: "Did you not say to me that you would not ask me** to produce **a sign?"** [19]His disciples **said to him:** "We remember what we said, **but even so,** please give us a sign." [20]Rabbi Yose the son of Kisma **said to them: "If it is as** I said, **the water in the Banyas cave will turn to blood."** [21]**And** that water did indeed **turn to blood.** [22]**As he was dying,** Rabbi

דִּילְמָא מִבָּעֵינָא, דְּלָא אִיעַכַּב״. [1]אֲזַל לְגַבֵּיהּ. אֲמַר לֵיהּ: ״שָׁלוֹם עָלֶיךָ רַבִּי וּמוֹרִי״! [2]אֲמַר לֵיהּ: ״שָׁלוֹם עָלֶיךָ בַּר לִיוָאִי״. [3]אֲמַר לֵיהּ: ״לְאֵימַת אָתֵי מָר״? [4]אֲמַר לֵיהּ: ״הַיּוֹם״. [5]אֲתָא לְגַבֵּי אֵלִיָּהוּ. [6]אֲמַר לֵיהּ: ״מַאי אֲמַר לָךְ״? [7]אֲמַר לֵיהּ: ״שָׁלוֹם עָלֶיךָ בַּר לִיוָאִי״. [8]אֲמַר לֵיהּ: ״אַבְטַחָךְ לָךְ וְלַאֲבוּךְ לְעָלְמָא דְּאָתֵי״. [9]אֲמַר לֵיהּ: ״שַׁקּוֹרֵי קָא שַׁקֵּר בִּי, [10]דַּאֲמַר לִי: ׳הַיּוֹם אָתֵינָא׳, וְלָא אֲתָא״! [11]אֲמַר לֵיהּ: ״הָכִי אֲמַר לָךְ: [12]׳הַיּוֹם אִם בְּקֹלוֹ תִשְׁמָעוּ׳ ״.

[13]שָׁאֲלוּ תַּלְמִידָיו אֶת רַבִּי יוֹסֵי בֶּן קִיסְמָא: ״אֵימָתַי בֶּן דָּוִד בָּא״? [14]אָמַר: ״מִתְיָירֵא אֲנִי שֶׁמָּא תְּבַקְשׁוּ מִמֶּנִּי אוֹת״. [15]אָמְרוּ לוֹ: ״אֵין אָנוּ מְבַקְשִׁין מִמְּךָ אוֹת״. [16]אָמַר לָהֶם: ״לִכְשֶׁיִּפּוֹל הַשַּׁעַר הַזֶּה וְיִבָּנֶה, וְיִפּוֹל, וְיִבָּנֶה, וְיִפּוֹל, וְאֵין מַסְפִּיקִין לִבְנוֹתוֹ עַד שֶׁבֶּן דָּוִד בָּא״. [17]אָמְרוּ לוֹ: ״רַבֵּינוּ, תֵּן לָנוּ אוֹת״! [18]אָמַר לָהֶם: וְלֹא כָּךְ אֲמַרְתֶּם לִי שֶׁאֵין אַתֶּם מְבַקְשִׁין מִמֶּנִּי אוֹת״? [19]אָמְרוּ לוֹ: ״וְאַף עַל פִּי כֵן״. [20]אָמַר לָהֶם: ״אִם כָּךְ, יֵהָפְכוּ מֵי מְעָרַת פַּמְיָיס לְדָם״. [21]וְנֶהֶפְכוּ לְדָם. [22]בִּשְׁעַת פְּטִירָתוֹ, אָמַר

LITERAL TRANSLATION

Perhaps I will be needed, [and] I should not be delayed." [1]He went to him. He said to him: "Peace be with you, my master, and my teacher." [2]He said to him: "Peace be with you, O son of Levi." [3]He said to him: "When will Master come?" [4]He said to him: "Today." [5]He came to Elijah. [6]He said to him: "What did he say to you?" [7]He said to him: "Peace be with you, O son of Levi." [8]He said to him: "He promised you and your father the World to Come." [9]He said to him: "He lied to me, [10]for he said to me: 'Today I am coming,' and he has not come." [11]He said to him: "Thus, he said to you: [12]'Today if you will only heed His voice.'"

[13]Rabbi Yose ben Kisma was asked by his disciples: "When will the son of David come?" [14]He said: "I am afraid that you will ask me for a sign." [15]They said to him: "We will not ask you for a sign." [16]He said to them: "When this gate falls and is rebuilt, and falls, and is rebuilt, and falls, and they do not manage to rebuild it before the son of David comes." [17]They said to him: "Our master, give us a sign." [18]He said to them: "Did you not say to me that you would not ask me for a sign?" [19]They said to him: "But even so." [20]He said to them: "If so, the water in the Banyas cave will turn to blood." [21]And it turned to blood. [22]At the time of his death, he said

RASHI

אמר ליה — רבי יהושע למשיח: לאימת אתי מר אמר ליה: היום. אבטחך לך ולאביך לעולם הבא — דאי לאו צדיקים גמורין אתם לא הוה יהיב לך שלמא, ולא הוה מדכר שמיה דאבוך. היום אם בקולו — של הקדוש ברוך הוא תשמעו. השער הזה — של עיר רומי, שבעיר רומי היה אותו שער. ואין מספיקין לבנותו — פעם שלישית. מי פמייס — שירדן נובע ממנו, כדתניא בבכורות (נה, א): ירדן יוצא ממערת

לָהֶן: ״הַעֲמִיקוּ לִי אֲרוֹנִי, [98B] 1שֶׁאֵין כָּל דֶּקֶל וְדֶקֶל שֶׁבְּבָבֶל שֶׁאֵין סוּס שֶׁל פַּרְסִיִּים נִקְשָׁר בּוֹ, 2וְאֵין לְךָ כָּל אָרוֹן וְאָרוֹן שֶׁבְּאֶרֶץ יִשְׂרָאֵל שֶׁאֵין סוּס מָדִי אוֹכֵל בּוֹ תֶּבֶן״.

3אָמַר רַב: אֵין בֶּן דָּוִד בָּא עַד שֶׁתִּתְפַּשֵּׁט הַמַּלְכוּת הָרְשָׁעָה עַל יִשְׂרָאֵל תִּשְׁעָה חֳדָשִׁים, 4שֶׁנֶּאֱמַר: ״לָכֵן יִתְּנֵם עַד עֵת יוֹלֵדָה יָלָדָה וְיֶתֶר אֶחָיו יְשׁוּבוּן עַל בְּנֵי יִשְׂרָאֵל״.

5אָמַר עוּלָּא: יֵיתֵי וְלָא אִיחְמִינֵיהּ. 6וְכֵן אָמַר [רַבָּה]: יֵיתֵי וְלָא אִיחְמִינֵיהּ. 7רַב יוֹסֵף אָמַר: יֵיתֵי, וְאִזְכֵּי דְּאֵיתִיב בְּטוּלָּא דְּכוּפִיתָא דַּחֲמָרֵיהּ.

8אֲמַר לֵיהּ אַבַּיֵּי לְרַבָּה: מַאי טַעְמָא? 9אִילֵימָא מִשּׁוּם חֶבְלוֹ שֶׁל מָשִׁיחַ — 10וְהָתַנְיָא: ״שָׁאֲלוּ תַּלְמִידָיו אֶת רַבִּי אֶלְעָזָר: מַה יַּעֲשֶׂה אָדָם וְיִנָּצֵל מֵחֶבְלוֹ שֶׁל מָשִׁיחַ? 11יַעֲסוֹק

LITERAL TRANSLATION

to them: "Set my coffin deep, [98B] [1]for there is no date-palm in Babylonia to which a horse of the Persians is not tied, [2]and there is no coffin in Eretz Israel out of which a horse of the Medes does not eat straw."

[3]Rav said: The son of David will not come until the wicked kingdom has spread over Israel for nine months, [4]for it is stated: "Therefore, will he give them, until the time when the woman in labor has given birth; then the remnant of his brethren shall return to the Children of Israel."

[5]Ulla said: Let him come, and I not see him. [6]And similarly Rabbah said: Let him come, and I not see him. [7]Rav Yosef said: Let him come, and let me be worthy to sit in the shadow of the dung of his ass.

[8]Abaye said to Rabbah: What is the reason? [9]If you say on account of the sufferings of the Messiah — [10]surely it was taught: "Rabbi Elazar's disciples asked him: What can a person do to save himself from the sufferings of the Messiah? [11]Let him engage

TRANSLATION AND COMMENTARY

Yose ben Kisma **said to** his disciples: "When you bury me, **set my coffin** very **deep** in the ground, [98B] [1]**for there is no date-palm in** all of **Babylonia to which a horse belonging to the Persians will not be tied,** as the Persian army will conquer all of Babylonia, and their soldiers and horses will be spread out all across the land, [2]**and there is no coffin in Eretz Israel out of which a horse belonging to the Medes will not eat straw,** for the Medes will disinter all the coffins in the country and use them as feeding troughs for their animals."

אָמַר רַב [3]**Rav said: The son of David will not come until the wicked kingdom** of Rome **has spread for nine months over** the whole world across which **Israel** is scattered, [4]**for the verse states** (Michah 5:2): **"Therefore, will he give them up, until the time when the woman in labor has given birth then the remnant of his brethren shall return to the Children of Israel."**

אָמַר עוּלָּא [5]**Ulla said:** Let the Messiah **come, but** let **me not see him,** for I fear the pain and suffering that will precede his arrival. [6]**And similarly Rabbah said: Let** the Messiah **come, but** let **me not see him.** [7]**Rav Yosef** adopted a different approach and **said:** Let the Messiah **come, and let me be worthy to sit in the shadow of the dung of his ass.**

אָמַר לֵיהּ [8]**Abaye said to Rabbah: What is the reason** that you prefer not to be there when the Messiah comes? [9]**If you say** that you do not wish to be there **on account of the sufferings** before the advent **of the Messiah,** you have nothing to fear, [10]for **surely it was taught** in a Baraita: **"Rabbi Elazar's disciples asked him: What can a person do to save himself from the sufferings** before the advent **of the Messiah?** [11]And Rabbi Elazar explained: **Let him**

RASHI

העמיקו ארוני — עשו לי קבר בקרקע עמוק. **שאין סוס מדי אוכל בו תבן** — שמוציאין הארונות חוץ לקרקע ועושין מהן אבוסים במלחמת גוג ומגוג. **שאין כל דקל וכו׳** — כלומר עתידין פרס ומדי לבא על בבל וללכדה ונתמלאה כל ארץ בבל חיילות פרסיים וסוסיהם, ומשם באים לארץ ישראל ולוכדים אותה. **עד שתפשוט מלכות הרשעה על ישראל תשעה חדשים שנאמר ״לכן יתנם לישראל עד עת יולדה ילדה״** — היינו תשעה חדשים כדמתרגמינן ״בכן יתמסרון כעידן דילדתא למילד״, וכתיב (מיכה ה) ״ועמד ורעה בעוז ה׳ וגו׳ וישבו כי עתה יגדל״ ומתרגמינן ״ויתיבון מביני גלוותהון״. **על בני ישראל** — היינו כל העולם שישראל מפוזרים בו. **ייתי** — משיח ולא אחמיניה. **בטולא דכופיתא דחמריה** — בצל הרעי של חמורו, כלומר אפילו בכך אני רוצה ובלבד שאראנו. **כופיתא** = רעי, כמו רמא כופתא וסכר ירדנא, בבבא בתרא (עג,ב). **מאי טעמא** — אמר לא אחמייה. **חבלו של משיח** — גורלו, ולקמן בעי מאי היא, לישנא אחרינא: חבלו — פחדים וחבלים שיהיו בימיו מחיל האומות.

NOTES

טוּלָּא דְּכוּפִיתָא **The shadow of the dung.** Rav Yosef's statement has been understood as intimating that even if someone is not able to reach the spiritual level of the Messianic age, he should nevertheless strive to attach himself to something related to the material — a play on the words חֲמוֹר, "ass," and חֹמֶר, "material" — aspects of that period (*Netzaḥ Yisrael*).

בַּתּוֹרָה וּבִגְמִילוּת חֲסָדִים״. [1]וּמָר — הָא תּוֹרָה, וְהָא גְּמִילוּת חֲסָדִים!

[2]אֲמַר לֵיהּ: שֶׁמָּא יִגְרוֹם הַחֵטְא, כִּדְרַבִּי יַעֲקֹב בַּר אִידִי. [3]דְּרַבִּי יַעֲקֹב בַּר אִידִי רָמֵי: [4]כְּתִיב: ״וְהִנֵּה אָנֹכִי עִמָּךְ וּשְׁמַרְתִּיךָ בְּכֹל אֲשֶׁר תֵּלֵךְ״. [5]וּכְתִיב: ״וַיִּירָא יַעֲקֹב מְאֹד וַיֵּצֶר לוֹ״. [6]שֶׁהָיָה מִתְיָירֵא שֶׁמָּא יִגְרוֹם הַחֵטְא. [7]כִּדְתַנְיָא: ״׳עַד יַעֲבֹר עַמְּךָ ה׳׳ — [8]זוֹ בִּיאָה רִאשׁוֹנָה; ׳עַד יַעֲבֹר עַם זוּ קָנִיתָ׳ — [9]זוֹ בִּיאָה שְׁנִיָּה. [10]אֱמוֹר מֵעַתָּה: רְאוּיִים הָיוּ יִשְׂרָאֵל לַעֲשׂוֹת לָהֶם נֵס בְּבִיאָה שְׁנִיָּה כְּבִיאָה רִאשׁוֹנָה, אֶלָּא שֶׁגָּרַם הַחֵטְא״.

[11]וְכֵן אֲמַר רַבִּי יוֹחָנָן: יֵיתֵי וְלָא אִיחְמִינֵיהּ. [12]אֲמַר לֵיהּ רֵישׁ לָקִישׁ: מַאי טַעְמָא? [13]אִילֵימָא מִשּׁוּם דִּכְתִיב: ״כַּאֲשֶׁר יָנוּס אִישׁ מִפְּנֵי הָאֲרִי וּפְגָעוֹ הַדֹּב [וּבָא הַבַּיִת] וְסָמַךְ יָדוֹ עַל הַקִּיר וּנְשָׁכוֹ הַנָּחָשׁ״ — [14]בֹּא וְאַרְאֲךָ דּוּגְמָתוֹ בָּעוֹלָם הַזֶּה: בִּזְמַן שֶׁאָדָם יוֹצֵא לַשָּׂדֶה וּפָגַע בּוֹ סַנְטָר, דּוֹמֶה כְּמִי שֶׁפָּגַע בּוֹ אֲרִי. [15]נִכְנַס לָעִיר פָּגַע בּוֹ גַּבַּאי,

LITERAL TRANSLATION

in the Torah and deeds of charity." [1]And Master — here is Torah, and here are deeds of charity!

[2]He said to him: Lest sin be a cause, like that [teaching] of Rabbi Ya'akov bar Idi. [3]For Rabbi Ya'akov bar Idi cast [together two verses]: [4]It is written: "And, behold, I am with you, and will keep you in all places to which you go." [5]And it is written: "Then Jacob was greatly afraid and distressed." [6]He was afraid lest sin be a cause. [7]As it was taught: "'Until Your people pass over, O Lord' — [8]this is the first coming; 'until Your people pass over, whom You have acquired' — [9]this is the second coming. [10]Say from now: [the people of] Israel were worthy of having a miracle performed for them in their second coming as in their first coming, but sin was a cause."

[11]And similarly Rabbi Yoḥanan said: Let him come, and I not see him. [12]Resh Lakish said to him: What is the reason? [13]If you say because it is written: "As when a man flees from a lion, and a bear meets him; or went into the house, and leaned his arm on the wall, and a snake bit him" — [14]come and I will show you its example in this world: When a person goes out to the field, and a guardsman meets him, it seems to him as if a lion met him. [15][When] he enters the city, [and] a tax-collector meets him,

TRANSLATION AND COMMENTARY

engage in the study of **Torah and** the performance of **charitable deeds."** [1]**And** you, **Master,** have a wealth of **Torah and charitable deeds** in your hands!

אֲמַר לֵיהּ [2]Rabbah **said to** Abaye: I am afraid **lest sin** undo the merits of my Torah study and good deeds. This is **like** what **Rabbi Ya'akov bar Idi** said, [3]**for Rabbi Ya'akov bar Idi raised the** following **contradiction:** [4]In one place, **the verse states** that God promised Jacob (Genesis 28:15): **"And, behold, I am with you, and will keep you in all places to which you go."** [5]**And** elsewhere **the verse states** (Genesis 32:8): **"Then Jacob was greatly afraid and distressed."** If God promised Jacob that He would remain with him, why was he afraid? [6]Rabbi Ya'akov bar Idi explains: Jacob **was afraid lest** his **sins cause** that promise to be canceled. [7]**As it was taught** in a Baraita regarding the verse (Exodus 15:16): "Until Your people pass over, O Lord; until Your people pass over, whom You have acquired": "The words, **'until Your people pass over, O Lord,'** [8]allude to Israel's **first entry** into the Land of Israel in the days of Joshua; and the words, **'until Your people pass over, whom You have acquired,'** [9]allude to their **second entry** into the Land of Israel in the days of Ezra. [10]**Infer from this** that the people of **Israel were** worthy of having **miracles performed for them** during **their second entry** into the Land of Israel, just **as** miracles were performed for them during **their first entry** into the land, **but** their **sins caused** those miracles not to be performed."

וְכֵן אֲמַר [11]**And similarly Rabbi Yoḥanan said:** Let the Messiah **come, but** let **me not see him,** for I do not wish to suffer the afflictions preceding his arrival. [12]**Resh Lakish said to him: What is the reason** for that declaration? [13]**If you say** that you do not wish to be there, **because the verse** describing that period **states** (Amos 5:19): **"As when a man flees from a lion, and a bear meets him; or went into the house, and leaned his arm on the wall, and a snake bit him"** — [14]**come and I will show you an example** of such troubles **in this world: When a person goes out to** his **field, and a guardsman meets him,** and demands a payment from him, **it seems to him as if a lion had met him.** [15]**When he** then **returns to the city, and a tax-collector meets him,** and demands additional payments, **it seems**

RASHI

לעשות להם נס — לעלות בזרוע על כרחם של מלכי פרס. **בביאה שניה** — בימי עזרא כביאה ראשונה בימי יהושע, מדהקישן הכתוב. **מאי טעמא** — איזו צרה באה בארץ בימיו שאתה אומר לא אחמיניה. **סנטר** — מפרש בבבא בתרא (סח,א) בר מחוזנייתא, שיודע מיצרי השדות וגבוליהן, עד כאן של פלוני מכאן ואילך של פלוני, ובידו לרבות לאחד ולמעט לאחר, וכשפוגעו אותו סנטר רוצה למדוד שדותיו לקצר מיצרי השדות, ודומה כמי שפגע בו ארי. **גבאי** — גובה מס המלך.

LANGUAGE

סַנְטָר Guardsman. Some commentators maintain that this is derived from the Hebrew root נטר, meaning "to guard." Other scholars believe that it derives from the Greek συντηρέω, *syntireo*, meaning "to guard." Others claim that it comes from the Latin *saltarius* (with an "l" substituted for an "n"), meaning "a watchman over fields."

דּוֹמֶה כְּמִי שֶׁפְּגָעוֹ דֹּב. [1]נִכְנַס לְבֵיתוֹ וּמָצָא בָּנָיו וּבְנוֹתָיו מוּטָּלִין בְּרָעָב, דּוֹמֶה כְּמִי שֶׁנְּשָׁכוֹ נָחָשׁ.

[2]אֶלָּא מִשּׁוּם דִּכְתִיב: ״שַׁאֲלוּ נָא, וּרְאוּ אִם יֹלֵד זָכָר מַדּוּעַ רָאִיתִי כָל גֶּבֶר יָדָיו עַל חֲלָצָיו כַּיּוֹלֵדָה וְנֶהֶפְכוּ כָל פָּנִים לְיֵרָקוֹן״. [3]מַאי ״רָאִיתִי כָל גֶּבֶר״? [4]אָמַר רָבָא בַּר יִצְחָק אָמַר רַב: מִי שֶׁכָּל גְּבוּרָה שֶׁלּוֹ. [5]וּמַאי ״וְנֶהֶפְכוּ כָל פָּנִים לְיֵרָקוֹן״? [6]אָמַר רַבִּי יוֹחָנָן: פָּמַלְיָא שֶׁל מַעְלָה וּפָמַלְיָא שֶׁל מַטָּה. [7]בְּשָׁעָה שֶׁאָמַר הַקָּדוֹשׁ בָּרוּךְ הוּא: הַלָּלוּ מַעֲשֵׂה יָדַי וְהַלָּלוּ מַעֲשֵׂה יָדַי — [8]הֵיאַךְ אֲאַבֵּד אֵלּוּ מִפְּנֵי אֵלּוּ?

[9]אָמַר רַב פַּפָּא, הַיְינוּ דְּאָמְרִי אֱינָשֵׁי: [10]רָהֵיט וְנָפֵל תּוֹרָא וְאָזֵיל וְשָׁדֵי לֵיהּ סוּסְיָא בְּאוּרְיֵיהּ.

LITERAL TRANSLATION

it seems to him as if a bear met him. [1][When] he enters his house, and he finds his sons and daughters prostrate with hunger, it seems as if a snake bit him.

[2]Rather, because it is written: "Ask now, and see whether a man gives birth; why, then, do I see every man with his hands on his loins, as a woman in labor, and all faces are turned green?" [3]What is "I see every man"? [4]Rava bar Yitzḥak said in the name of Rav: He who all might is His. [5]What is "and all faces are turned green"? [6]Rabbi Yoḥanan said: The heavenly company and the worldly company. [7]When the Holy One, blessed be He, said: These are My handiwork, and these are My handiwork — [8]how can I destroy these on account of these?

[9]Rav Pappa said: This is what people say: [10]An ox ran and fell, and [its owner] went and stood a horse at its trough.

TRANSLATION AND COMMENTARY

to him as if a bear had met him. [1]**When he** then **enters his house, and finds his sons and daughters prostrate with hunger, it seems to him as if a snake had bit him.** Thus, you see that even now one trouble follows upon another.

אֶלָּא [2]Rabbi Yoḥanan said to Resh Lakish: I prefer not to be there when the Messiah comes, **because the verse states:** (Jeremiah 30:6): **"Ask now, and see whether a man gives birth; why, then, do I see every man with his hands on his loins, as a woman in labor, and all faces are turned green?"** [3]The Gemara asks: **What is** the meaning of the words, **"I see every man** [כָל גֶּבֶר]"? [4]**Rava bar Yitzḥak said in the name of Rav:** This is an allusion to **Him who all might** [כָּל גְּבוּרָה] **is His.** God Himself will be in great distress, as a woman in labor, when He has to strike the other nations in order to deliver Israel. [5]**What is** the meaning of the words, **"and all faces are turned green"?** [6]**Rabbi Yoḥanan said:** This is an allusion to **the heavenly company** — the angels — **and the worldly company** — the people of Israel. [7]Both the angels and the people of Israel will be in great distress and their faces will turn green **when the Holy One, blessed be He, says:** The nations of the world **are My handiwork, and** the people of Israel **are My handiwork.** [8]**How,** then, **can I destroy** the nations of the world **on account of** the people of Israel? Thus, Rabbi Yoḥanan feared the period before the advent of the Messiah, for he saw it as a time when it would appear as if God no longer distinguished between the people of Israel and the other nations of the world.

אָמַר רַב פַּפָּא [9]**Rav Pappa said: This is** the meaning of **the popular adage:** [10]**When an ox runs and falls,** and its owner reluctantly **goes and stands a horse at its trough,** even though the horse is not as strong as the ox. But when the ox recovers, its owner has difficulty removing the horse and restoring the ox to its former place. So, too, when the people of Israel sinned, the Holy One, blessed be He, reluctantly transferred their greatness to the nations of the world. But when Israel repents and God sends the Messiah to deliver them, it will be difficult for Him to destroy the nations and restore the people of Israel to their former greatness.

RASHI

מי שכל הגבורה שלו — הקדוש ברוך הוא מצטער בעצמו כיולדה ואומר בשעה שמעביר העובדי כוכבים מפני ישראל: היאך אאביד אלו מפני אלו. **פמליא של מעלה ושל מטה** — מלאכים וישראל, אפילו הגרים לא גרסינן. **רהיט ונפיל תורא ואזיל ושדי סוסיא באורייה** — כשרץ השור ונפל מעמידין סוס במקומו באבוסו מה שלא היה רוצה לעשות קודם מפלתו של שור, שהיה חביב עליו שורו ביותר, וכשמתרפא השור היום או למחר ממפלתו קשה לו להוציא סוסו מפני השור לאחר שהעמידו שם, כך הקדוש ברוך הוא כיון שראה מפלתן של ישראל נותן גדולתו לעובדי כוכבים, וכשחוזרים ישראל בתשובה ונגאלין קשה לו לאבד עובדי כוכבים מפני ישראל. **אורייה** — כמו (מלכים א ה) ״ארוות סוסים״.

NOTES

מִי שֶׁכָּל גְּבוּרָה שֶׁלּוֹ He who all the might is His. Our commentary follows *Rashi,* who understands this expression as an allusion to God. *Ramah* utterly rejects this interpretation, and suggests instead that the verse means that in the period before the Messiah, even the mightiest among men will stand with his hands on his loins, as a woman in labor.

רָהֵיט וְנָפֵל תּוֹרָא If an ox ran and fell. *Ramah* understands the popular adage differently: Even when an ox is so tired that it falls while running, it is still powerful enough to collide with a horse and send it flying to its trough.

BACKGROUND

חִילָּק וּבִילָּק **Ḥilak and Bilak.** The Rishonim were unsure of the meaning of these names, which appear elsewhere in the Talmud as well (see *Rashi* here). According to a Geonic tradition, Ḥilak and Bilak were two violent good-for-nothings who were infamous in their generation. So that when the Sages of that generation wished to refer to worthless people, it mentioned those names.

TRANSLATION AND COMMENTARY

אָמַר רַב גִּידֵּל [1]**Rav Gidel said in the name of Rav: In the future,** the people of **Israel will enjoy** plenty during **the years of the Messiah.**

אָמַר רַב יוֹסֵף [2]**Rav Yosef said:** Surely, **this is obvious!** [3]**Rather,** if not the people of Israel, then **who** else **should enjoy** the Messianic period? [4]**Should Ḥilak and Bilak** (two proverbial fictitious names) **enjoy it?**

לְאַפּוֹקֵי [5]The Gemara answers: As obvious as Rav's statement may appear, it was necessary in order **to exclude** the position **of Rabbi Hillel, who said:** [6]**There will be no Messiah** for the people of **Israel, for they already enjoyed him in the days of Ḥezekiah.** Rav said that Israel will enjoy the years of the Messiah, in order to counter Rabbi Hillel, who claimed that all the prophecies regarding the Messiah were fulfilled in King Ḥezekiah.

אָמַר רַב [7]**Rav said: The world was only created for the sake of David,** King of Israel, who would sing psalms of praise to God. [8]**Shmuel said:** The world was only created **for the sake of Moses,** who would receive the Torah at Mount Sinai. [9]**And Rabbi Yoḥanan said:** The world was only created **for the sake of the Messiah,** who will bring the redemption.

מַה שְּׁמוֹ [10]The Gemara asks: **What is** the Messiah's **name?** [11]**A Sage of the School of Rabbi Shela said:** The Messiah's **name is Shilo** (a play on the name Shelah), [12]**as the verse states** (Genesis 49:10): **"Until Shilo comes."** [13]**A Sage of the School of Rabbi Yannai said:** The Messiah's **name is Yinon** (a play on the name Yannai), [14]**as the verse states** (Psalms 72:17): **"May his name endure forever; may his name continue** [*yinon*] **as long as the sun;** and may men bless themselves by him," which may also be understood as saying: His [= the Messiah's] name is Yinon from the beginning of time. [15]**A Sage of the School of Ḥaninah said:** The Messiah's **name is Ḥaninah,**

[1]אָמַר רַב גִּידֵּל אָמַר רַב: עֲתִידִין יִשְׂרָאֵל דְּאָכְלִי שְׁנֵי מָשִׁיחַ. [2]אָמַר רַב יוֹסֵף: פְּשִׁיטָא! [3]וְאֶלָּא מַאן אָכֵיל לְהוּ? [4]חִילָּק וּבִילָּק אָכְלֵי לְהוּ? [5]לְאַפּוֹקֵי מִדְּרַבִּי הִילֵּל, דְּאָמַר: [6]אֵין מָשִׁיחַ לְיִשְׂרָאֵל, שֶׁכְּבָר אֲכָלוּהוּ בִּימֵי חִזְקִיָּה. [7]אָמַר רַב: לֹא אִבְרֵי עָלְמָא אֶלָּא לְדָוִד. [8]וּשְׁמוּאֵל אָמַר: לְמֹשֶׁה. [9]וְרַבִּי יוֹחָנָן אָמַר: לַמָּשִׁיחַ. [10]מַה שְּׁמוֹ? [11]דְּבֵי רַבִּי שֵׁילָא אָמְרִי: שִׁילֹה שְׁמוֹ, [12]שֶׁנֶּאֱמַר: "עַד כִּי יָבֹא שִׁילֹה". [13]דְּבֵי רַבִּי יַנַּאי אָמְרִי: יִנּוֹן שְׁמוֹ, [14]שֶׁנֶּאֱמַר: "יְהִי שְׁמוֹ לְעוֹלָם לִפְנֵי שֶׁמֶשׁ יִנּוֹן שְׁמוֹ". [15]דְּבֵי רַבִּי חֲנִינָה אָמַר: חֲנִינָה שְׁמוֹ,

LITERAL TRANSLATION

[1]Rav Gidel said in the name of Rav: In the future Israel will enjoy [lit., "eat"] the years of the Messiah. [2]Rav Yosef said: It is obvious! [3]Rather, who should enjoy [lit., "eat"] them? [4]Should Ḥilak and Bilak enjoy [lit., "eat"] them?

[5]To exclude that of Rabbi Hillel, who said: [6]There is no Messiah for Israel, for they already enjoyed [lit., "ate"] him in the days of Ḥezekiah.

[7]Rav said: The world was only created for [the sake of] David. [8]And Shmuel said: For [the sake of] Moses. [9]And Rabbi Yoḥanan said: For [the sake of] the Messiah.

[10]What is his name? [11][A Sage] of the School of Rabbi Shela said: His name is Shilo, [12]as it is stated: "Until Shilo comes." [13][A Sage] of the School of Rabbi Yannai said: His name is Yinon, [14]as it is stated: "May his name endure forever; may his name continue [*yinon*] as long as the sun." [15][A Sage] of the School of Ḥaninah said: His name is Ḥaninah,

RASHI

דאבלי שני משיח — שובע שיהיה באותן הימים לישראל יהיה. **אלא חילק ובילק אבלי להו** — כך היו רגילין לומר, כאדם שאומר "וכי שדים ושדות יאכלוהו"? ובמסכת חולין (יט,א): לא חילק ידענא ולא בילק ידענא, ולי נראה דמשמעות לשון חילק ובילק לשון חורבה, כמו בוקה ומבוקה ומבולקה (נחום ב), ואמרינן בחולין (שם) לא חילק — דרבנן דמצריכין לחלק הסימן, שמצריכין לחלק כל הטבעת ולשייר על פני כולו, ולא בילק — לר׳ יוסי, שמחריב הסימן, שחותך קצת בתוך הטבעת והשאר חוץ לטבעת, ונראה למורי דאין לו משמעות לא הכא ולא התם, לישנא אחרינא: חילק ובילק — שני דייני סדום שהיו שמותיהן כך. **אין משיח לישראל** — שחזקיה היה משיח ועליו נאמרו כל הנבואות "אצמיח קרן לבית ישראל ועמד ורעה בעוז ה׳". **אלא לדוד** — בזכות דוד שהיה עתיד לומר כמה שירות ותושבחות. **למשה** — בשביל משה שהיה עתיד לקבל את התורה. **מה שמו** — של משיח. **ינון שמו** — כמו ינאי, כל אחד היה דורש אחר שמו. **לפני שמש** — עד שלא נברא היה שמו ינון, והיינו אחד משבעה דברים שעלו במחשבה ליבראות.

NOTES

Similarly, even when it appears that God might be hesitating to destroy Israel's enemies, He will in the end destroy them for the sake of His nation.

מַה שְּׁמוֹ? **What is his name?** It is clear that each of the Sages mentioned here was alluding to his own teacher when he suggested the name of the Messiah (Shela — Shilo; Yannai — Yinon; Ḥaninah — Ḥaninah). As is intimated below, there are people in every generation who possess messianic potential, but the time is not yet ripe. Hence the disciples saw their masters as potential Messiahs. It has also been noted that the initial letters of the words Menaḥem (*mem*), Shilo (*shin*), Yannai (*yod*), and Ḥaninah (*het*) spell

TRANSLATION AND COMMENTARY

as the verse states (Jeremiah 16:13): **"For I will show you no favor** [*ḥaninah*]," the favor of bringing the Messiah. [1]**And some say** that the Messiah's **name is Menaḥem the son of Ḥizkiyah,** [2]**as the verse states** (Lamentations 1:16): **"Because the comforter** [*menaḥem*] **that should relieve my soul is far from me,"** meaning that the Messiah named Menaḥem has still not come. [3]**And the Rabbis said:** The Messiah's **name is "The leper of the School of Rabbi** Yehudah HaNasi," [4]**as the verse states** (Isaiah 53:4): **"But in truth he has borne our sicknesses and endured our pain; yet we did esteem him injured, stricken by God, and afflicted."**

אָמַר רַב נַחְמָן [5]**Rav Naḥman said:** If the Messiah **comes from among those who are alive** today, he will be somebody **like me,** who already has a measure of dominion over Israel. [6]**As the verse states** (Jeremiah 30:21): **"And their prince shall be of themselves, and their governor shall proceed from their midst."**

אָמַר רַב [7]**Rav said:** If the Messiah comes **from among those who are alive** today, he will be **our holy Rabbi,** Rabbi Yehudah HaNasi, who towers above all his contemporaries in sanctity, piety, and Torah knowledge. [8]And **if** he comes **from among those who are dead,** he will be **Daniel, the beloved man,** who was endowed with similar qualities.

אָמַר רַב יְהוּדָה [9]**Rav Yehudah said in the name of Rav: In the future, the Holy One, blessed be He, will raise up another David over** the people of Israel, for the Messiah will also be named David, [10]**as the verse states** (Jeremiah 30:9): **"But they shall serve the Lord their God, and David their king, whom I will raise up for them."** [11]The verse **does not read:** "David their king whom **He raised up** for them," in the past tense, [12]**but rather:** "David their king whom **I will raise up** for them," in the future tense.

שֶׁנֶּאֱמַר: ״אֲשֶׁר לֹא אֶתֵּן לָכֶם חֲנִינָה״. [1]וְיֵשׁ אוֹמְרִים מְנַחֵם בֶּן חִזְקִיָּה שְׁמוֹ, [2]שֶׁנֶּאֱמַר: ״כִּי רָחַק מִמֶּנִּי מְנַחֵם מֵשִׁיב נַפְשִׁי״. [3]וְרַבָּנַן אָמְרִי: ״חִיוָּורָא דְּבֵי רַבִּי שְׁמוֹ״, [4]שֶׁנֶּאֱמַר: ״אָכֵן חֳלָיֵינוּ הוּא נָשָׂא וּמַכְאֹבֵינוּ סְבָלָם וַאֲנַחְנוּ חֲשַׁבְנֻהוּ נָגוּעַ מֻכֵּה אֱלֹהִים וּמְעֻנֶּה״.

[5]אָמַר רַב נַחְמָן: אִי מִן חַיָּיא הוּא, כְּגוֹן אֲנָא, [6]שֶׁנֶּאֱמַר: ״וְהָיָה אַדִּירוֹ מִמֶּנּוּ וּמֹשְׁלוֹ מִקִּרְבּוֹ יֵצֵא״.

[7]אָמַר רַב: אִי מִן חַיָּיא הוּא, כְּגוֹן רַבֵּינוּ הַקָּדוֹשׁ. [8]אִי מִן מֵתַיָּא הוּא, כְּגוֹן דָּנִיֵּאל אִישׁ חֲמוּדוֹת.

[9]אָמַר רַב יְהוּדָה אָמַר רַב: עָתִיד הַקָּדוֹשׁ בָּרוּךְ הוּא לְהַעֲמִיד לָהֶם דָּוִד אַחֵר, [10]שֶׁנֶּאֱמַר: ״וְעָבְדוּ אֵת ה׳ אֱלֹהֵיהֶם וְאֵת דָּוִד מַלְכָּם אֲשֶׁר אָקִים לָהֶם״. [11]״הֵקִים״ לֹא נֶאֱמַר, [12]אֶלָּא ״אָקִים״.

LITERAL TRANSLATION

as it is stated: "For I will show you no favor [*ḥaninah*]." [1]And some say his name is Menaḥem the son of Ḥizkiyah, [2]as it is stated: "Because the comforter [*menaḥem*] who will relieve my soul is far from me." [3]And the Rabbis said: His name is: "The leper of the School of Rabbi," [4]as it is stated: "But in truth he has borne our sicknesses and endured our pain; yet we thought him to be injured, stricken by God, and afflicted."

[5]Rav Naḥman said: If he is from among those who are alive, like me, [6]as it is stated: "And their prince shall be of themselves, and their governor shall proceed from their midst."

[7]Rav said: If from among those who are alive, like our holy Rabbi. [8]If from among those who are dead, like Daniel, the beloved man.

[9]Rav Yehudah said in the name of Rav: In the future, the Holy One, blessed be He, will raise up another David over them, [10]as it is stated: "But they shall serve the Lord their God, and David their king, whom I will raise up for them." [11]"He raised up" is not stated, [12]but rather "I will raise up."

RASHI

ולא אתן להם חנינה — עדיין לא יבא משיח. **מנחם** — בן חזקיה. **חיוורא דבי רבי** — מצורע של בית רבי. **אי מן חייא הוא כגון רבינו הקדוש** — אם משיח מאותן שחיים עכשיו ודאי היינו רבינו הקדוש, דסובל תחלואים וחסיד גמור הוה, כדאמרינן בבבא מציעא (פה, א), ואם היה מאותן שמתו כבר — היה דניאל איש חמודות שנדון ביסורין בגוב אריות וחסיד גמור היה, והאי כגון לאו דווקא, לישנא אחרינא: כגון רבינו הקדוש, כלומר, אם יש דוגמתו בחיים היינו רבינו הקדוש, ואם דוגמא הוא למתים, היינו כגון דניאל איש חמודות. **דוד אחר** — שעתיד למלוך עליהם. **אקים** — הקים לא נאמר אלא ״אקים״.

NOTES

מָשִׁיחַ, "the Messiah" (*Gaon of Vilna*). Even in later generations, Sages intimated in their writings that they saw themselves as fit to redeem Israel from their enemies and usher in the Messianic age.

חִיוָּורָא דְּבֵי רַבִּי **The leper of the house of Rabbi.** Some understand the expression חִיוָּורָא דְּבֵי רַבִּי as "the leper of the house of Rabbi [Yehudah HaNasi]." According to this, the Messiah will be one of the descendants of Rabbi Yehudah HaNasi, and also a leper, as is intimated in the verse cited in our passage. *Arukh* cites a different reading: חִיוָּורָא רַב — "great leper."

רַב נַחְמָן, רַבִּי, דָּנִיֵּאל **Rav Naḥman, Rabbi, Daniel.** According to *Rashi,* Rabbi Yehudah HaNasi and Daniel were suggested as possible Messiahs, for they were both totally righteous

BACKGROUND

קֵיסָר וּפַלְגֵי קֵיסָר Caesar and the Vice-Caesar. This title reflects a situation that existed for some time in the Roman empire, after the reforms in the political organization of Rome instituted by the Emperor Diocletian. At that time, and for several years afterward, not only was the empire divided among governors, but each governor, given the title "Augustus," had a vice-governor, given the title "caesar," who was also an independent ruler, though somewhat lower in rank. Here a future regime like that is described, in which there would be a "Caesar" and a "Vice-Caesar."

LANGUAGE (RASHI)

קלב״א שורי״ץ* comes from the Old French *chalve soriz*, meaning "a bat."

TRANSLATION AND COMMENTARY

אֲמַר לֵיהּ [1]**Rav Pappa said to Abaye: But surely** another **verse states** (Ezekiel 37:25): [2]**"And My servant David shall be their prince forever,"** implying that King David himself will reign over Israel in the future.

כְּגוֹן קֵיסָר [3]Abaye answered: During the Messianic age, there will be two leaders in Israel, **like the Caesar and the Vice-Caesar.** A second David will reign as the Messianic king, as the verse states: "David the king whom I will raise up for them," and King David will serve under him as his second in command ("prince"), as the verse states: "My servant David shall be their prince forever."

דָּרַשׁ רַבִּי שִׂמְלַאי [4]**Rabbi Simlai expounded: What is** meant by **the verse that states** (Amos 5:18): **"Woe to you who desire the day of the Lord! Why would you have this day of the Lord; it is darkness, and not light"?** The verse may be understood by way of the following illustration: [5]**It is like a rooster and a bat that were waiting** together **for the light** of day. [6]**The rooster said to the bat:** "It is clear why **I wait for the light** of day, for I am active during the day. [7]**But you, why do you need light,** since light and darkness are the same to you?" Similarly, the people of Israel await the day of the Lord, for that day will bring them light. But as for the nations of the world, why do they await the Lord's day, which will bring them only darkness?

[99A] וְהַיְינוּ [8]The Gemara adds: **This is** like **what a certain heretic said to Rabbi Abbahu: "When will the Messiah come?"** [9]Rabbi Abbahu **said to him:** "He will come **when darkness covers those people,"** people like yourself. [10]The heretic **said to** Rabbi Abbahu: "Why **do you curse me** for no reason?" [11]Rabbi Abbahu **said to him:** "It is not I who curse you, for **the verse states** explicitly (Isaiah 60:2): **'For, behold, the darkness shall cover the earth, and fog the peoples; but the Lord shall shine upon You, and His glory shall be seen upon you.'"**

תַּנְיָא [12]**It was taught** in a Baraita: **"Rabbi Eliezer says: The Messianic age** will last **for forty years,**

[1]אֲמַר לֵיהּ רַב פַּפָּא לְאַבַּיֵי: וְהָכְתִיב: [2]"וְדָוִד עַבְדִּי נָשִׂיא לָהֶם לְעוֹלָם"!

[3]כְּגוֹן קֵיסָר וּפַלְגֵי קֵיסָר.

[4]דָּרַשׁ רַבִּי שִׂמְלַאי: מַאי דִּכְתִיב: "הוֹי הַמִּתְאַוִּים אֶת יוֹם ה'! לָמָּה זֶּה לָכֶם יוֹם ה' הוּא חֹשֶׁךְ וְלֹא אוֹר"? [5]מָשָׁל לְתַרְנְגוֹל וַעֲטַלֵּף שֶׁהָיוּ מְצַפִּין לָאוֹר. [6]אָמַר לֵיהּ תַּרְנְגוֹל לַעֲטַלֵּף: "אֲנִי מְצַפֶּה לְאוֹרָה, שֶׁאוֹרָה שֶׁלִּי הִיא. [7]וְאַתָּה, לָמָּה לָךְ אוֹרָה"?

[99A] [8]וְהַיְינוּ דַּאֲמַר לֵיהּ הַהוּא מִינָא לְרַבִּי אַבָּהוּ: "אֵימָתַי אָתֵי מָשִׁיחַ"? [9]אֲמַר לֵיהּ: "לְכִי חָפֵי לְהוּ חֲשׁוֹכָא לְהָנְהוּ אֱינָשֵׁי". [10]אֲמַר לֵיהּ: "מֵילָט קָא לָטֵית לִי"? [11]אֲמַר לֵיהּ: "קְרָא כְּתִיב: 'כִּי הִנֵּה הַחֹשֶׁךְ יְכַסֶּה אֶרֶץ וַעֲרָפֶל לְאֻמִּים וְעָלַיִךְ יִזְרַח ה' וּכְבוֹדוֹ עָלַיִךְ יֵרָאֶה'".

[12]תַּנְיָא: "רַבִּי אֱלִיעֶזֶר אוֹמֵר: יְמוֹת הַמָּשִׁיחַ אַרְבָּעִים שָׁנָה,

LITERAL TRANSLATION

[1]Rav Pappa said to Abaye: But surely it is written: [2]"And My servant David shall be their prince forever."

[3]Like the Caesar and the Vice-Caesar.

[4]Rabbi Simlai expounded: What is that which is written: "Woe to you who desire the day of the Lord! Why would you have this day of the Lord; it is darkness, and not light"? [5]It is like a rooster and a bat that were waiting for the light. [6]The rooster said to the bat: "I wait for the light, for the light is mine. [7]But you, why do you need light?"

[99A] [8]And this is what a certain heretic said to Rabbi Abbahu: "When will the Messiah come?" [9]He said to him: "When darkness covers those people." [10]He said to him: "Do you curse me?" [11]He said to him: "The verse states: 'For, behold, the darkness shall cover the earth, and fog the peoples; but the Lord shall shine upon You, and His glory shall be seen upon you.'"

[12]It was taught: "Rabbi Eliezer says: The days of the Messiah are forty years,

RASHI

כגון קיסר ופלגי קיסר — מלך ושני לו, כן דוד החדש מלך, כדכתיב "ודוד מלכם אשר אקים" ודוד המלך שני לו, כדכתיב "נשיא להם" ולא כתוב מלך. עטלף — *קלב"א שורי"ץ בלעז, ואין לה עינים. שאורה שלי הוא — שיש לי עינים לראות, ונמצאתי נהנית בה, כך ישראל מצפין לגאולה, שיום ה' יהיה להם אור, אבל העובדי כוכבים — למה מקוים אותו? הרי הוא להם חשך ולא אור. הכי גרסינן — היינו דאמר ליה ההוא מינא לרבי אבהו וכו'.

NOTES

men and they both suffered severely from various afflictions. Others suggest that Rabbi Yehudah HaNasi and Daniel were suggested because they both fulfilled the verse cited by Rav Naḥman, according to which the Messiah will be someone who enjoyed a certain measure of dominion even before emerging as the Messiah (*Maharsha, Be'er Sheva*).

קֵיסָר וּפַלְגֵי קֵיסָר The Caesar and the Vice-Caesar. According to *Arukh*, King David will be the King of Israel during the Messianic period, and the Messiah — a second David — will serve under him.

יְמוֹת הַמָּשִׁיחַ The days of the Messiah. It has been argued that the Messianic age will serve as a period of preparation for Israel and the whole world for life in the World to Come. Hence, the dispute regarding the length of the Messianic age

TRANSLATION AND COMMENTARY

[1]as the verse states (Psalms 95:10): **'Forty years will I loathe the generation,'** meaning that God will loathe the nations of the world while the Messiah rules. [2]**Rabbi Elazar ben Azaryah says:** The Messianic age will last for **seventy years,** [3]**as the verse states** (Isaiah 23:15): **'And it shall come to pass on that day, that Tyre shall be forgotten seventy years, according to the days of one king,'** a king who stands out above all others. [4]**Who is this singular king?** [5]**Say** that **this is** a reference to **the Messiah,** whose rule shall last for seventy years. [6]**Rabbi** Yehudah HaNasi **says:** The Messianic age will last for **three generations,** [7]**as the verse states** (Psalms 72:5): **'May they fear You as long as the sun and moon endure, throughout all generations** [דור דורים].' The expression דור דורים, translated here as 'throughout all generations,' may be rendered as 'generation, generations,' the word 'generation' implying one generation, and the word 'generations' implying an additional two generations, for a total of three generations. [8]**Rabbi Hillel says: There will be no Messiah for** the people of **Israel, for they already enjoyed him in the days of Hezekiah,** when Israel was delivered from Sennacherib. In Rabbi Hillel's opinion, the Messiah will have no role in the final redemption, which will be brought about solely by God Himself."

אָמַר רַב יוֹסֵף [9]**Rav Yosef said: May** God **our Master pardon Rabbi Hillel,** for surely he is mistaken. [10]**When did Hezekiah** live? **During the First Temple period.** [11]**But** the Prophet **Zechariah prophesied during the Second Temple period, saying** (Zechariah 9:9): **"Rejoice greatly, O daughter of Zion, shout, O daughter of Jerusalem: behold, your king will come to you; he is just, and victorious; humble, and riding upon an ass, and upon a colt, the foal of an ass."**

[1]שֶׁנֶּאֱמַר: ׳אַרְבָּעִים שָׁנָה אָקוּט בְּדוֹר׳. [2]רַבִּי אֶלְעָזָר בֶּן עֲזַרְיָה אוֹמֵר: שִׁבְעִים שָׁנָה, [3]שֶׁנֶּאֱמַר: ״וְהָיָה בַּיּוֹם הַהוּא וְנִשְׁכַּחַת צֹר שִׁבְעִים שָׁנָה כִּימֵי מֶלֶךְ אֶחָד״. [4]אֵיזֶהוּ מֶלֶךְ מְיוּחָד? [5]הֱוֵי אוֹמֵר זֶה מָשִׁיחַ. [6]רַבִּי אוֹמֵר: שְׁלֹשָׁה דוֹרוֹת, [7]שֶׁנֶּאֱמַר: ׳יִירָאוּךָ עִם שָׁמֶשׁ וְלִפְנֵי יָרֵחַ דּוֹר דּוֹרִים׳. [8]רַבִּי הִילֵּל אוֹמֵר: אֵין לָהֶם מָשִׁיחַ לְיִשְׂרָאֵל, שֶׁכְּבָר אֲכָלוּהוּ בִּימֵי חִזְקִיָּה״.

[9]אָמַר רַב יוֹסֵף: שְׁרָא לֵיהּ מָרֵיהּ לְרַבִּי הִילֵּל! [10]חִזְקִיָּה אֵימַת הֲוָה — בְּבַיִת רִאשׁוֹן. [11]וְאִילּוּ זְכַרְיָה קָא מִתְנַבֵּי בְּבַיִת שֵׁנִי, וְאָמַר: ״גִּילִי מְאֹד בַּת צִיּוֹן הָרִיעִי בַּת יְרוּשָׁלַיִם הִנֵּה מַלְכֵּךְ יָבוֹא לָךְ צַדִּיק וְנוֹשָׁע הוּא עָנִי וְרֹכֵב עַל חֲמוֹר וְעַל עַיִר בֶּן אֲתֹנוֹת״.

LITERAL TRANSLATION

[1]as it is stated: 'Forty years will I loathe the generation.' [2]Rabbi Elazar ben Azaryah says: Seventy years, [3]as it is stated: 'And it shall come to pass on that day, that Zor shall be forgotten seventy years, according to the days of one king.' [4]Who is the singular king? [5]Say this is the Messiah. [6]Rabbi says: Three generations, [7]as it is stated: 'May they fear You with the sun and before the moon, throughout all generations.' [8]Rabbi Hillel says: There is no Messiah for Israel, for they already enjoyed [lit., 'ate'] him in the days of Hezekiah."

[9]Rav Yosef said: May our Master pardon Rabbi Hillel. [10]When was Hezekiah — during the First Temple [period]. [11]But Zechariah prophesied during the Second Temple [period], and said: "Rejoice greatly, O daughter of Zion, shout, O daughter of Jerusalem: behold, your king will come to you; he is just, and victorious; humble, and riding upon an ass, and upon a colt, the foal of an ass."

SAGES

רַבִּי הִילֵּל **Rabbi Hillel.** Apparently this Hillel was the grandson of Rabbi Yehudah HaNasi, and the younger brother of the Nasi in his generation, Rabbi Yehudah Nasia. Some authorities attribute the teachings of Hillel that are presented in the *Ethics of the Fathers* to this Hillel.

RASHI

אקוט בדור — אקח ישראל ואמלוך עליהם, כמו נקטיה, ״ארבעים שנה אקוט בדור״ — בדור קטן של ארבעים שנה שהוא משונה מדורות שלפניו, ומסתמא היינו משיח שעינין גדולים יהיו בדורו, ופשטיה דקרא מיהא גבי מתי מדבר, אבל מדכתיב ״אקוט״ — משמע אף להבא היה מתנבא. **מיוחד** — חשוב. הכי גרסינן: **רבי אומר שלשה דורות שנאמר ייראוך עם שמש** — כלומר בהדי משיח שכתב בו (תהלים עב) ״לפני שמש ינון שמו״ ייראוך ישראל, ״ולפני ירח״ — לפני מלכות בית דוד שנמשל כירח כדכתיב (שם פט) ״כירח יכון עולם וגו׳״ כמו כן ״ייראוך דור דורים, דור — אחד, דורים — שנים, הרי שלשה. **אין להם משיח לישראל** — אלא הקדוש ברוך הוא ימלוך בעצמו ויגאלם לבדו. **שרי ליה מריה** — ימחול לו הקדוש ברוך הוא, שאמר דברים אשר לא כן. **ואלו זכריה מיהא מתנבא על משיח בבית שני** — דכתיב בתרי עשר ״הנה מלכך יבא לך וגו׳״ ולאו היינו זכריה בן יהוידע הכהן שניבא בבית ראשון, אלא זכריה בן ברכיה שהיה במלכות דריוש.

NOTES

is essentially a dispute about how long it will take to prepare the world to rise to that level. Thus, the authorities who shorten the Messianic age (and all the more so, Rabbi Hillel, who says that there will be no Messiah) speak in praise of Israel, for they maintain that Israel will rise to the level of the World to Come relatively quickly (*Rabbi David Bonfils*).

רַבִּי הִילֵּל **Rabbi Hillel.** The Rishonim disagree about the meaning of Rabbi Hillel's statement that there will be no Messiah for the people of Israel. Our commentary follows *Rashi*, who understands that Rabbi Hillel means that the final redemption will not be brought by a human Messianic figure, but rather by God Himself. *Ramah* understands Rabbi Hillel as saying that Israel will not enjoy a comprehensive

[1]תַּנְיָא אִידָךְ: ״רַבִּי אֱלִיעֶזֶר אוֹמֵר: יְמוֹת הַמָּשִׁיחַ אַרְבָּעִים שָׁנָה. [2]כְּתִיב הָכָא: ׳וַיְעַנְּךָ וַיַּרְעִבֶךָ וַיַּאֲכִלְךָ״. [3]וּכְתִיב הָתָם: ׳שַׂמְּחֵנוּ כִּימוֹת עִנִּיתָנוּ שְׁנוֹת רָאִינוּ רָעָה׳. [4]רַבִּי דּוֹסָא אוֹמֵר: אַרְבַּע מֵאוֹת שָׁנָה. [5]כְּתִיב הָכָא: ׳וַעֲבָדוּם וְעִנּוּ אֹתָם אַרְבַּע מֵאוֹת שָׁנָה. [6]וּכְתִיב הָתָם: ׳שַׂמְּחֵנוּ כִּימוֹת עִנִּיתָנוּ׳. [7]רַבִּי אוֹמֵר: שְׁלֹשׁ מֵאוֹת וְשִׁשִּׁים וְחָמֵשׁ שָׁנָה, כְּמִנְיַן יְמוֹת הַחַמָּה, [8]שֶׁנֶּאֱמַר: ׳כִּי יוֹם נָקָם בְּלִבִּי וּשְׁנַת גְּאוּלַי בָּאָה׳ ״.
[9]מַאי ״יוֹם נָקָם בְּלִבִּי״? [10]אָמַר רַבִּי יוֹחָנָן: לְלִבִּי גִּלִּיתִי, לְאֵבָרַיי לֹא גִּלִּיתִי. [11]רַבִּי שִׁמְעוֹן בֶּן לָקִישׁ אָמַר: לְלִבִּי גִּלִּיתִי, לְמַלְאֲכֵי הַשָּׁרֵת לֹא גִּלִּיתִי.

LITERAL TRANSLATION

[1]It was taught in another [Baraita]: "Rabbi Eliezer says: The days of the Messiah are forty years. [2]It is written here: 'And He afflicted you, and suffered you to hunger, and fed you [with manna].' [3]And it is written there: 'Make us glad according to the days that You afflicted us the years we saw evil.' [4]Rabbi Dosa says: Four hundred years. [5]It is written here: 'And they shall serve them, and they shall afflict them four hundred years.' [6]And it is written there: 'Make us glad according to the days that You have afflicted us.' [7]Rabbi says: Three-hundred-and-sixty-five years, like the number of days of the sun, [8]for it is stated: 'For the day of vengeance is in My heart, and the year of My redeemed is come.'"
[9]What is: "For the day of vengeance is in My heart"? [10]Rabbi Yoḥanan said: To My heart I revealed [it], to My organs I did not reveal [it]. [11]Rabbi Shimon ben Lakish said: To My heart I revealed [it], to the ministering angels I did not reveal [it].

TRANSLATION AND COMMENTARY

תַּנְיָא אִידָךְ [1]**It was taught in another Baraita: "Rabbi Eliezer says: The Messianic age** will last **for forty years.** [2]**Here,** regarding the wandering of the people of Israel, **the verse states** (Deuteronomy 8:3): **'And He afflicted you, and suffered you to hunger, and fed you with manna.'** [3]**And elsewhere the verse states** (Psalms 90:15): **'Make us glad according to the days that You have afflicted us.'** This shows that the days of Israel's gladness — the Messianic age — will be equal to the time of their affliction in the wilderness. [4]**Rabbi Dosa says:** The Messianic age will last for **four hundred years.** [5]**Here,** regarding Israel's servitude in Egypt, **the verse states** (Genesis 15:13): **'And they shall serve them, and they shall afflict them four hundred years.'** [6]**And elsewhere the verse states** (Psalms 90:15): **'Make us glad according to the days that You have afflicted us.'** [7]**Rabbi** Yehudah HaNasi **says:** The Messianic age will last for **three-hundred-and-sixty-five years, equal to the number of days in a solar year,** [8]**as the verse states** (Isaiah 63:4): **'For the day of vengeance is in My heart, and the year of My redeemed is come.'** The 'day of vengeance' for the sin of the spies lasted forty years, one year for each day of their mission. Similarly, 'the year of My redeemed' will last one year for each day of the solar year."

מַאי [9]Having cited the verse, "For the day of vengeance is in My heart, and the year of My redeemed is come," the Gemara asks: **What is** the significance of the words, **"For the day of vengeance is in *My heart*"?** [10]**Rabbi Yoḥanan said:** Only **to My heart did I reveal** the hidden matters regarding the final redemption, but **to My organs, I did not reveal them.** [11]**Rabbi Shimon ben Lakish said:** Only **to My heart did I reveal** the hidden matters regarding the final redemption, but **to the ministering angels I did not reveal** them.

RASHI

רבי אומר שלש מאות ששים וחמש כמנין ימות החמה, דכתיב "כי יום נקם בלבי ושנת גאולי באה" — [ליום נקם של מרגלים ארבעים יום מה יום נקם של מרגלים] שנה אחת בכל יום כדכתיב (במדבר יד) "יום לשנה יום לשנה וגו'" כך שנת גאולי באה שנה ליום שנה ליום, שלכל יום ויום של שנה זו הכתובה שנת גאולי במקרא זה — נותנים שנה אחת, ואית דגרסי רבי אומר: שלש מאות ששים וחמשה אלפים שנה, דכתיב "שנת גאולי באה" ושנה של הקדוש ברוך הוא הכי הוי דכתיב (תהלים צ) "כי אלף שנים בעיניך כיום". **ועד עכשיו** — ימות המשיח. **לאיברי לא גליתי** — שלא הוצאתי דבר מפי שהיו איברי יכולין לשמוע, אלא בלבי היה טמון הדבר.

NOTES

redemption in the future, for whatever promises were made to Israel regarding their redemption were already fulfilled in the days of Hezekiah. Others have argued that Rabbi Hillel does not mean to deny that the Messiah will still come and redeem Israel. Rather he maintains that Israel will no longer merit the Messiah's arrival, and that when he comes, he will come only for the sake of God's glory (*Torat HaOlah*).

שְׁלֹשׁ מֵאוֹת וְשִׁשִּׁים וְחָמֵשׁ שָׁנָה **Three-hundred-and-sixty-five years.** Rabbi Yehudah HaNasi's position is based on the premise that, unless specified otherwise, a "year" is a solar year of three-hundred-and-sixty-five days (*Rashash*). According to some readings, Rabbi Yehudah HaNasi maintains that the Messianic age will last for three-hundred-and-sixty-five thousand years, each of God's days lasting a thousand years. In *Midrash Shoḥar Tov*, we find the figure of three-hundred-and-fifty-four thousand years — three-hundred-and-fifty-four being the number of days in a lunar year.

לְלִבִּי גִּלִּיתִי, לְאֵבָרַיי לֹא גִּלִּיתִי **To My heart I revealed it, to My organs I did not reveal it.** This passage is surely meant to be understood in a metaphoric sense, internal thought being attributed to the heart, and speech and revelation to the organs. The Amoraic dispute may be

TRANSLATION AND COMMENTARY

תָּנֵי [1]**Avimi the son of Rabbi Abbahu taught** a related Baraita: **"The Messianic age for Israel** will last **for seven thousand years,** [2]**as the verse states** (Isaiah 62:5): **'And as the bridegroom rejoices over the bride, so shall your God rejoice over you.'** A bridegroom rejoices over his bride for seven days, and each of God's days is a thousand years."

אָמַר רַב יְהוּדָה [3]**Rav Yehudah said in the name of Shmuel.** [4]**The Messianic age** will be as long **as from the day that the world was created until now,** [5]**as the verse states** (Deuteronomy 11:21): "That your days may be multiplied, and the days of your children, in the land which the Lord swore to your fathers to give them, **as the days of heaven upon the earth."** The Messianic age, when the people of Israel will dwell in the land which God swore to their fathers, will be as long as "the days of heaven upon the earth" that have passed before the Messiah's arrival.

רַב נַחְמָן בַּר יִצְחָק [6]**Rav Naḥman bar Yitzḥak said:** The Messianic age will be as long **as from the days of Noah until now,** [7]**as the verse states** (Isaiah 54:9): **"For this is as the seas of Noah to me: as I have sworn** that the seas of Noah shall no more go over the earth; so have I sworn that I will not be furious with you, nor rebuke you." Like the days of Noah [כִּימֵי נֹחַ, a play on the words כִּי מֵי נֹחַ, "as the waters of Noah"], i.e., the period that passed from the days of Noah until the Messiah's arrival — such will be the days of the Messiah, the period regarding which God swore that He would not destroy the world in His furor.

אָמַר [8]**Rabbi Ḥiyya bar Abba said in the name of Rabbi Yoḥanan: All the Prophets'** favorable **prophecies regarding** the redemption of Israel and the end of days refer to **the Messianic age.** [9]**But regarding the World to Come,** they did not prophesy, as the verse states (Isaiah 64:3): **"The eye has not seen, that a God beside You should do such a thing for him that waits for Him."**

[1] תָּנֵי אֲבִימִי בְּרֵיהּ דְּרַבִּי אַבָּהוּ: ״יְמוֹת הַמָּשִׁיחַ לְיִשְׂרָאֵל שִׁבְעַת אֲלָפִים שָׁנָה, [2] שֶׁנֶּאֱמַר: ׳וּמְשׂוֹשׂ חָתָן עַל כַּלָּה כֵּן יָשִׂישׂ עָלַיִךְ אֱלֹהָיִךְ׳״.

[3] אָמַר רַב יְהוּדָה אָמַר שְׁמוּאֵל. [4] יְמוֹת הַמָּשִׁיחַ — כְּמִיּוֹם שֶׁנִּבְרָא הָעוֹלָם וְעַד עַכְשָׁיו, [5] שֶׁנֶּאֱמַר: ״כִּימֵי הַשָּׁמַיִם עַל הָאָרֶץ״.

[6] רַב נַחְמָן בַּר יִצְחָק אָמַר: כִּימֵי נֹחַ עַד עַכְשָׁיו, [7] שֶׁנֶּאֱמַר: ״כִּי מֵי נֹחַ זֹאת לִי אֲשֶׁר נִשְׁבַּעְתִּי״.

[8] אָמַר רַבִּי חִיָּיא בַּר אַבָּא אָמַר רַבִּי יוֹחָנָן: כָּל הַנְּבִיאִים כּוּלָּן לֹא נִתְנַבְּאוּ אֶלָּא לִימוֹת הַמָּשִׁיחַ. [9] אֲבָל לָעוֹלָם הַבָּא — ״עַיִן לֹא רָאָתָה אֱלֹהִים זוּלָתְךָ יַעֲשֶׂה לִמְחַכֵּה לוֹ״.

LITERAL TRANSLATION

[1]Avimi the son of Rabbi Abbahu taught: "The days of the Messiah for Israel are seven thousand years, [2]as it is stated: 'And [as] the bridegroom rejoices over the bride, so shall your God rejoice over you.'"

[3]Rav Yehudah said in the name of Shmuel. [4]The days of the Messiah — as from the day that the world was created until now, [5]as it is stated: "As the days of heaven upon the earth."

[6]Rav Naḥman bar Yitzḥak said: As from the days of Noah until now, [7]as it is stated: "For this is as the seas of Noah to me: as I have sworn."

[8]Rabbi Ḥiyya bar Abba said in the name of Rabbi Yoḥanan: All the Prophets prophesied only about the days of the Messiah. [9]But regarding the World to Come — "The eye has not seen, that a God beside You, should do such a thing for him that waits for Him."

RASHI

למען ירבו ימיכם בימי השמים על הארץ – ולא עמדו בארץ כל כך, אבל עתידין לעמוד בשיבת משיח. במשוש חתן – שבעת ימי המשתה, כן ישיש עליך שבעת ימים, ויומו של הקדוש ברוך הוא אלף שנה. כי מי נח – כמו ״כימי נח״, כחשבון השנים שנמלא בידו לאותו זמן שנשבע ה׳ ״מעבור מי נח עוד על הארץ כן נשבעתי״ – כפי אותו חשבון נשבעתי ״מקצף עליך ומגער בך״ – שלא אחריב את עולמי לאחר ביאת משיח עד שיכלה זה הזמן.

NOTES

understood as follows: According to Rabbi Yoḥanan, the matter of Israel's final redemption was not expressed through speech or prophecy (for speech involves a revelation to some of the organs, such as the lips). According to Resh Lakish, the matter was not even revealed to the ministering angels, who could have been learned about the matter even without speech or prophecy (*Ramah*).

HALAKHAH

כָּל הַנְּבִיאִים כּוּלָּן לֹא נִתְנַבְּאוּ אֶלָּא לִימוֹת הַמָּשִׁיחַ **All the Prophets only prophesied regarding the days of the Messiah.** "All the good that the Prophets prophesied for Israel relate to the material good that Israel will enjoy during the Messianic age. But the good of the World to Come cannot be imagined or comprehended, and the Prophets did not prophesy about it." (*Rambam, Sefer Mada, Hilkhot Teshuvah* 8:7.)

TRANSLATION AND COMMENTARY

וּפְלִיגָא דִּשְׁמוּאֵל [1]The Gemara notes that Rabbi Yoḥanan's position **is in disagreement with** that of **Shmuel, for Shmuel said:** [2]**There is no difference** in the conditions of life **between** the present **world and the Messianic age except for** Israel's deliverance from **the oppression of** foreign **kingdoms.** When the Messiah comes, Israel will regain political independence, but the natural order will continue. According to Shmuel, who is in disagreement with Rabbi Yoḥanan, the prophecies that predict a drastic change in the world order are not referring to the Messianic age, but rather to the World to Come.

וְאָמַר [3]**Rabbi Ḥiyya bar Abba said in the name of Rabbi Yoḥanan: All the Prophets' prophecies regarding** future reward for the righteous refer to **repentant sinners.** [4]**But regarding** the even greater reward that awaits the **absolutely righteous people** who never sinned, the Prophets did not prophesy, as the verse states (Isaiah 64:3): **"The eye has not seen, that a God beside You** should do such a thing for him that waits for Him."

וּפְלִיגָא דְּרַבִּי אַבָּהוּ [5]The Gemara notes that Rabbi Yoḥanan's position on this matter **is in disagreement with** the view of **Rabbi Abbahu, for Rabbi Abbahu said in the name of Rav:** [6]**In a place where repentant sinners stand, righteous people cannot stand,** [7]**as the verse states** (Isaiah 57:14): **"Peace, peace, both for far and near"** — the verse **first** offers peace to **the far, and then** it offers peace to **the near.** [8]**What** does the verse mean by **"far"?** [9]It refers to sinners who were **at first far** from God, and then repented and came close to Him. [10]**And what** does the verse mean by **"near"?** [11]It refers to those who were **near** to God **from the beginning and now** remain righteous.

[1]וּפְלִיגָא דִּשְׁמוּאֵל, דְּאָמַר שְׁמוּאֵל: [2]אֵין בֵּין הָעוֹלָם הַזֶּה לִימוֹת הַמָּשִׁיחַ אֶלָּא שִׁעְבּוּד מַלְכֻיּוֹת בִּלְבַד.

[3]וְאָמַר רַבִּי חִיָּיא בַּר אַבָּא אָמַר רַבִּי יוֹחָנָן: כָּל הַנְּבִיאִים לֹא נִתְנַבְּאוּ אֶלָּא לְבַעֲלֵי תְשׁוּבָה. [4]אֲבָל צַדִּיקִים גְּמוּרִים — "עַיִן לֹא רָאָתָה אֱלֹהִים זוּלָתְךָ".

[5]וּפְלִיגָא דְּרַבִּי אַבָּהוּ, דְּאָמַר רַבִּי אַבָּהוּ אָמַר רַב: [6]מָקוֹם שֶׁבַּעֲלֵי תְשׁוּבָה עוֹמְדִין שָׁם, צַדִּיקִים אֵינָן עוֹמְדִין שָׁם, [7]שֶׁנֶּאֱמַר: "שָׁלוֹם שָׁלוֹם לָרָחוֹק וְלַקָּרוֹב" — בְּרֵישָׁא רָחוֹק, וַהֲדַר קָרוֹב. [8]מַאי "רָחוֹק"? [9]רָחוֹק דְּמֵעִיקָּרָא. [10]וּמַאי "קָרוֹב"? [11]קָרוֹב דְּמֵעִיקָּרָא וּדְהַשְׁתָּא.

LITERAL TRANSLATION

[1]And this is in disagreement with Shmuel, for Shmuel said: [2]There is no difference between this world and the days of the Messiah except for the oppression of kingdoms.

[3]And Rabbi Ḥiyya bar Abba said in the name of Rabbi Yoḥanan: All the prophets prophesied only about repentant sinners. [4]But regarding absolutely righteous people — "The eye has not seen, that a God beside You."

[5]And this is in disagreement with Rabbi Abbahu, for Rabbi Abbahu said in the name of Rav: [6]In a place where repentant sinners stand, righteous people do not stand there, [7]as it is stated: "Peace, peace, both for far and near" — first the far, and then the near. [8]What is "far"? [9]Far from the beginning. [10]And what is "near"? [11]Near from the beginning and now.

RASHI

לא נתנבאו — טובה לישראל. **עין לא ראתה** — דאין קץ לדבר. **צדיקים אינן עומדין** — דגדול כחן של בעלי תשובה שאין בריה יכולה לעמוד (לפניהם) [במחיצתם]. **ברישא לרחוק** — שנתרחק מן הקדוש ברוך הוא ואחר כך שב אליו בתשובה, והדר שלום לקרוב מעיקרא צדיק גמור, דגדול כחן של בעלי תשובה.

NOTES

מָקוֹם שֶׁבַּעֲלֵי תְשׁוּבָה עוֹמְדִין שָׁם In a place where repentant sinners stand. The Rishonim and Aḥaronim explain that repentant sinners are considered on a higher spiritual level than righteous people who have never sinned, because they have acquired a taste for sin and must work harder to overcome their evil inclinations (*Rambam, Akedah*, and others).

HALAKHAH

אֵין בֵּין הָעוֹלָם הַזֶּה לִימוֹת הַמָּשִׁיחַ There is no difference between this world and the days of the Messiah. "There is no difference between the present world and the Messianic age except that during the Messianic age the people of Israel will no longer be subject to foreign governments, and they will regain the independence they enjoyed during the days of David and Solomon." It has been pointed out that *Rambam* appears to rule in accordance with both the position of Shmuel cited in this Halakhah, and the position of Rabbi Yoḥanan cited in the previous Halakhah, while according to our Gemara, these two positions are in disagreement with each other (see *Kesef Mishneh, Leḥem Mishneh*, and others). (*Rambam, Sefer Mada, Hilkhot Teshuvah* 9:2.)

מָקוֹם שֶׁבַּעֲלֵי תְשׁוּבָה עוֹמְדִין In a place where repentant sinners stand. "Repentant sinners are on a higher spiritual level than righteous people who have never sinned," following Rabbi Abbahu. (*Rambam, Sefer Mada, Hilkhot Teshuvah* 7:4.)

TRANSLATION AND COMMENTARY

וְרַבִּי יוֹחָנָן אָמַר [1]And Rabbi Yoḥanan, who maintains that people who never sinned are greater than those who sinned and repented, said that the verse in Isaiah should be understood thus: [2]The words **"for far"** refer to those **who were far from sin** all their lives. [3]The word **"near"** refers to those **who were near to sin, but** later **distanced themselves from** it.

וְאָמַר [4]**Rabbi Ḥiyya bar Abba said in the name of Rabbi Yoḥanan: All the Prophets' prophecies regarding** the future reward for the righteous refer to the reward that awaits **someone who marries his daughter to a Torah scholar, or conducts business on behalf of a Torah scholar, or enables a Torah scholar to benefit from his property.** [5]**But as for** the even greater reward that awaits the **Torah scholars themselves,** the verse states (Isaiah 64:3): **"The eye has not seen, that a God beside You** should do such a thing for him that waits for Him."

מַאי [6]The Gemara asks: **What is** that reward which **"the eye has not seen"?** [7]**Rabbi Yehoshua ben Levi said: This** refers to **wine** that has been **preserved in its grapes from the six days of Creation.** Since it was never tasted, no one knows how delightful it tastes.

רֵישׁ לָקִישׁ אָמַר [8]**Resh Lakish said: This** refers to **Eden, which no eye has ever seen.** [9]**And if you should ask: Where did Adam live?** [10]Adam lived **in the garden.** [11]**And if you should say:** Surely **the garden** where Adam lived **was Eden,** that is wrong. [12]**Therefore the Torah states** (Genesis 2:10): **"And a river went out of Eden to water the garden,"** teaching you that "the garden" and "Eden" are different places.

וְהָאוֹמֵר [13]The Gemara now returns to our Mishnah: "Among those sinners who do not have a portion in the World to Come is **someone who says: 'The Torah was not** given **from Heaven** but was written by Moses.'" [14]**Our Rabbis taught** a related Baraita: "The verse that states (Numbers 15:31), **'Because he has despised the word of the Lord, and has broken His commandment, that soul shall be utterly cut off,'** [15]refers to **someone who says** that **the Torah was not** given **from Heaven** but was written by Moses. [16]According to **another explanation,** the words

[1]וְרַבִּי יוֹחָנָן אָמַר: [2]"לָרָחוֹק" — שֶׁהוּא רָחוֹק מֵעֲבֵירָה. [3]"קָרוֹב" — שֶׁהוּא קָרוֹב מֵעֲבֵירָה וְנִתְרַחֵק מִמֶּנָּה.

[4]וְאָמַר רַבִּי חִיָּיא בַּר אַבָּא אָמַר רַבִּי יוֹחָנָן: כׇּל הַנְּבִיאִים כּוּלָּן לֹא נִתְנַבְּאוּ אֶלָּא לְמַשִּׂיא בִּתּוֹ לְתַלְמִיד חָכָם, וּלְעוֹשֶׂה פְּרַקְמַטְיָא לְתַלְמִיד חָכָם, וּלְמְהַנֶּה תַּלְמִיד חָכָם מִנְּכָסָיו. [5]אֲבָל תַּלְמִידֵי חֲכָמִים עַצְמָן — "עַיִן לֹא רָאֲתָה אֱלֹהִים זוּלָתְךָ".

[6]מַאי "עַיִן לֹא רָאֲתָה"? [7]אָמַר רַבִּי יְהוֹשֻׁעַ בֶּן לֵוִי: זֶה יַיִן הַמְשׁוּמָּר בַּעֲנָבָיו מִשֵּׁשֶׁת יְמֵי בְרֵאשִׁית.

[8]רֵישׁ לָקִישׁ אָמַר: זֶה עֵדֶן, לֹא רָאֲתָה עַיִן מֵעוֹלָם. [9]וְאִם תֹּאמַר: אָדָם הֵיכָן דָּר? [10]בַּגָּן. [11]וְאִם תֹּאמַר: גַּן הוּא עֵדֶן — [12]תַּלְמוּד לוֹמַר: "וְנָהָר יֹצֵא מֵעֵדֶן לְהַשְׁקוֹת אֶת הַגָּן".

[13]"וְהָאוֹמֵר: 'אֵין תּוֹרָה מִן הַשָּׁמַיִם' וכו׳". [14]תָּנוּ רַבָּנַן: "'כִּי דְבַר ה׳ בָּזָה וּמִצְוָתוֹ הֵפַר הִכָּרֵת תִּכָּרֵת' — [15]זֶה הָאוֹמֵר: אֵין תּוֹרָה מִן הַשָּׁמַיִם. [16]דָּבָר אַחֵר: 'כִּי דְבַר ה׳ בָּזָה' —

LITERAL TRANSLATION

[1]And Rabbi Yoḥanan said: [2]"For far" — who was far from sin. [3]"Near" — who was near to sin and distanced himself from it.

[4]And Rabbi Ḥiyya bar Abba said in the name of Rabbi Yoḥanan: All the Prophets prophesied only about someone who marries his daughter to a Torah scholar, or conducts business on behalf of a Torah scholar, or benefits a Torah scholar with his property. [5]But regarding Torah scholars themselves — "The eye has not seen, that a God beside You."

[6]What is "The eye has not seen"? [7]Rabbi Yehoshua ben Levi said: This is wine preserved in its grapes from the six days of Creation.

[8]Resh Lakish said: This is Eden, [which] the eye has never seen. [9]And if you say: Where did Adam live? [10]In the garden. [11]And if you say: The garden is Eden — [12]therefore the Torah states: "And a river went out of Eden to water the garden."

[13]"And someone who says: 'The Torah is not from Heaven,' etc." [14]Our Rabbis taught: "'Because he has despised the word of the Lord, and has broken His commandment, that soul shall be utterly cut off' — [15]this is someone who says: The Torah is not from Heaven. [16]Another explanation: 'Because he has despised the word of the Lord' —

RASHI

שהיה רחוק מן העבירה — כל ימיו, דהיינו צדיק גמור.

LANGUAGE

פְּרַקְמַטְיָא **Business.** From the Greek πραγματεία, *pragmateia*, meaning "the transaction of business, commerce."

NOTES

יַיִן הַמְשׁוּמָּר **Wine that is preserved.** Wine symbolizes absolute joy and is used here as a metaphor for the unadulterated joy and gladness that await the righteous, which were preserved for them since the time of the Creation (*HaKotev*).

זֶה אֶפִּיקוֹרוֹס. [1]דָּבָר אַחֵר: ׳כִּי
דְבַר ה׳ בָּזָה׳ — [2]זֶה הַמְגַלֶּה
פָּנִים בַּתּוֹרָה. [3]׳וְאֶת מִצְוָתוֹ
הֵפַר׳ — זֶה הַמֵּפֵר בְּרִית בָּשָׂר.
[4]׳הִכָּרֵת תִּכָּרֵת׳. [5]׳הִכָּרֵת׳ —
בָּעוֹלָם הַזֶּה. [6]׳תִּכָּרֵת׳ —
לָעוֹלָם הַבָּא. [7]מִכָּאן אָמַר רַבִּי
אֱלְעָזָר הַמּוֹדָעִי: הַמְחַלֵּל אֶת
הַקֳּדָשִׁים, וְהַמְבַזֶּה אֶת
הַמּוֹעֲדוֹת וְהַמֵּפֵר בְּרִיתוֹ שֶׁל
אַבְרָהָם אָבִינוּ, [8]וְהַמְגַלֶּה פָּנִים
בַּתּוֹרָה שֶׁלֹּא כַּהֲלָכָה, וְהַמַּלְבִּין
פְּנֵי חֲבֵירוֹ בָּרַבִּים — אַף עַל
פִּי שֶׁיֵּשׁ בְּיָדוֹ תּוֹרָה וּמַעֲשִׂים
טוֹבִים, אֵין לוֹ חֵלֶק לָעוֹלָם
הַבָּא״.

[9]תַּנְיָא אִידָךְ: ״׳כִּי דְבַר ה׳ בָּזָה׳
— [10]זֶה הָאוֹמֵר אֵין תּוֹרָה מִן
הַשָּׁמַיִם. [11]וַאֲפִילּוּ אָמַר: כָּל
הַתּוֹרָה כּוּלָּהּ מִן הַשָּׁמַיִם, חוּץ

LITERAL TRANSLATION

this is an *apikoros*. [1]Another explanation: 'Because he has despised the word of the Lord' — [2]this is someone who acts impudently towards the Torah. [3]'And has broken His commandment' — this is someone who breaks the covenant of the flesh. [4]'[That soul] shall be utterly cut off.' [5]'Cut off' — in this world. [6]'Utterly [cut off]' — in the World to Come. [7]From here Rabbi Eliezer Hamoda'i said: Someone who desecrates holy things, or despises the intermediate days of the Festivals, or breaks the Covenant of Abraham our father, [8]or acts impudently toward the Torah, or puts his fellow to shame (lit., "whitens the face") in public — even if he has in his hand Torah and good deeds, he has no share in the World to Come."

[9]It was taught in another [Baraita]: "'Because he despised the word of the Lord' — [10]this is someone who says: The Torah is not from Heaven. [11]And even if he said: The entire Torah is from Heaven, except

TRANSLATION AND COMMENTARY

'because he has despised the word of the Lord' refer to **an *apikoros*,** a heretic who denigrates the Rabbis and their Torah. [1]According to yet **another explanation,** the words **'because he has despised the word of the Lord'** [2]refer to **someone who acts impudently towards the Torah.** [3]**'And has broken His commandment'** refers to **someone who breaks the covenant of the flesh,** and refuses to undergo circumcision. [4]The verse promises **'that soul shall be utterly cut off,'** using the double verb form *hikaret tikaret* [הִכָּרֵת תִּכָּרֵת]. That apparent superfluity teaches that the sinner will be cut off in two worlds. [5]He will be **'cut off'** [*hikaret*] — **in this world** and die a premature or sudden death; [6]and he will be **'utterly** [*tikaret*] cut off' — **in the World to Come.** [7]**From** this verse **Rabbi Eliezer Hamoda'i concluded:** If **someone desecrates holy things,** willfully defiling them, **or he despises the intermediate days of the Festivals,** treating them as ordinary days, **or he breaks the Covenant of the Patriarch Abraham,** refusing to undergo circumcision, [8]**or he acts impudently toward the Torah, or he puts another person to shame in public,** then **even if he has to his credit Torah** study **and** the performance of many other **good deeds, he** still **has no share in the World to Come."**

תַּנְיָא אִידָךְ [9]**It was taught in another Baraita:** "The verse (Numbers 15:31), **'because he has despised the word of the Lord,'** [10]refers to **someone who says** that **the Torah was not** given **from Heaven** but was written by Moses. [11]**Even if** a person **said: The entire Torah was** given

RASHI

אפיקורוס ומגלה פנים — מפורש לקמן. **ברית בשר** — מילה. **מכאן** — מן הפסוק הזה שכתוב כי דבר ה׳ בזה (אמר רבי אליעזר וכו׳ מחלל את הקדשים דמחלל קדשים ומבזה מועדות ומגלה פנים כו׳ היינו ״דבר ה׳ בזה״) דבזיון הוא. **מפר ברית** — היינו את בריתי הפר. **מועדות** — חולו של מועד.

NOTES

הַמְחַלֵּל אֶת הַקֳּדָשִׁים Someone who desecrates holy things. The present tense that is used in this Baraita to express the various actions — מְחַלֵּל, "desecrates," מְבַזֶּה, "disregards," מַלְבִּין, "puts to shame" — teaches us that only if a person commits these transgressions regularly does he forfeit his share in the World to Come (see *Rambam*).

הַמְבַזֶּה אֶת הַמּוֹעֲדוֹת Someone who despises the intermediate days of the Festivals. This refers to someone who plans from the outset to do work on the intermediate day of a Festival, thus demonstrating that he does not regard the day as important enough to honor with abstention from work (*Rabbenu Yehonatan*).

HALAKHAH

הַמְחַלֵּל אֶת הַקֳּדָשִׁים Someone who desecrates holy things. "Someone who desecrates holy things, or despises the intermediate days of the Festivals, or publicly puts another person to shame, or acts impudently towards the Torah, or refuses to undergo circumcision, does not have a share in the World to Come," following the Gemara. (*Rambam, Sefer Mada, Hilkhot Teshuvah* 3:14.)

הָאוֹמֵר אֵין תּוֹרָה מִן הַשָּׁמַיִם Someone who says: The Torah is not from Heaven. "Someone who says that the Torah was not given by God, referring to the whole Torah, or even a single verse, or even a single word, falls under the category of those who deny the Torah, and does not have a share in the World to Come." (*Rambam, Sefer Mada, Hilkhot Teshuvah* 3:8.)

מִפָּסוּק זֶה שֶׁלֹּא אֲמָרוֹ הַקָּדוֹשׁ בָּרוּךְ הוּא אֶלָּא מֹשֶׁה מִפִּי עַצְמוֹ — [1]זֶהוּ ׳כִּי דְבַר ה׳ בָּזָה׳. [2]וַאֲפִילּוּ אָמַר: כָּל הַתּוֹרָה כּוּלָּהּ מִן הַשָּׁמַיִם, חוּץ מִדִּקְדּוּק זֶה, מִקַּל וָחוֹמֶר זֶה, מִגְּזֵירָה שָׁוָה זוֹ — [3]זֶה הוּא ׳כִּי דְבַר ה׳ בָּזָה׳״.

[4]תַּנְיָא: ״הָיָה רַבִּי מֵאִיר אוֹמֵר: הַלּוֹמֵד תּוֹרָה וְאֵינוֹ מְלַמְּדָהּ — [5]זֶה הוּא ׳דְּבַר ה׳ בָּזָה׳. [6]רַבִּי נָתָן אוֹמֵר: כָּל מִי שֶׁאֵינוֹ מַשְׁגִּיחַ עַל הַמִּשְׁנָה. [7]רַבִּי נְהוֹרַאי אוֹמֵר: כָּל שֶׁאֶפְשָׁר לַעֲסוֹק בַּתּוֹרָה וְאֵינוֹ עוֹסֵק. [8]רַבִּי יִשְׁמָעֵאל אוֹמֵר: זֶה הָעוֹבֵד עֲבוֹדָה זָרָה״. [9]מַאי מַשְׁמָעֵהּ? [10]דְּתָנָא דְּבֵי רַבִּי יִשְׁמָעֵאל: ״׳כִּי דְבַר ה׳ בָּזָה׳ — [11]זֶה הַמְבַזֶּה דִּבּוּר שֶׁנֶּאֱמַר לוֹ לְמֹשֶׁה מִסִּינַי: ׳אָנֹכִי ה׳ אֱלֹהֶיךָ, לֹא יִהְיֶה לְךָ אֱלֹהִים אֲחֵרִים וגו׳״.

[12]״רַבִּי יְהוֹשֻׁעַ בֶּן קָרְחָה אוֹמֵר: כָּל הַלּוֹמֵד תּוֹרָה וְאֵינוֹ חוֹזֵר

LITERAL TRANSLATION

for this verse which the Holy One, blessed be He, did not say, but rather Moses [said it] on his own — [1]this is: 'Because he despised the word of the Lord.' [2]And even if he said: The entire Torah is from Heaven, except for this precision, this *kal vaḥomer*, this *gezerah shavah* — [3]this is: 'Because he despised the word of the Lord.'"

[4]It was taught: "Rabbi Meir said: Someone who studies Torah, but does not teach it — [5]this is: 'Because he despised the word of the Lord.' [6]Rabbi Natan says: Anyone who disregards the Mishnah. [7]Rabbi Nehorai says: Anyone who can engage in the Torah, but does not engage [in it]. [8]Rabbi Yishmael says: This is someone who worships idols." [9]What is its meaning? [10]For [a Sage] of the School of Rabbi Yishmael taught: "'Because he despised the word of the Lord' — [11]this is someone who disregards a word spoken to Moses at Sinai: 'I am the Lord your God.... You shall have no other gods [beside Me].'"

[12]"Rabbi Yehoshua ben Korḥah says: Anyone who studies Torah but does not review

TRANSLATION AND COMMENTARY

from Heaven, except for a certain verse which the Holy One, blessed be He, did not say, but rather Moses said that verse **on his own,** that person **is** included among those referred to by the verse: [1]**'Because he despised the word of the Lord.'** [2]**And even if** a person **said: The entire Torah was** given **from Heaven, except for a certain** law derived by a **deduction** based on a defective or plene spelling, or **a certain** law based on a *kal vaḥomer* argument, or **a certain** law based on a *gezerah shavah* — [3]that person **is** included among those referred to by the verse: **'Because he despised the word of the Lord.'"**

תַּנְיָא [4]**It was taught** in another related Baraita: **"Rabbi Meir said:** If **someone studies Torah, but does not teach it** to others, [5]he **is** included among those referred to by the verse (Numbers 15:31): **'Because he despised the word of the Lord.'** Since he does not teach others, he does not attach importance to his knowledge. [6]**Rabbi Natan says: Anyone who disregards the Mishnah,** and does not act in accordance with its teachings, 'has despised the word of the Lord.' [7]**Rabbi Nehorai says: Anyone who is capable of engaging in Torah** study, **but does not do** so, 'has despised the word of the Lord.' [8]**Rabbi Yishmael says:** The words, 'he despised the word of the Lord,' refer to **someone who worships idols."** [9]The Gemara asks: **How may the verse be expounded** as referring to someone who practices idolatry? [10]**As it was taught by a Sage of the School of Rabbi Yishmael:** "The verse, **'because he despised the word of the Lord,'** [11]refers to **someone who disregards the word spoken to Moses at Sinai** and heard directly by all of Israel (Exodus 20:2-3): **'I am the Lord your God....You shall have no other gods beside Me.'"**

רַבִּי יְהוֹשֻׁעַ בֶּן קָרְחָה [12]Having mentioned the importance of Torah study, the Gemara now cites a Baraita which expands on this topic: **"Rabbi Yehoshua ben Korḥah says: Anyone who studies Torah, but fails to review**

RASHI

דקדוק זה — חסרות ויתרות. מקל וחומר [זה] ומגזירה שוה [זו] — [ושאמר לו רבו גזירה שוה] לא גמר מרבו. המשנה — זה שעושה כמו שאינה עיקר. זה העובד עבודה זרה — היינו "דבר ה'" — דבור שדבר הקדוש ברוך הוא בעצמו לישראל, דאנכי ולא יהיה לך מפי הגבורה שמענום. חוזר — לשנותה.

NOTES

מִי שֶׁאֵינוֹ מַשְׁגִּיחַ עַל הַמִּשְׁנָה **Anyone who disregards the Mishnah.** Since the Mishnah is an explanation of the Written Law, someone who disregards the Mishnah demonstrates that the Torah is not important to him, and that he despises the word of the Lord (*Maharsha*).

HALAKHAH

כָּל שֶׁאֶפְשָׁר לַעֲסוֹק בַּתּוֹרָה **Anyone who is capable of engaging in the Torah.** "Someone who is capable of engaging in Torah study but forsakes it, is regarded as someone who despises the word of God." (*Rambam, Sefer Mada, Hilkhot Talmud Torah* 3:13; *Shulḥan Arukh, Yoreh De'ah* 246:25.)

עָלֶיהָ, דּוֹמֶה לְאָדָם שֶׁזּוֹרֵעַ וְאֵינוֹ קוֹצֵר. [1]רַבִּי יְהוֹשֻׁעַ אוֹמֵר: כָּל הַלּוֹמֵד תּוֹרָה וּמְשַׁכְּחָהּ דּוֹמֶה לְאִשָּׁה שֶׁיּוֹלֶדֶת וְקוֹבֶרֶת. [2]רַבִּי עֲקִיבָא אוֹמֵר: [99B] [3]זַמֵּר בְּכָל יוֹם, זַמֵּר בְּכָל יוֹם״.

[4]אָמַר רַב יִצְחָק בַּר אֲבוּדִימִי: מַאי קְרָא? [5]שֶׁנֶּאֱמַר: ״נֶפֶשׁ עָמֵל עָמְלָה לוֹ כִּי אָכַף עָלָיו פִּיהוּ״. [6]הוּא עָמֵל בְּמָקוֹם זֶה, וְתוֹרָתוֹ עוֹמֶלֶת לוֹ בְּמָקוֹם אַחֵר.

[7]אָמַר רַבִּי אֶלְעָזָר: כָּל אָדָם לְעָמָל נִבְרָא, שֶׁנֶּאֱמַר: ״כִּי אָדָם לְעָמָל יוּלָּד״. [8]אֵינִי יוֹדֵעַ אִם לַעֲמַל פֶּה נִבְרָא אִם לַעֲמַל מְלָאכָה נִבְרָא. [9]כְּשֶׁהוּא אוֹמֵר, ״כִּי אָכַף עָלָיו פִּיהוּ״, הֱוֵי אוֹמֵר לַעֲמַל פֶּה נִבְרָא. [10]וַעֲדַיִין אֵינִי יוֹדֵעַ אִם לַעֲמַל תּוֹרָה אִם לַעֲמַל שִׂיחָה. [11]כְּשֶׁהוּא אוֹמֵר, ״לֹא יָמוּשׁ סֵפֶר הַתּוֹרָה הַזֶּה מִפִּיךָ״, הֱוֵי אוֹמֵר לַעֲמַל תּוֹרָה נִבְרָא.

LITERAL TRANSLATION

it, is like a person who sows but does not reap. [1]Rabbi Yehoshua says: Anyone who studies Torah and forgets it, is like a woman who gives birth and buries. [2]Rabbi Akiva says: [99B] [3]Chant every day, chant every day."

[4]Rav Yitzḥak bar Avudimi said: What is the verse? [5]For it is stated: "The hunger of the laborer labors for him; for his mouth presses upon him." [6]He labors in this place, and his Torah labors for him in another place.

[7]Rabbi Eliezer said: Every man was created for toil, as it is stated: "Man is born for toil." [8]I do not know whether he was created for toil of the mouth, or whether he was created for toil of work. [9]Since it says, "For his mouth presses upon him," say that he was created for toil of the mouth. [10]But I still do not know whether for toil of Torah or for toil of talk. [11]Since it says: "This book of the Torah shall not depart from your mouth," say that he was created for the toil of Torah.

TRANSLATION AND COMMENTARY

what he has learned, **is like a person who sows** grain **and fails to reap** it, [1]**Rabbi Yehoshua says: Anyone who studies Torah, but** later **forgets it, is like a woman who gives birth, but** soon thereafter **buries** her newborn. [2]**Rabbi Akiva says:** [99B] [3]**Chant** your studies **every day, chant** your studies **every day**. Continually review them."

אָמַר [4]**Rav Yitzḥak bar Avudimi said: What** Biblical **verse** is the source for this statement? [5]It is **the verse** that **states** (Proverbs 16:26): **"The hunger of the laborer labors for him; for his mouth presses upon him."** [6]A slightly different reading allows for the interpretation: If a person **labors** in Torah **in this place,** the present world, **his Torah will labor for him in another place,** the World to Come. Why? Because he presses upon his mouth, forcing it to review what he has learned.

אָמַר רַבִּי אֶלְעָזָר [7]**Rabbi Eliezer said: Every man was created for toil, as the verse states** (Job 5:7): **"Man is born for toil."** [8]Had I only had this verse, **I would not know whether** man **was created for toil of the mouth, or whether he was created for the toil of** physical **work.** [9]**Since** another verse **states** (Proverbs 16:26): **"For his mouth presses upon him," say that** man **was created for toil of the mouth.** [10]**But** even with this second verse, **I still would not know whether** this toil of the mouth is the **toil of Torah** study **or the toil of** ordinary **talk.** [11]**Since** another verse **states** (Joshua 1:8): **"This book of the Torah shall not depart out of your mouth," say that** man was **created for the toil of Torah** study.

RASHI

זמר בכל יום — היה מסדר למודך, אף על פי שסדור בפיך כזמר, והוא יגרום לך שתהא לעולם הבא בשמחה ובשירים. **נפש עמל עמלה לו** — מפני שעמל בתורה — תורה עומלת לו. **כי אכף עליו פיהו** — מפני שהוא משים דברים בפיו תמיד כאוכף שעל החמור, לישנא אחרינא: זמר, כלומר שעוסק בשירים וזמירות תדיר תדיר נעשה זמר, כך החוזר על התורה נעשה לו סדורה בפיו. **תורה עומלת לו** — שמחזרת עליו, ומבקשת מאת קונה למסור לו טעמי תורה וסדריה, וכל כך למה — מפני שאכף = שכפף פיהו על דברי תורה.

NOTES

זַמֵּר בְּכָל יוֹם Chant every day. Some Rishonim had the reading: זַמֵּר בְּכָל יוֹם — זֶמֶר, "Chant every day — a chant." That is to say, sing your Torah studies every day, and it will keep for you in the future like a song. Alternatively: Sing your Torah studies every day in this world, and it will be a song for you in the World to Come (see *Ramah*).

אִם לַעֲמַל פֶּה אִם לַעֲמַל מְלָאכָה Whether for toil of the mouth, or for toil of work. There are those who have connected this question to the Tannaitic dispute as to whether it is preferable to devote all of one's time to Torah study and totally abandon all worldly pursuits, or it is preferable to spend most of one's time earning a livelihood, and devote only one's spare time to Torah study (*Ri'af*). Others have understood the passage in a homiletical sense, asking whether man was created for toil of the mouth — for Torah study and prayer — or for toil of work — for the fulfillment of the Torah's commandments. After concluding that man was created for toil of the mouth, the Gemara clarifies whether he was created for the toil of prayer (as the Rabbis have said that *siḥah* is one of the designations of prayer), or for the toil of Torah (*Ye'arot Devash*).

[1]וְהַיְינוּ דַּאֲמַר רָבָא: כּוּלְּהוּ גּוּפֵי דְּרוּפְתְּקֵי נִינְהוּ; טוּבֵי לִדְזָכֵי דְּהָוֵי דְּרוּפְתְּקֵי דְּאוֹרַיְיתָא. [2]״נֹאֵף אִשָּׁה חֲסַר לֵב״. [3]אָמַר רֵישׁ לָקִישׁ: זֶה הַלּוֹמֵד תּוֹרָה לִפְרָקִים, [4]שֶׁנֶּאֱמַר: ״כִּי נָעִים כִּי תִשְׁמְרֵם בְּבִטְנֶךָ, יִכֹּנוּ יַחְדָּו עַל שְׂפָתֶיךָ״.

[5]תָּנוּ רַבָּנַן: ״׳וְהַנֶּפֶשׁ אֲשֶׁר תַּעֲשֶׂה בְּיָד רָמָה׳ — [6]זֶה מְנַשֶּׁה בֶּן חִזְקִיָּה, שֶׁהָיָה יוֹשֵׁב וְדוֹרֵשׁ בְּהַגָּדוֹת שֶׁל דּוֹפִי. [7]אָמַר: ׳וְכִי לֹא הָיָה לוֹ לְמֹשֶׁה לִכְתּוֹב אֶלָּא: [8]״וַאֲחוֹת לוֹטָן תִּמְנָע״, [9]״וְתִמְנַע הָיְתָה פִּילֶגֶשׁ לֶאֱלִיפַז״, [10]״וַיֵּלֶךְ רְאוּבֵן בִּימֵי קְצִיר חִטִּים וַיִּמְצָא דוּדָאִים בַּשָּׂדֶה״?׳ [11]יָצְאָה בַּת קוֹל וְאָמְרָה לוֹ: ׳תֵּשֵׁב בְּאָחִיךָ תְדַבֵּר בְּבֶן אִמְּךָ תִּתֶּן דֹּפִי. [12]אֵלֶּה עָשִׂיתָ וְהֶחֱרַשְׁתִּי דִּמִּיתָ הֱיוֹת אֶהְיֶה כָמוֹךָ אוֹכִיחֲךָ וְאֶעֶרְכָה לְעֵינֶיךָ׳. [13]וְעָלָיו מְפוֹרָשׁ בַּקַּבָּלָה: ׳הוֹי מֹשְׁכֵי הֶעָוֹן בְּחַבְלֵי הַשָּׁוְא וְכַעֲבוֹת הָעֲגָלָה חַטָּאָה׳״.

LITERAL TRANSLATION

[1]And this is what Rava said: All bodies are bags; it is good for one who merits being a bag for Torah. [2]"He who commits adultery with a woman lacks understanding." [3]Resh Lakish said: This is someone who learns Torah irregularly, [4]as it is stated: "For it is a pleasant thing if you keep them within your belly, let them dwell together on your lips."

[5]Our Rabbis taught: "'But the soul who acts presumptuously' — [6]this is Manasseh the son of Hezekiah, who would sit and expound scornful interpretations. [7]He said: 'Did Moses not have [anything else] to write besides: [8]"And Lotan's sister was Timna," [9]"And Timna was concubine to Elifaz," [10]"And Reuben went in the days of the wheat harvest, and found mandrakes in the field"?' [11]A heavenly voice issued forth and said to him: 'You sit and speak against your brother; you slander your mother's son. [12]These things have you done, and if I kept silence, you imagined that I was altogether like you, but I will reprove you, and set the matter before your eyes.' [13]And about him it is stated explicitly in post-Mosaic Scripture: 'Woe to them that draw iniquity with cords of vanity, and sin as if with a cart rope.'"

TRANSLATION AND COMMENTARY

וְהַיְינוּ דַּאֲמַר רָבָא [1]**This is what Rava** meant when he **said: All** human **bodies are** like empty **bags** that are ready to be filled. Fortunate are they **who merit** to be **a bag** (a receptacle) **for Torah.**

נֹאֵף אִשָּׁה [2]The verse states (Proverbs 6:32): **"He who commits adultery with a woman lacks understanding."** [3]**Resh Lakish said: This** verse alludes to **someone who learns Torah** irregularly. He is compared to an unmarried man who engages in sexual intercourse with one woman or another from time to time. One cannot acquire Torah knowledge without regular study, [4]**as the verse states** (Proverbs 22:18): **"For it is a pleasant thing if you keep them in your belly; let them dwell on your lips."**

תָּנוּ רַבָּנַן [5]**Our Rabbis taught** the following Baraita: "The verse that states (Numbers 15:30): **'But the person who acts presumptuously,** whether he be born in the land, or a stranger, that person dishonors the Lord; and that soul shall be cut off from among his people,' [6]refers to **Manasseh the son of Hezekiah,** king of Judah, **who would sit and expound scornful interpretations,** mocking the Torah. [7]**He would say: 'Did Moses not have anything else to write** in the Torah **besides** unnecessary verses that do not teach us anything, like (Genesis 36:22): [8]**"And Lotan's sister was Timna"**; [9]and (Genesis 36:12): **"And Timna was concubine to Elifaz"**; [10]and (Genesis 30:14): **"And Reuben went in the days of the wheat harvest, and found mandrakes in the field"?'** [11]**A heavenly voice issued forth and said to** Manasseh: **'You sit and speak against your brother; you slander your own mother's son.** [12]**These things have you done, and if I kept silence, you would imagine that I was altogether like you, but I will reprove you, and set the matter before your eyes.'** [13]**And about** a person like Manasseh **it is stated explicitly in post-Mosaic Scripture** (Isaiah 5:18): **'Woe to them that draw iniquity with cords of vanity, and sin as if with a cart rope.'"**

RASHI

דרופתקי = טרחנין, כלומר, כל הגופין לעמל נבראו. **טוביה לדזכי** — אשריו למי שזכה והיה עמלו וטרחו בתורה, לשון אחר: דרפתקי = כיס ארוך שמשימין בו מעות, כל הגופין נרתקין הם לקבל ולהכניס דברים, אשריו למי שזוכה ונעשה נרתק לתורה. **לומד תורה לפרקים** — ואינו לומד תדיר, כמי שאין לו אשה ובועל פעמים זו פעמים זו. **שנאמר כי נעים כי תשמרם** — אימתי תשמרם בבטנך — [בזמן] שיכונו יחדיו על שפתיך. **לא היה לו למשה לכתוב אלא ואחות לוטן תמנע** — בתמיה, דבר שאינו צריך הוא, וכן היה מלגלג ואומר שכתבו משה שלא לצורך, ולקמיה מפרש דהיינו מגלה פנים בתורה. **וילך ראובן וגו׳** — והיינו נמי שלא לצורך. **בחבלי השוא** — בחנם, בלא שום הנאה היה חוטא.

NOTES

כִּי נָעִים כִּי תִשְׁמְרֵם **For it is a pleasant thing if you keep them.** According to the reading found in *Arukh*, this verse is brought as a proof text for Rava's statement that it is fortunate to become a "bag" for Torah. Regarding a person who allows his body to become a receptacle for Torah, the verse states: "For it is a pleasant thing if you keep them."

דּוֹרֵשׁ בְּהַגָּדוֹת שֶׁל דּוֹפִי **He would expound scornful interpretations.** Some suggest that Manasseh went beyond

LANGUAGE

כּוּבְיָא Embroidery. The *Arukh* contains the reading כביה which is probably derived from the Persian *kakiya,* meaning "a spider," thus the "thread of kuvya" is a spider web.

TRANSLATION AND COMMENTARY

מַאי ״כַּעֲבוֹת הָעֲגָלָה״ [1]The Gemara asks: **What is** meant by the words, **"as if with a cart rope"?** [2]**Rabbi Yose said: First the evil inclination resembles an embroidery thread, but in the end it resembles a cart rope.** So, too, Manasseh began with words of scorn about a few isolated verses, but eventually he violated the entire Torah.

דְּאָתֵן עֲלָהּ [3]The Gemara asks: **Now that we have come to** discuss the matter, the question **still** remains regarding the verse, **"and Lotan's sister was Timna." What** do those words teach us? [4]The Gemara explains: **Timna was of royal stock, as the verses state** (Genesis 36:29, 40): **"The chief Lotan," "the chief Timna."** [5]**And every "chief"** mentioned in this series of verses **was a king without a crown.** [6]Timna **wanted to convert** to the Jewish faith, [7]and **she approached** the Patriarchs **Abraham, Isaac, and Jacob, but they did not accept her** as a proselyte. [8]**She** then **went and became the concubine of Elifaz the son of Esau,** [9]**saying: "Better to be a maidservant of this nation and not a noblewoman of some other nation."** [10]**From her** and Elifaz **issued Amalek, who** later **vexed Israel.** [11]**What is the reason** that the Patriarchs and their descendants were punished with Amalek? [12]They were punished because **they should not have put** Timna **off** when she approached them to convert. Thus, we learn a number of important things from this verse which appears to be superfluous.

וַיֵּלֶךְ רְאוּבֵן [13]Regarding the verse (Genesis 30:14), **"And Reuben went in the days of the wheat harvest,"** [14]**Rava the son of Rabbi Yitzḥak said in the name of Rav: From here** we see **that righteous people do not extend their hands to commit robbery,** even regarding matters of little value. Reuben did not take wheat, which surely belonged to somebody. He took only a mandrake, that did not belong to anybody.

[1]מַאי ״כַּעֲבוֹת הָעֲגָלָה״? [2]אָמַר רַבִּי אַסִי: יֵצֶר הָרַע, בַּתְּחִלָּה דּוֹמֶה לְחוּט שֶׁל כּוּבְיָא וּלְבַסּוֹף דּוֹמֶה לַעֲבוֹת הָעֲגָלָה.

[3]דְּאָתָן עֲלַהּ, מִיהַת ״אֲחוֹת לוֹטָן תִּמְנַע״ מַאי הִיא? [4]תִּמְנַע בַּת מְלָכִים הֲוַאי, דִּכְתִיב: ״אַלּוּף לוֹטָן, אַלּוּף תִּמְנַע״. [5]וְכָל ״אַלּוּף״ מַלְכוּתָא בְּלָא תָּאגָא הִיא. [6]בָּעֲיָא לְאִיגַּיּוּרֵי. [7]בָּאתָה אֵצֶל אַבְרָהָם יִצְחָק וְיַעֲקֹב וְלֹא קִבְּלוּהָ. [8]הָלְכָה וְהָיְתָה פִּילֶגֶשׁ לֶאֱלִיפַז בֶּן עֵשָׂו. [9]אָמְרָה: ״מוּטָב תְּהֵא שִׁפְחָה לְאוּמָּה זוֹ, וְלֹא תְּהֵא גְּבִירָה לְאוּמָּה אַחֶרֶת״. [10]נְפַק מִינָּהּ עֲמָלֵק, דְּצַעֲרִינְהוּ לְיִשְׂרָאֵל. [11]מַאי טַעְמָא? [12]דְּלָא אִיבָּעֵי לְהוּ לְרַחֲקָהּ.

[13]״וַיֵּלֶךְ רְאוּבֵן בִּימֵי קְצִיר חִטִּים״. [14]אָמַר רָבָא בְּרַבִּי יִצְחָק אָמַר רַב: מִכָּאן לַצַּדִּיקִים שֶׁאֵין פּוֹשְׁטִין יְדֵיהֶן בְּגָזֵל.

LITERAL TRANSLATION

[1]What is "as if with a cart rope"? [2]Rabbi Assi said: The evil inclination, at first it resembles an embroidery thread, and at the end it resembles a cart rope.

[3]Now that we have come to it, [the question] still [remains]: "And Lotan's sister was Timna," what is it? [4]Timna was the daughter of kings, as it is written: "The chief Lotan," "the chief Timna." [5]And every "chief" is a king without a crown. [6]She wanted to convert. [7]She came before Abraham, Isaac, and Jacob, but they did not accept her. [8]She went and became the concubine of Elifaz the son of Esau. [9]She said: "It is better to be a maidservant of this nation, and not be a noblewoman of another nation." [10]Amalek issued from her, who vexed Israel. [11]What is the reason? [12]They should not have put her off.

[13]"And Reuben went in the days of the wheat harvest." [14]Rava the son of Rabbi Yitzḥak said in the name of Rav: From here [we see] that righteous people do not extend their hands in robbery.

RASHI

מלכותא בלא תגא — שר גדול אלא שאינו מעוטר, וכיון דתמנע היתה אחות מלך — ודאי בת מלך היא. **מוטב שאהיה שפחה לאומה זו** — לבני אברהם יצחק (ויעקב) שהן יראי שמים — ולא אהיה גברת לאומה אחרת, ולכך נעשית פילגש לאליפז בן עשו שהיה מזרע יצחק. **לרחקה** — מתחת כנפי השכינה, שהיה להם לגיירה. **בימי קציר חטים** — לאחר שקצרו השדה שהכל רשאין ליכנס בתוך שדה חבריהן.

NOTES

the claim that the verses under discussion are unnecessary. He added explanations of his own which fell into the category of "scornful interpretations" (*Or Kasalmah*).

וְלֹא קִבְּלוּהָ But they did not accept her. It has been suggested that Abraham, Isaac, and Jacob did not accept Timna as a convert because she was a *mamzeret*, the product of an adulterous or incestuous relationship, as we find in the Midrash (*Be'er Sheva,* and others). *Rabbi Ya'akov Emden* proposes that they did not accept her because she wished to convert only in order to marry one of the Patriarchs.

דְּלָא אִיבָּעֵי לְהוּ לְרַחֲקָהּ They should not have put her off. Even though we find a tendency to discourage conversion in Rabbinic literature, if a person comes on his own and asks to convert, attempts should be made to draw that person closer to God and the Jewish people (*Tosafot*).

TRANSLATION AND COMMENTARY

וַיִּמְצָא דוּדָאִים בַּשָּׂדֶה [1]That verse continues: **"And he found mandrakes [*duda'im*] in the field."** [2]The Gemara asks: **What are *duda'im*,** translated here as mandrakes? [3]**Rav said:** A plant called *yavruhei.* [4]**Levi said:** A plant called *siglei.* [5]**Rabbi Yonatan said:** A plant called *seviskei.*

אָמַר רַבִּי אֲלֶכְּסַנְדְּרִי [6]The Gemara returns to the importance of Torah study. **Rabbi Alexandri said: Whoever engages in Torah** study **for its own sake makes peace in the heavenly retinue and in the earthly retinue,** [7]**as the verse states** (Isaiah 27:5): **"Or let him take hold of My stronghold, that he may make peace with Me; and he shall make peace with Me."** Torah study is God's stronghold. By mentioning peace twice, the verse intimates that the study of Torah makes peace both in Heaven and on earth.

רַב אָמַר [8]**Rav said:** Someone who engages in Torah study for its own sake is regarded **as if he had built a palace** both **in Heaven and on earth,** [9]**as the verse states** (Isaiah 51:16): **"And I have put My words in your mouth, and I have covered you in the shadow of My hand, to plant the heavens, and lay the foundations of the earth,** and say to Zion, you are My people."

רַבִּי יוֹחָנָן אָמַר [10]**Rabbi Yoḥanan said:** Someone who engages in Torah study for its own sake **also protects the entire world** through his studies, [11]**as the verse states: "And I have covered you in the shadow of My hand."** Someone who has God's words in his mouth causes God to protect the entire world.

וְלֵוִי אָמַר [12]**And Levi said:** Someone who studies Torah for its own sake **also draws the redemption closer,** [13]**as the** same **verse states: "And say to Zion, you are My people."**

אָמַר רֵישׁ לָקִישׁ [14]In a similar vein, **Resh Lakish said: Whoever teaches someone else's son Torah, Scripture regards him as if he** himself **had made him,** [15]**as the verse states** (Genesis 12:5): "And Abram took Sarai his wife...**and the souls that they had acquired** [the Hebrew term עָשׂוּ may also be rendered as "made"] **in Haran,"** by teaching them Torah.

[1]״וַיִּמְצָא דוּדָאִים בַּשָּׂדֶה״. [2]מַאי דּוּדָאִים? [3]אָמַר רַב: יַבְרוּחֵי. [4]לֵוִי אָמַר: סִיגְלֵי. [5]רַבִּי יוֹנָתָן אָמַר: סְבִיסְקֵי.

[6]אָמַר רַבִּי אֲלֶכְּסַנְדְּרִי: כָּל הָעוֹסֵק בַּתּוֹרָה לִשְׁמָהּ מֵשִׂים שָׁלוֹם בְּפָמַלְיָא שֶׁל מַעְלָה וּבְפָמַלְיָא שֶׁל מַטָּה, [7]שֶׁנֶּאֱמַר: ״אוֹ יַחֲזֵק בְּמָעֻזִּי יַעֲשֶׂה שָׁלוֹם לִי שָׁלוֹם יַעֲשֶׂה לִּי״.

[8]רַב אָמַר: כְּאִילּוּ בָּנָה פַּלְטֵרִין שֶׁל מַעְלָה וְשֶׁל מַטָּה, [9]שֶׁנֶּאֱמַר: ״וָאָשִׂם דְּבָרַי בְּפִיךָ וּבְצֵל יָדִי כִּסִּיתִיךָ לִנְטֹעַ שָׁמַיִם וְלִיסֹד אָרֶץ״.

[10]רַבִּי יוֹחָנָן אָמַר: אַף מֵגֵין עַל כָּל הָעוֹלָם כּוּלּוֹ, [11]שֶׁנֶּאֱמַר: ״וּבְצֵל יָדִי כִּסִּיתִיךָ״.

[12]וְלֵוִי אָמַר: אַף מְקָרֵב אֶת הַגְּאוּלָּה, [13]שֶׁנֶּאֱמַר: ״וְלֵאמֹר לְצִיּוֹן עַמִּי אָתָּה״.

[14]אָמַר רֵישׁ לָקִישׁ: כָּל הַמְלַמֵּד אֶת בֶּן חֲבֵירוֹ תּוֹרָה מַעֲלֶה עָלָיו הַכָּתוּב כְּאִילּוּ עֲשָׂאוֹ, [15]שֶׁנֶּאֱמַר: ״וְאֶת הַנֶּפֶשׁ אֲשֶׁר עָשׂוּ בְחָרָן״.

LITERAL TRANSLATION

[1]"And he found mandrakes [*duda'im*] in the field." [2]What are *duda'im*? [3]Rav said: *Yavruhei.* [4]Levi said: *Siglei.* [5]Rabbi Yonatan said: *Seviskei.*

[6]Rabbi Alexandri said: Whoever engages in the Torah for its own sake makes peace in the heavenly retinue and in the earthly retinue, [7]as it is stated: "Or let him take hold of My stronghold, that he may make peace with Me; and he shall make peace with Me."

[8]Rav said: As if he built a palace in Heaven and on earth, [9]as it is stated: "And I have put My words in your mouth, and I have covered you in the shadow of My hand, to plant the heavens, and lay the foundations of the earth."

[10]Rabbi Yoḥanan said: He also protects the entire world, [11]as it is stated: "And I have covered you in the shadow of My hand."

[12]And Levi said: He also draws the redemption closer, [13]as it is stated: "And say to Zion, you are My people."

[14]Resh Lakish said: Whoever teaches his fellow's son Torah, Scripture regards him as if he made him, [15]as it is stated: "And the souls they made in Haran."

RASHI

יברוחי – כדמתרגמינן, ולא איתפרש מאי היא. סיגלי וסביסקי [וסבסוך] – מינין אחרים, סיגלי עיקרי עשבים והוא ממיני בשמים, ואמהות של אותן עשבים קרי סגלי, (וסבסך) [וסביסקי] נמי מין בשמים. מעוזי – תורה. שלום שלום – תרתי זימני, אחד למעלה ואחד למטה. פלטירין של מעלה ושלמטה – כדכתיב לנטוע שמים וליסוד ארץ. אשר עשו בחרן – דמתרגמינן דשעבידו לאורייתא בחרן, וקרי להו עשייה.

NOTES

בְּפָמַלְיָא שֶׁל מַעְלָה וּבְפָמַלְיָא שֶׁל מַטָּה In the heavenly retinue and in the earthly retinue. Someone who engages in Torah study for its own sake brings peace to Heaven, for there will be no need to impose any punishments upon him. He also brings peace to the earth, for his merits provide protection for the rest of the community as well (*Ramah*).

LANGUAGE

יַבְרוּחֵי *Yavruhei.* This is derived from the Arabic يبروج, meaning "mandrakes." The word derives from the Persian *sabizak,* meaning "mandrakes."

BACKGROUND

דּוּדָאִים Mandrakes.

A flowering mandrake plant.

Medicinal mandrake (*Mandragora officinalis*) belongs to the nightshade family, it is a perennial plant whose leaves form a crown on the ground. The fruit of the mandrake are small golden balls, each weighing about 25 grams, with a pleasant and pungent smell when they are ripe, usually around the months of May and June (the time of the wheat harvest). Many legends are attached to this plant, mainly to its root, which is strangely shaped, sometimes suggesting a human form. For many generations mandrake root was regarded as a fertility drug.

סִיגְלֵי Violet.

The fragrant violet, *viola odorata*, from the violet family, is a perennial whose leaves surround the stem at the base. It reaches a height of about 15 cm., its fragrant flowers blossom in the spring, and today it is mainly grown as an ornamental plant.

TRANSLATION AND COMMENTARY

רַבִּי אֶלְעָזָר אוֹמֵר [1]**Rabbi Elazar said:** Someone who engages in Torah study is regarded **as if he** himself **made** those **words of Torah,** [2]**as the verse states** (Deuteronomy 29:8): **"Keep the words of this covenant, and do them** [the Hebrew expression וַעֲשִׂיתֶם אֹתָם may also be rendered as 'make them']," implying that when a person studies Torah, he refashions what he learns.

רָבָא אָמַר [3]**Rava said:** Someone who engages in Torah study is regarded **as if he had made himself,** [4]**as the verse states:** "Keep the words of the covenant, **and do them." Do not read** the verse as it is written: "And do [=make] **them** [*otam*]." [5]**But rather,** read the verse as follows: "And do [=make] **yourselves** [*atem*]."

אָמַר רַבִּי אֲבָהוּ [6]**Rabbi Abbahu said: Whoever causes another person to perform a mitzvah, Scripture regards him as if he** himself **had performed** it, [7]**as the verse states** (Exodus 17:5): "And the Lord said to Moses...**and your rod, with which you struck the river,** take in your hand, and go." [8]The question arises: **Did Moses strike** the river? [9]**But surely** the Torah states explicitly that it was **Aaron** who **struck it!** [10]**Rather,** the verse comes **to teach you** that **whoever causes another person to perform a commandment, Scripture regards him as if he** himself **had performed** it. Since Moses told Aaron to take his rod and strike the river, Moses is regarded as if he had done the deed.

אֶפִּיקוֹרוֹס [11]Among those sinners who, according to our Mishnah, do not have a portion in the World to Come is the ***"apikoros." Rav and Rabbi Ḥanina both say:*** An *apikoros* **is someone who reviles a Torah scholar.** [12]**Rabbi Yoḥanan and Rabbi Yehoshua ben Levi say:** An *apikoros* **is someone who reviles another person before a Torah scholar.**

בִּשְׁלָמָא [13]The Gemara raises a question based on the following two premises: First, reviling a Torah scholar is a more serious offense than reviling another person in the Torah scholar's presence. And second, the offense of acting impudently toward the Torah is more serious than being an *apikoros*. Now, **granted that, according to those** authorities **who said that someone who reviles another person in a Torah scholar's presence is an** ***apikoros,***

[1]רַבִּי אֶלְעָזָר אוֹמֵר: כְּאִילּוּ עֲשָׂאָן לְדִבְרֵי תוֹרָה, [2]שֶׁנֶּאֱמַר: "וּשְׁמַרְתֶּם אֶת דִּבְרֵי הַבְּרִית הַזֹּאת וַעֲשִׂיתֶם אֹתָם".

[3]רָבָא אָמַר: כְּאִילּוּ עֲשָׂאוֹ לְעַצְמוֹ, [4]שֶׁנֶּאֱמַר: "וַעֲשִׂיתֶם אֹתָם". [5]אַל תִּקְרֵי: "אֹתָם", אֶלָּא "אַתֶּם".

[6]אָמַר רַבִּי אֲבָהוּ: כָּל הַמְעַשֶּׂה אֶת חֲבֵירוֹ לִדְבַר מִצְוָה — מַעֲלֶה עָלָיו הַכָּתוּב כְּאִילּוּ עֲשָׂאָהּ, [7]שֶׁנֶּאֱמַר: "וּמַטְּךָ אֲשֶׁר הִכִּיתָ בּוֹ אֶת הַיְאֹר". [8]וְכִי מֹשֶׁה הִכָּהוּ? [9]וַהֲלֹא אַהֲרֹן הִכָּהוּ! [10]אֶלָּא לוֹמַר לְךָ: כָּל הַמְעַשֶּׂה אֶת חֲבֵירוֹ לִדְבַר מִצְוָה, מַעֲלֶה עָלָיו הַכָּתוּב כְּאִילּוּ עֲשָׂאָהּ.

[11]"אֶפִּיקוֹרוֹס". רַב וְרַבִּי חֲנִינָא אָמְרִי תַּרְוַיְיהוּ: זֶה הַמְבַזֶּה תַּלְמִיד חָכָם. [12]רַבִּי יוֹחָנָן וְרַבִּי יְהוֹשֻׁעַ בֶּן לֵוִי אָמְרִי: זֶה הַמְבַזֶּה חֲבֵירוֹ בִּפְנֵי תַּלְמִיד חָכָם.

[13]בִּשְׁלָמָא לְמַאן דְּאָמַר הַמְבַזֶּה חֲבֵירוֹ בִּפְנֵי תַּלְמִיד חָכָם

LITERAL TRANSLATION

[1]Rabbi Elazar said: As if he made the words of Torah, [2]as it is stated: "Keep the words of this covenant, and do them."

[3]Rava said: As if he made himself, [4]as it is stated: "And do them." [5]Do not read: "Them [*otam*]," but rather "you [*atem*]."

[6]Rabbi Abbahu said: Whoever causes his fellow to [perform] a mitzvah, Scripture regards him as if he did it, [7]as it is stated: "And your rod, with which you struck the river." [8]Did Moses smite it? [9]But surely Aaron struck it! [10]Rather, to teach you: Whoever causes his fellow to [perform] a commandment, the verse regards him as if he did it.

[11]*"Apikoros."* Rav and Rabbi Ḥanina both say: This is someone who reviles a Torah scholar. [12]Rabbi Yoḥanan and Rabbi Yehoshua ben Levi say: This is someone who reviles his fellow before a Torah scholar.

[13]Granted, according to the one who said [that] he who reviles his fellow before a Torah scholar

RASHI

כאילו עשאו — לאותו דבר מצוה. **והלא אהרן הכה** — דכתיב (שמות ז) "(ויאמר) אל אהרן קח מטך ונטה ידך".

NOTES

הַמְבַזֶּה חֲבֵירוֹ בִּפְנֵי תַּלְמִיד חָכָם **Someone who reviles his fellow before a Torah scholar.** A person who reviles another person before a Torah scholar demonstrates that he feels no shame before the Torah scholar and acts as if he were not there at all. If the other person deserved rebuke, the Torah scholar should have rebuked him, and if

HALAKHAH

אֶפִּיקוֹרוֹס ***Apikoros.*** "The category of *apikoros* includes three offenders: Someone who denies prophecy, someone who denies the prophecy of Moses, and someone who denies God's knowledge of man's deeds." *Kesef Mishneh* notes that *Rambam* disregards the definitions of *apikoros* found in our Gemara. (*Rambam, Sefer Mada, Hilkhot Teshuvah* 3:8.)

אֶפִּיקוֹרוֹס הָוֵי, [1]מְבַזֶּה תַּלְמִיד חָכָם עַצְמוֹ — מְגַלֶּה פָּנִים בַּתּוֹרָה שֶׁלֹּא כַּהֲלָכָה הָוֵי. [2]אֶלָּא לְמַאן דְּאָמַר מְבַזֶּה תַּלְמִיד חָכָם עַצְמוֹ אֶפִּיקוֹרוֹס הָוֵי, [3]מְגַלֶּה פָּנִים בַּתּוֹרָה כְּגוֹן מַאי?

[4]כְּגוֹן מְנַשֶּׁה בֶּן חִזְקִיָּה.

[5]וְאִיכָּא דְּמַתְנֵי לַהּ אַסֵּיפָא: ״מְגַלֶּה פָּנִים בַּתּוֹרָה״. [6]רַב וְרַבִּי חֲנִינָא אָמְרִי: זֶה הַמְבַזֶּה תַּלְמִיד חָכָם. [7]רַבִּי יוֹחָנָן וְרַבִּי יְהוֹשֻׁעַ בֶּן לֵוִי אָמְרִי: זֶה הַמְבַזֶּה אֶת חֲבֵירוֹ בִּפְנֵי תַּלְמִיד חָכָם.

[8]בִּשְׁלָמָא לְמַאן דְּאָמַר הַמְבַזֶּה תַּלְמִיד חָכָם עַצְמוֹ מְגַלֶּה פָּנִים בַּתּוֹרָה הָוֵי, [9]מְבַזֶּה חֲבֵירוֹ בִּפְנֵי תַּלְמִיד חָכָם אֶפִּיקוֹרוֹס הָוֵי. [10]אֶלָּא לְמַאן דְּאָמַר מְבַזֶּה חֲבֵירוֹ בִּפְנֵי תַּלְמִיד חָכָם מְגַלֶּה פָּנִים בַּתּוֹרָה הָוֵי, [11]אֶפִּיקוֹרוֹס — כְּגוֹן מַאן?

[12]אָמַר רַב יוֹסֵף: כְּגוֹן הָנֵי דְּאָמְרִי: ״מַאי אַהֲנוּ לָן רַבָּנַן? [13]לְדִידְהוּ קָרוּ, לְדִידְהוּ תָּנוּ״.

LITERAL TRANSLATION

is an *apikoros*, [1]he who reviles the Torah scholar is himself someone who acts impudently toward the Torah. [2]But according to the one who says that he who reviles a Torah scholar is himself an *apikoros*, [3]someone who acts impudently toward the Torah — like what [is he]?

[4]Like Manasseh ben Hezekiah.

[5]And there are [some] who teach this regarding the last clause: "Someone who acts impudently toward the Torah." [6]Rav and Rabbi Ḥanina say: This is someone who reviles a Torah scholar. [7]Rabbi Yoḥanan and Rabbi Yehoshua ben Levi say: This is someone who reviles his fellow before a Torah scholar.

[8]Granted, according to the one who says that he who reviles a Torah scholar is himself someone who acts impudently toward the Torah, [9]he who reviles his fellow before a Torah scholar is an *apikoros*. [10]But according to the one who says that he who reviles his fellow before a Torah scholar is someone who acts impudently toward the Torah, [11]an *apikoros* — like what [is he]?

[12]Rav Yosef said: Like those who say: "How do the Rabbis benefit us? [13]They read [the Torah] for themselves, they study [the Mishnah] for themselves."

TRANSLATION AND COMMENTARY

[1]we can say that **someone who** commits the more serious offense and **reviles the Torah scholar is himself** an example of **someone who acts impudently toward the Torah.** [2]**But according to those** authorities **who say that someone who reviles the Torah scholar is himself an *apikoros*,** [3]then **what is an example of someone who acts impudently toward the Torah?**

כְּגוֹן [4]The Gemara answers: Someone who acts impudently toward the Torah is **like Manasseh ben Hezekiah,** King of Judah, who, as we saw above, interpreted the Torah in a mocking and scornful manner.

וְאִיכָּא דְּמַתְנֵי לַהּ [5]**There are some who taught this** Amoraic dispute **regarding the next clause** of the Baraita, which speaks of **"someone who acts impudently toward the Torah."** [6]**Rav and Rabbi Ḥanina** both **say: This** refers to **someone who reviles a Torah scholar.** [7]**Rabbi Yoḥanan and Rabbi Yehoshua ben Levi** disagree and **say: This** refers to **someone who reviles another person before a Torah scholar.**

בִּשְׁלָמָא [8]The Gemara asks: **Granted that, according to those** authorities **who said that someone who reviles a Torah scholar is himself** an example of **someone who acts impudently toward the Torah,** [9]we can say that **someone who** commits the less serious offense and **reviles another person in the Torah scholar's presence** is an example of **an *apikoros*.** [10]**But according to those** authorities **who say that someone who reviles another person in the Torah scholar's presence is** an example of **someone who acts impudently toward the Torah,** [11]**what is an example of an *apikoros*?**

אָמַר רַב יוֹסֵף [12]**Rav Yosef said:** An *apikoros* is **like those who say: "How do the Rabbis benefit us?** [13]It is only **for their own** benefit that **they read the Torah and study the Mishnah."**

RASHI

מגלה פנים בתורה — מעיז פניו כלפי עוסקי תורה, מגלה פנים משמע לן דחמיר מאפיקורוס, דאפיקורוס היינו דאית ביה אפקירותא בעלמא. **אלא למאן דאמר מבזה תלמידי חכמים עצמן אפיקורוס הוי** — כל שכן דמבזה חברו בפני תלמידי חכמים לאו מגלה פנים הוא — והשתא מאי ניהו מגלה פנים בתורה. **מנשה בן חזקיה** — שהיה דורש באגדות של דופי. **איכא דמתני לה אסיפא** — דברייתא, דקתני מכאן אמר רבי אלעזר וכו׳ המגלה פנים בתורה רב ורבי חנינא וכו׳. **מאי אהני לן** — והם אינן יודעין שעולם מתקיים עליהם.

NOTES

he did not deserve rebuke, then the scoffer should certainly have been embarrassed to revile him and thus violate a prohibition in the Torah scholar's presence.

HALAKHAH

מְגַלֶּה פָּנִים בַּתּוֹרָה **Someone who acts impudently toward the Torah.** "Someone who commits transgressions with presumption and arrogance, whether he violates relatively minor prohibitions or very serious prohibitions, is referred to as someone who acts impudently toward the Torah." (*Rambam, Sefer Mada, Hilkhot Teshuvah* 3:11.)

1אָמַר לֵיהּ אַבַּיֵי: הַאי מְגַלֶּה פָּנִים בַּתּוֹרָה נַמִּי הוּא, 2דִּכְתִיב: "אִם לֹא בְרִיתִי יוֹמָם וָלָיְלָה חֻקּוֹת שָׁמַיִם וָאָרֶץ לֹא שָׂמְתִּי". 3אָמַר רַב נַחְמָן בַּר יִצְחָק: מֵהָכָא נַמִּי שְׁמַע מִינָּהּ, 4שֶׁנֶּאֱמַר: "וְנָשָׂאתִי לְכָל הַמָּקוֹם בַּעֲבוּרָם". 5אֶלָּא, כְּגוֹן דְּיָתֵיב קַמֵּיהּ רַבֵּיהּ וְנָפְלָה לֵיהּ שְׁמַעְתָּא בְּדוּכְתָּא אַחֲרִיתִי, 6וְאָמַר: "הָכִי אָמְרִינַן הָתָם", וְלָא אָמַר: "הָכִי אָמַר מָר". 7רָבָא אָמַר: כְּגוֹן הָנֵי דְּבֵי בִנְיָמִין אָסְיָא, 8דְּאָמְרִי: "מַאי אַהֲנֵי לָן רַבָּנַן? 9מֵעוֹלָם [100A] לָא שָׁרוּ לָן עוֹרְבָא, וְלָא אָסְרוּ לָן יוֹנָה". 10רָבָא, כִּי הָווּ מַיְיתֵי טְרֵיפְתָּא דְּבֵי בִנְיָמִין קַמֵּיהּ — 11כִּי הֲוָה חָזֵי בָּהּ טַעְמָא לְהֶיתֵּירָא, אָמַר לְהוּ: "תֶּחֱזוּ דְּקָא שָׁרֵינָא לְכוּ עוֹרְבָא". 12כִּי הֲוָה חָזֵי לָהּ טַעְמָא לְאִיסּוּרָא, אָמַר לְהוּ: "תֶּחֱזוּ דְּקָא אָסַרְנָא לְכוּ יוֹנָה". 13רַב פַּפָּא אָמַר: כְּגוֹן דְּאָמַר: "הָנֵי רַבָּנַן".

LITERAL TRANSLATION

1Abaye said to him: That one is also someone who acts impudently toward the Torah, 2for it is written: "If not for My covenant, I would not have appointed day and night, the laws of heaven and earth."

3Rav Naḥman bar Yitzḥak said: From here, too, infer this, 4for it is stated: "Then I will spare all the place for their sake."

5Rather, like someone who was sitting before his master, and a teaching fell to him from another place, 6and he said: "Thus we said there," and he did not say: "Thus said Master."

7Rava said: Like those from the house of Binyamin the doctor, 8who say: "How have the Rabbis benefited us? 9They never [100A] permitted for us a raven, nor forbade for us a dove."

10Rava, when they brought before him a slaughtered animal [with a disease or a defect] from the house of Binyamin — 11when he saw a reason to permit [it], he would say to them: "See that I permit a raven for you." 12When he saw a reason to forbid [it], he would say to them: "See that I forbid a dove for you."

13Rav Pappa said: Like someone who says: "Those Rabbis."

TRANSLATION AND COMMENTARY

אָמַר לֵיהּ אַבַּיֵי 1**Abaye said to** Rav Yosef: **Such people also act impudently toward the Torah,** 2**for** they deny what **is written** explicitly in the verse (Jeremiah 33:25): **"If not for My covenant, I would not have appointed day and night, the laws of heaven and earth."**

אָמַר 3**Rav Naḥman bar Yitzḥak said: From here, too,** we may **infer this** idea that Torah scholars benefit the community at large, 4**for the verse states** (Genesis 18:26): "And the Lord said, If I find in Sodom fifty just men within the city, **then I will spare all the place for their sakes,"** demonstrating that the righteous provide protection for those who live where they do.

אֶלָּא 5The Gemara continues to search for an example of an *apikoros*: **Rather,** an *apikoros* is a disciple **who was sitting before his master and happened** to mention **a** certain **law from another place,** 6**saying** in an irreverent manner: **"Thus we said there," and he did not say: "Thus said Master."** Even if the disciple had not learned that law from his master, he should have introduced it that way, honoring his master.

רָבָא אָמַר 7**Rava said:** An *apikoros* is **like those from the house of Binyamin the doctor,** 8**who say: "How do the Rabbis benefit us** with all their learning? 9Surely, **they** have **never** [100A] **permitted us a raven, nor forbade us a dove!** They have never issued any rulings — neither leniencies nor stringencies — that are not stated explicitly in the Torah! What good are they, then, for us?"

רָבָא 10It is related that **when a** ritually **slaughtered animal that was suspected of being infected with an organic disease or of displaying a congenital defect was brought from the house of Binyamin to Rava** to rule whether the animal was fit to be eaten, he would act as follows: 11**When he found a reason to permit** the animal, **he would say to them: "See that I have permitted a raven for you** — a creature that you thought was forbidden." 12And **when he found a reason to forbid** the animal, **he would say to them: "See that I have forbidden for you a dove** — a creature that you thought was permitted."

רַב פַּפָּא אָמַר 13**Rav Pappa said:** An *apikoros* is **like someone who says** in a derogatory tone: **"Those Rabbis,"** rather than saying respectfully: "The Rabbis in such-and-such a place."

RASHI

מגלה פנים בתורה הוא — שכופר במה שכתוב בתורה. אם לא בריתי יומם ולילה וגו' — שמהנין לעולם ומקיימין [אותו], והוא אומר דלא מהני מידי. מהכא נמי שמעינן — שהצדיקים מהנין לאחרים. לא שרו לן עורבא — לא אמרו לנו שום חידוש שלא מצינו בתורה (דשרינן עורבא). [דקא שרינא לכו עורבא] — שהיתר זה אינו מצוי בתורה אלא סופרים אמרוהו. כגון דאמר הנהו רבנן — כאדם שאומר אותו תלמיד חכם, דלשון בזוי הוא זה, שהיה לו לומר "רבותינו שבמקום פלוני" לישנא אחרינא: כגון דאמר "הני" רבנן דכשהוא מספר שום דבר מרבנן אומר הני ולשון גנאי הוא הני, אבל "הנהו רבנן" אינו גנאי.

TRANSLATION AND COMMENTARY

רַב פַּפָּא [1]It was related that **Rav Pappa** himself **was** once **careless and said: "Like those Rabbis,"** [2]**and he observed a fast** to atone for his indiscretion.

לֵוִי בַּר שְׁמוּאֵל [3]It was further related that **Levi bar Shmuel and Rav Huna bar Ḥiyya were** once **making mantles for the** sacred **scrolls** found **in the house of Rav Yehudah.** [4]**When they reached the Scroll of Esther, they said** to Rav Yehudah: **"This Scroll of Esther does not require a mantle,** for it is not as holy as the rest of the Bible." [5]Rav Yehudah **said to them: "This** manner of speaking — 'this Scroll of Esther' — **also looks like irreverence."**

רַב נַחְמָן אָמַר [6]**Rav Naḥman said:** An *apikoros* **is someone who calls his master by his name.** [7]As **Rabbi Yoḥanan said: Why was Gehazi punished** with leprosy? [8]**Because he referred to his master,** Elisha, **by his name, as the verse states** (II Kings 8:5): **"And Gehazi said, My lord, O king, this is the woman, and this is her son, whom Elisha restored to life."**

יָתֵיב רַבִּי יִרְמְיָה [9]It was related that **Rabbi Yirmeyah** once **sat before Rabbi Zera, and said: In the future, the Holy One, blessed is He, will send out a stream from the Holy of Holies, and near it will grow all kinds of delicious fruit,** [10]**as the verse states** (Ezekiel 47:12): **"And by the stream upon its bank, on this side and on that side, shall grow all fruit trees, whose leaves shall not wither, neither shall**

[1]רַב פַּפָּא אִישְׁתְּלֵי וַאֲמַר: ״כְּגוֹן הָנֵי רַבָּנַן״, [2]וְאֵיתִיב בְּתַעֲנִיתָא. [3]לֵוִי בַּר שְׁמוּאֵל וְרַב הוּנָא בַּר חִיָּיא הָווּ קָא מְתַקְּנִי מִטְפְּחוֹת סִפְרֵי דְּבֵי רַב יְהוּדָה. [4]כִּי מְטוֹ מְגִילַּת אֶסְתֵּר אָמְרִי: ״הָא [מְגִילַּת אֶסְתֵּר] לָא בָּעֵי מִטְפַּחַת״. [5]אֲמַר לְהוּ: ״כִּי הַאי גַּוְונָא נַמִי מֶיחֱזֵי כִּי אַפְּקִירוּתָא״.

[6]רַב נַחְמָן אָמַר: זֶה הַקּוֹרֵא רַבּוֹ בִּשְׁמוֹ, [7]דְּאָמַר רַבִּי יוֹחָנָן: מִפְּנֵי מָה נֶעֱנַשׁ גֵּיחֲזִי? [8]מִפְּנֵי שֶׁקָּרָא לְרַבּוֹ בִּשְׁמוֹ, שֶׁנֶּאֱמַר: ״וַיֹּאמֶר גֵּחֲזִי אֲדֹנִי הַמֶּלֶךְ זֹאת הָאִשָּׁה וְזֶה בְּנָהּ אֲשֶׁר הֶחֱיָה אֱלִישָׁע״. [9]יָתֵיב רַבִּי יִרְמְיָה קַמֵּיהּ דְּרַבִּי זֵירָא, וְיָתֵיב וְקָאָמַר: עָתִיד הַקָּדוֹשׁ בָּרוּךְ הוּא לְהוֹצִיא נַחַל מִבֵּית קָדְשֵׁי הַקֳּדָשִׁים וְעָלָיו כָּל מִינֵי מְגָדִים, [10]שֶׁנֶּאֱמַר: ״וְעַל הַנַּחַל יַעֲלֶה עַל שְׂפָתוֹ מִזֶּה וּמִזֶּה כָּל עֵץ מַאֲכָל לֹא יִבּוֹל

LITERAL TRANSLATION

[1]Rav Pappa forgot and said: "Like those Rabbis," [2]and observed a fast.

[3]Levi bar Shmuel and Rav Huna bar Ḥiyya were making mantles for the scrolls in the house of Rav Yehudah. [4]When they reached the Scroll of Esther, they said: "This [Scroll of Esther] does not require a mantle." [5]He said to them: "This, too, looks like irreverence."

[6]Rav Naḥman said: This is someone who calls his master by his name, [7]for Rabbi Yoḥanan said: Why was Gehazi punished? [8]Because he called his master by his name, as it is stated: "And Gehazi said, My lord, O king, this is the woman, and this is her son, whom Elisha restored to life."

[9]Rabbi Yirmeyah sat before Rabbi Zera, and said: In the future, the Holy One, blessed be He, will send out a stream from the Holy of Holies, and near it will be all kinds of delicious fruit, [10]as it is stated: "And by the stream upon its bank, on this side and on that side, shall grow all fruit trees, whose leaves shall not wither,

LANGUAGE (RASHI)

דינטר״ס* This word should apparently be read as דיינטייר״ש, from the Old French *daintiers,* meaning "delicacies."

RASHI

כי מטו מגלת אסתר – לתקן לה מטפחת אמרי הא מגלת אסתר לא בעיא מטפחת, כלומר בלשון בעיא אמרו לו לרבי יהודה: הא ודאי לא צריכא מטפחת כגון האחרות, ולשון גנאי הוא דהוה להו למימר לרבס בלשון שאלה כך: צריכה או אינה צריכה. **מעיין בית ה׳** – יצא והשקה את נחל שטים (יואל ד). **מגדים** = *דינטר״ס בלעז, כל מיני פירות מתוקים.

NOTES

הָא מְגִילַּת אֶסְתֵּר **This Scroll of Esther.** *Rashi* and others understand the irreverence differently. Levi bar Shmuel and Rav Huna bar Ḥiyya should not have announced categorically that the Scroll of Esther does not require a mantle. Rather, they should have formulated their comment as a question: "Does the Scroll of Esther require a mantle?" to avoid the appearance of scorning the work. *Maharsha* suggests that our passage is related to the Tannaitic dispute in tractate *Megilah* regarding the sanctity of the Scroll of Esther.

מִפְּנֵי מָה נֶעֱנַשׁ גֵּיחֲזִי? **Why was Gehazi punished?** Our commentary follows those who understand that Rabbi Yoḥanan asks why Gehazi was punished with leprosy. *Ramah* points out the difficulties with this explanation: First, Gehazi's leprosy preceded the incident in which he referred to his master by name. Moreover, Gehazi was afflicted with leprosy because he took money from Na'aman. Rather,

HALAKHAH

הַקּוֹרֵא רַבּוֹ בִּשְׁמוֹ **Someone who calls his master by his name.** "One is forbidden to call his master by his name. If his master has an unusual name, he may not even call another person by that name. *Rama* adds that one may, however, say: 'My master and teacher, So-and-so.' According to *Shakh,* even this is only permitted when speaking about one's master when he is not present, but a person may not address his master in this manner. Others, however, disagree (see *Be'er Hetev*)." (*Shulḥan Arukh, Yoreh De'ah* 242:15.)

TRANSLATION AND COMMENTARY

their fruit fail; they shall bring forth new fruit every month, because their waters came out of the Sanctuary; and their fruit shall be for food, and their leaves for medicine." [1]A **certain old man** who was present at the discourse **said to** Rabbi Yirmeyah: "What you said is **correct."** [2]**And, similarly, Rabbi Yoḥanan said:** "What you said is **correct."** [3]**Rabbi Yirmeyah said to Rabbi Zera: Does** not **this** kind of talk **appear** to you **as irreverence?** Is it not disrespectful for a man of meager learning to tell a Torah Sage that what he said is correct? [4]Rabbi Zera **said to him: This** old man only meant to **support you.** [5]**But if you heard** that supporting the words of a Sage is construed as irreverence, **you heard** about an incident like this: **Rabbi Yoḥanan** once **sat** before his disciples **and lectured:** [6]**In the future, the Holy One, blessed be He, will bring precious stones and jewels which are thirty** cubits wide **and thirty cubits** high, **and hollow out in them openings that are ten cubits wide and twenty cubits high, and stand them at the gates of Jerusalem,** [7]**as the verse states** (Isaiah 54:12): **"And I will make your windows of rubies, and your gates of beryl,** and all your borders of choicest stones." [8]After Rabbi Yoḥanan finished his exposition, **a certain disciple mocked him, saying: "Now we do not** even **find jewels the size of the egg of a dove, and** you say that in the future **we shall find** jewels **of such size?"** [9]**One day** that disciple's **ship was sailing at sea,**

עָלֵהוּ וְלֹא יִתֹּם פִּרְיוֹ לָחֳדָשָׁיו
יְבַכֵּר כִּי מֵימָיו מִן הַמִּקְדָּשׁ
[הֵמָּה] יוֹצְאִים וְהָיָה פִרְיוֹ
לְמַאֲכָל וְעָלֵהוּ לִתְרוּפָה״. [1]אֲמַר
לֵיהּ הַהוּא סָבָא: ״יִישַׁר״! [2]וְכֵן
אֲמַר רַבִּי יוֹחָנָן: ״יִישַׁר״! [3]אֲמַר
לֵיהּ רַבִּי יִרְמְיָה לְרַבִּי זֵירָא: כִּי
הַאי גַּוְנָא מֶיחֱזֵי אַפְקְרוּתָא?
[4]אֲמַר לֵיהּ: הָא [הַאי] סַיּוֹעֵי
קָא מְסַיֵּיעַ לֵיהּ [לָךְ]. [5]אֶלָּא אִי
שְׁמִיעַ לָךְ, הָא שְׁמִיעַ לָךְ: כִּי
הָא דְּיָתֵיב רַבִּי יוֹחָנָן וְקָא
דָּרֵישׁ: [6]עָתִיד הַקָּדוֹשׁ בָּרוּךְ
הוּא לְהָבִיא אֲבָנִים טוֹבוֹת
וּמַרְגָּלִיּוֹת שֶׁהֵן שְׁלֹשִׁים עַל
שְׁלֹשִׁים אַמּוֹת, וְחוֹקֵק בָּהֶם
עֶשֶׂר בְּרוּם עֶשְׂרִים, וּמַעֲמִידָן
בְּשַׁעֲרֵי יְרוּשָׁלַיִם, [7]שֶׁנֶּאֱמַר:
׳וְשַׂמְתִּי כַּדְכֹּד שִׁמְשֹׁתַיִךְ
וּשְׁעָרַיִךְ לְאַבְנֵי אֶקְדָּח וגו׳״.
[8]לִגְלֵג עָלָיו אוֹתוֹ תַּלְמִיד,
אֲמַר: ״הָשְׁתָּא כְּבֵיעָתָא
דְּצִילְצְלָא לָא מַשְׁכְּחִינַן, כּוּלֵּי
הַאי מַשְׁכְּחִינַן״? [9]לְיָמִים
הִפְלִיגָה סְפִינָתוֹ בַּיָּם, חֲזֵינְהוּ

LITERAL TRANSLATION

neither shall their fruit fail; they shall bring forth new fruit every month, because their waters have come out of the Sanctuary; and their fruit shall be for food, and their leaves for medicine." [1]A certain old man said to him: "Correct!" [2]And similarly Rabbi Yoḥanan said: "Correct!" [3]Rabbi Yirmeyah said to Rabbi Zera: Like this, does it appear as irreverence? [4]He said to him: This one supports you. [5]But if you heard, you heard this: As when Rabbi Yoḥanan sat and lectured: [6]In the future, the Holy One, blessed be He, will bring precious stones and jewels which are thirty by thirty cubits, and hollow out in them [openings] that are ten [cubits] by twenty [cubits] high, and stand them at the gates of Jerusalem, [7]as it is stated: "And I will make your windows of rubies, and your gates of beryl, etc." [8]A certain disciple mocked him, [and] said: "Now we do not find [jewels] like the egg of a dove, [and] we shall find as large as that?" [9]One day his ship was sailing at sea, [and] he saw

RASHI

יבכר — בכל חדש וחדש יתבשלו בו פירות. בשמו — שאומר ״פלוני״ ואינו אומר ״מורי רבי פלוני״. אמר ליה ההוא סבא יישר וכן אמר רבי יוחנן — כדבריך, ורבי יוחנן נמי הכי קאמר כדאמרת, מפי רבי, ולא גרסינן וכן אמר רבי יוחנן יישר. כי האי גוונא — מי מיחזי כאפקרותא, אלא אי שמיע לך מידי הא שמיע לך. לגלג עליו אותו תלמיד — אדר׳ יוחנן, דהיינו אפקרותא. כדכד — אבן טובה, וכן שמה. שמשותיך — חלונות שהשמש זורח בהם, כמו (תהלים פד) ״שמש ומגן״ היינו שמש ממש, (לישנא אחרינא) לאבני אקדח — שהקדוש ברוך הוא חוקקן כבמקדח, עד שחוקק בהם עשר ברום עשרים. צילצלתא — עוף קטן.

BACKGROUND

צִילְצְלָא **Dove.**

The smallest variety of dove, quite common in the cities of Israel. Because it is so small, its eggs are also very small (20 x 40 mm.) and they became a symbol of tininess.

NOTES

Rabbi Yoḥanan asks why Gehazi was denied a share in the World to Come, and explains that he was punished so severely because he acted disrespectfully toward his master. *Rabbi Ya'akov Emden* suggests that Rabbi Yoḥanan asks why Gehazi never recovered from his leprosy.

אֲמַר לֵיהּ הַהוּא סָבָא **A certain old man said to him.** *Ramah* explains that the old man's act of irreverence was that he first spoke on his own, and only then did he mention that Rabbi Yoḥanan also said that Rabbi Yirmeyah's teaching was correct, instead of limiting himself to the words of Rabbi Yoḥanan.

יִישַׁר. וְכֵן אֲמַר רַבִּי יוֹחָנָן **Correct. And similarly Rabbi Yoḥanan said: Correct.** It may be asked: What is the novelty of Rabbi Yirmeyah's statement? Surely the verse states explicitly (Joel 4:18): "And a fountain shall issue from the house of the Lord"! *Maharsha* explains that Rabbi Yirmeyah teaches us that the verse should be understood literally. The old man agreed with Rabbi Yirmeyah and added that Rabbi Yoḥanan also said that the verse should be understood literally.

לִגְלֵג עָלָיו אוֹתוֹ תַּלְמִיד **A certain disciple mocked him.** Why was the disciple only punished after supporting Rabbi Yoḥanan's position, and not earlier when he mocked him? *Rashash* suggests that Rabbi Yoḥanan may not have heard his disciple's mocking words.

לְמַלְאֲכֵי הַשָּׁרֵת דְּקָא מְנַסְּרִי אֲבָנִים טוֹבוֹת וּמַרְגָּלִיּוֹת. [1]אֲמַר לְהוּ: "הָנֵי לְמַאן"? [2]אָמְרִי: "עָתִיד הַקָּדוֹשׁ בָּרוּךְ הוּא לְהַעֲמִידָן בְּשַׁעֲרֵי יְרוּשָׁלַיִם". [3]כִּי הֲדַר, אַשְׁכְּחֵיהּ לְרַבִּי יוֹחָנָן דְּיָתֵיב וְקָא דָּרֵישׁ. [4]אֲמַר לֵיהּ: "רַבִּי, דְּרוֹשׁ וּלְךָ נָאֶה לִדְרוֹשׁ, כְּשֵׁם שֶׁאָמַרְתָּ כָּךְ רָאִיתִי". [5]אֲמַר לוֹ: "רֵיקָה, אִם לֹא רָאִיתָ לֹא הֶאֱמַנְתָּ? [6]מְלַגְלֵג עַל דִּבְרֵי חֲכָמִים אַתָּה"! [7]יְהַב בֵּיהּ עֵינֵיהּ, וַעֲשָׂאוֹ גַּל שֶׁל עֲצָמוֹת. [8]מֵיתִיבֵי: [9]"'וָאוֹלֵךְ אֶתְכֶם קוֹמְמִיּוּת'. [10]רַבִּי מֵאִיר אוֹמֵר: מָאתַיִם אַמָּה, כִּשְׁתֵּי קוֹמוֹת שֶׁל אָדָם הָרִאשׁוֹן. [11]רַבִּי יְהוּדָה אוֹמֵר: מֵאָה אַמָּה, כְּנֶגֶד הֵיכָל וְכוֹתְלָיו, [12]שֶׁנֶּאֱמַר: 'אֲשֶׁר בָּנֵינוּ כִּנְטִעִים מְגֻדָּלִים בִּנְעוּרֵיהֶם בְּנוֹתֵינוּ כְזָוִיֹּת מְחֻטָּבוֹת תַּבְנִית הֵיכָל וגו'".
[13]כִּי קָאָמַר רַבִּי יוֹחָנָן, לְכַוֵּי דְּבֵי זִיקָא.

LITERAL TRANSLATION

that the ministering angels were cutting precious stones and jewels. [1]He said to them: "For whom are these?" [2]They said: "In the future, the Holy One, blessed be He, will stand them at the gates of Jerusalem." [3]When he returned, he found Rabbi Yoḥanan sitting and lecturing. [4]He said to him: "My master, lecture, for it is becoming for you to lecture. Just as you had said, I saw." [5]He said to him: "Good for nothing, had you not seen, would you not have believed? [6]You mock the words of the Sages." [7]He set his eyes upon him, and made him into a heap of bones.

[8]They raised an objection: [9]"'And I have made you walk upright.' [10]Rabbi Meir said: Two hundred cubits, like twice the height of the first man. [11]Rabbi Yehudah says: A hundred cubits, corresponding to the Sanctuary and its walls, [12]as it is stated: 'For our sons are as plants grown up in their youth; our daughters as corner stones, polished in the fashion of a palace.'"

[13]When Rabbi Yoḥanan said, openings for air.

TRANSLATION AND COMMENTARY

and he saw that the ministering angels were cutting huge **precious stones and jewels.** [1]The disciple **said to** the angels: **"For whom are these** precious stones and jewels?" [2]**They explained: "In the future, the Holy One, blessed be He, will stand them at the gates of Jerusalem."** [3]**When** the disciple **returned** home, **he found Rabbi Yoḥanan sitting and lecturing.** [4]**He said to him: "My master,** continue to **lecture, for it is becoming for you to lecture. What you said** would happen, I myself **saw** with my own eyes." [5]Rabbi Yoḥanan **said to him: "Good for nothing, had you not seen** what you saw, **would you not have believed** what I said? [6]If so, you **mock the words of the Sages."** [7]Rabbi Yoḥanan then **set his eyes upon** his disciple in anger, **and** caused him to die, **turning him into a heap of bones.**

מֵיתִיבֵי [8]**An objection was raised** from a Baraita against what Rabbi Yoḥanan said, that, in the future, God will make twenty-cubit-high openings in precious stones and stand them at the gates of Jerusalem: "Regarding the verse that states (Leviticus 26:13), [9]**'And I have made you walk upright** [קוֹמְמִיּוּת],' [10]**Rabbi Meir said:** The doubling of the letter *mem* in the word קוֹמְמִיּוּת indicates that in the future people will be **two hundred cubits** tall, **twice the height** [קוֹמוֹת] **of Adam.** [11]**Rabbi Yehudah said:** In the future, people will be **a hundred cubits** tall, **corresponding to** the height of the **Sanctuary and its walls,** [12]**as the verse states** (Psalms 144:12): **'For our sons are as plants grown up in their youth; our daughters as corner stones, polished in the fashion of a palace** [הֵיכָל = "sanctuary"].' If people will be a hundred cubits tall, how will they be able to pass through openings that are only twenty cubits high?"

כִּי קָאָמַר [13]The Gemara answers: **When Rabbi Yoḥanan said** that in the future God will make twenty-cubit-high apertures in the walls of Jerusalem, he was referring to **openings** in the walls **for air.**

RASHI

גל של עצמות – שמת, דאדם שמת נעשה גל של עצמות. **קוממיות** – שתי קומות של אדם הראשון, כדאמרינן בחגיגה (יב,א) שמיעטו הקדוש ברוך הוא והעמידו על מאה אמה שנאמר ותשת עלי כפך, כף בגימטריא הכי הוי. **כנגד היכל וכותליו** – שכך היה אורך כל ההיכל עם הכותלים דכתיב (מלכים א,ו) "והבית אשר בנה המלך שלמה לה' ששים אמה ארכו" וכותל מזרח שש אמות, וכותל מערב שש אמות, ואמה אחת טרקסין, הרי שלש עשרה אמות, ואולם עשר אמה רוחב, וכותל האולם שש, הרי עשרים ותשע, ומאחורי האולם תא אחד רחבו שש וכתלו חמש, הרי ארבעים, וששים אמה של אורך הבית הרי מאה, והיאך יכולין לכוף קומתן וליכנס בפתח שאין לו אלא רום עשרים כדאמרת. **אשר בנינו** – כלומר בנים שלנו יהיו לעתיד כאילנות גבוהין מגודלים. **ובנותינו** – ובנות שלנו כזויות המחוטבות לתבנית היכל, כלומר ככותל ההיכל מחוטבות כמו (דברים כט) "מחוטב עציך", לישנא אחרינא: אהיכל דבית שני קאמר, דקים לן – היכל ששים אורך ברום מאה הוא. **לכוי דבי זיקא** – לחלונות שהשמש והאור נכנסין בהן, אבל השערים גבוהים יותר.

NOTES

מָאתַיִם אַמָּה...מֵאָה אַמָּה Two hundred cubits...a hundred cubits. *Maharal* understands this passage as a metaphor. The Tannaim disagree here about the nature of man in the future. According to some, people will be two hundred cubits tall, twice the height of Adam and perfect in both body and soul. Others maintain that people will be only a hundred cubits tall, corresponding to the height of Adam, and they will only reach spiritual perfection.

TRANSLATION AND COMMENTARY

מַאי ״וְעָלֵהוּ לִתְרוּפָה״ [1]The Gemara returns now to the verse cited above regarding the stream that will flow from the Sanctuary. **What is** the meaning of the words **"and their leaves for medicine** [לִתְרוּפָה]**"**? [2]**Rabbi Yitzhak bar Avudimi and Rav Ḥisda** both said that the word לִתְרוּפָה should be understood as an acronym for the words לְהַתִּיר פֶּה, "to free the mouth," but they **disagreed** about how to understand these words. [3]**One** of the Amoraim **said:** The leaves will **free the upper mouths,** meaning that the mute will speak. [4]**And the other** Amora **said:** Those leaves will **free the lower mouths** — a euphemism for uteruses — of barren women.

אִיתְּמַר נַמִּי [5]**It was also stated** that other Amoraim disagreed about the same matter: **Ḥizkiyah said:** The leaves will **free the mouths of mutes,** and allow them to speak. [6]**Bar Kappara said:** Those leaves will **free the mouths** — uteruses — **of barren women,** and allow them to have children. [7]**Rabbi Yoḥanan said:** The word לִתְרוּפָה should be understood **in its literal sense,** as meaning **"for medicine."**

מַאי ״לִתְרוּפָה״ [8]The Gemara asks: **What is** the Midrashic meaning of the words **"for medicine** [לִתְרוּפָה]**"**? [9]**Rabbi Shmuel bar Naḥmani said:** The word לִתְרוּפָה should be understood as an acronym **"for brightening** [לְתוֹאַר] **the countenance of those with mouths** [פֶּה]." The leaves of the tree growing along the stream flowing from the Sanctuary will brighten the countenance and improve the appearance of Sages who labor with their mouths in the study of Torah.

דָּרַשׁ [10]But their faces will be bright only in the World to Come, as **Rabbi Yehudah the son of Rabbi Simon expounded: Whoever blackens his face for the words of Torah in this world, the Holy One, blessed be He, will brighten his looks in the World to Come,** [11]**as** the verse first states (Song of Songs 5:11): "His locks are curly, and black as a raven," and shortly thereafter **the verse states** (Song of Songs 5:15): **"His countenance is like the Lebanon, excellent as the cedars."**

אָמַר [12]**Rabbi Tanḥum the son of Rabbi Ḥanila'i said: Whoever starves himself for the words of Torah in this world, the Holy One, blessed be He, will satisfy him in the World to Come, as** the verse first states (Psalms 36:7): "Your judgments are a great deep," that is to say, God is very exacting with the righteous in this world. [13]Shortly thereafter **the verse** describes the reward that awaits the righteous in the World to Come, **stating** (Psalms 36:9):

LITERAL TRANSLATION

[1]What is "and their leaves for medicine"? [2]Rabbi Yitzhak bar Avudimi and Rav Ḥisda [disagreed]. [3]One said: To free the upper mouth. [4]And one said: To free the lower mouth.

[5]It was also stated: Ḥizkiyah said: To free the mouths of mutes. [6]Bar Kappara said: To free the mouths of barren women. [7]Rabbi Yoḥanan said: For medicine, literally.

[8]What is "for medicine"? [9]Rabbi Shmuel bar Naḥmani said: For brightening the countenance of those with mouths.

[10]Rabbi Yehudah the son of Rabbi Simon expounded: Whoever blackens his face for the words of Torah in this world, the Holy One, blessed be He, will brighten his looks in the World to Come, [11]as it is states: "His countenance is like the Lebanon, excellent as the cedars."

[12]Rabbi Tanḥum the son of Rabbi Ḥanila'i said: Whoever starves himself for the words of Torah in this world, the Holy One, blessed be He, will satisfy him in the World to Come, [13]as it is stated: "They are abundantly satisfied

[1]מַאי ״וְעָלֵהוּ לִתְרוּפָה״? [2]רַבִּי יִצְחָק בַּר אֲבוּדִימִי וְרַב חִסְדָּא. [3]חַד אָמַר: לְהַתִּיר פֶּה שֶׁל מַעְלָה. [4]וְחַד אָמַר: לְהַתִּיר פֶּה שֶׁל מַטָּה.

[5]אִיתְּמַר נַמִּי: חִזְקִיָּה אָמַר: לְהַתִּיר פֶּה אִילְּמִין. [6]בַּר קַפָּרָא אָמַר: לְהַתִּיר פֶּה עֲקָרוֹת. [7]רַבִּי יוֹחָנָן אָמַר: לִתְרוּפָה מַמָּשׁ.

[8]מַאי ״לִתְרוּפָה״? [9]רַבִּי שְׁמוּאֵל בַּר נַחְמָנִי אָמַר: לְתוֹאַר פָּנִים שֶׁל בַּעֲלֵי הַפֶּה.

[10]דָּרַשׁ רַבִּי יְהוּדָה בְּרַבִּי סִימוֹן: כָּל הַמַּשְׁחִיר פָּנָיו עַל דִּבְרֵי תוֹרָה בָּעוֹלָם הַזֶּה, הַקָּדוֹשׁ בָּרוּךְ הוּא מַבְהִיק זִיוָיו לָעוֹלָם הַבָּא, [11]שֶׁנֶּאֱמַר: ״מַרְאֵהוּ כַּלְּבָנוֹן בָּחוּר כָּאֲרָזִים״.

[12]אָמַר רַבִּי תַּנְחוּם בְּרַבִּי חֲנִילָאִי: כָּל הַמַּרְעִיב עַצְמוֹ עַל דִּבְרֵי תוֹרָה בָּעוֹלָם הַזֶּה, הַקָּדוֹשׁ בָּרוּךְ הוּא מַשְׂבִּיעוֹ לָעוֹלָם הַבָּא, [13]שֶׁנֶּאֱמַר: ״יִרְוְיֻן

RASHI

[להתיר פה של מטה] — להתיר פה אלמים שיהו מדברים. להתיר פה של מטה — רחם של העקרות, האוכלות מן העלין נפקדות. איתמר נמי חזקיה וכו' — והיינו הך דלעיל לתרופה. מראהו כלבנון — וכתיב לעיל מיניה ״שחורות כעורב״ וסמיך ליה ״חכו ממתקים״. ירויון מדשן ביתך — אמר לי רבי דלעיל

NOTES

יִרְוְיֻן מִדֶּשֶׁן בֵּיתֶךָ **They are abundantly satisfied with the fatness of Your house.** Most commentators understand that Rabbi Ḥanila'i's homily is based on the earlier verse (Psalms 36:7): "Your judgments are a great deep," which describes

TRANSLATION AND COMMENTARY

"They are abundantly satisfied with the fatness of Your house, and You let them drink of the river of Your pleasures."

כִּי אֲתָא [1]**When Rav Dimi arrived** in Babylonia from Eretz Israel, **he said: In the future, the Holy One, blessed be He, will give each and every righteous man as much** good **as He can put in His hand,** [2]**as the verse states** (Psalms 68:20): **"Blessed be the Lord who day by day bears our burden** [יַעֲמָס לָנוּ], **God is our salvation. Selah."** The words יַעֲמָס לָנוּ, translated here as: "He bears our burden," may also be read as: "He will load us with a handful."

אָמַר לֵיהּ אַבַּיֵי [3]**Abaye said to** Rav Dimi: **Is it possible to say this,** that the righteous will receive from God all the good that fits in His hand? [4]**But surely it was already stated** in another verse (Isaiah 40:12): **"Who has measured the waters in the hollow of His hand, and meted out Heaven with the span"!** If the entire world fits in God's hand, as it were, then how can man receive from God all the good that fits in His hand?

אָמַר [5]Rav Dimi **said: Why are you not familiar with the Aggadah?** [6]**For they say in** Eretz Israel **in the name of Rava bar Madi: In the future, the Holy One, blessed be He, will give each and every righteous man three-hundred-and-ten worlds,** [7]**as the verse states** (Proverbs 8:21): **"That I may cause those who love Me to inherit substance** [*yesh*]; **and I will fill their treasures."** [8]**The numerical value of the word** *yesh* [יֵשׁ: י = 10, ש = 300] **is three-hundred-and-ten.**

מִדֶּשֶׁן בֵּיתֶךָ וְנַחַל עֲדָנֶיךָ תַשְׁקֵם״.

[1]כִּי אֲתָא רַב דִּימִי אֲמַר: עָתִיד הַקָּדוֹשׁ בָּרוּךְ הוּא לִיתֵּן לְכָל צַדִּיק וְצַדִּיק מְלֹא עוּמְסוֹ, [2]שֶׁנֶּאֱמַר: ״בָּרוּךְ ה׳ יוֹם יוֹם יַעֲמָס לָנוּ, הָאֵל יְשׁוּעָתֵנוּ. סֶלָה״.

[3]אֲמַר לֵיהּ אַבַּיֵי: וְכִי אֶפְשָׁר לוֹמַר כֵּן? [4]וַהֲלֹא כְּבָר נֶאֱמַר: ״מִי מָדַד בְּשָׁעֳלוֹ מַיִם וְשָׁמַיִם בַּזֶּרֶת תִּכֵּן״!

[5]אָמַר: מַאי טַעְמָא לָא שְׁכִיחַתְּ בְּאַגַּדְתָּא? [6]דְּאָמְרִי בְּמַעֲרָבָא מִשְּׁמֵיהּ דְּרָבָא בַּר מָרִי: עָתִיד הַקָּדוֹשׁ בָּרוּךְ הוּא לִיתֵּן לְכָל צַדִּיק וְצַדִּיק שְׁלֹשׁ מֵאוֹת וַעֲשָׂרָה עוֹלָמוֹת, [7]שֶׁנֶּאֱמַר: ״לְהַנְחִיל אֹהֲבַי יֵשׁ וְאֹצְרֹתֵיהֶם אֲמַלֵּא״. [8]יֵשׁ בְּגִימַטְרִיָּא תְּלָת מְאָה וַעֲשָׂרָה הָוֵי.

LITERAL TRANSLATION

with the fatness of Your house, and You let them drink of the river of Your pleasures."

[1]When Rav Dimi came, he said: In the future, the Holy One, blessed be He, will give each and every righteous man as much as He can put in His hand, [2]as it is stated: "Blessed be the Lord who day by day bears our burden, God is our salvation. Selah."

[3]Abaye said to him: Is it possible to say this? [4]But surely it has been stated: "Who has measured the waters in the hollow of His hand, and meted out Heaven with the span"!

[5]He said: What is the reason that you are not familiar with the Aggadah? [6]For they say in the West in the name of Rava bar Madi: In the future, the Holy One, blessed be He, will give each and every righteous man three-hundred-and-ten worlds, [7]as it is stated: "That I may cause those who love Me to inherit substance [*yesh*]; and I will fill their treasures." [8]The numerical value of [the word] *yesh* is three-hundred-and-ten.

RASHI

מינה מהאי קרא איירי עניינא דמרעיב את עצמו וקאמר ״ירויון מדשן ביתך״ שהקדוש ברוך הוא משביען לעולם הבא. מלא עומסו — מלא חופנו של הקדוש ברוך הוא טובה. וכי אפשר לומר כן — היאך אדם יכול לקבל מלא עומסו של הקדוש ברוך הוא, והרי אין לו מקום ליתן, דכל העולם כולו אינו אלא כמזרת ועד אגודל, באותן עולמות יתן לצדיק את העומס.

NOTES

God's exactness with the righteous in this world, as opposed to what is stated in the later verse (Psalms 36:9): "They are abundantly satisfied with the fatness [*deshen*] of Your house," which describes the reward that awaits the righteous in the World to Come (see *Rashi, Maharsha,* and others). *Ramah* understands that the homily is based on the latter verse alone. He interprets the word *deshen* as "ashes," and regards it as a symbol of poverty. People who live in poverty and privation in this world will in the future "drink of the river of Your pleasures."

שְׁלֹשׁ מֵאוֹת וַעֲשָׂרָה עוֹלָמוֹת Three-hundred-and-ten worlds. The statement that in the future God will give each and every righteous man three-hundred-and-ten worlds is cited here in the name of the Amora Rava bar Madi. This is quite surprising since the same statement is cited in the Mishnah (*Uktzin* 3:12) in the name of Rabbi Yehoshua ben Levi. Some have distinguished between our passage, which reads לְהַנְחִיל, "cause to inherit," and the Mishnah, which reads לִיתֵּן, "give." But it would appear that the statement was not originally included in the Mishnah itself. Rather, it was a late addition, similar to the Gemara (see *Yesh Seder LaMishnah, Margoliyot HaYam*).

שְׁלֹשׁ מֵאוֹת וַעֲשָׂרָה עוֹלָמוֹת Three-hundred-and-ten worlds. Various suggestions have been offered as to the significance of the number three-hundred-and-ten. It has been argued that since there are six-hundred-and-twenty commandments (six-hundred-and-thirteen Biblical commandments, and seven Rabbinic decrees), and there are also six-hundred-and-twenty letters in the Ten Commandments, each righteous person should have received worlds equal in number to the commandments. But since man was first created as a double being — male and female — and separated later, each partner receives only half of the worlds, three-hundred-and-ten (*Torat Ḥayyim*).

TRANSLATION AND COMMENTARY

תַּנְיָא [1] **It was taught** in a related Baraita: **"Rabbi Meir says: According to the measure that a person measures out** to others, **they measure out to him** from above. If someone dispenses charity to the poor by the handful, God will reward him with a handful of His good, [2] **as the verse states** (Isaiah 27:8): **'By measure** [*besase'ah*], **by exile, You did contend with them.'** The word *besase'ah* (translated here as 'by measure') may be read homiletically as *bese'ah-se'ah* — that *se'ah* with which a person measures out to others will be the *se'ah* with which God measures out to him. [3] **Rabbi Yehoshua said** to Rabbi Meir: **Is it possible to say this, that if a person gives as much as he can put in his hand to a poor person in this world, the Holy One, blessed be He, will give him as much as He can put in His hand in the World to Come?** [4] **But surely the verse states** (Isaiah 40:12): 'Who has measured the waters in the hollow of His hand, **and meted out heaven with the span'!** If the entire world fits in God's hand, as it were, then how can man receive from God all the good that fits in His hand? Rabbi Meir said to Rabbi Yehoshua: [5] **Do you not say as** I have said? [6] **Which of** God's **measures is greater,** His **measure of good** reward, **or** His **measure of retribution?** [100B] [7] Surely you would **say** that God's **measure of good** reward, **is greater than** His **measure of retribution,** [8] **for regarding** God's **measure of good** reward, while the Israelites were wandering in the wilderness, **the verses state** (Psalms 78:23-24): **'He commanded the clouds from above, and opened the doors of Heaven, and rained down manna upon them to eat,'** [9] whereas **regarding** God's **measure of retribution** during the deluge, **the verse states** (Genesis 7:11): **'And the windows of Heaven were opened.'** Thus, we see that to provide reward, God

[1] תַּנְיָא: ״רַבִּי מֵאִיר אוֹמֵר:
בְּמִדָּה שֶׁאָדָם מוֹדֵד, מוֹדְדִין לוֹ,
[2] דִּכְתִיב: ׳בְּסַאסְּאָה בְּשַׁלְּחָהּ
תְּרִיבֶנָּה׳. [3] אָמַר רַבִּי יְהוֹשֻׁעַ:
וְכִי אֶפְשָׁר לוֹמַר כֵּן? אָדָם נוֹתֵן
מְלֹא עוּמְסוֹ לְעָנִי בָּעוֹלָם הַזֶּה,
הַקָּדוֹשׁ בָּרוּךְ הוּא נוֹתֵן לוֹ
מְלֹא עוּמְסוֹ לָעוֹלָם הַבָּא?
[4] וְהָכְתִיב: ׳שָׁמַיִם בַּזֶּרֶת תִּכֵּן׳!
[5] וְאַתָּה אִי אוֹמֵר כֵּן? [6] אֵיזוֹ
הִיא מִדָּה מְרוּבָּה? מִדַּת טוֹבָה
מְרוּבָּה, אוֹ מִדַּת פּוּרְעָנוּת?
[100B] [7] הֱוֵי אוֹמֵר: מִדָּה טוֹבָה
מְרוּבָּה מִמִּדַּת פּוּרְעָנוּת,
[8] בְּמִדָּה טוֹבָה כְּתִיב: ׳וַיְצַו
שְׁחָקִים מִמָּעַל וְדַלְתֵי שָׁמַיִם
פָּתָח וַיַּמְטֵר עֲלֵיהֶם מָן
לֶאֱכֹל׳, [9] וּבְמִידַּת פּוּרְעָנוּת הוּא
אוֹמֵר: ׳וַאֲרֻבֹּת הַשָּׁמַיִם נִפְתָּחוּ׳.

LITERAL TRANSLATION

[1] It was taught: "Rabbi Meir says: As the measure that a person measures out, they measure out to him, [2] as it is written: 'By measure, by exile, You did contend with them.' [3] Rabbi Yehoshua said: Is it possible to say this [that if] a person gives as much as he can put in his hand to a poor person in this world, the Holy One, blessed be He, gives him as much as He can put in His hand in the World to Come? [4] But surely it is written: 'And meted out heaven with the span'! [5] And you do not say this? [6] What is the greater measure? Is the measure of good greater, or the measure of retribution? [100B] [7] Say: The measure of good is greater than the measure of retribution. [8] Regarding the measure of good, it is written: 'He commanded the clouds from above, and opened the doors of heaven, and rained down manna upon them to eat.' [9] And regarding the measure of retribution, it is written: 'And the windows of Heaven were opened.'

RASHI

במדה שאדם מודד — אם מדד ונתן לצדקה לעני מלא חפניו — הקדוש ברוך הוא מודד בחפניו ונותן לו. **וכי אפשר לומר כן** — שיהא הקדוש ברוך הוא נותן לאדם מלא חפניו? והלא אינו יכול לסבול כל כך! **הוי אומר מדה טובה מרובה ממדת פורענות** — דבמידה טובה כתיב דלתות ובמדת פורענות כתיב "ארובות", ודלת גדול מארובה, דארבע ארובות יש בדלת, במסכת יומא בפרק "יום הכפורים" (עו,א), אלמא מדה טובה מרובה, ומעכשיו אין לתמוה היאך יש באדם כח לקבל שכר כל כך, שהרי למדת פורענות נותן הקדוש ברוך הוא כח באדם לקבלו — כל שכן שנותן כח באדם לקבל מדה טובה.

NOTES

מִדָּה טוֹבָה וּמִדַּת פּוּרְעָנוּת **The measure of good and the measure of retribution.** Elsewhere (*Yoma* 76a), *Rashi* notes that God's measure of reward is five hundred times as great as His measure of retribution, for the Torah states (Deuteronomy 5:9-10): "Punishing the iniquity of the fathers on the children, and on the children's children, to the third and the fourth generation of those who hate me, and showing mercy to the thousandth (lit., 'thousands') generation of those who love me and keep my commandments." We see from here that God's mercy lasts for at least two thousand generations (the smallest number of "thousands"), five hundred times as long as His retribution, which lasts for only four generations.

וַאֲרֻבֹּת הַשָּׁמַיִם נִפְתָּחוּ **And the windows of Heaven were opened.** An additional difference between God's measure of reward and His measure of retribution has been noted, for regarding God's blessing, the verse states, "And He opened the doors of heaven," that is to say, God Himself opened the doors, whereas regarding His retribution, the verse states, "And the windows of heaven were opened," that is to say, as if by themselves.

TRANSLATION AND COMMENTARY

opens the doors of Heaven, whereas to dispense punishment, He opens only the windows. [1]Now, **regarding** God's **measure of retribution,** another **verse states** (Isaiah 66:24): **'And they shall go forth, and look upon the carcasses of the men who have rebelled against me; for their worm shall not die, neither shall their fire be quenched; and they shall be an abhorrence to all flesh.'** [2]**But surely if a man** merely **sticks his finger into a fire in this world, he is immediately burned!** How, then, are the wicked able to withstand the eternal fire of damnation? [3]**Rather, just as the Holy One, blessed be He, gives the wicked** sufficient **strength to receive their retribution, so,** too, **the Holy One, blessed be He, gives the righteous** sufficient **strength to receive their reward. Therefore** the righteous are able to receive from God all the good that fits in His hand."

רַבִּי עֲקִיבָא אוֹמֵר [4]We have learned in our Mishnah: **"Rabbi Akiva says: Also** included among those who do not have a portion in the World to Come is **someone who reads heretical books** [*sefarim ḥitzonim*] containing heterodox interpretations of the Bible." The meaning of the expression, *sefarim ḥitzonim*, literally, "outside books," but translated here as "heretical books," [5]is clarified by a Baraita in which **it was taught** explicitly: **"The books of the heretics."**

רַב יוֹסֵף אָמַר [6]**Rav Yosef said:** Not only heretical books, but **also the book of Ben Sira one is forbidden to read.**

אֲמַר לֵיהּ אַבַּיֵי [7]**Abaye said to** Rav Yosef: **What is the reason** that you forbid the reading of the book of Ben Sira? [8]**You may say** that the book should not be read, **because it** contains a passage which **states: "Do not strip** the skin of **the** ***gildana*** [a type of fish] **from it gill, so that its skin will not go to waste.** [9]**Rather, roast** the fish with its skin **on a fire, and eat** the skin as

[1]בְּמִידַּת פּוּרְעָנוּת כְּתִיב: 'וְיָצְאוּ וְרָאוּ בְּפִגְרֵי הָאֲנָשִׁים הַפֹּשְׁעִים בִּי כִּי תוֹלַעְתָּם לֹא תָמוּת וְאִשָּׁם לֹא תִכְבֶּה וְהָיוּ דֵרָאוֹן לְכָל בָּשָׂר'. [2]וַהֲלֹא אָדָם מוֹשִׁיט אֶצְבָּעוֹ בָּאוּר בָּעוֹלָם הַזֶּה, מִיָּד נִכְוֶה! [3]אֶלָּא, כְּשֵׁם שֶׁנּוֹתֵן הַקָּדוֹשׁ בָּרוּךְ הוּא כֹּחַ בָּרְשָׁעִים לְקַבֵּל פּוּרְעָנוּתָם — כָּךְ נוֹתֵן הַקָּדוֹשׁ בָּרוּךְ הוּא כֹּחַ בַּצַּדִּיקִים לְקַבֵּל טוֹבָתָן".

[4]"רַבִּי עֲקִיבָא אוֹמֵר: אַף הַקּוֹרֵא בַּסְּפָרִים הַחִיצוֹנִים וכו'". [5]תָּנָא: "בְּסִפְרֵי מִינִים".

[6]רַב יוֹסֵף אָמַר: בְּסֵפֶר בֶּן סִירָא נַמִי אָסוּר לְמִיקְרֵי.

[7]אֲמַר לֵיהּ אַבַּיֵי: מַאי טַעְמָא? [8]אִילֵימָא מִשּׁוּם דִּכְתַב [בֵּיהּ]: "לָא תִינְטוֹשׁ גִּילְדָנָא מֵאוּדְנֵיהּ דְּלָא לֵיזִיל מַשְׁכֵּיהּ לְחַבְלָא. [9]אֶלָּא, צְלֵי יָתֵיהּ בְּנוּרָא, וְאֵיכוֹל בֵּיהּ תַּרְתֵּין גְּרִיצִים"

LITERAL TRANSLATION

[1]Regarding the measure of retribution, it is written: 'And they shall go forth, and look upon the carcasses of the men who have rebelled against me; for their worm shall not die, neither shall their fire be quenched; and they shall be an abhorrence to all flesh.' [2]But surely [if] a man extends his finger into a fire in this world, he is immediately burned! [3]Rather, just as the Holy One, blessed be He, gives the wicked the strength to receive their retribution, so the Holy One, blessed be He, gives the righteous the strength to receive their reward."

[4]"Rabbi Akiva says: Also someone who reads heretical books, etc." [5][A Sage] taught: "The books of the heretics."

[6]Rav Yosef said: It is also forbidden to read the book of Ben Sira.

[7]Abaye said to him: What is the reason? [8]If you say because it is written in it: "Do not strip the *gildana* from it gill, so that its skin will not go to waste. [9]Rather, roast it on a fire, and eat with it two loaves of bread"

RASHI

מינים — גלחים. רב יוסף אמר אף בספר בן סירא — שיש בו דברי הבאי, ובא עליהם לידי ביטול תורה. לא תיפשוט גילדנא מאודניה — כלומר לא תטול עורו של דג אפילו מעל אזנו, מפני שאתה מפסיד העור דאזיל משכיה לחבלא — להפסידא, אלא צלי יתיה בנורא ואכול ביה תרתין גרילין — שאתה יכול לצלות עור הדג עמו ולאכול בו שתי חלות דהוי לפתן לשתי חלות. גלדנא — שם הדג. לישנא אחרינא: להכי נקט מאודניה, שדרכו של דג להתחיל הפשטו מאזנו.

BACKGROUND

סֵפֶר בֶּן סִירָא **The Book of Ben Sira.** The Book of Ben Sira was very popular among the Jews of the Second Temple Period. It was composed by Yehoshua Ben Sira, perhaps a contemporary of the High Priest, Shimon the Righteous. The Sages refused to include this book in the Biblical canon, but in Egypt the translators of the Septuagint included the Book of Ben Sira in the Bible, and to this day it is found in many vernacular editions of the Bible which are based on that translation.

The book, as we now have it, was originally written entirely in Hebrew, and fragments of it have been found in Masada and the caves of the Judean Desert. Moreover, none of the doubtful passages attributed to it here, in Aramaic, have been discovered. Indeed it is known that another book existed, written in Aramaic mixed with Hebrew, called the "Wisdom of Ben Sira." That book includes various matters, including superstitions and entirely fanciful stories. Those two books were apparently joined together in a popular Aramaic edition, which is why the Sages were contemptuous of it, in addition to the main reason, which is that it was not included in the Bible.

It must be added that even in the Talmud the Book of Ben Sira is quoted as though it were Scripture, and in some places it is hinted that the passages are indeed scriptural. Thus the Sages did not object to the original book of Ben Sira, but rather to attributing too much sanctity to it, and the admixture of superstition and fancy.

NOTES

סְפָרִים הַחִיצוֹנִים **Heretical books.** It is not at all clear which "heretical books" (or "outside books") our Mishnah is referring to. But (see also the Jerusalem Talmud) the Mishnah appears to be referring to books that were written around the time that the Hebrew canon was closed, which some people wanted to include in that canon. (Certain "heretical books" were included in the Greek version of the canon, including the book of Ben Sira and others). But books that do not emanate from the milieu of Biblical culture were not included in this stringency, and each is judged on its own merits (for example, the Jerusalem Talmud notes that the prohibition does not apply to the epics of Homer).

HALAKHAH

סְפָרִים הַחִיצוֹנִים **Heretical books.** "One is forbidden to read books which explain how a person is to serve an idol." (*Rambam, Sefer Mada, Hilkhot Avodah Zarah* 2:2.)

TRANSLATION AND COMMENTARY

a relish **with two loaves of bread,"** which is trivial advice. However, [1]**if** you object to this passage **according to its plain sense,** a similar idea **is also found in the Torah** in the verse that states (Deuteronomy 20:19): **"You shall not destroy its trees."** Just as the Torah forbids the destruction of trees or anything else from which benefit might still be derived, so, too, the book of Ben Sira forbids the destruction of those parts of a fish which are still fit to be eaten. [2]And **if** you object to this passage **according to its** homiletical **interpretation,** Ben Sira meant to **teach us proper conduct,** [3]**that** a man **should not engage in** sexual **intercourse** with his wife **in an unnatural manner** (anal intercourse).

וְאֶלָּא [4]**Rather,** you must forbid the reading of the book of Ben Sira, **because of the verses** that **state** (Ben Sira 42:11-14): **"A daughter is a false treasure for her father; out of fear for her he is not able to sleep at night; when she is a minor,** he worries **lest she be seduced** by others; **when she is a young girl,** he is concerned **lest she be promiscuous; when she reaches maturity,** he is anxious **lest she not marry; when she is married,** he worries **lest she not have any sons,** and be sent back to her paternal home; **when she is old,** he is concerned **lest she** begin to **practice witchcraft."** [5]If you think that a father of girls should not be told this, **surely** we find that **our Rabbis also expressed** a similar idea, for they taught: **"The world cannot exist without males, nor** can it exist **without females.** [6]Nevertheless, **happy is he whose children are males;** and **woe to him whose children are females."**

אֶלָּא [7]**Rather,** you must think that the book of Ben Sira should not be read, **because of the verse** that **states** (Ben Sira 14:1; 30:29): **"Do not bring anxiety into your heart, for anxiety has killed mighty people."** [8]But **surely Solomon** already **said** this (Proverbs 12:25): **"Anxiety in a man's heart dejects it** [יַשְׁחֶנָּה]." [9]And **Rabbi Ammi and Rabbi Assi disagreed** about the meaning of the verse: [10]**One** of the two Amoraim **said** that the word יַשְׁחֶנָּה should be understood: **Let him banish** [יְשִׂיחֶנָּה] his anxiety **from his mind.** [11]**And the other** Amora **said** that the word should be understood: **Let him speak** [יְשִׂיחֶנָּה] about his anxiety **to others.**

— [1]אִי מִפְּשָׁטֵיהּ, בְּאוֹרַיְיתָא נַמִי כְּתַב: "לֹא תַשְׁחִית אֶת עֵצָהּ". [2]אִי מִדְּרָשָׁא, אוֹרַח אַרְעָא קָא מַשְׁמַע לָן, [3]דְּלָא לִיבְעוֹל שֶׁלֹּא כְּדַרְכָּהּ.

[4]וְאֶלָּא, מִשּׁוּם דִּכְתִיב: "בַּת לְאָבִיהָ מַטְמוֹנֶת שָׁוְא, מִפַּחְדָּהּ לֹא יִישַׁן בַּלַּיְלָה; בְּקַטְנוּתָהּ, שֶׁמָּא תִתְפַּתֶּה; בְּנַעֲרוּתָהּ, שֶׁמָּא תִזְנֶה; בָּגְרָה, שֶׁמָּא לֹא תִינָּשֵׂא; נִישֵּׂאת, שֶׁמָּא לֹא יִהְיוּ לָהּ בָּנִים; הִזְקִינָה, שֶׁמָּא תַּעֲשֶׂה כְּשָׁפִים". [5]הָא רַבָּנַן נַמִי אֲמָרוּהָ: "אִי אֶפְשָׁר לָעוֹלָם בְּלֹא זְכָרִים וּבְלֹא נְקֵבוֹת. [6]אַשְׁרֵי מִי שֶׁבָּנָיו זְכָרִים, אוֹי לוֹ לְמִי שֶׁבָּנָיו נְקֵבוֹת".

[7]אֶלָּא, מִשּׁוּם דִּכְתִיב: "לָא תָעִיל דַּוְיָא בְּלִבָּךְ דְּגַבְרֵי גִיבָּרִין קְטַל דַּוְיָא". [8]הָא שְׁלֹמֹה אֲמָרָהּ: "דְּאָגָה בְלֶב אִישׁ יַשְׁחֶנָּה". [9]רַבִּי אַמִּי וְרַבִּי אַסִּי: [10]חַד אָמַר: יְשִׂיחֶנָּה מִדַּעְתּוֹ. [11]וְחַד אָמַר: יְשִׂיחֶנָּה לַאֲחֵרִים.

LITERAL TRANSLATION

— [1]if [you object] according to its plain sense, in the Torah, too, it is written: "You shall not destroy its trees." [2]If [the objection arises] from its interpretation, it is teaching us proper conduct (lit., "the way of the world"), [3]that one should not engage in intercourse in an unnatural manner.

[4]Rather, because it is written: "A daughter is a false treasure for her father; out of fear for her he does not sleep at night; when she is a minor, lest she be seduced; when she is a young girl, lest she be promiscuous; when she reaches maturity, lest she not marry; when she is married, lest she not have any sons; when she is old, lest she practice witchcraft." [5]Surely our Rabbis also said it: "The world cannot exist without males, nor without females. [6]Happy is he whose children are males; woe to him whose children are females."

[7]Rather, because it is written: "Do not bring anxiety into your heart, for anxiety has killed mighty people." [8]Surely Solomon said it: "Anxiety in a man's heart dejects it." [9]Rabbi Ammi and Rabbi Assi disagreed: [10]One said: Let him banish it from his mind. [11]And one said: Let him speak it out to others.

RASHI

אי מפשטיה — אי ממשמעותיה קא מתמהת באורייתא נמי כתיב. דלא לבעול שלא כדרכה — דאין הגון לאדם לשנות את דרכו, והיינו דקאמר מאודניה. לא יישן — אינו יכול לישן. קטנה — קודם שהביאה שתי שערות. נערה — משהביאה שתי שערות עד שירבה שחור על הלבן הרי היא בוגרת. בנערותה שמא תזנה — משבגרה ראויה היא לנישואין, להכי אמר שלא תנשא. דויא — דאגה.

NOTES

בַּת לְאָבִיהָ מַטְמוֹנֶת שָׁוְא **A daughter is a false treasure to her father.** A father might have thought that since he has a right to his daughter's handiwork and her betrothal money, he should regard her as a treasure. Thus Ben Sira said that a daughter is but a vain treasure (*Maharsha*).

TRANSLATION AND COMMENTARY

וְאֶלָּא [1] **Rather,** you must object to the reading of the book of Ben Sira **because** of **the verse that states** (Ben Sira 11:36): **"Keep the multitudes from inside your house, and do not bring everybody into your house."** [2] **But surely Rabbi** Yehudah HaNasi **also said** this, **for it was taught** in a Baraita: **"Rabbi** Yehudah HaNasi **says: A person should never bring** too **many friends into his house,** [3] **for the verse states** (Proverbs 18:24): **'A man with friends will be shaken.'"**

אֶלָּא [4] **Rather,** you must forbid the reading of the book of Ben Sira, **because** of the nonsensical advice offered by **the verses** that **read:** "If you see **a thin-bearded man,** know that he **is sharp-minded;** and if you see **a thick-bearded man,** know that he **is stupid.** [5] If **someone blows on his cup** in order to remove the froth, he **is not** very **thirsty.** [6] And similarly, if **someone asks, 'With what** relish **shall I eat my bread?'** — **take the bread** away **from him,** for he cannot be very hungry. [7] If you see **someone with a gap in his beard,** know that he must be very cunning and that **the entire world cannot overcome him."**

אָמַר רַב יוֹסֵף [8] **Rav Yosef said:** Even though the book of Ben Sira as a whole should not be studied, **the good ideas that it contains may be expounded** even in public. The good advice includes the following passages: [9] **"A good wife is a good present; she will be given into the bosom of a God-fearing man** (Ben Sira 26:3)." [10] **"A bad wife is** like **leprosy for her husband. What is his remedy?** [11] **Let him send her from his house, and he will be healed from his leprosy**

[1] וְאֶלָּא, מִשּׁוּם דִּכְתִיב: ״מְנַע רַבִּים מִתּוֹךְ בֵּיתְךָ וְלֹא הַכֹּל תָּבִיא אֶל בֵּיתְךָ״. [2] וְהָא רַבִּי נַמִּי אֲמָרָהּ, דְּתַנְיָא: ״רַבִּי אוֹמֵר: לְעוֹלָם לֹא יַרְבֶּה אָדָם רֵעִים בְּתוֹךְ בֵּיתוֹ, [3] שֶׁנֶּאֱמַר: ׳אִישׁ רֵעִים לְהִתְרוֹעֵעַ׳״.
[4] אֶלָּא, מִשּׁוּם דִּכְתִיב: ״זַלְדְּקָן קוּרְטְמָן; עַבְדְּקָן סַכְסָן. [5] דְּנָפַח בְּכָסֵיהּ לָא צָחֵי. [6] אֲמַר, ׳בְּמַאי אֵיכוּל לַחְמָא?׳ — לַחְמָא סַב מִינֵּיהּ. [7] מַאן דְּאִית לֵיהּ מַעַבַּרְתָּא בְּדִיקְנֵיהּ — כּוּלֵּי עָלְמָא לָא יָכְלֵי לֵיהּ״.
[8] אָמַר רַב יוֹסֵף: מִילֵּי מַעַלְיָיתָא דְּאִית בֵּיהּ דָּרְשִׁינַן לְהוּ: [9] ״אִשָּׁה טוֹבָה מַתָּנָה טוֹבָה; בְּחֵיק יְרֵא אֱלֹהִים תִּנָּתֵן. [10] אִשָּׁה רָעָה — צָרַעַת לְבַעְלָהּ. מַאי תַּקַּנְתֵּיהּ? [11] יְגָרְשֶׁנָּהּ מִבֵּיתוֹ, וְיִתְרַפֵּא

LITERAL TRANSLATION

[1] Rather, because it is written: "Keep the multitudes from inside your house, and do not bring everybody into your house." [2] But surely Rabbi also said it, for it was taught: "Rabbi says: A person should never bring many friends into his house, [3] as it is stated: 'A man with friends will be shaken.'"

[4] Rather, because it is written: "A thin-bearded man is sharp-minded; a thick-bearded man is stupid. [5] He who blows on his cup is not thirsty. [6] He who says, 'With what shall I eat [my] bread?' — take the bread from him. [7] Someone who has a gap in his beard — the entire world cannot overcome him."

[8] Rav Yosef said: The good things that it has we expound: [9] "A good wife is a good present; she will be given into the bosom of a God-fearing man. [10] A bad wife is leprosy for her husband. What is his remedy? [11] Let him send her from his house, and he will be healed

RASHI

מנע רבים – אותם שאין לך עסק עמהם מנעם מתוך ביתך. ולא הכל תביא ביתך – אפילו אותם שאתה מתעסק עמהם לא תביאם תדיר לביתך אלא מבחוץ תדבר עמהם. איש רעים – שיש לו רעים הרבה. להתרועע – לסוף מריעים לו שמתקוטט עמהם. זלדקן – מי שזקנו דקה ותלושה. קורטמן – תדע שחכם וחריף הוא ביותר. עבדקן סכסן – מי שזקנו עבה שוטה הוא. סכסן – כמו: כל בר בר אנא סכסא בבבא בתרא (עד,א). נפח בכסיה – מי שנופח אופיא שבכוסו. לא צחי – בידוע שאינו צמא. אמר במאי איכול לחמא – האומר: באיזה לפתן אוכל פת זה. סב לחמא מיניה – בידוע שאינו רעב וקח הלחם מידו, שאילו היה רעב היה אוכל. מאן דאית ליה מעברתא בדקניה – שזקנו מחולק ומפולל ויש בין שני שבילות כמין מעבר. כולי עלמא לא יכלי ליה – בערמימותיה, דמתוך שחשב כל ימיו בערמות הוא משים ידו לזקנו ומושך, כאדם שמחשב, עד שנקרחה, לישנא אחרינא: גרסינן הכרתא, מי שיש לו היכר בזקנו שסעד, כולי עלמא שלא סעדו אין יכולין להגיע לכחו, לישנא אחרינא: גורתא, והוא לשון קרחה, וכל הני דברי רוח ולכך אין קורין בו. דרשינן – כלומר אמרינן להו בפרקא, ומשמעינן להו לכולי עלמא כגון כל הני אשה טובה כו׳, אשה רעה צרעת לבעלה – מה תקנתו – יגרשנה מביתו, כך הלשון של ספר בן סירא, אשה רעה מתנה רעה לא גרסינן.

NOTES

זַלְדְּקָן קוּרְטְמָן **A thin-bearded man is sharp-minded.** It has been suggested that the book of Ben Sira was forbidden not only because of this fallacious advice, but also because such advice might lead to problems of faith. For if someone believes that a person's external characteristics reflect internal deficiencies, he will think that everything is predestined, and he will not try to improve himself (*Ramah*).

עַבְדְּקָן סַכְסָן **A thick-bearded man is stupid.** According to the Geonim, the term סַכְסָן refers to a quarrelsome person, who is extreme in his opinions and does not tolerate the opinions of others.

מַעַבַּרְתָּא בְּדִיקְנֵיהּ **Someone who has a gap in his beard.** Some suggest that the expression מַעַבַּרְתָּא בְּדִיקְנֵיהּ refers to someone whose beard is of two colors (*Arukh*).

מִצָּרַעְתּוֹ. [1]אִשָּׁה יָפָה — אַשְׁרֵי בַּעְלָהּ; מִסְפַּר יָמָיו כִּפְלַיִם. [2]הַעְלֵם עֵינֶיךָ מֵאֵשֶׁת חֵן פֶּן תִּלָּכֵד בִּמְצוּדָתָהּ. [3]אַל תֵּט אֵצֶל בַּעְלָהּ לִמְסוֹךְ עִמּוֹ יַיִן וְשֵׁכָר, כִּי בְּתוֹאַר אִשָּׁה יָפְיָהּ רַבִּים הוּשְׁחָתוּ. [4]וַעֲצוּמִים כָּל הֲרוּגֶיהָ. [5]רַבִּים הָיוּ פִּצְעֵי רוֹכֵל הַמַּרְגִּילִים לִדְבַר עֶרְוָה כְּנִיצוֹץ מַבְעִיר גַּחֶלֶת. [6]כִּכְלוּב מָלֵא עוֹף כֵּן בָּתֵּיהֶם מְלֵאִים מִרְמָה. [7]מְנַע רַבִּים מִתּוֹךְ בֵּיתֶךָ וְלֹא הַכֹּל תָּבִיא בֵּיתֶךָ. [8]רַבִּים יִהְיוּ דּוֹרְשֵׁי שְׁלוֹמֶךָ, גַּלֵּה סוֹדְךָ לְאֶחָד מֵאֶלֶף. [9]מִשּׁוֹכֶבֶת חֵיקֶךָ שְׁמוֹר פִּתְחֵי פִיךָ. [10]אַל תֵּצַר צָרַת מָחָר כִּי לֹא תֵּלֵד מַה יֵּלֵד יוֹם. [11]שֶׁמָּא לְמָחָר אֵינֶנּוּ, וְנִמְצָא מִצְטַעֵר עַל עוֹלָם שֶׁאֵינוֹ שֶׁלּוֹ״.

[12]״כָּל יְמֵי עָנִי רָעִים״. [13]בֶּן סִירָא אוֹמֵר: אַף לֵילוֹת. [14]בְּשֵׁפֶל גַּגִּים גַּגּוֹ, וּבִמְרוֹם

TRANSLATION AND COMMENTARY

(Ben Sira 25:30)." [1]**"A pretty wife, her husband is happy;** he feels as if **the number of his days have been doubled** (Ben Sira 26:1)." [2]**"Hide your eyes from a woman of grace, lest you be caught in her snare.** [3]**Turn not to her husband to mix wine and strong drink with him, for many have been corrupted by the beauty of a pretty woman, and mighty are all those who have met their death through her** (Ben Sira 9:9-11)." [4]**Many are the wounds of a peddler,** who suffers blows from jealous husbands who catch him alone with their wives (Ben Sira 11:36)." [5]**"Those who accustom themselves to sexual offenses are like a spark that ignites a coal,** for all that they have will be consumed." [6]**"Like a cage filled with birds, so, too, their houses are filled with deceit** (Ben Sira 11:43)." [7]**"Keep the multitudes from inside your house, and do not bring everybody into your house.** [8]**Let many be those who greet you; but** nevertheless **reveal your secrets** to only **one in a thousand** (Ben Sira 11:36-37)." [9]"Even **from** your wife **who lies in your bosom, guard the doors of your mouth,** and do not tell her everything (see Michah 7:5)." [10]**"Grieve not about tomorrow's trouble, for you know not what today may bring forth** (see Proverbs 27:1). [11]**Perhaps tomorrow you will no longer be** alive, for you might die today, **and you will have been distressed about a world that is not yours."**

כָּל יְמֵי עָנִי רָעִים [12]The verse in Proverbs states (Proverbs 15:15): **"All the days of the poor are evil."** [13]**Ben Sira says: Even the nights** of the poor are evil, for they are filled with anxiety. [14]**Among the lowest roofs** in town **is the** poor man's **roof, and on the**

LITERAL TRANSLATION

from his leprosy. [1]A pretty wife — happy is her husband; the number of his days are doubled. [2]Hide your eyes from a woman of grace, lest you be caught in her snare. [3]Turn not to her husband to mix wine and strong drink with him, for by the beauty of a pretty woman many have been corrupted, and mighty are all those whom she has killed. [4]Many are the wounds of a peddler. [5]Those who accustom themselves to sexual offenses are like a spark that ignites a coal. [6]Like a cage filled with birds, so their houses are filled with deceit. [7]Keep the multitudes from inside your house, and do not bring everybody into your house. [8]Let many be those who greet you; [but] reveal your secrets to one in a thousand. [9]From her who lies in your bosom, guard the doors of your mouth. [10]Grieve not about tomorrow's trouble, for you know not what today may bring forth. [11]Perhaps tomorrow he will not be, and he will have been distressed about a world that is not his."

[12]"All the days of the poor are evil." [13]Ben Sira says: Even the nights. [14]Among the lowest of roofs is his roof, and at the height

RASHI

כפליים — מרוב הנאה חשובין ככפליים. **אל תט אצל בעלה** — למסוך עמו יין ושכר. **רבים היו פצעי רוכל** — כמה וכמה מכות מקבל רוכל המחזיר בעיר [ונושא] תכשיטי נשים ועסקו עמהם, שפעמים שמוצאו בעלה עמה מתיחד עם אשתו ומכהו ופוצעו. **המרגילים לדבר עבירה** — ניאוף, הרי הן כניצוץ מבעיר גחלת, כשביב המבעיר את הפחם כך כל אשר להם כלה והולך. **גחלת** — אקרי פחם, שאינו בוער, כדאמרינן (ברכות נג,ב): גחלים עוממות, מפי רבי. **בכלוב** — דירה של עופות. **רבים יהיו דורשי שלומך** — שתהא מתאהב עם הכל, ואף על פי כן לא תגלה סודך לכולם אלא לאחד מני אלף. **מה ילד יום** — מה אירע היום, שמא למחר איננו — שמת הוא היום. **ונמצא** — שמילר על יום שאינו עתיד לראות, והיינו עולם שאינו שלו שהוא מצטער עליו, ודואג על חנס מיום המחרת שלא תבא עליו צרה. **כל ימי עני רעים וטוב לב משתה** — פסוק הוא במשלי (טו). **בשפל גגים גגו** — שעני הוא ואינו יכול להגביהו, לפיכך ממטר גגים לגגו — שיורד מטר הגגים הגבוהים לגגו ומזלפים עליו הגשמים, ואין לו מנוחה אפילו בלילות. **במרום הרים כרמו** — שאין לו השגת יד לקנות כרסב שפלה בדמים יקרים, וקונה לו

NOTES

אִשָּׁה יָפָה — אַשְׁרֵי בַּעְלָהּ A pretty wife — happy is her husband. A man should marry a woman whom he finds attractive in his eyes. He should not marry for her money, or the like, for in the end he will be drawn to pretty women who are forbidden to him, and come to commit serious violations of the law (*Rabbi Ya'akov Emden*).

רַבִּים הָיוּ פִּצְעֵי רוֹכֵל Many are the wounds of a peddler. *Ramah* suggests that this statement should be understood

TRANSLATION AND COMMENTARY

highest hill in the surrounding area **is his vineyard.** [1]Since his house is the lowest, **the rain** falling on all **the** neighboring **roofs** flows off **onto his roof,** and into his house. **And** since his vineyard is on the highest hill, **the earth of his vineyard** gets washed away and carried off **to** all **the** other **vineyards.**

סִימָן [2][The Gemara offers **a mnemonic device** to remember the names of the authors of a series of Aggadic statements relating to the verse cited above, "All the days of the poor are evil." **Zera, Rava, Mesharshiya, Ḥanina is good, Yannai is easygoing, Yoḥanan is compassionate, Yehoshua makes narrow.**]

אָמַר רַבִּי זֵירָא [3]**Rabbi Zera said in the name of Rav: What is** meant by **the verse** that **states** (Proverbs 15:15): **"All the days of the poor are evil"?** [4]This is an allusion to **those who study the Talmud** in great depth and with great toil, and remain with many unanswered questions. [5]That same verse continues: **"But he that is of a merry heart has a continual feast"** — this is an allusion to **those who study** the plain meaning of **the Mishnah.**

רָבָא אָמַר אִיפְּכָא [6]**Rava said** just **the opposite,** that the first half of the verse, "all the days of the poor are evil," refers to those who study only the Mishnah, and the second half of the verse, "but he that is of a merry heart has a continual feast," refers to those who study the Talmud. [7]**And this is what Rav Mesharshiya said in the name of Rava: What is** meant by **the verse** that states (Ecclesiastes 10:9): "He who removes stones shall be hurt by them; and he who chops wood shall be endangered by that"? [8]**"He who removes stones shall be hurt by them"** — this is an allusion to **those who study Mishnah.** They do not benefit from their studies, for they are unable to draw practical conclusions from what they have learned. [9]**"And he who chops wood shall be endangered by that"** — this is an allusion to **those who study Talmud.** They invest great effort in their studies, but they see the fruit of their labors when they issue practical Halakhic rulings.

רַבִּי חֲנִינָא אוֹמֵר [10]**Rabbi Ḥanina says: "All the days of the poor are evil"** — **this** refers to **someone who has a bad wife.** [11]**"But he that is of a merry heart has a continual feast"** — **this** refers to **someone who has a good wife.**

LITERAL TRANSLATION

of the hills is his vineyard. [1]The rain of the roofs to his roof, and the earth of his vineyard to the vineyards.

[2][A sign: Zera, Rava, Mesharshiya, Ḥanina, Toviyah, Yannai is easygoing, Yoḥanan is compassionate, Yehoshua shortens.]

[3]Rabbi Zera said in the name of Rav: What is that which is written: "All the days of the poor are evil"? [4]They who study Talmud. [5]"But he that is of a merry heart has a continual feast" — they who study Mishnah.

[6]Rava said the opposite. [7]And this is what Rav Mesharshiya said in the name of Rava: What is that which is written: [8]"He who removes stones shall be hurt by them" — these are students of Mishnah; [9]"And he who chops wood shall be endangered by that" — these are students of Talmud.

[10]Rabbi Ḥanina says: "All the days of the poor are evil" — this is someone who has a bad wife. [11]"But he who is of a merry heart has a continual feast" — this is someone who has a good wife.

הָרִים כַּרְמוֹ. [1]מִמְּטַר גַּגִּים לְגַגּוֹ, וּמֵעֲפַר כַּרְמוֹ לַכְּרָמִים.

[2][סִימָן: זֵירָ״א רָבָ״א, מְשַׁרְשִׁיָּ״א חֲנִינָ״א טוֹבִיָּ״ה, יַנָּא״י יָפֶ״ה יוֹחָנָ״ן מְרַחֵ״ם, יְהוֹשֻׁ״ע מְקַצֵּ״ר].

[3]אָמַר רַבִּי זֵירָא אָמַר רַב: מַאי דִּכְתִיב: ״כָּל יְמֵי עָנִי רָעִים״? [4]אֵלּוּ בַּעֲלֵי תַלְמוּד. [5]״וְטוֹב לֵב מִשְׁתֶּה תָמִיד״ — אֵלּוּ בַּעֲלֵי מִשְׁנָה.

[6]רָבָא אָמַר אִיפְּכָא. [7]וְהַיְינוּ דְּאָמַר רַב מְשָׁרְשִׁיָּא מִשְּׁמֵיהּ דְּרָבָא: מַאי דִּכְתִיב: [8]״מַסִּיעַ אֲבָנִים יֵעָצֵב בָּהֶם״ — אֵלּוּ בַּעֲלֵי מִשְׁנָה; [9]״וּבוֹקֵעַ עֵצִים יִסָּכֶן בָּם״ — אֵלּוּ בַּעֲלֵי תַלְמוּד.

[10]רַבִּי חֲנִינָא אוֹמֵר: ״כָּל יְמֵי עָנִי רָעִים״ — זֶה מִי שֶׁיֵּשׁ לוֹ אִשָּׁה רָעָה. [11]״וְטוֹב לֵב מִשְׁתֶּה תָמִיד״ — זֶה שֶׁיֵּשׁ לוֹ אִשָּׁה טוֹבָה.

RASHI

באחד מן ההרים בזול, וכל עפר שהוא מוליא לזבל (ולדייר) מוליך הרוח מן ההר לשאר כרמים שבבקעה ונמצא העני נפסד. **בעלי תלמוד** — שקשה ללמוד מרוב קושיות וסוגיות שיש בו. **משנה** — נוחה ללמוד. **רבא אמר איפכא** — דבעלי תלמוד נהנין מיגיעו, שידעו להורות איסור והיתר, אבל בעלי משנה — שונה ואינו יודע מהו אומר, דאין מורין הלכה מתוך משנה. **יסכן** — יתחמם.

NOTES

differently: Many are the sins of the peddler, for with the adornments and perfumes that he sells, he tempts people to sin.

[1] רַבִּי יַנַּאי אוֹמֵר: ״כָּל יְמֵי עָנִי רָעִים״ — זֶה אִסְטְנִיס. [2] ״וְטוֹב לֵב מִשְׁתֶּה תָּמִיד״ — זֶה שֶׁדַּעְתּוֹ יָפָה.
[3] רַבִּי יוֹחָנָן אָמַר: ״כָּל יְמֵי עָנִי רָעִים״ — זֶה רַחֲמָנִי. [4] ״וְטוֹב לֵב מִשְׁתֶּה תָּמִיד״ — זֶה אַכְזָרִי.
[5] רַבִּי יְהוֹשֻׁעַ בֶּן לֵוִי אָמַר: ״כָּל יְמֵי עָנִי רָעִים״ — זֶה [101A] שֶׁדַּעְתּוֹ קְצָרָה. [6] ״וְטוֹב לֵב מִשְׁתֶּה תָּמִיד״ — זֶה שֶׁדַּעְתּוֹ רְחָבָה.
[7] וְאָמַר רַבִּי יְהוֹשֻׁעַ בֶּן לֵוִי: כָּל יְמֵי עָנִי רָעִים. [8] וְהָאִיכָּא שַׁבָּתוֹת וְיָמִים טוֹבִים!
[9] כְּדִשְׁמוּאֵל. דְּאָמַר שְׁמוּאֵל: שִׁינּוּי וֶסֶת תְּחִלַּת חוֹלִי מֵעַיִים.
[10] תָּנוּ רַבָּנַן: ״הַקּוֹרֵא פָּסוּק שֶׁל שִׁיר הַשִּׁירִים וְעוֹשֶׂה אוֹתוֹ כְּמִין זֶמֶר, וְהַקּוֹרֵא פָּסוּק בְּבֵית מִשְׁתָּאוֹת בְּלֹא זְמַנּוֹ, [11] מֵבִיא רָעָה לָעוֹלָם, מִפְּנֵי שֶׁהַתּוֹרָה חוֹגֶרֶת שַׂק, וְעוֹמֶדֶת לִפְנֵי הַקָּדוֹשׁ בָּרוּךְ הוּא, וְאוֹמֶרֶת לְפָנָיו: [12] ׳רִבּוֹנוֹ שֶׁל עוֹלָם! עֲשָׂאוּנִי בָּנֶיךָ כְּכִנּוֹר שֶׁמְּנַגְּנִין בּוֹ לֵצִים׳! [13] אָמַר לָהּ: ׳בִּתִּי, בְּשָׁעָה

LITERAL TRANSLATION

[1] Rabbi Yannai says: "All the days of the poor are evil" — this is a fastidious person. [2] "But he that is of a merry heart has a continual feast" — this is someone whose mind is good (lit., "beautiful").

[3] Rabbi Yoḥanan says: "All the days of the poor are evil" — this is a compassionate person. [4] "But he that is of a merry heart has a continual feast" — this is a cruel person.

[5] Rabbi Yehoshua ben Levi says: "All the days of the poor are evil" — this is someone [101A] whose mind is narrow. [6] "But he that is of a good heart has a continual feast" — this is someone whose mind is wide.

[7] And Rabbi Yehoshua ben Levi said: "All the days of the poor are bad." [8] But surely there are Sabbaths and the Festival days!

[9] As Shmuel said. For Shmuel said: A change in custom is the beginning of intestinal disease.

[10] Our Rabbis taught: "Someone who reads a verse of the Song of Songs and treats it like a song, and someone who reads a verse in a banquet house not at its time, [11] brings evil to the world, for the Torah puts on sackcloth, and stands before the Holy One, blessed be He, and says before Him: [12] 'Master of the universe! Your sons have turned me into a lyre upon which jokers play!' [13] He said to it: 'My daughter, while

TRANSLATION AND COMMENTARY

רַבִּי יַנַּאי אוֹמֵר [1] **Rabbi Yannai says: "All the days of the poor are evil" — this** refers to **a fastidious person.** [2] **"But he that is of a merry heart has a continual feast" — this** refers to **someone who has a** more **easygoing temperament.**

רַבִּי יוֹחָנָן אָמַר [3] **Rabbi Yoḥanan says: "All the days of the poor are evil" — this** refers to **a compassionate person,** who is always distressed by the suffering that he sees in the world. [4] **"But he that is of a merry heart has a continual feast" — this** refers to **a cruel person,** who is not touched by the suffering of others.

רַבִּי יְהוֹשֻׁעַ בֶּן לֵוִי [5] **Rabbi Yehoshua ben Levi says: "All the days of the poor are evil" — this** alludes to **someone** [101A] **whose mind is narrow,** meaning someone who cannot tolerate things being done against his will. [6] **"But he that is of a merry heart has a continual feast" — this** alludes to **someone whose mind is open,** and who can tolerate other opinions.

וְאָמַר [7] **Rabbi Yehoshua ben Levi said:** The verse states: **"All the days of the poor are bad."** [8] **But surely there are the Sabbaths and the Festival days,** when even a poor man can rest and enjoy himself with food and drink!

כְּדִשְׁמוּאֵל [9] The Gemara answers: For a poor man, even the Sabbath and the Festival days are bad, **as Shmuel said. For Shmuel said: A change in custom is the beginning of intestinal disease.** A poor person is unable to enjoy the Sabbath and Festival days, because the change in his regular diet will damage his health.

תָּנוּ רַבָּנַן [10] **Our Rabbis taught** the following Baraita: "If **someone reads a verse** from **the Song of Songs and treats it like an** ordinary secular **song,** rather than like a sacred work, **or** if **someone reads a verse in a banquet house at an inappropriate time,** [11] he **brings evil to the world, for the Torah,** as it were, **puts on sackcloth, and stands before the Holy One, blessed be He, and says to Him:** [12] **'Master of the universe! Your sons have turned me into a lyre upon which jokers play,** and trifle with me as if I were a toy!' [13] And God **says to** the Torah: **'My daughter,** what

LANGUAGE

אִסְטְנִיס **Fastidious person.** From the Greek ασθενής, *asthenis*, meaning "weak," "sickly." As used by the Sages, it often means someone who is hypersensitive and spoiled.

RASHI

שדעתו קצרה — משים ללבו כל דאגות חבירו ודואג על כל מה שעתיד לבא עליו. **רחבה** — ואינו משים ללבו דאגה כל כך, לישנא אחרינא: דעתו קצרה — רגזן. **והא איכא שבתות וימים טובים** — שאין לך עני בישראל שאין לו מעדנים. **שנוי וסת** — משנה וסת ואוכל יותר, שאינו רגיל לאכול, היינו תחילת חולי מעיים, לפיכך אפילו שבתות וימים טובים רעים לו. **הכי גרסינן: הקורא שיר השירים ועושה אותו כמין זמר** — שקורא בנגינה אחרת שאינו נקוד בה, ועושה אותה כמין שיר, אף על פי שמשיר השירים הוא ועיקרו שיר אסור לעשותו כמין שיר, אלא בקריאתו. **הקורא פסוק בבית המשתאות בלא זמנו** — במיסב על יינו עושה שחיקותיו בדברי תורה וקורא פסוקים בקול רם לשחק בהם בני המשתה, אבל אם אומרו בזמנו על המשתה כגון שהוא יום טוב ונוטל כוס בידו, ואומר עליו דברי הגדה

שֶׁאוֹכְלִין וְשׁוֹתִין, בַּמֶּה יִתְעַסְּקוּ׳? [1] אָמְרָה לְפָנָיו: ׳רִבּוֹנוֹ שֶׁל עוֹלָם, אִם בַּעֲלֵי מִקְרָא הֵן, יַעַסְקוּ בְּתוֹרָה וּבִנְבִיאִים וּבִכְתוּבִים. אִם בַּעֲלֵי מִשְׁנָה הֵן, יַעַסְקוּ בְּמִשְׁנָה בַּהֲלָכוֹת וּבְהַגָּדוֹת. וְאִם בַּעֲלֵי תַלְמוּד הֵן, יַעַסְקוּ בְּהִלְכוֹת פֶּסַח בַּפֶּסַח, בְּהִלְכוֹת עֲצֶרֶת בָּעֲצֶרֶת, בְּהִלְכוֹת חַג בֶּחָג׳. [2] הֵעִיד רַבִּי שִׁמְעוֹן בֶּן אֶלְעָזָר מִשּׁוּם רַבִּי שִׁמְעוֹן בֶּן חֲנַנְיָא: כָּל הַקּוֹרֵא פָּסוּק בִּזְמַנּוֹ מֵבִיא טוֹבָה לָעוֹלָם, [3] שֶׁנֶּאֱמַר: ׳וְדָבָר בְּעִתּוֹ, מַה טּוֹב׳״.

[4] ״וְהַלּוֹחֵשׁ עַל הַמַּכָּה וכו׳״. [5] אָמַר רַבִּי יוֹחָנָן: וּבְרוֹקֵק בָּהּ, [6] לְפִי שֶׁאֵין מַזְכִּירִין שֵׁם שָׁמַיִם עַל הָרְקִיקָה.

[7] אִיתְּמַר: רַב אָמַר: אֲפִילּוּ ״נֶגַע צָרַעַת״. [8] רַבִּי חֲנִינָא אָמַר:

LITERAL TRANSLATION

they are eating and drinking, with what should they deal?' [1] It said before Him: 'Master of the universe, if they are versed in the Scriptures, let them engage in the Torah, the Prophets, and the Writings. If they are versed in the Mishnah, let them engage in the Mishnah, laws and Aggadah. If they are versed in the Talmud, let them deal with the laws of Pesaḥ on Pesaḥ, the laws of Shavuot on Shavuot, [and] the laws of the holiday [of Sukkot] on the holiday [of Sukkot].' [2] Rabbi Shimon ben Elazar testified in the name of Rabbi Shimon ben Ḥananya: Whoever reads a verse in its time brings good to the world, [3] as it is stated: 'And a word in due season, how good it is!'"

[4] "And someone who mutters an incantation over a wound, etc." [5] Rabbi Yoḥanan said: And when he spits on it, [6] for we do not mention the name of Heaven in connection with spitting.

[7] It was stated: Rav said: Even "a plague of leprosy." [8] Rabbi Ḥanina said:

TRANSLATION AND COMMENTARY

do you suggest that **they engage in while they eat and drink?'** [1] And the Torah **answers** God: **'Master of the universe, if they are versed in the Scriptures, they should study the Torah, the Prophets, and the Writings. If they are versed in the Mishnah, they should study Mishnah, laws and Aggadah. If they are versed in the Talmud, they should engage in the laws of Pesaḥ on Pesaḥ, the laws of Shavuot on Shavuot, and the laws of the holiday of Sukkot on the holiday of Sukkot.'** [2] **Rabbi Shimon ben Elazar testified in the name of Rabbi Shimon ben Ḥananya: Whoever reads a verse at its** proper **time,** and in a fitting manner, **brings good to the world,** [3] **as the verse states** (Proverbs 15:23): 'A man has joy in the answer of his mouth; **and a word in due season, how good it is!'"**

וְהַלּוֹחֵשׁ עַל הַמַּכָּה [4] Our Mishnah lists among those who do not have a share in the World to Come: **"Someone who mutters an incantation over a wound** as a remedy, reciting the verse (Exodus 15:26): 'I will put none of these diseases upon you, which I have brought upon Egypt, for I am the Lord that heals you.'" [5] **Rabbi Yoḥanan said:** The Mishnah is referring to when someone **spits upon** the wound while muttering the incantation. Such a person forfeits his share in the World to Come, [6] **for one may not mention the name of God in connection with spitting.**

אִיתְּמַר [7] **It was stated** that **Rav said: This applies even** to a verse which does not mention God's name, like (Leviticus 13:9): "When **the plague of leprosy** is in a man, then he shall be brought to the priest." One may not mutter that over a wound. [8] **Rabbi Ḥanina said: Even** a verse which is not at all

RASHI

ופסוקים מענינו של יום — מביא טובה לעולם. וברוקק — שכן דרך מלחשים לרקק קודם הלחש, ואסור להזכיר פסוק על הלחישה, ויש לחשים שדרכן לרקק אחריהם ואומר אותן בלשון לעז ומזכירין להם שם בלשון לעז ואמר לי רבי דמותר, דאין אסור אלא לוחש אחר הרקיקה דנראה שמזכיר השם על הרקיקה, ועוד, לא נאסר אלא בלשון הקודש אבל בלעז לא. אפילו נגע צרעת — אפילו לוחש (אחרי האי) קרא דלית ביה שם שמים על הרקיקה, שקורא "נגע צרעת כי תהיה באדם והובא אל הכהן" (ויקרא יג) לשם רפואה — אין לו חלק לעולם הבא.

NOTES

כָּל הַקּוֹרֵא פָּסוּק בִּזְמַנּוֹ **Whoever reads a verse in its time.** Rabbi Shimon ben Ḥananya teaches us that even if a person recites Biblical verses during a meal, if he recites them at the proper time, such as verses relating to the Sabbath or a Festival during the Sabbath or Festival meal — not only is the activity permitted, but it brings good to the world (see *Rabbenu Yehonatan, Ri Almandri*).

אֲפִילּוּ ״נֶגַע צָרַעַת״ **Even "a plague of leprosy."** According to *Ramah,* Rav teaches us that one may not even mutter as an incantation over a wound a verse which portends evil and is therefore unfit to serve as a healing charm, like "a plague of leprosy."

HALAKHAH

הַלּוֹחֵשׁ...וּבְרוֹקֵק בָּהּ **And someone who mutters...where he spits upon it.** "If someone mutters an incantation over a wound, or over a sick person, and then spits upon the wound or the patient, and then reads a verse from the Torah, he does not have a portion in the World to Come. Even if he did not spit, he has violated a prohibition. According to some, a person is permitted to mutter the incantation in a language other than Hebrew (*Rashi,* in the name of his teacher). But there is reason to be stringent and forbid the practice, especially if Divine Names are mentioned." (*Shulḥan Arukh, Yoreh De'ah* 179:8.)

אֲפִילּוּ ״וַיִּקְרָא אֶל מֹשֶׁה״.
[1]תָּנוּ רַבָּנַן: ״סָכִין וּמְמַשְׁמְשִׁין בִּבְנֵי מֵעַיִם בַּשַּׁבָּת, וְלוֹחֲשִׁין לְחִישַׁת נְחָשִׁים וַעֲקְרַבִּים בַּשַּׁבָּת, וּמַעֲבִירִין כְּלִי עַל גַּב הָעַיִן בַּשַּׁבָּת. [2]אָמַר רַבָּן שִׁמְעוֹן בֶּן גַּמְלִיאֵל: בַּמֶּה דְּבָרִים אֲמוּרִים? [3]בִּכְלִי הַנִּיטָּל. [4]אֲבָל בִּכְלִי שֶׁאֵינוֹ נִיטָּל אָסוּר. [5]וְאֵין שׁוֹאֲלִין בִּדְבַר שֵׁדִים בַּשַּׁבָּת. [6]רַבִּי יוֹסֵי אוֹמֵר: אַף בַּחוֹל אָסוּר״.
[7]אָמַר רַב הוּנָא: אֵין הֲלָכָה כְּרַבִּי יוֹסֵי.
[8]וְאַף רַבִּי יוֹסֵי לֹא אָמְרָהּ אֶלָּא מִשּׁוּם סַכָּנָה. [9]כִּי הָא דְּרַב

TRANSLATION AND COMMENTARY

connected to an illness or a wound, like (Leviticus 1:1): **"And the Lord called to Moses,** and spoke to him out of the Tent of Meeting, saying...," one may not mutter over a wound.

תָּנוּ רַבָּנַן [1]**Our Rabbis taught: "One may apply oil and rub the stomach** of a sick person **on the Sabbath** in order to reduce the patient's discomfort; **and** similarly **one may mutter an incantation against snake and scorpion** bites **on the Sabbath** in order to reduce the victim's pain; **and** similarly if a person is suffering from an eye infection, **one may apply a** cold **utensil to the** infected **eye on the Sabbath.** [2]**Rabban Shimon ben Gamliel said: When does this** last **law apply?** [3]It applies to **a utensil which is permitted to be picked up** and handled on the Sabbath, like a key, a knife, or a ring. [4]**But a utensil which is not permitted to be picked up** and handled on the Sabbath, because its normal use involves an activity that is not permitted on that day, **is forbidden** to be used for such a purpose. [5]If one has lost a certain article, **one may not inquire** about its location **with demons on the Sabbath,** for the verse states (Isaiah 58:13), 'If you...call the Sabbath a delight...and honor it, not doing your ways, nor finding your possessions.' [6]**Rabbi Yose says: Even on a weekday, it is forbidden** to ask demons about lost articles."

אָמַר רַב הוּנָא [7]**Rav Huna said: The law is not in accordance with** the position of **Rabbi Yose.**

וְאַף רַבִּי יוֹסֵי [8]**Even Rabbi Yose** did not mean to say that the practice is included under the Biblical prohibition against sorcery, but **only** that questioning demons is forbidden **because of the danger** involved. [9]**For example, Rav Yitzḥak bar Yosef** once consulted with

LITERAL TRANSLATION

Even "And He called to Moses."

[1]Our Rabbis taught: "We may apply oil and rub a stomach on the Sabbath, and we may mutter an incantation against snakes and scorpions on the Sabbath, and we may pass a utensil over an eye on the Sabbath. [2]Rabban Shimon ben Gamliel said: In what are these things said? [3]Regarding a utensil which may be picked up. [4]But a utensil which may not be picked up is forbidden. [5]And we may not inquire with demons on the Sabbath. [6]Rabbi Yose says: Even on a weekday it is forbidden."

[7]Rav Huna said: The law is not like (the position of) Rabbi Yose.

[8]And even Rabbi Yose only said this because of danger. [9]Like that of Rav

RASHI

ואפילו ויקרא אל משה — שאין בו לא חולי ולא נגע, דאין ראוי ללחשו על המכה, ואין מזכירו לשם רפואה אלא כסבור הוא להנצל בזכות דברי תורה שהוא הזכיר — אסור ללוחשו. **וממשמשין במעיים** — של חולה בשבת, ואין בכך משום רפואה, דסיכה איתקש לשתיה. **ולוחשין על נחשים ועל עקרבים בשבת** — בשביל שלא יזיקו, ואין בכך משום צידה. **כלי על העין** — שכן דרך ליתן כלי מתכות על העין כדי לקרר העין, אי נמי: כגון שעושין לאדם שחש בעינו, מקיפים עינו בטבעת. **כלי הניטל** — כגון מפתח סכין וטבעת. **בדבר שדים** — שכן עושין כשאובדין שום דבר שואלין במעשה שדים והם מגידים להם, ואסור לעשות בשבת משום ״ממצוא חפצך״ (ישעיה נח). **אף בחול אסור** — לשאול בשדים, כדמפרש לקמן משום סכנה. **כי הא דרב יצחק** — היה שואל במעשה שדים ויקש השד להזיקו ונעשה לו נס ובלעו הארז.

HALAKHAH

סָכִין וּמְמַשְׁמְשִׁין בִּבְנֵי מֵעַיִם בַּשַּׁבָּת **We may apply oil and rub a stomach on the Sabbath.** "One may apply oil and rub the stomach of a sick person on the Sabbath in order to reduce his discomfort, provided that one does so in a different manner than usual. For example, one should apply the oil and rub at the same time," following Rabbi Yoḥanan. (*Shulḥan Arukh, Oraḥ Ḥayyim* 327:2.)

לְחִישַׁת נְחָשִׁים וַעֲקְרַבִּים בַּשַּׁבָּת **An incantation against snakes and scorpions on the Sabbath.** "One is permitted to mutter an incantation against snake and scorpion bites on the Sabbath, and this is not included under the prohibition of entrapping animals (following *Rashi*'s understanding of the Gemara)." (*Shulḥan Arukh, Oraḥ Ḥayyim* 328:45.)

If someone was bitten by a snake or a scorpion, he is permitted to mutter an incantation over the bite, even on the Sabbath. Even though the incantation is ineffective, he is permitted to mutter it to put his mind at rest (following *Rambam*'s understanding of the Gemara). (*Shulḥan Arukh, Yoreh De'ah* 179:6).

וּמַעֲבִירִין כְּלִי עַל גַּב הָעַיִן בַּשַּׁבָּת **And we may pass a utensil over an eye on the Sabbath.** "One is permitted to apply a cold utensil to an infected eye on the Sabbath, provided that it is a utensil which may be picked up and handled on that day." (*Shulḥan Arukh, Oraḥ Ḥayyim* 328:46.)

וְאֵין שׁוֹאֲלִין בִּדְבַר שֵׁדִים **And we may not inquire with demons.** Inquiring of demons is forbidden. "There are those who permit consulting with demons in cases of robbery, following Rabbi Yose, in accordance with the interpretation of Rav Huna that the prohibition exists because of the danger posed to the inquirer, and not because of sorcery. *Rema* adds that, even so, one should not rely on this allowance." (*Shulḥan Arukh, Yoreh De'ah* 179:16.)

TRANSLATION AND COMMENTARY

a demon, and it caused him to **be swallowed up inside a cedar** tree, [1]**and** he was only saved when **a miracle was performed for him, and the cedar split open and spat him out.**

תָּנוּ רַבָּנַן [2]**Our Rabbis taught** a related Baraita: **"One may apply oil and rub the stomach** of a sick person **on the Sabbath, provided that one does not do it in the** same **manner as one would do it on an** ordinary **weekday."**

הֵיכִי עָבִיד [3]The Gemara asks: **How should** a person apply oil and rub the stomach of a sick person on the Sabbath? [4]**Rabbi Ḥama the son of Rabbi Ḥanina said: He should apply the oil** first, **and afterwards** he should **rub** the sick person's stomach. [5]**Rabbi Yoḥanan said: He should apply the oil and rub** the sick person's stomach **at the same time.**

תָּנוּ רַבָּנַן [6]**Our Rabbis taught** the following Baraita: **"Spirits** who are consulted with **oil and spirits** who are consulted with **eggs — one is permitted to make inquiries of them** on the Sabbath, **but** people refrain from doing so **because they answer falsely.** [7]Those who are accustomed to muttering incantations **mutter incantations over oil** that is found **in a utensil, but they do not mutter incantations over oil** that is found **in** someone's **hand,** for such incantations are ineffective. [8]**Therefore,** a person **may apply oil** brought to him **in** someone's **hand, but he may not apply oil** brought to him **in a utensil,** for a harmful incantation may have been muttered over that oil."

רַב יִצְחָק בַּר שְׁמוּאֵל [9]It was related that **Rav Yitzḥak bar Shmuel bar Marta** once **happened upon a certain inn where they brought him oil in a utensil.** [10]**He applied** the oil, **and boils broke out on his face.** [11]**He went out to the market, where a certain woman**

יִצְחָק בַּר יוֹסֵף דְּאִיבְלַע בְּאַרְזָא, [1]וְאִתְעֲבִיד לֵיהּ נִיסָּא פָּקַע אַרְזָא וּפַלְטֵיהּ.

[2]תָּנוּ רַבָּנַן: ״סָכִין וּמְמַשְׁמְשִׁין בִּבְנֵי מֵעַיִים בְּשַׁבָּת, וּבִלְבַד שֶׁלֹּא יַעֲשֶׂה כְּדֶרֶךְ שֶׁהוּא עוֹשֶׂה בַּחוֹל״.

[3]הֵיכִי עָבִיד? [4]רַבִּי חָמָא בְּרַבִּי חֲנִינָא אָמַר: סָךְ, וְאַחַר כָּךְ מְמַשְׁמֵשׁ. [5]רַבִּי יוֹחָנָן אָמַר: סָךְ וּמְמַשְׁמֵשׁ בְּבַת אַחַת.

[6]תָּנוּ רַבָּנַן: ״שָׂרֵי שֶׁמֶן וְשָׂרֵי בֵיצִים — מוּתָּרִין לִשְׁאוֹל בָּהֶן, אֶלָּא מִפְּנֵי שֶׁמְּכַזְּבִין. [7]לוֹחֲשִׁין עַל שֶׁמֶן שֶׁבַּכְּלִי, וְאֵין לוֹחֲשִׁין עַל שֶׁמֶן שֶׁבַּיָּד. [8]לְפִיכָךְ סָכִין מִשֶּׁמֶן שֶׁבַּיָּד, וְאֵין סָכִין מִשֶּׁמֶן שֶׁבַּכְּלִי״.

[9]רַב יִצְחָק בַּר שְׁמוּאֵל בַּר מָרְתָא אִיקְּלַע לְהַהוּא אוּשְׁפִּיזָא, אַיְיתִי לֵיהּ מִישְׁחָא בְּמָנָא. [10]שָׁף, נְפַקָן לֵיהּ צִימְחֵי בְּאַפֵּיהּ. [11]נְפַק לַשּׁוּק, חֲזִיתֵיהּ הַהִיא אִיתְּתָא,

LITERAL TRANSLATION

Yitzḥak bar Yosef, who was swallowed up in a cedar, [1]and a miracle was performed for him, [and] the cedar split open and spat him out.

[2]Our Rabbis taught: "We may apply oil and rub a stomach on the Sabbath, except that he may not do it in the way he does it on a weekday."

[3]How does he do it? [4]Rabbi Ḥama the son of Rabbi Ḥanina said: He applies oil, and afterwards he rubs. [5]Rabbi Yoḥanan said: He applies oil and rubs at the same time.

[6]Our Rabbis taught: "Spirits of oil and spirits of eggs — we are permitted to inquire of them, except that they are false. [7]We mutter [an incantation] over oil in a utensil, but we do not mutter [an incantation] over oil in the hand. [8]Therefore, we may apply oil in a hand, but we may not apply oil in a utensil."

[9]Rav Yitzḥak bar Shmuel bar Marta happened upon a certain inn, [where] they brought him oil in a utensil. [10]He applied [it, and] boils broke out on his face. [11]He went out to the market, [where] a certain woman saw him,

RASHI

סך ואחר כך ממשמש – הוי שנוי, דבחול דרך למשמש ואחר כך לסוך. שרי שמן – יש מעשה שדים ששואלין על ידי שמן וקרי להו שרי שמן, והיינו שרי בוהן, ויש ששואלין בשפופרת של ביצה וקרי להו שרי ביצים. אלא שמכזבין – לכך נמנעו מלשאול בהן. לוחשים על שמן שבכלי – אותן העושין מעשה שדים דרכן ללחוש על שמן שבכלי, ואין דרכן ללחוש על שמן שביד שאינו מועיל, לפיכך אדם יכול לסוך על ידו משמן שביד ואין לחוש שמא נעשה בו מעשה שדים ואין בו סכנת השד. שף – סך שמן בפניו. צמחין – אבעבועות *מלנ״ץ.

LANGUAGE (RASHI)

מלנ״ץ* From the Old French *malantz*, meaning "swellings from an illness."

NOTES

דְּאִיבְלַע בְּאַרְזָא **Who was swallowed up in a cedar.** *Rashi* understands that when Rav Yitzḥak bar Yosef consulted with a demon, the demon tried to harm him, but he was miraculously saved when he was swallowed up by a cedar tree which protected him from the demon.

שָׂרֵי שֶׁמֶן **Spirits of oil.** Some sources read שֵׁדֵי שֶׁמֶן, "demons of oil," and some sources identify these "spirits of oil" with שָׂרֵי בוֹהֶן, "thumb spirits." Various sources (*Sefer Hasidim* and others) mention details regarding the way these spirits are summoned and administered an oath.

אֶלָּא מִפְּנֵי שֶׁמְּכַזְּבִין **Except that they are false.** Many Rishonim read מִפְּנֵי שֶׁמְּכַזְּבִין, "because they are false." According to this reading, one is permitted to make inquiries of these spirits of oil and eggs, because they answer falsely, and no benefit can be derived from their answers. If the spirits provided true answers, there might be a problem of sorcery (see *Ramah, She'elot U'Teshuvot HaRamban, She'elot U'Teshuvot HaRivash*).

¹אֲמַרָה: ״זִיקָא דַּחֲמָת קָא חָזֵינָא הָכָא״. ²עָבְדָא לֵיהּ מִלְּתָא וְאִיתַּסֵּי.

³אֲמַר לֵיהּ רַבִּי אַבָּא לְרַבָּה בַּר מָרִי: כְּתִיב: ״כָּל הַמַּחֲלָה אֲשֶׁר שַׂמְתִּי בְּמִצְרַיִם לֹא אָשִׂים עָלֶיךָ כִּי אֲנִי ה׳ רֹפְאֶךָ״. ⁴וְכִי מֵאַחַר שֶׁלֹּא שָׂם, רְפוּאָה לָמָּה? ⁵אֲמַר לֵיהּ: הָכִי אֲמַר רַבִּי יוֹחָנָן: מִקְרָא זֶה מֵעַצְמוֹ נִדְרָשׁ, ⁶שֶׁנֶּאֱמַר: ״וַיֹּאמֶר אִם שָׁמוֹעַ תִּשְׁמַע לְקוֹל ה׳ אֱלֹהֶיךָ״. ⁷אִם תִּשְׁמַע, לֹא אָשִׂים; ⁸וְאִם לֹא תִּשְׁמַע, אָשִׂים. ⁹אַף עַל פִּי כֵן, ״כִּי אֲנִי ה׳ רֹפְאֶךָ״.

¹⁰אָמַר רַבָּה בַּר בַּר חָנָה: כְּשֶׁחָלָה רַבִּי אֱלִיעֶזֶר נִכְנְסוּ תַּלְמִידָיו לְבַקְּרוֹ. ¹¹אָמַר לָהֶן: ״חֵמָה עַזָּה יֵשׁ בָּעוֹלָם״. ¹²הִתְחִילוּ הֵן בּוֹכִין, וְרַבִּי עֲקִיבָא מְשַׂחֵק. ¹³אָמְרוּ לוֹ: ״לָמָּה אַתָּה מְשַׂחֵק״? ¹⁴אָמַר לָהֶן: ״וְכִי מִפְּנֵי מָה אַתֶּם בּוֹכִים״? ¹⁵אָמְרוּ לוֹ: ״אֶפְשָׁר סֵפֶר תּוֹרָה שָׁרוּי בְּצַעַר, וְלֹא נִבְכֶּה״? ¹⁶אָמַר לָהֶן: ״לְכָךְ אֲנִי

LITERAL TRANSLATION

¹[and] said: "The spirit of Ḥamat I see here." ²She did something for him, and he was cured.

³Rabbi Abba said to Rabbah bar Mari: It is written: "I will put none of these diseases upon you, which I have brought upon Egypt, for I am the Lord who heals you." ⁴Now if He did not put [them], why [is there] healing? ⁵He said to him: Thus said Rabbi Yoḥanan: This verse is interpreted by itself, ⁶for it is stated: "And he said, If you diligently heed the voice of the Lord." ⁷If you heed, I will not put; ⁸but if you do not heed, I will put. ⁹But even so, "For I am the Lord who heals you."

¹⁰Rabbah bar bar Ḥannah said: When Rabbi Eliezer became ill, his disciples went in to visit him. ¹¹He said to them: "There is fierce anger in the world." ¹²They began to weep, and Rabbi Akiva laughed. ¹³They said to him: "Why are you laughing?" ¹⁴He said to them: "And why are you weeping?" ¹⁵They said to him: "Is it possible that a Torah scroll is in distress, and we will not cry?" ¹⁶He said to them: "Therefore I

TRANSLATION AND COMMENTARY

who was an expert on demons **saw him,** ¹**and said: "I see here** in your face the mark of **the** evil **spirit of** that demon named **Ḥamat."** ²**She did something for him** (meaning that she muttered an incantation), **and he was cured.**

אֲמַר לֵיהּ רַבִּי אַבָּא ³**Rabbi Abba said to Rabbah bar Mari: The verse states** (Exodus 15:26): **"I will put none of these diseases upon you, which I have brought upon Egypt, for I am the Lord who heals you."** ⁴The question may be raised: **If** God **will not inflict** upon Israel any of those diseases that He brought upon Egypt, **why,** then, **is healing** necessary?

אֲמַר לֵיהּ ⁵Rabbah bar Mari **said to** Rabbi Abba: **Rabbi Yoḥanan said as follows:** The solution to the difficulty in **this verse is learned from** the verse **itself,** ⁶**for** the beginning of this very **verse states: "And he said, If you diligently heed the voice of the Lord."** ⁷**If you heed** the voice of the Lord, **I will put** upon you **none** of those diseases that I brought upon Egypt. ⁸**But if you do not heed** God's voice, **I will put** those diseases upon you. ⁹**But even so** — even if you do not heed God's voice, and I am forced to inflict those diseases on you — know that **"I am the Lord who heals you,"** and I will supply you with a remedy.

אָמַר ¹⁰**Rabbah bar bar Ḥannah said: When Rabbi Eliezer became ill, his disciples went in to visit him,** ¹¹and **he said to them: "There is fierce anger in the world.** God must be very angry with the world, otherwise I would not suffer such afflictions." ¹²Hearing their master talk about his suffering, most of Rabbi Eliezer's disciples **began to weep, but Rabbi Akiva** began to **laugh** with joy. ¹³The other disciples **said to** Rabbi Akiva: **"Why are you laughing?"** ¹⁴Rabbi Akiva turned the question around and **asked** his colleagues: **"Why are you** all **weeping?"** ¹⁵**They said to him: "Is it possible that a Torah scroll** — our master, Rabbi Eliezer, **is in distress, and we do not weep?"** ¹⁶Rabbi Akiva **said to them:** "It is precisely **for that reason** that I am happy and **laugh.**

RASHI

זיקא דחמת — רוח של אותו שד ששמו חמת אני רואה בפניך שאחזתך. **חמה עזה יש בעולם** — על עצמו היה אומר, שכעס עליו המקום והכביד חוליו.

NOTES

זִיקָא דַּחֲמָת The spirit of Ḥamat. Some Rishonim read: רוֹקָא דַּחֲמָת, "the spittle of Ḥamat," meaning the spittle of the sorceress named Ḥamat (*Rabbenu Ḥananel*).

חֵמָה עַזָּה יֵשׁ בָּעוֹלָם There is fierce anger in the world. Some explain that Rabbi Eliezer was sure that he was not suffering for his own sins but for the sins of his generation, for the Talmud states in several places that a righteous man may suffer on account of the sins of his generation. The Rabbinic scholars who went to visit him in hospital thought so, too, and therefore they cried. Rabbi Akiva maintains that Rabbi Eliezer was punished for his small number of flaws, and so it was good for him to suffer (*Ri'af, Maharsha, Iyyun Ya'akov*).

מְשַׂחֵק. [1] כָּל זְמַן שֶׁאֲנִי רוֹאֶה רַבִּי, שֶׁאֵין יֵינוֹ מַחְמִיץ וְאֵין פִּשְׁתָּנוֹ לוֹקֶה, וְאֵין שַׁמְנוֹ מַבְאִישׁ, וְאֵין דּוּבְשָׁנוֹ מַדְבִּישׁ, אָמַרְתִּי: [2] ׳שֶׁמָּא חַס וְשָׁלוֹם קִיבֵּל רַבִּי עוֹלָמוֹ׳. [3] וַעַכְשָׁיו שֶׁאֲנִי רוֹאֶה רַבִּי בְּצַעַר, אֲנִי שָׂמֵחַ״. [4] אָמַר לוֹ: ״עֲקִיבָא, כְּלוּם חִיסַּרְתִּי מִן הַתּוֹרָה כּוּלָּהּ״? [5] אָמַר לוֹ: ״לִימַּדְתָּנוּ רַבֵּינוּ: ׳כִּי אָדָם אֵין צַדִּיק בָּאָרֶץ אֲשֶׁר יַעֲשֶׂה טּוֹב וְלֹא יֶחֱטָא׳״.

[6] תָּנוּ רַבָּנַן: ״כְּשֶׁחָלָה רַבִּי אֱלִיעֶזֶר נִכְנְסוּ אַרְבָּעָה זְקֵנִים לְבַקְּרוֹ — רַבִּי טַרְפוֹן וְרַבִּי יְהוֹשֻׁעַ וְרַבִּי אֶלְעָזָר בֶּן עֲזַרְיָה וְרַבִּי עֲקִיבָא. [7] נַעֲנָה רַבִּי טַרְפוֹן וְאָמַר: ׳טוֹב אַתָּה לְיִשְׂרָאֵל מִטִּיפָּה שֶׁל גְּשָׁמִים, שֶׁטִּיפָּה שֶׁל גְּשָׁמִים בָּעוֹלָם הַזֶּה, וְרַבִּי בָּעוֹלָם הַזֶּה וּבָעוֹלָם הַבָּא׳. [8] נַעֲנָה רַבִּי יְהוֹשֻׁעַ וְאָמַר: ׳טוֹב אַתָּה לְיִשְׂרָאֵל יוֹתֵר מִגַּלְגַּל חַמָּה, שֶׁגַּלְגַּל חַמָּה בָּעוֹלָם הַזֶּה, וְרַבִּי בָּעוֹלָם הַזֶּה וּבָעוֹלָם הַבָּא׳. [9] נַעֲנָה רַבִּי אֶלְעָזָר בֶּן עֲזַרְיָה וְאָמַר: ׳טוֹב אַתָּה לְיִשְׂרָאֵל יוֹתֵר מֵאָב וָאֵם, שֶׁאָב וָאֵם בָּעוֹלָם הַזֶּה, וְרַבִּי בָּעוֹלָם הַזֶּה וּבָעוֹלָם הַבָּא׳. [10] נַעֲנָה רַבִּי

TRANSLATION AND COMMENTARY

[1] **As long as I saw Master, that his wine did not sour, and his flax was not afflicted, and his oil did not turn rancid, and his honey did not spoil, I said** to myself: [2] **'Perhaps, Heaven forbid, Master** has already **received his world,** and no further reward awaits him in the World to Come.' [3] **But now that I see Master in distress, I am happy** and laugh, for surely he is being punished now for his few misdeeds, so that he will receive the rest of his reward in the World to Come." [4] Rabbi Eliezer **said to** Rabbi Akiva: **"Akiva, did I omit anything of the entire Torah,** that you say that I am being punished for my misdeeds?" [5] Rabbi Akiva **said to him:** "Surely **Master** himself **has taught us** (Ecclesiastes 7:20): **'For there is not a just man upon earth, who does good, and sins not.'"**

תָּנוּ רַבָּנַן [6] **Our Rabbis taught** a similar Baraita: **"When Rabbi Eliezer became ill, four elders went in to visit him — Rabbi Tarfon, and Rabbi Yehoshua, and Rabbi Elazar ben Azaryah, and Rabbi Akiva.** [7] When asked to speak, **Rabbi Tarfon answered** with words of encouragement, **saying: 'You,** O Master, **are better for Israel than a drop of rain, for a drop of rain** only brings benefit **in this world,** whereas **Master** brings benefit here **in this world and** also **in the World to Come.'** [8] **Rabbi Yehoshua answered and said: 'You,** O Master, **are better for Israel than the wheel of the sun, for the wheel of the sun** only brings benefit in **this world,** whereas **Master** brings benefit here **in this world and** also **in the World to Come.'** [9] **Rabbi Elazar ben Azaryah answered and said: 'You,** O Master, **are better for Israel than a father and a mother, for a father and a mother** bring benefit only **in this world,** whereas **Master** brings benefit **in this world and** also **in the World to Come.'** [10] **Rabbi**

LITERAL TRANSLATION

laugh. [1] As long as I see Master, that his wine does not sour, and his flax is not afflicted, and his oil does not turn rancid, and his honey does not spoil, I said: [2] 'Perhaps, Heaven forbid, Master has received his world.' [3] But now that I see Master in distress, I am happy." [4] He said to him: "Akiva, did I omit anything of the entire Torah?" [5] He said to him: "Master has taught us: 'For there is not a just man upon earth, who does good, and sins not.'"

[6] Our Rabbis taught: "When Rabbi Eliezer became ill, four elders went in to visit him — Rabbi Tarfon, and Rabbi Yehoshua, and Rabbi Elazar ben Azaryah, and Rabbi Akiva. [7] Rabbi Tarfon answered and said: 'You are better for Israel than a drop of rain, for a drop of rain is in this world, and Master is in this world and in the World to Come.' [8] Rabbi Yehoshua answered and said: 'You are better for Israel than the wheel of the sun, for the wheel of the sun is in this world, and Master is in this world and in the World to Come.' [9] Rabbi Elazar ben Azaryah answered and said: 'You are better for Israel than a father and a mother, for a father and a mother are in this world, and Master is in this world and in the World to Come.' [10] Rabbi

RASHI

שכל זמן שהייתי רואה את רבי שאין יינו מחמיץ וכו׳ — כלומר שהיתה הצלחה בכל מעשיו. אמרתי קבל רבי את עולמו — כל שכרו. רואה רבי בצער — ושכרו משתמר להבא, לכך אני שמח. מדביש — מתקלקל ונעשה צלול מחמת חמימות. כלום חסרתי — שאתה אומר אני סובל עונותי. שגלגל חמה בעולם הזה — ולא לעתיד שמאורות מתחדשות.

NOTES

שֶׁמָּא קִיבֵּל רַבִּי עוֹלָמוֹ **Perhaps...Master has received his world.** Even though there were many righteous people who lived lives of ease and success in this world, since Rabbi Eliezer was successful in an almost unnatural way, and no obstacles impeded him, one might have thought he had already received his reward (*Be'er Sheva*).

לִימַּדְתָּנוּ רַבֵּינוּ **Master has taught us.** It has been inferred from here that whenever a disciple speaks before his master, he must say, "Master has taught us," even if he did not learn the matter from his master, for even when Rabbi Akiva cited a Biblical verse, he introduced it with the words, "Master has taught us" (*Tzofnat Pa'ane'ah*).

TRANSLATION AND COMMENTARY

Akiva answered and said: 'Sufferings are dear, for they allow a person to achieve atonement for his sins.' [1]Rabbi Eliezer **said to** his attendants: **'Support me, so that I may** sit up and **hear the words of Rabbi Akiva my disciple, who said: "Sufferings are dear."'** [2]Rabbi Eliezer **said to** Rabbi Akiva: **'Akiva, from where do you know this,** that sufferings are dear?' [3]Rabbi Akiva **said: 'I learn this from the verse** which states (II Kings 21:1-2): **"Manasseh was twelve years old when he began to reign, and He reigned fifty-five years in Jerusalem....And he did that which was evil in the sight of the Lord."** [4]**And** another **verse states** (Proverbs 25:1): [101B] [5]**"These also are the proverbs of Solomon, which the men of Hezekiah, King of Judah copied,"** implying that Hezekiah actively engaged in the public study and dissemination of the Torah. [6]Now, is it possible that **Hezekiah the King of Judah taught Torah to the general public, but did not teach Torah to his** own **son Manasseh?** [7]**Rather,** we must conclude that **despite all the trouble that** Hezekiah **took with** Manasseh to teach him Torah, **and all the toil that he toiled with him** to guide him along the correct path — **only suffering restored** Manasseh **to the right way,** [8]**as the verses state** (II Chronicles 33:10-11): **"And the Lord spoke to Manasseh, and to his people, but they would not heed.** [9]**So the Lord brought upon them the captains of the host of the King of Assyria, who took Manasseh among the thorns, and bound him with fetters, and carried him to Babylon."** [10]**And the** next **verses continue** (II Chronicles 33:12-13): **"And when he** [= Manasseh] **was in affliction, he besought the Lord his God, and humbled himself greatly before the God of his fathers, and he prayed to him. And he entreated Him, and He heard his supplication, and brought him back to Jerusalem into his kingdom; then Manasseh knew that the Lord was God."** [11]**Thus, you have learned that sufferings are dear,** for they can change a person for the better.'"

LITERAL TRANSLATION

Akiva answered and said: 'Sufferings are dear.' [1]He said to them: 'Support me, so that I may hear the words of Rabbi Akiva my disciple, who said: "Sufferings are dear."' [2]He said to him: 'Akiva, from where do you [know] this?' [3]He said: 'I interpret a verse: "Manasseh was twelve years old when he began to reign, and he reigned fifty-five years in Jerusalem....And he did that which was evil in the sight of the Lord." [4]And it is written: [101B] [5]"These also are the proverbs of Solomon, which the men of Hezekiah, King of Judah, copied." [6]Did Hezekiah the King of Judah teach the entire world Torah, and to his son Manasseh he did not teach Torah? [7]Rather, despite all the trouble that he took with him, and all the toil that he toiled with him — only suffering restored him to the right way, [8]as it is stated: "And the Lord spoke to Manasseh, and to his people, but they would not heed. [9]So the Lord brought upon them the captains of the host of the King of Assyria, who took Manasseh among the thorns, and bound him with fetters, and carried him to Babylon." [10]And it is written: "And when he was in affliction, he besought the Lord his God, and humbled himself greatly before the God of his fathers, and he prayed to him. And he entreated Him, and He heard his supplication, and brought him back to Jerusalem into his kingdom; then Manasseh knew that the Lord was God." [11]Thus, you have learned that sufferings are dear.'"

עֲקִיבָא וְאָמַר: ׳חֲבִיבִין יִסּוּרִין׳. [1]אָמַר לָהֶם: ׳סַמְכוּנִי וְאֶשְׁמְעָה דִּבְרֵי עֲקִיבָא תַלְמִידִי, שֶׁאָמַר: חֲבִיבִין יִסּוּרִין׳. [2]אָמַר לוֹ: ׳עֲקִיבָא, זוֹ מִנַּיִן לְךָ׳? [3]אָמַר: ׳מִקְרָא אֲנִי דוֹרֵשׁ: ״בֶּן שְׁתֵּים עֶשְׂרֵה שָׁנָה מְנַשֶּׁה בְּמָלְכוֹ וַחֲמִשִּׁים וְחָמֵשׁ שָׁנָה מָלַךְ בִּירוּשָׁלָיִם [וגו׳] וַיַּעַשׂ הָרַע בְּעֵינֵי ה׳״. [4]וּכְתִיב: [101B] [5]״גַּם אֵלֶּה מִשְׁלֵי שְׁלֹמֹה, אֲשֶׁר הֶעְתִּיקוּ אַנְשֵׁי חִזְקִיָּה, מֶלֶךְ יְהוּדָה״. [6]וְכִי חִזְקִיָּה מֶלֶךְ יְהוּדָה לְכָל הָעוֹלָם כּוּלּוֹ לִימֵּד תּוֹרָה, וְלִמְנַשֶּׁה בְּנוֹ לֹא לִימֵּד תּוֹרָה? [7]אֶלָּא, מִכָּל טוֹרַח שֶׁטָּרַח וּמִכָּל עָמָל שֶׁעָמַל בּוֹ — לֹא הֶעֱלָהוּ לַמּוּטָב אֶלָּא יִסּוּרִין, [8]שֶׁנֶּאֱמַר: ״וַיְדַבֵּר ה׳ אֶל מְנַשֶּׁה וְאֶל עַמּוֹ וְלֹא הִקְשִׁיבוּ. [9]וַיָּבֵא ה׳ עֲלֵיהֶם אֶת שָׂרֵי הַצָּבָא אֲשֶׁר לְמֶלֶךְ אַשּׁוּר וַיִּלְכְּדוּ אֶת מְנַשֶּׁה בַּחֹחִים וַיַּאַסְרֻהוּ בַּנְחֻשְׁתַּיִם וַיּוֹלִיכֻהוּ בָּבֶלָה״. [10]וּכְתִיב: ״וּכְהָצֵר לוֹ, חִלָּה אֶת פְּנֵי ה׳ אֱלֹהָיו, וַיִּכָּנַע מְאֹד מִלִּפְנֵי אֱלֹהֵי אֲבוֹתָיו, וַיִּתְפַּלֵּל אֵלָיו. וַיֵּעָתֶר לוֹ, וַיִּשְׁמַע תְּחִנָּתוֹ, וַיְשִׁיבֵהוּ יְרוּשָׁלַיִם לְמַלְכוּתוֹ. וַיֵּדַע מְנַשֶּׁה כִּי ה׳ הוּא הָאֱלֹהִים״. [11]הָא, לָמַדְתָּ שֶׁחֲבִיבִין יִסּוּרִין׳״.

RASHI

חביבין יסורין — שמכפרין עליך. גם לא משלי שלמה אשר העתיקו אנשי חזקיה — היינו תלמידי חזקיה כדקיימא לן בהשותפין בבבא בתרא (טו,א) חזקיה וסיעתו כתבו משלי, מכלל דחזקיה היה מלמד לכל, וכדאמרן (סנהדרין לד,א): נעץ חרב על פתח בית המדרש, וכל שכן שלמנשה בנו לימד. מכל טורח שטרח בו — ללמדו.

תָּנוּ רַבָּנַן: [1]״שְׁלֹשָׁה בָּאוּ בַּעֲלִילָה: אֵלּוּ הֵן: קַיִן, עֵשָׂו, וּמְנַשֶּׁה. [2]קַיִן, דִּכְתִיב: ׳גָּדוֹל עֲוֹנִי מִנְּשׂוֹא׳. [3]אָמַר לְפָנָיו: ׳רִבּוֹנוֹ שֶׁל עוֹלָם! [4]כְּלוּם גָּדוֹל עֲוֹנִי מִשִּׁשִּׁים רִיבּוֹא שֶׁעֲתִידִין לַחֲטוֹא לְפָנֶיךָ, וְאַתָּה סוֹלֵחַ לָהֶם׳? [5]עֵשָׂו, דִּכְתִיב: ׳הַבְרָכָה אַחַת הִיא לְךָ אָבִי׳? [6]מְנַשֶּׁה — בַּתְּחִילָּה קָרָא לֶאֱלוֹהוּת הַרְבֵּה, [7]וּלְבַסּוֹף קָרָא לֵאלֹהֵי אֲבוֹתָיו״.

[8]״אַבָּא שָׁאוּל אוֹמֵר: אַף הַהוֹגֶה אֶת הַשֵּׁם בְּאוֹתִיּוֹתָיו וכו׳״. [9]תָּנָא: ״וּבַגְּבוּלִין, וּבִלְשׁוֹן עֲגָה״.

[10]״שְׁלֹשָׁה מְלָכִים וְאַרְבָּעָה הֶדְיוֹטוֹת וכו׳״. [11]תָּנוּ רַבָּנַן:

LITERAL TRANSLATION

[1]Our Rabbis taught: "Three came with an argument: Cain, Esau, and Manasseh. [2]Cain, as it is written: 'My sin is greater than I can bear.' [3]He said before Him: 'Master of the universe! [4]Is my sin greater than [that of] the six-hundred thousand who will sin before You, and [yet] You will forgive them?' [5]Esau, as it is written: 'Have you but one blessing, my father?' [6]Manasseh — at first he called to many gods, [7]and at the end he called to the God of his fathers."

[8]"Abba Shaul says: Also someone who pronounces the [Divine] Name according to its letters, etc." [9][A Tanna] taught: "That is in the country, and in conversation."

[10]"Three kings and four ordinary people, etc." [11]Our Rabbis taught:

TRANSLATION AND COMMENTARY

תָּנוּ רַבָּנַן [1]Having alluded to Manasseh's repentance, the Gemara now cites a Baraita in which **our Rabbis taught: "Three** Biblical figures **came with** irrefutable **arguments: Cain, Esau, and Manasseh.** [2]**Cain, as the verse states** (Genesis 4:13): **'My sin is greater than I can bear.'** [3]Cain **said to** God: **'Master of the universe!** [4]**Is my sin greater than that of the six-hundred thousand** Israelites **who will sin before You** and worship the golden calf, **and yet You will forgive them?** Faced with that argument, God was compelled to set a mark upon Cain, to protect him. [5]**Esau, as the verse states** (Genesis 27:38): **'Have you but one blessing, my father?'** And Isaac was compelled to bestow a blessing upon his son, Esau. [6]**Manasseh,** as the verse states (II Chronicles 33:12): 'And when he [= Manasseh] was in affliction, he besought the Lord his God, and humbled himself greatly before the God of his fathers' — implying that Manasseh had **at first called upon many gods,** but they did not answer him, [7]**and now he called upon the God of his fathers,** arguing that if God does not answer him, He will prove to be no different than the other gods."

אַבָּא שָׁאוּל [8]Our Mishnah continues: **"Abba Shaul says: Also** included among those who do not have a share in the World to Come is **someone who pronounces the Divine Name** of four letters **as it is written."** [9]**A Tanna taught** a Baraita which explains: "We are dealing here with a person who pronounces the Divine Name as it is written **in the country** outside the Temple in Jerusalem. But in the Temple, the Divine Name was indeed pronounced as it is written. Moreover, we are dealing here with a person who pronounces the Divine Name **in** casual **conversation."**

שְׁלֹשָׁה מְלָכִים [10]Our Mishnah continues: **"Three** important **kings** mentioned in the Bible **and four ordinary people** who reached distinction do not have a portion in the World to Come because of their failures in matters of faith. The three kings are Jeroboam ben Nebat and Ahab, Kings of Israel, and Manasseh, King of Judah, all of whom did evil in the sight of God." [11]**Our Rabbis taught** the following Baraita: **"Jeroboam**

RASHI

שבאו בעלילה — שלא באו לבקש לפני הקדוש ברוך הוא בתפלה, אלא באו בעלילה, שאמרו דברים של גנאון שאין להם תשובה. **הברכה אחת היא** — וכי אין לך ברכה יותר תשובה ניצחת השיבו ועלתה לו. **מנשה** — בא בעלילה שלא להתפלל למקום, אלא לבסוף, אם לא תושיעני מה הועיל לי שקראתי לך יותר משאר אלהות, והיינו דכתיב ״ויכנע לפני (ה׳) אלהי אבותיו״ מכלל דעד השתא לפני אלוהות אחרים נכנע. **תנא** — כי אמרינן דהוגה את השם באותיותיו אין לו חלק לעולם הבא — בגבולין, אבל במקדש לא, שהרי בשם היו מברכין. **ובלשון עגה** — אפילו במקדש לא, לשון עגה — לעז, שאינו הוגה באותיותיו בלשון הקדש שלנו אלא שאר לועזין, עגה לשון ״בלעגי שפה״ (ישעיהו כח) מפי רבי, לישנא אחרינא: עגה לשון עוגה, מקום שיש בו חבורת בני אדם שמדברין דברי חול, גבולין קרי חוץ למקדש, ואסור לפרש שם בן ארבעים ושתים בלשון עגה חוץ למקדש, ואי עבד אין לו חלק, אבל בלשון קדש אינו נענש כל כך, ובמקדש הואיל ונהגו להזכיר פירושו — אינו נענש.

LANGUAGE

עֲגָה **Unnecessary conversation.** This appears to be related to the Arabic root علج, meaning "stammering, blemished." *Bertinuro* interprets it as coming from the Greek ἀγη, *agi*, or αγα, *aga*, meaning "hatred," "hostility."

NOTES

בָּאוּ בַּעֲלִילָה **They came with an argument.** It has been suggested that the arguments put forward by the three Biblical personalities mentioned here were in fact flawed, even though they themselves thought that they were irrefutable. They were answered not because they were right, but so that they would not think that God acts unjustly (*Maharsha*).

בִּלְשׁוֹן עֲגָה **In conversation.** A number of interpretations have been offered for the expression בִּלְשׁוֹן עֲגָה (see *Rashi*, and others). *Ramah* suggests that we are dealing here with a person who vocalizes the Divine Name in an improper manner. Alternatively, he proclaims the Divine Name in a foreign language.

“יָרָבְעָם — שֶׁרִיבַּע עַם. [1]דָּבָר אַחֵר: יָרָבְעָם — שֶׁעָשָׂה מְרִיבָה בָּעָם. [2]דָּבָר אַחֵר: יָרָבְעָם — שֶׁעָשָׂה מְרִיבָה בֵּין יִשְׂרָאֵל לַאֲבִיהֶם שֶׁבַּשָּׁמַיִם. [3]בֶּן נְבָט — בֶּן שֶׁנִּיבַּט וְלֹא רָאָה”. [4]תָּנָא: “הוּא נְבָט, הוּא מִיכָה, הוּא שֶׁבַע בֶּן בִּכְרִי. [5]נְבָט — שֶׁנִּיבַּט וְלֹא רָאָה, [6]מִיכָה — שֶׁנִּתְמַכְמֵךְ בַּבִּנְיָן, [7]וּמַה שְּׁמוֹ — שֶׁבַע בֶּן בִּכְרִי שְׁמוֹ”. [8]תָּנוּ רַבָּנַן: “שְׁלֹשָׁה נִיבְּטוּ וְלֹא רָאוּ, [9]וְאֵלּוּ הֵן: נְבָט, וַאֲחִיתוֹפֶל, וְאִיצְטַגְנִינֵי פַּרְעֹה”. [10]נְבָט רָאָה אֵשׁ שֶׁיּוֹצֵאת מֵאַמָּתוֹ. [11]הוּא סָבַר אִיהוּ מָלֵיךְ, וְלָא הִיא — יָרָבְעָם הוּא דִּנְפַק מִינֵּיהּ. [12]אֲחִיתוֹפֶל רָאָה צָרַעַת שֶׁזָּרְחָה לוֹ עַל אַמָּתוֹ,

LITERAL TRANSLATION

“Jeroboam — who caused the people to lie low. [1]Another explanation: Who caused a quarrel among the people. [2]Another explanation: Who caused a quarrel between [the people of] Israel and their Father in Heaven. [3]The son of Nebat — a son who looked, but did not see.”

[4][A Tanna] taught: “He is Nebat, he is Michah, he is Sheba ben Bichri. [5]Nebat — who looked, but did not see. [6]Michah — who was crushed in a building. [7]And what is his name? Sheba ben Bichri is his name.”

[8]Our Rabbis taught: “Three looked, but did not see, [9]and they are: Nebat, and Achitofel, and Pharaoh’s astrologers.” [10]Nebat saw fire issuing from his penis. [11]He thought that he would reign, but it was not so — it was Jeroboam who would issue from him. [12]Achitofel saw leprosy that broke out on his penis.

TRANSLATION AND COMMENTARY

[*Yarav'am*] was called by that name because he **caused the people** of Israel **to lie low** [*riba am*]. [1]**Another explanation** of that name may also be suggested: Jeroboam was called by that name because he **caused a quarrel** [*merivah*] **among the people** [*am*] of Israel. [2]Yet **another explanation** of that name may be offered: Jeroboam was called by that name because he fashioned golden calves, and **caused a quarrel** [*merivah*] **between** the people [*am*] of **Israel and their Father in Heaven.** [3]**The** appellation **son of Nebat** intimates that Jeroboam’s father was **someone who** thought that he had **looked** [*nibat*] carefully, and understood what he had seen, **but** in fact he **did not see** properly [as will be explained below].”

תָּנָא [4]**A Tanna taught** a related Baraita: **“Nebat, Michah, and Sheba ben Bichri** were the same person. [5]He was called **Nebat, because** he thought that he had **looked** carefully and understood what he had seen, **but** in fact he **did not see** properly. [6]He was called **Michah,** because he was **crushed** [*nitmachmech*] when he was used as a brick **in a building** in Egypt, but later he was miraculously saved. The Aggadah relates that when the Israelites were slaves in Egypt, and they had no more bricks to build Pharaoh’s treasure cities, the bodies of Jewish children were used instead of bricks. When Moses complained about this to God, God explained that he was ridding Israel of its thorns, for were these children to live they would grow up to lead wicked lives. God told Moses to remove one of them, so that he might see for himself, and he removed Michah, who in fact grew up to become a sinner. [7]**And what was his** real **name? His** real name was **Sheba ben Bichri.”**

תָּנוּ רַבָּנַן [8]**Our Rabbis taught: “Three** Biblical figures thought that they had **looked** carefully, and understood what they had seen, **but** in fact they **did not see** properly. [9]Those three **are:** Jeroboam’s father **Nebat, Achitofel, and Pharaoh’s astrologers.”** [10]The Gemara explains: **Nebat saw fire issuing from his penis,** and **he thought** that this was a sign **that he would reign** as king, and so he (= Sheba ben Bichri; see II Samuel 20) gathered all of Israel to him, hoping to take the kingship from David. [11]**But it was not so,** for **it was** a sign that his son **Jeroboam who would issue forth from him** would become king. [12]**Achitofel saw that leprosy had broken out on his penis,** and **he thought** this was a sign **that he would reign** as king. Achitofel advised Absalom to

RASHI

שריבע עם — שריבן את ישראל והשפילם. עשה מריבה בעם — הריבם אלו עם אלו בעסק עבודת כוכבים, זה עובד וזה מוחה בידו — ובאו לידי מחלוקת. שניבט ולא ראה — היה סבור להביט יפה ולעמוד על דבר עיקר ולא ראה שטעה, כדאמרינן לקמן ראה אש יוצאה מאמתו וכו׳. נתמכמך בבנין — של מצרים, שנתנוהו בבנין במקום לבנה, כדמפרש באגדה, שאמר לו משה להקדוש ברוך הוא: אתה הרעות לעם הזה — שעכשיו אם אין להם לבנים משימין בניהם של ישראל בבנין, אמר לו הקדוש ברוך הוא: קוצים הם מכלין, שגלוי לפני אילו הם חיים היו רשעים [גמורים], ואם תרצה, תנסה והוציא אחד מהן, הלך והוציא את מיכה, לישנא אחרינא: נתמכמך — עסק בבנין עד שנעשה מך, כדאמרינן (סוטה יא,א) כל העוסק בבנין מתמסכן. הוא סבר איהו מליך — ולכן נתאמץ שבע בן בכרי וקבץ כל ישראל אליו והיה רוצה למלוך, כדכתיב במקרא. איהו מליך — ולכן נעשה

NOTES

הוּא נְבָט, הוּא מִיכָה **He is Nebat, he is Michah.** The Baraita might not mean to say that Nebat, Michah, and Sheba ben Bichri were all the same person, but rather that their conduct was similar, as if they were all one person, and that therefore it is possible to learn about one from the other (*Ein Eliyahu*).

אֲחִיתוֹפֶל **Achitofel.** Achitofel knew that he would not be able to lead a successful revolt against the mighty, wise, and God-fearing David, and so he supported Absalom’s revolt against his father. Achitofel thought that once

LITERAL TRANSLATION

[1]He thought that he would reign, but it was not so — it was Batsheba his daughter from whom Solomon would issue. [2]Pharaoh's astrologers, for Rabbi Ḥama the son of Rabbi Ḥanina said: [3]What is that which is written: "This is the water of Merivah"? — [4]this is what Pharaoh's astrologers saw and erred. [5]They saw that the savior of Israel would be struck by water. [6]He said: "Every son that is born you shall cast into the river." But they did not know he would be punished because of the matter of the water of Merivah.

[7]And from where do we [know] that he will not go to the World to Come? [8]For it is written: "And this thing became a sin to the house of Jeroboam, even to cut it off, and to destroy it from the face of the earth." [9]"To cut it off" — in this world. [10]"And to destroy it" — in the World to Come.

[11]Rabbi Yoḥanan said: How did Jeroboam merit the kingship? [12]Because he rebuked Solomon. [13]And why was he punished? [14]Because he rebuked him in public. As it is stated: "And this was the cause that he lifted up his hand against the king: Solomon built the Millo, and repaired the breaches of the city of David his father."

[1]הוּא סָבַר אִיהוּ מָלַךְ, וְלָא הִיא — בַּת שֶׁבַע בִּתּוֹ הוּא דְּנָפְקָא מִינָּהּ שְׁלֹמֹה. [2]אִיצְטַגְנִינֵי פַּרְעֹה — דְּאָמַר רַבִּי חָמָא בְּרַבִּי חֲנִינָא: [3]מַאי דִּכְתִיב: "הֵמָּה מֵי מְרִיבָה"? — [4]הֵמָּה שֶׁרָאוּ אִיצְטַגְנִינֵי פַּרְעֹה וְטָעוּ. [5]רָאוּ שֶׁמּוֹשִׁיעָן שֶׁל יִשְׂרָאֵל בַּמַּיִם הוּא לוֹקֶה, [6]אָמַר: "כָּל הַבֵּן הַיִּלּוֹד הַיְאֹרָה תַּשְׁלִיכֻהוּ". וְהֵן לֹא יָדְעוּ שֶׁעַל עִסְקֵי מֵי מְרִיבָה לוֹקֶה.

[7]וּמְנָא לָן דְּלָא אָתֵי לְעָלְמָא דְּאָתֵי? [8]דִּכְתִיב: "וַיְהִי בַּדָּבָר הַזֶּה לְחַטַּאת בֵּית יָרָבְעָם וּלְהַכְחִיד וּלְהַשְׁמִיד מֵעַל פְּנֵי הָאֲדָמָה." [9]"לְהַכְחִיד" — בָּעוֹלָם הַזֶּה, [10]"וּלְהַשְׁמִיד" — לָעוֹלָם הַבָּא.

[11]אָמַר רַבִּי יוֹחָנָן: מִפְּנֵי מָה זָכָה יָרָבְעָם לְמַלְכוּת? [12]מִפְּנֵי שֶׁהוֹכִיחַ אֶת שְׁלֹמֹה. [13]וּמִפְּנֵי מָה נֶעֱנַשׁ? [14]מִפְּנֵי שֶׁהוֹכִיחוֹ בָּרַבִּים. שֶׁנֶּאֱמַר: "וְזֶה הַדָּבָר אֲשֶׁר הֵרִים יָד בַּמֶּלֶךְ: שְׁלֹמֹה בָּנָה אֶת הַמִּלּוֹא, סָגַר אֶת פֶּרֶץ עִיר דָּוִד אָבִיו".

TRANSLATION AND COMMENTARY

rebel against David, hoping that after Absalom rose to the throne, he would be able to supplant him. [1]**But it was not so,** but rather **it was** a sign that **from his** grand**daughter Batsheba, Solomon would issue forth** and become king. [2]**Pharaoh's astrologers** also thought that they had looked carefully, and understood what they had seen, but they were mistaken, **for Rabbi Ḥama the son of Rabbi Ḥanina said:** [3]**What is** the meaning of **the** verse that **states** (Numbers 20:13): **"This is the water of Merivah"?** [4]**This is** the water that **Pharaoh's astrologers saw and** about which **they made a mistake.** [5]**They saw** in the stars **that the** person who was destined to become the **savior of Israel would be smitten with water,** and so Pharaoh **ordered** that (Exodus 1:22): **"Every son that is born you shall cast into the river."** [6]**But they did not understand that** the stars were warning that Moses **would be punished because of the sin** connected with **the water of Merivah,** when Moses referred to the congregation of Israel as rebels and thus was barred from entering the Land of Israel.

וּמְנָא לָן [7]The Gemara asks: **From where do we know that** Jeroboam **will not go to the World to Come?** [8]**For the verse states** (I Kings 13:34): **"And this thing became a sin to the house of Jeroboam, even to cut it off, and to destroy it from the face of the earth."** [9]**"To cut it off"** — refers to Jeroboam's punishment **in this world.** [10]**"And to destroy it"** — refers to his punishment **in the World to Come.**

אָמַר רַבִּי יוֹחָנָן [11]**Rabbi Yoḥanan said: How did** a wicked person like **Jeroboam merit the kingship?** [12]Jeroboam became king **because he rebuked Solomon** for his wrongdoing, as will be explained below. [13]**And why was** Jeroboam **punished** and brought to idolatry, so that he would lose his share in the World to Come? [14]**Because he rebuked** Solomon **in public, as the verse states** (I Kings 11:27): **"And this was the cause that he lifted up his hand against the king: Solomon built the Millo, and repaired the breaches of the city of David his father."**

RASHI

יועץ לאבשלום כדי שתשוב המלוכה מדוד לאבשלום, ובין כך ובין כך יתגלגל הדבר ותשוב אליו. על מי מריבה — שבעון שאמר "שמעו נא המורים" נענש ולא נכנס לארץ ישראל. ומנא לן דלא אתי — ירבעם לעלמא דאתי, והכי נמי מפרש לקמן בכלהו שלשה מלכים וארבעה הדיוטות. הוכיח את שלמה — כדמפרש ואזיל דאמר דוד אביך וכו׳. ומפני מה נענש שהוכיחו ברבים — לביישו.

NOTES

Absalom rose to the throne, he would be able to take the kingship away from him and rule in his place (*Ramah*).

LANGUAGE

אַנְגַּרְיָא **Levies.** This derives from the Greek αγγαρεία, *aggareia*, meaning "forced labor for the authorities."

TRANSLATION AND COMMENTARY

אָמַר לוֹ [1]Jeroboam **said to** Solomon: **"David your father made breaches in the wall in order** to make it easier **for** the people of **Israel to make Festival pilgrimages. And you closed** those breaches **in order** to force the people to enter the city through the gates, so that you can **collect levies for** your wife, **the daughter of Pharaoh?"** [2]**And what is** the meaning of the words: **"And this was the cause that he lifted up his hand against the king"?** What exactly did Jeroboam do? [3]**Rav Naḥman said: He** lifted up his hand and **removed his tefillin in** Solomon's **presence,** thus demonstrating that he no longer held him in high regard.

אָמַר רַב נַחְמָן [4]**Rav Naḥman said: Jeroboam's haughtiness drove him out of the World** to Come, [5]**as the verses state** (I Kings 12:26-27): **"And Jeroboam said in his heart, Now shall the kingdom return to the House of David. If this people goes up to do sacrifice in the house of the Lord in Jerusalem, then shall the heart of this people turn again to their lord, namely to Rehoboam, King of Judah, and they shall kill me, and return to Rehoboam, King of Judah."** [6]Jeroboam **said** to himself: **"We have learned** by tradition that **sitting in the Temple Courtyard is only permitted to**

[1]אָמַר לוֹ: "דָּוִד אָבִיךָ פָּרַץ פְּרָצוֹת בַּחוֹמָה כְּדֵי שֶׁיַּעֲלוּ יִשְׂרָאֵל לָרֶגֶל. וְאַתָּה גָּדַרְתָּ אוֹתָם כְּדֵי לַעֲשׂוֹת אַנְגַּרְיָא לְבַת פַּרְעֹה?" [2]וּמַאי "וְזֶה אֲשֶׁר הֵרִים יָד בַּמֶּלֶךְ"? [3]אָמַר רַב נַחְמָן: שֶׁחָלַץ תְּפִילָּיו בְּפָנָיו. [4]אָמַר רַב נַחְמָן: גַּסּוּת הָרוּחַ שֶׁהָיָה בּוֹ בְּיָרָבְעָם טְרָדַתּוּ מִן הָעוֹלָם, [5]שֶׁנֶּאֱמַר: "וַיֹּאמֶר יָרָבְעָם בְּלִבּוֹ עַתָּה תָּשׁוּב הַמַּמְלָכָה לְבֵית דָּוִד. אִם יַעֲלֶה הָעָם הַזֶּה לַעֲשׂוֹת זְבָחִים בְּבֵית ה' בִּירוּשָׁלַיִם, וְשָׁב לֵב הָעָם הַזֶּה אֶל אֲדֹנֵיהֶם, אֶל רְחַבְעָם מֶלֶךְ יְהוּדָה, וַהֲרָגֻנִי, וְשָׁבוּ אֶל רְחַבְעָם מֶלֶךְ יְהוּדָה". [6]אָמַר, "גְּמִירִי: דְּאֵין יְשִׁיבָה בָּעֲזָרָה

LITERAL TRANSLATION

[1]He said to him: "David your father made breaches in the wall so that Israel would make Festival pilgrimages. And you fenced them in order to collect levies for the daughter of Pharaoh?" [2]And what is: "And this was the cause that he lifted up his hand against the king"? [3]Rav Naḥman said: He removed his tefillin before him.

[4]Rav Naḥman said: The coarse spirit that was in Jeroboam harassed him out of the world, [5]as it is stated: "And Jeroboam said in his heart, Now shall the kingdom return to the House of David. If this people goes up to do sacrifice in the house of the Lord in Jerusalem, then shall the heart of this people turn again to their lord, to Rehoboam, King of Judah, and they shall kill me, and return to Rehoboam, King of Judah." [6]He said: "We have learned: Sitting in the Temple Courtyard

RASHI

פרץ פרצות בחומה כדי שיעלו — (וירדו) [ויכנסו] בריות. **ואתה גדרת אותם כדי לעשות אנגריא** — כדי שיכנסו בשערים, לידע מי נכנס כדי לגבות מס לבת פרעה, מפי רבי, לישנא אחרינא: שסגר השערים ועשה מגדל לבת פרעה על אחד מן השערים, וכולם עוברים דרך שם כדי שיהיו מלויין עמה לכבדה ולעבדה, כל עבודת בית המלך קרי אנגריא, לישנא אחרינא: שהיה רגיל שלמה לסגור דלתות העזרה ומצניע מפתחות בידו, ודרכו של מלך לישן שלש שעות ביום וישראל עומדין על העזרה עד שיעמוד המלך, ואמר לו ירבעם: אתה רוצה שיתנו לך אנגריא לבת פרעה אשתך שתתן להם מפתחות. (בית) [את] המלוא — אחת מן הפרצות גדר, ומלאו לכותל החומה ובנה שם מגדל לבת פרעה ולאנשים שעובדין לה, לעיל מהאי קרא כתיב וירם יד במלך כלומר קם בדברים כנגד המלך ומרד בו. **שחלץ תפילין בפניו** — שהיה לו לפנות לצד אחר מפני אימת מלכותו ולחלוץ שלא בפניו, לישנא אחרינא: חולץ תפילין בפניו — לבא להתרים כנגדו בחזקה. **חלץ תפילין** — אין נכון להיות בגלוי ראש לפני המלך, [והוא התחיל במרד בכך להראות ולומר לו שאינו נוהג כמלך]. **גמירי דאין ישיבה** — הלכה למשה מסיני, ולא מקרא.

NOTES

שֶׁחָלַץ תְּפִילָּיו בְּפָנָיו **He removed his tefillin before him.** It follows from here that a disciple is forbidden to remove his tefillin in his master's presence. This prohibition has been understood in a number of ways. Some suggest that when a person bares his head before his superior, he expresses his refusal to accept the other person's authority (*Rashi*). Others explain that when a disciple attends to his master, he must wear his tefillin so that people should know that he is his disciple, and not his slave. A disciple who removes his tefillin before his master intimates that he no longer wishes to serve his master, and thus signals that he wishes to rebel against him (*Maharsha, Be'er Sheva*). Yet others propose that, since it was customary in those days to wear tefillin all day long, a person would not ordinarily remove his tefillin unless he wished to turn to some mundane task. Thus, it is inappropriate for a person to remove his tefillin in front of his master, for he should not demonstrate before him that he is about to suspend his Torah studies and turn to other pursuits (*Iyyun Ya'akov*).

יְשִׁיבָה בָּעֲזָרָה **Sitting in the Temple Courtyard.** Elsewhere, *Rashi* explains that the prohibition against sitting in the Temple Courtyard is derived from a verse relating to the

HALAKHAH

יְשִׁיבָה בָּעֲזָרָה **Sitting in the Temple Courtyard.** "Only the kings of the House of David are permitted to sit in the Temple Courtyard." (*Rambam, Sefer Avodah, Hilkhot Bet HaBeḥirah* 7:6; *Sefer Shofetim, Hilkhot Sanhedrin* 14:12; *Hilkhot Melakhim* 2:4.)

TRANSLATION AND COMMENTARY

the legitimate **kings of the House of Judah.** If I go with the people to sacrifice in the Temple in Jerusalem, and the people **see Rehoboam sitting and me standing, they will think that this one** — Rehoboam — **is the king, and this one** — Jeroboam — **is** but **a slave. And if I sit** down, too, **I will be** regarded as **a rebel against the king** of the House of Judah, **and** the people **will kill me, and follow** Rehoboam." [1]**Immediately: "The king took counsel, and made two calves of gold, and said to them, It is too much for you to go up to Jerusalem; behold your gods, O Israel, who brought you up from the land of Egypt. And he set the one in Beth-El, and the other he put in Daniel** (I Kings 12:25-29)."

מַאי "וַיִּוָּעַץ" [2]The Gemara asks: **What is** the meaning of the words: "The king **took counsel**"? [3]**Rabbi Yehudah said:** Jeroboam **sat a wicked man next to a righteous man** of the elders of Israel, and consulted with them. [4]**He said to them: "Will you sign on everything that I will do?"** [5]**They said to him: "Yes,** we will." [6]**He said to them: "I want to be king."** [7]**They said to him: "Yes,** we will accept you as king." [8]He asked them: **"Will you do whatever I ask you** to do?" [9]**They said to him: "Yes,** we will." He asked them: "Will you obey me **even** if I ask you **to worship an idol?"** [10]**The righteous man said: "God forbid,** I will never agree to idol worship!" [11]**The wicked man said to the righteous man** sitting next to him: **"Do you** really **think that a man like Jeroboam would** actually **worship an idol?** [12]**Rather, he** merely **wishes to test you** and see **whether you will accept what he says.** Thus the wicked man convinced the righteous man to sign that he would follow Jeroboam even if he asked him to worship an idol. Later, when Jeroboam asked the righteous man to practice idolatry, he was unable to refuse.

אֶלָּא לְמַלְכֵי בֵּית יְהוּדָה בִּלְבַד, כֵּיוָן דְּחָזוּ לֵיהּ לִרְחַבְעָם דְּיָתֵיב וַאֲנָא קָאֵימְנָא, סָבְרִי: הָא מַלְכָּא וְהָא עַבְדָּא. וְאִי יָתֵיבְנָא — מוֹרֵד בַּמַּלְכוּת הֲוַאי, וְקָטְלִין לִי, וְאָזְלוּ בָּתְרֵיהּ". [1]מִיָּד: "וַיִּוָּעַץ הַמֶּלֶךְ, וַיַּעַשׂ שְׁנֵי עֶגְלֵי זָהָב, וַיֹּאמֶר אֲלֵהֶם, רַב לָכֶם מֵעֲלוֹת יְרוּשָׁלַיִם הִנֵּה אֱלֹהֶיךָ יִשְׂרָאֵל אֲשֶׁר הֶעֱלוּךָ מֵאֶרֶץ מִצְרָיִם. וַיָּשֶׂם אֶת הָאֶחָד בְּבֵית אֵל וְאֶת הָאֶחָד נָתַן בְּדָן".

[2]מַאי "וַיִּוָּעַץ"? [3]אָמַר רַבִּי יְהוּדָה: שֶׁהוֹשִׁיב רָשָׁע אֵצֶל צַדִּיק, [4]אֲמַר לְהוּ: "חָתְמִיתוּ עַל כָּל דְּעָבֵידְנָא"? [5]אֲמַרוּ לֵיהּ: "הֵין". [6]אֲמַר לְהוּ: "מַלְכָּא בָּעֵינָא לְמֶיהֱוֵי". [7]אֲמַרוּ לֵיהּ: "הֵין". [8]"כָּל דְּאָמֵינָא לְכוּ עָבְידִתּוּ? [9]אֲמַרוּ לֵיהּ: "הֵין". "אֲפִילּוּ לְמִפְלַח לַעֲבוֹדָה זָרָה"? [10]אֲמַר לֵיהּ צַדִּיק: "חַס וְחָלִילָה"! [11]אֲמַר לֵיהּ רָשָׁע לְצַדִּיק: "סָלְקָא דַּעְתָּךְ דְּגַבְרָא כְּיָרָבְעָם פָּלַח לַעֲבוֹדָה זָרָה? [12]אֶלָּא לְמִינְסִינְהוּ הוּא דְּקָא בָּעֵי, אִי קַבְּלִיתוּ לְמֵימְרֵיהּ".

LITERAL TRANSLATION

is only [permitted] to the kings of the House of Judah. When they see Rehoboam sitting and me standing, they will think: This one is the king, and this one is a slave. And if I sit, I will be a rebel against the kingdom, and they will kill me and go after him." [1]Immediately: "The king took counsel, and made two calves of gold, and said to them, It is too much for you to go up to Jerusalem; behold your gods, O Israel, who brought you up from the land of Egypt. And he set the one in Beth-El, and the other he put in Daniel."

[2]What is "he took counsel"? [3]Rabbi Yehudah said: He sat a wicked man next to a righteous man, [4][and] said to them: "Will you sign on everything that I will do?" [5]They said to him: "Yes." [6]He said to them: "I want to be king." [7]They said to him: "Yes." [8]Whatever I say to you, you will do?" [9]They said to him: "Yes." "Even to worship an idol?" [10]The righteous man said: "God forbid!" [11]The wicked man said to the righteous man: "Do you think that a man like Jeroboam would worship an idol? [12]Rather, he wishes to test you, whether you will accept his words."

RASHI

שהושיב רשע אצל צדיק – ואומר להם להעמיד להם אלם אחד בבית אל, ואחד בדן, הסכימו עמו. אמר לו רשע לצדיק – סלקא דעתך גברא כירבעם פלח לעבודת כוכבים, אלא לנסיונהו בעי, אם דעתנו שלם עמו, נתרצה בדבר, וכך היה מטעה רשע לצדיק, עד שהיו כולן חתומים שהן היו רוצים ושוב לא היו יכולים לחזור בהן.

NOTES

priests (Deuteronomy 18:5): "To stand to minister." The allowance granted to the kings of the Davidic dynasty is not learned from the Torah, but from what is reported about David (II Samuel 7:18), that he sat before God. According to tradition, this means that he sat in the Temple Courtyard. According to the Jerusalem Talmud, the allowance granted to the Davidic kings to sit in the Temple Courtyard is the matter of an Amoraic dispute.

TRANSLATION AND COMMENTARY

[102A] [1]**And even Achiyah the Shiloni erred** in this matter, **and signed** that he accepted Jeroboam as king, and that he agreed to follow his orders. How do we know this? [2]**For Jehu was an exceedingly righteous man, as the verse states** (II Kings 10:30): **"And the Lord said to Jehu, Because you have done well what is right in My eyes, and have done to the house of Ahab according to all that was in My heart, your children of the fourth generation shall sit on the throne of Israel."** [3]**And the** next **verse states** (II Kings 10:31): **"But Jehu took no care to walk in the Torah of the Lord God of Israel with all his heart; for he departed not from the sins of Jeroboam, who made Israel sin."** [4]**What caused** Jehu to do this? [5]**Abaye said:** A **covenant is made with the lips,** that is to say, words are liable to come true, even if the speaker had no intention of doing what he said. [6]**For the verse states** that Jehu said (II Kings 10:18): **"Ahab served the Baal a little, but Jehu shall serve him much."** Even though Jehu said those words in cunning, so that he could destroy the worshipers of the Baal (see verse 19), once they were uttered they drew Jehu to the Baal. [7]**Rava said:** Jehu **saw the seal of Achiyah the Shiloni** on the document pledging allegiance to Jeroboam and obedience to his commands, **and he erred,** thinking that Achiyah had even agreed to worship an idol.

דִּכְתִיב [8]**The verse states** (Hosea 5:2): **"And the apostates are deep in slaughter** [וְשַׁחֲטָה שֵׂטִים הֶעְמִיקוּ], **and I am rejected by them all."** [9]**Rabbi Yoḥanan said: The Holy One, blessed be He, said: "They** — Jeroboam's followers — **went deeper than I,** in enforcing

[102A] [1]וְאַף אֲחִיָּה הַשִּׁילוֹנִי טָעָה, וְחָתַם, [2]דְּהָא יֵהוּא צַדִּיקָא רַבָּה הֲוָה, שֶׁנֶּאֱמַר: "וַיֹּאמֶר ה' אֶל יֵהוּא, יַעַן אֲשֶׁר הֱטִיבֹתָ לַעֲשׂוֹת הַיָּשָׁר בְּעֵינַי כְּכֹל אֲשֶׁר בִּלְבָבִי עָשִׂיתָ לְבֵית אַחְאָב בְּנֵי רְבִעִים יֵשְׁבוּ לְךָ עַל כִּסֵּא יִשְׂרָאֵל". [3]וּכְתִיב: "וְיֵהוּא לֹא שָׁמַר לָלֶכֶת בְּתוֹרַת ה' אֱלֹהֵי יִשְׂרָאֵל בְּכָל לְבָבוֹ, לֹא סָר מֵעַל חַטֹּאות יָרָבְעָם אֲשֶׁר הֶחֱטִיא אֶת יִשְׂרָאֵל". [4]מַאי גָּרְמָא לֵיהּ? [5]אָמַר אַבַּיֵי: בְּרִית כְּרוּתָה לַשְּׂפָתַיִם, [6]שֶׁנֶּאֱמַר: "אַחְאָב עָבַד אֶת הַבַּעַל מְעָט, יֵהוּא יַעַבְדֶנּוּ הַרְבֵּה". [7]רָבָא אָמַר: חוֹתָמוֹ שֶׁל אֲחִיָּה הַשִּׁילוֹנִי רָאָה, וְטָעָה. [8]דִּכְתִיב: "וְשַׁחֲטָה שֵׂטִים הֶעְמִיקוּ וַאֲנִי מוּסָר לְכֻלָּם". [9]אָמַר רַבִּי יוֹחָנָן: אָמַר הַקָּדוֹשׁ בָּרוּךְ הוּא: "הֵם הֶעְמִיקוּ

LITERAL TRANSLATION

[102A] [1]And even Achiyah the Shiloni erred, and signed, [2]for Jehu was an exceedingly righteous man, as it is stated: "And the Lord said to Jehu, Because you have done well what is right in My eyes, and have done to the house of Ahab according to all that was in My heart, your children of the fourth generation shall sit on the throne of Israel." [3]And it is written: "But Jehu took no care to walk in the Torah of the Lord God of Israel with all his heart; for he departed not from the sins of Jeroboam, who made Israel sin." [4]What caused him? [5]Abaye said: A covenant is made with the lips, [6]as it is stated: "Ahab served the Baal a little, but Jehu shall serve him much." [7]Rava said: He saw the seal of Achiyah the Shiloni, and he erred.

[8]As it is written: "And the apostates are deep in slaughter, and I am rejected by them all." [9]Rabbi Yoḥanan said: The Holy One, blessed be He, said: "They went deeper

RASHI

ואף אחיה השילוני טעה בדבר — דסבר לנסוייהו אתי, וחתם באותו מעשה. **שנאמר ויאמר ה' אל יהוא וגו' לעשות הישר וכתיב ויהוא לא שמר ללכת בתורת ה'** — ואמרינן מאי גרמא ליה, — ואמר רבא: חותמו של אחיה השילוני ראה, וטעה, — מכלל דהוא טעה. **ושחטה שטים העמיקו** — שטים — עובדי עבודה זרה על שם שסטים אחריה לשחוט לעבודה זרה. **העמיקו** — והחמירו, שאמרו שכל מי שעולה לרגל ידקר בחרב כדי שילכו וישחטו לפני העגלים. **ואני מוסר לכולם** — כלומר אנכי לא חשתי כל כך לכבוד עצמי לומר כל מי שאינו עולה לרגל ידקר בחרב, כמו שחשו הם לכבוד עבודה זרה, אלא יסורין בעלמא יסרתים, כלומר דעבר בעשה, לישנא אחרינא: שטים — כלומר שטיות שלהם, שסרו מאחרי, העמיקו עד שחיטה, שחייבו מיתה כל מי שעולה לרגל ומניח את העגלים. **ושחטה** — לשון שחיטה.

NOTES

וְאַף אֲחִיָּה הַשִּׁילוֹנִי טָעָה, וְחָתַם **And even Achiyah the Shiloni erred, and signed.** *Ramah* explains that Achiyah never signed a statement that he agreed to worship an idol, but rather he signed that he agreed to the crowning of Jeroboam as king. His mistake was that he did not condition his approval upon Jeroboam's fidelity to God's path, as we find regarding Joshua (Joshua 1:18): "Whoever rebels against your commandment, and will not hearken to your words in all that you command him, he shall be put to death; only be strong and of good courage."

הֵם הֶעְמִיקוּ מִשֶּׁלִּי **They went further than me.** They went further and imposed stricter punishments upon those who violate their commandments than I did upon those who violate My commandments. Had they imposed a lesser punishment upon those who make a pilgrimage to the Temple on a Festival, those who fear God would not have violated a positive commandment by not making such a pilgrimage. But since they imposed the death penalty upon those who make the pilgrimage, even the God-fearing people do not come, for saving a human life supersedes all the commandments (*Maharsha*).

מִשֶּׁלִּי, אֲנִי אָמַרְתִּי כָּל שֶׁאֵינוֹ עוֹלֶה לָרֶגֶל עוֹבֵר בַּעֲשֵׂה, וְהֵם אָמְרוּ: כָּל הָעוֹלֶה לָרֶגֶל — יִדָּקֵר בַּחֶרֶב״.

[1] ״וַיְהִי בָּעֵת הַהִיא וְיָרָבְעָם יָצָא מִירוּשָׁלַיִם, וַיִּמְצָא אֹתוֹ אֲחִיָּה הַשִּׁילוֹנִי הַנָּבִיא בַּדֶּרֶךְ, וְהוּא מִתְכַּסֶּה בְּשַׂלְמָה חֲדָשָׁה״. [2] תָּנָא מִשּׁוּם רַבִּי יוֹסֵי: ״עֵת הִיא מְזוּמֶּנֶת לְפוּרְעָנוּת״.

[3] ״בְּעֵת פְּקֻדָּתָם יֹאבֵדוּ״. [4] תָּנָא מִשּׁוּם רַבִּי יוֹסֵי: ״עֵת מְזוּמֶּנֶת לְפוּרְעָנוּת״.

[5] ״בְּעֵת רָצוֹן עֲנִיתִיךָ״. [6] תָּנָא מִשּׁוּם רַבִּי יוֹסֵי: ״עֵת מְזוּמֶּנֶת לְטוֹבָה״.

[7] ״וּבְיוֹם פָּקְדִי וּפָקַדְתִּי עֲלֵהֶם חַטָּאתָם״. [8] תָּנָא מִשּׁוּם רַבִּי יוֹסֵי: ״עֵת הִיא מְזוּמֶּנֶת לְפוּרְעָנוּת״.

[9] ״וַיְהִי בָּעֵת הַהִיא, וַיֵּרֶד יְהוּדָה מֵאֵת אֶחָיו״. [10] תָּנָא מִשּׁוּם רַבִּי

LITERAL TRANSLATION

than I. I said [that] whoever does not go up for a Festival violates a positive commandment, and they said [that] whoever goes up for the Festival will be pierced by a sword."

[1] "And it came to pass at that time, when Jeroboam left Jerusalem, that the Prophet Achiyah the Shiloni found him on the way, and he was covered with a new garment." [2] [A Tanna] taught in the name of Rabbi Yose: "It was a time designated for tribulation."

[3] "In the time of their punishment, they shall perish." [4] [A Tanna] taught in the name of Rabbi Yose: "A time designated for tribulation."

[5] "In an acceptable time I have answered you." [6] [A Tanna] taught in the name of Rabbi Yose: "A time designated for good."

[7] "In the day when I punish, I will punish their sin upon them." [8] [A Tanna] taught in the name of Rabbi Yose: "It was a time designated for tribulation."

[9] "And it came to pass at that time, that Judah went down from his brothers." [10] [A Tanna] taught in the name of Rabbi

TRANSLATION AND COMMENTARY

their idolatrous worship. I only **said that whoever does not make a pilgrimage** to the Temple **on a Festival violates a positive commandment, and they said that,** on the contrary, **whoever makes a pilgrimage** to the Temple **on a Festival will be pierced by a sword,** for he forsakes his idols and worships God in the Temple." Rabbi Yoḥanan understands the verse as follows: They who deviated [שֵׂטִים] from my service to practice idolatry went as far and deep [הֶעְמִיקוּ] as imposing slaughter [וְשַׁחֲטָה] upon anybody who forsakes his idol and makes a pilgrimage to the Temple. It should be noted that the literal meaning of this verse is very obscure.

וַיְהִי בָּעֵת הַהִיא [1] The verse states (I Kings 11:29): **"And it came to pass at that time [בָּעֵת] when Jeroboam left Jerusalem, that the Prophet Achiyah the Shiloni found him in the way, and he was covered with a new garment."** [2] **A Tanna taught** a Baraita **in the name of Rabbi Yose:** "The words 'at that time' intimate that it **was a time designated for tribulation,** for the Davidic kingdom was rent into two."

בְּעֵת פְּקֻדָּתָם יֹאבֵדוּ [3] And similarly, the verse states (Jeremiah 51:18): **"In the time [בְּעֵת] of their punishment, they shall perish."** [4] **A Tanna taught** a Baraita **in the name of Rabbi Yose:** "The words 'in the time' intimate that it was **a time designated for tribulation,** when the Temple was to be destroyed."

בְּעֵת רָצוֹן עֲנִיתִיךָ [5] In contrast, the verse states (Isaiah 49:8): **"In an acceptable time [בְּעֵת] I have answered you."** [6] And **a Tanna taught** a Baraita **in the name of Rabbi Yose:** "The words 'in a time' intimate **a time designated for good,** the arrival of the Messiah."

וּבְיוֹם פָּקְדִי [7] The verse states (Exodus 32:34): **"In the day [בְּיוֹם] when I punish, I will punish their sin upon them."** [8] **A Tanna taught** a Baraita **in the name of Rabbi Yose:** "The words 'in the day' intimate **a time designated for tribulation,** the Ninth of Av, when our forefathers were banned from entering Eretz Israel, when both the First Temple and the Second Temple were destroyed, the city of Betar fell, and the city of Jerusalem was plowed over."

וַיְהִי בָּעֵת הַהִיא [9] Similarly, the verse states (Genesis 38:1): **"And it came to pass at that time, that Judah went down from his brothers."** [10] **A Tanna taught** a Baraita **in the name of Rabbi Yose:** "The words 'at that

RASHI

מזומנת לפורענות — שבו נחלקה מלכות ישראל, דסמיך ליה ויקח את השלמה ויקרעה לשנים עשר קרעים וגו׳. **וביום פקדי** — בתשעה באב, שבכל השנה מאותן ארבעים שנה שעמדו במדבר יום מזומן לפורענות, בו חזרו מרגלים, בו נחרב הבית בראשונה ובשניה. **ויהי בעת ההיא וירד יהודה** — מזומנת לפורענות, שתמר נתחייבה שריפה ומתו שני בניו.

HALAKHAH

עוֹלֶה לָרֶגֶל **Going up for a Festival.** "There is a positive Biblical commandment to go up to the Temple in Jerusalem on each of the three Pilgrim Festivals (Pesaḥ, Shavuot, and Sukkot). Whoever does not go up to Jerusalem on those occasions violates a positive Biblical commandment." (*Rambam, Sefer Korbanot, Hilkhot Ḥagigah* 1:1.)

TRANSLATION AND COMMENTARY

time' intimate that it was **a time designated for tribulation,** for Tamar was sentenced to burning, and almost put to death."

וַיֵּלֶךְ רְחַבְעָם שְׁכֶם [1]The verse states (I Kings 12:1): **"And Rehoboam went to Shechem; for all Israel came to Shechem, to make him king."** [2]A **Tanna taught** a Baraita **in the name of Rabbi Yose:** "Shechem was **a place designated for tribulation. In Shechem Dina was raped.** [3]**In Shechem Joseph was sold by his brothers.** [4]And **in Shechem the kingdom of the House of David was divided** into two."

וְיָרָבְעָם יָצָא [5]The verse cited above states (I Kings 11:29): "And it came to pass at that time **when Jeroboam left Jerusalem."** [6]**Rabbi Ḥanina bar Pappa said:** Jeroboam **distanced himself from the destiny of Jerusalem,** never to return or to take part once again in the divine service performed there.

וַיִּמְצָא אֹתוֹ [7]The verse continues: **"That the Prophet Achiyah the Shiloni found him on the way, and he was covered with a new garment, and the two were alone in the field."** [8]The Gemara asks: **What** do the words **"with a new garment"** teach us? [9]**Rav Naḥman said:** Those words teach us that Jeroboam was **like a new garment. Just as a new garment has no defect, so, too, did Jeroboam's Torah have no defects.** [10]**Another explanation** may also be offered: The words **"a new garment"** teach us that the two of them — Achiyah and Jeroboam — [11]**proposed new points** of law to each other **that no ear had ever heard** before.

מַאי [12]The Gemara asks: **What** do the words **"and the two were alone in the field"** teach us? [13]**Rav Yehudah said in the name of Rav:** Those words teach us that **all** the other **Torah scholars** of that generation **appeared next to them as plants of the field,** for Achiyah and Jeroboam were superior to them all in their Torah knowledge.

יוֹסֵי: ״עֵת מְזוּמֶּנֶת לְפוּרְעָנוּת״. [1]״וַיֵּלֶךְ רְחַבְעָם שְׁכֶם, כִּי שְׁכֶם בָּא כָל יִשְׂרָאֵל לְהַמְלִיךְ אֹתוֹ״. [2]תָּנָא מִשּׁוּם רַבִּי יוֹסֵי: ״מָקוֹם מְזוּמָּן לְפוּרְעָנוּת. [3]בִּשְׁכֶם עִינּוּ אֶת דִּינָה. [4]בִּשְׁכֶם מָכְרוּ אֶחָיו אֶת יוֹסֵף. בִּשְׁכֶם נֶחְלְקָה מַלְכוּת בֵּית דָּוִד״. [5]״וְיָרָבְעָם יָצָא מִירוּשָׁלַיִם״. [6]אָמַר רַבִּי חֲנִינָא בַּר פַּפָּא: שֶׁיָּצָא מִפִּיתְקָהּ שֶׁל יְרוּשָׁלַיִם. [7]״וַיִּמְצָא אֹתוֹ אֲחִיָּה הַשִּׁילוֹנִי הַנָּבִיא בַּדֶּרֶךְ, וְהוּא מִתְכַּסֶּה בְּשַׂלְמָה חֲדָשָׁה וּשְׁנֵיהֶם לְבַדָּם בַּשָּׂדֶה״. [8]מַאי ״בְּשַׂלְמָה חֲדָשָׁה״? [9]אָמַר רַב נַחְמָן: כְּשַׂלְמָה חֲדָשָׁה. מַה שַּׂלְמָה חֲדָשָׁה אֵין בָּהּ שׁוּם דּוֹפִי, אַף תּוֹרָתוֹ שֶׁל יָרָבְעָם לֹא הָיָה בָּהּ שׁוּם דּוֹפִי. [10]דָּבָר אַחֵר: ״שַׂלְמָה חֲדָשָׁה״, [11]שֶׁחִידְּשׁוּ דְּבָרִים שֶׁלֹּא שָׁמְעָה אֹזֶן מֵעוֹלָם. [12]מַאי ״וּשְׁנֵיהֶם לְבַדָּם בַּשָּׂדֶה״? [13]אָמַר רַב יְהוּדָה אָמַר רַב: שֶׁכָּל תַּלְמִידֵי חֲכָמִים דּוֹמִין לִפְנֵיהֶם כְּעִשְׂבֵי הַשָּׂדֶה.

LITERAL TRANSLATION

Yose: "A time designated for tribulation."

[1]"And Rehoboam went to Shechem; for all Israel came to Shechem, to make him king." [2][A Tanna] taught in the name of Rabbi Yose: "A place designated for tribulation. [3]In Shechem they raped Dina. [4]In Shechem his brothers sold Joseph. In Shechem the kingdom of the House of David was divided."

[5]"When Jeroboam left Jerusalem." [6]Rabbi Ḥanina bar Pappa said: That [means] he left the destiny of Jerusalem.

[7]"That the Prophet Achiyah the Shiloni found him on the way, and he was covered with a new garment, and the two of them were alone in the field." [8]What is [the meaning of] "with a new garment"? [9]Rav Naḥman said: Like a new garment. Just as a new garment has no defect, so, too, the Torah of Jeroboam had no defect. [10]Another explanation: "A new garment." [11]That they innovated things that an ear never heard.

[12]What is: "And the two of them were alone in the field"? [13]Rav Yehudah said in the name of Rav: Because all Torah scholars appeared before them as plants of the field.

RASHI

בשכם מכרו אחיו את יוסף — כדכתיב (בראשית ל״ז) הלא אחיך רועים בשכם ודותן דכתיב בקרא היינו כפר הסמוך לשכם, ונקראת על שם שכם, אי נמי: כמדרשו, שהיו דנין עליו להרגו. **בשכם נחלקה מלכות בית דוד** — כדכתיב במלכים (א׳ י״ב). **מפתקה של ירושלים** — מכללה, שלא לחזור בה לעולם ולא ליטול חלק בעבודה. **מפתקה** — כגון (בבא מציעא פו,א) נפל פתקה מרקיעא, כלומר מחזקת של ירושלים הכתוב וחתום בה. **שום דופי** — גימגום בגמרא. **שחדשו** — דרשו דברי תורה בין ירבעם לאחיה.

NOTES

פִּיתְקָהּ שֶׁל יְרוּשָׁלַיִם **The destiny of Jerusalem.** Some explain: Jeroboam left those who are included among the righteous who will merit redemption in the future, as the verse states (Isaiah 4:3): "Everyone in Jerusalem that is written to life" (see *Arukh*).

שַׂלְמָה חֲדָשָׁה **A new garment.** "A new garment" symbolizes power and high position, as in (Isaiah 3:6): "You have clothing, be our ruler" (*Maharsha*).

דְּבָרִים שֶׁלֹּא שָׁמְעָה אֹזֶן מֵעוֹלָם **New points that an ear never heard.** Some suggest that Achiyah and Jeroboam discussed crowning Jeroboam as king, a secret matter that had never been discussed before (*Ramah*).

[1]וְאִיכָּא דְּאָמַר: שֶׁכָּל טַעֲמֵי תוֹרָה מְגוּלִּין לָהֶם כְּשָׂדֶה.
[2]"לָכֵן תִּתְּנִי שִׁלּוּחִים עַל מוֹרֶשֶׁת גַּת; בָּתֵּי אַכְזִיב לְאַכְזָב לְמַלְכֵי יִשְׂרָאֵל". [3]אָמַר רַבִּי חֲנִינָא בַּר פַּפָּא: יָצְאָה בַּת קוֹל, [4]וְאָמְרָה לָהֶן: "מִי שֶׁהָרַג אֶת הַפְּלִשְׁתִּי וְהוֹרִישׁ אֶתְכֶם גַּת תִּתְּנוּ שִׁילּוּחִים לְבָנָיו? [5]'בָּתֵּי אַכְזִיב לְאַכְזָב לְמַלְכֵי יִשְׂרָאֵל'".
[6]אָמַר רַב חֲנִינָא בַּר פַּפָּא: כָּל הַנֶּהֱנֶה מִן הָעוֹלָם הַזֶּה בְּלֹא בְּרָכָה כְּאִילּוּ גּוֹזֵל לְהַקָּדוֹשׁ בָּרוּךְ הוּא וּכְנֶסֶת יִשְׂרָאֵל, [7]שֶׁנֶּאֱמַר: "גּוֹזֵל אָבִיו וְאִמּוֹ, וְאֹמֵר אֵין פָּשַׁע חָבֵר הוּא לְאִישׁ מַשְׁחִית". [8]וְאֵין "אָבִיו" אֶלָּא הַקָּדוֹשׁ בָּרוּךְ הוּא, [9]שֶׁנֶּאֱמַר: "הֲלֹא הוּא אָבִיךָ קָּנֶךָ"? [10]וְאֵין "אִמּוֹ" אֶלָּא כְּנֶסֶת יִשְׂרָאֵל, [11]שֶׁנֶּאֱמַר: "שְׁמַע בְּנִי מוּסַר אָבִיךָ וְאַל תִּטֹּשׁ תּוֹרַת אִמֶּךָ".

LITERAL TRANSLATION

[1]And there is [one] who says: All the meanings of the Torah were revealed to them like a field.

[2]"Therefore shall you give presents to Moreshet-gat; the houses of Achziv are a dried up stream for the Kings of Israel." [3]Rabbi Ḥanina bar Pappa said: A heavenly voice issued, [4]and said to them: "He who slew the Philistine and bequeathed you Gat — will you give dismissal to his sons? [5]'The houses of Achziv are a dried-up stream for the Kings of Israel.'"

[6]Rav Ḥinena bar Pappa said: Whoever enjoys this world without a blessing is [regarded] as if he robbed the Holy One, blessed be He, and the congregation of Israel, [7]as it is stated: "He who robs his father or his mother, and says, It is no transgression, he is [the] companion of a corrupter." [8]And "his father" is none other than the Holy One, blessed be He, [9]as it is stated: "Is not He your father who bought you?" [10]And "his mother" is none other than the congregation of Israel, [11]as it is stated: "My son, hear the instruction of your father, and do not forsake the Torah of your mother."

TRANSLATION AND COMMENTARY

וְאִיכָּא דְּאָמַר [1]**And there is** someone **who says** that those words teach us **that all the meanings** underlying the laws **of the Torah were revealed to them like a field.**

לָכֵן תִּתְּנִי שִׁלּוּחִים [2]The verse states (Michah 1:14): **"Therefore shall you give presents** [שִׁלּוּחִים] **to Moreshet-gat** [מוֹרֶשֶׁת גַּת]; **the houses of Achziv are a dried up stream for the Kings of Israel."** [3]**Rabbi Ḥanina bar Pappa said** that the verse should be understood as follows: When Jeroboam was crowned as king, **a heavenly voice issued** from above, [4]**and said to** the people of Israel: **"He who slew the Philistine,** Goliath, **and** thereby **gave you Gat** [גַּת] **as a possession** [מוֹרֶשֶׁת], that is to say, David — **will you give dismissal** [שִׁילּוּחִים] **to his sons,** forsaking the kingdom of the House of David, and accepting another king? If so, then the rest of the verse will be fulfilled in you: [5]**'The houses of Achziv are a dried-up stream** [לְאַכְזָב] **for the Kings of Israel.'** The Kings of Israel will be disappointed [אַכְזִיב] by their subjects, who will betray them as well."

אָמַר [6]In an apparent digression, the Gemara quotes what **Rav Ḥinena bar Pappa said: Whoever enjoys this world without** first reciting **a blessing is regarded as if he has robbed** both **the Holy One, blessed be He,** to whom everything in the world belongs, **and** also **the congregation of Israel,** upon whom he brings a curse if he fails to recite a blessing, [7]**as the verse states** (Proverbs 28:24): **"He who robs his father or his mother, and says, It is no transgression, he is the companion of a corrupter."** [8]**And** here, in this context, the words **"his father" refer to the Holy One, blessed be He,** [9]**as the verse states** (Deuteronomy 32:6): **"Is not He your father who bought you?"** [10]**And** the words **"his mother" refer to the congregation of Israel,** [11]**as the verse states** (Proverbs 1:8): **"My son, hear the instruction of your father, and do not forsake the Torah of your mother."**

RASHI

יצתה בת קול ואמרה – כשהמליכו את ירבעם. **מי שהרג** – דוד. **את הפלשתי** – ועל ידי כן היה מורים לכם גת, לכן תתנו שלוחים לבניו שתעזבו מלכות בית דוד ותמליכו אחרים. **בתי אכזיב לאכזב** – למלכי בית דוד אתם מכזבים והלכתם אחר מלכי ישראל – לפיכך תהיו נמסרין לאכזב ביד נכרים שהן שטי כזב. **אין אביו אלא הקדוש ברוך הוא שנאמר וכו'** – ואין גזילה כלפי מעלה וכלפי כנסת ישראל אלא זו בלבד, שמונע מלברך כנסת ישראל הוא גוזל להקדוש ברוך הוא, שחכמים תקנו על כל דבר ודבר ברכה כדאמר התם (ברכות לה,א): כל הטועם ואינו מברך נקרא גזלן, שנאמר לה' הארץ ומלואה.

NOTES

יָצְאָה בַּת קוֹל A heavenly voice issued forth. The Rishonim ask about this heavenly voice: Surely, Jeroboam was crowned king by a Prophet sent by God! Why, then, did a heavenly voice issue, admonishing Israel for abandoning the House of David and accepting another king? *Ramah* explains that the heavenly voice issued in order to rebuke the people of Israel for rebelling against the House of David and to warn them that the matter would end badly. *Rabbi Ya'akov Emden* suggests that Jeroboam was crowned on condition that he would conduct himself in a fit manner, but once he strayed from God's path he lost his legitimacy, and the people should have returned to the Davidic monarchy.

[1]מַאי ״חָבֵר הוּא לְאִישׁ מַשְׁחִית״? [2]חָבֵר הוּא לְיָרָבְעָם בֶּן נְבָט, שֶׁהִשְׁחִית יִשְׂרָאֵל לַאֲבִיהֶם שֶׁבַּשָּׁמַיִם.

[3]״וַיַּדַּח יָרָבְעָם (בֶּן נְבָט) אֶת יִשְׂרָאֵל מֵאַחֲרֵי ה׳, וְהֶחֱטִיאָם חֲטָאָה גְדוֹלָה״. [4]אָמַר רַבִּי חָנִין: כִּשְׁתֵּי מַקְלוֹת הַמַּתִּיזוֹת זוֹ אֶת זוֹ.

[5]״וְדִי זָהָב״. [6]אָמְרוּ דְּבֵי רַבִּי יַנַּאי: אָמַר מֹשֶׁה לִפְנֵי הַקָּדוֹשׁ בָּרוּךְ הוּא: [7]״רִבּוֹנוֹ שֶׁל עוֹלָם, בִּשְׁבִיל כֶּסֶף וְזָהָב שֶׁהִשְׁפַּעְתָּ לָהֶן לְיִשְׂרָאֵל עַד שֶׁיֹּאמְרוּ ׳דַּיי׳ גָּרַם לָהֶם לַעֲשׂוֹת לָהֶם אֱלֹהֵי זָהָב. [8]מָשָׁל: אֵין אֲרִי דּוֹרֵס וְנוֹהֵם מִתּוֹךְ קוּפָּה שֶׁל תֶּבֶן, אֶלָּא מִתּוֹךְ קוּפָּה שֶׁל בָּשָׂר״.

[9]אָמַר רַבִּי אוֹשַׁעְיָא: עַד יָרָבְעָם הָיוּ יִשְׂרָאֵל יוֹנְקִים מֵעֵגֶל אֶחָד. [10]מִכָּאן וְאֵילָךְ מִשְּׁנַיִם וּשְׁלֹשָׁה עֲגָלִים.

[11]אָמַר רַבִּי יִצְחָק: אֵין לְךָ כָּל פּוּרְעָנוּת וּפוּרְעָנוּת שֶׁבָּאָה לָעוֹלָם שֶׁאֵין בָּהּ אֶחָד מֵעֶשְׂרִים וְאַרְבָּעָה בְּהֶכְרֵעַ לִיטְרָא שֶׁל עֵגֶל הָרִאשׁוֹן,

TRANSLATION AND COMMENTARY

מַאי [1]Now the Gemara relates the saying to this discussion: **What is** the meaning of the words: **"He is the companion** [חָבֵר] **of a corrupter** [לְאִישׁ מַשְׁחִית]"? [2]The Gemara explains: Someone who enjoys this world without first reciting a blessing **is a companion** [חָבֵר] **of Jeroboam ben Nebat, who corrupted** [הִשְׁחִית] **the people of Israel** in the eyes of **their Father in Heaven.**

וַיַּדַּח יָרָבְעָם [3]The verse states (II Kings 17:21): **"And Jeroboam drove Israel from following the Lord, and made them sin a great sin."** [4]**Rabbi Ḥanin said:** This verse teaches that Jeroboam was **like** a person with **two sticks** in his hand. He strikes the one against the other, **causing it to fly off.** Jeroboam drove the people of Israel away from the Lord against their will.

וְדִי זָהָב [5]Having mentioned the golden calves made by Jeroboam, the Gemara now discusses the golden calf made by the Israelites in the wilderness. The verse states (Deuteronomy 1:1): **"And Di-zahav."** [6]**The Sages of the House of Rabbi Yannai said: Moses said before the Holy One, blessed be He:** [7]**"Master of the Universe,** it is **the silver and the gold** [*zahav*] **that You gave** the people of **Israel in** such **abundance until they said, 'Enough** [*dai*],**' that caused them to make themselves gods of gold.** They do not bear exclusive responsibility for their transgression. [8]**An example** may be offered to illustrate what happened to the people of Israel in the wilderness: **A lion does not tear apart** animals **and roar** after it has been fed **from a basket of straw, but rather** it tears apart animals and roars after it has been fed **from a basket of meat.** So, too, did the people of Israel turn to an idol after You gave them gold in such great abundance."

אָמַר רַבִּי אוֹשַׁעְיָא [9]**Rabbi Oshaya said: Until** the time of **Jeroboam,** the people of **Israel suckled from** only **one calf,** that is to say, they bore guilt for the one golden calf that they made in the wilderness. [10]**From now on,** they suckled **from two or three calves,** that is to say, they bore the guilt for the two golden calves that Jeroboam made, and the third golden calf which was made years earlier in the wilderness.

אָמַר רַבִּי יִצְחָק [11]**Rabbi Yitzḥak said: No tribulation comes into the world that does not include** a small amount of punishment — **one twenty-fourth of the surplus of a litra** (a tiny weight that is added to tip the

LITERAL TRANSLATION

[1]What is: "He is [the] companion of a corrupter"? [2]He is a companion of Jeroboam ben Nebat, who corrupted [the people of] Israel for their Father in Heaven.

[3]"And Jeroboam drove Israel from following the Lord, and made them sin a great sin." [4]Rabbi Ḥanin said: Like two sticks, one causing the other to fly off.

[5]"And Di-zahav." [6][The Sages] of the House of Rabbi Yannai said: Moses said before the Holy One, blessed be He: [7]"Master of the Universe, because of the silver and the gold that You gave [the people of] Israel in abundance until they said, 'Enough,' that caused them to make gods of gold for themselves. [8]An example: A lion does not tear apart and roar from a basket of straw, but rather from a basket of meat."

[9]Rabbi Oshaya said: Until Jeroboam [the people of] Israel suckled from one calf. [10]From now on, from two or three calves.

[11]Rabbi Yitzḥak said: There is no tribulation that comes to the world that does not have one twenty-fourth of the surplus of a litra of the first calf,

LANGUAGE

לִיטְרָא Litra. This derives from the Greek λίτρα, *litra*, a unit of weight roughly equivalent to the pound, approximately 450 grams.

RASHI

כשתי מקלות המתיזות זו את זו — כאדם שיש בידו מקל אחד ומכה בו מקל אחר ומתיזו ומשליכו ברחוק, כך הדיח ירבעם את ישראל מאחרי ה׳ בעל כרחם. **ודי זהב** — אידי דאיירי עד השתא בעגלים של ירבעם מפרש האי קרא. **מתוך קופה של בשר** — כשיש לו הרבה לאכול הוא נוהם. **עד ירבעם היו ישראל יונקים מעגל אחד** — לוקין על חטא עגל אחד שעשו במדבר. הכי גרסינן: **מכאן ואילך היו יונקין משלשה עגלים** — שנים מירבעם, ושלישי של המדבר, ולפי מה שכתוב בספרים שנים ושלשה עגלים ניחא, כלומר משנים שעשה ירבעם ושלישי שנעשה במדבר, ושלשה היינו שלישי, כמו (משלי ל) שלשה המה נפלאו ממנו וארבעה לא ידעתים. **אחד מעשרים וארבעה בהכרע ליטרא** — לאו דוקא, אלא כלומר דבר מועט מאד כמה שכף המשקל נוטה לצד זה יותר

TRANSLATION AND COMMENTARY

scale) — for the sin **of the first** golden **calf** that the Israelites had made in the wilderness, [1]**as the verse states** (Exodus 32:34): **"In the day when I punish, I will punish their sin upon them."** The sin of the golden calf was never forgiven completely, and a small amount of punishment for that offense is added every time that God punishes Israel.

אָמַר רַבִּי חֲנִינָא [2]**Rabbi Ḥanina said: After twenty-four generations** the debt created by **this verse,** "In the day when I punish [פָּקְדִי], I will punish [וּפָקַדְתִּי] their sin upon them," **was** finally **collected,** [3]**as the verse states** (Ezekiel 9:1): **"And He cried in my ears with a loud voice, saying, Bring near those who have charge** [פְּקֻדּוֹת] **over the city, every man with his deadly weapon in his hand."** The word פְּקֻדּוֹת alludes to the words פָּקְדִי and וּפָקַדְתִּי. Twenty-four generations passed between Israel's wandering in the wilderness and the destruction of the Temple. Only at the end of that period did God call in the debt of punishment that was owed him since the time that Israel made the golden calf in the wilderness.

אַחַר הַדָּבָר הַזֶּה [4]Regarding Jeroboam, the verse states (I Kings 13:33): **"After this thing Jeroboam returned not from his evil way."** [5]The Gemara asks: To **which** event do the words **"after** this thing" allude? [6]**Rabbi Abba said: After the Holy One, blessed be He, seized Jeroboam by his garment,** sending him Prophets to admonish him — [7]**and** after He himself **said to him: "Repent, and** then **I, and you, and the son of Jesse will walk about** together **in the Garden of Eden."** [8]Jeroboam **said to** God: **"Who will walk at the head?"** [9]God answered: **"The son of Jesse will be at the head."** [10]With spiteful pride Jeroboam rejected the offer and said: **"If so, I want no** part of it."

רַבִּי אַבָּהוּ [11]It was related that **Rabbi Abba was accustomed to expound** at length **about the three kings** mentioned in our Mishnah who do not have a portion in the World to Come, for he regarded as

LITERAL TRANSLATION

[1]as it is stated: "In the day when I punish, I will punish their sin upon them."

[2]Rabbi Ḥanina said: After twenty-four generations this verse was collected, [3]as it is stated: "And He cried in my ears with a loud voice, saying, Bring near those who have charge over the city, every man with his deadly weapon in his hand."

[4]"After this thing Jeroboam returned not from his evil way." [5]What is "after"? [6]Rabbi Abba said: After the Holy One, blessed be He, seized Jeroboam by his garment, [7]and said to him: "Repent, and I, and you, and the son of Jesse will walk about in the Garden of Eden." [8]He said to him: "Who will be at the head?" [9]"The son of Jesse will be at the head." [10]"If so, I do not want."

[11]Rabbi Abba was accustomed to expound about the three kings.

[1]שֶׁנֶּאֱמַר: "וּבְיוֹם פָּקְדִי וּפָקַדְתִּי עֲלֵיהֶם חַטָּאתָם".

[2]אָמַר רַבִּי חֲנִינָא: לְאַחַר עֶשְׂרִים וְאַרְבָּעָה דּוֹרוֹת נִגְבָּה פָּסוּק זֶה, [3]שֶׁנֶּאֱמַר: "וַיִּקְרָא בְאָזְנַי קוֹל גָּדוֹל, לֵאמֹר, קָרְבוּ פְּקֻדּוֹת הָעִיר, וְאִישׁ כְּלִי מַשְׁחֵתוֹ בְּיָדוֹ".

[4]"אַחַר הַדָּבָר הַזֶּה לֹא שָׁב יָרָבְעָם מִדַּרְכּוֹ הָרָעָה". [5]מַאי "אַחַר"? [6]אָמַר רַבִּי אַבָּא: אַחַר שֶׁתְּפָשׂוֹ הַקָּדוֹשׁ בָּרוּךְ הוּא לְיָרָבְעָם בְּבִגְדוֹ, [7]וְאָמַר לוֹ: "חֲזוֹר בָּךְ, וַאֲנִי וְאַתָּה וּבֶן יִשַׁי נְטַיֵּיל בְּגַן עֵדֶן", [8]אָמַר לוֹ: "מִי בָּרֹאשׁ"? [9]"בֶּן יִשַׁי בָּרֹאשׁ". [10]"אִי הָכִי, לָא בָּעֵינָא".

[11]רַבִּי אַבָּהוּ הֲוָה רָגִיל דַּהֲוָה קָא דָרֵישׁ בִּשְׁלֹשָׁה מְלָכִים.

RASHI

אלא זה, בבא בתרא (פט,א): כמה הוי הכרע ליטרא. **לאחר עשרים וארבעה דורות** — למעשה העגל. **פסוק זה** — דכתיב בעגל וביום פקדי, והכא בימי צדקיה כשחרב הבית כתוב קרבו פקודות העיר — קרב אותו מעשה שנאמר וביום פקדי, וממעשה העגל עד צדקיה עשרים וארבעה דורות, דבימי נחשון נעשה העגל, צא וחשוב כמה דורות מנחשון עד צדקיה: נחשון שלמון בנו, בועז בנו, עובד בנו, ישי בנו, דוד בנו, שלמה בנו, רחבעם בנו, אביה בנו, אסא בנו, יהושפט בנו, יורם בנו, אחזיה בנו, יואש בנו, אמציה בנו, עוזיה בנו, יותם בנו, אחז בנו, חזקיה בנו, מנשה בנו, אמון בנו, יאשיה בנו, יהואחז ויהויקים בניו, ומלכו זה אחר זה ודור אחד הם, יהויכין בנו של יהויקים — הרי עשרים וארבעה, יהויקים לא סיים מלכותו שהוגלה לבבל עם החרש והמסגר והמליכו לצדקיהו דודו במקומו, והלכך לא קא חשיב לצדקיה דור באפיה נפשיה, דהוא מלך בדור עשרים וארבע. **דהוה דריש בשלשה מלכים** — דהוה קאי במתניתין דשלשה מלכים אין להם חלק.

NOTES

שֶׁתְּפָשׂוֹ הַקָּדוֹשׁ בָּרוּךְ הוּא לְיָרָבְעָם בְּבִגְדוֹ **The Holy One, blessed be He, seized Jeroboam by his garment.** God seized Jeroboam by his garment, as it were, like someone who grasps another person's clothing when he wishes to talk to him about something important (see *Ramah*). Some suggest that the word בְּבִגְדוֹ, "by his garment," be understood as בְּבִגִידָתוֹ, "in his treachery" (*Rabbi Ya'akov Emden*). Alternatively, just as Jeroboam's "new garment" symbolized his Torah, so, too, did God seize Jeroboam by the garment in order to intimate that He wished to draw him back to Him by virtue of his Torah (*Iyyun Ya'akov*).

וַאֲנִי וְאַתָּה וּבֶן יִשַׁי **And I, and you, and the son of Jesse.** David was a repentant sinner, for he atoned for his sin with Batsheba. Thus he deserves to be in the Garden of Eden. If you, Jeroboam, repent, you will have proved that even someone who sinned and caused others to sin can repent and gain a place with God in the Garden of Eden. But David will nevertheless be at the head, for it was he who first demonstrated the power of repentance (*Ri'af*).

TRANSLATION AND COMMENTARY

meritorious to speak ill of the wicked. [1]It once happened that **he became sick,** and was close to dying, **and he accepted upon himself not to expound** about those kings. But **as soon as** [102B] **he recovered** from his illness, Rabbi Abba began once **again** to **expound** on that topic. [2]His disciples **said** to him: **"Did you not take it upon yourself not to expound about** those kings?" [3]Rabbi Abba **said** to them: **"Did** those kings ever **go back** from their evil ways and repent, **that I should** now **go back** on myself, and stop talking about their wicked lives?"

רַב אַשִׁי [4]It was further related that **Rav Ashi** once **ended** his discourse for the day with the matter of **the three kings** who do have a portion in the World to Come. [5]**He** closed his lecture and **said** to his disciples: **"Tomorrow, we will open** our studies **with our colleagues** — the three wicked kings, implying that they were nonetheless Torah scholars, too." [6]That night, **Manasseh,** the King of Judah, **came, and appeared to** Rav Ashi **in his dream.** [7]Manasseh **said** to Rav Ashi in anger: "Did **you refer to us as 'your colleagues,' and 'the colleagues of your father'?** How do you compare yourself to us? You probably cannot even answer the question: [8]**Where** on the loaf **should** a person **break his bread before** reciting **the** ***HaMotzi*** **blessing,** the blessing recited before partaking of bread?" [9]Rav Ashi **said to him: "I do not know** the answer." [10]Manasseh **said to him: "You have not** even **learned where** on the loaf a person **should break his bread before** reciting **the** ***HaMotzi*** **blessing, and you refer to us as 'your colleagues'?"** [11]Rav Ashi **said to** Manasseh: **"Teach me** the law, **and tomorrow I will teach** the law **in your name at** my **public lecture."** [12]Manasseh **said to him:** "One should cut into his loaf of bread in a place **where**

[1]חֲלַשׁ, קַבֵּיל עֲלֵיהּ דְּלָא דָּרֵישׁ. כֵּיוָן [102B] דְּאִתְפַּח הֲדַר קָא דָּרֵישׁ. [2]אָמְרִי: "לָא קַבִּילַתְּ עֲלָךְ דְּלָא דָּרְשַׁתְּ בְּהוּ"? [3]אֲמַר: "אִינְהוּ מִי הֲדַרוּ בְּהוּ, דַּאֲנָא אַהְדַּר בִּי"?

[4]רַב אַשִׁי אוֹקִי אַשְּׁלֹשָׁה מְלָכִים, [5]אֲמַר: "לְמָחָר נִפְתָּח בְּחַבְרִין". [6]אֲתָא מְנַשֶּׁה אִיתְחֲזֵי לֵיהּ בְּחֶלְמֵיהּ, [7]אֲמַר: "'חַבְרָךְ' 'וַחֲבִירֵי דַּאֲבוּךְ' קָרֵית לָן? [8]מֵהֵיכָא בָּעֵית לְמִישְׁרָא הַמּוֹצִיא"? [9]אֲמַר לֵיהּ: "לָא יָדַעְנָא". [10]אֲמַר לֵיהּ: "מֵהֵיכָא דְּבָעֵית לְמִישְׁרָא הַמּוֹצִיא לָא גְּמִירַתְּ, וְ'חַבְרָךְ' קָרֵית לָן"? [11]אֲמַר לֵיהּ: "אַגְמְרֵיהּ לִי, וּלְמָחָר דָּרֵישְׁנָא לֵיהּ מִשְּׁמָךְ בְּפִירְקָא". [12]אֲמַר לֵיהּ: "מֵהֵיכָא

LITERAL TRANSLATION

[1]He fell ill, [and] accepted upon himself not to expound. When [102B] he recovered, he again expounded. [2]They said: "Did you not accept upon yourself not to expound about them?" [3]He said: "Did they go back, that I should go back?"

[4]Rav Ashi stood at the three kings. [5]He said: "Tomorrow, we will open with our colleagues." [6]Manasseh came, [and] appeared to him in his dream. [7]He said: "You call us 'your colleagues,' and 'the colleagues of your father'? [8]Where must you break the bread before the *HaMotzi* [blessing]?" [9]He said to him: "I do not know." [10]He said to him: "You did not learn where you must break the bread before the *HaMotzi* [blessing], and you call us 'your colleagues'?" [11]He said to him: "Teach me, and tomorrow I will teach it in your name at the public lecture." [12]He said to him: "Where

RASHI

איתפח – נתרפא. **אמרו לו** – תלמידיו, לא קבלת עילווך וכו׳. **אמר: אינהו מי הדרו בהו** – מדרכם הרעה דאנא אהדר לי מלדרוש? **אוקי אשלשה מלכים** – אוקי סיום הך פירקא עד שהגיעו לשלשה מלכים. **אמר למחר נפתח בחברין** – נדרוש בחברינו שהיו תלמידי חכמים כמותנו ואין להם חלק לעתיד. **אמר ליה** – מנשה בחלום: חברך וחברא דאביך אנן – כלומר וכי סבור אתה שנהיה חבירך וחבירי דאבוך? **מהיכא בעית למשרא המוציא** – אינך יודע מאיזה מקום בפת אתה צריך לבצוע המוציא. **וחבירך קרית לן** – ואתה קורא אותנו חבירך?! **מהיכא דקרים בשולא** – דרפתא, ממקום שנקרמין פניה של פת בתנור דהיינו מלמעלה, או מסביבות הפת, או משוליו, אבל באמצע – לא, שאם הביאו לפניו פרוסה של

NOTES

הֲדַר קָא דָּרֵישׁ **He again expounded.** Rabbi Abba preached about those kings in order to restore their souls, for he thought that by preaching about their evil ways he might be able to achieve atonement for their sins (*Ḥida*).

מֵהֵיכָא בָּעֵית לְמִישְׁרָא הַמּוֹצִיא? **Where must you break the bread before the *HaMotzi* blessing?** Attempts have been made to explain both the question and the answer as metaphors, and to find some connection between Manasseh's sin and the matter of the *HaMotzi* blessing (see *Akedah, Maharsha,* and others). According to the Gemara's plain sense, it would appear that Manasseh asked Rav Ashi a question that he should certainly have encountered in his daily life, but nevertheless Rav Ashi did not know the answer.

HALAKHAH

מֵהֵיכָא דְּקָרֵים בִּישׁוּלָא **Where it formed a crust and was well baked.** "A person should break his bread in a place where

TRANSLATION AND COMMENTARY

it formed a thick crust and was well baked." [1]Rav Ashi said to him: "If you were so smart, why then did you worship idols?" [2]Manasseh said to him: "Had you been around in the early generations, you would have taken up the trail of your cloak, and run after me to worship the idols." [3]The next day Rav Ashi returned to the Academy, and said to the Rabbis as he began his lecture: "Let us open our studies with our masters — the three wicked kings, who were greater Torah scholars than we, but nonetheless forfeited their place in the World to Come."

אַחְאָב [4]The Gemara now offers a Midrashic interpretation of the name Ahab, the second king mentioned in the Mishnah as having no portion in the World to Come: Ahab was called by that name because he was like a brother (*aḥ*) and a father (*av*) — like a brother to Heaven, but like a father to his idols. [5]Ahab was like a brother to Heaven, as the verse states (Proverbs 17:17): "And a brother is born for adversity" — in times of adversity he was a brother to Heaven, turning to God for help. [6]But he was like a father to his idols, as the verse states (Psalms 103:13): "As a father pities his children" — he loved his idols the way a father pities his children.

וַיְהִי הֲנָקֵל [7]It is stated about Ahab (I Kings 16:31): "And it came to pass, as if it had been a light thing for him to walk in the sins of Jeroboam the son of Nebat." [8]Rabbi Yoḥanan said: Ahab was so much more wicked than Jeroboam, that the relatively minor sins that Ahab committed were like the most severe sins that Jeroboam committed. [9]Why, then, do the verses in various places hang the sins of the other Kings of Israel on Jeroboam? [10]Rabbi Yoḥanan explains: Those verses mention Jeroboam because it was he who initiated corruption, being the first King of Israel to practice idolatry.

דְקָרֵים בִּישׁוּלָא״. [1]אֲמַר לֵיהּ: ״מֵאַחַר דְּחַכִּימְתּוּ כּוּלֵּי הַאי, מַאי טַעְמָא קָא פָּלְחִתּוּ לַעֲבוֹדָה זָרָה״? [2]אֲמַר לֵיהּ: ״אִי הֲוַת הָתָם, הֲוַת נָקִיטְנָא בְּשִׁיפּוּלֵי גְּלִימָא, וּרְהָטַתְּ אַבַּתְרַאי״. [3]לְמָחָר אֲמַר לְהוּ לְרַבָּנַן: ״נִפְתַּח בְּרַבְוָותָא״.

[4]אַחְאָב — אָח לַשָּׁמַיִם, אָב לַעֲבוֹדָה זָרָה. [5]אָח לַשָּׁמַיִם, דִּכְתִיב: ״אָח לְצָרָה יִוָּלֵד״. [6]אָב לַעֲבוֹדָה זָרָה, דִּכְתִיב: ״כְּרַחֵם אָב עַל בָּנִים״.

[7]״וַיְהִי הֲנָקֵל לֶכְתּוֹ בְּחַטֹּאות יָרָבְעָם בֶּן נְבָט״. [8]אָמַר רַבִּי יוֹחָנָן: קַלּוֹת שֶׁעָשָׂה אַחְאָב כַּחֲמוּרוֹת שֶׁעָשָׂה יָרָבְעָם. [9]וּמִפְּנֵי מָה תָּלָה הַכָּתוּב בְּיָרָבְעָם? [10]מִפְּנֵי שֶׁהוּא הָיָה תְּחִילָּה לְקַלְקָלָה.

LITERAL TRANSLATION

it formed a crust and was well baked." [1]He said to him: "If you were so smart, what is the reason that you worshiped idols?" [2]He said to him: "Had you been there, you would have taken up the trail of your cloak, and run after me." [3]The next day he said to the Rabbis: "Let us open with our masters."

[4]Ahab — a brother to Heaven, a father to idols. [5]A brother to Heaven, as it is written: "And a brother is born for adversity." [6]A father to idols, as it is written: "As a father pities his children."

[7]"And it came to pass, as if it were a light thing for him to walk in the sins of Jeroboam the son of Nebat." [8]Rabbi Yoḥanan said: The light [sins] that Ahab did were like the severe [sins] that Jeroboam did. [9]And why does the verse hang [them] on Jeroboam? [10]Because he was the beginning of corruption.

RASHI

לחם לא יהא בולע ומברך אלא משולי הפת ולא מאמצעיתו, לישנא אחרינא: מהיכא דקדים — כלומר מהיכא שמקדים לאפות, והיינו הך, לישנא אחרינא: מהיכא דגמר בשולא — ממקום שהלחם אפוי יפה ולא מאותו מקום שקורין בשו״ל, וראשון נראה. הוית נקוט שיפולי גלימך = היית מגבה שפת חלוקך מבין רגליך כדי שתהא קל לרוץ, והיית רץ לשם מפני יצר עבודה זרה שהיה שולט. נפתח ברבוותא — נתחיל לדרוש ברבותינו, ולא אמר בחבירינו. אח לשמים — רע לשמים, כדאמרינן (מגילה יא,א) באחשורוש: אח וראש. דכתיב ואח לצרה יולד — [ווי לצרה], אלמא: אח לשון רעה, ווי. אב לעבודה זרה — שהיה אוהבה ביותר, דכתיב ״כרחם אב״, אלמא: אב מרחם, והני קראי בכדי נקט להו. ויהי הנקל — באחאב כתוב, [כלומר: קלות היו לאחאב כל חטאותיו של ירבעם]. מפני מה תלה הכתוב בירבעם — דבכמה מקומות כתיב ״לא סר מכל חטאת ירבעם״ ולא כתיב אחאב, אף על פי שהיה רשע ממנו. תחלה לקלקלה — שהיה מלך ראשון שהקדים את תבשילו.

NOTES

אָח לַשָּׁמַיִם **A brother to Heaven.** *Rashi* and *Arukh* understand the word אָח as a cry of distress, "woe." According to this, אָח לַשָּׁמַיִם means "woe to Heaven." He explains the verse אָח לְצָרָה יִוָּלֵד in a similar manner: "Woe, he is born for adversity." Others understand the word אָח according to its plain sense, as "brother." They understand the proof text as follows: When he faces adversity, he turns to God as a brother (*Maharsha*). Some explain: A brother to Heaven — slightly related; but a father to idols — closely related (*Iyyun Ya'akov*).

HALAKHAH

it is well baked (following the third explanation cited by *Rashi*). *Rama* adds that with our loaves, one should break the bread on the side of the loaf, at the bottom, and at the top." (*Shulḥan Arukh, Oraḥ Ḥayyim* 167:1.)

TRANSLATION AND COMMENTARY

גַּם מִזְבְּחוֹתָם [1]The verse states (Hosea 12:12): **"Their altars are like droppings on the furrows of the field."** [2]**Rabbi Yoḥanan said: There was no furrow in** all of **Eretz Israel in which Ahab did not set up an idol, and bow down to it.**

וּמְנָא לָן [3]The Gemara asks: **From where do we know that** Ahab **will not go to the World to Come?** [4]The Gemara explains: **The verse states** (I Kings 21:21): **"And I will cut off from Ahab every man, and him that is shut up and him that is abandoned in Israel."** The redundancy in the verse suggests the following interpretation: [5]The words, **"him that is shut up,"** refer to Ahab's punishment **in this world.** [6]The words, **"and him that is abandoned,"** refer to his punishment **in the World to Come.**

אָמַר רַבִּי יוֹחָנָן [7]**Rabbi Yoḥanan said: How did** a wicked person like **Omri merit the kingship?** [8]Omri became king **because he added a city to Eretz Israel, as it is stated: "And he bought the hill Shomron from Shemer for two talents of silver, and built on the hill, and called the name of the city which he built, after the name of Shemer, owner of the hill, Shomron."**

אָמַר רַבִּי יוֹחָנָן [9]**Rabbi Yoḥanan said: How did** a wicked person like **Ahab merit the kingship for twenty-two years?** [10]Ahab reigned for twenty-two years **because he honored the Torah that was given with twenty-two letters.** Where do we see that Ahab honored the Torah? [11]**The verses state** (I Kings 20: 2, 3, 6, 9): **"And he sent messengers to Ahab King of Israel into the city, and said to him, Thus says Ben-Hadad, Your silver and your gold are mine; your wives also and your good children, are mine.... Yet I will send my**

[1]״גַּם מִזְבְּחוֹתָם כְּגַלִּים עַל תַּלְמֵי שָׂדָי״. [2]אָמַר רַבִּי יוֹחָנָן: אֵין לְךָ כָּל תֶּלֶם וָתֶלֶם בְּאֶרֶץ יִשְׂרָאֵל שֶׁלֹּא הֶעֱמִיד עָלָיו אַחְאָב עֲבוֹדָה זָרָה, וְהִשְׁתַּחֲוָה לָהּ.

[3]וּמְנָא לָן דְּלָא אָתֵי לְעָלְמָא דְּאָתֵי? [4]דִּכְתִיב: ״וְהִכְרַתִּי לְאַחְאָב מַשְׁתִּין בְּקִיר וְעָצוּר וְעָזוּב בְּיִשְׂרָאֵל״. [5]״עָצוּר״ — בָּעוֹלָם הַזֶּה, [6]״וְעָזוּב״ — לָעוֹלָם הַבָּא.

[7]אָמַר רַבִּי יוֹחָנָן: מִפְּנֵי מָה זָכָה עָמְרִי לְמַלְכוּת? [8]מִפְּנֵי שֶׁהוֹסִיף כְּרַךְ אֶחָד בְּאֶרֶץ יִשְׂרָאֵל, שֶׁנֶּאֱמַר: ״וַיִּקֶן אֶת הָהָר שֹׁמְרוֹן מֵאֶת שֶׁמֶר בְּכִכְּרַיִם כָּסֶף וַיִּבֶן אֶת הָהָר וַיִּקְרָא [אֶת] שֵׁם הָעִיר אֲשֶׁר בָּנָה עַל שֵׁם שֶׁמֶר אֲדֹנֵי הָהָר שֹׁמְרוֹן״.

[9]אָמַר רַבִּי יוֹחָנָן: מִפְּנֵי מָה זָכָה אַחְאָב לְמַלְכוּת עֶשְׂרִים וּשְׁתַּיִם שָׁנָה? [10]מִפְּנֵי שֶׁכִּיבֵּד אֶת הַתּוֹרָה שֶׁנִּיתְּנָה בְּעֶשְׂרִים וּשְׁתַּיִם אוֹתִיּוֹת, [11]שֶׁנֶּאֱמַר: ״וַיִּשְׁלַח מַלְאָכִים אֶל אַחְאָב מֶלֶךְ יִשְׂרָאֵל הָעִירָה, וַיֹּאמֶר לוֹ, כֹּה אָמַר בֶּן הֲדַד, כַּסְפְּךָ וּזְהָבְךָ לִי הוּא וְנָשֶׁיךָ וּבָנֶיךָ הַטּוֹבִים לִי הֵם...כִּי אִם כָּעֵת מָחָר אֶשְׁלַח

LITERAL TRANSLATION

[1]"Their altars are like droppings on the furrows of my field." [2]Rabbi Yoḥanan said: There is no furrow in Eretz Israel in which Ahab did not set up an idol, and bow down to it.

[3]And from where do we [know] that he will not go to the World to Come? [4]For it is written: "And I will cut off from Ahab every man [lit., who urinates against the wall], and him that is shut up and him that is abandoned in Israel." [5]"Him that is shut up" — in this world. [6]"And him that is left abandoned — in the World to Come.

[7]Rabbi Yoḥanan said: How did Omri merit the kingship? [8]Because he added one city to Eretz Israel, as it is stated: "And he bought the hill Shomron from Shemer for two talents of silver, and built on the hill, and called the name of the city which he built, after the name of Shemer, owner of the hill, Shomron."

[9]Rabbi Yoḥanan said: Why did Ahab merit the kingship for twenty-two years? [10]Because he honored the Torah that was given with twenty-two letters, [11]as it is stated: "And he sent messengers to Ahab King of Israel into the city, and said to him, Thus says Ben-Hadad, Your silver and your gold are mine; your wives also and your good children are mine.... Yet I will send

RASHI

גם מזבחותם — הכי רישיה דקרא "בגלגל שוורים זבחו גם מזבחותם כגלים על תלמי שדי". **משתין בקיר** — תלמיד חכם משית בקירות לבו, ומניין שכבד את התורה דכתיב "והיה כל מחמד עיניך ישימו בידם" והיינו ספר תורה ועל זה השיבו את "הדבר הזה לא אוכל לעשות".

NOTES

מִפְּנֵי מָה זָכָה עָמְרִי לְמַלְכוּת? **How did Omri merit the kingship?** The objection has been raised: Surely Omri rose to the throne before he built the city of Shomron! Some suggest that God knew that Omri would build the city, and so he allowed him to become king (see *Maharsha*). Others propose that Rabbi Yoḥanan meant to ask: Why did Omri's reign span several generations? This was a reward for the city that he had built in Israel (*Iyyun Ya'akov*).

TRANSLATION AND COMMENTARY

servants to you tomorrow about this time, and they shall search your house, and the houses of your servants; and it shall be, that they shall put in their hand all the delight of your eyes and take them....And he said to the messengers of Ben-Hadad, Tell my lord the king, All that you did send for to your servant at the first I will do; but this thing I may not do." [1] It may be asked: What is "the delight of your eyes" which Ahab refused to hand over to Ben-Hadad after agreeing to surrender his wives and his gold? [2] Is this not a reference to a Torah scroll? Hence Ahab's reign continued for twenty-two years.

דִּילְמָא עֲבוֹדָה זָרָה [3] The Gemara asks: But perhaps the expression, "the delight of your eyes," refers to Ahab's idols?

לָא סָלְקָא דַּעְתָּךְ [4] The Gemara rejects this suggestion: You cannot possibly think so, for the verse states (I Kings 20:8): "And all the elders and all the people said to him, Do not consent and heed him not." The expression "the elders" refers to Torah scholars, who would surely not have encouraged Ahab to refuse Ben-Hadad's order to hand over his idols!

וְדִילְמָא סָבֵי [5] The Gemara asks: Who says that the expression "the elders" refers to Torah scholars? Perhaps it refers to the disgraceful elders who worshiped idols! [6] Does not the verse state elsewhere (II Samuel 17:4): "And the saying pleased Absalom well, and all the elders of Israel"? [7] And Rabbi Yosef said: Here the expression, "the elders," refers to wicked and disgraceful elders.

הָתָם לָא כְּתִיב [8] The Gemara rejects this argument: There, regarding Absalom, the verse does not state: "And all the people." [9] But here, regarding Ahab, the verse states: "And all the people." [10] And it is impossible that among "all the people" there were no righteous people, [11] for elsewhere the verse states (I Kings 19:18): "Yet I will leave seven thousand in Israel; all the knees that have not bent to the Baal, and every mouth that has not kissed him."

אָמַר רַב נַחְמָן [12] Rav Naḥman said: Ahab himself was balanced, partly righteous and partly wicked, [13] as the

LITERAL TRANSLATION

my servants to you tomorrow about this time, and they shall search your house, and the houses of your servants; and it shall be, that they shall put in their hand all the delight of your eyes and take them....And he said to the messengers of Ben-Hadad, Tell my lord the king, All that you did send for to your servant at the first I will do; but this thing I may not do." [1] What is "the delight of your eyes"? [2] Is it not a Torah scroll? [3] Perhaps an idol? [4] This cannot enter your mind, for it is written: "And all the elders and all the people said to him, Do not consent and heed him not." [5] Perhaps elders of disgrace? [6] Is it not written: "And the saying pleased Absalom well, and all the elders of Israel." [7] And Rabbi Yosef said: Elders of disgrace. [8] There, it is not written: "And all the people." [9] Here, it is written: "And all the people." [10] For it is impossible that there were no righteous people among them. [11] And it is written: "Yet I will leave seven thousand in Israel; all the knees that have not bent to the Baal, and every mouth that has not kissed him." [12] Rav Naḥman said: Ahab was balanced, [13] as it is stated: "And the Lord said, Who

אֶת עֲבָדַי אֵלֶיךָ וְחִפְּשׂוּ אֶת בֵּיתְךָ וְאֵת בָּתֵּי עֲבָדֶיךָ וְהָיָה כָּל מַחְמַד עֵינֶיךָ יָשִׂימוּ בְיָדָם וְלָקָחוּ...וַיֹּאמֶר לְמַלְאֲכֵי בֶן הֲדַד, אִמְרוּ לַאדֹנִי הַמֶּלֶךְ, כֹּל אֲשֶׁר שָׁלַחְתָּ (לְעַבְדְּךָ) [אֶל עַבְדְּךָ] בָרִאשׁוֹנָה אֶעֱשֶׂה, וְהַדָּבָר הַזֶּה לֹא אוּכַל לַעֲשׂוֹת". [1] מַאי "מַחְמַד עֵינֶיךָ"? [2] לָאו סֵפֶר תּוֹרָה. [3] דִּילְמָא עֲבוֹדָה זָרָה. [4] לָא סָלְקָא דַּעְתָּךְ, דִּכְתִיב: "וַיֹּאמְרוּ אֵלָיו כָּל הַזְּקֵנִים וְכָל הָעָם לֹא תֹאבֶה וְלֹא תִשְׁמַע". [5] וְדִילְמָא סָבֵי דְּבַהֲתָא הֲווֹ? [6] מִי לָא כְּתִיב: "וַיִּישַׁר הַדָּבָר בְּעֵינֵי אַבְשָׁלֹם (וְהַזְּקֵנִים) [וּבְעֵינֵי כָּל זִקְנֵי יִשְׂרָאֵל]". [7] וְאָמַר רַב יוֹסֵף: סָבֵי דְּבַהֲתָא. [8] הָתָם לָא כְּתִיב: "וְכָל הָעָם". [9] הָכָא כְּתִיב: "וְכָל הָעָם", [10] דְּאִי אֶפְשָׁר דְּלָא הֲווֹ בְּהוֹן צַדִּיקֵי. [11] וּכְתִיב: "וְהִשְׁאַרְתִּי בְיִשְׂרָאֵל שִׁבְעַת אֲלָפִים כָּל הַבִּרְכַּיִם אֲשֶׁר לֹא כָרְעוּ לַבַּעַל וְכָל הַפֶּה אֲשֶׁר לֹא נָשַׁק לוֹ". [12] אָמַר רַב נַחְמָן: אַחְאָב שָׁקוּל הָיָה, [13] שֶׁנֶּאֱמַר: "וַיֹּאמֶר ה', מִי

RASHI

וְדִילְמָא — מחמד עיניו היינו עבודה זרה. לא סלקא דעתך — מדקאמרי ליה זקנים "לא תשמע ולא תאבה", ואי עבודה זרה מי הוו אמרו ליה הכי. סבי דבהתא — זקנים שפלים, שהיו רשעים כמו שמצינו באבשלום דקרי ליה לסבי דבהתא: זקנים. שקול היה — מחלה עונות ומחלה זכיות, מדמהדרי כולי האי מי יפתה את אחאב משמע דבקושי גדול נענש.

NOTES

שָׁקוּל הָיָה He was balanced. According to Rashi, the proof that Ahab was balanced, partly righteous and partly wicked, is that Ahab had to be enticed to go up to Ramot Gilead where he was to receive his punishment. Others understand that the proof is from the words, "And one said in this manner, and another said in that manner." The heavenly

TRANSLATION AND COMMENTARY

verse states (I Kings 22:20): **"And the Lord said, Who shall entice Ahab, that he may go up and fall at Ramot Gilead? And one said in this manner, and another said in that manner."** Since punishment could only be imposed upon him in this roundabout manner, Ahab could not have been entirely wicked.

מַתְקִיף לַהּ [1]**Rav Yosef strongly objected** to what Rav Naḥman said: **About** Ahab **the verse states** (I Kings 21:25): **"But there was none like Ahab, who gave himself over to do evil in the eyes of the Lord, whom Jezebel his wife incited."** [2]**And we have learned** in a Baraita: **"Every day** Jezebel **would weigh out golden shekels** according to Ahab's weight, and dedicate them **for idol worship."** [3]**And you say that** Ahab **was balanced,** partly righteous and partly wicked?

אֶלָּא [4]**Rather, Ahab** was a thoroughly wicked man, but he **was** nevertheless **liberal with his money,** and dispensed it freely. **Since he** also **benefitted Torah scholars with his property, he achieved partial atonement.**

וַיֵּצֵא [5]The passage dealing with tempting Ahab continues (I Kings 22:21-22): **"And there came forth a spirit, and stood before the Lord, and said, I will entice him. And the Lord said to him, With what? And he said, I will go out, and I will be a lying spirit in the mouth of all his Prophets. And He said, You shall entice him, and also prevail; go out, and do so."** [6]The Gemara asks: **What is meant by** the words, **"a spirit"**? [7]**Rabbi Yoḥanan said: The spirit of Naboth the Jezreelite** came to take vengeance against Ahab, by tempting him to wage war against Aram in order to recapture Ramot Gilead.

מַאי "צֵא" [8]The Gemara raises another question: And **what is meant by** the words: **"Go out"?** Why did God not say merely: "Do so"? [9]**Ravina said:** God meant to say: **Go out from My presence,** for any being who proposes to execute deceit is not fit to stand before God, [10]**as the verse states** (Psalms 101:7): **"He that tells lies shall not dwell in My sight."**

אָמַר רַב פַּפָּא [11]**Rav Pappa said: This is** the meaning of **the popular adage:** [12]**He who takes his vengeance** ends up **destroying his** own **house.** The spirit of Naboth came to take vengeance against Ahab, and was banished from God's presence.

יְפַתֶּה אֶת אַחְאָב וְיַעַל וְיִפֹּל בְּרָמֹת גִּלְעָד? וַיֹּאמֶר זֶה בְּכֹה וְזֶה אֹמֵר בְּכֹה".

[1]מַתְקִיף לַהּ רַבִּי יוֹסֵף: מַאן דִּכְתַב בֵּיהּ: "רַק לֹא הָיָה כְאַחְאָב אֲשֶׁר הִתְמַכֵּר לַעֲשׂוֹת הָרַע בְּעֵינֵי ה' אֲשֶׁר הֵסַתָּה אֹתוֹ אִיזֶבֶל אִשְׁתּוֹ". [2]וְתָנֵינָא: "בְּכָל יוֹם הָיְתָה שׁוֹקֶלֶת שִׁקְלֵי זָהָב לַעֲבוֹדָה זָרָה". [3]וְאַתְּ אָמְרַתְּ שָׁקוּל הָיָה?

[4]אֶלָּא, אַחְאָב וַותְּרָן בְּמָמוֹנוֹ הָיָה, וּמִתּוֹךְ שֶׁהֶהֱנָה תַּלְמִידֵי חֲכָמִים מִנְּכָסָיו, כִּיפְּרוּ לוֹ מֶחֱצָה.

[5]"וַיֵּצֵא הָרוּחַ וַיַּעֲמֹד לִפְנֵי ה' וַיֹּאמֶר אֲנִי אֲפַתֶּנּוּ. וַיֹּאמֶר ה' אֵלָיו, בַּמָּה? וַיֹּאמֶר, אֵצֵא, וְהָיִיתִי רוּחַ שֶׁקֶר בְּפִי כָּל נְבִיאָיו. וַיֹּאמֶר, תְּפַתֶּה וְגַם תּוּכָל, צֵא וַעֲשֵׂה כֵן". [6]מַאי רוּחַ? [7]אָמַר רַבִּי יוֹחָנָן: רוּחוֹ שֶׁל נָבוֹת הַיִּזְרְעֵאלִי.

[8]מַאי "צֵא"? [9]אָמַר רָבִינָא: צֵא מִמְּחִיצָתִי, [10]שֶׁכֵּן כְּתִיב: "דֹּבֵר שְׁקָרִים לֹא יִכּוֹן לְנֶגֶד עֵינָי".

[11]אָמַר רַב פַּפָּא: הַיְינוּ דְּאָמְרִי אֱינָשֵׁי: [12]דְּפָרַע קִינֵיהּ מַחֲרִיב בֵּיתֵיהּ.

LITERAL TRANSLATION

shall entice Ahab, that he may go up and fall at Ramot Gilead? And one said in this manner, and another said in that manner."

[1]Rav Yosef strongly objected: He about whom it is written: "But there was none like Ahab, who gave himself over to do evil in the eyes of the Lord, whom Jezebel his wife incited." [2]And we have learned: "Every day she weighed out golden shekels for idol worship." [3]And you said [that] he was balanced?

[4]Rather, Ahab was liberal with his money, and since he benefitted Torah scholars with his property, this atoned for him in part.

[5]"And there came forth a spirit, and stood before the Lord, and said, I will entice him. And the Lord said to him, With what? And he said, I will go out, and I will be a lying spirit in the mouth of all his Prophets. And He said, You shall entice him, and also prevail; go out, and do so." [6]What is [meant by] "a spirit"? [7]Rabbi Yoḥanan said: The spirit of Naboth the Jezreelite.

[8]What is [meant by:] "Go out"? [9]Ravina said: Go out from My presence, [10]as it is written: "He that tells lies shall not dwell in My sight."

[11]Rav Pappa said: This is what people say: [12]He who takes his vengeance destroys his house.

RASHI

רוחו של נבות – שלפי שהוא הרג נבות היה רוחו מחזר לפתותו ולהפילו. **דפרע קיניה** – קנאה,

NOTES

court disagreed about his verdict, because he was balanced, and the matter was only decided by the spirit of Nabot, because the sin of murder is so great and has no atonement (*Maharsha, Torat Ḥayyim*).

דְּפָרַע קִינֵיהּ מַחֲרִיב בֵּיתֵיהּ **He who takes his vengeance destroys his house.** The popular adage is based on a play

TRANSLATION AND COMMENTARY

וַיַּעַשׂ אַחְאָב [1]The verse states (I Kings 16:33): **"And Ahab made a pagan shrine; and Ahab did more to provoke the Lord God of Israel to anger than all the Kings of Israel that were before him."** [2]**Rabbi Yoḥanan said:** Ahab **wrote on the doors of Shomron: "Ahab denies the God of Israel."** [3]**Therefore, he does not have a portion in the God of Israel.**

וַיְבַקֵּשׁ אֶת אֲחַזְיָהוּ [4]The verse states (II Chronicles 22:9): **"And he sought Ahaziah; and they caught him, for he was hiding in Shomron."** [5]**Rabbi Levi said:** What was Ahaziah doing in hiding? [6]**He was cutting out the Divine Names** found in the Torah, **and writing the names of idols in their place.**

מְנַשֶּׁה [7]The Gemara now offers a Midrashic interpretation of the name Manasseh, the third king mentioned in the Mishnah as having no portion in the World to Come: **Manasseh** was called by that name, because he **forgot** (*nashah*) **God.** [8]**Another explanation** may also be offered. He was called Manasseh because he **caused the people of Israel to forget** [*hinshi*] **their Father in Heaven.**

וּמְנָלַן [9]The Gemara asks: **From where do we know that** Manasseh **will not go to the World to Come?** [10]**For the verse states** (II Kings 21:1-3): **"Manasseh was twelve years old when he began to reign, and he reigned fifty-five years in Jerusalem....And he did that which was evil in the sight of the Lord...as did Ahab King of Israel."** [11]We may infer from here that **just as Ahab does not have a portion in the World to Come, so, too, does Manasseh not have a portion in the World to Come.**

רַבִּי יְהוּדָה אוֹמֵר [12]We have learned in our Mishnah: **"Rabbi Yehudah says: Manasseh has a portion in the World to Come,** for he repented of his evil ways, [13]**as the verse states** (II Chronicles 33:13):

[1]"וַיַּעַשׂ אַחְאָב אֶת הָאֲשֵׁרָה וַיּוֹסֶף אַחְאָב לַעֲשׂוֹת לְהַכְעִיס אֶת ה׳ אֱלֹהֵי יִשְׂרָאֵל מִכֹּל מַלְכֵי יִשְׂרָאֵל אֲשֶׁר הָיוּ לְפָנָיו". [2]אָמַר רַבִּי יוֹחָנָן: שֶׁכָּתַב עַל דַּלְתוֹת שׁוֹמְרוֹן: "אַחְאָב כָּפַר בֵּאלֹהֵי יִשְׂרָאֵל". [3]לְפִיכָךְ, אֵין לוֹ חֵלֶק בֵּאלֹהֵי יִשְׂרָאֵל.

[4]"וַיְבַקֵּשׁ אֶת אֲחַזְיָהוּ וַיִּלְכְּדֻהוּ וְהוּא מִתְחַבֵּא בְשֹׁמְרוֹן". [5]אָמַר רַבִּי לֵוִי: [6]שֶׁהָיָה קוֹדֵר אַזְכָּרוֹת, וְכוֹתֵב עֲבוֹדָה זָרָה תַּחְתֵּיהֶן.

[7]מְנַשֶּׁה — שֶׁנָּשָׁה יָהּ. [8]דָּבָר אַחֵר: מְנַשֶּׁה — שֶׁהִנְשִׁי אֶת יִשְׂרָאֵל לַאֲבִיהֶם שֶׁבַּשָּׁמַיִם.

[9]וּמְנָלַן דְּלָא אָתֵי לְעָלְמָא דְּאָתֵי? [10]דִּכְתִיב: "בֶּן שְׁתֵּים עֶשְׂרֵה שָׁנָה מְנַשֶּׁה בְמָלְכוֹ וַחֲמִשִּׁים וְחָמֵשׁ שָׁנָה מָלַךְ בִּירוּשָׁלָיִם...וַיַּעַשׂ (הָרַע) [אֲשֵׁרָה] (בְּעֵינֵי ה׳) כַּאֲשֶׁר עָשָׂה אַחְאָב מֶלֶךְ יִשְׂרָאֵל". [11]מָה אַחְאָב אֵין לוֹ חֵלֶק לָעוֹלָם הַבָּא, אַף מְנַשֶּׁה אֵין לוֹ חֵלֶק לָעוֹלָם הַבָּא.

[12]"רַבִּי יְהוּדָה אוֹמֵר: מְנַשֶּׁה יֵשׁ לוֹ חֵלֶק לָעוֹלָם הַבָּא, [13]שֶׁנֶּאֱמַר:

LITERAL TRANSLATION

[1]"And Ahab made a pagan shrine; and Ahab did more to anger the Lord God of Israel than all the Kings of Israel that were before him." [2]Rabbi Yoḥanan said: He wrote on the doors of Shomron: "Ahab denies the God of Israel." [3]Therefore, he has no portion in the God of Israel.

[4]"And he sought Ahaziah; and they caught him, for he was hiding in Shomron." [5]Rabbi Levi said: [6]He was cutting out mention [of the Divine Names], and writing [the names of] idols in their place.

[7]Manasseh — who forgot God. [8]Another explanation: Who caused the people of Israel to forget their Father in Heaven.

[9]And from where do we [know] that he will not go to the World to Come? [10]For it is written: "Manasseh was twelve years old when he began to reign, and he reigned fifty-five years in Jerusalem....And he did that which was evil in the sight of the Lord...as did Ahab King of Israel." [11]Just as Ahab has no portion in the World to Come, so, too, does Manasseh have no portion in the World to Come.

[12]"Rabbi Yehudah says: Manasseh has a portion in the World to Come, [13]as it is stated:

RASHI

הפורע נוקם חמתו וקנאתו מחריב ביתיה, כרוח של נבות שנקם כעסו מאחאב ויצא ממחילתו של הקדוש ברוך הוא. קודר אזכרות — מוחק שמות שבתורה. וכותב שם עבודה זרה תחתיהן — לפיכך היה מתחבא, שאילו היה עושה בפרהסיא לא היו מניחין [אותו] לעשות כן, קודר — כמו (עירובין נח,א) מקדרין בהרים לשון (נוקב) [מחטט ונוקר]. שנשה יה — ששכח הקדוש ברוך הוא. שהנשי — השכיח. מה אחאב אין לו חלק — כדאמרן עזוב לעולם הבא.

NOTES

of words, for the word קִינֵיהּ, "his vengeance," also alludes to קֵן in the sense of "nest, house." Some sources record a variant reading: דְּפָרַע קִינֵיהּ מַחֲרִיב קִינֵיהּ, where the play on words is explicit.

לְפִיכָךְ, אֵין לוֹ חֵלֶק **Therefore, he does not have a portion in the God of Israel.** It is not clear whether the clause beginning with the word "therefore" is part of Ahab's statement, that he waives his portion in the God of Israel, or whether it is Rabbi Yoḥanan's conclusion. We find a variant reading: "Gabriel came, and wrote: 'Therefore, he shall not have a portion in the God of Israel.'"

'וַיִּתְפַּלֵּל אֵלָיו וַיֵּעָתֵר לוֹ וגו׳ ".
[1]אָמַר רַבִּי יוֹחָנָן: וּשְׁנֵיהֶם מִקְרָא אֶחָד דָּרְשׁוּ, [2]שֶׁנֶּאֱמַר: "וּנְתַתִּים לְזַוֲעָה לְכֹל מַמְלְכוֹת הָאָרֶץ בִּגְלַל מְנַשֶּׁה בֶּן יְחִזְקִיָּהוּ". [3]מָר סָבַר: בִּגְלַל מְנַשֶּׁה, שֶׁעָשָׂה תְּשׁוּבָה, וְאִינְהוּ לָא עֲבוּד. [4]וּמָר סָבַר: [103A] [5]בִּגְלַל מְנַשֶּׁה, דְּלָא עֲבַד תְּשׁוּבָה.

[6]אָמַר רַבִּי יוֹחָנָן: כָּל הָאוֹמֵר מְנַשֶּׁה אֵין לוֹ חֵלֶק לָעוֹלָם הַבָּא מְרַפֶּה יְדֵיהֶן שֶׁל בַּעֲלֵי תְשׁוּבָה, [7]דְּתָנֵי תַּנָּא קַמֵּיהּ דְּרַבִּי יוֹחָנָן: "מְנַשֶּׁה עָשָׂה תְּשׁוּבָה (לִשְׁלֹשִׁים) [שְׁלֹשִׁים] וְשָׁלֹשׁ שָׁנִים, דִּכְתִיב: "בֶּן שְׁתֵּים עֶשְׂרֵה שָׁנָה מְנַשֶּׁה בְּמָלְכוֹ וַחֲמִשִּׁים וְחָמֵשׁ שָׁנָה מָלַךְ בִּירוּשָׁלָיִם....וַיַּעַשׂ (הָרַע) [אֲשֵׁרָה] וכו׳ כַּאֲשֶׁר עָשָׂה אַחְאָב מֶלֶךְ יִשְׂרָאֵל". [8]כַּמָּה מָלַךְ אַחְאָב? עֶשְׂרִין וְתַרְתֵּין שְׁנִין. [9]מְנַשֶּׁה, כַּמָּה מָלַךְ? חֲמִשִּׁים וְחָמֵשׁ. [10]דַּל מִינַּיְיהוּ עֶשְׂרִים וְתַרְתֵּין — פָּשׁוּ לְהוּ תְּלָתִין וּתְלָת.

LITERAL TRANSLATION

'And he prayed to Him and he healed him, etc.'" [1]Rabbi Yoḥanan said: And the two of them expounded one verse, [2]for it is stated: "And I will make them into a horror for all the kingdoms of the earth, on account of Manasseh the son of Hezekiah." [3]This Sage maintains: On account of Manasseh, because he repented, and they did not. [4]And this Sage maintains: [103A] [5]On account of Manasseh, because he did not repent.

[6]Rabbi Yoḥanan said: Whoever says [that] Manasseh does not have a portion in the World to Come weakens the hands of repentant sinners, [7]for a Tanna taught before Rabbi Yoḥanan: "Manasseh repented for thirty-three years, for it is written: 'Manasseh was twelve years old when he began to reign, and he reigned fifty-five years in Jerusalem....And he did evil....And he made a pagan altar, as did Ahab King of Israel.'" [8]How long did Ahab reign? Twenty-two years. [9]Manasseh, how long did he reign? Fifty-five. [10]Deduct from them twenty-two — thirty-three are left.

TRANSLATION AND COMMENTARY

'And he [Manasseh] **prayed to Him, and He received his entreaty,** and heard his supplication, and brought him back to Jerusalem into his kingdom.'" [1]**Rabbi Yoḥanan said: The two of them** — the Sages who say that Manasseh does not have a portion in the World to Come, and Rabbi Yehudah, who says that he does — both **expounded the same verse,** arriving at opposite conclusions. [2]**For the verse states** (Jeremiah 15:4): **"And I will make them into a horror for all the kingdoms of the earth, on account of Manasseh the son of Hezekiah."** [3]**One Sage,** Rabbi Yehudah, **maintains:** God will make the people of Israel into a horror for all the kingdoms of the earth **on account of Manasseh, because he repented, and they did not.** [4]**And the** other **Sages maintain:** [103A] [5]God will make the people of Israel into a horror for all of the kingdoms of the earth **on account of Manasseh, because he did not repent.** Rather he dragged all of Israel into sin after him.

אָמַר רַבִּי יוֹחָנָן [6]**Rabbi Yoḥanan said: Whoever says that Manasseh does not have a portion in the World to Come weakens the hands of repentant sinners** and discourages them, for it implies that sometimes a sinner's repentance is not accepted. [7]We know that Manasseh repented, **for a Tanna taught** the following Baraita **before Rabbi Yoḥanan: "Manasseh repented for thirty-three years, for the verse states** (II Kings 21:1-3): **'Manasseh was twelve years old when he began to reign, and he reigned fifty-five years in Jerusalem....And he did that which was evil....And he made a pagan altar, as did Ahab King of Israel."** These verses imply that Manasseh sinned for as long as Ahab ruled as King of Israel. [8]**How long did Ahab reign** as king? **Twenty-two years.** [9]And **how long did Manasseh reign? Fifty-five** years. [10]**Deduct twenty-two from** fifty-five, and you **are left** with **thirty-three** — the number of years after Manasseh repented and refrained from sinning.

RASHI

ושניהם — רבי יהודה דאמר יש לו חלק, ורבנן דאמרי אין לו חלק. **בגלל מנשה דלא עשה תשובה** — והמשיכן כולן אחריו. **כאשר עשה אחאב** — דמשמע כשיעור השנים שחטא אחאב במלכו חטא מנשה, והיינו עשרים ושתים שנה שחטא בהם, כנגד עשרים ושתים שנים שמלך אחאב. **פשו להו שלשים ושלש** — שעשה תשובה. **וישמע אליו ויחתר לו** — ומבחוץ כתיב ויעתר לו כך שמעתי.

NOTES

מְרַפֶּה יְדֵיהֶן שֶׁל בַּעֲלֵי תְשׁוּבָה **Weakens the hands of repentant sinners.** If a sinner is truly repentant, nothing should stand in the way of divine pardon. If we say that Manasseh is denied his portion in the World to Come, even though he repented for thirty years, other sinners guilty of serious transgressions are liable to give up hope, thinking that they will derive no benefit from their repentance.

TRANSLATION AND COMMENTARY

אָמַר רַבִּי יוֹחָנָן [1] **Rabbi Yoḥanan said in the name of Rabbi Shimon ben Yoḥai: What is meant by the** verse relating to Manasseh **that states** (II Chronicles 33:13) **"And he prayed to Him; and He made an opening for him** [וַיֵּחָתֵר לוֹ]"? [2] **The verse should have stated:** "And he prayed to him, **and He heeded him** [וַיֵּעָתֵר לוֹ]"! [3] **This** verse **teaches** us **that the Holy One, blessed be He, made** Manasseh **an opening in Heaven in order to receive him as a repentant.** It was necessary for God to do this **on account of the divine attribute of justice** that did not want to receive Manasseh. God made an opening in Heaven, stretched out His hand, and received Manasseh without the knowledge of the divine attribute of justice.

וְאָמַר רַבִּי יוֹחָנָן [4] **Rabbi Yoḥanan said in the name of Rabbi Shimon ben Yoḥai: What is meant by the verse that states** (Jeremiah 26:1): **"In the beginning of the reign of Jehoiakim son of Josiah,"** [5] **and the verse that states** (Jeremiah 28:1): **"In the beginning of the reign of Zedekiah"?** [6] Doesn't the phrase, "in the beginning" imply that **until now there were no kings** in Israel? For Jeremiah could have written: "In the first year of his reign." [7] **Rather, the Holy One, blessed be He, wanted to return the entire world to chaos,** as it was "in the beginning," because **of** the wicked King **Jehoiakim.** [8] But **He looked at** the people of **his generation,** saw that they were righteous, **and was pacified.** [9] And similarly, **the Holy One, blessed be He, wanted to return the entire world to chaos,** as "in the beginning," because **of the** sinful **generation of Zedekiah.** [10] But **He looked at Zedekiah,** saw that he was righteous, **and was pacified.**

[1] אָמַר רַבִּי יוֹחָנָן מִשּׁוּם רַבִּי שִׁמְעוֹן בֶּן יוֹחַי: מַאי דִּכְתִיב: "וַיִּשְׁמַע אֵלָיו; וַיֵּחָתֵר לוֹ". [2] "וַיֵּעָתֵר לוֹ" מִיבָּעֵי לֵיהּ! [3] מְלַמֵּד שֶׁעָשָׂה לוֹ הַקָּדוֹשׁ בָּרוּךְ הוּא כְּמִין מַחְתֶּרֶת בָּרָקִיעַ, כְּדֵי לְקַבְּלוֹ בִּתְשׁוּבָה, מִפְּנֵי מִדַּת הַדִּין.

[4] וְאָמַר רַבִּי יוֹחָנָן מִשּׁוּם רַבִּי שִׁמְעוֹן בֶּן יוֹחַי: מַאי דִּכְתִיב: "בְּרֵאשִׁית מַמְלֶכֶת יְהוֹיָקִים בֶּן יֹאשִׁיָּהוּ". [5] וּכְתִיב: "בְּרֵאשִׁית מַמְלֶכֶת צִדְקִיָּה". [6] וְכִי עַד הָאִידָּנָא לָא הֲווּ מַלְכֵי? [7] אֶלָּא, בִּקֵּשׁ הַקָּדוֹשׁ בָּרוּךְ הוּא לְהַחֲזִיר אֶת הָעוֹלָם כּוּלּוֹ לְתוֹהוּ וָבוֹהוּ בִּשְׁבִיל יְהוֹיָקִים. [8] נִסְתַּכֵּל בְּדוֹרוֹ, וְנִתְקָרְרָה דַּעְתּוֹ. [9] בִּקֵּשׁ הַקָּדוֹשׁ בָּרוּךְ הוּא לְהַחֲזִיר אֶת הָעוֹלָם כּוּלּוֹ לְתוֹהוּ וָבוֹהוּ בִּשְׁבִיל דּוֹרוֹ שֶׁל צִדְקִיָּה. [10] נִסְתַּכֵּל בְּצִדְקִיָּה, וְנִתְקָרְרָה דַּעְתּוֹ.

LITERAL TRANSLATION

[1] Rabbi Yoḥanan said in the name of Rabbi Shimon ben Yoḥai: What is that which is written: "And he prayed to Him; and He made an opening for him"? [2] It should [have been written]: "And He heeded him"! [3] This teaches that the Holy One, blessed be He, made him an opening in Heaven in order to receive him as a repentant, on account of the [divine] attribute of justice.

[4] And Rabbi Yoḥanan said in the name of Rabbi Shimon ben Yoḥai: What is that which is written: "In the beginning of the reign of Jehoiakim son of Josiah"? [5] And [what does it mean where] it is written: "In the beginning of the reign of Zedekiah"? [6] Until now there were no kings? [7] Rather, the Holy One, blessed be He, wanted to return the entire world to chaos because of Jehoiakim. [8] He looked at his generation, and His mind was appeased. [9] The Holy One, blessed be He, wanted to return the entire world to chaos because of the generation of Zedekiah. [10] He looked at Zedekiah, and His mind was appeased.

RASHI

מדת הדין – היתה מעכבת שלא להקביל פני מנשה בתשובה, ועשה הקדוש ברוך הוא מחתרת ברקיע ופשט ידו וקבלו בלא ידיעת מדת הדין. מאי דכתיב בראשית ממלכות יהויקים ובראשית ממלכת צדקיה – מאי טעמא כתיב בהני בראשית יותר מאחריני. וכי עד האידנא לא הוו מלכי – ואי משום תחלת ממלכתו קאמר – הוה ליה למכתב: בשנה ראשונה למלכותו אלא להכי שני קרא בדיבוריה וכתיב בראשית – ללמדך מעשה בראשית היה בימי יהויקים, שבקש הקדוש ברוך הוא להחזיר את עולמו לתהו ובהו כמו שהיה מבראשית. כיון שנסתכל בדורו – של יהויקים שהיו צדיקים, שעדיין לא גלו החרש והמסגר. דורו של צדקיהו – היו רשעים, שכל הצדיקים הגלו כבר עם יהויכין.

NOTES

וַיֵּחָתֵר לוֹ **He made an opening for him.** Many commentators have expressed their astonishment at this passage, for the verse in fact reads: וַיֵּעָתֵר לוֹ "And He received his entreaty," and nowhere do we find: וַיֵּחָתֵר לוֹ "And He made an opening for him," neither in the way the verse is written, nor in the way the verse is read. Some suggest that there may have been a tradition during the Tannaitic period that the word should be written or read as וַיֵּחָתֵר. Most commentators suggest that the Talmudic text is corrupt, and that the Gemara really means to say that the words וַיֵּעָתֵר לוֹ are used here in the sense of וַיֵּחָתֵר לוֹ. The Jerusalem Talmud states explicitly that there are places where חֲתִירָה is referred to as עֲתִירָה.

עָשָׂה לוֹ מַחְתֶּרֶת **He made him an opening.** *Ramah* notes that this passage must be understood as a metaphor, for nothing can possibly stand in God's way and make it necessary for Him to act secretly. Rabbi Yoḥanan means to say that, according to God's attribute of justice, Manasseh should have been denied the opportunity to repent. Therefore He turned to His attribute of mercy

דּוֹרוֹ שֶׁל יְהוֹיָקִים וְצִדְקִיָּה **The generation of Jehoiakim and Zedekiah.** *Ramah* accounts for the change in the generations

1 בְּצִדְקִיָּה נַמִי, כְּתִיב: ״וַיַּעַשׂ הָרַע בְּעֵינֵי ה׳״!
2 שֶׁהָיָה בְּיָדוֹ לִמְחוֹת, וְלֹא מִיחָה.
3 וְאָמַר רַבִּי יוֹחָנָן מִשּׁוּם רַבִּי שִׁמְעוֹן בֶּן יוֹחַי: מַאי דִּכְתִיב: 4 ״אִישׁ חָכָם נִשְׁפָּט אֶת אִישׁ אֱוִיל וְרָגַז וְשָׂחַק וְאֵין נָחַת״? 5 אָמַר הַקָּדוֹשׁ בָּרוּךְ הוּא: ״כָּעַסְתִּי עַל אָחָז וּנְתַתִּיו בְּיַד מַלְכֵי דַמֶּשֶׂק. 6 זִיבַּח וְקִיטֵּר [לֶאֱלֹהֵיהֶם], 7 שֶׁנֶּאֱמַר: ׳וַיִּזְבַּח לֵאלֹהֵי דַרְמֶשֶׂק הַמַּכִּים בּוֹ וַיֹּאמֶר [כִּי] אֱלֹהֵי מַלְכֵי אֲרָם הֵם מַעְזְרִים אֹתָם לָהֶם אֲזַבֵּחַ וְיַעְזְרוּנִי וְהֵם הָיוּ [לוֹ] לְהַכְשִׁילוֹ וּלְכָל יִשְׂרָאֵל׳. 8 שָׂחַקְתִּי עִם אֲמַצְיָה, וְנָתַתִּי מַלְכֵי אֱדוֹם בְּיָדוֹ — הֵבִיא אֱלֹהֵיהֶם וְהִשְׁתַּחֲוָה לָהֶם, 9 שֶׁנֶּאֱמַר: ׳וַיְהִי אַחֲרֵי (כן) בּוֹא אֲמַצְיָהוּ מֵהַכּוֹת אֶת אֲדוֹמִים וַיָּבֵא אֶת אֱלֹהֵי בְּנֵי שֵׂעִיר וַיַּעֲמִידֵם [לוֹ] לֵאלֹהִים וְלִפְנֵיהֶם יִשְׁתַּחֲוֶה וְלָהֶם יְקַטֵּר׳״.
10 אָמַר רַב פַּפָּא: הַיְינוּ דְּאָמְרִי אֱינָשֵׁי: בָּכְיֵי לֵיהּ לְמָר, דְּלָא יָדַע; חָיְיכֵי לְמָר, דְּלָא יָדַע.

LITERAL TRANSLATION

1 Regarding Zedekiah also, it is written: "And he did evil in the eyes of the Lord"!
2 He could have objected, but he did not object.
3 And Rabbi Yoḥanan said in the name of Rabbi Shimon ben Yoḥai: What is that which is written: 4 "If a wise man contends with a foolish man, whether he rages or laughs, there is no ease"? 5 The Holy One, blessed be He, said: "I was angry with Ahaz, and gave him into the hand of the Kings of Damascus. 6 He sacrificed and burned incense [to their gods], 7 as it is stated: 'He sacrificed to the gods of Damascus, who struck him; and he said, Because the gods of the Kings of Aram help them, I will sacrifice to them, and they will help me. But they were the ruin of him, and of all Israel.' 8 I was happy with Amaziah, and I gave the Kings of Edom into his hand. He brought their gods, and prostrated himself before them, 9 as it is stated: 'Now it came to pass, after Amaziah came from striking the Edomites, that he brought the gods of the children of Se'ir, and set them up to be his gods, and prostrated himself before them, and burned incense to them.'"
10 Rav Pappa said: This is what people say: I wept for my master, but he did not know; I laughed for my master, but he did not know.

TRANSLATION AND COMMENTARY

בְּצִדְקִיָּה 1 The Gemara asks: Why was God pacified when He saw Zedekiah? Surely **regarding Zedekiah as well, the verse states** (II Kings 24:19): **"And he did evil in the sight of the Lord"!**

שֶׁהָיָה בְּיָדוֹ 2 The Gemara answers: Zedekiah himself was not wicked. But **he could have objected** to the behavior of his generation, **but did not do so.** Consequently the evil that was perpetrated by his generation is attributed to him.

וְאָמַר רַבִּי יוֹחָנָן 3 **Rabbi Yoḥanan said in the name of Rabbi Shimon ben Yoḥai: What is meant by the verse that states** (Proverbs 29:9): 4 **"If a wise man contends with a foolish man, whether he rages or laughs, there is no rest"?** The "wise man" alludes to God, and the "foolish man" alludes to Kings Ahaz and Amaziah. 5 **The Holy One, blessed be He, said: "I was angry with Ahaz, and** so I **handed him over to the Kings of Damascus.** What did he do? 6 **He sacrificed and burned incense to their gods,** 7 **as the verse states** (II Chronicles 28:23): **'He sacrificed to the gods of Damascus, who struck him; and he said, Because the gods of the Kings of Aram help them, I will sacrifice to them, and they will help me. But they were the ruin of him, and of all Israel.'** When God is angry with the people of Israel, and causes them to fall in battle, they worship idols. 8 **I was happy with Amaziah, and I handed the Kings of Edom over to him.** What did he do? **He brought their gods** back with him, **and prostrated himself before them,** 9 **as the verse states** (II Chronicles 25:14): **'Now it came to pass, after Amaziah came from striking the Edomites, that he brought the gods of the children of Se'ir, and set them up to be his gods, and prostrated himself before them, and burned incense to them.'** Even when God brings Israel success in battle, they worship idols."

אָמַר רַב פַּפָּא 10 **Rav Pappa said: This is** the meaning of **the popular adage: I wept for my master, but he did not understand; I laughed for my master, but**

RASHI

איש חכם נשפט — זה הקדוש ברוך הוא, שנקרא ״ה׳ איש מלחמה״ (שמות טו) **איש אויל** — אלו מלכים שבסמוך, אחז ואמציה, **ורגז ושחק ואין נחת**, בין שהוא כועס עמהם בין שהוא שוחק עמהם — אינן יראין מלפניו, ואינם חתים לחזור למוטב. **בכי ליה למר כו׳** — לאו דוקא נקט מר אלא משום דהכי מילי דאינשי: כשהוא חכם כשהוא רוצה להישפט ולהתווכח עמהן, בין שהוא שוחק עליהם בין שהוא כועס עמהן אינם יראים מלפניו ואינם חתים לחזור למוטב.

NOTES

as follows: During the days of Jehoiachin the son of Jehoiakim, the noblemen and the Sages were exiled to Babylonia. Thus, the Sages who were living at the time of Jehoiakim were all gone by the time of Zedekiah, and Zedekiah was left with people of low standing and little learning.

TRANSLATION AND COMMENTARY

he did not understand. [1]**Woe to my master who does not understand the difference between good and evil.** So, too, the people of Israel — whether God acts favorably toward them or punishes them, they worship idols.

וַיָּבֹאוּ כֹּל [2]The verse states (Jeremiah 39:3): **"And all the princes of the King of Babylonia came in, and sat in the middle** [הַתָּוֶךְ] **gate."** [3]**Rabbi Yoḥanan said in the name of Rabbi Shimon ben Yoḥai:** The word הַתָּוֶךְ may be understood as חָתוּךְ (the letter *heh* substituting for the letter *het*), "deciding." The princes of the King of Babylonia came in, sat at the Temple gate, **the place where** the Sanhedrin sat and **decided about the laws.**

אָמַר רַב פַּפָּא [4]**Rav Pappa said: This is** the meaning of **the popular adage:** [5]**Where the master of the house** once **hung his weapon, there the mean shepherd** who succeeded to his distinguished predecessor's position now **hangs up his pitcher.** The former seat of the Sanhedrin is now occupied by the princes of Babylonia.

סִימָן [6](The Gemara offers **a mnemonic device** for a series of Midrashic statements made by Rav Ḥisda in the name of Rabbi Yirmeyah bar Abba: **By the field, houses, shall not befall.)**

אָמַר רַב חִסְדָּא [7]**Rav Ḥisda said in the name of Rabbi Yirmeyah bar Abba: What is meant by the verse that states** (Proverbs 24:30-31): [8]**"I passed by the field of a lazy man, and by the vineyard of a man without understanding; and, lo, it was overgrown with thorns, and nettles covered it, and its stone wall was broken"?** The entire verse may be understood as a description of the political and spiritual decline of the last Kings of Judah: [9]**"I passed by the field of a lazy man" — this is** an allusion to **Ahaz;** [10]**"and by the vineyard of a man without understanding" — this is** an allusion to **Manasseh;** [11]**"and, lo, it was overgrown with thorns" — this is** an allusion to **Amon;** [12]**"and nettles covered it" — this is** an allusion to **Jehoiakim;** [13]**"and its stone wall was broken" — this is** an allusion to **Zedekiah, in whose days the Temple was destroyed.**

[1]וַוי לֵיהּ לְמָר דְּלָא יָדַע בֵּין טַב לְבִישׁ.

[2]"וַיָּבֹאוּ כֹּל [שָׂרֵי] מֶלֶךְ בָּבֶל (וַיָּבֹאוּ) [וַיֵּשְׁבוּ] בְּשַׁעַר הַתָּוֶךְ". [3]אָמַר רַבִּי יוֹחָנָן מִשּׁוּם רַבִּי שִׁמְעוֹן בֶּן יוֹחַי: מָקוֹם שֶׁמְּחַתְּכִין בּוֹ הֲלָכוֹת.

[4]אָמַר רַב פַּפָּא: הַיְינוּ דְּאָמְרִי אֱינָשֵׁי: [5]בְּאַתְרָא דְּמָרֵיהּ תָּלָא לֵיהּ זַיְינֵיהּ, תַּמָּן קוּלְבָּא רָעֲיָא קוּלְתֵּיהּ תָּלָא.

[6](סִימָן: עַל שְׂדֵה, בָּתִּים, לֹא תְאוּנֶּה).

[7]אָמַר רַב חִסְדָּא אָמַר רַבִּי יִרְמְיָה בַּר אַבָּא: מַאי דִּכְתִיב: [8]"עַל שְׂדֵה אִישׁ עָצֵל עָבַרְתִּי, וְעַל כֶּרֶם אָדָם חֲסַר לֵב; וְהִנֵּה עָלָה כֻלּוֹ קִמְּשׂוֹנִים כָּסּוּ פָנָיו חֲרֻלִּים, וְגֶדֶר אֲבָנָיו נֶהֱרָסָה"? [9]"עַל שְׂדֵה אִישׁ עָצֵל עָבַרְתִּי" — זֶה אָחָז; [10]"וְעַל כֶּרֶם אָדָם חֲסַר לֵב" — זֶה מְנַשֶּׁה; [11]"וְהִנֵּה עָלָה כֻלּוֹ קִמְּשׂוֹנִים" — זֶה אָמוֹן; [12]"כָּסּוּ פָנָיו חֲרֻלִּים" — זֶה יְהוֹיָקִים; [13]"וְגֶדֶר אֲבָנָיו נֶהֱרָסָה" — זֶה צִדְקִיָּהוּ, שֶׁנֶּחֱרַב בֵּית הַמִּקְדָּשׁ בְּיָמָיו.

LITERAL TRANSLATION

[1]Woe to my master who does not know [the difference] between good and evil.

[2]"And all the princes of the King of Babylonia came in, and sat in the middle gate." [3]Rabbi Yoḥanan said in the name of Rabbi Shimon ben Yoḥai: The place where they decide laws.

[4]Rav Pappa said: This is what people say: [5]In the place where the master of the house hangs his weapon, there the mean shepherd hangs up his pitcher.

[6](A sign: By the field, houses, shall not befall.)

[7]Rav Ḥisda said in the name of Rabbi Yirmeyah bar Abba: What is that which is written: [8]"I passed by the field of a lazy man, and by the vineyard of a man without understanding (lit., 'lacking a heart'); and, lo, it was overgrown with thorns, and nettles covered it, and its stone wall was broken"? [9]"I passed by the field of a lazy man" — this is Ahaz; [10]"and by the vineyard of a man without understanding" — this is Manasseh; [11]"and, lo, it was overgrown with thorns" — this is Amon; [12]"and nettles covered it" — this is Jehoiakim; [13]"and its stone wall was broken down" — this is Zedekiah, in whose days the Temple was destroyed.

RASHI

מקום שהיו מחתכין בו — ודורשין הלכות, נהפך למושב לגיס של שרי מלך בבל. **בשער התוך** — לשון חותך, והיינו בהר הבית ובעזרה ששם היו יושבים סנהדרין, וכדאמר בעלמא (סנהדרין פו,ב): שלשה בתי דינין היו שם אחד בלשכת הגזית, ואחד על פתח העזרה, ואחד על פתח הר הבית. **קולתיה תלא** — כלומר במקום שהיו חותכין הלכות — בו דנין שרי בבל דינים שלהם. **באתרא דמריה תלא זייניה** — מקום שהאדון תולה כליו. **קולבא רעיא** — נבל רועה. **קולתיה תלא** — כדו תלה לשם כמו (בראשית כד) "כדה" דמתרגמינן קולתא, לישנא אחרינא: קודתיה — מקדתו, כמו (סוטה ט,א): מקדה של חרס. **והנה עלה כולו קמשונים זה אמון** — שהעלה שממית על גבי המזבח, לקמן. **כסו פניו חרולים זה יהויקים** — שכסה פניו מאורו של הקדוש ברוך הוא, כדאמר לקמן כלום אנו צריכים אלא לאורו — יטול אורו. **על שדה איש עצל עברתי זה אחז** — ולהכי קרי ליה עצל — שחתם את התורה ובטל את העבודה, לקמן. **ועל כרם אדם חסר לב זה מנשה** — שקדר אזכרות והרס את המזבח (לישנא אחרינא): **חרולים** — *אורטיג"ש. **זה צדקיה** — שהיה צדיק ונהרס בית המקדש בימיו.

LANGUAGE

קוּלְבָּא Mean. Some authorities believe this is related to the Arabic قلب meaning "a forger," or "cheat."

LANGUAGE (RASHI)

אורטיג"ש* Apparently it should be read as אורטיא"ש, from the Old French *orties*, meaning "nettles."

¹וְאָמַר רַב חִסְדָּא אָמַר רַבִּי יִרְמְיָה בַּר אַבָּא: אַרְבַּע כִּיתּוֹת אֵין מְקַבְּלוֹת פְּנֵי שְׁכִינָה: ²כַּת לֵצִים, כַּת שַׁקְרָנִים, כַּת חֲנֵיפִים, כַּת מְסַפְּרֵי לָשׁוֹן הָרָע. ³כַּת לֵצִים, דִּכְתִיב: ״מָשַׁךְ יָדוֹ אֶת לֹצְצִים״. ⁴כַּת שַׁקְרָנִים, דִּכְתִיב: ״דֹּבֵר שְׁקָרִים לֹא יִכּוֹן לְנֶגֶד עֵינָי״. ⁵כַּת חֲנֵיפִים, דִּכְתִיב: ״כִּי לֹא לְפָנָיו חָנֵף יָבוֹא״. ⁶כַּת מְסַפְּרֵי לָשׁוֹן הָרַע, דִּכְתִיב: ״כִּי לֹא אֵל חָפֵץ רֶשַׁע אָתָּה לֹא יְגֻרְךָ רָע״. ⁷צַדִּיק אַתָּה, וְלֹא יִהְיֶה בִּמְגוּרְךָ רַע.

⁸וְאָמַר רַב חִסְדָּא אָמַר רַבִּי יִרְמְיָה בַּר אַבָּא: מַאי דִּכְתִיב: ⁹״לֹא תְאֻנֶּה אֵלֶיךָ רָעָה וְנֶגַע לֹא יִקְרַב בְּאָהֳלֶךָ״? ¹⁰״לֹא תְאֻנֶּה אֵלֶיךָ רָעָה״ — שֶׁלֹּא יִשְׁלוֹט בָּהֶן יֵצֶר הָרַע. ¹¹״וְנֶגַע לֹא יִקְרַב בְּאָהֳלֶךָ״ — שֶׁלֹּא תִּמְצָא אִשְׁתְּךָ סָפֵק נִדָּה בְּשָׁעָה שֶׁתָּבֹא מִן הַדֶּרֶךְ. ¹²דָּבָר אַחֵר: ״לֹא תְאֻנֶּה אֵלֶיךָ רָעָה״ — שֶׁלֹּא יְבַעֲתוּךָ חֲלוֹמוֹת רָעִים

TRANSLATION AND COMMENTARY

וְאָמַר רַב חִסְדָּא ¹**Rav Ḥisda said in the name of Rabbi Yirmeyah bar Abba: Four classes of people will not greet the Divine Presence:** ²**The class of scoffers, the class of liars, the class of flatterers,** and **the class of slanderers.** ³**The class of scoffers, as the verse states** (Hosea 7:5): **"He stretched out his hand with scoffers"** — God drew His hand away from the scoffers to avoid them. ⁴**The class of liars, as the verse states** (Psalms 101:7): **"He that tells lies shall not remain in Your sight."** ⁵**The class of flatterers, as the verse states** (Job 13:16): **"For a flatterer shall not come before him."** ⁶**The class of slanderers, as the verse states** (Psalms 5:5): **"For You are not a God who desires wickedness; nor shall evil dwell with You."** ⁷You, God, **are righteous, and there shall be no** words of **evil in Your dwelling.**

וְאָמַר רַב חִסְדָּא ⁸The Gemara now discusses another verse that uses the term "your tent." **Rav Ḥisda said in the name of Rabbi Yirmeyah bar Abba: What is meant by the verse that states** (Psalms 91:10): ⁹**"No evil shall befall you, nor shall any plague come near your tent"?** ¹⁰**"No evil shall befall you"** — this means **that the evil inclination shall not rule over you.** ¹¹**"Nor shall any plague come near your tent"** — this teaches **that you shall not find your wife** ("your tent") **in doubt about whether she is** forbidden to you because she is **menstruating when you come** home **from a journey.** It is more difficult for a man returning home after a long journey to find his wife in doubt about her menstrual status than to find her forbidden to him with certainty. When she is in doubt, he is not sure that he must abstain from relations with her. ¹²**Another explanation** may be offered: **"No evil shall befall you"** — this also means **that bad dreams and evil**

LITERAL TRANSLATION

¹And Rav Ḥisda said in the name of Rabbi Yirmeyah bar Abba: Four classes [of people] do not greet the Divine Presence: ²The class of scoffers, the class of liars, the class of flatterers, the class of slanderers. ³The class of scoffers, as it is written: "He stretched out his hand with scoffers." ⁴The class of liars, as it is written: "He that tells lies shall not remain in My sight." ⁵The class of flatterers, as it is written: "For a flatterer shall not come before him." ⁶The class of slanderers, as it is written: "For You are not a God who desires wickedness; nor shall evil dwell with You." ⁷You are righteous, and there shall be no evil in Your dwelling.

⁸And Rav Ḥisda said in the name of Rabbi Yirmeyah bar Abba: What is that which is written: ⁹"No evil shall befall you, nor shall any plague come near your tent"? ¹⁰"No evil shall befall you" — that the evil inclination shall not rule them. ¹¹"Nor shall any plague come near your tent" — that you shall not find your wife in doubt about whether she is menstruating when you come from the road. ¹²Another explanation: "No evil shall befall you" — that bad dreams

RASHI

משך ידו את לוצצים — משך הקדוש ברוך הוא את ידיו מן הלוצצים שלא להתקרב אצלם. **לא יגורך רע** — היינו מספרי לשון הרע דכתיב בתריה ״תאבד דוברי כזב איש דמים וגו׳״, ועוד: דכתיב בתריה ״קבר פתוח גרונם וגו׳״. **שלא תמצא אשתך ספק נדה וכו׳** — והיינו באהלך = באשתך, כדאמרינן אין אהלו אלא אשה, ובשעה שאדם בא מן הדרך קשה לו כשימצא את אשתו ספק נדה יותר מנדה ודאית, שעל ספק הוא מיצר ויצרו תקפו ואומר טהורה היא, ועל אנס אני מונע.

NOTES

אַרְבַּע כִּיתּוֹת **Four classes.** As for the four classes of people mentioned here, even though they have other qualities which assure them a portion in the World to Come, since they scoff, or lie, or flatter, or slander, they will never greet the Divine Presence and behold God in "a clear mirror" (*Ramah*).

מְסַפְּרֵי לָשׁוֹן הָרַע **Slanderers.** *Rashi* argues that we know that the verse, "For You are not a God who desires wickedness; nor shall evil dwell with You," refers to slanderers from the verses that follow (Psalms 5:7): "You destroy those who speak falsehood," and (Psalms 5:10):

TRANSLATION AND COMMENTARY

thoughts shall not alarm you. [1]**"Nor shall any plague come near your tent"** — this means **that you shall not have a son or a student who disgraces his education in public** and misapplies his learning, **like Jesus the Nazarene.**

עַד כָּאן [2]The Gemara reads Psalms 91 as a series of blessings that were bestowed upon Solomon: From the beginning of the psalm **until here** (the end of verse 10), Solomon's **father** David **blessed him** the way a father blesses his son. [3]**From here on** — verses 11-13 — Solomon's **mother blessed him,** saying: **"For He shall order His angels to preserve you in all your ways. They shall bear you in their hands,** lest you dash your foot against a stone. **You shall tread upon the lion and the adder;** the young lion and the crocodile shall you trample under foot." It is the way of a mother to bless her son that he be spared injury from stones and evil spirits. [4]**Up until here, his mother blessed him.** [5]**From here on, Heaven blessed him,** for the rest of the psalm speaks in the name of God in the first person (Psalms 91:14-16): [103B] [6]**"Because he has desired Me, therefore I will deliver him; I will set him on high, because he has known My name. He shall call upon Me, and I will answer him; I will be with him in trouble; I will deliver him, and honor him. With long life I will satisfy him, and show him My salvation."**

אָמַר [7]**Rabbi Shimon ben Lakish said: What is meant by the verse that states** (Job 38:15): [8]**"And from the wicked** [*resha'im*] **their light is withheld, and the high arm shall be broken"?** [9]**Why is the** letter ***ayin*** **in the** word ***resha'im*** **suspended** slightly above the rest of the line? This teaches that the word *resha'im* should be interpreted as if it were written without the *ayin* as *rashim*, the plural of the word *rash*, "poor." [10]And the verse comes to teach that **if a person is poor** and has many enemies **below,** in this world, **he is** surely a sinner who **is** also **poor above,** in Heaven.

וְהִרְהוּרִים רָעִים. [1]״וְנֶגַע לֹא יִקְרַב בְּאָהֳלֶךָ״ — שֶׁלֹּא יְהֵא לְךָ בֵּן אוֹ תַּלְמִיד שֶׁמַּקְדִּיחַ תַּבְשִׁילוֹ בָּרַבִּים, כְּגוֹן יֵשׁוּ הַנּוֹצְרִי.

[2]עַד כָּאן בֵּרְכוֹ אָבִיו. [3]מִכָּאן וְאֵילָךְ בֵּרַכְתּוֹ אִמּוֹ. ״כִּי מַלְאָכָיו יְצַוֶּה לָּךְ לִשְׁמָרְךָ בְּכָל דְּרָכֶיךָ. עַל כַּפַּיִם יִשָּׂאוּנְךָ וגו׳. עַל שַׁחַל וָפֶתֶן תִּדְרֹךְ וגו׳״. [4]עַד כָּאן בֵּרַכְתּוֹ אִמּוֹ. [5]מִכָּאן וְאֵילָךְ בֵּרַכְתּוּ שָׁמַיִם: [103B] [6]״כִּי בִי חָשַׁק וַאֲפַלְּטֵהוּ; אֲשַׂגְּבֵהוּ כִּי יָדַע שְׁמִי. יִקְרָאֵנִי וְאֶעֱנֵהוּ, עִמּוֹ אָנֹכִי בְצָרָה, אֲחַלְּצֵהוּ וַאֲכַבְּדֵהוּ. אוֹרֶךְ יָמִים אַשְׂבִּיעֵהוּ, וְאַרְאֵהוּ בִּישׁוּעָתִי״.

[7]אָמַר רַבִּי שִׁמְעוֹן בֶּן לָקִישׁ: מַאי דִּכְתִיב: [8]״וְיִמָּנַע מֵרְשָׁעִים אוֹרָם, וּזְרוֹעַ רָמָה תִּשָּׁבֵר״? [9]מִפְּנֵי מָה עַיִ״ן שֶׁל רְשָׁעִים תְּלוּיָה? [10]כֵּיוָן שֶׁנַּעֲשָׂה אָדָם רָשׁ מִלְּמַטָּה, נַעֲשֶׂה רָשׁ מִלְמַעְלָה.

LITERAL TRANSLATION

and evil thoughts shall not alarm you. [1]"Nor shall any plague come near your tent" — that you shall not have a son or a student who disgraces his education (lit., "spoils the cooking") in public, like Jesus the Nazarene.

[2]Until here his father blessed him. [3]From here on his mother blessed him. "For He shall order His angels to preserve you in all your ways. They shall bear you in their hands....You shall tread upon the lion and the adder, etc." [4]Until here his mother blessed him. [5]From here on, Heaven blessed him: [103B] [6]"Because he desired Me, I will deliver him; I will set him on high, because he has known My name. He shall call upon Me, and I will answer him; I will be with him in trouble; I will deliver him, and honor him. With long life I will satisfy him, and show him My salvation."

[7]Rabbi Shimon ben Lakish said: What is that which is written: [8]"And from the wicked their light is withheld, and the high arm shall be broken"? [9]Why is the *ayin* in *resha'im* suspended? [10]When a person is poor below, he is poor above.

RASHI

עד כאן ברכו אביו — דוד אביו לשלמה בנו, מסתמא לפי ענין הברכות יש לידע סדור ברכות, שכן דרך האב בדברים האלו בספק נדה, וביצר הרע, ובהרהורים רעים, ובבנים ותלמידים שלא יקדיחו תבשילם ברבים, אבל אשה אינה נותנת דעת בכך אלא מהמרכת הלב שיש לה מתפללה על בנה שינצל מאבן נגף, ומרוחין ושדין, לפיכך קא דריש לפי הענין, שאלו ברכות ברכתו אמו "כי מלאכיו יצוה לך" מפי רבי, ועוד: משום דכתיב כי מלאכיו — משמע ליה דסליק ענין אחד דברכה, ומ"כי מלאכיו" עד כי בי חשק סליק חד ענין, הלכך מוקים דמי לדמי, דעד כאן ברכו אביו וכו׳. מפי רבי. **כי בי חשק** — לא שייך אלא ברבונא דעלמא, כלומר: אותו שחפץ בי ובירא
תי אפלטהו. **ע׳ שברשעים תלויה** — שאינה כתובה בשיטת אותיות התיבה, אלא תלויה היא למעלה, ונראה ככתוב רשים. **ביון שנעשה אדם רש מלמטה** — שיש לו שונאין, ואין רוח הבריות נוחה הימנו. **נעשה רש מלמעלה** — בידוע ששונאין אותו מלמעלה, להכי כתוב רשים, שני מיני רשות.

BACKGROUND

עי״ן תְּלוּיָה A suspended ***ayin.***

כְּמוֹ לְבוּשׁ: טו וְיִמָּנַע מֵרְשָׁעִים אוֹרָם וּזְרוֹעַ רָמָה תִּשָּׁבֵר: טז הֲבָאתָ

As this verse is customarily printed, the letter *ayin* in the word רְשָׁעִים is raised above the other letters and stands out from them on the line.

NOTES

"Their throat is an open sepulcher; they flatter with their tongue." According to *Ramah*, the words "wickedness" and "evil" mentioned in the verse itself show that the verse must be referring to slanderers who are not only wicked toward Heaven, but evil toward their fellow men as well.

מִפְּנֵי מָה עַיִ״ן שֶׁל רְשָׁעִים תְּלוּיָה? Why is the *ayin* in *resha'im* suspended? *Ramah* had the following reading: "Whenever a person becomes a leader [רֹאשׁ — רָשׁ] below, he becomes

TRANSLATION AND COMMENTARY

וְלָא נִכְתְּבֵיהּ כְּלָל [1]The Gemara raises an objection: If so, then the letter *ayin* **should not have been written at all!**

רַבִּי יוֹחָנָן [2]**Rabbi Yoḥanan and Rabbi Elazar** said that the letter *ayin* intimates that we are dealing here with *rashim*, "poor people," who are in fact *resha'im*, "wicked." [3]**One** of these Amoraim **said:** The word *resha'im* is written **to** protect **the honor of David,** who was hated by many people, but nevertheless loved and desired by God. [4]**And the other** Amora **said:** The word *resha'im* is written **to** protect **the honor of Nehemiah ben Hachaliah,** for he, too, was hated by many people for no reason.

תָּנוּ רַבָּנַן [5]**Our Rabbis taught** a Baraita: **"Manasseh** king of Judah **taught** *Torat Kohanim* ('the priests' Torah,' the Talmudic name for the Book of Leviticus), **in fifty-five ways, corresponding to the** fifty-five **years of his kingdom.** Manasseh was a great Torah scholar who would offer novel interpretations of the Book of Leviticus every year. [6]**Ahab** was an even greater scholar, for he taught Leviticus in **eighty-five** ways. [7]**Jeroboam** was the greatest scholar of all, for he taught Leviticus in **a hundred-and-three** ways."

תַּנְיָא [8]**It was taught** in a Baraita: **"Rabbi Meir said: Absalom does not have a portion in the World to Come,** [9]**as the verse states** (II Samuel 18:15): **'And they struck Absalom, and killed him.'** [10]**'And they struck him'** — killing him **in this world.** [11]**'And they killed him'** — so that he would not enter **the World to Come."**

תַּנְיָא [12]**It was taught** in another Baraita: **"Rabbi Shimon ben Elazar said in the name of Rabbi Meir:** [13]**Ahaz and Ahaziah** from among the Kings of Judah, **and all the Kings of Israel regarding whom it is stated: 'And he**

[1]וְלָא נִכְתְּבֵיהּ כְּלָל!
[2]רַבִּי יוֹחָנָן וְרַבִּי אֶלְעָזָר — [3]חַד אָמַר: מִפְּנֵי כְּבוֹדוֹ שֶׁל דָּוִד.
[4]וְחַד אָמַר: מִשּׁוּם כְּבוֹדוֹ שֶׁל נְחֶמְיָה בֶּן חֲכַלְיָה.
[5]תָּנוּ רַבָּנַן: ״מְנַשֶּׁה הָיָה שׁוֹנֶה חֲמִשִּׁים וַחֲמִשָּׁה פָּנִים בְּתוֹרַת כֹּהֲנִים, כְּנֶגֶד שְׁנֵי מַלְכוּתוֹ.
[6]אַחְאָב — שְׁמֹנִים וַחֲמִשָּׁה.
[7]יָרָבְעָם — מֵאָה וּשְׁלֹשָׁה״.
[8]תַּנְיָא: ״הָיָה רַבִּי מֵאִיר אוֹמֵר: אַבְשָׁלוֹם אֵין לוֹ חֵלֶק לָעוֹלָם הַבָּא, [9]שֶׁנֶּאֱמַר: ׳וַיַּכּוּ אֶת אַבְשָׁלוֹם וַיְמִיתֻהוּ׳. [10]׳וַיַּכּוּהוּ׳ — בָּעוֹלָם הַזֶּה. [11]׳וַיְמִיתֻהוּ׳ — לָעוֹלָם הַבָּא״.
[12]תַּנְיָא: ״רַבִּי שִׁמְעוֹן בֶּן אֶלְעָזָר אוֹמֵר מִשּׁוּם רַבִּי מֵאִיר: [13]אָחָז וַאֲחַזְיָה וְכָל מַלְכֵי יִשְׂרָאֵל

LITERAL TRANSLATION

[1]Let it not write it at all!

[2]Rabbi Yoḥanan and Rabbi Elazar — [3]one said: Because of the honor of David. [4]And one said: Because of the honor of Nehemiah ben Hachaliah.

[5]Our Rabbis taught: "Manasseh taught *Torat Kohanim* in fifty-five ways, corresponding to the years of his kingdom. [6]Ahab — eighty-five. [7]Jeroboam — a hundred-and-three."

[8]It was taught: "Rabbi Meir said: Absalom has no portion in the World to Come, [9]as it is stated: 'And they struck Absalom and killed him.' [10]'And they struck him' — in this world. [11]'And killed him' — in the World to Come."

[12]It was taught: "Rabbi Shimon ben Elazar says in the name of Rabbi Meir: [13]Ahaz and Ahaziah and all the Kings of Israel

RASHI

ולא נכתביה — לעי״ן כלל. **משום כבודו של דוד** — שאין הדבר נוהג בצדיקים, ודוד היו לו שונאים הרבה. **ונחמיה בן חכליה** — שהיו לו שונאים הרבה מנכרים שמבקשין להרגו, על שהיה בונה בית המקדש, כדכתיב בעזרא (נחמיה ד), ״ואחת מחזקת השלח וגו׳״. לישנא אחרינא: היו לו קנאים מישראל, דכתיב (שם ו) ״רבים ביהודה בעלי שבועה לו כי הוא חתן לשכניה בן ארח״, שהיו מבזין אותו, בקדושין (ע,א) מפרש להאי קרא, ולהכי איכתבא, לומר שברשעים אמרינן ולא בצדיקים. **היה שונה חמשים וחמשה פנים בתורת כהנים** — ספר ויקרא היה מחדש בו כל שנה ושנה, ודורשו מפלפולו.

NOTES

a wicked man [רָשָׁע] above," for power corrupts. The letter *ayin*, which is suspended above the rest of the line, in order to intimate that while below he may be a leader, above he is a wicked man. This only applies to a person who acquired power on his own, but not to someone who inherited his high position from his father (like the Kings of Judah). Thus, it was necessary to exclude David and Nehemiah from the rule (see also *Rambam*'s *Commentary to the Mishnah*).

פָּנִים בְּתוֹרַת כֹּהֲנִים ***Torat Kohanim* in fifty-five ways.** *Torat Kohanim* is cited here as an example because it deals with the sacred matters of the Temple, and also because it is considered a particularly difficult book. Thus, the accomplishments of Manasseh, Ahab, and Jeroboam are even more impressive. The Baraita tells of these kings' greatness in Torah in order to explain why they do not have a portion in the World to Come. Since they were masters of the Torah, they must have sinned intentionally and with premeditation (*Maharsha*).

כְּנֶגֶד שְׁנֵי מַלְכוּתוֹ **Corresponding to the years of his kingdom.** According to *Rashi*, Manasseh offered a new interpretation of the Book of Leviticus in each of the fifty-five years of his reign. According to *Ramah*, the Baraita means to say that Manasseh ruled for fifty-five years, because he had once been a great Torah scholar who taught *Torat Kohanim* in fifty-five different ways.

אָחָז וַאֲחַזְיָה **Ahaz and Ahaziah.** The other Kings of Judah were either so wicked that they were sentenced to eternal punishment in Gehinom (Amon and Jehoiakim), or else they were less wicked and had a portion in the World to Come, like Jehoiachin. The kings mentioned here were spared eternal punishment in Gehinom because they fought the wars of the people of Israel, and shared in their sorrow and pain (*Ramah*).

TRANSLATION AND COMMENTARY

did evil in the sight of the Lord' — [1]**will not live** in the World to Come, **but** they **will** also **not be sentenced** to eternal punishment in Gehinom."

וְגַם דָּם נָקִי [2]The verse states (II Kings 21:16): **"Moreover, Manasseh shed a great deal of innocent blood, until he filled Jerusalem from one end to another; beside his sin which he made Judah sin, to do evil in the eyes of the Lord."** What is meant by the words "until he filled Jerusalem from one end to another," literally, "from mouth to mouth"? [3]**Here** in Babylonia **they explain that** this means that Manasseh **killed** the Prophet **Isaiah,** who spoke to God mouth to mouth. [4]**In Eretz Israel, they say that** this means that Manasseh **made an idol that was** so big and heavy that it was **a load for a thousand people, and every day it would kill all of them,** crushing them under its great weight, and filling Jerusalem with blood from one end to another.

כְּמַאן אָזְלָא [5]The Gemara asks: **According to whose position did Rabbah bar Bar Ḥannah say: The soul of one righteous man is balanced against the entire world?** [6]The Gemara answers: This was said **according to** those authorities **who said** that Manasseh **killed** the Prophet **Isaiah,** and that his blood filled Jerusalem from one end to another.

כְּתִיב [7]The Gemara points out the following contradiction: In one place (II Chronicles 33:7) **the verse states** that Manasseh made **"a carved idol,"** in the singular. [8]**And** elsewhere (II Chronicles 33:19) **the verse states** that he made **"carved idols,"** in the plural. [9]**Rabbi Yoḥanan said: At first,** Manasseh **made** his idol with **one face, but later he made** that idol with **four faces** as a provocation, **so that the Divine Presence would see** the idol's face from all directions, **and become angry.**

אָחָז הֶעֱמִידוֹ [10]The Gemara continues: **Ahaz stood** an idol **up in the upper chamber** of the Temple, **as the verse states** (II Kings 23:12): **"And the altars that were on the top of the upper chamber of Ahaz."** [11]**Manasseh stood** the idol **up in the Sanctuary** itself, **as the verse states** (II Kings 21:7): **"And he set the carved**

שֶׁכָּתוּב בָּהֶן: 'וַיַּעַשׂ הָרַע בְּעֵינֵי ה' ' — [1]לֹא חַיִּין וְלֹא נִידּוֹנִין.

[2]"וְגַם דָּם נָקִי שָׁפַךְ מְנַשֶּׁה הַרְבֵּה מְאֹד, עַד אֲשֶׁר מִלֵּא אֶת יְרוּשָׁלַיִם פֶּה לָפֶה לְבַד מֵחַטָּאתוֹ אֲשֶׁר הֶחֱטִיא אֶת יְהוּדָה, לַעֲשׂוֹת הָרַע בְּעֵינֵי ה' ". [3]הָכָא תַּרְגִּימוּ: שֶׁהָרַג יְשַׁעְיָה. [4]בְּמַעֲרְבָא אָמְרִי: שֶׁעָשָׂה צֶלֶם מַשּׂאוֹי אֶלֶף בְּנֵי אָדָם, וּבְכָל יוֹם וָיוֹם הוֹרֵג (אֶת) כּוּלָּם.

[5]כְּמַאן אָזְלָא הָא דַּאֲמַר רַבָּה בַּר בַּר חָנָה: שְׁקוּלָה נְשָׁמָה שֶׁל צַדִּיק אֶחָד כְּנֶגֶד כָּל הָעוֹלָם כּוּלּוֹ? [6]כְּמַאן דַּאֲמַר: יְשַׁעְיָה הָרַג.

[7]כְּתִיב: "פֶּסֶל". [8]וּכְתִיב: "פְּסִילִים". [9]אָמַר רַבִּי יוֹחָנָן: בַּתְּחִלָּה עָשָׂה לוֹ פַּרְצוּף אֶחָד, וּלְבַסּוֹף עָשָׂה לוֹ אַרְבָּעָה פַּרְצוּפִים, כְּדֵי שֶׁתִּרְאֶה שְׁכִינָה וְתִכְעוֹס.

[10]אָחָז הֶעֱמִידוֹ בָּעֲלִיָּיה, שֶׁנֶּאֱמַר: "וְאֶת הַמִּזְבְּחוֹת אֲשֶׁר עַל הַגַּג עֲלִיַּת אָחָז וגו' ". [11]מְנַשֶּׁה הֶעֱמִידוֹ בַּהֵיכָל, שֶׁנֶּאֱמַר: "וַיָּשֶׂם אֶת פֶּסֶל

LITERAL TRANSLATION

regarding whom it is written: 'And he did evil in the eyes of the Lord' — [1]will not live but will not be sentenced.

[2]"Moreover Manasseh shed a great deal of innocent blood, until he filled Jerusalem from one end to another (lit., 'from mouth to mouth'); beside his sin which he made Judah sin, to do evil in the eyes of the Lord." [3]Here they explain: That he killed Isaiah. [4]In Eretz Israel (lit., "the West") they say: That he made an idol that was a load for a thousand people, and every day it would kill all of them.

[5]According to whose position was Rabbah bar Bar Ḥannah basing himself when he said: The soul of one righteous man is balanced against the entire world? [6]According to the one who said: He killed Isaiah.

[7]It is written: "A carved idol." [8]And it is written: "Carved idols." [9]Rabbi Yoḥanan said: At first he made it one face, and in the end he made it four faces, so that the Divine Presence would see and become angry.

[10]Ahaz stood it up in the upper chamber, as it is stated: "And the altars that were on the top of the upper chamber of Ahaz, etc." [11]Manasseh stood it up in the Sanctuary, as it is stated: "And he set the carved idol

RASHI

לא חיין — לא יחיו לעולם הבא עם הצדיקים, ואין נדונין נמי בגיהנם, ודוקא קאמר מלכי ישראל, אבל שלמה וצדקיה מבית דוד אתו, ואף על גב דכתיב בהו "ויעש הרע" — חיין הן לעתיד. **אחז ואחזיה** — ממלכי יהודה, וקים להו שהיו רשעים, ואמון ויהויקים לא חשיב, ואף על גב דהוו רשעים מאד, כדלקמן, בהנהו קים להו דחיין. **הורג את כולן** — שהיו נבקעין בכובד המשאוי. **כמאן דאמר שהרג ישעיה** — והא קאמר קרא "מלא את ירושלים פה לפה", שנשמתו של צדיק שקולה כמו שמלא את ירושלים חללים. **כתוב** — (במלכים) [דברי הימים ב' לג] "וישם את פסל הסמל אשר עשה בבית האלהים", וכתיב "והעמיד את האשרים והפסילים" בדברי הימים (שם). **ולבסוף עשה** — מנשה לאותו דמות ארבעה פרצופים. **כדי שתראה שכינה מכל צד** — שתכנס להיכל תראה פרצוף כנגדו ותכעוס.

LANGUAGE

פַּרְצוּף Face. This derives from the Greek πρόσωπον, *prosopon,* meaning "a face," also "a mask in the form of a face."

BACKGROUND

שְׁמָמִית **A gecko.**

Some authorities maintain that the שְׁמָמִית mentioned in the Bible and other ancient sources is this small nocturnal lizard, about fifteen cm. long and grey in color. Geckoes are found in hilly areas of the Mediterranean region, often inside houses. Geckoes can climb almost anywhere, on smooth walls and even on ceilings, and they live on insects, which they catch. The repulsive look of the gecko, in some people's opinion, has given rise to beliefs connected to it and to revulsion from it in ancient times as well. Thus to offer a gecko as a sacrifice on the altar was a deliberate and flagrant act of desecration.

TRANSLATION AND COMMENTARY

idol of the fertility goddess that he had made, in that house, of which the Lord said to David, and to Solomon his son, In this house, and in Jerusalem, which I have chosen from all the tribes of Israel, will I put My name forever." [1]**Amon** brought the idol **into the Holy of Holies, as the verse states** (Isaiah 28:20): **"For the bed is too short for spreading; and the covering too narrow to wrap oneself."** [2]**What is** the meaning of the words, **"For the bed is too short for spreading** [מֵהִשְׂתָּרֵעַ]"? [3]**Rabbi Shmuel bar Naḥmani said in the name of Rabbi Yonatan: For this bed is too narrow for two lovers to lie down together** [מִלְּהִשְׂתָּרֵר רֵעִים]. The Holy of Holies in the Temple cannot be used both for the service of God and the worship of idols. [4]**What is** the meaning of the words, **"And the covering** [וְהַמַּסֵּכָה] **too narrow** [צָרָה] to wrap oneself [כְּהִתְכַּנֵּס]"? [5]**Rabbi Shmuel bar Naḥmani said: When Rabbi Yonatan reached this verse, he would weep,** interpreting the verse as follows: [6]**"He about whom the verse states** (Psalms 33:7): **'He gathers** [כֹּנֵס] **the waters of the sea like a rampart' — shall an idol** [מַסֵּכָה] **become a second wife to him** [צָרָה]?"

אָחָז בִּטֵּל [7]The Gemara now lists the crimes of the later Kings of Judah: **Ahaz canceled the** divine **service** in the Temple, **and sealed** up **the Torah,** forbidding its study, [8]**as the verse states** (Isaiah 8:16): **"Bind up the testimony, seal the Torah among my disciples."** [9]**Manasseh cut out the Divine Names** found in the Torah scrolls, **and destroyed the altar.** [10]**Amon burned the Torah, and offered a gecko** as a sacrifice **on the altar.** [11]**Ahaz allowed forbidden sexual relationships.** [12]**Manasseh** followed this permissiveness and **had intercourse with his sister.** [13]**Amon** went further and **had intercourse with his mother, as the verse states** (II Chronicles 33:23): **"But Amon trespassed more and more."**

הָאֲשֵׁרָה אֲשֶׁר עָשָׂה בַּבַּיִת אֲשֶׁר אָמַר ה׳ אֶל דָּוִד וְאֶל שְׁלֹמֹה [בְנוֹ] בַּבַּיִת הַזֶּה וּבִירוּשָׁלַיִם אֲשֶׁר בָּחַרְתִּי מִכֹּל שִׁבְטֵי יִשְׂרָאֵל אָשִׂים אֶת שְׁמִי לְעוֹלָם״. [1]אָמוֹן הִכְנִיסוֹ לְבֵית קָדְשֵׁי הַקֳּדָשִׁים, שֶׁנֶּאֱמַר: ״כִּי קָצַר הַמַּצָּע מֵהִשְׂתָּרֵעַ וְהַמַּסֵּכָה צָרָה כְּהִתְכַּנֵּס״. [2]מַאי ״כִּי קָצַר הַמַּצָּע מֵהִשְׂתָּרֵעַ״? [3]אָמַר רַבִּי שְׁמוּאֵל בַּר נַחְמָנִי אָמַר רַבִּי יוֹנָתָן: [כִּי] קָצַר הַמַּצָּע זֶה מִלְּהִשְׂתָּרֵר עָלָיו שְׁנֵי רֵעִים כְּאֶחָד. [4]מַאי ״וְהַמַּסֵּכָה צָרָה וגו׳״? [5]אָמַר רַבִּי שְׁמוּאֵל בַּר נַחְמָנִי: רַבִּי יוֹנָתָן כִּי הֲוָה מָטֵי לְהַאי קְרָא הֲוָה קָא בָּכֵי: [6]״מִי שֶׁכָּתַב בּוֹ: ׳כֹּנֵס כַּנֵּד מֵי הַיָּם׳ — תֵּעָשֶׂה לוֹ מַסֵּכָה צָרָה״? [7][אָחָז בִּטֵּל אֶת הָעֲבוֹדָה] וְחָתַם אֶת הַתּוֹרָה, [8]שֶׁנֶּאֱמַר: ״צוֹר תְּעוּדָה, חֲתוֹם תּוֹרָה בְּלִמּוּדָי״. [9]מְנַשֶּׁה קָדַר אֶת הָאַזְכָּרוֹת, וְהָרַס אֶת הַמִּזְבֵּחַ. [10]אָמוֹן שָׂרַף אֶת הַתּוֹרָה, וְהֶעֱלָה שְׁמָמִית עַל גַּבֵּי הַמִּזְבֵּחַ. [11]אָחָז הִתִּיר אֶת הָעֶרְוָה. [12]מְנַשֶּׁה בָּא עַל אֲחוֹתוֹ. [13]אָמוֹן בָּא עַל אִמּוֹ, שֶׁנֶּאֱמַר: ״כִּי הוּא אָמוֹן הִרְבָּה אַשְׁמָה״.

LITERAL TRANSLATION

of the fertility goddess that he had made, in that house, of which the Lord said to David, and to Solomon his son, In this house, and in Jerusalem, which I have chosen from all the tribes of Israel, will I put My name forever." [1]Amon brought it into the Holy of Holies, as it is stated: "For the bed is too short for spreading out; and the covering too narrow to wrap oneself." [2]What is: "For the bed is too short for spreading out"? [3]Rabbi Shmuel bar Naḥmani said in the name of Rabbi Yonatan: For this bed is too narrow for two lovers to lie down together. [4]What is: "And the covering too narrow, etc."? [5]Rabbi Shmuel bar Naḥmani said: When Rabbi Yonatan reached this verse, he would weep: [6]"He about whom it is written: 'He gathers the waters of the sea like a rampart' — shall an idol become a second wife to him?"

[7][Ahaz canceled the service] and sealed the Torah, [8]as it is stated: "Bind up the testimony, seal the Torah among my disciples." [9]Manasseh cut out mentions [of the Divine Names], and destroyed the altar. [10]Amon burned the Torah, and offered a gecko on the altar. [11]Ahaz allowed forbidden sexual relationships. [12]Manasseh had intercourse with his sister. [13]Amon had intercourse with his mother, as it is stated: "But Amon increased guilt."

RASHI

מלהשתרר עליו שני רעים — שכינה ודמות הפרצוף. **מצע** — בית המקדש. **תעשה לו מסכה צרה** — כאשה שנעשית צרה לחברתה. **העלה שממית** — קורי עכביש, שבטל עבודה מכל וכל, עד שארגו עכביש קוריהן על גבי המזבח. **היתר** — נעשה לו כהיתר.

NOTES

הֶעֱלָה שְׁמָמִית **He offered a gecko.** The Hebrew word *semamit* has been variously identified as an unclean bird (perhaps a parrot) (*Ramah*); or else a type of monkey (*Rambam*); or else a type of lizard (see *Arukh*). In modern Hebrew it refers to the gecko. In any event, Amon offered an unclean creature as a sacrifice on the altar in order to show his scorn for God.

בָּא עַל אִמּוֹ **He had intercourse with his mother.** Amon's act of intercourse with his mother might have been derived from his name אָמוֹן, which alludes to אֵם, "mother." Free

[1]רַבִּי יוֹחָנָן וְרַבִּי אֶלְעָזָר. [2]חַד אָמַר: שֶׁשָּׂרַף אֶת הַתּוֹרָה. [3]וְחַד אָמַר: שֶׁבָּא עַל אִמּוֹ. [4]אָמְרָה לוֹ אִמּוֹ: ״כְּלוּם יֵשׁ לְךָ הֲנָאָה מִמָּקוֹם שֶׁיָּצָאתָ מִמֶּנּוּ״? [5]אָמַר לָהּ: ״כְּלוּם אֲנִי עוֹשֶׂה אֶלָּא לְהַכְעִיס אֶת בּוֹרְאִי״.

[6]כִּי אֲתָא יְהוֹיָקִים, אֲמַר: ״קַמָּאֵי לָא יָדְעִי לְאַרְגּוֹזֵי. [7]כְּלוּם אָנוּ צְרִיכִין אֶלָּא לְאוֹרוֹ — יֵשׁ לָנוּ זְהַב פַּרְוַיִים שֶׁאָנוּ מִשְׁתַּמְּשִׁין בּוֹ. [8]יִטּוֹל אוֹרוֹ״. [9]אָמְרוּ לוֹ: ״וַהֲלֹא כֶּסֶף וְזָהָב שֶׁלּוֹ הוּא, שֶׁנֶּאֱמַר: ׳לִי הַכֶּסֶף וְלִי הַזָּהָב נְאֻם ה׳ צְבָאוֹת׳״. [10]אָמַר לָהֶם: ״כְּבָר נְתָנוֹ לָנוּ, [11]שֶׁנֶּאֱמַר: ׳הַשָּׁמַיִם שָׁמַיִם לַה׳; וְהָאָרֶץ נָתַן לִבְנֵי אָדָם׳״.

[12]אֲמַר לֵיהּ רָבָא לְרַבָּה בַּר מָרִי: מִפְּנֵי מָה לֹא מָנוּ אֶת יְהוֹיָקִים? [13]מִשּׁוּם דִּכְתִיב בֵּיהּ: ״וְיֶתֶר דִּבְרֵי יְהוֹיָקִים וְתֹעֲבֹתָיו אֲשֶׁר עָשָׂה וְהַנִּמְצָא עָלָיו״. [14]מַאי ״וְהַנִּמְצָא עָלָיו״? [15]רַבִּי יוֹחָנָן וְרַבִּי אֶלְעָזָר. [16]חַד אָמַר: שֶׁחָקַק שֵׁם עֲבוֹדָה זָרָה עַל אַמָּתוֹ. [17]וְחַד אָמַר: שֶׁחָקַק שֵׁם שָׁמַיִם עַל אַמָּתוֹ.

LITERAL TRANSLATION

[1]Rabbi Yoḥanan and Rabbi Elazar [disagreed]. [2]One said: That he burned the Torah. [3]And one said: That he had intercourse with his mother. [4]His mother said to him: "Do you have pleasure from the place from which you came?" [5]He said to her: "I do it only in order to anger my Creator."

[6]When Jehoiakim came, he said: "The first ones did not know how to provoke. [7]We do not need His light — we have Paravim gold, which we use. [8]Let Him take His light!" [9]They said to him: "But surely the silver and gold is His, as it is stated: 'The silver is mine, and the gold is mine, says the Lord of hosts.'" [10]He said to them: "He has already given it to us, [11]as it is stated: 'The Heavens are the Heavens of the Lord; but He has given the Earth to the children of men.'"

[12]Rava said to Rabbah bar Mari: Why did they not count Jehoiakim? [13]Because it is written about him: "Now the rest of the acts of Jehoiakim, and his abominations which he did, and that which was found in him." [14]What is "and that which was found in him"? [15]Rabbi Yoḥanan and Rabbi Elazar [disagreed]. [16]One said: That he engraved the name of an idol on his penis. [17]And one said: That he engraved the name of Heaven on his penis.

TRANSLATION AND COMMENTARY

רַבִּי יוֹחָנָן [1]**Rabbi Yoḥanan and Rabbi Elazar disagreed** about the matter. [2]**One** of the Amoraim **said that** Amon **burned the Torah.** [3]**And the other** Amora **said that he had intercourse with his mother.** [4]Amon's **mother said to him: "Do you** actually **derive pleasure from the place you came from?"** [5]Amon **said to** his mother: **"I only do it in order to** provoke and **anger my Creator."**

כִּי אֲתָא יְהוֹיָקִים [6]It was related that **when Jehoiakim** ascended to the throne and **came** to power, **he said: "The** kings **who reigned before me did not know how to provoke** God as well as I do. Listen to how I provoke Him: [7]**We do not need the light** that God provides us through the sun, for **we have** magical **Paravim gold** which shines, and **which we can use** for illumination. [8]So **let Him take His light** from this world!" [9]The righteous people of his generation **said to him: "But surely** all **the silver and** all **the gold is** also **His, as the verse states** (Ḥaggai 2:8): **'The silver is mine, and the gold is mine, says the Lord of hosts.'"** [10]Jehoiakim **said to them:** "God **has already given us** whatever is found here on earth, [11]**as the verse states** (Psalms 115:16): **'The Heavens are the Heavens of the Lord; but He has given the Earth to the children of men.'"**

אֲמַר לֵיהּ [12]**Rava said to Rabbah bar Mari: Why was Jehoiakim not counted** among the kings who do not have a portion in the World to Come? [13]**The verse states about him** (II Chronicles 36:8): **"Now the rest of the acts of Jehoiakim, and his abominations which he did, and that which was found in him."** And the Rabbis explained: [14]**What is** meant by the words, **"and that which was found in him"**? What abomination was "found in him"? [15]**Rabbi Yoḥanan and Rabbi Elazar disagreed.** [16]**One** of the Amoraim **said:** This means **that** in his devotion to his idol, **he inscribed the name of the idol on his penis.** [17]**And the other** Amora **said:** This means **that** in his attempt to show his contempt for God, **he inscribed the name of Heaven on his penis.**

RASHI

ממקום שיצאת משם — מקום שאדם יוצא ממנו שבע הוא ממנו ואינו מתאוה להנאת אותו מקום. **קמאי לא ידעי לארגוזי** — מלכים ראשונים שלפנינו לא היו יודעים להכעיס המקום כמו שהוא חרף ואמר: כלום אנו צריכין אלא לאורו, שמאיר לנו השמש — יבא ויטול אורו. **שאנו משתמשין בו** — שמאיר ביותר. **אמרו לו** — בני דורו והלא כסף וכו׳, דבני דורו צדיקים היו כדאמרן: נסתכל בדורו של יהויקים ונתקררה דעתו. **מפני מה לא מנו את יהויקים** — בהדי הנך שאין להם חלק לעולם הבא. **משום דכתיב ויתר דברי יהויקים** — בתמיהה, משום דכתיב ביה רשע כזה לא מנאוהו. **שם עבודה זרה על אמתו** — מתוך שהיה אדוק בה. **שם שמים** — משום בזיון.

NOTES

permission was given here to interpret the name as alluding to the worst imaginable offenses (see *Margoliyot HaYam*).

TRANSLATION AND COMMENTARY

אֲמַר לֵיהּ [1]Rabbah bar Mari **said to** Rava: **Regarding** the **kings** who do not have a portion in the World to Come, **I did not hear** anything; but **regarding the ordinary people** who do not have a share in the World to Come, **I did hear** something. [2]**Why was Michah not counted** in that group? [3]**Because** he made **his bread available to** all the **travelers** who were guests in his house, **as it is stated: "All who pass by the Levites."**

וְעָבַר בַּיָּם צָרָה [4]The verse states (Zechariah 10:11): **"And He shall pass through the sea with affliction, and shall strike the waves in the sea."** [5]**Rabbi Yoḥanan said: This is** an allusion to **the idol** ("the affliction") **of Michah,** which he brought with him when the Israelites passed through the Red Sea during the Exodus from Egypt.

תַּנְיָא [6]**It was taught** in a Baraita: **"Rabbi Natan says: From Gerav** — where Michah lived and set up his idol — **to Shiloh** — the seat of the Sanctuary — **was** a distance of only **three miles.** [7]Consequently, **the smoke of the fire** rising from **the altar in the Sanctuary** in Shiloh **and the smoke of** the fire rising from the altar erected before **the idol of Michah were mingled.** [8]**The ministering Angels wanted to remove** Michah from the world. [9]But **the Holy One, blessed be He, said to them:** [10]**'Leave him, for** he makes **his bread available to** all the **travelers** who are guests in his house.' [11]**And because of this** — the idol set up by Michah — **the members** of the other tribes, who waged war against the tribe of Benjamin because of the affair **of the concubine in Gibeah, were punished.** Forty thousand of them died in battle before they finally emerged victorious. [12]**The Holy One, blessed be He, said to them: 'For My honor you did not** raise any **protests** or take any action to destroy the idol erected by Michah; [13]but **for the honor of flesh and blood, you protested** when the concubine of the Levite traveler who spent the night in Gibeah was abused!'"

LITERAL TRANSLATION

[1]He said to him: Regarding kings I did not hear; regarding ordinary people I heard. [2]Why did they not count Michah? [3]Because his bread was available for travelers, as it is stated: "All who pass by the Levites."

[4]"And He shall pass through the sea with affliction, and shall strike the waves in the sea." [5]Rabbi Yoḥanan said: This is the idol of Michah.

[6]It was taught: "Rabbi Natan says: From Gerav to Shiloh it is three miles. [7]And the smoke of the fire on the altar in the Sanctuary and the smoke from the idol of Michah mingled. [8]The ministering Angels wanted to remove him. [9]The Holy One, blessed be He, said to them: [10]'Leave him, for his bread is found for travelers.' [11]And because of this thing, the people of the concubine in Gibeah were punished. [12]The Holy One, blessed be He, said to them: 'For My honor you did not protest; [13]for the honor of flesh and blood you protested!'"

[1]אֲמַר לֵיהּ: בִּמְלָכִים לֹא שָׁמַעְתִּי, בְּהֶדְיוֹטוֹת שָׁמַעְתִּי. [2]מִפְּנֵי מָה לֹא מָנוּ אֶת מִיכָה? [3]מִפְּנֵי שֶׁפִּתּוֹ מְצוּיָה לְעוֹבְרֵי דְרָכִים, שֶׁנֶּאֱמַר: "כָּל הָעוֹבֵר וְשָׁב אֶל הַלְוִיִּם".

[4]"וְעָבַר בַּיָּם צָרָה, וְהִכָּה בַיָּם גַּלִּים". [5]אָמַר רַבִּי יוֹחָנָן: זֶה פִּסְלוֹ שֶׁל מִיכָה.

[6]תַּנְיָא: "רַבִּי נָתָן אוֹמֵר: מִגָּרֵב לְשִׁילֹה שְׁלֹשָׁה מִילִין. [7]וְהָיָה עֲשַׁן הַמַּעֲרָכָה וַעֲשַׁן פֶּסֶל מִיכָה מִתְעָרְבִין זֶה בָּזֶה. [8]בִּקְּשׁוּ מַלְאֲכֵי הַשָּׁרֵת לְדוֹחֲפוֹ. [9]אָמַר לָהֶן הַקָּדוֹשׁ בָּרוּךְ הוּא: [10]'הַנִּיחוּ לוֹ, שֶׁפִּתּוֹ מְצוּיָה לְעוֹבְרֵי דְרָכִים'. [11]וְעַל דָּבָר זֶה נֶעֶנְשׁוּ אַנְשֵׁי פִּלֶגֶשׁ בְּגִבְעָה. [12]אָמַר לָהֶן הַקָּדוֹשׁ בָּרוּךְ הוּא: 'בִּכְבוֹדִי לֹא מְחִיתֶם; [13]עַל כְּבוֹדוֹ שֶׁל בָּשָׂר וָדָם מְחִיתֶם'"!

RASHI

במלכים לא שמעתי — מפני מה לא מנו את יהויקים. **בהדיוטות שמעתי** — מפני מה לא מנו מיכה בהדי ארבעה הדיוטות דמתניתין. **פתו מצויה לעוברי דרכים** — שהיו כל העולם מתארחין אצלו, כדכתיב (במקרא) "כל העובר ושב אל הלוים" — זה מיכה. **זה פסלו של מיכה** — כשכתב משה את השם והשליכו על נילוס להעלות ארונו של יוסף, בא מיכה ונטלו בהחבא, והיינו דכתיב "ועבר בים צרה" — כשהעביר הקדוש ברוך הוא לישראל עבר מיכה עמהם שבידו השם — לעשות העגל, לישנא אחרינא: מיכה עשה פסל והביאו עמו כשעברו ישראל הים. **גרב** — מקומו של מיכה בגרב הוה פסלו של מיכה קבוע, ובשילה היה המשכן. **לדוחפו** — למיכה. **ועל דבר זה** — על פסלו של מיכה שלא מיחו ישראל בידו נענשו אנשי פילגש בגבעה, שנפלו ביד בנימין והרגו מהם ארבעים אלף.

NOTES

הָעוֹבֵר וְשָׁב אֶל הַלְוִיִּם **All who pass by the Levites.** These words are not a Biblical verse. They appear to summarize the incident involving Michah, for the Bible recounts how guests would arrive at Michah's house (the Levite boy, the Dan tribesmen), and Michah would host them all.

בִּקְּשׁוּ לְדוֹחֲפוֹ **They wanted to remove him.** It has been suggested that the ministering Angels tried to push away the smoke rising from the altar erected before Michah's idol, to prevent it from mingling with the smoke rising from the altar at Shiloh.

[1]אָמַר רַבִּי יוֹחָנָן מִשּׁוּם רַבִּי יוֹסֵי בֶּן קִסְמָא: גְּדוֹלָה לְגִימָה, [2]שֶׁהִרְחִיקָה שְׁתֵּי מִשְׁפָּחוֹת מִיִּשְׂרָאֵל, שֶׁנֶּאֱמַר: ״עַל דְּבַר אֲשֶׁר לֹא קִדְּמוּ אֶתְכֶם בַּלֶּחֶם וּבַמַּיִם״.

[3]וְרַבִּי יוֹחָנָן דִּידֵיהּ אָמַר: מַרְחֶקֶת אֶת הַקְּרוֹבִים, וּמְקָרֶבֶת אֶת הָרְחוֹקִים, וּמַעֲלֶמֶת עֵינַיִם מִן הָרְשָׁעִים, וּמַשְׁרָה שְׁכִינָה עַל נְבִיאֵי הַבַּעַל, [4]וְשִׁגְגָתוֹ עוֹלָה זָדוֹן. [5]מַרְחֶקֶת אֶת הַקְּרוֹבִים — [104A] מֵעַמּוֹן וּמוֹאָב. [6]וּמְקָרֶבֶת אֶת הָרְחוֹקִים — מִיִּתְרוֹ. [7]דְּאָמַר רַבִּי יוֹחָנָן: בִּשְׂכַר: ״קִרְאֶן לוֹ, וְיֹאכַל לָחֶם״, [8]זָכוּ בְּנֵי בָנָיו וְיָשְׁבוּ בְּלִשְׁכַּת הַגָּזִית, [9]שֶׁנֶּאֱמַר: ״וּמִשְׁפְּחוֹת סוֹפְרִים יֹשְׁבֵי יַעְבֵּץ; תִּרְעָתִים שִׁמְעָתִים שׂוּכָתִים הֵמָּה הַקִּינִים הַבָּאִים מֵחַמַּת אֲבִי בֵית רֵכָב״. [10]וּכְתִיב

LITERAL TRANSLATION

[1]Rabbi Yoḥanan said in the name of Rabbi Yose ben Kisma: A mouthful [of food] is great, [2]for it estranged two families from Israel, as it is stated: "Because they met you not with bread and with water."

[3]And Rabbi Yoḥanan himself said: It estranges those who are near, and draws close those who are far, and averts the eyes from the wicked, and causes the Divine Presence to rest upon the Prophets of Baal, [4]and its inadvertent violation is regarded as an intentional violation. [5]It estranges those who are near — [104A] from Amon and Moab. [6]And draws close those who are far — from Jethro. [7]For Rabbi Yoḥanan said: In reward for: "Call him, that he may eat bread," [8]the sons of his sons merit to sit in the Chamber of Hewn Stone, [9]as it is stated: "And the families of the scribes who dwelt at Jabez; the Tiratuites, the Shimeathites, the Sucathites. These were the Kenites who came of Ḥamat, the father of the house of Rechav." [10]And it is written

TRANSLATION AND COMMENTARY

אָמַר רַבִּי יוֹחָנָן [1]**Rabbi Yoḥanan said in the name of Rabbi Yose ben Kisma:** Offering guests **refreshments is of great** importance, [2]**for** refusing to do so **estranged two families** of people **from Israel, as the verse states** (Deuteronomy 23:4-5): "An Ammonite or a Moabite shall not enter into the congregation of the Lord...**because they met you not with bread and with water.**"

וְרַבִּי יוֹחָנָן [3]**And Rabbi Yoḥanan himself said:** Offering or refusing to offer refreshments may **estrange those who are near, or draw close those who are far, or avert the eyes** of God, as it were, **from the wicked** so that they are not punished in proportion to the rest of their actions, **or cause the Divine Presence to rest upon the Prophets of Baal.** [4]**The inadvertent** refusal of refreshments **may** sometimes even **be regarded as intentional,** and punished accordingly. [5]The Gemara explains: The refusal to offer refreshments may **estrange those who are near** — [104A] as we see **from** the nations of **Amon and Moab.** As descendants of the sons of Abraham's nephew Lot, the peoples of Amon and Moab were once close to Israel, but because they did not meet Israel with bread or water on their way from Egypt, they were banned from marrying into the Jewish people. [6]Offering refreshments may also **draw close those who are far,** as we see **from Jethro.** [7]**For Rabbi Yoḥanan said: In reward for** what Jethro said to his daughters regarding Moses (Exodus 2:20): **"Call him, that he may eat bread,"** [8]**his descendants merited to sit** as members of the Sanhedrin which met **in the Chamber of Hewn Stone,** [9]**as the verse states** (I Chronicles 2:55): **"And the families of the scribes who dwelt at Jabez; the Tirathites, the Shimeathites, the Sucathites. These were the Kenites who came of Ḥamat, the father of the house of Rechab."** [10]**And** elsewhere **it is explained**

RASHI

לגימה — אכילה שמאכילין אורחים. **שתי משפחות** — עמון ומואב, שלפי שלא קדמו ישראל בלחם ובמים נכתב שלא יבאו בקהל. **מעלמת עינים מן הרשעים** — מעלמת מעיני המקום שלא להביט ברשעו לשלם לו כדרכו הרעה, אלא עושה כאילו אינו רואה במעשיו. **עמון ומואב** — קרובין לישראל, שבאו מלוט בן אחי אברהם, ורחקן המקום שלא יבאו בקהל, לישנא אחרינא: קרובין ממש ליכא למימר, דהא מדין מבני קטורה היו בני אברהם וקרובים היו בני מדין לישראל יותר מעמון ומואב, שהם בני אברהם, אלא עמון ומואב שכנים וקרובים היו לארץ ישראל, ומדין רחוקים להם היו. **וישבו בלשכת הגזית** — ממשפחות סופרים, והאי קרא מפרש ליה כולו בסיפרי בפרשת ״ויאמר משה לחובב״. **המה הקינים הבאים מחמת אבי בית רכב** — וקינים אלו בניו של יתרו, דכתיב ״ובני קיני חותן משה״, ובניו של יתרו הן הן בניו של רכב, דכתיב ״הקינים הבאים מחמת אבי בית רכב״ וכתיב (ירמיהו לה) ״ולבית הרכבים אמר ירמיהו כי כה אמר ה׳ [וגו׳] יען אשר שמעתם [על] מצות [יהונדב] אביכם [וגו׳] לא יכרת איש ליונדב בן רכב [עומד] לפני כל הימים״ ואמרינן בסיפרי

NOTES

וְיָשְׁבוּ בְּלִשְׁכַּת הַגָּזִית **To sit in the Chamber of Hewn Stone.** The Midrash deduces that Jethro's descendants served as members of the Sanhedrin, which sat in the Chamber of Hewn Stone, from the word Tirathites [תִּרְעָתִים, *Tir'atim*], which it interprets to mean, "the elders who sit at the gate [תַּרְעָא, in Aramaic] to judge the people." Some suggest that the word תִּרְעָתִים refers to "two gates," for the Chamber of Hewn Stone had two gates, one leading to a sacred area, the other leading to a secular area (*Margoliyot HaYam*).

TRANSLATION AND COMMENTARY

who the Kenites were (Judges 1:16): **"And the children of the Keni, Moses's father-in-law, went up from the city of palm trees with the children of Judah into the wilderness of Judah, which lies to the south of Arad; and he went and dwelt among the people."** The Kenites — descendants of Moses's father-in-law Jethro — served as scribes — members of the Sanhedrin which met in the Chamber of Hewn stone. [1]Offering refreshments may also **avert the eyes** of God, as it were, **from the wicked** so that they will not be punished as much as they deserve, as we see **from Michah,** whose hospitality saved him from punishment for erecting an idol. [2]Offering refreshments may also **cause the Divine Presence to rest upon the Prophets of Baal,** as we see **from the friend of Ido the Prophet.** When Ido the Prophet was sent by God to Jeroboam to prophesy about the destruction of the altar in Beth-El, a false Prophet tricked him into returning with him to his house to eat bread and drink water, contrary to God's explicit instructions. The false Prophet's hospitality caused a true prophetic spirit to rest upon him, [3]**as the verse states** (I Kings 13:20): **"And it happened, as they sat at the table, that the word of the Lord came to the Prophet that brought him back."** [4]**The inadvertent** refusal of refreshments **may** sometimes even **be regarded as intentional,** and punished accordingly, **as Rav Yehudah said in the name of Rav:** [5]**Had Jonathan sent David off with two loaves of bread** when he fled from Saul, David would not have had to seek food in Nob, and the people of **Nob, the city of the priests, would not have been slain, Doeg the Edomite would not have been displaced** from the World to Come for his role in the slaughter, **and Saul and his three sons would not have been slain** for their part in the crime. Even though Jonathan's failure to send David off with ample provisions was inadvertent, this lapse was treated as intentional, and led to dire results.

הָתָם: "וּבְנֵי קֵינִי חֹתֵן מֹשֶׁה עָלוּ מֵעִיר הַתְּמָרִים אֶת בְּנֵי יְהוּדָה מִדְבַּר יְהוּדָה אֲשֶׁר בְּנֶגֶב עֲרָד וַיֵּלֶךְ וַיֵּשֶׁב אֶת הָעָם". [1]וּמַעְלֶמֶת עֵינַיִם מִן הָרְשָׁעִים — מִמִּיכָה. [2]וּמַשְׁרָה שְׁכִינָה עַל נְבִיאֵי הַבַּעַל — מֵחֲבֵירוֹ שֶׁל עִדּוֹ הַנָּבִיא, [3]דִּכְתִיב: "וַיְהִי הֵם יֹשְׁבִים אֶל הַשֻּׁלְחָן וַיְהִי דְּבַר ה׳ אֶל הַנָּבִיא אֲשֶׁר הֱשִׁיבוֹ". [4]וְשִׁגְגָתָהּ עוֹלָה זָדוֹן, דְּאָמַר רַב יְהוּדָה אָמַר רַב: [5]אִלְמָלֵי הִלְוָוהוּ יְהוֹנָתָן לְדָוִד שְׁתֵּי כִּכְּרוֹת לֶחֶם לֹא נֶהֶרְגָה נוֹב עִיר הַכֹּהֲנִים, וְלֹא נִטְרַד דּוֹאֵג הָאֲדֹמִי, וְלֹא נֶהֱרַג שָׁאוּל וּשְׁלֹשֶׁת בָּנָיו.

[6]וּמִפְּנֵי מָה לֹא מָנוּ אֶת אָחָז? [7]אָמַר רַבִּי יִרְמְיָה בַּר אַבָּא:

LITERAL TRANSLATION

there: "And the children of the Keni, Moses's father-in-law, went up from the city of palm trees with the children of Judah into the wilderness of Judah, which lies to the south of Arad; and he went and dwelt among the people." [1]And averts the eyes from the wicked — from Michah. [2]And causes the Divine Presence to rest upon the Prophets of Baal — from the friend of Ido the Prophet, [3]as it is written: "And it happened, as they sat at the table, that the word of the Lord came to the Prophet that brought him back." [4]And its inadvertent violation is regarded as an intentional violation, as Rav Yehudah said in the name of Rav: [5]Had Jonathan sent David off with two loaves of bread, [the people of] Nob, the city of the priests, would not have been slain, and Doeg the Edomite would not have been displaced, and Saul and his three sons would not have been slain.

[6]And why did they not count Ahaz? [7]Rabbi Yirmeyah bar Abba said:

RASHI

אפשר נכרים הם ונכנסין להיכל — והרי כל ישראל לא נכנסו להיכל — אלא שהיו יושבין בסנהדרין ומורין בדברי תורה, מפי רבי. ממיכה — דאמרינן לעיל: הניחו לו, שפתו מצויה לעוברי דרכים. **ומשרה שכינה על נביאי הבעל מחברו של עדו הנביא** — דעדו הנביא נתנבא על מזבח בית אל שיחרב מפני שהעמיד בו ירבעם צלמים, דכתיב (במלכים א׳ יג) "והנה איש האלהים בא מיהודה וגו׳ ויאמר מזבח מזבח" ומפרש בסדר עולם דהיינו עדו הנביא, ובא נביא השקר והטעהו לעדו והשיבו לבית אל והעבירו על מצות הקדוש ברוך הוא שאמר לו לא תשוב לבית אל, והאכילו, ובזכות שהאכילו שרתה עליו שכינה שנאמר ויהי דבר ה׳ אל האיש הנביא אשר השיבו" להאכילו אצלו. **ושגגתה עולה זדון** — שהרי מצינו ביהונתן ששגג ולא הלוהו לדוד שתי ככרות ונענש, דאמר רב יהודה וכו׳. **לווהו** — לשון לויה. **לא נהרגה נוב** — שלא היה צריך דוד לשאול לחם מכהני נוב, ולא היה דואג מלשין עליהם. **ולא היה שאול נהרג** — על אותו עון.

וּמִפְּנֵי מָה [6]The Gemara asks: **Why was** the wicked King **Ahaz not counted** among the kings who are denied a portion in the World to Come? [7]**Rabbi Yirmeyah bar Abba said: Because he was cast between**

NOTES

וְלֹא נֶהֱרַג שָׁאוּל **And Saul would not have been slain.** Although Saul was liable for other offenses, those crimes would only have caused him to forfeit his kingship. The death sentence was only imposed upon Saul for his part in the killing of the priests at Nob (*Maharsha*).

TRANSLATION AND COMMENTARY

two righteous kings, **between** his father **Jotham and** his son **Hezekiah,** whose good deeds protected him.

רַב יוֹסֵף אָמַר [1]**Rav Yosef said:** Ahaz was not counted among the kings who are denied a portion in the World to Come, **because he displayed shame before** the Prophet **Isaiah,** [2]**as the verse states** (Isaiah 7:3): **"Then said the Lord to Isaiah, Go out now to meet Ahaz, you, and She'ar-jashub your son, at the end of the aqueduct of the upper pool in the highway of the washer's** [*koves*] **field."** [3]**What is** meant by the word ***koves***? [4]**There are** those **who say** that Ahaz **hid** [*kavash*] **his face and passed by** Isaiah in shame. [5]**And there are** others **who say** that Ahaz **inverted a washer's** [*koves*] **trough over his head** as he **passed by** Isaiah, so that the Prophet would not recognize him.

מִפְּנֵי מָה [6]Similarly, the Gemara asks: **Why was** the wicked king **Amon not counted** among the kings who are denied a portion in the World to Come? [7]**Because of the honor of** his righteous son, **Josiah,** whose merits saved his father.

מְנַשֶּׁה נַמִּי [8]The Gemara comments: If so, then **Manasseh, too, should not have been counted** among the kings who are denied a portion in the World to Come, **because of the honor of** his righteous father, **Hezekiah!**

בְּרָא מְזַכֵּי אַבָּא [9]The Gemara explains: A righteous **son** may **clear his** wicked **father,** and save him from punishment, but **a** righteous **father cannot clear his** wicked **son,** and spare him of the same, [10]**as the verse states** (Deuteronomy 32:39): **"No one saves from My hand"** — [11]**Abraham cannot save Ishmael** from divine punishment, **nor can Isaac save Esau.**

מִפְּנֵי שֶׁמּוּטָּל בֵּין שְׁנֵי צַדִּיקִים, בֵּין יוֹתָם לְחִזְקִיָּהוּ.
[1]רַב יוֹסֵף אָמַר: מִפְּנֵי שֶׁהָיָה לוֹ בֹּשֶׁת פָּנִים מִישַׁעְיָהוּ, [2]שֶׁנֶּאֱמַר: ״וַיֹּאמֶר ה׳ אֶל יְשַׁעְיָהוּ צֵא נָא לִקְרַאת אָחָז אַתָּה וּשְׁאָר יָשׁוּב בְּנֶךָ אֶל קְצֵה תְּעָלַת הַבְּרֵכָה הָעֶלְיוֹנָה אֶל מְסִלַּת שְׂדֵה כוֹבֵס״. [3]מַאי כּוֹבֵס? [4]אִיכָּא דְּאָמְרִי: דְּכַבְשִׁינְהוּ לְאַפֵּיהּ וַחֲלַף. [5]וְאִיכָּא דְּאָמְרִי: אוּכְלָא דְּקַצְרֵי סְחַף אַרֵישֵׁיהּ וַחֲלַף.
[6]מִפְּנֵי מָה לֹא מָנוּ אֶת אָמוֹן? [7]מִפְּנֵי כְבוֹדוֹ שֶׁל יֹאשִׁיָּהוּ.
[8]מְנַשֶּׁה נַמִּי לָא נִמְנֵי, מִפְּנֵי כְבוֹדוֹ שֶׁל חִזְקִיָּהוּ!
[9]בְּרָא מְזַכֵּי אַבָּא; אַבָּא לָא מְזַכֵּי בְּרָא, [10]דִּכְתִיב: ״וְאֵין מִיָּדִי מַצִּיל״, [11]אֵין אַבְרָהָם מַצִּיל אֶת יִשְׁמָעֵאל, אֵין יִצְחָק מַצִּיל אֶת עֵשָׂו.

LITERAL TRANSLATION

Because he was cast between two righteous people, between Jotham and Hezekiah.

[1]Rav Yosef said: Because he had shame before Isaiah, [2]as it is stated: "Then said the Lord to Isaiah, Go out now to meet Ahaz, you, and She'ar-jashub your son, at the end of the aqueduct of the upper pool in the highway of the washer's [*koves*] field." [3]What is *koves*? [4]There are [those] who say: He hid his face and passed by. [5]And there are [those] who say: He inverted a washer's trough over his head and passed by.

[6]Why did they not count Amon? [7]Because of the honor of Josiah.

[8]Manasseh, too, they should not have counted because of the honor of Hezekiah!

[9]A son clears [his] father; a father does not clear [his] son, [10]as it is written: "No one saves from my hand" — [11]Abraham cannot save Ishmael, Isaac cannot save Esau.

RASHI

שמוטל — לאביו יותם ובנו חזקיה, ושאר מישראל ששבו להיות בניך ותלמידיך, וכל מי שישוב לביתך דהיינו תלמידיו, כדמתרגמינן ״ושאר דלא חטאו ודתבו חטיאי תלמידוהי״. מאי כובס דכבשינהו לאפיה — שכבש את פניו והיה מתבייש מפני ישעיה. כובס — כמו כובש. אוכלא דקצרי סחף ארישיה — כלי מנוקב של כובסין שמזלפין בו מים על הבגדים ואותו כלי הפך אחז על ראשו כדי שלא יכירו ישעיה, שהיה מתבייש [ממנו]. יאשיהו — בן אמון. חזקיהו — אבי מנשה. [ברא מזכה אבא וכו׳] — יאשיה מזכה אמון אביו, ולא חזקיה מנשה בנו, דכתיב ״אין מידי מציל״ ודרשינן ליה בהגדה: אין אברהם מציל וכו׳.

NOTES

מַאי כּוֹבֵס? What is *koves*? The question appears to be: What was the king doing in a despicable place like a washer's field? The Gemara answers that the term *koves* should be understood as an allusion to the shame that Ahaz displayed before the Prophet Isaiah.

בְּרָא מְזַכֵּי אַבָּא A son clears his father. A righteous son may clear his wicked father, and save him from punishment, because his father must have guided him in that direction, or at least not hindered him from taking that path. Thus, the father may take a portion of the credit. But if the son of a righteous man turns wicked, his righteous father cannot clear him. Surely his father educated him properly, yet he turned wicked (*Maharsha*).

The question has been raised: Why does the Gemara say here that a righteous father cannot clear his wicked son, when other sources speak of *zekhut avot,* "the merits of fathers," which can be of assistance to their descendants? It has been suggested that "the merits of fathers" only helps their descendants achieve success in this world. But regarding the World to Come, the wicked father of a righteous son may share in the merits of his son, for it was he who brought him to the world; but a righteous father cannot help his wicked son (see *Be'er Sheva*).

[1]הָשְׁתָּא דְּאָתֵית לְהָכִי — אָחָז נַמִי לָא אִימְנֵי מִשּׁוּם כְּבוֹדוֹ שֶׁל חִזְקִיָּהוּ.

[2]וּמִפְּנֵי מָה לֹא מָנוּ אֶת יְהוֹיָקִים? [3]מִשּׁוּם דְּרַבִּי חִיָּיא בְּרַבִּי אֲבוּיָה, דְּאָמַר רַבִּי חִיָּיא בְּרַבִּי אֲבוּיָה: [4]כְּתִיב עַל גּוּלְגָּלְתּוֹ [שֶׁל] יְהוֹיָקִים: ״זֹאת וְעוֹד אַחֶרֶת״. [5]זְקֵינוֹ דְּרַבִּי פְּרִידָא אַשְׁכַּח גּוּלְגָּלְתָּא דַּהֲוָה קָא שַׁדְיָא בְּשַׁעֲרֵי יְרוּשָׁלַיִם, [6]וּכְתִיב בָּהּ: ״זֹאת וְעוֹד אַחֶרֶת״. [7]קְבָרָהּ, וְלָא אִיקַּבְּרָא; [8]קְבָרָהּ, וְלָא אִיקַּבְּרָא. [9]אֲמַר: גּוּלְגָּלְתּוֹ שֶׁל יְהוֹיָקִים הִיא, דִּכְתִיב בֵּיהּ: ״קְבוּרַת חֲמוֹר יִקָּבֵר סָחוֹב וְהַשְׁלֵךְ וגו׳״. [10]אָמַר: מַלְכָּא הוּא, וְלָא אִיכַּשַּׁר לְזַלְזוֹלֵי בֵּיהּ. [11]כְּרָכָהּ בְּשִׁירָאֵי, וְאוֹתְבָהּ בְּסִיפְתָּא. [12]חֲזֵיתָא דְּבֵיתְהוּ. [13]סְבָרָא: הָא דְּאִיתְּתָא קַמַּיְיתָא הֲוָה, דְּהָא לָא קָא מִנְשֵׁי לָהּ. [14]שְׁגַרָא תַּנּוּרָא וְקַלְתָּהּ. [15]הַיְינוּ דִּכְתִיב: ״זֹאת, וְעוֹד אַחֶרֶת״.

[16]תַּנְיָא: ״אָמַר רַבִּי שִׁמְעוֹן בֶּן אֶלְעָזָר: [17]בִּשְׁבִיל ׳וְהַטּוֹב בְּעֵינֶיךָ עָשִׂיתִי׳, [18]׳מָה אוֹת׳?

LITERAL TRANSLATION

[1]Now that you have come to this — Ahaz, too, was not counted because of the honor of Hezekiah.

[2]And why did they not count Jehoiakim? [3]Because of that of Rabbi Ḥiyya the son of Rabbi Avuyah, for Rabbi Ḥiyya the son of Rabbi Avuyah said: [4]It is written on Jehoiakim's skull: "This and yet another." [5]Rabbi Perida's grandfather found a skull that had been cast aside at the gates of Jerusalem, [6]and it was written on it: "This, and yet another." [7]He buried it, but it would not be buried; [8]he buried it, but it would not be buried. [9]He said: This is the skull of Jehoiakim, about whom it is written: "He shall be buried with the burial of an ass, drawn and cast forth." [10]He said: He was the king, and it is not proper to belittle him. [11]He wrapped it in silk, and placed it in a cupboard. [12]His wife saw [it]. [13]She thought: This is from his first wife, whom he cannot forget. [14]She heated the oven, and burned it. [15]That is what was written: "This, and yet another."

[16]It was taught: "Rabbi Shimon ben Elazar said: [17]Because of 'And I have done what is good in Your eyes,' [18]'What shall be the sign?'

TRANSLATION AND COMMENTARY

הָשְׁתָּא [1]The Gemara asks: **Now that you have come to this** explanation, you can **also** say that the wicked King **Ahaz was not denied** a portion in the World to Come, **because of the honor of** his righteous son, **Hezekiah.**

וּמִפְּנֵי מָה [2]The Gemara asks: **Why was** the wicked King **Jehoiakim not denied** a share in the World to Come? [3]**Because of what Rabbi Ḥiyya the son of Rabbi Avuyah** said, **for Rabbi Ḥiyya the son of Rabbi Avuyah said:** The following words **were inscribed on Jehoiakim's skull:** [4]**"This and yet another,"** alluding to the fact that Jehoiakim would suffer a double punishment. [5]**Rabbi Perida's grandfather** — Rabbi Ḥiyya bar Avuyah — once **found a skull that had been cast aside at the gates of Jerusalem,** [6]**and on it were inscribed** the words: **"This, and yet another."** [7]Out of respect for the dead, **he buried** the skull, **but** no sooner had he buried it than **it rose** once **again** from the grave. [8]**He** tried again to **bury** the skull, **but again it came up** from the grave. [9]Rabbi Ḥiyya bar Avuyah **said** to himself: **This must be the skull of Jehoiakim, about whom the verse states** (Jeremiah 22:19): **"He shall be buried with the burial of an ass, drawn and cast forth** beyond the gates of Jerusalem." [10]**He said:** As evil as he may have been, Jehoiakim **was** nevertheless **the king, and it is not proper that he should be degraded** in this manner. [11]And so he took the skull home with him, **wrapped it in silk, and placed it in a cupboard.** [12]**His wife saw** the skull. [13]**She thought** to herself: Surely **that** skull **must belong to** my husband's **first wife, whom he cannot forget.** [14]Enraged, she **heated the oven, and burned** the skull. When Rabbi Ḥiyya bar Avuyah came home, and saw what his wife had done, he said: [15]Thus was fulfilled **that which was inscribed on** the skull: **"This, and yet another,"** for Jehoiakim's skull was cast out of the grave, and then consumed by fire. Because he was deprived of a proper burial, some of his sins were forgiven, and he kept his portion in the World to Come.

תַּנְיָא [16]**It was taught** in a Baraita: **"Rabbi Shimon ben Elazar said:** [17]**Because** Hezekiah boasted (II Kings 20:3): **'And I have done what is good in Your eyes,'** he came to say (II Kings 20:8): [18]**'What shall be the sign** that the Lord will heal me?' One misdeed leads to another. In this case, conceit led to his asking God for a sign.

RASHI

השתא דאתית להכי — דברא מזכה לאבא. **אחז נמי** — לא תימא דכבשינהו [לאפיה], אלא מפני כבודו של חזקיה לא מנאוהו. **מפני מה לא מנו את יהויקים** — באותן שאין להם חלק [לעולם הבא]. **משום דרבי חייא בר אבויה** — שנתכפר על שלא ניתן לקבורה, וכל הני מפני מה לא מנו לא בעי אלא מהנך דהוו רשעים גמורים, כדחשיבנא להו לעיל: אחז חתם את התורה וכו׳. [**זאת ועוד כו׳** — נקמה נעשית בה כבר, ועוד אחרת תעשה בה]. **פרידא** — כך שמו. **סיפתא** = ארגז. **בשביל הטוב מה אות** — בשביל חזקיה [ששיבח את] עצמו, דאמר ״הטוב בעיניך עשיתי״ גרם לו שאמר ״מה אות״ כי אעלה בית ה׳, ששאל אות מהקדוש ברוך הוא, שעבירה גוררת עבירה.

[1]בִּשְׁבִיל ׳מָה אוֹת׳? נָכְרִים אָכְלוּ עַל שׁוּלְחָנוֹ. [2]בִּשְׁבִיל שֶׁנָּכְרִים אָכְלוּ עַל שׁוּלְחָנוֹ, גָּרַם גָּלוּת לְבָנָיו״.

[3]מְסַיֵּיעַ לֵיהּ לְחִזְקִיָּה, דְּאָמַר חִזְקִיָּה: כָּל הַמְזַמֵּן עוֹבֵד עֲבוֹדָה זָרָה לְתוֹךְ בֵּיתוֹ וּמְשַׁמֵּשׁ עָלָיו, גּוֹרֵם גָּלוּת לְבָנָיו, [4]שֶׁנֶּאֱמַר: ״וּמִבָּנֶיךָ אֲשֶׁר יֵצְאוּ מִמְּךָ [אֲשֶׁר תּוֹלִיד] יִקָּחוּ וְהָיוּ סָרִיסִים בְּהֵיכַל מֶלֶךְ בָּבֶל״.

[5]״וַיִּשְׂמַח עֲלֵיהֶם חִזְקִיָּהוּ וַיַּרְאֵם אֶת בֵּית נְכֹתֹה אֶת הַכֶּסֶף וְאֶת הַזָּהָב וְאֶת הַבְּשָׂמִים וְאֵת הַשֶּׁמֶן הַטּוֹב וגו׳ ״. [6]אָמַר רַב: מַאי בֵּית נְכֹתֹה? [7]אִשְׁתּוֹ הִשְׁקְתָה עֲלֵיהֶם. [8]וּשְׁמוּאֵל אָמַר: בֵּית גְּנָזָיו הֶרְאָה לָהֶם. [9]וְרַבִּי יוֹחָנָן אָמַר: זַיִן אוֹכֵל זַיִן הֶרְאָה לָהֶן.

[10]״אֵיכָה יָשְׁבָה בָדָד״. [11]אָמַר רָבָא אָמַר רַבִּי יוֹחָנָן: מִפְּנֵי מָה לָקוּ יִשְׂרָאֵל בְּאֵיכָה? [12]מִפְּנֵי

LITERAL TRANSLATION

[1]Because of 'What shall be the sign?' Gentiles ate at his table. [2]Because Gentiles ate at his table, he brought exile to his sons."

[3]This supports Ḥizkiyah, for Ḥizkiyah said: Whoever invites an idol worshiper into his house and serves him, brings exile to his sons, [4]as it is stated: "And from your sons who shall issue from you, whom you shall beget, will be taken away; and they shall be eunuchs in the palace of the King of Babylonia."

[5]"And Hezekiah was glad of them, and showed them his treasure house [*bet nekhoto*], the silver, and the gold, and the spices, and the precious ointment, etc." [6]Rav said: What is *bet nekhoto*? [7]He had his wife pour for them. [8]And Shmuel said: He showed them his treasure house. [9]And Rabbi Yoḥanan said: He showed them a weapon that eats a weapon.

[10]"How does the city sit solitary." [11]Rava said in the name of Rabbi Yoḥanan: Why was Israel punished with *eikhah*? [12]Because

TRANSLATION AND COMMENTARY

[1]**Because of** what Hezekiah said: **'What shall be the sign** that the Lord will heal me?' **Gentiles ate at his table.** Those were the messengers sent by the King of Babylonia with letters and a present after God gave Hezekiah a sign that He would heal him. [2]**Because Gentiles ate at** Hezekiah's **table, he caused his sons to go into exile."**

מְסַיֵּיעַ לֵיהּ [3]The Gemara notes that **this** Baraita **supports** the position of the Amora **Ḥizkiyah, for Ḥizkiyah said: "Whoever invites an idol worshiper into his house and serves him,** as did Hezekiah, **causes his sons to go into exile,** [4]**as the verse states** (II Kings 20:13): "And he [= Hezekiah] showed them the house of his treasures, the silver, and the gold," and several verses later, the Prophet Isaiah says to the king: (II Kings 20:18): **"And of your sons who shall issue from you, whom you shall beget, shall they take away; and they shall be eunuchs in the palace of the King of Babylonia."**

וַיִּשְׂמַח עֲלֵיהֶם [5]The verse states (Isaiah 39:2): **"And Hezekiah was glad of them, and showed them his treasure house [*bet nekhoto*], the silver, and the gold, and the spices, and the precious ointment."** [6]**Rav said: What is** meant by the words *bet nekhoto*, translated here as "house of his treasures"? [7]Hezekiah **had his wife** — who would ordinarily not be seen for reasons of modesty — **pour them** their wine. [8]**Shmuel said** that the phrase should be understood literally: Hezekiah **showed** his guests **his treasure house.** [9]**And Rabbi Yoḥanan said:** Hezekiah **showed** his guests **a weapon that** was strong enough to **break** another **weapon.**

אֵיכָה יָשְׁבָה בָדָד [10]Having mentioned the Babylonian exile, the Gemara presents a series of Midrashic statements relating to the opening verses of the Book of Lamentations. Most of the statements are made by Rava in the name of Rabbi Yoḥanan. The Book of Lamentations opens (Lamentations 1:1): **"How [*Eikhah*] does the city sit solitary."** [11]**Rava said in the name of Rabbi Yoḥanan: Why was Israel punished,** and a lamentation recited over the people that begins **with** the word *eikhah* [Lamentations 1:1]? [12]**Because they**

RASHI

אכלו נכרים על שולחנו — אותם ששלח לו מרודך בלאדן ספרים ומנחה על ידם. **ומשמש עליו** — כגון חזקיה דאמרינן לקמן: אשתו השקתה עליהם. **גורם גלות** — דכתיב ״וישמח עליהם חזקיהו ויראם את (כל) בית נכתה״ וכתיב בתריה ״ומבניך אשר יצאו ממך יקחו והיו סריסים בהיכל מלך בבל״. **אשתו השקתה עליהם** — היא עצמה מוזגת להם, והיינו ״בית נכתה״ לשון מנכה על שם צלע שנפתחה מן האדם וממנה נברא אשה. **בית גנזיו** — והכי מתרגמינן ״בית גניזוהי״ ומנחם פתר במחברתו לשון סממנים כמו (בראשית לז) ״נכאת וצרי ולוט״. **זין אוכל זין** — כגון פרזלא דשליט בפרזלא. **איכה** — שלושים ושש בגימטריא.

NOTES

בֵּית נְכֹתֹה **The house of his treasures.** According to *Ramah*, Rav's interpretation of the words *bet nekhoto* as alluding to Hezekiah's wife is based on the word בַּיִת, "house," which often means "wife" in the Gemara. Alternatively, the expression *bet nekhoto* refers to "his treasure house," which is ordinarily hidden from the public eye, i.e., his wife (*Maharsha*). According to Shmuel, who explains the expression *bet nekhoto* as referring to "a weapon that breaks a weapon," the word *nekhoto* [נְכֹתֹה] is derived from the root הכה, "strike," and thus alludes to a weapon. Some have the reading, זוּן הֶרְאָה לָהֶן: "He showed them all types of food [מָזוֹן] and spices."

TRANSLATION AND COMMENTARY

violated the thirty-six — the numerical value of the word *eikhah* [א = 1, י = 10, כ = 20, ה = 5] — **Torah prohibitions punishable by excision.**

אָמַר רַבִּי יוֹחָנָן [1] **Rabbi Yoḥanan said: Why was** Israel **punished,** and lamentations recited in verses that are arranged in accordance **with the** Hebrew **alphabet?** [2] **Because the people violated the Torah which was written with the** Hebrew **alphabet.**

יָשְׁבָה בָדָד [3] The Book of Lamentations opens with (Lamentations 1:1): "How does the city **sit solitary."** [4] **Rava said in the name of Rabbi Yoḥanan: The Holy One, blessed be He, said:** [5] **I said** (Deuteronomy 33:28): **"Israel then shall dwell in safety alone; the fountain of Jacob shall dwell upon a land of corn and wine; also his Heavens shall drop down dew"** — the people of Israel shall dwell alone in their wealth and power. [6] **Now** that they do not wish to accept My words and have joined the nations of the world to learn from them, **their seat shall be solitary.**

הָעִיר רַבָּתִי עָם [7] The verse continues (Lamentations 1:1): **"The city that was full of people."** [8] **Rava said in the name of Rabbi Yoḥanan: They would marry off a young woman** who had not yet reached her most fertile years **to an older man** who had already reached the peak of his fertility, [9] **and an older woman** who had already reached her most fertile years **to a younger man** who had not yet reached the peak of his fertility, **in order to increase the number of children.**

הָיְתָה כְּאַלְמָנָה [10] The verse continues (Lamentations 1:1): **"She became like a widow."** [11] **Rav Yehudah said in the name of Rav:** The city of Jerusalem has become **like a widow, but not actually a widow.** [12] **Rather,** the city has become **like a woman whose husband went abroad, but intends to return.** Jerusalem, the city that was once full of people, is now empty, but those who have been cast out will once again be gathered within its gates.

שֶׁעָבְרוּ עַל שְׁלֹשִׁים וְשֵׁשׁ כְּרִיתוֹת שֶׁבַּתּוֹרָה.
[1] אָמַר רַבִּי יוֹחָנָן: מִפְּנֵי מָה לָקוּ בְּאָלֶ״ף בֵּי״ת? [2] מִפְּנֵי שֶׁעָבְרוּ עַל הַתּוֹרָה, שֶׁנִּיתְּנָה בְּאָלֶ״ף בֵּי״ת.
[3] ״יָשְׁבָה בָדָד״. [4] אָמַר רָבָא אָמַר רַבִּי יוֹחָנָן: אָמַר הַקָּדוֹשׁ בָּרוּךְ הוּא: [5] אֲנִי אָמַרְתִּי: ״וַיִּשְׁכֹּן יִשְׂרָאֵל בֶּטַח בָּדָד עֵין יַעֲקֹב אֶל אֶרֶץ דָּגָן וְתִירוֹשׁ אַף שָׁמָיו יַעַרְפוּ טָל״. [6] עַכְשָׁיו יִהְיֶה בָּדָד מוֹשָׁבָם.
[7] ״הָעִיר רַבָּתִי עָם״. [8] אָמַר רָבָא אָמַר רַבִּי יוֹחָנָן: שֶׁהָיוּ מַשִּׂיאִין קְטַנָּה לְגָדוֹל, [9] וּגְדוֹלָה לְקָטָן, כְּדֵי שֶׁיִּהְווּ לָהֶם בָּנִים הַרְבֵּה.
[10] ״הָיְתָה כְּאַלְמָנָה״. [11] אָמַר רַב יְהוּדָה אָמַר רַב: כְּאַלְמָנָה, וְלֹא אַלְמָנָה מַמָּשׁ, [12] אֶלָּא כְּאִשָּׁה שֶׁהָלַךְ בַּעְלָהּ לִמְדִינַת הַיָּם, וְדַעְתּוֹ לַחֲזוֹר אֵלֶיהָ.

LITERAL TRANSLATION

they violated the thirty-six prohibitions punishable by excision in the Torah.

[1] Rabbi Yoḥanan said: Why were they punished with the alphabet? [2] Because they violated the Torah which was given with the alphabet.

[3] "Sit solitary." [4] Rava said in the name of Rabbi Yoḥanan: The Holy One, blessed be He, said: [5] I said: "Israel then shall dwell in safety alone; the fountain of Jacob shall dwell upon a land of corn and wine; also his Heavens shall drop down dew." [6] Now their seat shall be solitary.

[7] "The city that was full of people." [8] Rava said in the name of Rabbi Yoḥanan: That they would marry off a young woman to an old man, [9] and an old woman to a young man, so that they would have many children.

[10] "She became like a widow." [11] Rav Yehudah said in the name of Rav: Like a widow, but not actually a widow, [12] but rather like a woman whose husband went overseas, and has it in mind to return.

RASHI

שלושים ושש כריתות — בכריתות (ב,א) חשיב להו. **לקו בא״ב** — שכל מגילת איכה סדורה באלפא ביתא. **בטח בדד** — שיושבין יחידים ואינן מתיראין לא מן הנכרים ולא מן חיות רעות. **רבתי עם** — עם שמתרבה והולך יותר משאר עם. **קטנה לגדול** — שכבת זרע של קטן אינו מבושל ואינו מזריע מהר כשל גדול, וכן רחם של קטנה אינה קולטת מהר כשל גדולה, לפיכך משיאין גדולה לקטן כדי לכשתהא זרעו [מבושל] קולט מהר וקטנה לגדול כדי שיהא שכבת זרעו קולט מהר, ולא קטנה לקטן שעוהין להוליד, ולא קטן וקטנה ממש, אלא שעומדין על פרקן ורלויין הם להוליד ומיהו אין זרע שלהם מבושל כל כך.

NOTES

שֶׁעָבְרוּ עַל הַתּוֹרָה, שֶׁנִּיתְּנָה בְּאָל״ף בֵּי״ת **Because they violated the Torah which was given with the alphabet.** The verses in Lamentations are arranged in alphabetical order to intimate that the people of Israel committed every type of sin that can be expressed by the letters of the alphabet, and that they were also punished with every type of punishment that can be expressed by the letters of the alphabet (*Rabbi M. Almosnino*).

1"רַבָּתִי בַגּוֹיִם שָׂרָתִי בַּמְּדִינוֹת". 2אָמַר רָבָא אָמַר רַבִּי יוֹחָנָן: כָּל מָקוֹם שֶׁהֵן הוֹלְכִין, נַעֲשִׂין שָׂרִים לַאֲדוֹנֵיהֶן.
3תָּנוּ רַבָּנַן: "מַעֲשֶׂה בִּשְׁנֵי בְּנֵי אָדָם שֶׁנִּשְׁבּוּ בְּהַר הַכַּרְמֶל, וְהָיָה שַׁבַּאי מְהַלֵּךְ אַחֲרֵיהֶם. [104B] 4אָמַר לוֹ אֶחָד מֵהֶם לַחֲבֵירוֹ: 'גָּמָל שֶׁמְּהַלֶּכֶת לְפָנֵינוּ סוּמָא בְּאַחַת מֵעֵינֶיהָ, וּטְעוּנָה שְׁתֵּי נוֹדוֹת, אַחַת שֶׁל יַיִן וְאַחַת שֶׁל שֶׁמֶן, וּשְׁנֵי בְנֵי אָדָם הַמַּנְהִיגִים אוֹתָהּ — אֶחָד יִשְׂרָאֵל וְאֶחָד נָכְרִי'. 5אָמַר לָהֶן [שַׁבַּאי]: 'עַם קְשֵׁה עוֹרֶף! 6מֵאַיִן אַתֶּם יוֹדְעִין? 7אָמְרוּ לוֹ: 'גָּמָל — מֵעֲשָׂבִים שֶׁלְּפָנֶיהָ. מִצַּד שֶׁרוֹאָה, אוֹכֶלֶת; מִצַּד שֶׁאֵינָהּ רוֹאָה, אֵינָהּ אוֹכֶלֶת. 8וּטְעוּנָה שְׁתֵּי נוֹדוֹת אַחַת שֶׁל יַיִן וְאַחַת שֶׁל שֶׁמֶן. 9שֶׁל יַיִן — מְטַפְטֵף וְשׁוֹקֵעַ, 10וְשֶׁל שֶׁמֶן — מְטַפְטֵף וְצָף. 11וּשְׁנֵי בְנֵי אָדָם הַמַּנְהִיגִים אוֹתָהּ, אֶחָד נָכְרִי וְאֶחָד יִשְׂרָאֵל. 12נָכְרִי נִפְנָה לַדֶּרֶךְ, וְיִשְׂרָאֵל נִפְנָה לַצְּדָדִין'. 13רָדַף אַחֲרֵיהֶם, וּמָצָא כְּדִבְרֵיהֶם. 14בָּא וּנְשָׁקָן עַל רֹאשָׁן, וֶהֱבִיאָן לְבֵיתָן וְעָשָׂה

LITERAL TRANSLATION

1"She that was great among the nations, and a princess among the provinces." 2Rava said in the name of Rabbi Yoḥanan: Wherever they go, they become princes to their lords.

3Our Rabbis taught: "It happened that two people were taken captive on Mount Carmel, and the captor walked behind them. [104B] 4One of them said to the other person: 'The camel that is walking before us is blind in one of its eyes, and it is laden with two bottles, one of wine, and one of oil, and the two people leading it — one is a Jew, and one is a Gentile.' 5[The captor] said to them: 'Stiff-necked people! 6From where do you know [these things]?' 7They said to him: 'The camel from the plants that are in front of it. From the side that it sees, it eats; from the side that it does not see, it does not eat. 8And it is laden with two bottles, one of wine, and one of oil. 9[The one] of wine — it drips and sinks; 10[the one] of oil — it drips and floats. 11And the two people leading it — one is a Gentile, and one is a Jew. 12The Gentile relieves himself on the road, and the Jew relieves himself on the side.' 13He ran after them, and found it was like their words. 14He came and kissed them on their heads, and brought them to their houses, and made

TRANSLATION AND COMMENTARY

רַבָּתִי בַגּוֹיִם 1The verse continues (Lamentations 1:1): **"She that was great among the nations, and a princess among the provinces."** 2**Rava said in the name of Rabbi Yoḥanan: Wherever** the city's former residents **go** in their exile, **they become princes to their lords** because of their wisdom and understanding.

תָּנוּ רַבָּנַן 3**Our Rabbis taught** a Baraita which illustrates this last point: **"It** once **happened that two** Jews **were taken captive on Mount Carmel, and** their **captor walked behind them,** leading them away into captivity. [104B] 4**One of** the two captives **said to the other:** 'I can tell that **the camel that is walking ahead of us is blind in one eye, and is laden with two bottles, one of wine, and one of oil, and** as for **the two people** who are **leading** the animal, **one is a Jew, and the other is a Gentile.'** 5**The captor said to them:** 'O you **stiff-necked people!** 6**How do you know these things** when you cannot see that far ahead?' 7The captives **said to** their captor: 'We deduced that **the camel** walking ahead of us is blind in one eye **from** the way that it ate **the plants in front of it. It only ate the plants on one side of it,** showing that it could only see out of that eye. 8**And** furthermore, we know that the camel **is laden with two bottles, one of wine, and one of oil,** from the drops that we see on the ground behind it. On one side, the drops have sunk into the ground, while on the other side, they have stuck to the surface. 9Drops leaking from the bottle **of wine dripped** onto the ground, **and sank** in, 10whereas drops leaking from the bottle **of oil** clung **to the surface.** 11**And** furthermore, we know about **the two people** who are **leading** the animal that **one is a Gentile, and the other is a Jew** from the way that they relieved themselves. 12**The Gentile relieved himself on the road** itself, **whereas the Jew relieved himself on the side of the road.'** 13The captor immediately **ran** ahead to catch up with the camel and **found** that the situation **was** indeed exactly **as** his captives had **said.** 14**He went** back to them, **and kissed them on their heads** as a sign of honor, **and brought them to his house, and made them**

RASHI

אחד — מן הנשבים לחברו. גמל — זו שמהלכת לפנינו סומא וכו׳. [מצד שרואה — שאינה אוכלת, פעמים מצד ימין ופעמים מצד שמאל, כבהמה הרועה שאוכלת מכאן ומכאן, אלא מצד שרואה אוכלת]. יין מטפטף ושוקע — בקרקע, ורואין אנו בין רגלינו הטיפין שנפלו כשעברה הגמל במקום זה, מצד אחד שקועין, ומצד אחר הטיפין של שמן שצפים. נפנה לצדדין — שכן דרך ישראל להיות צנוע. רדף — השבאי דרך הגמל והמנהיג ומצא כדבריהם, ואמרו אותם יהודים על אותו שבאי אדוניהם שהוא בן קלסתר מלך *אשקנ״ק בלעז, שהיה דיוקנו דומה למגמת פניו של אותו קלסתר של מלך שבזנות הולידו.

LANGUAGE (RASHI)

אשקנ״ק* Apparently this should be read as אישקינ״א, from the Old French *eschange*, meaning "duplicate, identical."

TRANSLATION AND COMMENTARY

a great feast, and danced before them, and said: [1]**'Blessed be He who chose the seed of Abraham, and gave them of His wisdom, and wherever they go, they become princes to their lords** because of their great wisdom and understanding.' [2]**And** the captor **sent** his captives **off, and they went** back **to their houses in peace."**

בָּכֹה תִבְכֶּה בַּלַּיְלָה [3]The verse in Lamentations states (Lamentations 1:2): **"She weeps and weeps** [בָּכֹה תִבְכֶּה] **at night."** [4]**Why** does the verse use the double-verb form, בָּכֹה תִבְכֶּה, alluding to **two weepings?** [5]**Rabbah said in the name of Rabbi Yoḥanan:** Jerusalem wept **once for** the destruction of **the First Temple,** which already took place, [6]**and** wept a second time **for** the destruction of **the Second Temple,** which was still to take place.

בַּלַּיְלָה [7]The verse states: "She weeps **at night."** What is meant by "at night"? [8]She weeps **because of what happened at night** after the Israelites heard the spies' report after scouting of the land, **as the verse states** (Numbers 14:1): **"And all the congregation lifted up their voice, and cried, and the people wept all night."**

אָמַר רַבָּה [9]**Rabbah said in the name of Rabbi Yoḥanan: That day** that the Israelites wept all night **was the night of the Ninth of Av.** [10]**The Holy One, blessed be He, said to Israel:** "Because you **wept** today **for no cause,** since the Promised Land is a land of milk and honey, [11]**I will** therefore **give you** reason **to weep** on this day **throughout the generations,** for on the Ninth of Av both the First and the Second Temples will be destroyed."

דָּבָר אַחֵר [12]The Gemara offers **another explanation** of the words, **"at night."** [13]When **someone weeps at night, his voice is** more **audible** than during the day.

דָּבָר אַחֵר [14]The Gemara offers yet **another explanation** of the words, **"at night"**: [15]When **someone weeps at night, the stars and the constellations cry** along **with him.**

לָהֶן סְעוּדָה גְּדוֹלָה, וְהָיָה מְרַקֵּד לִפְנֵיהֶם, וְאָמַר: [1]'בָּרוּךְ שֶׁבָּחַר בְּזַרְעוֹ שֶׁל אַבְרָהָם, וְנָתַן לָהֶם מֵחָכְמָתוֹ, וּבְכָל מָקוֹם שֶׁהֵן הוֹלְכִין נַעֲשִׂין שָׂרִים לַאֲדוֹנֵיהֶם'. [2]וּפְטָרָן [וְהָלְכוּ] לְבָתֵּיהֶם לְשָׁלוֹם".

[3]"בָּכֹה תִבְכֶּה בַּלַּיְלָה". [4]שְׁתֵּי בְכִיּוֹת הַלָּלוּ — לָמָּה? [5]אָמַר רַבָּה אָמַר רַבִּי יוֹחָנָן: אֶחָד עַל מִקְדָּשׁ רִאשׁוֹן, [6]וְאֶחָד עַל מִקְדָּשׁ שֵׁנִי.

[7]"בַּלַּיְלָה". [8]עַל עִסְקֵי לַיְלָה, שֶׁנֶּאֱמַר: "וַתִּשָּׂא כָּל הָעֵדָה וַיִּתְּנוּ אֶת קוֹלָם וַיִּבְכּוּ הָעָם בַּלַּיְלָה הַהוּא".

[9]אָמַר רַבָּה אָמַר רַבִּי יוֹחָנָן: אוֹתוֹ (הַיּוֹם) לֵיל תִּשְׁעָה בְּאָב הָיָה. [10]אָמַר לָהֶן הַקָּדוֹשׁ בָּרוּךְ הוּא לְיִשְׂרָאֵל: "אַתֶּם בְּכִיתֶם בְּכִיָּה שֶׁל חִנָּם, [11]וַאֲנִי אֶקְבַּע לָכֶם בְּכִיָּה לְדוֹרוֹת".

[12]דָּבָר אַחֵר: "בַּלַּיְלָה". [13]שֶׁכָּל הַבּוֹכֶה בַּלַּיְלָה קוֹלוֹ נִשְׁמָע.

[14]דָּבָר אַחֵר: "בַּלַּיְלָה". [15]שֶׁכָּל הַבּוֹכֶה בַּלַּיְלָה, כּוֹכָבִים וּמַזָּלוֹת בּוֹכִין עִמּוֹ.

LITERAL TRANSLATION

them a great feast, and danced before them, and said: [1]'Blessed be He who chose the seed of Abraham, and gave them of His wisdom, and wherever they go, they become princes to their lords.' [2]And he sent them off [and they went] to their houses in peace."

[3]"She weeps and weeps at night." [4]These two weepings — why? [5]Rabbah said in the name of Rabbi Yoḥanan: One for the First Temple, [6]and one for the Second Temple.

[7]"At night." [8]Because of matters of the night, as it is stated: "And all the congregation raised and gave voice, and the people wept all night."

[9]Rabbah said in the name of Rabbi Yoḥanan: That day was the night of the Ninth of Av. [10]The Holy One, blessed be He, said to Israel: "You wept a weeping for no cause, [11]and [so] I will establish for you a weeping for generations."

[12]Another explanation: "At night." [13]For anyone who weeps at night, his voice is heard.

[14]Another explanation: "At night." [15]For anyone who weeps at night, the stars and the constellations cry with him.

RASHI

על עסקי לילה — לפי שבכו אותו לילה בכיית חנם. **קולו נשמע יותר מביום** — כדאמרינן בעלמא (יומא כ,א) מפני מה אין הקול נשמע ביום כבלילה — מפני גלגל חמה המנסר ברקיע, והיינו דכתיב "בכה תבכה בלילה" כדי שיהא קולה נשמע וירחמו עליה — ואף על פי כן "אין מנחם לה". **כוכבים ומזלות בוכים** — שנכמרו רחמים עליו.

NOTES

לֵיל תִּשְׁעָה בְּאָב הָיָה **It was the night of the Ninth of Av.** Elsewhere, a calculation is made about how much time had passed since the last time that the Israelites set out on a journey (the twentieth of Iyyar). If you add the month that they stayed at Kivrot Hata'avah, the week that they waited for Miriam, and the days of traveling, it turns out that the spies set out on their mission on the first of Tamuz. If Tamuz was a full month (with thirty days), then the spies returned to Moses on the eighth of Av. Thus, the Israelites wept on the night of the Ninth of Av because of the stories that were told to them by the spies.

TRANSLATION AND COMMENTARY

דָּבָר אַחֵר [1]The Gemara suggests **one** final **explanation** of the words, **"at night"**: [2]When **someone weeps at night, others who hear him** are touched by his crying and **weep** along **with him.**

מַעֲשֶׂה בְּאִשָּׁה אַחַת [3]Indeed, **it** once **happened that the son of a certain woman who** happened to **be Rabban Gamliel's neighbor died, and** the woman **wept over** him all **night.** [4]**Rabban Gamliel heard** his neighbor weeping, **and wept** along **with her,** crying so much **that his eyelashes fell out.** [5]**The next day, his disciples observed** that their master had been up all night crying, **and** so they **removed** the grieving woman **from his neighborhood** so he could sleep.

וְדִמְעָתָהּ עַל לֶחֱיָהּ [6]The verse in Lamentations continues (Lamentations 1:2): **"And her tears are on her cheeks."** [7]**Rava said in the name of Rabbi Yoḥanan:** Jerusalem weeps **like a woman who weeps for the husband of her youth,** [8]**as the verse states** (Joel 1:5): **"Lament like a virgin girded with sackcloth for the husband of her youth."**

הָיוּ צָרֶיהָ לְרֹאשׁ [9]The verse in Lamentations states (Lamentations 1:5): **"Her adversaries have become the chief."** [10]**Rava said in the name of Rabbi Yoḥanan: Whoever** is designated to **persecute Israel is** first **made a chief,** [11]**as the verse states** (Isaiah 8:23): **"For there is no weariness [מוּעָף] to Him that is set against [מוּצָק] her; at the first He lightly afflicted the land of Zebulun, and the land of Naftali and afterwards He afflicted her more grievously by the way of the sea, beyond the Jordan in the Galilee of the nations."**

אָמַר רָבָא [12]**Rava said in the name of Rabbi Yoḥanan:** This verse teaches us that **whoever** is designated to **persecute** (מֵצִיק) **Israel** completes its mission and **does not become weary** (עָיֵף).

לֹא אֲלֵיכֶם [13]The verse in Lamentations states (Lamentations 1:12): **"Is it nothing to you, all you who pass by."** [14]**Rava said in the name of Rabbi Yoḥanan:**

[1]דָּבָר אַחֵר: ״בַּלַּיְלָה״. [2]שֶׁכָּל הַבּוֹכֶה בַּלַּיְלָה הַשּׁוֹמֵעַ קוֹלוֹ בּוֹכֶה כְּנֶגְדּוֹ.

[3]מַעֲשֶׂה בְּאִשָּׁה אַחַת, שְׁכֶנְתּוֹ שֶׁל רַבָּן גַּמְלִיאֵל שֶׁמֵּת בְּנָהּ, וְהָיְתָה בּוֹכָה עָלָיו בַּלַּיְלָה. [4]שָׁמַע רַבָּן גַּמְלִיאֵל קוֹלָהּ וּבָכָה כְּנֶגְדָּהּ, עַד שֶׁנָּשְׁרוּ רִיסֵי עֵינָיו. [5]לְמָחָר הִכִּירוּ בּוֹ תַּלְמִידָיו וְהוֹצִיאוּהָ מִשְּׁכוּנָתוֹ.

[6]״וְדִמְעָתָהּ עַל לֶחֱיָהּ״. [7]אָמַר רָבָא אָמַר רַבִּי יוֹחָנָן: כְּאִשָּׁה שֶׁבּוֹכָה עַל בַּעַל נְעוּרֶיהָ, [8]שֶׁנֶּאֱמַר: ״אֱלִי כִּבְתוּלָה חֲגֻרַת שַׂק עַל בַּעַל נְעוּרֶיהָ״.

[9]״הָיוּ צָרֶיהָ לְרֹאשׁ״. [10]אָמַר רָבָא אָמַר רַבִּי יוֹחָנָן: כָּל הַמֵּיצֵר לְיִשְׂרָאֵל נַעֲשֶׂה רֹאשׁ, [11]שֶׁנֶּאֱמַר: ״כִּי לֹא מוּעָף לַאֲשֶׁר מוּצָק לָהּ כָּעֵת הָרִאשׁוֹן הֵקַל אַרְצָה זְבֻלוּן וְאַרְצָה נַפְתָּלִי וְהָאַחֲרוֹן הִכְבִּיד דֶּרֶךְ הַיָּם עֵבֶר הַיַּרְדֵּן גְּלִיל הַגּוֹיִם״.

[12]אָמַר רָבָא אָמַר רַבִּי יוֹחָנָן: כָּל הַמֵּצִיק לְיִשְׂרָאֵל אֵינוֹ עָיֵף.

[13]״לֹא אֲלֵיכֶם, כָּל עֹבְרֵי דֶרֶךְ״. [14]אָמַר רָבָא אָמַר רַבִּי יוֹחָנָן:

LITERAL TRANSLATION

[1]Another explanation: "At night." [2]For anyone who weeps at night, whoever hears his voice weeps with him.

[3]It happened to a certain woman, the neighbor of Rabban Gamliel, whose son died, and she wept over him at night. [4]Rabban Gamliel heard her voice, and wept with her, until his eyelashes fell out. [5]The next day, his disciples noticed [it] in him, and removed her from his neighborhood.

[6]"And her tears are on her cheeks." [7]Rava said in the name of Rabbi Yoḥanan: Like a woman who weeps for the husband of her youth, [8]as it is stated: "Lament like a virgin girded with sackcloth for the husband of her youth."

[9]"Her adversaries have become the chief." [10]Rava said in the name of Rabbi Yoḥanan: Whoever persecutes Israel becomes a chief, [11]as it is stated: "For there is no weariness to Him that is set against her; first He lightly afflicted the land of Zebulun, and the land of Naftali, and later He afflicted [her] more grievously by the way of the sea, beyond the Jordan in the Galilee of the nations."

[12]Rava said in the name of Rabbi Yoḥanan: Whoever persecutes Israel does not become weary.

[13]"Is it nothing to you, all you who pass by." [14]Rava said in the name of Rabbi Yoḥanan:

RASHI

בוכה כנגדו — מתוך שנשמע בהדיא מרכך לבו של אדם השומע קולו לבכות עמו. **ריסי עיניו** — שער שבשפת העין היה נופל ונכפל על העין מרוב דמעות. **אלי** — ״קונו קינה״ מתרגמינן אליא. **על בעל נעוריה** — שבוכה תמיד ומלויה דמעות. **על לחיה** — לשון לחות ונערות, כגון לח ויבש.

NOTES

וּבָכָה כְּנֶגְדָּהּ And he wept with her. According to the Midrash, Rabban Gamliel was reminded of the destruction of the Temple, and wept in sorrow over that loss.

כָּל הַמֵּיצֵר לְיִשְׂרָאֵל נַעֲשֶׂה רֹאשׁ Whoever persecutes Israel becomes a chief. *Tosafot* explains that before a king persecutes Israel, God first raises him to a position of great power, so that Israel will be spared the dishonor of falling into the hands of an insignificant leader.

מִכָּאן לְקוּבְלָנָא מִן הַתּוֹרָה. [1]״כָּל עֹבְרֵי דֶרֶךְ״. [2]אָמַר רַב עַמְרָם אָמַר רַב: עֲשָׂאוּנִי כְּעוֹבְרֵי עַל דָּת, [3]דְּאִילּוּ בִּסְדוֹם, כְּתִיב: ״וַה׳ הִמְטִיר עַל סְדֹם״. [4]וְאִילּוּ בִּירוּשָׁלַיִם, כְּתִיב: ״מִמָּרוֹם שָׁלַח אֵשׁ בְּעַצְמֹתַי וַיִּרְדֶּנָּה וגו׳״. [5]וּכְתִיב: ״וַיִּגְדַּל עֲוֹן בַּת עַמִּי מֵחַטַּאת סְדֹם״. [6]וְכִי מַשּׂוֹא פָּנִים יֵשׁ בַּדָּבָר? [7]אָמַר רָבָא אָמַר רַבִּי יוֹחָנָן: מִדָּה יְתֵירָה הָיְתָה בִּירוּשָׁלַיִם שֶׁלֹּא הָיְתָה בִּסְדוֹם, [8]דְּאִילּוּ בִּסְדוֹם כְּתִיב: ״הִנֵּה זֶה הָיָה עֲוֹן סְדֹם אֲחוֹתֵךְ; גָּאוֹן שִׂבְעַת לֶחֶם...וְיַד עָנִי וְאֶבְיוֹן לֹא הֶחֱזִיקָה וגו׳״. [9]וְאִילּוּ בִּירוּשָׁלַיִם

LITERAL TRANSLATION

From here regarding a complaint from the Torah. [1]"All you that pass by." [2]Rav Amram said in the name of Rav: They have made me like those who violate the law, [3]for regarding Sodom, it is written: "Then the Lord rained upon Sodom." [4]And regarding Jerusalem, it is written: "From above He has sent fire into my bones, and it prevails, etc." [5]And it is written: "For the iniquity of the daughter of my people is greater than the sin of Sodom." [6]Is there partiality in the matter? [7]Rava said in the name of Rabbi Yoḥanan: Jerusalem had a greater measure that Sodom did not have, [8]for regarding Sodom it is written: "Behold this was the iniquity of your sister Sodom; pride, surfeit of bread...and yet she did not strengthen the hand of the poor and needy, etc." [9]And regarding Jerusalem,

TRANSLATION AND COMMENTARY

Here we have support **from the Torah for** voicing one's **complaint** about troubles to other people. A person in distress should tell others, so they will offer help.

כָּל עֹבְרֵי דֶרֶךְ [1]**"All you that pass [עֹבְרֵי] by."** [2]**Rav Amram said in the name of Rav:** Jerusalem said: **They have made me like those who violate [עוֹבְרֵי]** not only the Torah, but even natural **law,** [3]**for regarding Sodom, the verse states** (Genesis 19:24): **"Then the Lord rained upon Sodom** and Gomorra brimstone and fire from the Lord out of Heaven." [4]**And regarding Jerusalem, the verse states** (Lamentations 1:13): **"From above He has sent fire into my bones, and it prevails** against them," teaching that both Sodom and Jerusalem were punished with fire."

וּכְתִיב [5]Another **verse states** (Lamentations 4:6): **"For the iniquity of the daughter of my people is greater than the sin of Sodom,"** teaching that the offenses committed in Jerusalem were even greater than those committed in Sodom." [6]The Gemara asks: **Does** God show **partiality in the matter?** Why was Jerusalem not overturned, like Sodom?

אָמַר רָבָא [7]**Rava said in the name of Rabbi Yoḥanan:** No partiality was shown to Jerusalem. On the contrary, **Jerusalem suffered a greater measure** of punishment **than did Sodom,** [8]**for regarding Sodom the verse states** (Ezekiel 16:49): **"Behold this was the iniquity of your sister Sodom; pride, surfeit of bread...and yet she did not strengthen the hand of the poor and needy,"** teaching that the people of Sodom did not suffer the afflictions of poverty and hunger. [9]**But regarding Jerusalem, the verse states**

RASHI

מכאן לקובלנא מן התורה — כשאדם מודיע צערו לאחר צריך שיאמר לו לא תבא זאת לך כמו שבאה אלי, כי קשה הוא לשמוע, שפעמים חוזרת עליו, והמקפיד על כך אין בו משום ניחוש, לישנא אחרינא: לקובלנא — כשיש לו צרה יודיענה לרבים, קובלנא = צעקה, לישנא אחרינא: נגד, דמתרגמינן "קבל", כאדם שאומר לחברו לא כנגדך אני אומר. **וירדנה** — ושרף אותה, והיינו עשאוני כעוברי דת שדנני באש כסדום. **לא עליכם** — נביא היה מתנודד על החורבן כאילו באה עליו צרה ומהפכה לאחרים ואומר להם לישראל לא תהא לכם צרה כזו, כמדומה לי נביא היה מדבר כנגד בני משה, או כנגד עשרת השבטים שלא הגלה נבוכדנצר. **וירדנה** — לשון שבירה, כמו (במדבר כד) "וירד מיעקב". כאדם המושל בחברו להלקותו ולשברו. הכי גרסינן: **"ויגדל עון בת עמי מחטאת סדום" וכי משוא פנים יש בדבר?** — והואיל וישראל רעים יותר מסדום למה לא נהפכו כסדום? לשון אחר: וכי משוא פנים יש בדבר — דהתם כתיב "וה׳ המטיר" — הוא בעצמו, והכא כתיב "שלח" — על ידי שליח. **מדה יתירה לטובה** — דבירושלים כתיב "ידי נשים רחמניות בשלו ילדיהן היו לברות למו" שהיתה מזומנת חברתה ואוכלת בנה, אלמא רחמניות היו, ואילו בסדום כתיב "יד עני ואביון לא החזיקה" ומדה זו כפרה עליהם שלא נהפכו, לשון אחר: מדה יתירה — פורענות גדולה היתה בירושלים, שילדיהם היו אוכלות זו עם זו דכתיב "היו לברות למו", ואילו בסדום כתיב "גאון שבעת לחם" שלא טעמו טעם עוני, הא למדת גדול פורענות ירושלים מפורענות סדום, ולא היה משוא פנים בדבר.

NOTES

לְקוּבְלָנָא מִן הַתּוֹרָה **A complaint from the Torah.** *Rashi* offers three different interpretations of this passage. *Meiri* adds that from here we have Biblical support for the idea that a person may complain about his troubles, and such a person does not appear to be rejecting the afflictions that God sent upon him.

כְּעוֹבְרֵי עַל דָּת **Like those who violate the Torah.** They have made me like those who violate not only the Torah which contains laws and statutes that man cannot understand, but also natural law, whose statutes are rational and natural — that is to say, they have made me like the people of Sodom (*Maharsha*).

כְּתִיב: ״יְדֵי נָשִׁים רַחֲמָנִיּוֹת בִּשְּׁלוּ יַלְדֵיהֶן״.
[1]״סִלָּה כָל אַבִּירַי ה׳ בְּקִרְבִּי״. [2]כְּאָדָם שֶׁאוֹמֵר לַחֲבֵרוֹ: ״נִפְסְלָה מַטְבֵּעַ זוֹ״.
[3]״פָּצוּ עָלַיִךְ פִּיהֶם״. [4]אָמַר רָבָא אָמַר רַבִּי יוֹחָנָן: בִּשְׁבִיל מָה הִקְדִּים פ״א לְעַי״ן? [5]בִּשְׁבִיל מְרַגְּלִים שֶׁאָמְרוּ בְּפִיהֶם מַה שֶּׁלֹּא רָאוּ בְּעֵינֵיהֶם.
[6]״אֹכְלֵי עַמִּי אָכְלוּ לֶחֶם ה׳ לֹא קָרָאוּ״. [7]אָמַר רָבָא אָמַר רַבִּי יוֹחָנָן: כָּל הָאוֹכֵל מִלַּחְמָן שֶׁל יִשְׂרָאֵל טוֹעֵם טַעַם לֶחֶם, [8]וְשֶׁאֵינוֹ אוֹכֵל מִלַּחְמָן שֶׁל יִשְׂרָאֵל אֵינוֹ טוֹעֵם טַעַם לֶחֶם.
[9]״ה׳ לֹא קָרָאוּ״. [10]רַב אָמַר: אֵלּוּ הַדַּיָּינִין. [11]וּשְׁמוּאֵל אָמַר: אֵלּוּ מְלַמְּדֵי תִינוֹקוֹת.

LITERAL TRANSLATION

it is written: "Hands of compassionate women cooked their children."

[1]"The Lord has spurned all my mighty men in the midst of me." [2]Like someone who says to his fellow: "This coin was invalidated."

[3]"They have opened their mouths against you." [4]Rava said in the name of Rabbi Yoḥanan: Why does the letter pe come before the letter ayin? [5]Because of the spies who said with their mouths what they did not see with their eyes.

[6]"The eaters of My people ate bread, and call not upon the Lord." [7]Rava said in the name of Rabbi Yoḥanan: Whoever eats of the bread of Israel tastes the taste of bread, [8]and whoever does not eat of the bread of Israel does not taste the taste of bread.

[9]"And call not upon the Lord." [10]Rav said: These are the judges. [11]And Shmuel said: These are the teachers of children.

TRANSLATION AND COMMENTARY

(Lamentations 4:10): **"Hands of compassionate women have cooked their own children,"** testifying to the abject hunger that afflicted the city.

סִלָּה כָל אַבִּירַי ה׳ [1]The verse states (Lamentations 1:15): **"The Lord has spurned all my mighty men in the midst of me."** [2]God spurned and rejected the mighty leaders of Jerusalem, **like someone who says to his fellow: "This coin was invalidated,** and is now worthless."

פָּצוּ עָלַיִךְ פִּיהֶם [3]The verse states (Lamentations 2:16): **"They have opened** [פָּצוּ] **their mouths against you."** And the next verse states (Lamentations 2:17): "The Lord has done [עָשָׂה] that which He devised." [4]**Rava said in the name of Rabbi Yoḥanan: Why does** the verse beginning with the **letter pe** (verse 16) **come before** the verse beginning with **the letter ayin** (verse 17)? The verses in chapters 1 through 4 in Lamentations follow the order of the Hebrew alphabet, but in chapters 2 through 4, the verses beginning with the letter pe, which means mouth, precede the verses beginning with the letter ayin, which means eye. [5]This is **because the spies who** were sent to scout out the Land of Israel returned and **said with their mouths what they had not seen with their eyes.**

אֹכְלֵי עַמִּי [6]The verse states (Psalms 14:4): **"The eaters of My people ate bread, and call not upon the Lord."** [7]**Rava said in the name of Rabbi Yoḥanan:** This verse teaches that **any** non-Jew **who** steals and **eats of the bread of Israel** feels that he **tastes the taste of bread,** [8]**and any** non-Jew **who does not** steal and **eat of the bread of Israel** feels that he **does not taste the taste of bread,** for a non-Jew only enjoys his bread if he knows that it was stolen from Israel.

ה׳ לֹא קָרָאוּ [9]The second half of the verse reads (Psalms 14:4): **"And they call not upon the Lord."** [10]**Rav said: This** refers to **judges** who have no fear of God, and therefore pervert justice. [11]**Shmuel said: This** refers to **teachers** of children who do not teach their charges properly. Bad judges and teachers cause the bread of Israel to become the food of their enemies.

RASHI

סלה — לשון מסלה, כלומר כל האבירים פסלם הקדוש ברוך הוא ועשאם פסולים וכבושים כמסלה זו, והיינו דמיא למטבע שנפסל ואין לו תקנה. מפני מה הקדים פ״א לעי״ן — ברוב האלפא ביתא שבאיכה. מפני מרגלים — שהקדימו מאמר פיהם עד שלא ראו בעין. טועם טעם לחם — שהגויים מוצאים טעמם בלחמם של ישראל, שהנאה הוא להם כשגוזלין אותן. אלו הדיינין — מטה משפט בשביל עונותיהם היו לחם עמי למאכל אויביו. מלמדי תינוקות — שעושין מלאכתן רמיה.

NOTES

יְדֵי נָשִׁים רַחֲמָנִיּוֹת **Hands of compassionate women.** According to *Rashi*, Rabbi Yoḥanan means to say that Jerusalem was spared from being overturned, not because God showed partiality in the matter, but because Jerusalem had a greater measure of compassion than Sodom. Following this approach, *Ramah* adds that the verse shows that there were compassionate women in Jerusalem, whereas regarding Sodom there is no mention of anybody showing compassion.

ה׳ לֹא קָרָאוּ **And call not upon the Lord.** The Amoraim explain that this verse refers to teachers of children and to judges, because those people should certainly have remembered God while they were teaching their pupils or issuing rulings; but even they failed to do so. All the more so, did the rest of the people forget about God, and fail to call upon Him (*Ramah*).

TRANSLATION AND COMMENTARY

מִי מְנָאָן [1]The Gemara now leaves the Midrashic commentary on Lamentations and raises a question about the Mishnah: **Who formulated the count** of kings and ordinary people who do not have a portion in the World to Come? [2]**Rav Ashi said: The members of the Great Assembly,** the supreme council of Sages established in the days of Ezra and Nehemiah, **formulated the count.**

אָמַר רַב יְהוּדָה [3]**Rav Yehudah said in the name of Rav: They wanted to count another** king — Solomon — among the kings who do not have a portion in the World to Come. [4]First, **a likeness of the image of his father,** David, **came and prostrated itself before them,** and pleaded on Solomon's behalf, **but they did not regard it.** [5]Then, **a fire came** down **from Heaven, and singed the benches** on which the members of the Great Assembly sat, **but they did not regard it.** [6]And then, **a heavenly voice issued forth, and said to them** (Proverbs 22:29): **"Do you see a man diligent in his business? he shall stand before kings; he shall not stand before obscure men."** [7]**Someone who** was diligent in his business, and **put** the construction of **My house before** the construction of **his house, and moreover, My house he built in seven years, and his house he built in thirteen years** — [8]surely **he shall stand before kings** in the World to Come, and **he shall not stand before obscure men — but they did not regard it.** [9]Finally, **a heavenly voice issued forth, and said** (Job 34:33): **"Shall He recompense it according to your mind, when you refuse His judgment? shall He say, You shall choose, and not I; and speak what you know."** God alone decides who has a portion in the World to Come, and His decision does not depend on your list.

דּוֹרְשֵׁי רְשׁוּמוֹת [10]The Gemara notes: **Those who interpret the Torah metaphorically said: All of** the people listed among those who do not have a share in the World to Come **will go** in the end **to the World to Come,**

[1]מִי מְנָאָן? [2]אָמַר רַב אַשִׁי: אַנְשֵׁי כְּנֶסֶת הַגְּדוֹלָה מְנָאוּם. [3]אָמַר רַב יְהוּדָה אָמַר רַב: בִּקְשׁוּ עוֹד לִמְנוֹת אֶחָד. [4]בָּאָה דְּמוּת דְּיוֹקְנוֹ שֶׁל אָבִיו וְנִשְׁתַּטְּחָה לִפְנֵיהֶם, וְלֹא הִשְׁגִּיחוּ עָלֶיהָ. [5]בָּאָה אֵשׁ מִן הַשָּׁמַיִם וְלִחֲכָה אֵשׁ בְּסַפְסְלֵיהֶם, וְלֹא הִשְׁגִּיחוּ עָלֶיהָ. [6]יָצְאָה בַּת קוֹל, וְאָמְרָה לָהֶם: ״חָזִיתָ אִישׁ מָהִיר בִּמְלַאכְתּוֹ, לִפְנֵי מְלָכִים יִתְיַצָּב; בַּל יִתְיַצֵּב לִפְנֵי חֲשֻׁכִּים״. [7]מִי שֶׁהִקְדִּים בֵּיתִי לְבֵיתוֹ, וְלֹא עוֹד, אֶלָּא שֶׁבֵּיתִי בְּנָה בְּשֶׁבַע שָׁנִים, וּבֵיתוֹ בָּנָה בִּשְׁלֹשׁ עֶשְׂרֵה שָׁנָה — [8]לִפְנֵי מְלָכִים יִתְיַצָּב; [בַּל יִתְיַצֵּב] לִפְנֵי חֲשֻׁכִּים — וְלֹא הִשְׁגִּיחַ עָלֶיהָ. [9]יָצְאָה בַּת קוֹל וְאָמְרָה: ״הֲמֵעִמְּךָ יְשַׁלְּמֶנָּה, כִּי מָאַסְתָּ? כִּי אַתָּה תִבְחַר, וְלֹא אָנִי; וגו׳״. [10]דּוֹרְשֵׁי רְשׁוּמוֹת הָיוּ אוֹמְרִים: כּוּלָּן בָּאִין לָעוֹלָם הַבָּא,

LITERAL TRANSLATION

[1]Who counted them? [2]Rav Ashi said: The members of the Great Assembly counted them.

[3]Rav Yehudah said in the name of Rav: They wanted to count another one. [4]A likeness of his father's image came and prostrated itself before them, but they did not regard it. [5]A fire came from Heaven, and the fire licked their benches, but they did not regard it. [6]A heavenly voice issued, and said to them: "Do you see a man diligent in his business? He shall stand before kings; he shall not stand before obscure men." [7]Someone who put My house before his house, and moreover, My house he built in seven years, and his house he built in thirteen years — [8]he shall stand before kings; he shall not stand before obscure men — but [they] did not regard it. [9]A heavenly voice issued, and said: "Shall He recompense it according to you, when you refuse His judgment? You shall choose, and not I; etc."

[10]Those who interpret the Torah metaphorically said: All of them will come to the World to Come,

RASHI

מי מנאן — להנך מלכים והדיוטות דקתני במתניתין אין להם חלק. **עוד אחד** — שלמה. **דיוקנו** — של דוד אביו נשתטח לפניהם, שלא למנותו עמהם. **בל יתיצב לפני חשוכים** — בגיהנם. **לפני מלכים יתיצב** — בגן עדן ולא לפני חשוכים. **המעמך ישלמנה** — וכי עליכם לשלם תשלומי עונשו לאדם, שאתם נמאסים בו בשלמה לומר שאין לו חלק לעולם הבא. **כי אתה תבחר ולא אני** — וכי הבחירה בכם תלויה ולא בי, לומר מי שיש לו חלק ומי אין לו חלק הלא בי הדבר תלוי. **דורשי רשומות** — דורשי פסוקים כדכתיב (דניאל י) ״את הרשום בכתב אמת״ היו אומרים שלכולם יש להם חלק, אפילו למנשה וירבעם ולאחאב.

NOTES

מִי מְנָאָן **Who counted them.** *Be'er Sheva* explains that the question whether a certain person has a portion in the World to Come cannot be answered by way of rational analysis, and so the Gemara asks who formulated the list of kings and ordinary people who do not have a portion in the World to Come. Rav Ashi answers that the members of the Great Assembly which included the last Prophets formulated the list, with prophetic inspiration.

דּוֹרְשֵׁי רְשׁוּמוֹת **Those who interpret the Torah metaphorically.** *Ramah* explains this expression in two ways: Those who interpret important matters, and those who interpret esoteric verses (as in Daniel 10:21: "But I will tell you that which is inscribed [רָשׁוּם] in the true record").

[1]שֶׁנֶּאֱמַר: ״לִי גִלְעָד וְלִי מְנַשֶּׁה וְאֶפְרַיִם מָעוֹז רֹאשִׁי; יְהוּדָה מְחֹקְקִי, מוֹאָב סִיר רַחְצִי עַל אֱדוֹם אַשְׁלִיךְ נַעֲלִי; עָלַי פְּלֶשֶׁת הִתְרוֹעָעִי״. [2]״לִי גִלְעָד (וְלִי מְנַשֶּׁה)״ — זֶה אַחְאָב שֶׁנָּפַל בְּרָמוֹת גִּלְעָד; [3]״מְנַשֶּׁה״ — כְּמַשְׁמָעוֹ; [4]״אֶפְרַיִם מָעוֹז רֹאשִׁי״ — זֶה יָרָבְעָם דְּקָאָתֵי מֵאֶפְרַיִם; [5]״יְהוּדָה מְחֹקְקִי״ — זֶה אֲחִיתוֹפֶל [105A] דְּקָאָתֵי מִיהוּדָה; [6]״מוֹאָב סִיר רַחְצִי״ — זֶה גֵּחֲזִי שֶׁלָּקָה עַל עִסְקֵי רְחִיצָה; [7]״עַל אֱדוֹם אַשְׁלִיךְ נַעֲלִי״ — זֶה דּוֹאֵג הָאֲדוֹמִי; [8]״עָלַי פְּלֶשֶׁת הִתְרוֹעָעִי״ — אָמְרוּ מַלְאֲכֵי הַשָּׁרֵת לִפְנֵי הַקָּדוֹשׁ בָּרוּךְ הוּא: [9]״רִבּוֹנוֹ שֶׁל עוֹלָם, אִם יָבֹא דָּוִד שֶׁהָרַג אֶת הַפְּלִשְׁתִּי, וְהוֹרִישׁ אֶת בָּנֶיךָ גַּת, מָה אַתָּה עוֹשֶׂה לוֹ?״ [10]אָמַר לָהֶן: ״עָלַי לַעֲשׂוֹתָן רֵיעִים זֶה לָזֶה״.

[11]״מַדּוּעַ שׁוֹבְבָה הָעָם הַזֶּה יְרוּשָׁלַיִם מְשֻׁבָה נִצַּחַת וגו׳״. [12]אָמַר רַב: תְּשׁוּבָה נִצַּחַת 9הֱשִׁיבָה כְּנֶסֶת יִשְׂרָאֵל לַנָּבִיא.

LITERAL TRANSLATION

[1]as it is stated: "Gilead is Mine, and Manasseh is Mine; Ephraim also is the strength of My head; Judah is My scepter; Moab is My washingpot; on Edom I will cast my shoe; Philistia, acclaim Me." [2]"Gilead is Mine, and Manasseh is Mine" — this is Ahab who fell at Ramot Gilead; [3]"Manasseh" — literally; [4]"Ephraim also is the strength of My head" — this is Jeroboam who came from Ephraim; [5]"Judah is My scepter" — this is Achitofel [105A] who came from Judah; [6]"Moab is My washingpot" — this is Gehazi who was punished for matters relating to washing; [7]"On Edom I will cast my shoe" — this is Doeg the Edomite; [8]"Philistia, acclaim Me" — the ministering Angels said to the Holy One, blessed be He: [9]"Master of the Universe, if David comes, who killed the Philistine, and caused Your sons to inherit Gat, what will You do for him?" [10]He said to them: "It is upon me to make them friends with one another."

[11]"Why is this people of Jerusalem turned away in perpetual backsliding, etc.?" [12]Rav said: The congregation of Israel gave the Prophet an irrefutable answer.

TRANSLATION AND COMMENTARY

even Manasseh, Jeroboam, and Ahab, [1]**as the verses state** (Psalms 60:9-10): **"Gilead is Mine, and Manasseh is Mine; Ephraim also is the strength of My head; Judah is My scepter; Moab is My washingpot; over Edom I will cast my shoe; Philistia, acclaim Me."** [2]**"Gilead is Mine, and Manasseh is Mine" — this is** a reference to **Ahab who fell in Ramot Gilead;** [3]**"Manasseh"** — this should be understood **literally** as referring to Manasseh, King of Judah; [4]**"Ephraim also is the strength of My head" — this is** a reference to **Jeroboam, who came from** the tribe of **Ephraim;** [5]**"Judah is My scepter" — this is** an allusion to **Achitofel** [105A], **who came from** the tribe of **Judah;** [6]**"Moab is My washingpot" — this is** an allusion to **Gehazi, who was punished** with leprosy **for the incident involving** Naaman's **washing** seven times in the Jordan River (see II Kings 5); [7]**"On Edom I will cast my shoe" — this is** an allusion to **Doeg the Edomite;** [8]**"Philistia** [פְּלֶשֶׁת], **acclaim** [הִתְרוֹעָעִי] **Me** [עָלַי]**" — the ministering Angels said to the Holy One, blessed be He:** [9]**"Master of the Universe, if David, who killed the Philistine** [הַפְּלִשְׁתִּי], **and caused Your sons to inherit Gat, comes** and complains to You for granting a portion in the World to Come to his enemies, Doeg and Achitofel, **what will You do for him** in order to appease him?" [10]God **said to** the Angels: **"It will be** incumbent **upon me** [עָלַי] to create good feelings between them and **reconcile them as friends** [רֵיעִים, alluded to by the word הִתְרוֹעָעִי]."

מַדּוּעַ שׁוֹבְבָה הָעָם [11]The verse states (Jeremiah 8:5): **"Why is this people of Jerusalem turned away in perpetual backsliding?"** [12]**Rav said:** When **the congregation of Israel** was admonished by the Prophet to repent, they **gave the Prophet an irrefutable answer**

RASHI

לי גלעד ולי מנשה — עלי לסבול עונש כדי שיהו הם זוכים. **מנשה במשמעו** — מנשה בן חזקיהו. **דקא אתי מיהודה** — דקאמר לו דוד ואתה אנוש כערכי אלופי ומיודעי, שהיה קורא לאחיתופל מיודעי, קרובי, שהיה משבט יהודה כדוד. **מואב סיר רחצי** — דוד דקא אתי ממואב. **סיר רחצי** — גחזי שסר ונצטרע על עסקי רחילה. **על אדום אשליך נעלי** — אנעיל אותם בגן עדן. **אם יבוא דוד שהרג את הפלשתי** — ויצעק לפניך על שאתה נותן חלק לדואג ואחיתופל לעולם הבא, מה אתה עושה להפיס דעתו — שהם היו שונאין אותו. **אמר להם** — עלי לפייסן ולעשותן ריעים ואהובים זה לזה, והיינו "התרועעי" לשון ריעות.

NOTES

אֲחִיתוֹפֶל דְּקָאָתֵי מִיהוּדָה **Achitofel, who came from Judah.** Achitofel is referred to as (II Samuel 15:12) "Hagiloni," that is to say, from the city of Gilo, which according to the book of Joshua was in the territory of Judah. The term מְחֹקְקִי, translated here as "scepter," but which may also be understood as "lawgiver," aptly applies to Achitofel, for he was the greatest scholar of his generation, a judge, and a counselor.

תְּשׁוּבָה נִצַּחַת **An irrefutable answer.** The Gemara understands the word מְשֻׁבָה, "backsliding," in the sense of תְּשׁוּבָה, "answer." The word נִצַּחַת seems to have been understood in the sense of נֶצַח, "eternal," since the first question raised by the congregation of Israel (according to Rav) relates to

[1]אָמַר לָהֶן נָבִיא לְיִשְׂרָאֵל: ״חִזְרוּ בִּתְשׁוּבָה! [2]אֲבוֹתֵיכֶם שֶׁחָטְאוּ, הֵיכָן הֵם?״ [3]אָמְרוּ לָהֶן: ״וּנְבִיאֵיכֶם שֶׁלֹּא חָטְאוּ, הֵיכָן הֵם״? [4]שֶׁנֶּאֱמַר: ״אֲבוֹתֵיכֶם, אַיֵּה הֵם? וְהַנְּבִאִים הַלְעוֹלָם יִחְיוּ?״ [5]אָמַר לָהֶן: ״(אֲבוֹתֵיכֶם) חָזְרוּ וְהוֹדוּ, [6]שֶׁנֶּאֱמַר: ׳אַךְ דְּבָרַי וְחֻקַּי אֲשֶׁר צִוִּיתִי אֶת עֲבָדַי הַנְּבִיאִים וגו׳ ׳ ״.

[7]שְׁמוּאֵל אָמַר: בָּאוּ עֲשָׂרָה בְּנֵי אָדָם וְיָשְׁבוּ לְפָנָיו. [8]אָמַר לָהֶן: ״חִזְרוּ בִּתְשׁוּבָה״. [9]אָמְרוּ לוֹ: ״עֶבֶד שֶׁמְּכָרוֹ רַבּוֹ, וְאִשָּׁה שֶׁגֵּרְשָׁהּ בַּעֲלָהּ, כְּלוּם יֵשׁ לָזֶה עַל זֶה כְּלוּם״? [10]אָמַר לוֹ הַקָּדוֹשׁ בָּרוּךְ הוּא לַנָּבִיא: [11]״לֵךְ אֱמוֹר לָהֶן: ׳אֵי זֶה סֵפֶר כְּרִיתוּת אִמְּכֶם אֲשֶׁר שִׁלַּחְתִּיהָ? אוֹ מִי מִנּוֹשַׁי אֲשֶׁר מָכַרְתִּי אֶתְכֶם לוֹ? הֵן בַּעֲוֹנוֹתֵיכֶם נִמְכַּרְתֶּם וּבְפִשְׁעֵיכֶם שֻׁלְּחָה אִמְּכֶם׳ ״.

[12]וְהַיְינוּ דְּאָמַר רֵישׁ לָקִישׁ: מַאי דִּכְתִיב: ״דָּוִד, עַבְדִּי״. ״נְבוּכַדְנֶצַּר...עַבְדִּי״? [13]גָּלוּי וְיָדוּעַ לִפְנֵי מִי שֶׁאָמַר וְהָיָה

LITERAL TRANSLATION

[1]The Prophet said to Israel: "Repent! [2]Your fathers who sinned, where are they?" [3]They said to them: "And your Prophets who did not sin, where are they?" [4]As it is stated: "Your fathers, where are they? and the Prophets, will they live forever?" [5]He said to them: "Your fathers returned and confessed, [6]as it is stated: 'But My words and My statutes, which I commanded My servants the Prophets, etc.' "

[7]Shmuel said: Ten people came and sat before him. [8]He said to them: "Repent." [9]They said to him: "A slave who was sold by his master, and a woman who was divorced by her husband, does one have anything on the other?" [10]The Holy One, blessed be He, said to the Prophet: [11]"Go, say to them: 'Where is your mother's bill of divorce, with which I have sent her away? Or to which of My creditors have I sold you? Behold, for your iniquities you sold yourselves, and for your transgressions was your mother sent away.' "

[12]And this is what Resh Lakish said: What is written: "David, My servant," "Nebuchadnezzar ...My servant"? [13]It is revealed and known to Him who spoke and

TRANSLATION AND COMMENTARY

[תְּשׁוּבָה נִצַּחַת, a play on the expression מְשֻׁבָה נִצַּחַת, "perpetual backsliding"]. [1]**The Prophet said to** the people of **Israel: "Repent!** [2]**Your fathers who sinned, where are they** now? Surely they have all died on account of their wrongdoing!" [3]**They answered** the Prophets, saying: **"And your Prophets who did not sin, where are they** now? Surely they, too, have died!" [4]The Prophet's argument and the people's reply are alluded to by **the verse** that **states** (Zechariah 1:5): **"Your fathers, where are they? and the Prophets, do they live forever?"** [5]The Prophet **said to them: "Your fathers later admitted** that the words of the Prophets had been fulfilled, [6]**as the** very next **verse states** (Zechariah 1:6): **'But My words and My statutes, which I commanded My servants the Prophets,** did they not overtake your fathers? so that they repented and said, As the Lord of hosts intended to do to us, according to our ways, and according to our doings, so has He dealt with us.'"

שְׁמוּאֵל אָמַר [7]**Shmuel said:** Israel's irrefutable answer was: **Ten people came and sat before** the Prophet Ezekiel. [8]**He admonished them,** saying: **"Repent."** [9]**They answered him: "If a slave was sold by his master, or a woman was divorced by her husband, does one** still **have a** claim **against the other?** Surely not. Since God handed us over to Nebuchadnezzar, and sent us out of His land, our relationship is over, and He can no longer claim that we are bound by His Torah and commandments." [10]**The Holy One, blessed be He, said to the Prophet:** [11]**"Go, say to them** (Isaiah 50:1): **'Where is your mother's bill of divorce, with which I have sent her away? or to which of My creditors have I sold you? Behold, for your iniquities you sold yourselves, and for your transgressions was your mother sent away.'** Divine punishment for Israel's sins does not rescind the Covenant."

וְהַיְינוּ דְּאָמַר [12]The Gemara notes that **this is what Resh Lakish said: What is** the meaning of **the verse that states** (II Samuel 3:18): **"David, My servant,"** and the verse that states (Jeremiah 43:10): **"Nebuchadnezzar...My servant"?** Why was the wicked King Nebuchadnezzar referred to as God's servant, just like David? [13]Rather, **it was revealed and known to Him who spoke and brought the world into being**

RASHI

ושמואל אמר: מאי תשובה נצחת — כהאי גוונא: [באו] עשרה בני אדם וכו׳. **עבד שמכרו רבו** — ומאחר שמכרנו הקדוש ברוך הוא לנבוכדנצר וגרשנו מעליו יש לו עלינו כלום. **מאי דכתיב ודוד עבדי נבוכדנצר עבדי** — שקראו לאותו רשע עבד כמו שקראו לדוד דכתיב בסוף ירמיה (מג) ״הנני שולח ולקחתי את נבוכדנצר עבדי״ — לא מפני שדומה זה לזה, אלא גלוי וידוע לפני מי שאמר והיה העולם שעתידין ישראל לומר: כבר מכרנו הקדוש ברוך הוא לנבוכדנצר לפיכך הקדים הקדוש ברוך הוא וקרא ״עבדי״ לנבוכדנצר — כדי להחזיר להן תשובה.

NOTES

the eternal existence of the Prophets, and the second question (according to Shmuel) also relates to the eternal relationship between God and Israel (*Ri'af*).

TRANSLATION AND COMMENTARY

that the people of Israel would speak this way, arguing that once God delivered them to their enemies, they were no longer bound by His commandments. [1]**Therefore, the Holy One, blessed be He, called** Nebuchadnezzar, **His servant,** first, in order to encourage Israel to repent. [2]Israel's argument can indeed be refuted as follows: If **a slave purchased property, to whom** does **the slave** belong, and **to whom** does **the property belong?** Both the slave and the property belong to the slave's master. Thus, even if God delivered the people of Israel to Nebuchadnezzar, they never left God's possession. Nebuchadnezzar is God's servant, and whatever is acquired by a servant belongs to his master.

וְהָעֹלָה עַל רוּחֲכֶם [3]The verses state (Ezekiel 20:32-33): **"And what comes into your mind shall never come to be, that you say, We will be like the nations, like the families of the countries, to serve wood and stone. As I live, says the Lord God, surely with a mighty hand, and with an outstretched arm, and with wrath poured out, will I rule over you."** [4]**Rav Naḥman said:** If only **God would become angry with us with all His anger, and redeem us** against our will, and rule over us as king.

וְיִסְּרוֹ לַמִּשְׁפָּט [5]The verse in Isaiah states (Isaiah 28:26): **"And chastise it in judgment; his God will instruct him."** [6]**Rabbah bar Bar Ḥannah said:** This is the irrefutable answer which the people of Israel gave the Prophet: When **the Prophet said to the people of Israel: "Repent** of your sins," [7]**they said to him: "We cannot** repent, for **the evil impulse controls us."** [8]The Prophet then **said to them: "Chastise your evil impulse,** and overcome it." [9]The people **answered: "'His God will instruct him'** — let God show us how to overcome our evil impulses, for by ourselves we cannot."

אַרְבָּעָה הֶדְיוֹטוֹת [10]The Gemara now returns to our Mishnah, still the first Mishnah of this chapter: "The **four ordinary people** who do not have a portion in the World to Come are **Balaam** the son of Be'or, who was invited by Balak to curse the people of Israel; **Doeg** the Edomite, who slandered David before Saul and caused the death of the priests of Nob; **Achitofel,** who offered Absalom evil counsel against his father; **and Gehazi,** Elisha's

הָעוֹלָם שֶׁעֲתִידִין יִשְׂרָאֵל לוֹמַר כָּךְ. [1]לְפִיכָךְ הִקְדִּים הַקָּדוֹשׁ בָּרוּךְ הוּא וּקְרָאוֹ עַבְדּוֹ. [2]עֶבֶד שֶׁקָּנָה נְכָסִים — עֶבֶד לְמִי, נְכָסִים לְמִי?

[3]״וְהָעֹלָה עַל רוּחֲכֶם הָיוֹ לֹא תִהְיֶה אֲשֶׁר אַתֶּם אֹמְרִים נִהְיֶה כַגּוֹיִם כְּמִשְׁפְּחוֹת הָאֲרָצוֹת לְשָׁרֵת עֵץ וָאָבֶן. חַי אָנִי נְאֻם ה׳ אֱלֹהִים אִם לֹא בְּיָד חֲזָקָה וּבִזְרוֹעַ נְטוּיָה וּבְחֵמָה שְׁפוּכָה אֶמְלוֹךְ עֲלֵיכֶם״. [4]אָמַר רַב נַחְמָן: כָּל כִּי הַאי רִיתְחָא לִירְתַּח רַחֲמָנָא עֲלַן וְלִפְרוֹקִינַן. [5]״וְיִסְּרוֹ לַמִּשְׁפָּט; אֱלֹהָיו יוֹרֶנּוּ״. [6]אָמַר רַבָּה בַּר בַּר חָנָה: אָמַר לָהֶן נָבִיא לְיִשְׂרָאֵל: ״חִזְרוּ בִּתְשׁוּבָה״. [7]אָמְרוּ לוֹ: ״אֵין אָנוּ יְכוֹלִין, יֵצֶר הָרַע שׁוֹלֵט בָּנוּ״. [8]אָמַר לָהֶם: ״יַסְּרוּ יִצְרֵיכֶם״. [9]אָמְרוּ לוֹ: ״אֱלֹהָיו יוֹרֶנּוּ״. [10]״אַרְבָּעָה הֶדְיוֹטוֹת: בִּלְעָם וְדוֹאֵג וַאֲחִיתוֹפֶל וְגֵחֲזִי״.

LITERAL TRANSLATION

the world came into being that Israel would speak this way. [1]Therefore the Holy One, blessed be He, called him His servant first. [2]A slave who purchased property — the slave to whom, the property to whom?

[3]"And what comes into your mind shall never come to be, that you say, We will be like the nations, like the families of the countries, to serve wood and stone. As I live, says the Lord God, surely with a mighty hand, and with an outstretched arm, and with wrath poured out, will I rule over you." [4]Rav Naḥman said: With all this anger, let the Merciful be angry with us, and redeem us.

[5]"And chastise it in judgment; his God will instruct him." [6]Rabbah bar Bar Ḥannah said: The Prophet said to Israel: "Repent." [7]They said to him: "We cannot. The evil impulse controls us." [8]He said to them: "Chastise your [evil] impulse." [9]They said to him: "His God will instruct him."

[10]"Four ordinary people: Balaam, and Doeg, and Achitofel, and Gehazi."

RASHI

עבד למי נכסים למי — כלומר נבוכדנצר עבדי הוא וכל מה שקנה לי הוא, ועדיין לא יצאתם מרשותי. **והעולה על רוחכם היה לא תהיה** — כל מה שאתם סבורים לא יהיה. **כל כי האי ריתחא** — מי יתן ויבא לנו זה הכעס ״בחימה שפוכה אמלוך עליכם״ — שיגאלנו בעל כרחנו וימלוך עלינו. **אמר רבי אבא בר כהנא** — היינו תשובה נצחת דאמרו ליה: ״אלהים יורנו״, שאין אנו יכולין ליסר אותו.

NOTES

אֱלֹהָיו יוֹרֶנּוּ **His God will instruct him.** Some understand the word יוֹרֶנּוּ in the sense of "casting, throwing." The people of Israel argued that they had no way of controlling their evil impulse, and so God had to cast it away from them (*Rabbi Ya'akov Emden*). As for the argument itself, *Ramah* noted that this was merely an excuse offered by the people of Israel for their wrongdoing, for God gives everyone the strength to choose between right and wrong, and to overcome his evil impulse, if he so desires.

TRANSLATION AND COMMENTARY

servant, who denigrated Rabbinic scholars." [1]**Balaam's** name shows that he was **without** [*belo*] **a people** [*am*], that is to say, he does not share a portion in the World to Come along with the people of Israel. [2]**Another explanation** of that name may also be suggested: **Balaam destroyed** [*bilah*] **a people** [*am*], offering Balak advice which led to the death of twenty-four thousand Israelites. [3]The appellation **son of Be'or** intimates that Balaam's father **engaged in bestiality with an animal** (*be'ir*).

תָּנָא [4]**A Tanna taught** a related Baraita: **"Be'or** the father of Balaam, **Kushan Rish'atayim, and Laban the Aramean** were the same man. [5]He was called **Be'or because he engaged in intercourse with an animal** (*be'ir*). [6]He was called **Kushan Rish'atayim** ("double wickedness"), **because he performed two wicked deeds against Israel, one in the days of Jacob,** when he (Laban the Aramean) pursued Jacob in order to kill him, **and one** after the death of Joshua **at the time of the judges,** as the verse states (Judges 3: 8): "And He [= God] sold them into the hand of Kushan Rish'atayim." [7]**And what was his** real **name?** [8]**His** real **name was Laban the Aramean.**

כְּתִיב [9]The Gemara points out the following contradiction: One **verse states** (Numbers 22:5): "Balaam **the son of Be'or,"** implying that Be'or was Balaam's father. [10]**And** another **verse states** (Numbers 24:3): "Balaam **his son Be'or,"** implying that Be'or was Balaam's son! [11]**Rabbi Yoḥanan said:** This second verse teaches that Balaam's biological **father was** like **his son in prophecy,** meaning that Balaam was a much greater Prophet than his father.

בִּלְעָם הוּא [12]The Gemara draws a conclusion from the Mishnah: Since the Mishnah lists the non-Jew Balaam among those who do not have a portion in the World to Come, it implies that among non-Jews **it is** only **Balaam who will not go to the World to Come, but other** non-Jews **will** indeed **go** there.

[1]בִּלְעָם — בְּלֹא עַם. [2]דָּבָר אַחֵר: בִּלְעָם — שֶׁבִּלָּה עַם. [3]בֶּן בְּעוֹר — שֶׁבָּא עַל בְּעִיר. [4]תָּנָא: "הוּא בְּעוֹר, הוּא כּוּשַׁן רִשְׁעָתַיִם הוּא לָבָן הָאֲרַמִּי". [5]בְּעוֹר — שֶׁבָּא עַל בְּעִיר. [6]כּוּשַׁן רִשְׁעָתַיִם — דַּעֲבַד שְׁתֵּי רִשְׁעִיּוֹת בְּיִשְׂרָאֵל, אַחַת בִּימֵי יַעֲקֹב, וְאַחַת בִּימֵי שְׁפוֹט הַשּׁוֹפְטִים. [7]וּמַה שְּׁמוֹ? [8]לָבָן הָאֲרַמִּי שְׁמוֹ.

[9]כְּתִיב: "בֶּן בְּעוֹר". [10]וּכְתִיב: "בְּנוֹ בְעֹר". [11]אָמַר רַבִּי יוֹחָנָן: אָבִיו בְּנוֹ הוּא לוֹ בִּנְבִיאוּת.

[12]בִּלְעָם הוּא דְּלָא אָתֵי לְעָלְמָא דְּאָתֵי, הָא אַחֲרִינֵי אָתוּ.

LITERAL TRANSLATION

[1]Balaam — without a people. [2]Another explanation: Balaam — who destroyed a people. [3]The son of Be'or — who had intercourse with an animal.

[4][A Tanna] taught: "He is Be'or, he is Kushan Rish'atayim, he is Laban the Aramean. [5]Be'or — because he had intercourse with an animal. [6]Kushan Rish'atayim — because he performed two wicked deeds against Israel, one in the days of Jacob, and one in the days when the judges judged. [7]And what is his name? [8]His name is Laban the Aramean.

[9]It is written: "The son of Be'or." [10]And it is written: "His son Be'or." [11]Rabbi Yoḥanan said: His father was his son in prophecy.

[12]Balaam is the one who will not come to the World to Come, but others will come.

RASHI

בלא עם — שאין לו חלק עם עם. **שבלה עם** — שבלבל ישראל בעצתו שהשיאו לבלק כדבעינן למימר לקמן, והפיל מהם עשרים וארבעה אלפים. **בעור שבא על בעיר** — שבא על אתונו, כמו בהמה דמתרגמינן בעיר. **תנא הוא בעור** — אביו של בלעם הוא כושן רשעתים הוא לבן הארמי. **אחת בימי יעקב** — שרדף אחריו ובקש לעקור הכל. **ואחת בימי שופטים** — לאחר מיתת יהושע, דכתיב (שופטים ג) "ויחר אף ה' בישראל ויתנם ביד כושן רשעתים". **בנו בעור** — משמע בעור בנו של בלעם היה. **בנו הוא** — לבלעם בנביאות, שבלעם גדול מאביו היה בנביאות. **הא שאר נכרים אתו** — כלומר מדקא חשיב תנא דמתניתין דבלעם שהיה נכרי בהדי הדיוטות, וקאמר דאין לו חלק — מכלל דשאר נכרים יש להם חלק.

NOTES

בְּלֹא עַם Without a people. Some explain that Balaam left the country of his birth — Aram Naharayim — and thus remained without a people and without a country (*Arukh*).

הוּא בְּעוֹר, הוּא כּוּשַׁן רִשְׁעָתַיִם He is Be'or, he is Kushan Rish'atayim. This statement, according to its plain meaning, is difficult to understand, since it implies that the wicked Laban=Be'or=Kushan Rish'atayim lived an extremely long life. The Baraita might mean that these three men are similar, for they all came from Aram Naharayim, and they all oppressed and afflicted Israel. Thus one may learn about one from what is said about the other (see *Rabbi Ya'akov Emden*, and others).

בִּלְעָם הוּא דְּלָא אָתֵי It is Balaam who will not come. It was necessary for the Mishnah to teach us that Balaam was not one of the righteous members of the other nations, even though that is evident from what is said about him in the Bible, because Balaam was nevertheless a Prophet (and according to some a Prophet of the stature of Moses). Thus one might have thought that he was a righteous non-Jew whose portion awaits him in the World to Come (*Meiri*).

HALAKHAH

הָא אַחֲרִינֵי אָתוּ But others will come. "The righteous members of the other nations have a portion in the World to Come," following Rabbi Yehoshua. (*Rambam, Sefer Mada, Hilkhot Teshuvah* 3:5.)

[1]מַתְנִיתִין מַנִּי? [2]רַבִּי יְהוֹשֻׁעַ הִיא, דְּתַנְיָא: [3]"רַבִּי אֱלִיעֶזֶר אוֹמֵר: 'יָשׁוּבוּ רְשָׁעִים לִשְׁאוֹלָה כָּל גּוֹיִם שְׁכֵחֵי אֱלֹהִים'. [4]'יָשׁוּבוּ רְשָׁעִים לִשְׁאוֹלָה' — אֵלּוּ פּוֹשְׁעֵי יִשְׂרָאֵל; 'כָּל גּוֹיִם שְׁכֵחֵי אֱלֹהִים' — אֵלּוּ פּוֹשְׁעֵי גוֹיִם, [5]דִּבְרֵי רַבִּי אֱלִיעֶזֶר. [6]אָמַר לוֹ רַבִּי יְהוֹשֻׁעַ: וְכִי נֶאֱמַר 'בְּכָל גּוֹיִם'? [7]וַהֲלֹא לֹא נֶאֱמַר אֶלָּא: 'כָּל גּוֹיִם שְׁכֵחֵי אֱלֹהִים'. [8]אֶלָּא: 'יָשׁוּבוּ רְשָׁעִים לִשְׁאוֹלָה' — מַאן נִינְהוּ? [9]'כָּל גּוֹיִם שְׁכֵחֵי אֱלֹהִים'".

[10]וְאַף אוֹתוֹ רָשָׁע נָתַן סִימָן בְּעַצְמוֹ. [11]אָמַר: "תָּמֹת נַפְשִׁי מוֹת יְשָׁרִים". [12]אִם תָּמוּת נַפְשִׁי מוֹת יְשָׁרִים, תְּהֵא אַחֲרִיתִי כָּמוֹהוּ. [13]וְאִם לָאו, הִנְנִי הוֹלֵךְ לְעַמִּי".

[14]"וַיֵּלְכוּ זִקְנֵי מוֹאָב וְזִקְנֵי מִדְיָן". [15]תָּנָא: "מִדְיָן וּמוֹאָב לֹא הָיָה לָהֶם שָׁלוֹם מֵעוֹלָם. [16]מָשָׁל לִשְׁנֵי כְלָבִים שֶׁהָיוּ בָּעֵדֶר, וְהָיוּ

LITERAL TRANSLATION

[1]Our Mishnah is in accordance with whom? [2]It is Rabbi Yehoshua, for it was taught: [3]"Rabbi Eliezer says: 'The wicked shall return to Sheol, all the nations that forget God.' [4]'The wicked return to Sheol' — these are the sinners of Israel; 'all the nations that forget God' — these are the sinners of the nations; [5][these are] the words of Rabbi Eliezer. [6]Rabbi Yehoshua said to him: Is it stated 'among all the nations'? [7]But surely it was only stated: 'All the nations that forget God.' [8]Rather: 'The wicked shall return to Sheol' — who are they? [9]'All the nations that forget God.'"

[10]And even that wicked man gave a sign about himself. [11]He said: "Let me die the death of the righteous." [12]If I die the death of the righteous, my end will be like his. [13]And if not, I will go to my people.

[14]"And the elders of Moab and the elders of Midian set out." [15][A Tanna] taught: "Midian and Moab were never [before] at peace. [16]It is like two watchdogs who were with a flock, and they

TRANSLATION AND COMMENTARY

[1]The Gemara asks: **In accordance with whose** position was **our Mishnah** taught? [2]The Gemara explains: Our Mishnah follows the position of **Rabbi Yehoshua, for it was taught** in a Baraita: [3]**"Rabbi Eliezer says:** The verse states (Psalms 9:18): **'The wicked shall be turned back to Sheol, all the nations that forget God.'** [4]**'The wicked shall be turned back to Sheol' — this is** a reference to **the sinners of Israel** who are sentenced to Sheol; **'all the nations that forget God' — this is** a reference to **the sinners of the nations,** all of whom are denied a place in the World to Come — [5]**this is the position of Rabbi Eliezer.** [6]**Rabbi Yehoshua said to** Rabbi Eliezer: **Does the verse state: 'Like all the nations** that forget God'? Had the verse been formulated that way, I would indeed understand that the wicked of Israel are like all the nations, and have no place in the World to Come. [7]**But surely the verse states only: 'All the nations that forget God,'** implying that those members of the nations who forget God have no place in the World to Come, but the others do. [8]**Rather,** the second half of the verse should be understood as explaining the first half: **'The wicked shall be turned back to Sheol' — who are they?** [9]**'All the nations that forget God.'"**

וְאַף אוֹתוֹ רָשָׁע [10]The Gemara adds: **Even that wicked man** himself — Balaam — **gave a sign about himself** that he does not have a share in the World to Come, [11]for **he said** (Numbers 23:10): **"Let me die the death of the righteous,** and let my last end be like his!" [12]**If I die the death of the righteous,** that is to say, if I die a natural death, **my end will be like his,** and I will have a place in the World to Come. [13]**But if** I do **not** die a natural death, but rather I am slain, then surely **I will go to my** own **people** in Gehinom.

וַיֵּלְכוּ [14]The verse states (Numbers 22:7): **"And the elders of Moab and the elders of Midian set out"** to consult Balaam. [15]**A Tanna taught** a Baraita: **"Midian and Moab had never before** been **at peace** with each other. [16]**They were like two watchdogs who were** guarding **a flock** together, even though **they hated one another.**

RASHI

מתניתין מני וכו' — אמר ליה רבי יהושע אלו נאמר "ישובו רשעים לשאולה ככל הגוים" — משמע כדקאמרת, השתא דכתיב "כל גוים שכחי אלהים" לא משמע אלא אותן השוכחים אלוה, כגון בלעם וישו [ושכמותו], אבל אחריני אתו, כדאמרינן בריש פרקין (לא,ב) "ורעו זרים לאנכם ובני נכר אכריכם" — לעולם הבא. **מאי נינהו כל גוים שכחי אלהים** — דמשום הכי בורר הקדוש ברוך הוא הרשעים שבהם ונותן אותם בגיהנם ואין להם חלק לעתיד, אבל השאר יש להם חלק. **ואף אותו רשע נתן סימן בעצמו** — שאין לו חלק לעתיד. **תמות נפשי מות ישרים** — אם ימות מיתת עצמו "תהא אחריתי כמוהו", דודאי יש לו חלק עמהם. **ואם לאו** — דלא ימות אלא יהרג — "הנני הולך לעמי", לגיהנם. **לא היה להם שלום** — דכתיב "המכה את מדין בשדה מואב".

NOTES

וְכִי נֶאֱמַר "בְּכָל גּוֹיִם"? Is it stated "among all the nations"? There are various readings of this line, but according to all of them, Rabbi Yehoshua means that the words "that forget God," are not to be understood as comprising a non-restrictive clause describing "all the nations," but rather should be taken as a restrictive clause, limiting the punishment of the

צְהוּבִין זֶה לָזֶה. [1]בָּא זְאֵב עַל הָאֶחָד. [2]אָמַר הָאֶחָד: ׳אִם אֵינִי עוֹזְרוֹ, הַיּוֹם הוֹרֵג אוֹתוֹ, וּלְמָחָר בָּא עָלַי׳. [3]הָלְכוּ שְׁנֵיהֶם וְהָרְגוּ הַזְּאֵב״.

[4]אָמַר רַב פַּפָּא: הַיְינוּ דְּאָמְרִי אֱינָשֵׁי: [5]כַּרְכּוּשְׁתָּא וְשׁוּנְרָא עֲבַדוּ הִלּוּלָא מִתַּרְבָּא דְבִישׁ גַּדָּא.

[6]״וַיֵּשְׁבוּ שָׂרֵי מוֹאָב עִם בִּלְעָם״. [7]וְשָׂרֵי מִדְיָן לְהֵיכָן אֲזוּל? [8]כֵּיוָן דַּאֲמַר לְהוּ: ״לִינוּ פֹה הַלַּיְלָה וַהֲשִׁבֹתִי אֶתְכֶם דָּבָר״, [9]אָמְרוּ: ״כְּלוּם יֵשׁ אָב שֶׁשּׂוֹנֵא אֶת בְּנוֹ״?

[10]אָמַר רַב נַחְמָן: חוּצְפָּא, אֲפִילּוּ כְּלַפֵּי שְׁמַיָּא מְהַנֵּי. [11]מֵעִיקָּרָא כְּתִיב: ״לֹא תֵלֵךְ עִמָּהֶם״. [12]וּלְבַסּוֹף כְּתִיב: ״קוּם, לֵךְ אִתָּם״.

[13]אָמַר רַב שֵׁשֶׁת: חוּצְפָּא מַלְכוּתָא בְּלֹא תָּאגָא הִיא, [14]דִּכְתִיב: ״וְאָנֹכִי הַיּוֹם רַךְ וּמָשׁוּחַ מֶלֶךְ; וְהָאֲנָשִׁים הָאֵלֶּה בְּנֵי צְרוּיָה קָשִׁים מִמֶּנִּי וגו׳״.

[15]אָמַר רַבִּי יוֹחָנָן: בִּלְעָם חִיגֵּר בְּרַגְלוֹ אַחַת הָיָה, שֶׁנֶּאֱמַר:

TRANSLATION AND COMMENTARY

[1]When **a wolf came** and attacked **one of them,** [2]**the other** dog **said: 'If I do not help** my fellow now, **today** the wolf **will kill him, and tomorrow he will come** back and attack **me.'** [3]**The two** dogs set aside their differences and **went and killed the wolf.** So, too, did Midian and Moab make peace with each other to fight against Israel."

אָמַר רַב פַּפָּא [4]**Rav Pappa said: This is** the meaning of **the popular adage:** [5]**A weasel and a cat made a wedding from the fat of bad luck.** Even though the weasel and the cat hate each other, they are ready to make peace and celebrate at the expense of a third party.

וַיֵּשְׁבוּ שָׂרֵי מוֹאָב [6]The verse states (Numbers 22:8): **"And the princes of Moab stayed with Balaam."** [7]The Gemara asks: **And where did the princes of Midian** mentioned in the previous verse **go?** [8]The Gemara explains: **When** Balaam **said to them** (Numbers 22:8): **"Lodge here this night, and I will bring you word,"** [9]the princes of Midian **said** to themselves: **"Is there a father who hates his son?** Surely God will not allow Balaam to curse the people of Israel." Seeing that their plan would not succeed, the princes of Midian went home.

אָמַר רַב נַחְמָן [10]**Rav Naḥman said: Impudence, even toward Heaven, may bring** the desired **results.** [11]**At first the verse states** that God told Balaam (Numbers 22:12): **"You shall not go with them."** [12]**But in the end,** after Balaam impudently sought God's permission a second time, **the verse states** that God answered (Numbers 22:20): **"Rise up, and go with them."**

אָמַר רַב שֵׁשֶׁת [13]**Rav Sheshet said: Impudence is royal power without a crown,** [14]**as the verse states** (II Samuel 3:39): **"And I am this day weak, though anointed king; and these men the sons of Zeruiah are too hard for me."** The sons of Zeruiah, with their insolence, were as strong as David himself, and David's only advantage was that he had been anointed king.

אָמַר רַבִּי יוֹחָנָן [15]**Rabbi Yoḥanan said: Balaam was lame in one leg, as the verse states** (Numbers 23:3):

LITERAL TRANSLATION

hated one another. [1]A wolf came upon one [of them]. [2][The other] one said: 'If I do not help him, today he will kill him, and tomorrow he will come upon me.' [3]The two of them went and killed the wolf."

[4]Rav Pappa said: This is what people say: [5]A weasel and a cat made a wedding from the fat of bad luck.

[6]"And the princes of Moab stayed with Balaam." [7]And where did the princes of Midian go? [8]When he said to them: "Lodge here this night, and I will bring you word," [9]they said: "Is there a father who hates his son?"

[10]Rav Naḥman said: Impudence, even toward Heaven, is beneficial. [11]At first it is written: "You shall not go with them." [12]And in the end it is written: "Rise up, and go with them."

[13]Rav Sheshet said: Impudence is kingship without a crown, [14]as it is written: "And I am this day weak, [though] anointed king; and these men the sons of Zeruiah are harder than I, etc."

[15]Rabbi Yoḥanan said: Balaam was lame in one leg, as it is stated:

RASHI

צהובין — כעוסין, כאדם שכועס פניו להובין. ברכושתא = חולדה. ברכושתא ושונרא — אין להם שלום מעולם. ביש גדא = מזל רע. כלום יש אב ששונא את בנו — שהוא סבור שיאמר לו הקדוש ברוך הוא קלל את בני, דקאמר בלעם לינו פה [הלילה]. חוצפא אפילו כלפי שמיא מהני — דאהני ליה מה שהאליף פניו לומר לשלוחי בלק "לינו פה", שאמר לו הקדוש ברוך הוא בתחילה לא תלך — והדר אמר לך. מלכותא בלא תגא — כלומר, שררה גדולה, ואינו חסר אלא כתר מלכות. אנכי היום רך ומשוח מלך והאנשים האלה קשים ממני — כלומר: איני גדול מהם אלא משיחת מלכות.

NOTES

underworld to those nations that forget God, but granting a portion in the World to Come to those nations that do not forget Him (see *Ramah*).

חִיגֵּר בְּרַגְלוֹ...בִּשְׁתֵּי רַגְלָיו **Lame in one leg...in both legs.** These deformities are mentioned in order to emphasize the character of these two personalities. Balaam was lame in

"וַיֵּלֶךְ שֶׁפִי". [1]שִׁמְשׁוֹן בִּשְׁתֵּי רַגְלָיו, שֶׁנֶּאֱמַר: "שְׁפִיפֹן עֲלֵי אֹרַח, הַנֹּשֵׁךְ עִקְּבֵי סוּס". [2]בִּלְעָם סוּמָא בְּאַחַת מֵעֵינָיו הָיָה, שֶׁנֶּאֱמַר: "שְׁתֻם הָעָיִן". [3]קוֹסֵם בְּאַמָּתוֹ הָיָה. [4]כְּתִיב הָכָא: "נֹפֵל, וּגְלוּי עֵינָיִם". [5]וּכְתִיב הָתָם: "וְהָמָן נֹפֵל עַל הַמִּטָּה וגו׳".

[6]אִיתְּמַר: מָר זוּטְרָא אָמַר: קוֹסֵם בְּאַמָּתוֹ הָיָה. [7]מָר בְּרֵיהּ דְּרָבִינָא אָמַר: שֶׁבָּא עַל אֲתוֹנוֹ. [8]מַאן דַּאֲמַר קוֹסֵם בְּאַמָּתוֹ הָיָה, כְּדַאֲמָרַן. [9]וּמַאן דַּאֲמַר בָּא עַל אֲתוֹנוֹ הָיָה — כְּתִיב הָכָא: "כָּרַע, שָׁכַב", [10]וּכְתִיב הָתָם: "בֵּין רַגְלֶיהָ [105B] כָּרַע נָפַל שָׁכָב וגו׳".

[11]"וְיֹדֵעַ דַּעַת עֶלְיוֹן". [12]הָשְׁתָּא

LITERAL TRANSLATION

"And he went limping." [1]Samson in two of his legs, as it is stated: "An adder in the path, that bites the horse's heels." [2]Balaam was blind in one of his eyes, as it is stated: "Whose eye is open." [3]He performed magic with his penis. [4]It is written here: "Falling down, but having his eyes open." [5]And it is written there: "And Haman fell upon the divan, etc."

[6]It was stated: Mar Zutra said: He performed magic with his penis. [7]Mar the son of Ravina said: He had intercourse with his ass. [8]The one who said he performed magic with his penis, as we said. [9]And the one who said he had intercourse with his ass — it is written here: "He crouched, he lay down." [10]And it is written there: "Between her legs [105B] he bent, he fell, he lay down, etc."

[11]"And he knows the knowledge of the Most High." [12]Now

TRANSLATION AND COMMENTARY

"And he went limping [שֶׁפִי]," for his leg was dislocated [שָׁפִי]. [1]**Samson** was lame **in both legs, as the verse** alluding to Samson in Jacob's blessing **states** (Genesis 49:17): "Dan shall be a serpent by the way, **an adder** [שְׁפִיפֹן] **in the path, that bites the horse's heels."** Samson, who came from the tribe of Dan, will be doubly lame [שְׁפִיפֹן, interpreted here as a doubling of the word שָׁפִי, used with regard to Balaam]. [2]**Balaam was blind in one eye, as the verse states** (Numbers 24:3): **"Whose eye is open,"** implying that only one of his eyes was open, but the other eye was closed. [3]Balaam **performed magic with his penis.** [4]**Here the verse states** (Numbers 24:4): **"Falling down, but having his eyes open."** [5]**And elsewhere** (Esther 7:8), **the verse states: "And Haman fell upon the divan."** Just as the word "fallen" regarding Haman has sexual connotations, so, too, does the word "falling" regarding Balaam have sexual connotations.

אִיתְּמַר [6]**It was stated** that the Amoraim disagreed about the following matter: **Mar Zutra said:** Balaam **performed magic with his penis.** [7]**Mar the son of Ravina said: He engaged in bestiality with his ass.** [8]The Gemara explains: The Amora **who said** that Balaam **performed magic with his penis,** interpreted the verses **as we just said.** [9]**And the** Amora **who said he engaged in bestiality with his ass** derived that as follows: **Here,** regarding Balaam, **the verse states** (Numbers 24:9): **"He crouched, he lay down."** [10]**And elsewhere** in the song of Deborah, **the verse states** (Judges 5:27): **"Between her legs** [105B] **he bent, he fell, he lay down."** Just as, there, "lying down" alludes to sexual relations, so, too, here, "lying down" alludes to sexual relations with his ass.

וְיֹדֵעַ דַּעַת עֶלְיוֹן [11]Regarding Balaam, the verse states (Numbers 24:16): **"And he knows the knowledge of the Most High."** [12]The Gemara asks: **Now** if Balaam **did not know** how to respond to questions **regarding his**

RASHI

שפי — כמו (חולין נד,ב) "בוקא דאטמא דשף מדוכתיה". שפיפון — משמעו שתים. שתום העין — שתום — פתוח, כמו "שתומו ניכר", כלומר: עינו אחת פתוחה, מכלל דהאחרת סתומה, והכי נמי מתרגמינן "דשפיר חזי", אית דמפרשי: שתום כמו סתום, ולאו מילתא היא. קוסם באמתו — כגון מעלה בזכורו. כרע נפל — מה כריעה דהתם דאית ביה נפילה — בעילה היא, אף כריעה דהכא דכתיב נופל — בעילה היא, שבא על בהמתו.

NOTES

one leg, but he traveled a great distance over difficult terrain because of his hatred of Israel. Samson was lame in both legs, but he delivered Israel with his great might (*Maharsha*).

בִּלְעָם בָּא עַל אֲתוֹנוֹ Balaam had intercourse with his ass. This statement might be understood metaphorically as intimating that Balaam eagerly followed his lowest animal-like instincts, pursuing glory and lucre. It was in this sense that "he had intercourse with his ass." But Mar the son of Ravina probably meant it literally (*Milḥemet Mitzvah* of *Rashbatz*).

כְּתִיב הָכָא: "כָּרַע, שָׁכַב" It is written here: "He crouched, he lay down." The difficulty has been pointed out that this verse was said by Balaam as a blessing in praise of Israel: "He crouched, he lay down like a lion, and like a great lion." Some therefore suggest that the text should read: "It is written here: 'Falling down.'" Some accept the standard reading, suggesting that since Balaam was so involved in satisfying his perverted desires, even when he bestowed a blessing upon Israel, he used an expression reflecting his degenerate lifestyle (*Rashash*; see also *Midrash Rabbah*).

וְיֹדֵעַ דַּעַת עֶלְיוֹן And he knows the knowledge of the Most High. The expression, "And he knows the knowledge of the Most High," was understood as reflecting Balaam's boast that in addition to his prophetic powers, he was also endowed with heavenly knowledge. The Gemara demonstrates that

TRANSLATION AND COMMENTARY

own **animal,** is it possible that **he knew the knowledge of the Most High?** [1]The Gemara explains: **What knowledge regarding his** own **animal** was Balaam missing? [2]**For** when Balak's officers saw Balaam riding on his ass, **they asked him: "Why are you not riding a horse?"** [3]Balaam **answered them: "I sent** my horses out **to pasture,** to eat and to rest." [4]The ass immediately **said to him** (Numbers 22:30): **"Am I not your ass?"** [5]Balaam answered: "You are my ass **only** to carry **loads,** but not for riding." [6]The ass countered (Numbers 22:30): "Am I not your ass **upon which you have ridden?"** [7]Balaam answered: "It was **only by chance** that I rode you, when I had no horse." The ass countered (Numbers 22:30): [8]"Am I not your ass upon which you have ridden **all your life to this day?"** [9]**"And moreover, I perform a carnal act with you at night."** Where is the allusion to bestiality in this verse? [10]**Here the verse states** (Numbers 22:30): **"I always acquiesced** to do so to you?" [11]**And elsewhere the verse states** (I Kings 1:2): **"And let her be his attendant** [סֹכֶנֶת]." Just as, there, the word סֹכֶנֶת alludes to carnal relations, so, too, here, the words הַהַסְכֵּן הִסְכַּנְתִּי allude to carnal relations. Now, if Balaam could not win an argument with his ass, how could he have knowledge of the Most High?

אֶלָּא מַאי [12]**Rather, what is** meant by the words: **"And he knows the knowledge of the Most High"?** [13]Balaam **knew how to determine the** precise **time when the Holy One, blessed be He, is angry.** At that precise moment he would proclaim his curses, and they would be fulfilled. [14]**And this is** the meaning of **what the Prophet** Michah **said to Israel** (Michah 6:5): **"O my people, remember now what Balak King of Moab devised, and what Balaam, the son of Be'or, answered him; from Shittim to Gilgal; that you may know the righteous acts of the Lord."** [15]**What is** meant by the words: **"That you may know the righteous acts of the Lord"?** [16]**The Holy One, blessed be He, said to the people of Israel: "Know, please, how many righteous acts I performed for you, that I was not angry all those days during the time of the wicked Balaam,** from the time that the people of Israel

דַּעַת בְּהֶמְתּוֹ לָא הֲוָה יָדַע, דַּעַת עֶלְיוֹן הֲוָה יָדַע? [1]מַאי דַּעַת בְּהֶמְתּוֹ? [2]דְּאָמְרִי לֵיהּ: "מַאי טַעְמָא לָא רְכַבְתְּ סוּסְיָא"? [3]אֲמַר לְהוּ: "שְׁדַאי לְהוּ בִּרְטִיבָא". [4]אֲמַרָה לֵיהּ: "הֲלֹא אָנֹכִי אֲתֹנְךָ". [5]"לִטְעִינָא בְּעָלְמָא". [6]"אֲשֶׁר רָכַבְתָּ עָלַי". [7]"אַקְרַאי בְּעָלְמָא". [8]"'מֵעוֹדְךָ עַד הַיּוֹם הַזֶּה'. [9]וְלֹא עוֹד, אֶלָּא שֶׁאֲנִי עוֹשָׂה [לְךָ] מַעֲשֵׂה אִישׁוּת בַּלַּיְלָה". [10]כְּתִיב הָכָא: "הַהַסְכֵּן הִסְכַּנְתִּי". [11]וּכְתִיב הָתָם: "וּתְהִי לוֹ סֹכֶנֶת".
[12]אֶלָּא מַאי "וְיֹדֵעַ דַּעַת עֶלְיוֹן"? [13]שֶׁהָיָה יוֹדֵעַ לְכַוֵּין אוֹתָהּ שָׁעָה שֶׁהַקָּדוֹשׁ בָּרוּךְ הוּא כּוֹעֵס בָּהּ. [14]וְהַיְינוּ דְּקָאָמַר לְהוּ נָבִיא לְיִשְׂרָאֵל: "עַמִּי זְכָר נָא, מַה יָּעַץ בָּלָק מֶלֶךְ מוֹאָב וּמֶה עָנָה אֹתוֹ בִּלְעָם בֶּן בְּעוֹר מִן הַשִּׁטִּים עַד הַגִּלְגָּל לְמַעַן דַּעַת צִדְקוֹת ה׳". [15]מַאי "לְמַעַן דַּעַת צִדְקוֹת ה׳"? [16]אָמַר לָהֶן הַקָּדוֹשׁ בָּרוּךְ הוּא לְיִשְׂרָאֵל: "דְּעוּ נָא כַּמָּה צְדָקוֹת עָשִׂיתִי עִמָּכֶם, שֶׁלֹּא כָּעַסְתִּי כָּל אוֹתָן הַיָּמִים בִּימֵי

LITERAL TRANSLATION

he does not know the knowledge of his animal, [but] the knowledge of the Most High he knows? [1]What is the knowledge of his animal? [2]For they said to him: "Why do you not ride horses?" [3]He said to them: "I sent them to pasture." [4]It said to him: "Am I not your ass." [5]"Only for a load." [6]"Upon which you have ridden." [7]"Only by chance." [8]"'All your life to this day.' [9]And not only this, but I perform a carnal act with you at night." [10]It is written here: "I always acquiesced." [11]And it is written there: "And let her be his attendant."

[12]Rather, what is: "And he knows the knowledge of the Most High"? [13]That he knew how to determine the hour when the Holy One, blessed be He, is angry. [14]And this is what the Prophet said to Israel: "O my people, remember now what Balak King of Moab devised, and what Balaam, the son of Be'or answered him; from Shittim to Gilgal; that you may know the righteous acts of the Lord." [15]What is, "that you may know the righteous acts of the Lord"? [16]The Holy One, blessed be He, said to Israel: "Know, please, how many righteous acts I performed for you, that I was not angry all those days in the days

RASHI

דעת בהמתו לא הוה ידע – מאי בעיא לאהדורי, כדמפרש דאמרי ליה שרי בלק: מאי טעמא לא רכבת אסוסיא. **ברטיבא** – באחו לרעות עשבים לחים. **אמר להו לטעינא בעלמא** – לישא משאות ולא לרכוב. **אמרה ליה** – אשר רכבת עלי. **אקראי בעלמא** – כשאין לי סוס מזומן. **אמרה לו** – מעודך. **מעשה אישות** – שאתה בועלי. **סוכנת** – מחממת. **מן השטים ועד הגלגל** – משחטאו בשטים ועד שנכנסו לארץ וחטאו בגלגל עשיתי עמהם צדקות הרבה. **כל אותן הימים** – שהיה בלעם מצפה לקללכם בשעה שהקדוש ברוך הוא כועס בה כל הקללות מתקיימות.

NOTES

Balaam was not wise at all, and that his "knowledge of the Most High" was limited to knowledge regarding the best time to proclaim a curse (*Tosafot, Avodah Zarah*).

[1] בִּלְעָם הָרָשָׁע. שֶׁאִילְמָלֵא כָּעַסְתִּי כָּל אוֹתָן הַיָּמִים — לֹא נִשְׁתַּיֵּיר מִשּׂוֹנְאֵיהֶן שֶׁל יִשְׂרָאֵל שָׂרִיד וּפָלִיט. [2] הַיְינוּ דְּקָאָמַר לֵיהּ בִּלְעָם לְבָלָק: ״מָה אֶקֹּב לֹא קַבֹּה אֵל וגו׳״ (אוֹתָן הַיּוֹם [הַיָּמִים] לֹא זָעַם ה׳).

[3] ״אֵל זֹעֵם בְּכָל יוֹם״. [4] ״וְכַמָּה זַעְמוֹ״? [5] רֶגַע, שֶׁנֶּאֱמַר: ״כִּי רֶגַע בְּאַפּוֹ חַיִּים בִּרְצוֹנוֹ וגו׳״. [6] אִיבָּעֵית אֵימָא: ״לֵךְ עַמִּי בֹּא בַחֲדָרֶיךָ וּסְגֹר דְּלָתְיךָ בַּעֲדֶךָ; חֲבִי כִמְעַט רֶגַע עַד יַעֲבָר זָעַם״. [7] אֵימַת רָתַח? [8] בִּתְלַת שָׁעֵי קַמַּיְיתָא, כִּי חִוָּורָא כַּרְבַּלְתָּא דְּתַרְנְגוֹלָא.

[9] כָּל שַׁעְתָּא וְשַׁעְתָּא נַמִי חִוָּורָא!

[10] כָּל שַׁעְתָּא וְשַׁעְתָּא אִית בֵּיהּ סוּרַיְקֵי סוּמָּקֵי. [11] הַהִיא שַׁעְתָּא, לֵית בֵּיהּ סוּרַיְקֵי סוּמָּקֵי.

[12] הַהוּא מִינָא דַּהֲוָה בְּשִׁיבָבוּתֵיהּ דְּרַבִּי יְהוֹשֻׁעַ בֶּן לֵוִי דַּהֲוָה קָא מְצַעֵר לֵיהּ. [13] יוֹמָא חַד נְקַט תַּרְנְגוֹלְתָּא, וַאֲסַר לֵיהּ בְּכַרְעֵיהּ, וְאוֹתִיב. [14] אֲמַר: ״כִּי מְטָא הַהוּא

LITERAL TRANSLATION

of the wicked Balaam. [1] For had I been angry all those days, a remnant or a survivor would not have been left of the enemies of Israel. [2] This is what Balaam said to Balak: "How shall I curse, whom God has not cursed, etc.?"

[3] "And a God who is angry every day." [4] And how long is His indignation? [5] A moment, as it is stated: "For His anger endures but a moment; in His favor is life, etc." [6] If you wish, say: "Go, my people, come into your chambers, and shut your doors about you; hide yourself for a little moment, until the anger passes."

[7] When is He angry? [8] In the first three hours, when the crest of the rooster is white.

[9] Every hour it is white!

[10] Every hour it has red streaks. [11] At that hour, it does not have red streaks.

[12] [There was] a certain heretic in the neighborhood of Rabbi Yehoshua ben Levi who distressed him. [13] One day he took a rooster, and tied it by its legs, and set it down. [14] He said: "When that

TRANSLATION AND COMMENTARY

sinned at Shittim and until they entered into Eretz Israel and sinned at Gilgal. [1] **For had I been angry all those days, not a remnant or a survivor would have been left of the enemies of Israel** — a euphemism for 'Israel' — for had Balaam succeeded in cursing Israel while I was angry, his curse would have been fulfilled. [2] **This is what Balaam** meant when he **said to Balak** (Numbers 23:8): **"How shall I curse, whom God has not cursed?** or how shall I be angry when the Lord has not been angry?" If God is not angry, I cannot curse.

אֵל זֹעֵם [3] The verse states (Psalms 7:12): **"And a God who is angry every day."** [4] The Gemara asks: **And how long does** God's **indignation** last? [5] The Gemara answers: Just for **a moment, as the verse states** (Psalms 30:6): **"For His anger endures but a moment; in His favor is life."** [6] And **if you wish,** you can **bring** support from a different verse which states (Isaiah 26:20): **"Go, my people, come into your chambers, and shut your doors about you; hide yourself for a little moment, until the anger passes."**

אֵימַת רָתַח [7] The Gemara asks: **When** precisely **is** God **angry?** [8] God becomes angry during **the first three hours** of the day **when the crest of the rooster appears white,** this whiteness symbolizing God's anger.

כָּל שַׁעְתָּא [9] The Gemara asks: But surely the rooster's crest may **appear white any hour** of the day!

כָּל שַׁעְתָּא [10] The Gemara answers: **Any** other **hour** of the day, even though the rooster's crest might appear white, **it** is still **marked by red streaks.** [11] But **in those** first three **hours** of the day, **it** appears completely white and **is not marked by** any **red streaks** at all.

הַהוּא מִינָא [12] **There was a certain heretic** living **in Rabbi Yehoshua ben Levi's neighborhood who distressed him.** [13] **One day** Rabbi Yehoshua ben Levi decided to put an end to the matter. **He took a rooster, tied it by its legs, and set it down** before him. [14] **He said:** "I will watch the rooster, and wait until its crest turns completely white, and **when that hour arrives, I will curse** my wicked neighbor and be rid of him forever."

RASHI

הכי גרסינן: לא זעם ה׳ — אותן הימים לא זעם ה׳. אל זועם בכל יום — קרא הוא. כמה זעמו רגע — כדמפיק ליה מקרא ״כי רגע באפו חיים ברצונו״. בתלת שעי קמייתא — של יום זמן קימה, שכל שלש שעות זמן קימה לעמוד ממטתו, וכועס הקדוש ברוך הוא בשעה שרואה המלכים שמשתחוים לחמה בשעה שמניחין כתריהם בראשם כדלקמן. כרבלתא — *קירשת״א בלעז. כל שעתא נמי חיורא — רוב שעות מתלבנות ומכספת, שאינה כל שעה בחוזק אדמימות. סורייקי סומקי — אפילו כשמכספת יש בה שורות שורות אדומות מאד כרגילותם, אבל אותה שעה — כולה מכספת.

LANGUAGE (RASHI)

קירשת״א* This apparently should be קרישט״א, from the Old French *creste*, meaning "crest."

NOTES

כִּי חִוָּורָא כַּרְבַּלְתָּא דְּתַרְנְגוֹלָא **When the crest of the rooster is white.** The Gemara does not mean to imply that the rooster knows when God is angry. Rather, there is a time when God is angry with the world, and God refrains from bestowing His bounty, and that change finds expression in the color of the rooster's crest (*Ramah*).

[1] שַׁעְתָּא, אִילַטְיֵיהּ״. [1] כִּי מְטָא הַהוּא שַׁעְתָּא נְמְנֵם. [2] אֲמַר: שְׁמַע מִינָּהּ לָאו אוֹרַח אַרְעָא, [3] דִּכְתִיב: ״גַּם עֲנוֹשׁ לַצַּדִּיק לֹא טוֹב״ — [4] אֲפִילּוּ בְּמִינֵי לָא אִיבָּעֵי לֵיהּ לְמֵימַר הָכִי.

[5] תָּנָא מִשְּׁמֵיהּ דְּרַבִּי מֵאִיר: ״בְּשָׁעָה שֶׁהַחַמָּה זוֹרַחַת וְהַמְּלָכִים מַנִּיחִין כִּתְרֵיהֶן עַל רָאשֵׁיהֶן וּמִשְׁתַּחֲוִים לַחַמָּה, מִיָּד כּוֹעֵס״.

[6] ״וַיָּקָם בִּלְעָם בַּבֹּקֶר וַיַּחֲבֹשׁ אֶת אֲתֹנוֹ״. [7] תָּנָא מִשּׁוּם רַבִּי שִׁמְעוֹן בֶּן אֶלְעָזָר: ״אַהֲבָה מְבַטֶּלֶת שׁוּרָה שֶׁל גְּדוּלָּה — [8] מֵאַבְרָהָם, דִּכְתִיב: ׳וַיַּשְׁכֵּם אַבְרָהָם בַּבֹּקֶר׳. [9] שִׂנְאָה מְבַטֶּלֶת שׁוּרָה שֶׁל גְּדוּלָּה — [10] מִבִּלְעָם, שֶׁנֶּאֱמַר: ׳וַיָּקָם בִּלְעָם בַּבֹּקֶר וַיַּחֲבֹשׁ אֶת אֲתֹנוֹ׳״.

[11] אָמַר רַב יְהוּדָה אָמַר רַב: לְעוֹלָם יַעֲסוֹק אָדָם בְּתוֹרָה וּבְמִצְוָה, אֲפִילּוּ שֶׁלֹּא לִשְׁמָהּ,

LITERAL TRANSLATION

hour comes, I will curse him." [1] When that hour came, he was asleep. [2] He said: Infer from this that it is not proper conduct, [3] as it is written: "Nor is it good to punish a righteous man" — [4] even regarding heretics he should not have said that.

[5] [A Tanna] taught in the name of Rabbi Meir: "When the sun shines, and the kings place their crowns on their heads, and bow down to the sun, He immediately becomes angry."

[6] "And Balaam rose in the morning, and saddled his ass." [7] [A Tanna] taught in the name of Rabbi Shimon ben Elazar: "Love undoes a wall of distinction — [8] from Abraham, as it is written: 'And Abraham rose early in the morning, and saddled his ass.' [9] Hatred undoes a wall of distinction — [10] from Balaam, as it is stated: 'And Balaam rose in the morning, and saddled his ass.'"

[11] Rav Yehudah said in the name of Rav: A person should always engage in Torah and commandments, even not for its own sake,

TRANSLATION AND COMMENTARY

[1] But **when the** designated **hour arrived, he was asleep.** [2] When Rabbi Yehoshua ben Levi awoke, **he said:** One may **infer from this** incident **that it is not right** to cause another person to be punished, [3] **as the verse states** (Proverbs 17:26): **"Nor is it good to punish a righteous man,"** which might also be read as: "Nor is it good for a righteous person to punish." [4] **Even regarding heretics, one should not utter** curses.

תָּנָא מִשְּׁמֵיהּ [5] **A Tanna taught** the following Baraita **in the name of Rabbi Meir: "When the sun shines** in the morning, **and kings** rise from their sleep, and **place their crowns on their heads, and bow down to the sun,** God **immediately becomes angry."**

וַיָּקָם בִּלְעָם [6] Regarding Balaam, the verse states (Numbers 22:21): **"And Balaam rose in the morning, and saddled his ass."** [7] A **Tanna taught** a Baraita **in the name of Rabbi Shimon ben Elazar:** "Intense **love can knock down a wall of distinction,** causing a distinguished person to waive his elevated status. [8] This is learned **from Abraham, as the verse states** (Genesis 22:3): **'And Abraham rose early in the morning, and saddled his ass.'** Abraham's love of God and desire to fulfill His command were so strong that he himself went out to saddle his ass. [9] **Hatred can** also **knock down a wall of distinction.** [10] This is learned **from Balaam, as the verse states** (Numbers 22:21): **'And Balaam rose in the morning, and saddled his ass.'** His hatred for Israel was so strong that he himself went out to saddle his ass."

אָמַר רַב יְהוּדָה [11] **Rav Yehudah said in the name of Rav: A person should always engage in** the study of the **Torah and** the performance of the **commandments, even** if **not for** their **own sake, for through** Torah

RASHI

גם ענוש לצדיק לא טוב — אין נכון לצדיק שיהא מעניש ולא הוה ליה איניש נענש בשבילו. אהבה — שאהב הקדוש ברוך הוא את אברהם ביטלה שורה של גדולה — שחבש הוא בעצמו. ושנאה — ששנא בלעם הרשע את ישראל — ביטלה שורה של גדולה, שחבש הוא בעצמו.

NOTES

אֲפִילּוּ בְּמִינֵי **Even regarding heretics.** Even though the law regarding heretics is that we may lower them into a pit and let them die there, and there is no obligation to save their lives, it is improper to ask God to punish them if for some reason He does not appear to be doing so (*Tosafot, Avodah Zarah*).

שׁוּרָה שֶׁל גְּדוּלָּה **A wall of distinction.** According to *Maharsha*, Abraham's saddling of his own ass does not prove that intense love can undo a wall of distinction. Rather, the proof is that he rose up early in the morning, in contrast to the custom of men of distinction to sleep late.

שֶׁלֹּא לִשְׁמָהּ **Not for its own sake.** The commentators distinguish between two types of "not for its own sake." Learning Torah in order to vex and provoke is absolutely forbidden. But learning Torah for some selfish purpose, so as to gain honor and recognition, rather than for its own sake, is permitted, and encouraged, for it will eventually lead to learning Torah for its own sake (see *Be'er Sheva*).

HALAKHAH

תּוֹרָה וּמִצְוָה, אֲפִילּוּ שֶׁלֹּא לִשְׁמָהּ **Torah and commandments, even not for its own sake.** "A person should always engage in the study of the Torah, even if not for its own sake, for through Torah study that is not for its own sake, a person will come to study Torah for its own sake." (*Shulḥan Arukh, Yoreh De'ah* 246:20.)

TRANSLATION AND COMMENTARY

study and the fulfillment of the commandments that **are not for their own sake,** a person will **come to do** these same things **for their own sake.** [1]Know that this is true, **for as a reward for the forty-two sacrifices that Balak offered, he earned merit so that Ruth would issue from him,** even though he offered those sacrifices for the downfall of the people of Israel. [2]This is in keeping with what **Rabbi Yose bar Huna said: Ruth was the daughter of Eglon,** who was **the grandson of Balak, King of Moab.**

אֲמַר לֵיהּ רָבָא [3]Having mentioned Ruth, from whom the House of David is descended, the Gemara now cites what **Rava said to Rabbah bar Mari: The verse states** that David's servants said to him (I Kings 1:47): **"May God make the name of Solomon better than your name** [מִשְּׁמֶךָ], **and make his throne greater than your throne** [מִכִּסְאֶךָ]." [4]**Is it proper to speak this way to the king?**

אֲמַר לֵיהּ [5]Rabbah bar Mari **said to** Rava: When David's servants said מִשְּׁמֶךָ and מִכִּסְאֶךָ, they **meant** to say that God should make Solomon's name **"similar to,"** but not greater than, David's name, and that He should make his throne "similar to," but not greater than, David's throne. [6]**For if you do not say this,** then there is a difficulty with another verse (Judges 5:24): **"Blessed above women is Jael, the wife of Heber the Kenite; blessed is she more than women** [מִנָּשִׁים] **in the tent."** [7]**Who are the women in the tent** alluded to in this verse? [8]**Sarah, Rebecca, Rachel, and Leah.** [9]Now, **is it proper to speak this way?** [10]**Rather,** when Deborah said מִנָּשִׁים, **she meant** to say that Jael is **similar to** the women in the tent, but not more blessed than they are. [11]**Here, too,** David's servants **meant** that God should make Solomon **similar to** his father David, but not greater.

וּפְלִיגָא [12]The Gemara notes that Rabbah bar Mari **disagrees with** the view **of Rav Yose bar Ḥoni, for Rav Yose bar Ḥoni said: A person is** liable to be **envious of all** other **people, except his** own **son and his** own

שֶׁמִּתּוֹךְ שֶׁלֹּא לִשְׁמָהּ בָּא לִשְׁמָהּ. [1]שֶׁבִּשְׂכַר אַרְבָּעִים וּשְׁתַּיִם קָרְבָּנוֹת שֶׁהִקְרִיב בָּלָק, זָכָה וְיָצְאָה מִמֶּנּוּ רוּת. [2]אָמַר רַבִּי יוֹסֵי בַּר הוּנָא: רוּת בִּתּוֹ שֶׁל עֶגְלוֹן, בֶּן בְּנוֹ שֶׁל בָּלָק מֶלֶךְ מוֹאָב, הָיְתָה.

[3]אֲמַר לֵיהּ רָבָא לְרַבָּה בַּר מָרִי: כְּתִיב: "יֵיטֵב אֱלֹהִים אֶת שֵׁם שְׁלֹמֹה מִשְּׁמֶךָ וִיגַדֵּל [אֶת] כִּסְאוֹ מִכִּסְאֶךָ". [4]אוֹרַח אַרְעָא לְמֵימְרָא לֵיהּ לְמַלְכָּא הָכִי? [5]אֲמַר לֵיהּ: "מֵעֵין" קָאָמְרָה לֵיהּ. [6]דְּאִי לָא תֵּימָא הָכִי, "תְּבֹרַךְ מִנָּשִׁים יָעֵל אֵשֶׁת חֶבֶר הַקֵּינִי; מִנָּשִׁים בָּאֹהֶל תְּבֹרָךְ". [7]נָשִׁים בָּאֹהֶל מַאן נִינְהוּ? [8]שָׂרָה רִבְקָה רָחֵל וְלֵאָה. [9]אוֹרַח אַרְעָא לְמֵימַר הָכִי? [10]אֶלָּא: "מֵעֵין" קָאָמַר. [11]הָכִי נַמִּי "מֵעֵין" קָאָמַר.

[12]וּפְלִיגָא דְּרַב יוֹסֵי בַּר חוֹנִי, דְּאָמַר רַב יוֹסֵי בַּר חוֹנִי: בַּכֹּל

LITERAL TRANSLATION

for out of [acting] not for its own sake, he comes to [act] for its own sake. [1]For as a reward for the forty-two sacrifices that Balak offered, he earned merit and Ruth issued from him. [2]Rabbi Yose bar Huna said: Ruth was the daughter of Eglon, the son of the son of Balak, King of Moab.

[3]Rava said to Rabbah bar Mari: It is written: "May God make the name of Solomon better than your name, and make his throne greater than your throne." [4]Is it proper conduct to speak this way to the king?

[5]He said to him: He said, "Similar to." [6]For if you do not say thus, [there is a problem with] "Blessed above women is Jael, the wife of Heber the Kenite; blessed is she more than women in the tent." [7]Who are the women in the tent? [8]Sarah, Rebecca, Rachel, and Leah. [9]Is it proper conduct to speak thus? [10]Rather, he said, "Similar to." [11]Here, too, he said: "Similar to."

[12]And this is in disagreement with the view (lit., "that") of Rav Yose bar Ḥoni, for Rav Yose bar Ḥoni said:

RASHI

ארבעים ושתים קרבנות — בין פרים לאילים, שבעה פרים, ושבעה אילים, שלש פעמים — הרי ארבעים ושתים, בין פרים ואילים. **אורח ארעא למימר הכי** — וכי דרך ארץ כן שיאמרו "וייטב אלהים שם שלמה משמך"? — והא חלשא דעתיה דאמרי ליה שיהא גדול מאביו. **מעין שמך** — קאמר ליה, ומעין כסאך ולא גדול ממש. **נשים באהל** — שרה רבקה רחל ולאה, שרה ורבקה דכתיב "ויביאה יצחק האהלה שרה אמו וגו'" רחל ולאה דכתיב (בראשית לא) "ויצא מאהל לאה ויבא באהל רחל". **אורח ארעא** — שאמרה דבורה ליעל [שתהא] ברוכה משרה ורבקה, אלא מעין ברכת שרה קאמרה. **ופליגא** — האי דמשנינן שם שלמה משמך — מעין — פליגא דרבי יוסי בר חוני.

NOTES

בֶּן בְּנוֹ The son of his son. The Rishonim point out that the expressions "the son of his son" and "the daughter of his son" do not always refer specifically to a person's grandchildren, but rather to any of his descendants (*Tosafot, Nazir*).

"מֵעֵין" קָאָמְרָה He said: "Similar to." The Gemara's discussion revolves around the meaning of the letter mem in the words מִשְּׁמֶךָ, מִכִּסְאֶךָ, and מִנָּשִׁים. The Gemara first thinks that the mem is used here in the sense of "more than." Thus, מִכִּסְאֶךָ means "greater than your throne," and מִנָּשִׁים means "more than women." The Gemara then explains that the mem is actually used in a diminutive sense — "out of," "from." Thus, מִכִּסְאֶךָ means "out of, next to your throne," and מִנָּשִׁים means "by way of, through women" (see *Ramah*).

TRANSLATION AND COMMENTARY

pupil. [1]We learn that a father is not envious of **his** own **son from Solomon,** for David's servants wished that God should make Solomon greater than David himself. [2]As for not being envious of **one's** own **pupil — if you wish,** you can **say** that this is derived from what Elisha said to his master Eliahu (II Kings 2:9): **"I pray you, let a double portion of your spirit be upon me."** [3]**And if you wish,** you can **say** that this is derived from what is said about Moses and Joshua (Numbers 27:23): **"And he laid his hands upon him, and commanded him."** Even though God only instructed Moses to lay one of his hands upon Joshua, Moses laid both his hands upon him.

וַיָּשֶׂם דָּבָר [4]Regarding Balaam, the verse states (Numbers 23:5): **"And the Lord put a word in Balaam's mouth."** [5]**Rabbi Eliezer said:** God sent **an Angel to pronounce** a blessing, rather than a curse. [6]**Rabbi Yonatan said:** God placed **a hook** in his mouth so he could not curse.

אָמַר רַבִּי יוֹחָנָן [7]**Rabbi Yoḥanan said: From the blessings** uttered **by that wicked man, you** may **learn what** curses **he had in his heart** to proclaim, had God not turned his curses into blessings. [8]He **had wanted to say that** Israel **would not have** any **synagogues** or **study halls,** but God turned the curse into a blessing, so that he said (Numbers 24:5): **"How goodly are your tents, O Jacob,"** an allusion to synagogues and study halls." [9]He had wanted to say that **the Divine Presence** [שְׁכִינָה] **would not rest upon** Israel, but he said (Numbers 24:5): **"And your tabernacles** [מִשְׁכְּנֹתֶיךָ] — the seat of the Divine Presence — **O Israel."** [10]He wanted to say that Israel's **kingdom would not last** very **long,** but he said (Numbers 24:6): **"Like the winding brooks"** which flow continuously. [11]He wanted to say that Israel **would not have** any **olive trees or vineyards,** but he said (Numbers 24:6): **"Like gardens by the river's side."** [12]He wanted to say that Israel's **smell would not go forth,** the fragrance of the commandments, but he said (Numbers 24:6): **"Like aloes** — fragrant plants — **which the Lord has planted."** [13]Balaam wanted to say that Israel **would not have** any **kings of stature,** but he said (Numbers 24:6): **"And cedar trees beside the waters."** [14]He wanted to say that

LITERAL TRANSLATION

A person is envious of all people, except his son and his pupil. [1]His son — from Solomon. [2]And his pupil, if you wish say: "I pray you, let a double portion of your spirit be upon me." [3]And if you wish say: "And he laid his hands upon him, and commanded him."

[4]"And the Lord put a word in Balaam's mouth." [5]Rabbi Eliezer says: An Angel. [6]Rabbi Yonatan said: A hook.

[7]Rabbi Yoḥanan said: From the blessing of that wicked man you learn what was in his heart. [8]He had wanted to say that they will have no synagogues or study halls — "How goodly are your tents, O Jacob." [9]The Divine Presence will not rest upon them — "And your tabernacles, O Israel." [10]Their kingdom will not last long — "Like the winding brooks." [11]They will not have olive trees and vineyards — "Like gardens by the river's side." [12]Their smell will not go forth — "Like aloes which the Lord has planted." [13]They will not have kings of stature — "And cedar trees beside the waters." [14]They will not

אָדָם מִתְקַנֵּא, חוּץ מִבְּנוֹ וְתַלְמִידוֹ. [1]בְּנוֹ — מִשְּׁלֹמֹה. [2]וְתַלְמִידוֹ, אִיבָּעֵית אֵימָא: "וִיהִי נָא פִּי שְׁנַיִם בְּרוּחֲךָ אֵלָי". [3]וְאִיבָּעֵית אֵימָא: "וַיִּסְמֹךְ אֶת יָדָיו עָלָיו וַיְצַוֵּהוּ".

[4]וַיָּשֶׂם דָּבָר בְּפִי בִלְעָם". [5]רַבִּי אֶלְעָזָר אוֹמֵר: מַלְאָךְ. [6]רַבִּי יוֹנָתָן אָמַר: חַכָּה.

[7]אָמַר רַבִּי יוֹחָנָן: מִבִּרְכָתוֹ שֶׁל אוֹתוֹ רָשָׁע אַתָּה לָמֵד מֶה הָיָה בְּלִבּוֹ. [8]בִּיקֵּשׁ לוֹמַר שֶׁלֹּא יְהוּ לָהֶם בָּתֵּי כְנֵסִיּוֹת וּבָתֵּי מִדְרָשׁוֹת — "מַה טֹּבוּ אֹהָלֶיךָ יַעֲקֹב". [9]לֹא תִּשְׁרֶה שְׁכִינָה עֲלֵיהֶם — "וּמִשְׁכְּנֹתֶיךָ יִשְׂרָאֵל". [10]לֹא תְּהֵא מַלְכוּתָן נִמְשֶׁכֶת — "כִּנְחָלִים נִטָּיוּ". [11]לֹא יְהֵא לָהֶם זֵיתִים וּכְרָמִים — "כְּגַנֹּת עֲלֵי נָהָר". [12]לֹא יְהֵא רֵיחָן נוֹדֵף — "כַּאֲהָלִים נָטַע ה׳". [13]לֹא יִהְיוּ לָהֶם מְלָכִים בַּעֲלֵי קוֹמָה — "כַּאֲרָזִים עֲלֵי מָיִם". [14]לֹא יִהְיֶה

RASHI

בנו מניין — שאינו מקנא בו. **משלמה** — דקאמרי ליה לדוד "ייטב אלהים שם שלמה משמך". **ותלמידו** — איבעית אימא דקאמר ליה לאליהו "ויהי נא פי שנים ברוחך אלי" ונתן לו אליהו ולא נתקנא בו. **ויסמוך את ידיו עליו ויצוהו** — אף על גב דהקדוש ברוך הוא לא אמר ליה אלא "וסמכת את ידך עליו" חדא, אזיל איהו וסמך תרתי. **מלאך** — שמסרו הקדוש ברוך הוא למלאך שלא יניחנו לקלל. **חכה** — נתן בפי בלעם שלא היה מניחו לקלל והיינו "וישם". **מברכותיו אתה למד מה היה בלבו** — דכתיב "ויהפוך ה׳ אלהיך לך את הקללה לברכה" — הוא היה רוצה לקללם בכך שלא יהיו בתי כנסיות, ולא נתן רשות ואמר "מה טובו אוהליך". **ריחו נודף** — ממלות.

NOTES

רֵיחָן נוֹדֵף **Their smell will not go forth.** *Maharsha* explains this differently: Balaam wanted to say that Israel's kingdom will not be well known throughout the world.

לָהֶם מֶלֶךְ בֶּן מֶלֶךְ — ״יִזַּל מַיִם מִדָּלְיָו״. [1]לֹא תְּהֵא מַלְכוּתָן שׁוֹלֶטֶת בָּאוּמּוֹת — ״וְזַרְעוֹ בְּמַיִם רַבִּים״. [2]לֹא תְּהֵא עַזָּה מַלְכוּתָן — ״וְיָרֹם מֵאֲגַג מַלְכּוֹ״. [3]לֹא תְּהֵא אֵימַת מַלְכוּתָן — ״וְתִנַּשֵּׂא מַלְכֻתוֹ״. [4]אָמַר רַבִּי אַבָּא בַּר כָּהֲנָא: כּוּלָּם חָזְרוּ לִקְלָלָה, חוּץ מִבָּתֵּי כְנֵסִיּוֹת וּמִבָּתֵּי מִדְרָשׁוֹת, [5]שֶׁנֶּאֱמַר: ״וַיַּהֲפֹךְ ה׳ אֱלֹהֶיךָ לְּךָ אֶת הַקְּלָלָה לִבְרָכָה כִּי אֲהֵבְךָ ה׳ אֱלֹהֶיךָ״. [6]קְלָלָה, וְלֹא קְלָלוֹת.

[7]אָמַר רַבִּי שְׁמוּאֵל בַּר נַחְמָנִי אָמַר רַבִּי יוֹנָתָן: [8]מַאי דִּכְתִיב: ״נֶאֱמָנִים פִּצְעֵי אוֹהֵב וְנַעְתָּרוֹת נְשִׁיקוֹת שׂוֹנֵא״? [9]טוֹבָה קְלָלָה שֶׁקִּילֵּל אֲחִיָּה הַשִּׁילוֹנִי אֶת יִשְׂרָאֵל, יוֹתֵר מִבְּרָכָה שֶׁבֵּרְכָם בִּלְעָם הָרָשָׁע. [10]אֲחִיָּה הַשִּׁילוֹנִי קִילֵּל אֶת יִשְׂרָאֵל בְּקָנֶה, שֶׁנֶּאֱמַר: ״וְהִכָּה ה׳ אֶת יִשְׂרָאֵל כַּאֲשֶׁר יָנוּד הַקָּנֶה בַּמַּיִם וגו׳״. [11]מַה קָּנֶה זֶה עוֹמֵד בִּמְקוֹם מַיִם, וְגִיזְעוֹ [106A] מַחֲלִיף, וְשָׁרָשָׁיו מְרוּבִּין, [12]וַאֲפִילּוּ כָּל רוּחוֹת שֶׁבָּעוֹלָם בָּאוֹת וְנוֹשְׁבוֹת בּוֹ אֵין מְזִיזוֹת אוֹתוֹ מִמְּקוֹמוֹ, [13]אֶלָּא הוּא הוֹלֵךְ וּבָא עִמָּהֶן, כֵּיוָן שֶׁדּוּמְמוּ הָרוּחוֹת, עָמַד קָנֶה בִּמְקוֹמוֹ. [14]אֲבָל בִּלְעָם הָרָשָׁע

LITERAL TRANSLATION

have a king the song of a king — "He shall pour the water out of his buckets." [1]Their kingdom will not rule the nations — "And his seed in great waters." [2]Their kingdom will not be fierce — "And his king shall be higher than Agag." [3]There will be no fear of their kingdom — "And his kingdom shall be exalted."

[4]Rabbi Abba bar Kahana said: They all returned as curses, except for the synagogues and study halls, [5]for it is stated: "But the Lord your God turned the curse into a blessing for you, because the Lord your God loved you." [6]The curse, but not the curses.

[7]Rabbi Shmuel bar Naḥmani said in the name of Rabbi Yonatan: [8]What is that which is written: "Faithful are the wounds of a friend; but the kisses of an enemy are profuse"? [9]The curse with which Achiah the Shiloni cursed Israel is better than the blessing with which the wicked Balaam blessed them. [10]Achiah the Shiloni cursed Israel with a reed, as it is stated: "For the Lord shall smite Israel as a reed is shaken in the water." [11]Just as a reed stands in a place of water, and its stump [106A] renews itself, and its roots are many, [12]and even [if] all the winds in the world come and blow at it, they do not move it from its place, [13]but rather it moves with them, [and] once the winds abate, the reed stands in its place. [14]But the wicked Balaam

TRANSLATION AND COMMENTARY

Israel **would not have a king** who was also **the son of a king,** but he said (Numbers 24:6): **"He shall pour the water out of his buckets."** [1]Balaam wanted to say that Israel's **kingdom will not rule the nations,** but he said (Numbers 24:6): **"And his seed in great waters."** [2]Balaam wanted to say that Israel's **kingdom will not be fierce,** but he said (Numbers 24:6): **"And his king shall be higher than Agag."** [3]He wanted to say that **there will be no fear of** Israel's **kingdom,** but he said (Numbers 24:6): **"And his kingdom shall be exalted."**

אָמַר [4]**Rabbi Abba bar Kahana said: All** of Balaam's curses, which were turned into blessings, **returned** in the end **as the curses** that he had originally intended. They all came true, **except for** the destruction of **synagogues and study halls,** [5]**for the verse states** (Deuteronomy 23:6): **"But the Lord your God turned the curse into a blessing unto you, because the Lord your God loved you."** [6]The Lord your God turned a single **curse** into a permanent blessing, **but not** all **the curses.**

אָמַר [7]**Rabbi Shmuel bar Naḥmani said in the name of Rabbi Yonatan:** [8]**What is** meant by **the verse that states** (Proverbs 27:6): **"Faithful are the wounds of a friend; but the kisses of an enemy are profuse"?** [9]**The curse with which Achiah the Shiloni cursed the people of Israel is better than the blessing with which the wicked Balaam blessed them.** [10]**Achiah the Shiloni cursed the people of Israel** by comparing them **to a reed, as the verse states** (I Kings 14:15): **"For the Lord shall smite Israel as a reed is shaken in the water."** But this curse contains within it a certain blessing. [11]**Just as a reed** grows **in a place** with a lot **of water,** and the water irrigates it all the time, **and** if it is cut off, **its stump** [106A] **can renew itself, and its roots are many,** [12]**and even** when **all the winds in the world come and blow** upon the reed, **they** are **not** able **to move it from its place,** [13]**but rather the** reed **moves with the** wind, **and once the winds abate, the reed stands** firm **in its place** — so, too, Israel. [14]**But the**

RASHI

וירם מאגג מלכו — מתרגמינן ״ותתקף מאגג״ — שתהא מלכותו עזה. **וכולם** — כל הברכות של בלעם חזרו לקללה, כמו שהיה כוונתו מתחילה. **חוץ מבתי כנסיות ובתי מדרשות** — שלא יפסקו מישראל לעולם. **הקללה לברכה** — אחת מן הקללות הפך לברכה, שלא חזרה לעולם, ולא כל הקללות לברכות שחזרו. **נעתרות** — נהפכות, כמו עתר שמהפך התבואה, כלומר: נאמנים פצעי אוהב ונהפכות מנאמנות נשיקות שונא. **מחליף** — לאחר שנקצץ.

קָנֶה **Reeds.**

Reeds in a Swamp

The reeds referred to in the sources are apparently Egyptian reeds, *Phragmites communis*, or the common cane, *Arundo dopax*. These are perennial grasses whose stalks rise to a height of two to four meters. These reeds usually grow in dense clumps along rivers and on the banks of lakes. They are used to make fences and for weaving coarse mats. Pens for writing were also made from reeds, mainly for writing large letters with ink.

בֵּרְכָן בָּאֶרֶז. [1]מָה אֶרֶז זֶה אֵינוֹ עוֹמֵד בִּמְקוֹם מַיִם, וְשָׁרָשָׁיו מוּעָטִין, וְאֵין גִּזְעוֹ מַחֲלִיף, [2]אֲפִילּוּ כָּל הָרוּחוֹת שֶׁבָּעוֹלָם בָּאוֹת וְנוֹשְׁבוֹת בּוֹ, אֵין מְזִיזוֹת אוֹתוֹ מִמְּקוֹמוֹ, כֵּיוָן שֶׁנָּשְׁבָה בּוֹ רוּחַ דְּרוֹמִית — מִיָּד עוֹקַרְתּוֹ וְהוֹפַכְתּוֹ עַל פָּנָיו. [3]וְלֹא עוֹד אֶלָּא שֶׁזָּכָה קָנֶה לִיטּוֹל מִמֶּנּוּ קוּלְמוֹס לִכְתּוֹב מִמֶּנּוּ סִפְרֵי תוֹרָה נְבִיאִים וּכְתוּבִים.

[4]״וַיַּרְא אֶת הַקֵּינִי וַיִּשָּׂא מְשָׁלוֹ״. [5]אָמַר לוֹ בִּלְעָם לְיִתְרוֹ: ״קֵינִי, לֹא הָיִיתָ עִמָּנוּ בְּאוֹתָהּ עֵצָה? [6]מִי הוֹשִׁיבְךָ אֵצֶל אֵיתָנֵי עוֹלָם״?

[7]וְהַיְינוּ דְּאָמַר רַבִּי חִיָּיא בַּר אַבָּא אָמַר רַבִּי סִימָאי: [8]שְׁלֹשָׁה הָיוּ בְּאוֹתָהּ עֵצָה, אֵלּוּ הֵן: בִּלְעָם, אִיּוֹב, וְיִתְרוֹ. בִּלְעָם שֶׁיָּעַץ — נֶהֱרַג. [9]אִיּוֹב שֶׁשָּׁתַק — נִידּוֹן בְּיִסּוּרִין. [10]וְיִתְרוֹ שֶׁבָּרַח — זָכוּ בְּנֵי בָנָיו לֵישֵׁב בְּלִשְׁכַּת הַגָּזִית, [11]שֶׁנֶּאֱמַר: ״וּמִשְׁפְּחוֹת סוֹפְרִים יוֹשְׁבֵי יַעְבֵּץ; תִּרְעָתִים שִׁמְעָתִים שׂוּכָתִים. [12]הֵמָּה הַקִּינִים הַבָּאִים מֵחַמַּת אֲבִי

LITERAL TRANSLATION

blessed them with a cedar. [1]Just as this cedar does not stand in a place of water, and its roots are few, and its stump does not renew itself, [2][and] even [if] all the winds in the world come and blow at it, they do not move it from its place, [but] if a southern wind blows at it, immediately it uproots it and turns it over. [3]Moreover, the reed merited that the stylus is taken from it with which to write the scrolls of the Torah, the Prophets, and the Writings. [4]"And he looked on the Kenites, and took up his theme." [5]Balaam said to Jethro: "Kenite, were you not with us in that counsel? [6]Who set you with the strong men of the world?"

[7]And this is what Rabbi Ḥiyya bar Abba said in the name of Rabbi Sima'i: [8]Three were in that counsel, [and] they are: Balaam, Job, and Jethro. Balaam, who counseled, was slain. [9]Job, who remained silent, was punished with afflictions. [10]And Jethro, who fled — the sons of his sons merited sitting in the Chamber of Hewn Stone, [11]as it is stated: "And the families of the scribes who dwelt at Jabez: the Tirathites, the Shimeathites, the Sucathites. [12]These are the Kenites who came of Hamat, the father of

TRANSLATION AND COMMENTARY

wicked Balaam blessed them by comparing them **to a cedar.** [1]**Just as a cedar does not stand in a place of water, and its roots are few** in proportion to its great size, **and** if it is felled, **its stump does not renew itself,** [2]**and even** though **when all the winds in the world come and blow upon** the cedar, **they** are **not** able to **move it from its place, when** a strong **southern wind blows upon it, immediately it uproots** the tree **and turns it over** — so, too, Israel. [3]**Moreover, the reed merited that the stylus is taken from it with which to write the scrolls of the Torah, the Prophets, and the Writings.** Thus, Achiah's curse was better for Israel than Balaam's blessing.

וַיַּרְא אֶת הַקֵּינִי [4]Regarding Balaam, the verse states (Numbers 24:21): **"And he looked on the Kenites, and took up his theme,"** and said, Strong is your dwelling place, and you put your nest in a rock." [5]**Balaam said to Jethro** (also known as Keni): **"Keni, were you not with us in that counsel,** when we advised Pharaoh to cast the newborn sons of Israel into the Nile? [6]**Who,** then, **set you** next **to the strong men of the world** ("strong is your dwelling place")?

וְהַיְינוּ דְּאָמַר [7]**And this is what Rabbi Ḥiyya bar Abba said in the name of Rabbi Sima'i:** [8]**Three** people **were in that counsel: Balaam, Job, and Jethro. Balaam, who counseled** Pharaoh to drown the Jewish babies in the Nile, **was** eventually **slain.** [9]**Job, who remained silent,** afraid to express his opinion, **was** later **punished with afflictions.** [10]As for **Jethro, who fled** after stating his opposition to the plan, so that Pharaoh wanted to kill him, **his descendants merited sitting** as members of the Sanhedrin which met **in the Chamber of Hewn Stone,** [11]**as the verse states** (I Chronicles 2:55): **"And the families of the scribes who dwelt at Jabez: the Tirathites, the Shimeathites, the Sucathites.** [12]**These are the Kenites who came of Hamat, the father of the House of**

RASHI

אינו עומד במקום מים — והאי דכתיב ״כארזים עלי מים״ שכינה היא דאמרה, איהו אמר ״כארזים״ כלומר שאין עומדין במקום מים, שכינה אמרה ״עלי מים״, וכן כולהו מפרש באגדה בכהאי גוונא ״כנחלים נטיו״ הוא אמר: ״כנחלים״ פוסקין לפעמים, יצאה בת קול [אמרה]: ״נטיו״, הוא אמר ״כגנות״ — אמרה בת קול: ״עלי נהר״, הוא אמר: ״כאהלים״ — יצאה בת קול ואמרה: ״נטע ה׳״. **רוח דרומית** — קשה. **לא עמנו היית באותה עצה** — שגזר פרעה כל הבן הילוד היאורה, בתמיה, — ודאי היית, כדלקמן. **ומי הושיבך אצל איתני עולם** — שעתידים בניך לישב בלשכת הגזית, והיינו דכתיב ״איתן מושבך״, וכי בין איתני עולם אתה יושב, מי הזקיקך לכך.

BACKGROUND

רוּחַ דְּרוֹמִית עוֹקַרְתּ **Southern wind uproots it.** The cedar grows in mountainous regions, and its roots are relatively few and not deep. Generally the tree is anchored in the earth against the prevalent winds, which blow from the west in the winter and the east in the summer. Wind from the north is quite rare, and winds from the south often appear very suddenly, attacking the cedar from a direction in which it is not anchored. Therefore, a south wind is liable to uproot it.

LANGUAGE

קוּלְמוֹס **Stylus.** This word derives from the Greek κάλαμος, *kalamos*, meaning "a cane," but it also refers to "a cane used for writing, a stylus."

NOTES

וְלֹא עוֹד אֶלָּא שֶׁזָּכָה קָנֶה **Moreover, the reed merited.** Even when the reed is uprooted from its place, it merits serving elsewhere as a stylus for the writing of sacred scrolls. So, too, the people of Israel — even when they are uprooted from their land, they merit studying Torah in exile (*Maharsha*).

TRANSLATION AND COMMENTARY

Rechab." [1]**And elsewhere it is explained** who the Kenites were (Judges 1:16): **"And the children of the Kenite, Moses's father-in-law, went up from the city of palm trees** with the children of Judah into the wilderness of Judah, which lies in the south of Arad; and they went and dwelt among the people."

וַיִּשָּׂא מְשָׁלוֹ [2]Among Balaam's words, we also find (Numbers 24:23): **"And he took up his theme, and said, Alas, who shall live** [יְחְיֶה] **except God has willed it** [מִשֻּׂמוֹ אֵל]?" [3]**Rabbi Shimon ben Lakish** interpreted the last two words homiletically, and **said: Woe to him who sustains himself** [מְּחַיֶּה] **with the name of God** [בְּשֵׁם אֵל], earning his livelihood by speaking in God's name like Balaam.

אָמַר רַבִּי יוֹחָנָן [4]**Rabbi Yoḥanan said** that the verse means: **Woe to the nation that will** stand in Israel's way **when the Holy One, blessed be He, brings redemption** [פִּדְיוֹן] **to His sons,** [5]for **who** would dare to **place his cloak between a lion and a lioness while they are mating?**

וְצִים מִיַּד [6]Balaam continues (Numbers 24:24): **"And ships shall come from the coast of Kittim."** [7]**Rav said:** This is a reference to **the Roman legion** that will advance against Assyria.

וְעִנּוּ אַשּׁוּר [8]The verse continues (Numbers 24:24): **"And they shall afflict Assyria, and they shall afflict Ever."** [9]**Until** the Roman legion reaches **Assyria, they will kill** all those that they meet along the way. [10]But **from there on, they will** spare their lives, and only **subjugate them** as their slaves.

הִנְנִי הוֹלֵךְ [11]Balaam said to Balak (Numbers 24:14): **"Behold, I go to my people; come therefore, and I shall advise you what this people shall do to**

בֵּית רֵכָב". [1]וּכְתִיב: "וּבְנֵי קֵינִי חֹתֵן מֹשֶׁה עָלוּ מֵעִיר הַתְּמָרִים".

[2]"וַיִּשָּׂא מְשָׁלוֹ וַיֹּאמַר אוֹי מִי יִחְיֶה מִשֻּׂמוֹ אֵל"? [3](אָמַר רַבִּי שִׁמְעוֹן בֶּן לָקִישׁ: אוֹי מִי שֶׁמְּחַיֶּה עַצְמוֹ בְּשֵׁם אֵל).

[4]אָמַר רַבִּי יוֹחָנָן: אוֹי לָהּ לָאוּמָּה שֶׁתִּמָּצֵא בְּשָׁעָה שֶׁהַקָּדוֹשׁ בָּרוּךְ הוּא עוֹשֶׂה פִּדְיוֹן לְבָנָיו, [5]מִי מֵטִיל כְּסוּתוֹ בֵּין לָבִיא לִלְבִיאָה בְּשָׁעָה שֶׁנִּזְקָקִין זֶה עִם זֶה?

[6]"וְצִים מִיַּד כִּתִּים". [7]אָמַר רַב: לִיבּוּן אַסְפִּיר.

[8]"וְעִנּוּ אַשּׁוּר וְעִנּוּ עֵבֶר". [9]עַד אַשּׁוּר — קָטְלִי מִיקְטַל. [10]מִכָּאן וְאֵילָךְ, מְשַׁעְבְּדִי שִׁיעְבּוּדֵי.

[11]"הִנְנִי הוֹלֵךְ לְעַמִּי, לְכָה אִיעָצְךָ אֲשֶׁר יַעֲשֶׂה הָעָם הַזֶּה

LITERAL TRANSLATION

the House of Rechab." [1]And it is written: "And the children of the Kenites, Moses's father-in-law, went up from the city of palm trees."

[2]"And he took up his theme, and said, Alas, who shall live except God has willed it?" [3]Rabbi Shimon ben Lakish said: Woe to him who sustains himself with the name of God.

[4]Rabbi Yoḥanan said: Woe to the nation that will be found when the Holy One, blessed be He, brings redemption to His sons, [5][for] who places his cloak between a lion and a lioness at the time that they are mating?

[6]"And ships shall come from the coast of Kittim." [7]Rav said: Libbun Aspir.

[8]"And they shall afflict Assyria, and they shall afflict Ever." [9]Until Assyria — they will kill [them]. [10]From there on, they will subjugate [them].

[11]"Behold, I go to my people; come therefore, and I shall advise you what this people shall do

LANGUAGE

לִיבּוּן אַסְפִּיר Libbun Aspir. The manuscripts indicate that this form should be revised to **לְגִיוֹן אַסְפִּיר**, apparently deriving from the Latin *legio*, meaning "legion," a large unit in the Roman army contaning about three thousand soldiers. **אַסְפִּיר** might derive from the middle Persian *asowar*, which derives from the Greek σπειρα, *speira*, meaning "a Greek military unit."

RASHI

שמחיה עצמו בשם אל — עושה עצמו אלוה, לשון אחר: מי שמחיה עצמו — כלומר אוי להם לאותן בני אדם שמחיין ומעדנין עצמן בעולם הזה, ופורקין עול תורה מעל צוארם ומשמנין את עצמן. **משמו אל** — כשמשים הקדוש ברוך הוא פדיון לעצמו ומשלם גמול לצדיקים לעתיד לבא, כך שמעתי. **אוי לה לאומה שתמצא** — אוי לה לאומה שתהיה באותן הימים שיעלה על דעתה לעכב ישראל. **מי מטיל כסות בין לביא וכו׳** — לעכבן שלא יזדקקו זה לזה, דמסוכן הוא, כלומר, מי הוא שיכול לעכב את ישראל והקדוש ברוך הוא מכניסם. **ציים** — ספינות גדולות כמו (ישעיה לג) "וצי אדיר (בל) יעברנו". **וצים מיד כתים אמר רב ליבא אספיר** — דכתים היינו מקום ששמו כך. **עד אשור מקטל קטילי** — ומאשור ואילך משעבדי להו שעבודי. **וצים מיד כתים וענו אשור** — דקטלי להו, וענו עבר דמשעבדי להן עד אשור. **כתים** — רומים, כלומר אותן אומות שהביא הקדוש ברוך הוא בצים — עתידין להרוג את כל האומות עד אשור, ומאשור ואילך מניחין אותן ומשעבדין בהם (ומניחין אותן), ולעתיד קא איירי. הן הנה היו לבני ישראל לא גרסינן, אלא הכי גרסינן: **הנני הולך לעמי לכה איעצך אשר יעשה**

NOTES

מִי שֶׁמְּחַיֶּה עַצְמוֹ בְּשֵׁם אֵל Who sustains himself with the name of God. Some explain that Rabbi Shimon ben Lakish is referring to people who try to save themselves by invoking Divine Names. Those who are unfit to engage in such matters will ultimately suffer injury and even die (see *Maharsha, Vilna Gaon*). According to *Rashi*'s second explanation, he refers to those people who pamper themselves in this world, and cast off the yoke of Torah. This is similar to the idea expressed in the Rabbinic teaching: "What does a person do so that he will die? — he sustains himself." A person who dedicates himself to the physical pleasures of life does not attain a true life (*Tzofnat Pa'ane'aḥ*).

לִיבּוּן אַסְפִּיר Libun Aspir. *Rashi* interprets these words as a place-name identifying Kittim. The Geonim had the reading לְגִיוֹן אַסְפִּיר, which they interpreted as referring to the Roman legion that fought against the Persian Empire. Until the

לְעַמְּךָ״. [1]״עַמְּךָ לָעָם הַזֶּה״ מִיבְּעֵי לֵיהּ!

[2]אָמַר רַבִּי אַבָּא בַּר כָּהֲנָא: כְּאָדָם שֶׁמְּקַלֵּל אֶת עַצְמוֹ וְתוֹלֶה קִלְלָתוֹ בַּאֲחֵרִים. [3]אָמַר לָהֶם: ״אֱלֹהֵיהֶם שֶׁל אֵלּוּ שׂוֹנֵא זִימָּה הוּא, וְהֵם מִתְאַוִּים לִכְלֵי פִשְׁתָּן. [4]בּוֹא וְאַשִּׂיאֲךָ עֵצָה: עֲשֵׂה לָהֶן קְלָעִים, וְהוֹשֵׁיב בָּהֶן זוֹנוֹת, [5]זְקֵינָה מִבַּחוּץ וְיַלְדָּה מִבִּפְנִים, וְיִמְכְּרוּ לָהֶן כְּלֵי פִשְׁתָּן״. [6]עָשָׂה לָהֶן קְלָעִים מֵהַר שֶׁלֶג עַד בֵּית הַיְשִׁימוֹת, וְהוֹשִׁיב בָּהֶן זוֹנוֹת, זְקֵינָה מִבַּחוּץ וְיַלְדָּה מִבִּפְנִים. [7]וּבְשָׁעָה שֶׁיִּשְׂרָאֵל אוֹכְלִין וְשׁוֹתִין וּשְׂמֵחִין וְיוֹצְאִין לְטַיֵּיל בַּשּׁוּק, אוֹמֶרֶת לוֹ הַזְּקֵינָה: ״אִי אַתָּה מְבַקֵּשׁ כְּלֵי פִשְׁתָּן״? [8]זְקֵינָה אוֹמֶרֶת לוֹ בְּשָׁוֶה, וְיַלְדָּה אוֹמֶרֶת לוֹ בְּפָחוֹת. [9]שְׁתַּיִם וְשָׁלֹשׁ פְּעָמִים. [10]וְאַחַר כָּךְ אוֹמֶרֶת לוֹ: ״הֲרֵי אַתְּ כְּבֶן בַּיִת; שֵׁב, בְּרוֹר לְעַצְמְךָ״. [11]וְצַרְצוּרֵי שֶׁל יַיִן עַמּוֹנִי מוּנָּח אֶצְלָהּ,

LITERAL TRANSLATION

to your people." [1]He should have [said]: "Your people to this people"!

[2]Rabbi Abba bar Kahana said: Like a person who curses himself and hangs his curse on others. [3]He said to them: "The God of these [people] hates lewdness, and they long for linen garments. [4]Come, and I will offer you advice: Put up booths for them, and place prostitutes in them. [5]An old woman outside, and a young woman inside, and let them sell them linen garments." [6]He put up booths for them from the mountain of snow to Bet Hayeshimot, and he placed prostitutes in them. An old woman outside, and a young woman inside. [7]And when Israel was eating, and drinking, and merry, and going out to walk in the marketplace, the old woman said to him: "Do you not want linen garments?" [8]The old woman said to him at its value, and the young woman said to him at less. [9]Two or three times. [10]And afterwards she said to him: "You are like a member of the household; sit down, [and] select for yourself." [11]A pitcher of Ammonite wine stood next to her,

TRANSLATION AND COMMENTARY

your people." [1]Surely Balaam **should have said:** "And I shall advise you what **your people** shall do **to this people,"** for he was about to advise Balak about how to subvert Israel!

אָמַר רַבִּי אַבָּא [2]**Rabbi Abba bar Kahana said:** Balaam formulated his words **like a person who curses himself, but hangs his curse on other** people so that he does not realize he has cursed himself. Balaam formulated what he said as if Israel had asked for his advice on how to lead Moab astray, so that Balak would take preemptive measures. [3]Balaam **said to** Moab as follows: **"The God of** Israel **hates lewdness, and** the people of Israel **long for** new **linen garments,** which you can use as a lure to corrupt them. [4]**Come, and I will offer you advice: Set up booths for them, and place prostitutes in them.** [5]Have **an old woman** stand **outside** each of the booths, **and** let **a young woman** sit **inside** each of them, **and let them sell them linen garments."** [6]Balak **set up booths for them from the mountain of snow,** the Hermon, **to Bet Hayeshimot, and placed prostitutes in them,** setting **an old woman** on the **outside, and a young woman** on the **inside.** [7]**And when** the people of **Israel ate, drank, and merrily went out to walk in the marketplace,** one of **the old women would** approach an Israelite man and **say: "Would you not like** to buy new **linen garments?"** [8]After he went in to examine the merchandise, and asked for the price, **the old woman would say to him** that she would sell him the garment **at its** fair market **value, whereas the younger woman would say to him** that he could buy the garment **at less** than its value. [9]This would be repeated **two or three times,** [10]until **finally** the young woman **said to him: "You are** already **like a member of the household; sit down, and select for yourself** whatever you like." [11]**A pitcher of Ammonite**

RASHI

העם הזה לעמך, עמך לעם הזה מבעי ליה – שהשיא עצה לבלק שנכשלו בה ישראל – ״הן הנה היו לבני ישראל בדבר בלעם״. **ותולה קללתו בחברו** – וכך בלעם לא רצה לתלות שפלות זה בבלק שיהא הוא צריך לבקש עצה היאך יכשלו בה ישראל, אלא בישראל תלה השפלות, לומר שהן צריכין לעצה שיכשלו בה בני מואב, שלא תתקוף ידי מואב על ישראל, והיינו דכתיב ״אשר יעשה העם הזה לעמך״, מפי רבי, לישנא אחרינא: תולה קללתו בחברו – כלומר, שתלה הכתוב קללה במואב ולא רצה לכתוב כלפי ישראל כמו שאמר בלעם הרשע. **קלעים** – אהלים של קלעים כמו שעושין בשוקים. **בערבות מואב מהר שלג** – שניר. **כשהיה אומר לה** – ישראל: כלי פשתן זה בכמה, זקנה אומרת לו דמי שוויו, וילדה אומרת לו בפחות מכדי שוויו, וכן עושין עד שתים או עד שלש פעמים. **ברור לעצמך** – כל תכשיטין שאתה רוצה. **צרצרי** – נודות.

NOTES

Roman legion reached Assyria, it killed all the Jews. But from there on, given the much larger size of the Jewish communities, the Romans did not kill the Jews but only subjugated them.

מִתְאַוִּים לִכְלֵי פִשְׁתָּן **They long for linen garments.** The Israelites had become used to linen garments in Egypt, where they were readily available, and now longed for them in the wilderness, where they could no longer be obtained (*Maharsha*).

TRANSLATION AND COMMENTARY

wine stood next to her, and in those days, **neither Ammonite wine nor Gentile wine had yet been prohibited** to a Jew. [1]The young woman would **say to him: "Would you like to drink a cup of wine?"** [2]**He would drink,** and become drunk, and begin to **burn with lust. He would say to** the young woman: **"Surrender yourself to me."** [3]**She would** then **withdraw her idol from her bosom, and say to him:** "If you want me, you must first **worship this** idol." [4]**He would say to her:** "But **surely, I am a Jew,** and idol worship is forbidden to me." [5]**She would say to him: "What do you care?** [6]**All that we ask you** to do **is to relieve yourself before it."** [7]**And** the Israelite would accede to the woman's request, **not knowing that** the idol Pe'or **was** ordinarily **worshiped in that manner.** [8]The woman would then say to him: **"And moreover, I will not let go of you until you deny the Torah of Moses your master,** [9]**as the verse states** (Hosea 9:10): **'But when they came to Baal-Peor, they dedicated themselves to that shame; and they became detestable in their love'** — because of their love of fornication, they became detestable, and denied God."

וַיֵּשֶׁב יִשְׂרָאֵל [10]The verse states (Numbers 25:1): **"And Israel abode in Shittim."** [11]**Rabbi Eliezer says: Shittim was** in fact **the name** of that place. [12]**Rabbi Yehoshua** disagrees and **says:** The name means that the Israelites **engaged in matters of foolishness** there, harlotry and idolatry.

וַתִּקְרֶאןָ לָעָם [13]The passage continues (Numbers 25:2): **"And they called** [וַתִּקְרֶאןָ] **the people to the sacrifices of their gods."** [14]**Rabbi Eliezer says:** The word וַתִּקְרֶאןָ, translated here as "they called," might also be understood in the sense of "meet, happen upon." [15]**Naked women met them** on the way, and lured them to sin. **Rabbi Yehoshua says:** The word וַתִּקְרֶאןָ might also be understood in the sense of "ejaculation." In their lust for the daughters of Moab, the men of Israel **all ejaculated.**

וַעֲדַיִין לֹא נֶאֱסַר (יַיִן שֶׁל עַמּוֹנִי וְלֹא) יַיִן שֶׁל נָכְרִים. [1]אָמְרָה לוֹ: "רְצוֹנְךָ שֶׁתִּשְׁתֶּה כּוֹס שֶׁל יַיִן"? [2]כֵּיוָן שֶׁשָּׁתָה, בָּעַר בּוֹ. [3]אָמַר לָהּ: "הַשְׁמִיעִי לִי". הוֹצִיאָה יִרְאָתָהּ מִתּוֹךְ חֵיקָהּ, אָמְרָה לוֹ: "עֲבוֹד לָזֶה"! [4]אָמַר לָהּ: "הֲלֹא יְהוּדִי אֲנִי". [5]אָמְרָה לוֹ: "וּמַה אִיכְפַּת לָךְ? [6]כְּלוּם מְבַקְּשִׁים מִמְּךָ אֶלָּא פִּיעוּר". [7][וְהוּא אֵינוֹ יוֹדֵעַ שֶׁעֲבוֹדָתָהּ בְּכָךְ]. [8]וְלֹא עוֹד אֶלָּא שֶׁאֵינִי מַנַּחְתְּךָ עַד שֶׁתִּכְפּוֹר בְּתוֹרַת מֹשֶׁה רַבְּךָ, [9]שֶׁנֶּאֱמַר: 'הֵמָּה בָּאוּ בַעַל פְּעוֹר וַיִּנָּזְרוּ לַבֹּשֶׁת וַיִּהְיוּ שִׁקּוּצִים כְּאָהֳבָם' ".

[10]"וַיֵּשֶׁב יִשְׂרָאֵל בַּשִּׁטִּים". [11]רַבִּי אֱלִיעֶזֶר אוֹמֵר: שִׁטִּים שְׁמָהּ. [12]רַבִּי יְהוֹשֻׁעַ אוֹמֵר: שֶׁנִּתְעַסְּקוּ בְּדִבְרֵי שְׁטוּת.

[13]"וַתִּקְרֶאןָ לָעָם לְזִבְחֵי אֱלֹהֵיהֶן". [14]רַבִּי אֱלִיעֶזֶר אוֹמֵר: עֲרוּמּוֹת פָּגְעוּ בָּהֶן. [15]רַבִּי יְהוֹשֻׁעַ אוֹמֵר: שֶׁנַּעֲשׂוּ כּוּלָּן בַּעֲלֵי קְרָיִין.

LITERAL TRANSLATION

and neither Ammonite wine nor Gentile wine had been prohibited yet. [1]She said to him: "Is it your desire to drink a cup of wine?" [2]When he drank, [his lust] ignited in him. [3]He said to her: "Surrender yourself to me." She withdrew her idol from her bosom, [and] said to him: "Worship this!" [4]He said to her: "Surely, I am a Jew." [5]She said to him: "What do you care? [6]We only ask you to relieve yourself [before it]." [7]And he does not know that its service is like that. [8]"And moreover, I will not let go of you until you deny the Torah of Moses your master, [9]as it is stated: 'But when they came to Baal-Peor, they dedicated themselves to that shame; and they became detestable in their love.'"

[10]"And Israel abode in Shittim." [11]Rabbi Eliezer says: Shittim was its name. [12]Rabbi Yehoshua says: They engaged in matters of foolishness.

[13]"And they called the people to the sacrifices of their gods." [14]Rabbi Eliezer says: Naked women met them. [15]Rabbi Yehoshua says: They all had emissions.

RASHI

בוער בו – שהיה משתכר ובוער בו יצר הרע. **השמיעי** – הוי שומעת לתשמיש. **פיעור** – כך היתה עבודתו של פעור, שמתריזין לפניו. הכי גרסינן: **כלום מבקשין ממך אלא פיעור** – והוא עושה, ושוב אומרת לו: כפור בתורת משה רבך – **והוא** – עושה. **וינזרו לבשת** – סרו מדרכם והלכו אחר הבשת. **באהבם** – מתוך תאות אהבתם לזנות היו משוקצים, שכופרין בהקדוש ברוך הוא. **ותקראן** – בגופן, ותקראן – [משמע] לשון מקרה.

NOTES

וַעֲדַיִין לֹא נֶאֱסַר יַיִן שֶׁל עַמּוֹנִי **Ammonite wine had not yet been prohibited.** There are two levels of prohibition regarding non-Jewish wine. "Wine poured as a libation," which was actually used in idol worship, is forbidden to be drunk (and to derive benefit from) by Torah law. The Sages extended the scope of the prohibition and forbade drinking any wine touched by non-Jews, even though it was not used, or intended, for idol worship. This Rabbinic decree is very ancient, for Daniel did not drink non-Jewish wine, even when he was in exile and in captivity (see Daniel 1:8). But in the days of Moses, non-Jewish wine had not yet been prohibited.

TRANSLATION AND COMMENTARY

מַאי לְשׁוֹן [1]Having cited a disagreement about the meaning of the place-name Shittim, the Gemara now asks about the name of another place: **What is** the meaning of **the term Refidim** (Exodus 17:1)? [2]**Rabbi Eliezer says: Refidim was** in fact **the name** of that place. [3]**Rabbi Yehoshua says:** The name Refidim [רְפִידִים] recalls that the Israelites **let go** [רִיפּוּ] there **of the words of the Torah,** [4]**as the verse states** (Jeremiah 47:3): **"The fathers do not look back to their children for feebleness** [מֵרִפְיוֹן] **of hands."** The name Refidim intimates that Amalek attacked the Israelites because they abandoned the Torah.

אָמַר רַבִּי יוֹחָנָן [5]**Rabbi Yoḥanan said: Wherever** the expression, **"And he abode,** he lived, he dwelt [וַיֵּשֶׁב]," **is used, it is always an indication of** impending **trouble,** [6]**as the verse states** (Numbers 25:1): **"And Israel abode** [וַיֵּשֶׁב] **in Shittim, and the people began to commit harlotry with the daughters of Moab."** [7]And similarly (Genesis 37:1): **"And Jacob dwelt** [וַיֵּשֶׁב] **in the land where his father had sojourned in the land of Canaan,"** which is immediately followed by (verse 2): **"And Joseph brought to his father their evil report,"** and the rest of the story of the sale of Joseph. [8]And similarly (Genesis 47:27): **"And Israel dwelt** in the land of Egypt **in the country of Goshen,"** which is followed by (verse 29): **"And the time drew near for Israel to die."** [9]And similarly (I Kings 5:5): **"And Judah and Israel dwelt in safety, every man under his vine and under his fig tree,"** and later we find (I Kings 11:14): **"And the Lord stirred up an adversary to Solomon, Hadad the Edomite; he was of the king's seed in Edom."**

וְאֶת מַלְכֵי [10]Returning to Balaam, the Gemara cites a verse (Numbers 31:8): **"And they slew the Kings of Midian, beside the rest of them that were slain...Balaam also, the son of Be'or, they slew with the sword."** [11]The Gemara asks: **Why was Balaam needed there?** [12]**Rabbi Yoḥanan said:** He **had gone to collect payment** from Balak **for the twenty-four thousand** members **of Israel whose downfall he had caused.**

[1]מַאי לְשׁוֹן רְפִידִים? [2]רַבִּי אֱלִיעֶזֶר אוֹמֵר: רְפִידִים שְׁמָהּ. [3]רַבִּי יְהוֹשֻׁעַ אוֹמֵר: שֶׁרִיפּוּ עַצְמָן מִדִּבְרֵי תוֹרָה, [4]שֶׁנֶּאֱמַר: "לֹא הִפְנוּ אָבוֹת אֶל בָּנִים מֵרִפְיוֹן יָדָיִם". [5]אָמַר רַבִּי יוֹחָנָן: כָּל מָקוֹם שֶׁנֶּאֱמַר: "וַיֵּשֶׁב", אֵינוֹ אֶלָּא לְשׁוֹן צַעַר, [6]שֶׁנֶּאֱמַר: "וַיֵּשֶׁב יִשְׂרָאֵל בַּשִּׁטִּים וַיָּחֶל הָעָם לִזְנוֹת אֶל בְּנוֹת מוֹאָב". [7]"וַיֵּשֶׁב יַעֲקֹב בְּאֶרֶץ מְגוּרֵי אָבִיו בְּאֶרֶץ כְּנָעַן...וַיָּבֵא יוֹסֵף אֶת דִּבָּתָם רָעָה אֶל אֲבִיהֶם". [8]וְנֶאֱמַר: "וַיֵּשֶׁב יִשְׂרָאֵל...בְּאֶרֶץ גֹּשֶׁן...וַיִּקְרְבוּ יְמֵי יִשְׂרָאֵל לָמוּת". [9]"וַיֵּשֶׁב יְהוּדָה וְיִשְׂרָאֵל לָבֶטַח אִישׁ תַּחַת גַּפְנוֹ וְתַחַת תְּאֵנָתוֹ...וַיָּקֶם ה׳ שָׂטָן לִשְׁלֹמֹה אֵת הֲדַד הָאֲדֹמִי; מִזֶּרַע הַמֶּלֶךְ הוּא בֶּאֱדוֹם". [10]"וְאֶת מַלְכֵי מִדְיָן הָרְגוּ עַל חַלְלֵיהֶם וגו׳ וְאֵת בִּלְעָם בֶּן בְּעוֹר הָרְגוּ בֶּחָרֶב". [11]בִּלְעָם — מַאי בָּעֵי הָתָם? [12]אָמַר רַבִּי יוֹחָנָן: שֶׁהָלַךְ לִיטּוֹל שְׂכַר עֶשְׂרִים וְאַרְבָּעָה אֶלֶף [שֶׁהִפִּיל מִיִּשְׂרָאֵל].

LITERAL TRANSLATION

[1]What is the term Refidim? [2]Rabbi Eliezer says: Refidim was its name. [3]Rabbi Yehoshua says: They slackened from the words of Torah, [4]as it stated: "The fathers do not look back to their children for feebleness of hands."

[5]Rabbi Yoḥanan said: Wherever it is stated: "And he abode," it is always an expression of trouble, [6]as it is stated: "And Israel abode in Shittim, and the people began to fornicate with the daughters of Moab." [7]"And Jacob dwelt in the land where his father had sojourned in the land of Canaan....And Joseph brought to his father their evil report." [8]"And Israel dwelt...in the country of Goshen....And the time drew near for Israel to die." [9]"And Judah and Israel dwelt in safety, every man under his vine and under his fig tree....And the Lord stirred up an adversary to Solomon, Hadad the Edomite; he was of the king's seed in Edom." [10]"And they slew the Kings of Midian, beside the rest of them that were slain... Balaam also, the son of Be'or, they slew with the sword." [11]Balaam — why was he needed there? [12]Rabbi Yoḥanan said: He went to collect payment for the twenty-four thousand in Israel that he caused to fall.

RASHI

מאי רפידים — איידי דלעיל איפליגו ביה רבי אליעזר ורבי יהושע במשמעות דשטים, נקיט נמי רפידים דפליגי בה בכי האי גוונא. **לא הפנו אבות אל בנים** — להטיב להם. **מפני רפיון ידים** — של תורה ומצות, והכי נמי רפידים רפיון ידים הוא, כלומר מפני שרפו ידים מן התורה בא עליהם עמלק. **שכר עשרים וארבע אלפים מישראל** — שהרגו בעצתו, הלך ליטול מבלק ומזקני מדין.

NOTES

"וַיֵּשֶׁב", אֵינוֹ אֶלָּא לְשׁוֹן צַעַר "And he abode" is always an expression of trouble. This teaches that Israel is not destined to live a life of peace and serenity, a life which might lead people to think that nothing remains to be done to improve the world. Whenever people become too complacent, trouble overcomes them (see *Maharsha, Torat Ḥayyim, Rashi* to the beginning of *Vayeshev*).

TRANSLATION AND COMMENTARY

אָמַר מָר זוּטְרָא [1]**Mar Zutra bar Toviyah said in the name of Rav: This is** the meaning of **the popular adage:** [2]**The camel went to look for horns,** and **his ears were cut off.** When Balaam went to Balak to collect his fee, not only did he not receive any payment, but he himself paid with his life.

וְאֶת בִּלְעָם [3]The verse states (Joshua 13:22): **"Balaam also, of the son of Be'or, the sorcerer,** did the Children of Israel slay with the sword among them that were slain by them." [4]The Gemara asks: Was Balaam **a** mere **sorcerer?** But surely **he was a Prophet!**

אָמַר רַבִּי יוֹחָנָן [5]**Rabbi Yoḥanan said:** Balaam was **at first a** true **Prophet, but later,** when he wished to curse Israel, the prophetic spirit left him, and he became **a sorcerer.**

אָמַר רַב פַּפָּא [6]**Rav Pappa said: This is** the meaning of **the popular adage:** [7]**She came from** a family of **princes and governors,** but **played the harlot with carpenters.**

[106B] הָרְגוּ בְנֵי יִשְׂרָאֵל [8]The verse states (Joshua 13:22): "Balaam also, of the son of Be'or, the sorcerer, **did the Children of Israel slay with the sword among them that were slain by them** [אֶל חַלְלֵיהֶם]." [9]**Rav said:** The plural term חַלְלֵיהֶם intimates that the Israelites **fulfilled** all **four modes** of judicial **execution in** Balaam: **Stoning, burning, slaying, and strangulation.** They hanged him (strangulation), and chopped off his head (slaying), letting it fall to the ground (stoning), and into a fire (burning).

אָמַר לֵיהּ [10]It was related that **a certain heretic** once **said to Rabbi Ḥanina: "Do you know how old Balaam was** when he was killed?" [11]Rabbi Ḥanina **said to him:** "The Torah **does not state** explicitly how old he was when he died. [12]**But from that which is written** elsewhere (Psalms 55:24): **'Bloody and deceitful men**

LITERAL TRANSLATION

[1]Mar Zutra bar Toviyah said in the name of Rav: This is what people say: [2]The camel went to look for horns; the ears he had were cut off from him.

[3]"Balaam also, of the son of Be'or, the sorcerer." [4]A sorcerer? He was a Prophet!

[5]Rabbi Yoḥanan said: At first a Prophet, and at the end a sorcerer.

[6]Rav Pappa said: This is what people say: [7]She came from princes and governors, [and] played the harlot with carpenters.

[106B] [8]"The Children of Israel slew with the sword among them that were slain by them." [9]Rav said: They fulfilled four [modes] of execution in him: Stoning, and burning, slaying, and strangulation.

[10]A certain heretic said to Rabbi Ḥanina: "Do you know how old Balaam was?" [11]He said to him: "It is not written. [12]But from what is written: 'Bloody and deceitful men

[1]אָמַר מָר זוּטְרָא בַּר טוֹבִיָּה אָמַר רַב: הַיְינוּ דְּאָמְרִי אֱינָשֵׁי: [2]גַּמְלָא אָזְלָא לְמִיבְעֵי קַרְנֵי; אוּדְנֵי דַהֲווּ לֵיהּ גְּזִיזַן מִינֵּיהּ. [3]״וְאֶת בִּלְעָם בֶּן בְּעוֹר הַקּוֹסֵם״. [4]קוֹסֵם? נָבִיא הוּא! [5]אָמַר רַבִּי יוֹחָנָן: בַּתְּחִלָּה נָבִיא, וּלְבַסּוֹף קוֹסֵם. [6]אָמַר רַב פַּפָּא: הַיְינוּ דְּאָמְרִי אֱינָשֵׁי: [7]״מִסְּגְנֵי וְשִׁילְטֵי הֲוַאי, אַיְיזָן לְגַבְרֵי נַגָּרֵי״. [106B] [8]״הָרְגוּ בְנֵי יִשְׂרָאֵל [בַּחֶרֶב] אֶל חַלְלֵיהֶם״. [9]אָמַר רַב: שֶׁקִּיְּימוּ בּוֹ אַרְבַּע מִיתוֹת, סְקִילָה וּשְׂרֵיפָה הֶרֶג וָחֶנֶק. [10]אֲמַר לֵיהּ הַהוּא מִינָא לְרַבִּי חֲנִינָא: ״מִי שְׁמִיעַ לָךְ, בִּלְעָם בַּר כַּמָּה הֲוָה״? [11]אֲמַר לֵיהּ: ״מִיכְתַּב לָא כְּתִיב. [12]אֶלָּא מִדִּכְתִיב: ׳אַנְשֵׁי דָמִים וּמִרְמָה

RASHI

גמלא תבע קרני — כך בלעם שאל שכר ונהרג. גזו מיניה = חתכו ממנו. בלעם בן בעור הקוסם הרגו בחרב — ההוא קרא ביהושע כתיב. ולבסוף — שנתן עיניו לקלל את ישראל, ניטלה ממנו נבואה ונעשה קוסם. מסגני ושילטא הואי — אשת סגנים ושרים היתה. אייזן לגברא נגר — זינתה למושכי חבל ספינה, לישנא אחרינא: נגרי = חרשים. הרגו אל חלליהם — מיתות הרבה, משמע שתלאוהו והציתו אש תחת הצליבה, וחתכו ראשו ונפל לתוך האש, תלייה היינו חנק, חתיכת הראש הרג, כשנפל לארץ — סקילה, כשנפל לאור היינו שריפה.

NOTES

מִסְּגְנֵי וְשִׁילְטֵי הֲוַאי **She came from princes and governors.** *Rashi* offers two interpretations of the word נַגָּרֵי: Ship draggers (which seems to be based on the reading נַגְּדֵי), and carpenters. Instead of אַיְיזָן, the Geonim read אֵיוָאן, which they understood as a woman's name in Persian. Thus, the adage goes: Eivan (a name) came from a family of princes and governors, but still played the harlot with a ship dragger.

Ramah understands the adage in an entirely different manner: When a woman who was married to a mighty soldier is widowed, she can no longer marry a man who does not carry a weapon. If she cannot find another soldier, she marries a carpenter, whose tools resemble weapons. So, too, regarding Balaam, who was initially a Prophet — even after the prophetic spirit left him, he still wanted to predict the future, and so he turned to sorcery.

שֶׁקִּיְּימוּ בּוֹ אַרְבַּע מִיתוֹת **They fulfilled four modes of execution in him.** Our commentary follows *Rashi,* who understands that Rav infers from the plural term חַלְלֵיהֶם that all four modes of judicial execution were administered to Balaam. *Ramah* explains that this is derived from the superfluous expression, "the Children of Israel," which teaches that they administered to Balaam all the modes of execution that were practiced by the Children of Israel (see also *Maharsha*).

TRANSLATION AND COMMENTARY

shall not live out half their days' — [1]it may be inferred that **he was** not more than **thirty-three or thirty-four years old** when he died." [2]The heretic **said to** Rabbi Ḥanina: **"You have said well,** for **I myself** once **saw Balaam's account book,** [3]in which **it was written: 'Thirty-three years old was the lame Balaam when Pineḥas the robber killed him.'"**

אֲמַר לֵיהּ [4]**Mar the son of Ravina said to his son: Regarding all** the kings and ordinary people who do not have a portion in the World to Come, **do not preach excessively** against them, **except for the wicked Balaam,** [5]**for as many** shameful and disgraceful things **that you can find about him, preach about him.**

כְּתִיב [6]The Gemara now moves on to Doeg, noting that, in one place, his name **is spelled** (I Samuel 22:9): **"Doeg** [דּוֹאֵג]," [7]**and** in another place, the same name **is spelled** (I Samuel 22:18): **"Doyeg** [דּוֹיֵיג]." [8]**Rabbi Yoḥanan said: At first the Holy One, blessed be He, sat and worried** [דּוֹאֵג] **lest** Doeg turn out badly, and become a heretic. [9]**After** His fears came true, and Doeg went astray, God **said: "Woe** [וַוי], **that he** took to bad ways."

סִימָן [10][The Gemara offers **a mnemonic device** to help the student remember a series of statements made by Rabbi Yitzḥak: **Mighty man, and wicked man, and righteous man, riches, and scribe.**]

אָמַר רַבִּי יִצְחָק [11]**Rabbi Yitzḥak said: What is** the meaning of **the verse which states** (Psalms 52:3): [12]**"Why boast you of evil O mighty man? the love of God endures for all time"?** [13]**The Holy One, blessed be He, said to Doeg: "Are you not a mighty man in**

לֹא יֶחֱצוּ יְמֵיהֶם׳ — [1]בַּר תְּלָתִין וּתְלָת שְׁנִין אוֹ בַּר תְּלָתִין וְאַרְבַּע״. [2]אֲמַר לֵיהּ: ״שַׁפִּיר קָאָמְרַתְּ. לְדִידִי חָזֵי לִי פִּנְקְסֵיהּ דְּבִלְעָם, [3]וַהֲוָה כְּתִיב בֵּיהּ: ׳בַּר תְּלָתִין וּתְלָת שְׁנִין בִּלְעָם חֲגִירָא כַּד קָטֵיל יָתֵיהּ פִּנְחָס לִיסְטָאָה׳״.

[4]אֲמַר לֵיהּ מָר בְּרֵיהּ דְּרָבִינָא לִבְרֵיהּ: בְּכוּלְּהוּ לָא תַּפֵּישׁ לְמִדְרַשׁ, לְבַר מִבִּלְעָם הָרָשָׁע, [5]דְּכַמָּה דְּמַשְׁכַּחַתְּ בֵּיהּ, דְּרוֹשׁ בֵּיהּ.

[6]כְּתִיב: ״דּוֹאֵג״. [7]וּכְתִיב: ״דּוֹיֵיג״. [8]אָמַר רַבִּי יוֹחָנָן: בַּתְּחִילָּה יוֹשֵׁב הַקָּדוֹשׁ בָּרוּךְ הוּא וְדוֹאֵג שֶׁמָּא יֵצֵא זֶה לְתַרְבּוּת רָעָה. [9]לְאַחַר שֶׁיָּצָא, אֲמַר: ״וַוי שֶׁיָּצָא זֶה״.

[10](סִימָן: גִּבּוֹר רָשָׁע וְצַדִּיק חַיִל וְסוֹפֵר).

[11]אָמַר רַבִּי יִצְחָק: מַאי דִּכְתִיב: [12]״מַה תִּתְהַלֵּל בְּרָעָה הַגִּבּוֹר? חֶסֶד אֵל כָּל הַיּוֹם״? [13]אָמַר לוֹ הַקָּדוֹשׁ בָּרוּךְ הוּא לְדוֹאֵג: ״לֹא

LITERAL TRANSLATION

shall not live out half their days' — [1]he was thirty-three or thirty-four years old." [2]He said to him: "You have said well. I myself saw Balaam's account book, [3]and it was written: 'Thirty-three years old was the lame Balaam when Pineḥas the robber killed him.'"

[4]Mar the son of Ravina said to his son: Regarding all of them, do not preach excessively, except for the wicked Balaam, [5]for as much as you find about him, preach about him.

[6]It is written: "Doeg." [7]And it is written: "Doyeg." [8]Rabbi Yoḥanan said: At first the Holy One, blessed be He, sat and worried lest he turn out badly (lit., "go out to evil culture"). [9]After he went out, He said: "Woe, that he went out."

[10][A sign: Mighty man, and wicked man, and righteous man, riches, and scribe.]

[11]Rabbi Yitzḥak said: What is that which is written: [12]"Why boast you of evil O mighty man? the love of God endures for all time?" [13]The Holy One, blessed be He, said to Doeg: "Are you not

RASHI

בר תלתין ותלת – ורבי חנינא לית ליה דרבי סימאי, דאמר לעיל שלשה היו באותה עצה דפרעה, בלעם ואיוב ויתרו, דלרבי סימאי בלעם חיה יותר מן מאתים ועשר שנים, דהא היה בעצת פרעה ד״כל הבן הילוד היאורה תשליכוהו״, דלרבי סימאי כל אותן מאתים ועשר שנים שהיו ישראל בגלות מצרים עד מלחמת מדין חיה בלעם. **חגירא** – תרגום של פיסח. **כד קטל יתיה פנחס ליסטאה** = שר צבא, ואפילו קטליה אחר כל המלחמה נקראת על שמו. **בכלהו** – מלכים והדיוטות. **לא תפיש ותדרוש** – לגנאי. **לבר מבלעם** – דכל מה דמשכחת ליה לגנאי – דרוש. **(שמא יצא זה לתרבות רעה) לאחר שיצא לתרבות רעה אמר ווי** – לכך כתוב דויג. **אמר לו הקדוש ברוך הוא לדואג והלא**

NOTES

בְּכוּלְּהוּ לָא תַּפֵּישׁ לְמִדְרַשׁ **Regarding all of them, do not preach excessively.** As we learned above (104b), those who interpret the Torah metaphorically said that all of the people included in the Mishnah among those who do not have a share in the World to Come will reach the World to Come. Only regarding Balaam did they find no Scriptural support suggesting he might reach the World to Come. Thus, one may not preach excessively against the other Biblical figures mentioned in the Mishnah. However, against Balaam one may preach as much as one pleases (*Iyyun Ya'akov*).

בַּתְּחִילָּה יוֹשֵׁב וְדוֹאֵג **At first He sat and worried.** *Ramah* appears to have had a different reading, according to which Rabbi Yoḥanan said as follows: At first, before Doeg was born, the Holy One, blessed be He, sat and worried lest that wicked man be born, and after Doeg was born, God said, "Woe."

TRANSLATION AND COMMENTARY

Torah? [1] **Why,** then, **do you boast of evil** and speak ill of David? [2] **Is not the love of God spread over you all day** when you engage in the study of His Torah?"

וְאָמַר רַבִּי יִצְחָק [3] **And Rabbi Yitzḥak said: What is** the meaning of **the verse that states** (Psalms 50:16): [4] **"But to the wicked man God says, What have you to do to declare My statutes?"** [5] **The Holy One, blessed be He, said to the wicked Doeg: "What** business **have you to declare** and discuss **My statutes** and commandments? [6] **When you reach the passage regarding killers and the passage regarding those who speak evil, how do you interpret them?** You yourself are guilty of both offenses!"

וַתִּשָּׂא בְרִיתִי [7] That same verse continues (Psalms 50:16): **"Or that you should take my covenant in your mouth"?** [8] **Rabbi Ammi said:** "In your mouth" — but not in your heart. [9] **Doeg's Torah was only from the lips outward,** but not in his heart, for he never fully understood or internalized what he had learned.

וְאָמַר רַבִּי יִצְחָק [10] **And Rabbi Yitzḥak said: What is** the meaning of **the verse that states** (Psalms 52:8): [11] **"The righteous also shall see, and fear, and shall laugh at him"?** [12] **At first** the righteous **saw** that, despite his wrongdoings, Doeg continued to prosper. [13] **But in the end** — after Doeg died young — **they laughed** and rejoiced.

וְאָמַר רַבִּי יִצְחָק [14] **And Rabbi Yitzḥak said: What is** the meaning of **the verse that states** (Job 20:15): [15] **"He has swallowed riches; and he shall vomit them up again; God shall cast them out of his belly"?** [16] **David said to the Holy One, blessed be He: "Master of the Universe, let Doeg die** now, and do not give him another opportunity to repent." [17] God **said to him: "'He has swallowed down riches, and he shall vomit them up again.'** Doeg is still filled with Torah, and wisdom, and so it is better to wait until he has forgotten it all." [18] David **said to** God: **"'God shall cast them out of his belly.'** Make him forget his Torah, so that he can be put to death immediately."

גִּבּוֹר בַּתּוֹרָה אַתָּה? [1] מַה
תִּתְהַלֵּל בְּרָעָה? [2] לֹא חֶסֶד אֵל
נָטוּי עָלֶיךָ כָּל הַיּוֹם״?
[3] וְאָמַר רַבִּי יִצְחָק: מַאי דִּכְתִיב:
[4] ״וְלָרָשָׁע אָמַר אֱלֹהִים מַה לְּךָ
לְסַפֵּר חֻקָּי״. [5] אָמַר לוֹ הַקָּדוֹשׁ
בָּרוּךְ הוּא לְדוֹאֵג הָרָשָׁע: ״מַה
לְּךָ לְסַפֵּר חֻקָּי? [6] כְּשֶׁאַתָּה
מַגִּיעַ לְפָרָשַׁת מְרַצְּחִים וּפָרָשַׁת
מְסַפְּרֵי לָשׁוֹן הָרַע מָה אַתָּה
דּוֹרֵשׁ בָּהֶם״?
[7] ״וַתִּשָּׂא בְרִיתִי עֲלֵי פִיךָ״?
[8] אָמַר רַבִּי אַמִי: [9] אֵין תּוֹרָתוֹ
שֶׁל דּוֹאֵג אֶלָּא מִשָּׂפָה וְלַחוּץ.
[10] וְאָמַר רַבִּי יִצְחָק: מַאי
דִּכְתִיב: [11] ״וְיִרְאוּ צַדִּיקִים
וְיִירָאוּ וְעָלָיו יִשְׂחָקוּ״?
[12] בַּתְּחִילָּה יִירְאוּ, [13] וּלְבַסּוֹף
יִשְׂחָקוּ.
[14] וְאָמַר רַבִּי יִצְחָק: מַאי
דִּכְתִיב: [15] ״חַיִל בָּלַע וַיְקִאֶנּוּ
מִבִּטְנוֹ יֹרִשֶׁנּוּ אֵל״? [16] אָמַר דָּוִד
לִפְנֵי הַקָּדוֹשׁ בָּרוּךְ הוּא: ״רִבּוֹנוֹ
שֶׁל עוֹלָם, יָמוּת דּוֹאֵג״. [17] אָמַר
לוֹ: ״חַיִל בָּלַע וַיְקִיאֶנּוּ״. [18] אָמַר
לְפָנָיו: ״מִבִּטְנוֹ יוֹרִישֶׁנּוּ אֵל״.

LITERAL TRANSLATION

a mighty man in Torah? [1] Why do you boast of evil? [2] Is not the love of God spread out over you all day?" [3] And Rabbi Yitzḥak said: What is that which is written: [4] "But to the wicked man God says, What have you to declare My statutes?" [5] The Holy One, blessed be He, said to the wicked Doeg: "What have you to declare My statutes? [6] When you reach the passage about killers and the passage about slanderers, what do you expound about them?"

[7] "Or that you should take my covenant in your mouth"? [8] Rabbi Ammi said: [9] Doeg's Torah was only from the lips outward.

[10] And Rabbi Yitzḥak said: What is that which is written: [11] "The righteous also shall see, and fear, and shall laugh at him"? [12] At first they shall see, [13] but in the end they shall laugh.

[14] And Rabbi Yitzḥak said: What is that which is written: [15] "He has swallowed riches; and he shall vomit them up again; God shall cast them out of his belly"? [16] David said before the Holy One, blessed be He: "Master of the universe, let Doeg die." [17] He said to him: "He has swallowed riches, and he shall vomit them up again." [18] He said before Him: "God shall cast them out of his belly."

RASHI

גבור אתה בתורה — למה תתהלל לספר לשון הרע על דוד. **לא חסד תורה עליך** — לא חכם בתורה אתה — דכתיב (משלי לא) ״ותורת חסד על לשונה״. **מרצחים** — שהרג נוב. **עלי פיך** — ולא בלב. **בתחלה ייראו** — הצדיקים היו יראים שלא ילמד אדם ממעשיו של דואג, שהולך וחוטא ומצליח. **ולבסוף** — כשמת בחצי ימיו ושב גמולו בראשו — ישחקו. **חיל בלע יקיאנו** — המתן עד שתשכח תורתו. **אמר לפניו ומבטנו יורישנו אל** — אל תמתין לו עד שתשכח, אלא תמהר ותשכיחנו.

NOTES

יִרְאוּ וְיִשְׂחָקוּ **They shall see and laugh.** Alternatively: At first, when people saw Doeg's greatness in Torah, they were in awe of him. But in the end when it became clear that his Torah was only from the lips outward, and not in his heart, they laughed (*Iyyun Ya'akov*).

LANGUAGE

אֲוִיר **Air.** This word derives from the Greek ἀήρ, *ari*, meaning "air," or "space."

TRANSLATION AND COMMENTARY

וְאָמַר רַבִּי יִצְחָק [1]**And Rabbi Yitzḥak said: What is** the meaning of **the verse that states** (Psalms 52:7): **"God shall likewise destroy you forever"?** [2]**The Holy One, blessed be He, said to David: "Let Doeg enter the World to Come."** [3]David **said to Him: "God shall likewise destroy you forever"** — deny Doeg eternal life.

מַאי דִּכְתִיב [4]**What is** meant by **the** end of that **verse, which states** (Psalms 52:7): **"He shall take you away, and pluck you from your tent, and root you out of the land of the living. Selah"?** [5]**The Holy One, blessed be He, said** to David: "Even if Doeg is barred from entering the World to Come, **let** the Sages at least **recite a law in the study hall in** Doeg's **name."** [6]David **said to Him: "He shall take you away, and pluck you out of your tent"** — let Doeg be totally plucked out of the tent of Torah, the study hall. [7]God then said to David: **"Let Doeg** at least **have sons who will be Sages."** [8]David said to Him: "He shall **root you out of the land of the living. Selah."**

וְאָמַר רַבִּי יִצְחָק [9]**And Rabbi Yitzḥak said: What is** meant by **the verse that states** (Isaiah 33:18): **"Where is the scribe? where is the receiver? where is he who counted the towers?"** [10]The verse refers to Torah scholars who went astray: **"Where is the scribe?"** — one who is familiar with **all the letters in the Torah,** and all the plene and defective spellings. [11]**"Where is the receiver** [שֹׁקֵל]**?" — one who weighs** [שׁוֹקֵל] **all the leniencies and the stringencies in the Torah,** and knows how to put forward *kal vaḥomer* arguments. [12]**"Where is he that counted the towers?" — he** who **could count** out **three hundred fixed laws pertaining** to the ritual impurity **of a tower flying in the air.**

[1]וְאָמַר רַבִּי יִצְחָק: מַאי דִּכְתִיב: "גַּם אֵל יִתָּצְךָ לָנֶצַח"? [2]אָמַר הַקָּדוֹשׁ בָּרוּךְ הוּא לְדָוִד: "נֵיתֵי דּוֹאֵג לְעָלְמָא דְּאָתֵי". [3]אָמַר לְפָנָיו: "גַּם אֵל יִתָּצְךָ לָנֶצַח". [4]"מַאי דִּכְתִיב: "יַחְתְּךָ וְיִסָּחֲךָ מֵאֹהֶל וְשֵׁרֶשְׁךָ מֵאֶרֶץ חַיִּים. סֶלָה"? [5]אָמַר הַקָּדוֹשׁ בָּרוּךְ הוּא: "לֵימְרוּ שְׁמַעְתָּא בֵּי מִדְרָשָׁא מִשְּׁמֵיהּ". [6]אָמַר לְפָנָיו: "יַחְתְּךָ וְיִסָּחֲךָ מֵאֹהֶל". [7]"לֶיהֱוֵי לֵיהּ בְּנִין רַבָּנַן". [8]"וְשֵׁרֶשְׁךָ מֵאֶרֶץ חַיִּים. סֶלָה".

[9]וְאָמַר רַבִּי יִצְחָק: מַאי דִּכְתִיב: "אַיֵּה סֹפֵר? אַיֵּה שֹׁקֵל? אַיֵּה סֹפֵר אֶת הַמִּגְדָּלִים?" [10]"אַיֵּה סֹפֵר?" — כָּל אוֹתִיּוֹת שֶׁבַּתּוֹרָה. [11]"אַיֵּה שֹׁקֵל?" — שֶׁשּׁוֹקֵל כָּל קַלִּים וַחֲמוּרִים שֶׁבַּתּוֹרָה. [12]"אַיֵּה סֹפֵר אֶת הַמִּגְדָּלִים?" — שֶׁהָיָה סוֹפֵר שְׁלֹשׁ מֵאוֹת הֲלָכוֹת פְּסוּקוֹת בְּמִגְדָּל הַפּוֹרֵחַ בָּאֲוִיר.

LITERAL TRANSLATION

[1]And Rabbi Yitzḥak said: What is that which is written: "God shall likewise destroy you forever"? [2]The Holy One, blessed be He, said to David: "Let Doeg enter the World to Come." [3]He said before Him: "God shall likewise destroy you forever."

[4]What is that which is written: "He shall take you away, and pluck you from your tent, and root you out of the land of the living. Selah"? [5]The Holy One, blessed be He, said: "Let them say a law in the study hall in his name." [6]He said before Him: "He shall take you away, and pluck you from your tent." [7]"Let him have sons who are Sages." [8]"And root you out of the land of the living. Selah."

[9]And Rabbi Yitzḥak said: What is that which is written: "Where is the scribe? where is the receiver? where is he who counted the towers?" [10]"Where is the scribe?" — all the letters in the Torah. [11]"Where is the receiver?" — who weighs all the leniencies and the stringencies in the Torah. [12]"Where is he who counted the towers?" — he would count three hundred fixed laws regarding a tower flying in the air.

RASHI

בי מדרשא — מאהל, זה בית המדרש. **ושרשך מארץ חיים סלה** — שורש שלו תכסח מארץ חיים, דלא להוו ליה בנין רבנן. **כל אותיות שבתורה** — שהיה בקי בחסירות ויתירות. **שוקל קלים וחמורים** — יודע לדרוש בקל וחומר. **במגדל הפורח באויר** — מתג עליונה שלמעלה מן הלמ״ד מפני מה כפופה למטה, לשון מורי ורבי מפי השמועה, לישנא אחרינא: במגדל הפורח באויר הנכנס לארץ העמים, בשידה תיבה ומגדל אם הוא טמא אם לאו, לישנא אחרינא: שלש מאות הלכות במגדל הפורח באויר — לעשות כישוף להעמיד מגדל באויר, כגון "שלש מאות הלכות בנטיעות קשואין", דאמרן בפירקין דלעיל (סח,א), ולמורי נראה דהכי

NOTES

שֶׁשּׁוֹקֵל כָּל קַלִּים וַחֲמוּרִים **Who weighs all the leniencies and the stringencies.** *Maharsha* adds that the term *shokel*, "weigh," implies that the verse is referring to someone who knows how to weigh the lenient and the stringent factors of a case against each other, for a *kal vaḥomer* argument can often be put forward in contrary ways, depending upon which factor is taken into consideration.

שְׁלֹשׁ מֵאוֹת הֲלָכוֹת **Three hundred laws.** The Rishonim note that the numbers three hundred and four hundred are exaggerations, which are used in the sense of "many" (see *Arukh*).

מִגְדָּל הַפּוֹרֵחַ בָּאֲוִיר **A tower flying in the air.** *Rashi* offers several explanations of this expression. *Rav Hai Gaon* explains that the Gemara is referring to a wooden box or closet that is suspended in the air — either miraculously or mechanically or by a magnet — and the Halakhic questions that may arise regarding the ritual purity of what is found inside.

TRANSLATION AND COMMENTARY

אָמַר רַבִּי [1]**Rabbi** Yehudah HaNasi **said:** Both **Doeg and Achitofel asked four hundred questions regarding a tower flying in the air, and not one of them was resolved** for them — evidence of the sharpness of their minds.

אָמַר רָבָא [2]**Rava said: Is there greatness in asking questions?** [3]For back **in the years of Rav Yehudah, all their study was in** the order of *Nezikin* (damages), **whereas** today **we teach** all six orders of the Mishnah, and even devote **a lot** of attention to the difficult tractate of *Uktzin*. [4]**And when Rav Yehudah reached** the Mishnah (*Taharot* 2:1): **"A woman who was preserving vegetables in a pot,"** [5]**and some say** when he reached the Mishnah (*Uktzin* 2:1): **"Olives which he preserved in their leaves are ritually pure,"** [6]**he** would have great difficulty with the material taught there, and **say: I see here problems** the likes of which were tackled by my masters, **Rav and Shmuel.** [7]**And we,** on the other hand, **teach** tractate ***Uktzin* in thirteen ways,** for we know the tractate backwards and forwards. [8]**But** this has not made us into greater people, for **Rav Yehudah** would merely **remove his shoe** at the beginning of a fast called in a time of drought, **and** immediately **it began to rain** by virtue of his great righteousness, **whereas we** today **cry out** in prayer, **and nobody takes heed of us.** [9]**Rather, the Holy One, blessed be He, desires** a pious and righteous **heart, as the verse states** (I Samuel 16:7): **"But the Lord looks on the heart."**

[1]אָמַר רַבִּי: אַרְבַּע מְאָה בַּעְיָיא בָּעוּ דוֹאֵג וַאֲחִיתוֹפֶל בְּמִגְדָּל הַפּוֹרֵחַ בָּאֲוִיר, [וְלָא אִיפְּשַׁט לְהוּ חַד].

[2]אָמַר רָבָא: רְבוּתָא לְמִבְעֵי בָּעֲיֵי? [3]בִּשְׁנֵי דְּרַב יְהוּדָה כּוּלֵּי תְּנוּיֵי בִּנְזִיקִין, וַאֲנַן קָא מַתְנִינַן טוּבָא בְּעוּקְצִין. [4]וְכִי הֲוָה מָטֵי רַב יְהוּדָה: ״אִשָּׁה שֶׁכּוֹבֶשֶׁת יָרָק בַּקְּדֵירָה״, [5]וְאָמְרִי לָהּ: ״זֵיתִים שֶׁכְּבָשָׁן בְּטַרְפֵיהֶן טְהוֹרִים״, [6]אָמַר: הֲוָיוֹת דְּרַב וּשְׁמוּאֵל קָא חָזֵינָא הָכָא. [7]וַאֲנַן קָא מַתְנִינַן בְּעוּקְצִין תְּלָת סְרֵי מְתִיבָתָא. [8]וְרַב יְהוּדָה שָׁלֵיף מְסָאנֵי וְאָתָא מִטְרָא, וַאֲנַן צָוְחִינַן וְלֵיכָּא דְּמַשְׁגַּח בָּן. [9]אֶלָּא הַקָּדוֹשׁ בָּרוּךְ הוּא לִיבָּא בָּעֵי, דִּכְתִיב: ״וַה׳ יִרְאֶה לַלֵּבָב״.

LITERAL TRANSLATION

[1]Rabbi said: Doeg and Achitofel asked four hundred questions regarding a tower flying in the air, [and not one of them was resolved].

[2]Rava said: Is there greatness in asking questions? [3]In the years of Rav Yehudah, all their study was in *Nezikin*, and we teach a lot in *Uktzin*. [4]And when Rav Yehudah reached, "A woman who was preserving vegetables in a pot," [5]and some say, "Olives which he preserved in their leaves are ritually pure," [6]he said: I see here problems of Rav and Shmuel. [7]And we teach *Uktzin* in thirteen ways. [8]But Rav Yehudah removes his shoe, and rain comes, and we cry out and nobody takes heed of us. [9]Rather, the Holy One, blessed be He, desires the heart, as it is written: "But the Lord looks on the heart."

RASHI

גרסינן: שלש מאות הלכות במגדל העומד [באויר], ומשנה אחת באהלות (פרק ד׳ משנה א׳), דמשתעי בהכי: מגדל העומד באויר וטומאה בתוכה, כלים שבתוכו טמאים, וכן נראה לרבי. רבותא למבעא בעיי — וללמוד תורה רחמנא לבא בעי, דהא בשני דרב יהודה כולהו תנויי בסדר נזיקין היה, כל הגמרא שלהן לא הוה אלא בסדר נזיקין, שלא היו מרבין כל כך [לדרוש]. האשה שכובשת ירק בקדירה — לא אשכחתיה במסכת עוקצין. שכובשת ירק — בחומץ או בציר — טהורים, דאין מקבלין טומאה על ידי עוקצין, שאם נגע טומאה בשרשיו העלין טהורין שאין נעשין יד לעלין מאחר שכבשם שאין מניחין לשם אלא למראה. זיתים שכבשן בטרפיהן — איתא במסכת עוקצין (פרק ב׳ משנה א׳). טרפיהן — עלין שלהן — טהורין הזיתים, שאין נעשין להם בית יד להכניס להם טומאה. הויות דרב ושמואל קא חזינא הכא — דלא הוה ידע מאי טעמא הן טהורין. תליסר מתיבתא — שלש עשרה ישיבות שאנו עוסקין כולן במסכת עוקצין ויודעין אותה יפה, ואפילו הכי בהם היו חסידים יותר ממנו, דאלו רבי יהודה כו׳.

NOTES

עוּקְצִין ***Uktzin.*** *Uktzin,* "stems, stalks," is the last tractate in the order of Purities, and deals with the ritual purity of fruits and the inedible stalks or stems to which they are attached. At issue is which inedible parts of a fruit are considered parts of the fruit itself when it comes to contracting ritual impurity.

אִשָּׁה שֶׁכּוֹבֶשֶׁת יָרָק **A woman who was preserving vegetables.** According to *Rashi,* we are dealing here with the issue of "stems." If vegetables or olives are placed in vinegar or some other liquid for pickling, they do not contract ritual impurity by their stems, which are no longer considered as parts of the vegetables or the olives. Consequently, if the stems come into contact with something that is ritually impure, the vegetables and the olives do not become ritually impure. *Ramah* understands that when the Gemara refers to "a woman who was preserving vegetables in a pot," it is referring to the law taught in *Taharot* 2:1 regarding a woman who was preserving vegetables which were terumah, and she touched one of the leaves of the vegetable with her hand. The Mishnah distinguishes between touching a dry portion of the leaf and touching a wet portion, and between touching a leaf the size of an egg and touching a leaf of a smaller size.

TRANSLATION AND COMMENTARY

אָמַר רַב מְשָׁרְשִׁיָּא [1] **Rav Mesharshiya said: Doeg and Achitofel did not** properly **understand the law.**

מַתְקִיף לָהּ [2] **Mar Zutra raised an objection:** Doeg and Achitofel, **about whom the verse states** (Isaiah 33:18): **"Where is the scribe? where is the receiver? where is he who counted the towers?"** — [3] **you say that they did not** properly **understand the law!** [4] **Rather, their traditions did not prove to be in agreement with the law, as the verse states** (Psalms 25:14): **"The counsel of the Lord is with them that fear Him."** Even though Doeg and Achitofel were brilliant scholars, since they did not fear God, their Halakhic conclusions were not accepted as the law.

אָמַר רַבִּי אַמִי [5] **Rabbi Ammi said: Doeg did not die until he forgot his learning,** [6] **as the verse states** (Proverbs 5:23): **"He shall die for want of instruction; and in the greatness of his folly he shall go astray."**

רַב (אַשִׁי) [7] **Rav Ashi said:** Before he died, Doeg **was afflicted with leprosy, as the verse states** (Psalms 73:27): **"You have destroyed** [הִצְמַתָּה] **all those who go astray from You."** [8] The significance of the term הִצְמַתָּה is learned from what **is stated elsewhere** (Leviticus 25:23): לִצְמִתֻת, **"forever,"** which **is translated** into Aramaic as לַחֲלוּטִין, **"absolutely."** [9] **And we have learned** in the Mishnah (*Megilah* 8b): **"There are no differences between a confined leper,** one who has not yet been conclusively declared ritually impure by a priest — **and a confirmed leper** [מוּחְלָט], one who has already been conclusively declared ritually impure by a priest, **except** for the obligations to **let one's hair grow** long **and rend one's garments,** which fall upon a confirmed leper, but not upon a confined leper (see Leviticus 13:4-5)." Thus, there is a connection between הִצְמַתָּה, "You have destroyed," pertaining to Doeg, and לִצְמִתֻת, "forever," which is connected to לַחֲלוּטִין, "absolutely," which alludes to a confirmed leper [מוּחְלָט]. Thus, we may conclude that Doeg was afflicted with leprosy before he died.

סִימָּן [10] (The Gemara offers **a mnemonic device** to help the student remember a series of statements made by Rabbi Yoḥanan: **Three, they saw, and half, and he called him.)**

אָמַר רַבִּי יוֹחָנָן [11] **Rabbi Yoḥanan said: Three Angels of destruction met Doeg:** [12] **One who made him forget his**

[1] אָמַר רַב מְשָׁרְשִׁיָּא: דּוֹאֵג וַאֲחִיתוֹפֶל לָא [הָווּ] סָבְרִי שְׁמַעֲתָא.

[2] מַתְקִיף לָהּ מָר זוּטְרָא: מַאן דִּכְתִיב בֵּיהּ: ״אַיֵּה סֹפֵר? אַיֵּה שֹׁקֵל? אַיֵּה סֹפֵר אֶת הַמִּגְדָּלִים?״ — [3] וְאַתְּ אָמְרַתְּ לָא הָווּ סָבְרִי שְׁמַעֲתָא? [4] אֶלָּא, דְּלָא הֲוָה סָלְקָא לְהוּ שְׁמַעֲתָא אַלִּיבָּא דְּהִלְכְתָא, דִּכְתִיב: ״סוֹד ה׳ לִירֵאָיו״.

[5] אָמַר רַבִּי אַמִי: לֹא מֵת דּוֹאֵג עַד שֶׁשָּׁכַח תַּלְמוּדוֹ, [6] שֶׁנֶּאֱמַר: ״הוּא יָמוּת בְּאֵין מוּסָר וּבְרֹב אִוַּלְתּוֹ יִשְׁגֶּה״.

[7] רַב (אַשִׁי) אָמַר: נִצְטָרַע, שֶׁנֶּאֱמַר: ״הִצְמַתָּה כָּל זוֹנֶה מִמֶּךָּ״. [8] כְּתִיב הָתָם: ״לִצְמִתֻת״. וּמְתַרְגְּמִינַן: ״לַחֲלוּטִין״. [9] וּתְנַן: ״אֵין בֵּין מוּסְגָּר וּמוּחְלָט אֶלָּא פְּרִיעָה וּפְרִימָה״.

[10] (סִימָּן: שְׁלֹשָׁה רָאוּ וַחֲצִי וּקְרָאוֹ).

[11] אָמַר רַבִּי יוֹחָנָן: שְׁלֹשָׁה מַלְאֲכֵי חַבָּלָה נִזְדַּמְּנוּ לוֹ לְדוֹאֵג, [12] אֶחָד שֶׁשִּׁכַּח תַּלְמוּדוֹ,

LITERAL TRANSLATION

[1] Rav Mesharshiya said: Doeg and Achitofel did not understand the law.

[2] Mar Zutra strongly objected: He about whom it is written: "Where is the scribe? where is the receiver? where is he who counted the towers?" — [3] and you say they did not understand the law! [4] Rather, [their] traditions did not prove to be in agreement with the law, as it is written: "The counsel of the Lord is with them that fear Him."

[5] Rabbi Ammi said: Doeg did not die until he forgot his learning, [6] as it is stated: "He shall die for want of instruction; and in the greatness of his folly he shall go astray."

[7] Rav Ashi said: He was afflicted with leprosy, as it is stated: "You have destroyed all those who go astray from You." [8] It is written there: "Forever." And we translate: "Absolutely." [9] And we have learned: "There is no [difference] between a confined leper and a confirmed leper except regarding letting the hair grow and rending garments."

[10] (A sign: Three, they saw, and half, and he called him.)

[11] Rabbi Yoḥanan said: Three Angels of destruction met Doeg: [12] One who made him forget his learning,

RASHI

לא סבירי — לא היו יודעין הלכה לפרשה כתקנה בטעמא. **דלא סלקא להו שמעתתא כו׳** — שלא זכו לקבוע הלכה כמותן. **ומתרגמינן לחלוטין** — ואנן תנן לשון חלוטין גבי מצורע.

HALAKHAH

מוּסְגָּר וּמוּחְלָט A confined leper and a confirmed leper. "There is no difference between a confined leper and a confirmed leper regarding their ritual impurity. The sole difference between them is that a confirmed leper is obligated to let his hair grow long and rend his garments, whereas a confined leper is not bound by those obligations." (*Rambam, Sefer Taharah, Hilkhot Tum'at Tzara'at* 10:10.)

TRANSLATION AND COMMENTARY

learning, one who burned his soul, and one who scattered his ashes in synagogues and study halls, so that he would be stepped upon by the righteous.

אָמַר רַבִּי [1]**Rabbi Yoḥanan said: Doeg and Achitofel did not see each other,** for both died at an early age, and their lives did not overlap. [2]**Doeg lived in the days of Saul,** when David was still a young man, **and Achitofel lived in the days of David,** toward the end of his life.

וְאָמַר רַבִּי יוֹחָנָן [3]**Rabbi Yoḥanan said: Doeg and Achitofel did not live out half their days.**

תַּנְיָא נַמִּי הָכִי [4]**The same thing was also taught** in a Baraita: "The verse states (Psalms 55:24): **'"Bloody and deceitful men shall not live out half their days.'** [5]Doeg lived for **only thirty-four years, and Achitofel for only thirty-three** years."

וְאָמַר רַבִּי יוֹחָנָן [6]**Rabbi Yoḥanan said: At first David called Achitofel his master, and later he called him his colleague, and at the end he called him his disciple.** How so? [7]**At first** David **called** Achitofel **his master,** as the verse states (Psalms 55:14): **"But it was you, a man my equal, my master, and my familiar friend."** [8]**And later** David **called** Achitofel **his colleague,** as the verse states (Psalms 55:15): **"We took sweet counsel together, and walked to the house of God in company"** — the word "together" implying friendship. [9]**And in the end he called him his disciple,** as the verse states (Psalms 41:10): **"Even my own familiar friend, in whom I trusted, [107B] who did eat of my bread, has lifted up his heel against me"** — the words "eating of my bread" symbolizing the master-disciple relationship ("eat of my bread" = "study my Torah").

אָמַר רַב יְהוּדָה [10]**Rav Yehudah said in the name of Rav: A person should never bring himself to the test, for David, King of Israel, brought himself to the test and failed.** How so? [11]David **said to God: "Master of the**

וְאֶחָד שֶׁשָּׂרַף נִשְׁמָתוֹ, וְאֶחָד שֶׁפִּיזֵּר עֲפָרוֹ בְּבָתֵּי כְנֵסִיּוֹת וּבְבָתֵּי מִדְרָשׁוֹת.

[1](אָמַר רַבִּי) יוֹחָנָן: דּוֹאֵג וַאֲחִיתוֹפֶל לֹא רָאוּ זֶה אֶת זֶה. [2]דּוֹאֵג בִּימֵי שָׁאוּל וַאֲחִיתוֹפֶל בִּימֵי דָוִד.

[3]וְאָמַר רַבִּי יוֹחָנָן: דּוֹאֵג וַאֲחִיתוֹפֶל לֹא חָצוּ יְמֵיהֶם. [4]תַּנְיָא נַמִּי הָכִי: "'אַנְשֵׁי דָמִים וּמִרְמָה לֹא יֶחֱצוּ יְמֵיהֶם'. [5]כָּל שְׁנוֹתָיו שֶׁל דּוֹאֵג לֹא הָיוּ אֶלָּא שְׁלֹשִׁים וְאַרְבַּע, וְשֶׁל אֲחִיתוֹפֶל אֵינָן אֶלָּא שְׁלֹשִׁים וְשָׁלֹשׁ".

[6]וְאָמַר רַבִּי יוֹחָנָן: בַּתְּחִלָּה קָרָא דָוִד לַאֲחִיתוֹפֶל רַבּוֹ, וּלְבַסּוֹף קְרָאוֹ חֲבֵירוֹ, וּלְבַסּוֹף קְרָאוֹ תַּלְמִידוֹ. [7]בַּתְּחִלָּה קְרָאוֹ רַבּוֹ — "וְאַתָּה אֱנוֹשׁ כְּעֶרְכִּי אַלּוּפִי וּמְיֻדָּעִי". [8]וּלְבַסּוֹף קְרָאוֹ חֲבֵרוֹ — "אֲשֶׁר יַחְדָּו נַמְתִּיק סוֹד בְּבֵית אֱלֹהִים נְהַלֵּךְ בְּרָגֶשׁ". [9]וּלְבַסּוֹף קְרָאוֹ תַּלְמִידוֹ — "גַּם אִישׁ שְׁלוֹמִי אֲשֶׁר בָּטַחְתִּי בוֹ, [107A] אוֹכֵל לַחְמִי הִגְדִּיל עָלַי עָקֵב".

[10]אָמַר רַב יְהוּדָה אָמַר רַב: לְעוֹלָם אַל יָבִיא אָדָם עַצְמוֹ לִידֵי נִסָּיוֹן, שֶׁהֲרֵי דָּוִד מֶלֶךְ יִשְׂרָאֵל הֵבִיא עַצְמוֹ לִידֵי נִסָּיוֹן וְנִכְשַׁל. [11]אָמַר לְפָנָיו: "רִבּוֹנוֹ

LITERAL TRANSLATION

and one who burned his soul, and one who scattered his ashes in synagogues and study halls.

[1]Rabbi Yoḥanan said: Doeg and Achitofel did not see one another. [2]Doeg was in the days of Saul and Achitofel was in the days of David.

[3]And Rabbi Yoḥanan said: Doeg and Achitofel did not reach half their days.

[4]It was also taught thus: "'Bloody and deceitful men shall not live out half their days.' [5]All the years of Doeg were only thirty-four, and of Achitofel were only thirty-three."

[6]And Rabbi Yoḥanan said: At first David called Achitofel his master, and later he called him his colleague, and at the end he called him his disciple. [7]At first he called him his master — "But it was you, a man my equal, my master, and my familiar friend." [8]And later he called him his colleague — "We took sweet counsel together, and walked to the house of God in company." [9]And in the end he called him his disciple — "Even my own familiar friend, in whom I trusted, [107A] who did eat of my bread, has lifted up his heel against me."

[10]Rav Yehudah said in the name of Rav: A person should never bring himself to the test, for David, King of Israel, brought himself to the test and failed. [11]He said before Him: "Master

RASHI

אלופי — היינו רבי. אבל לחמי לומד תורתי.

NOTES

שֶׁפִּיזֵּר עֲפָרוֹ **Which scattered his ashes.** Doeg's ashes were scattered in synagogues and study halls in order to fulfill through him the verse (Malachi 3:21): "And you shall tread down the wicked; for they shall be ashes under the soles of your feet" (*Maharsha, Torat Ḥayyim*).

שֶׁל עוֹלָם, מִפְּנֵי מָה אוֹמְרִים, ׳אֱלֹהֵי אַבְרָהָם אֱלֹהֵי יִצְחָק וֵאלֹהֵי יַעֲקֹב׳, [1]וְאֵין אוֹמְרִים, ׳אֱלֹהֵי דָּוִד׳?״ [2]אָמַר: ״אִינְהוּ מִינְּסוּ לִי, וְאַתְּ לָא מִינְּסִית לִי״. [3]אָמַר לְפָנָיו: ״רִבּוֹנוֹ שֶׁל עוֹלָם, בְּחָנֵנִי וְנַסֵּנִי, [4]שֶׁנֶּאֱמַר: ׳בְּחָנֵנִי ה׳ וְנַסֵּנִי וגו׳ ׳״. [5]אָמַר: ״מִינַּסְנָא לָךְ, וְעָבִידְנָא מִילְּתָא בַּהֲדָךְ, דִּלְדִידְהוּ לָא הוֹדַעְתִּינְהוּ, וְאִילּוּ אֲנָא קָא מוֹדַעֲנָא לָךְ, דִּמְנַסֵּינָא לָךְ בִּדְבַר עֶרְוָה״. [6]מִיָּד, ״וַיְהִי לְעֵת הָעֶרֶב וַיָּקָם דָּוִד מֵעַל מִשְׁכָּבוֹ וגו׳ ״. [7]אָמַר רַב יְהוּדָה: שֶׁהָפַךְ מִשְׁכָּבוֹ שֶׁל לַיְלָה לְמִשְׁכָּבוֹ שֶׁל יוֹם, [8]וְנִתְעַלְּמָה מִמֶּנּוּ הֲלָכָה: אֵבֶר קָטָן יֵשׁ בָּאָדָם, מַשְׂבִּיעוֹ, רָעֵב; [9]וּמַרְעִיבוֹ, שָׂבֵעַ.

[10]״וַיִּתְהַלֵּךְ עַל גַּג בֵּית הַמֶּלֶךְ וַיַּרְא אִשָּׁה רוֹחֶצֶת מֵעַל הַגָּג וְהָאִשָּׁה טוֹבַת מַרְאֶה מְאֹד״. [11]בַּת שֶׁבַע הֲוָה קָא חָיְיפָא רֵישָׁא תּוּתֵי חַלְתָּא. [12]אֲתָא שָׂטָן אִידַּמֵּי לֵיהּ כְּצִיפַּרְתָּא. [13]פְּתַק בֵּיהּ גִּירָא, פַּתְקָהּ

LITERAL TRANSLATION

of the Universe, why do we say, 'the God of Abraham, the God of Isaac, and the God of Jacob,' [1]and we do not say, 'the God of David'?" [2]He said: "They were tested by Me, but you have not been tested by Me." [3]He said before Him: "Master of the Universe, examine me, and test me, [4]as it is stated: 'Examine me, O Lord, and prove me, etc.' " [5]He said: "I will test you, and I will do something for you, for them I did not inform, but you I inform that I will test you with a forbidden sexual matter." [6]Immediately, "And it came to pass one evening, that David arose from his bed, etc." [7]Rav Yehudah said: He turned his nighttime bed into his daytime bed, [8]but a law escaped him: Man has a small organ — if he satiates it, it is hungry; [9]but if he starves it, it is satisfied. [10]"And he walked upon the roof of the king's house; and from the roof he saw a woman bathing; and the woman was very fair to look upon." [11]Bathsheba was washing her hair behind a screen. [12]Satan came, [and] appeared to him like a bird. [13]He shot an arrow at it, it hit the screen, she was ex posed,

TRANSLATION AND COMMENTARY

Universe, why do we say in the Amidah prayer, 'Blessed are You, O Lord, our God, and the God of our fathers, **the God of Abraham, the God of Isaac, and the God of Jacob,'** [1]**but we do not** also **say, 'the God of David'**? Why is my name not mentioned alongside the names of our forefathers?" [2]God **answered:** "Abraham, Isaac, and Jacob **were tested by Me,** and they passed the test, **but you have never been tested by Me.**" [3]David **said to** God: **"Master of the Universe, examine me, and test me,** and see that I, too, will pass Your test, [4]**as the verse states** (Psalms 26:2): **'Examine me, O Lord, and prove me;** try my reins and my heart.' " [5]God **said** to David: **"I will test you** as you wish, **and I will** even **do something for you** that I did not do for the Patriarchs. **For I did not tell** the Patriarchs how I would test them, **but I will tell you** now how I will test you. **I will test you with forbidden sex."** [6]**Immediately** (II Samuel 11:2), **"And it came to pass one evening, that David arose from his bed."** [7]**Rav Yehudah said:** When David was told how he would be tested, he tried to guard himself, and so **he turned his nighttime bed into his daytime bed.** He had sexual intercourse with his many wives during the day, so he would not lust after any other woman. [8]**But a** simple **law** of human nature **escaped him: Man has a small organ — if he satiates it** with many acts of intercourse, **it will become** more **hungry;** [9]**but if he starves it, it will be satisfied.**

וַיִּתְהַלֵּךְ עַל גַּג [10]The verse describes the test to which David was put (II Samuel 11:2): **"And he walked upon the roof of the king's house; and from the roof he saw a woman bathing; and the woman was very fair to look upon."** [11]**Bathsheba was washing her hair behind a screen.** [12]But **Satan came, and appeared to** David **in the form of a bird** flying in front of the screen. [13]David **shot an arrow at** the bird, but the arrow **hit the screen,** and knocked it over. Bathsheba **was thus exposed,**

RASHI

שהפך משכבו של לילה לשל יום — שהיה משמש מטתו ביום כדי שיהא שבע מתשמיש ולא יהרהר אחר אשה כל היום. **ונתעלמה ממנו [הלכה]** — שהמשביע אברו בתשמיש — רעב ומרבה תאוה. **הכי גרסינן** — מתהלך על גג המלך, ולא גרסינן והיינו. **חלתא** — כוורת. **פתיק [ביה] גירא** — בכוורת, כלומר שהכה ושברה, לישנא אחרינא: **פתחה** — שברה ונפתחה.

NOTES

מִפְּנֵי מָה אוֹמְרִים? Why do we say? Some connect this passage with what God said to David (II Samuel 7:9): "And I have made you a great name, like the name of the great men that are on the earth." The Rabbis understood that God promised David that people would say "the shield of David" (in the blessing following the *Haftarah*) just as they say "the shield of Abraham (in the Amidah prayer). Therefore, David also asked God to have his name mentioned alongside the names of Abraham, Isaac, and Jacob at the beginning of the Amidah prayer.

אֵבֶר קָטָן יֵשׁ בָּאָדָם Man has a small organ. *Akedat Yitzhak* notes that this statement does not refer only to man's sexual organ, but also to his eyes and his heart, for the more their desires are fulfilled, the greater their lust for more.

TRANSLATION AND COMMENTARY

and David **saw her,** and lusted after her. [1]**Immediately** (II Samuel 11:3-4), **"And David sent and inquired after the woman. And one said, Is not this Bathsheba, the daughter of Eli'am, the wife of Uriah the Hittite? And David sent messengers, and took her, and she came to him, and he lay with her, for she had purified herself from her uncleanness, and then she returned to her house."** [2]**And this is** the meaning of **the** verse **that states** (Psalms 17:3): **"You have proved my heart; You have visited it in the night: You have tried me, but You find nothing; let no presumptuous thought pass my lips."** [3]After succumbing to temptation, David **said:** "O God, You tested me with a matter of the night — with sexual temptation. You tried me, but did not find me innocent. [4]**Oh that a muzzle had been put into the mouth of him who hates me** (a euphemism for 'my mouth'), **and he** — that is, I — **would never have said this** — that God should test me."

דָּרַשׁ רָבָא [5]**Rava expounded: What is** meant by **the verse that states** (Psalms 11:1): [6]**"To the leader, of David. In the Lord I put my trust; how can you say to my soul, Flee like a bird to your mountain?"** [7]**David said to the Holy One, blessed be He: "Master of the Universe, pardon me for that iniquity** involving Bathsheba, [8]**so that** the wicked will **not say: 'The mountain among you,** David, the leading figure of his generation, **was driven out** of the world **by a bird,** by Satan who appeared to him in the form of a bird.

דָּרַשׁ רָבָא [9]**Rava expounded: What is** meant by **the verse that states** (Psalms 51:6): [10]**"Against You, You alone, have I sinned, and done what is evil in Your eyes; so that You are justified in Your sentence, and clear in Your judgment"?** [11]**David said to the Holy One, blessed be He: "It is revealed and known to You that had I wished to overcome my** evil **inclination,** I could **have overcome it** and resisted the temptation presented by Bathsheba. [12]**But I said** to myself that it is better for me to succumb to temptation and sin, **so that** the wicked will **not say** that **the servant defeated his master** by passing the test imposed upon him, even though God thought that he would fail."

לְחַלְתָּא, אִיגַּלְיָה וְחַזְיֵיה. [1]מִיָּד, "וַיִּשְׁלַח דָּוִד וַיִּדְרֹשׁ לָאִשָּׁה וַיֹּאמֶר הֲלוֹא זֹאת בַּת שֶׁבַע בַּת אֱלִיעָם אֵשֶׁת אוּרִיָּה הַחִתִּי וַיִּשְׁלַח דָּוִד מַלְאָכִים וַיִּקָּחֶהָ וַתָּבוֹא אֵלָיו וַיִּשְׁכַּב עִמָּהּ וְהִיא מִתְקַדֶּשֶׁת מִטֻּמְאָתָהּ וַתָּשָׁב אֶל בֵּיתָהּ". [2]וְהַיְינוּ דִּכְתִיב: "בָּחַנְתָּ לִבִּי; פָּקַדְתָּ לַּיְלָה צְרַפְתַּנִי בַל תִּמְצָא זַמֹּתִי בַּל יַעֲבָר פִּי". [3]אָמַר: [4]"אִיכּוּ זְמָמָא נְפַל בְּפוּמֵּיהּ דְּמַאן דְּסָנֵי לִי, וְלָא אֲמַר כִּי הָא מִילְּתָא".

[5]דָּרַשׁ רָבָא: מַאי דִּכְתִיב: [6]"לַמְנַצֵּחַ לְדָוִד בַּה' חָסִיתִי אֵיךְ תֹּאמְרוּ לְנַפְשִׁי נוּדִי הַרְכֶם צִפּוֹר". [7]אָמַר דָּוִד לִפְנֵי הַקָּדוֹשׁ בָּרוּךְ הוּא: "רִבּוֹנוֹ שֶׁל עוֹלָם, מְחוֹל לִי עַל אוֹתוֹ עָוֹן, [8]שֶׁלֹּא יֹאמְרוּ: 'הַר שֶׁבָּכֶם צִפּוֹר נְדָדַתּוּ'".

[9]דָּרַשׁ רָבָא: מַאי דִּכְתִיב: [10]"לְךָ לְבַדְּךָ חָטָאתִי וְהָרַע בְּעֵינֶיךָ עָשִׂיתִי לְמַעַן תִּצְדַּק בְּדָבְרֶךָ תִּזְכֶּה בְשָׁפְטֶךָ". [11]אָמַר דָּוִד לִפְנֵי הַקָּדוֹשׁ בָּרוּךְ הוּא: "גַּלְיָא וִידִיעָא קַמָּךְ דְּאִי בָּעֵינָא לְמִכְפְּיֵיהּ לְיִצְרִי, הֲוָה כָּיְיפִינָא. [12]אֶלָּא אָמִינָא, דְּלָא לֵימְרוּ: 'עַבְדָּא זָכֵי לְמָרֵיהּ'".

LITERAL TRANSLATION

and he saw her. [1]Immediately, "And David sent and inquired after the woman. And one said, Is not this Bathsheba, the daughter of Eli'am, the wife of Uriah the Hittite? And David sent messengers, and took her, and she came to him, and he lay with her, for she had purified herself from her uncleanness, and then she returned to her house." [2]And this is what is written: "You have proved my heart; You have visited it in the night: You have tried me, but You find nothing; let no presumptuous thought pass my lips." [3]He said: [4]"Oh that a muzzle had fallen into the mouth of him who hates me, and he had not said this word."

[5]Rava expounded: What is that which is written: [6]"To the leader, of David. In the Lord I put my trust; how can you say to my soul, Flee to your mountain like a bird?" [7]David said before the Holy One, blessed be He: "Master of the Universe, pardon me for that iniquity, [8]so that they will not say: 'The mountain among you — a bird drove him out.'"

[9]Rava expounded: What is that which is written: [10]"Against You, You alone, have I sinned, and done what is evil in Your eyes; so that You are justified in Your sentence, and clear in Your judgment"? [11]David said before the Holy One, blessed be He: "It is revealed and known before You that had I wished to force my inclination, I could have forced it. [12]But I said, so that they not say: 'The servant defeated his master.'"

RASHI

מתקדשת מטומאתה — אותה שעה פסק טומאתה, ולא בא עליה כשהיא נדה. פקדת לילה — על מעשה לילה פקדתני אם אוכל לעמוד בנסיון של דבר עבירה. צרפתני בל תמצא — חשבת לצרפני ולא מצאתני נקי. (זמותי בל יעבר פי) איכו זממא נפל — מי יתן והיה בפי רסן, ואפשר לעכב את דברי שלא אומר דבר זה [של] "בחנני". הר שבכם — מלך שלכם. צפור נדדתו — דעל ידי צפור נטרד, כדאמר אדמי ליה כצפור. למריה — העבד נצחו לאדוניו בתוכחתו.

TRANSLATION AND COMMENTARY

דָּרַשׁ רָבָא [1]**Rava expounded: What is** meant by **the verse that states** (Psalms 38:18): [2]**"For I am ready to stumble** [לְצֶלַע]**; and my pain is continually before me"?** [3]**Bathsheba the daughter of Eli'am was** designated **for David from the six days of creation** — that woman (צֶלַע, in the sense of "rib," an allusion to the formation of Eve from Adam's rib) was ready for David from the beginning of time. [4]**But she came to him with** great **pain.**

וְכֵן תָּנָא [5]**And similarly a Sage of the House of Rabbi Yishmael taught** a Baraita that stated: **"Bathsheba the daughter of Eli'am was** designated **for David** from the beginning of time. [6]**But he enjoyed her as an unripe fruit,** while she was still married to Uriah the Hittite."

דָּרַשׁ רָבָא [7]**Rava expounded: What is** meant by **the verse that states** (Psalms 35:15): [8]**"But when I stumble they gleefully gather; wretches gather against me, I know not why; they tear at me** [קָרְעוּ] **without end** [וְלֹא דָמּוּ]**"?** [9]**David said to the Holy One, blessed be He: "Master of the Universe, it is revealed and known to you that had** my enemies **torn** apart **my flesh** [קוֹרְעִין]**, I would not have bled** [לֹא הָיָה דָמִי שׁוֹתֵת]**,** for my flesh has wasted away, and my blood has dried up because of all the fasts that I have observed to atone for my transgression with Bathsheba. [10]**And furthermore, when they are engaged in** the study of the laws regarding **the four modes of judicial execution, they interrupt their studies, and say to me:** [11]**'David, if someone engages in intercourse with a married woman, by which** mode of execution is he put to **death?'** [12]**I say to them:** 'If **someone engages in intercourse with a married woman,** he is liable to **death by strangulation, but he** still **has a portion in the World to Come.** After conceding my guilt, I reproached the scholars: [13]**But** if **someone puts another person to public shame, he does not have a portion in the World to Come.'"**

[1]דָּרַשׁ רָבָא: מַאי דִּכְתִיב: [2]"כִּי אֲנִי לְצֶלַע נָכוֹן וּמַכְאוֹבִי נֶגְדִּי תָמִיד"? [3]רְאוּיָה הָיְתָה בַּת שֶׁבַע בַּת אֱלִיעָם לְדָוִד מִשֵּׁשֶׁת יְמֵי בְרֵאשִׁית. [4]אֶלָּא שֶׁבָּאָה אֵלָיו בְּמַכְאוֹב.

[5]וְכֵן תָּנָא דְּבֵי רַבִּי יִשְׁמָעֵאל: "רְאוּיָה הָיְתָה לְדָוִד בַּת שֶׁבַע בַּת אֱלִיעָם. [6]אֶלָּא שֶׁאֲכָלָהּ פַּגָּה".

[7]דָּרַשׁ רָבָא: מַאי דִּכְתִיב: [8]"וּבְצַלְעִי שָׂמְחוּ וְנֶאֱסָפוּ נֶאֶסְפוּ עָלַי נֵכִים [וְלֹא יָדַעְתִּי] קָרְעוּ וְלֹא דָמּוּ"? [9]אָמַר דָּוִד לִפְנֵי הַקָּדוֹשׁ בָּרוּךְ הוּא: "רִבּוֹנוֹ שֶׁל עוֹלָם, גָּלוּי וְיָדוּעַ לְפָנֶיךָ שֶׁאִם הָיוּ קוֹרְעִין בְּשָׂרִי — לֹא הָיָה דָמִי שׁוֹתֵת. [10]וְלֹא עוֹד אֶלָּא, בְּשָׁעָה שֶׁהֵם עוֹסְקִין בְּאַרְבַּע מִיתוֹת בֵּית דִּין — פּוֹסְקִין מִמִּשְׁנָתָן וְאוֹמְרִים לִי: [11]'דָּוִד, הַבָּא עַל אֵשֶׁת אִישׁ, מִיתָתוֹ בַּמֶּה'? [12]אָמַרְתִּי לָהֶם: 'הַבָּא עַל אֵשֶׁת אִישׁ, מִיתָתוֹ בְּחֶנֶק, וְיֵשׁ לוֹ חֵלֶק לָעוֹלָם הַבָּא. [13]אֲבָל הַמַּלְבִּין פְּנֵי חֲבֵירוֹ בָּרַבִּים — אֵין לוֹ חֵלֶק לָעוֹלָם הַבָּא'".

LITERAL TRANSLATION

[1]Rava expounded: What is that which is written: [2]"For I am ready to limp; and my pain is continually before me"? [3]Bathsheba the daughter of Eli'am was worthy of David from the six days of creation. [4]But she came to him with pain.

[5]And similarly [a Sage] of the House of Rabbi Yishmael taught: "Bathsheba the daughter of Eli'am was worthy of David. [6]But he ate her as an unripe fruit."

[7]Rava expounded: What is that which is written: [8]"But when I stumble they gleefully gather; wretches gather against me, I know not why; they tear at me without end"? [9]David said before the Holy One, blessed be He: "Master of the Universe, it is revealed and known before you that had they torn my flesh, I would not have bled. [10]And not only [this], but when they are engaged in the four [modes of] judicial execution — they interrupt their study, and say to me: [11]'David, someone who has intercourse with a married woman, his death is with what?' [12]I say to them: 'Someone who has intercourse with a married woman, his death is by strangulation, but he has a portion in the World to Come. [13]But someone who whitens the face of his fellow in public has no portion in the World to Come.'"

RASHI

כי אני לצלע נכון — אותו צלע היה נכון לי. **שאכלה פגה** — שקפץ את השעה ליזקק על ידי עבירה. **נאספו עלי נכים** — בעלי מומין, כמו "פרעה נכה" (מלכים ב' כג) והיו מלעיגים עלי ואני כלא יודע, לישנא אחרינא: **ולא ידעתי** — לא הייתי יודע כשמלעיגים, כלומר פתאום בא עלי אותו עון, שלא ידעתי (עד) שניתן פתחון פה לביישני. **הכי גרסינן** — בשעה שעוסקין במיתות בית דין אומרים הבא על אשת איש מיתתו וכו'.

NOTES

שֶׁאֲכָלָהּ פַּגָּה **He enjoyed her as an unripe fruit.** It has been suggested that we have here a play on words, for Bathsheba is also the name of a type of fig. Thus the expression, "he enjoyed her as an unripe fruit," is particularly appropriate when used in connection with her (*Likkutei HaShas* of *Ari*).

TRANSLATION AND COMMENTARY

אָמַר רַב יְהוּדָה [1]**Rav Yehudah said in the name of Rav: Even when he was** old and **sick, David fulfilled his marital duty with** his **eighteen** wives, [2]**as the verse states** (Psalms 6:7): **"I am weary with my groaning; all the night I make my bed to swim, I water my couch with my tears."** Even when David groaned with disease, he made his bed to swim, a euphemism for his many acts of sexual intercourse.

וְאָמַר רַב יְהוּדָה [3]**And Rav Yehudah said in the name of Rav:** After his son Absalom rebelled against him, **David wanted to** go and **worship an idol,** [4]**as the verse states** (II Samuel 15:32): **"And it came to pass, that when David was come to the top** [*rosh*] **of the hill, where he bowed down to God."** [5]**And** the word *rosh* in this context **refers to idol worship, as the verse states** (Daniel 2:32): **"The image's head** [*rosh*] **was of fine gold."** The verse cited above continues (II Samuel 15:32): [6]**"Behold, Hushai the Arkite came to meet him with his coat rent, and earth upon his head."** [7]Hushai **said to David: "Shall** people **say that a** pious **king like you worships an idol?"** [8]David **said to** Hushai: "Is it better that people say about a righteous **king like me** that **my son** seeks to **kill me?** People might reproach God for allowing a righteous man to be mistreated, and the name of Heaven would suffer public desecration. [9]Thus, **it is better that I should worship an idol,** and I alone desecrate God's name, **for then the name of Heaven will not be desecrated in public.** People will think that I was rightfully punished for my idol worship." [10]Hushai **said** to David: **"Why did you marry** a non-Jewish captive woman, Absalom's mother, Ma'achah the daughter of Talmai, the King of Geshur — **a woman of beautiful appearance?"** [11]David **said to him:**

[1]אָמַר רַב יְהוּדָה אָמַר רַב: אֲפִילּוּ בִּשְׁעַת חָלְיוֹ שֶׁל דָּוִד, קִיֵּים שְׁמוֹנֶה עֶשְׂרֵה עוֹנוֹת, [2]שֶׁנֶּאֱמַר: ״יָגַעְתִּי בְּאַנְחָתִי אַשְׂחֶה בְכָל לַיְלָה מִטָּתִי בְּדִמְעָתִי עַרְשִׂי אַמְסֶה״. [3]וְאָמַר רַב יְהוּדָה אָמַר רַב: בִּקֵּשׁ דָּוִד לַעֲבוֹד עֲבוֹדָה זָרָה, [4]שֶׁנֶּאֱמַר: ״וַיְהִי דָוִד בָּא עַד הָרֹאשׁ אֲשֶׁר יִשְׁתַּחֲוֶה שָׁם לֵאלֹהִים״. [5]וְאֵין רֹאשׁ אֶלָּא עֲבוֹדָה זָרָה, שֶׁנֶּאֱמַר: ״וְהוּא צַלְמָא רֵישֵׁיהּ דִּי דְהַב טָב״. [6]״וְהִנֵּה לִקְרָאתוֹ חוּשַׁי הָאַרְכִּי קָרוּעַ כֻּתָּנְתּוֹ וַאֲדָמָה עַל רֹאשׁוֹ״. [7]אָמַר לוֹ לְדָוִד: ״יֹאמְרוּ מֶלֶךְ שֶׁכְּמוֹתְךָ יַעֲבוֹד עֲבוֹדָה זָרָה״! [8]אָמַר לוֹ: ״מֶלֶךְ שֶׁכְּמוֹתִי — יַהַרְגֶנּוּ בְּנוֹ? [9]מוּטָּב יַעֲבוֹד עֲבוֹדָה זָרָה וְאַל יִתְחַלֵּל שֵׁם שָׁמַיִם בְּפַרְהֶסְיָא״. [10]אֲמַר: ״מַאי טַעְמָא קָנְסִיבַת יְפַת תּוֹאַר״? [11]אֲמַר לֵיהּ:

LITERAL TRANSLATION

[1]Rav Yehudah said in the name of Rav: Even at the time of his sickness, David fulfilled his marital duty with eighteen women, [2]as it is stated: "I am weary with my groaning; all the night I make my bed to swim, I water my couch with my tears."

[3]And Rav Yehudah said in the name of Rav: David wanted to worship an idol, [4]as it is stated: "And it came to pass, that when David was come to the top of the hill, where he bowed down to God." [5]And the top [*rosh*] is only idol worship, as it is stated: "The image's head was of fine gold." [6]"Behold, Hushai the Arkite came to meet him with his coat rent, and earth upon his head." [7]He said to David: "Shall they say [that] a king like you worships an idol?" [8]He said to him: "A king like me — shall his son kill him? [9]It is better that he should worship an idol, and that the name of Heaven not be desecrated in public." [10]He said: "What is the reason that you married a woman of beautiful appearance?" [11]He said to him:

RASHI

שמנה עשרה עונות — לשמונה עשרה נשיו, שלא לעגנן. **באנחתי אשחה** — אפילו בשעת אנחתי אשחה בכל לילה. **מטתי** — תשמיש המטה, ענין ״סחי ומאוס״ (איכה ג) קרי ליה. **בדמעתי ערשי אמסה** — שבשעת דמעתי אני ממאיס את מטתי בתשמיש. **יאמרו מלך שכמותי** — חסיד שכמותי הרגו בנו, ויהו מתרעמין על מדותיו של הקדוש ברוך הוא — ונמצא שם שמים מתחלל בפרהסיא. **מוטב אעבוד עבודה זרה** — ואחלל את השם ואני לבדי, ולא יחללו [אותו] כל העם. **אמר ליה** — חושי הארכי לדוד: הקדוש ברוך הוא לא עביד דינא בלא דינא, שמעמיד בנך להרגך, דאת מאי

NOTES

אַשְׂחֶה בְכָל לַיְלָה All the night I make my bed to swim. *Rashi* understands the word אַשְׂחֶה, translated here as "make to swim," in the sense of (Lamentations 3:45) סְחִי, "refuse, dirt," a reference to sexual intercourse. Others interpret the word in the sense of שִׂיחָה, "conversation," for the sexual act is often described euphemistically as "speech."

בִּקֵּשׁ דָּוִד לַעֲבוֹד עֲבוֹדָה זָרָה David wanted to worship an idol. *Ramah* and others explain that David did not really believe in the idol, nor did he truly mean to serve it. But rather, he wished to sin in public, in order to prevent the desecration of God's name if people thought that God allowed a righteous man like himself to suffer such abuse and affliction. Others explain that in his moments of great distress, David did in fact begin to think that there was no judge or justice in the world, nor was there divine providence. These heretical thoughts are referred to here as "idol worship." Hushai therefore came and told him that whatever he had undergone came upon him by right (*Hiddushei Aggadot* of *Rashba*).

TRANSLATION AND COMMENTARY

"Surely **the Torah permitted a woman of beautiful appearance** (see Deuteronomy 21:10-14)!" [1]Hushai **said to** David: **"Do you not derive** Halakhic conclusions from **the juxtaposition of** two **verses, for juxtaposed to** the verse permitting a man to marry a captive woman, we find the verse (Deuteronomy 21:18): **'If a man has a stubborn and rebellious son'?"** [2]This teaches us that **whoever marries a woman of beautiful appearance** will **have a stubborn and rebellious son.**

דָּרַשׁ רַבִּי דּוֹסְתַּאי [3]**Rabbi Dostai from** the city of **Biri expounded: To whom may David be compared?** [4]**To a Cuthean merchant** who bargains cleverly. [5]**David said to the Holy One, blessed be He** (Psalms 19:12-13): "Who can discern errors? Cleanse You me from secret faults. Keep back Your servant also from presumptuous sins; let them not have dominion over me; then shall I be upright, and I shall be clear of much transgression." First David asked God to pardon his unwitting sins: [6]**"Master of the Universe, who can discern errors?"** [7]God **said to him:** "Your unwitting sins **are pardoned."** Then David asked God to pardon the sins that he had knowingly committed, though in secret: [8]**"Cleanse You me from secret faults."** [9]God said to him: "Those sins **are** also **pardoned."** Then David asked God to pardon the rest of the sins that he had knowingly committed: [10]**"Keep back Your servant also from intentional sins."** [11]God said to him: "Those sins **are** also **pardoned."** [12]Then David said to God: **"Let them not have dominion over me; then shall I be upright — let the Rabbis** of future generations **not discuss me** and my transgression." [13]God said to him: "Your sins **are pardoned,** and so the Rabbis will not refer to you when they preach about sinners." [14]Finally David requested: **"And I shall**

"יְפַת תּוֹאַר רַחֲמָנָא שַׁרְיָיהּ". [1]אֲמַר לֵיהּ: "לֹא דָּרְשַׁתְּ סְמוּכִין, דִּסְמִיךְ לֵיהּ: 'כִּי יִהְיֶה לְאִישׁ בֵּן סוֹרֵר וּמוֹרֶה'?". [2]כָּל הַנּוֹשֵׂא יְפַת תּוֹאַר יֵשׁ לוֹ בֵּן סוֹרֵר וּמוֹרֶה.

[3]דָּרַשׁ רַבִּי דּוֹסְתַּאי דְּמִן בִּירִי: לְמָה דָּוִד דּוֹמֶה? [4]לְסוֹחֵר כּוּתִי. [5]אָמַר דָּוִד לִפְנֵי הַקָּדוֹשׁ בָּרוּךְ הוּא: [6]"רִבּוֹנוֹ שֶׁל עוֹלָם, שְׁגִיאוֹת מִי יָבִין"? [7][אֲמַר לֵיהּ:] "שְׁבִיקִי לָךְ". [8]"וּמִנִּסְתָּרוֹת נַקֵּנִי". [9]"שְׁבִיקִי לָךְ". [10]"גַּם מִזֵּדִים חֲשֹׂךְ עַבְדֶּךָ". [11]"שְׁבִיקִי לָךְ". [12]"אַל יִמְשְׁלוּ בִי אָז אֵיתָם — דְּלָא לִישְׁתָּעוּ בִּי רַבָּנַן". [13]"שְׁבִיקִי לָךְ". [14]"וְנִקֵּיתִי

LITERAL TRANSLATION

"The Torah permitted a woman of beautiful appearance." [1]He said to him: "Do you not interpret juxtaposed verses, for juxtaposed to it is: 'If a man has a stubborn and rebellious son'?" [2]Whoever marries a woman of beautiful appearance has a stubborn and rebellious son.

[3]Rabbi Dostai from Biri expounded: What is David like? [4]Like a Cuthean merchant. [5]David said before the Holy One, blessed be He: [6]"Master of the Universe, who can discern errors?" [7]He said to him: "They are pardoned for you." [8]"Cleanse You me from secret faults." [9]"They are pardoned for you." [10]"Keep back Your servant also from intentional sins." [11]"They are pardoned for you." [12]"Let them not have dominion over me; then shall I be upright — that the Rabbis should not discuss me." [13]"They are pardoned for you." [14]"And I shall be clear

RASHI

טעמא נסבת יפת תואר — דאמו של אבשלום מעכה בת תלמי מלך גשור (שמואל ב׳ ג), ותפסה דוד במלחמה, דאין לומר בעבירה באה לו דהא כתיב (מלכים א טו) "רק בדבר אוריה החתי". סוחר כותי — דרכו לפנות את סחורתו מעט מעט, להעמידה על דמים מועטים. שגיאות מי יבין — מי יכול להשמר משגגות. אמר לו — הקדוש ברוך הוא. שביקא לך — מחול לך. נסתרות — [מזיד] של צנעה. זדים — מזיד של פרהסיא. הכי גרסינן: אל ימשלו בי דלא לישתעו בי רבנן — והיינו אל ימשלו — לשון משל, שלא ידרשו בחטאתי חכמי הדורות, ואז איתם.

NOTES

לְסוֹחֵר כּוּתִי **To a Cuthean merchant.** Our commentary follows *Arukh*, who understands that a Cuthean merchant is a sharp bargainer. So, too, David first asked God to pardon his unwitting offenses, and then persuaded Him to pardon also his intentional sins. Others explain that a Cuthean merchant is willing to pay more, provided that he receives all the merchandise that he ordered. So, too, David was willing to accept afflictions, provided that this allowed him to achieve atonement for his sin with Bathsheba without detracting from his merits (*Ramah*). The Midrash compares David to a Cuthean beggar (סוֹחֵר = "around," someone who goes around begging from house to house), who first asks for water to drink, and then asks for an onion to eat, and then asks for a piece of bread to eat with his onion. So, too, David started with a small request, and slowly asked for more and more.

דְּלָא לִישְׁתָּעוּ בִּי רַבָּנַן **That the Rabbis should not discuss me.** According to *Ramah*, David did not want the Rabbis to include him among the kings who have no portion in the World to Come. Others explain that when a man suspects his wife of being unfaithful, and has her drink the bitter waters, the Rabbis first try to persuade her to confess by telling her of the sins of the great people of earlier generations, as is explained in tractate *Sotah*. David did not want the Rabbis to mention him in that context, or use his transgression as an example (*Tzofnat Pa'ane'ah*).

מִפֶּשַׁע רַב — שֶׁלֹּא יִכָּתֵב סִרְחוֹנִי״. [1]אָמַר לוֹ: ״אִי אֶפְשָׁר. [2]וּמַה יו״ד שֶׁנָּטַלְתִּי מִשָּׂרַי עוֹמֵד וְצוֹוֵחַ כַּמָּה שָׁנִים, עַד שֶׁבָּא יְהוֹשֻׁעַ וְהוֹסַפְתִּי לוֹ, [3]שֶׁנֶּאֱמַר: ׳וַיִּקְרָא מֹשֶׁה לְהוֹשֵׁעַ בִּן נוּן יְהוֹשֻׁעַ׳ — [4]כָּל הַפָּרָשָׁה כּוּלָּהּ עַל אַחַת כַּמָּה וְכַמָּה״.

[5]״וְנִקֵּיתִי מִפֶּשַׁע רַב״. [6]אָמַר לְפָנָיו: ״רִבּוֹנוֹ שֶׁל עוֹלָם, מְחוֹל לִי עַל אוֹתוֹ עָוֹן כּוּלּוֹ!״ [7]אָמַר: ״כְּבָר עָתִיד שְׁלֹמֹה בִּנְךָ לוֹמַר בְּחָכְמָתוֹ: ׳הֲיַחְתֶּה אִישׁ אֵשׁ בְּחֵיקוֹ וּבְגָדָיו לֹא תִשָּׂרַפְנָה? [8]אִם יְהַלֵּךְ אִישׁ עַל הַגֶּחָלִים וְרַגְלָיו לֹא תִכָּוֶינָה? [9]כֵּן הַבָּא עַל אֵשֶׁת רֵעֵהוּ לֹא יִנָּקֶה כָּל הַנֹּגֵעַ בָּהּ״. [10]אָמַר לֵיהּ: ״כָּל הָכִי נִטְרַד הַהוּא גַּבְרָא״? [11]אָמַר לוֹ: ״קַבֵּל עָלֶיךָ יִסּוּרִין״. [12]קִבֵּל עָלָיו.

[13]אָמַר רַב יְהוּדָה אָמַר רַב: שִׁשָּׁה חֳדָשִׁים נִצְטָרַע דָּוִד, וְנִסְתַּלְּקָה הֵימֶנּוּ שְׁכִינָה, וּפֵירְשׁוּ מִמֶּנּוּ סַנְהֶדְרִין. [14]נִצְטָרַע, דִּכְתִיב: ״תְּחַטְּאֵנִי בְאֵזוֹב וְאֶטְהָר תְּכַבְּסֵנִי וּמִשֶּׁלֶג אַלְבִּין״. [15]נִסְתַּלְּקָה הֵימֶנּוּ שְׁכִינָה, דִּכְתִיב: ״הָשִׁיבָה לִּי שְׂשׂוֹן יִשְׁעֶךָ וְרוּחַ נְדִיבָה תִסְמְכֵנִי״. [16]וּפֵירְשׁוּ מִמֶּנּוּ סַנְהֶדְרִין,

LITERAL TRANSLATION

of much transgression — that my sin not be recorded." [1]He said to him: "[That is] impossible. [2]If the yod that I took from Sarai stood and shouted for many years until Joshua came and I added it to his [name], [3]as it is stated: 'And Moses called Hosea son of Nun, Joshua' — [4]an entire passage all the more so."

[5]"And I shall be clear of much transgression." [6]He said before Him: "Master of the Universe, pardon me for that entire sin." [7]He said: "Solomon your son is already destined to say in his wisdom: 'Can a man take fire in his bosom, and his clothes not be burned? [8]Can one walk upon hot coals, and his feet not be scorched? [9]So he who lies with his neighbor's wife; whoever touches her shall not go unpunished.'" [10]He said to him: "That man will be so troubled?" [11]He said to him: "Accept afflictions upon yourself." [12]He accepted [them] upon himself.

[13]Rav Yehudah said in the name of Rav: For six months David was afflicted with leprosy, and the Shekhinah (lit., "Divine Presence") was removed from him, and the Sanhedrin withdrew from him. [14]He was afflicted with leprosy, as it is written: "Purge me with hyssop, and I shall be clean; wash me, and I shall be whiter than snow." [15]The Shekhinah was removed from him, as it is written: "Restore to me the joy of Your salvation; and uphold me with a willing spirit." [16]And the Sanhedrin withdrew from him,

TRANSLATION AND COMMENTARY

be clear of much transgression — let my sin be totally expunged, so that it **not** even **be recorded** in the Bible." [1]God **said to him: "That** last request I **cannot possibly** fulfill. [2]**If the** letter **yod that I took from Sarai's** name when I changed her name from Sarai [שָׂרַי] to Sarah [שָׂרָה] **continued to shout for many years,** because it was omitted from the Torah, and the protest continued **until Joshua came, and I added** the letter yod **to his name** [3]**as the verse states** (Numbers 13:16): **'And Moses called Hosea** [הוֹשֵׁעַ] **son of Nun, Joshua** [יְהוֹשֻׁעַ]**'** — [4]then **all the more so** would it be impossible for Me to expunge **the entire passage** describing your transgression."

וְנִקֵּיתִי מִפֶּשַׁע רַב [5]The verse states (Psalms 19:13): **"And I shall be clear of much transgression."** [6]David **said to** God: **"Master of the Universe, pardon me entirely for that sin** of mine involving Bathsheba." [7]God **said** to him in reply: **"Your son Solomon is already destined to say in his wisdom** (Proverbs 6:27-29): **'Can a man take fire in his bosom, and his clothes not be burned? [8]Can one walk upon hot coals, and his feet not be scorched? [9]So he who lies with his neighbor's wife; whoever touches her shall not go unpunished.'"** [10]David **said to** God: **"Will that man** — a euphemism for 'I' — really **be so troubled** by his transgression, and not be given any opportunity to atone for what he did?" [11]God **said to him: "Accept afflictions upon yourself,** and you will achieve atonement." [12]And indeed David **accepted** afflictions **upon himself.**

אָמַר רַב יְהוּדָה [13]**Rav Yehudah said in the name of Rav: For six months David was afflicted with leprosy, and the Shekhinah was removed from him, and the** Sages of **the Sanhedrin withdrew from him.** [14]David **was afflicted with leprosy, as the verse states** (Psalms 51:9): **"Purge me with hyssop, and I shall be clean; wash me, and I shall be whiter than snow,"** implying that he required purification by means of a hyssop, like a leper. [15]**The Shekhinah was removed from him, as the verse states** (Psalms 51:14): **"Restore to me the joy of Your salvation; and uphold me with a willing spirit."** [16]The Sages of **the Sanhedrin withdrew from him, as the**

RASHI

שלא יכתב סורחני — שתמחוק אותה פרשה מן המקרא, וישתכח הדבר לעולמים. כל הפרשה — שכתובה כבר, שעשית אותו חטא. על אחת כמה וכמה — שלא תעקור. תחטאני באזוב — מכלל שהיה צריך טהרת אזוב כמצורע.

TRANSLATION AND COMMENTARY

verse states (Psalms 119:79): **"Let those who fear You turn to me,** and those who have known Your testimonies." [1]**From where do we know** that these punitive measures lasted for **six months?** [2]**For the verse states** (I Kings 2:11): **"And the days that David reigned over Israel were forty years;** [107B] **seven years he reigned in Hebron, and thirty-three years he reigned in Jerusalem."** [3]**And** elsewhere **the verse states** (II Samuel 5:5): **"In Hebron he reigned over Judah seven years and six months;** and in Jerusalem he reigned thirty-three years over all Israel and Judah." [4]**Now those six** extra **months** that were mentioned in the Book of Samuel **were not counted** in the Book of Kings. [5]**Infer from this that** there were six months during which David's kingship was incomplete — those six months during which David **was afflicted with leprosy.**

אָמַר לְפָנָיו [6]At some later point, David once again **said to** God: **"Master of the Universe, pardon me for that iniquity** of mine with Bathsheba." God said to him: "Your sin **is pardoned."** [7]David then said to God (Psalms 86:17): **"Show me a sign for good, that they who hate me may see it, and be ashamed; because You, Lord, have helped me, and comforted me."** [8]God **said to** David: **"During your** own **lifetime, I will not** yet **make it known** to all that your sin has been pardoned, **but I will make** that **known during the lifetime of your son Solomon."** How did this take place? [9]**When Solomon** first **built the Temple, he wanted to bring the Ark into the Holy of Holies, but the** Temple **gates stuck together.** [10]**He recited twenty-four** different **prayers, but he was not answered.** [11]**He** then **said** (Psalms 24:7-8): **"'Lift up your heads,**

דִּכְתִיב: ״יָשׁוּבוּ לִי יְרֵאֶיךָ וגו׳״.
[1]שִׁשָּׁה חֳדָשִׁים מְנָלַן? [2]דִּכְתִיב:
״וְהַיָּמִים אֲשֶׁר מָלַךְ דָּוִד עַל
יִשְׂרָאֵל אַרְבָּעִים שָׁנָה; [107B]
בְּחֶבְרוֹן מָלַךְ שֶׁבַע שָׁנִים
וּבִירוּשָׁלַיִם מָלַךְ שְׁלֹשִׁים וְשָׁלֹשׁ
שָׁנִים״. [3]וּכְתִיב: ״בְּחֶבְרוֹן מָלַךְ
עַל יְהוּדָה שֶׁבַע שָׁנִים וְשִׁשָּׁה
חֳדָשִׁים וגו׳״. [4]וְהָנֵי שִׁשָּׁה
חֳדָשִׁים — לָא קָחָשֵׁיב. [5]שְׁמַע
מִינָּהּ נִצְטָרַע.
[6]אָמַר לְפָנָיו: ״רִבּוֹנוֹ שֶׁל עוֹלָם,
מְחוֹל לִי עַל אוֹתוֹ עָוֹן״. ״מָחוּל
לָךְ״. [7]״עֲשֵׂה עִמִּי אוֹת לְטוֹבָה,
וְיִרְאוּ שׂנְאַי וְיֵבֹשׁוּ כִּי אַתָּה ה׳
עֲזַרְתַּנִי וְנִחַמְתָּנִי״. [8]אָמַר לֵיהּ:
״בְּחַיֶּיךָ אֵינִי מוֹדִיעַ, אֲבָל אֲנִי
מוֹדִיעַ בְּחַיֵּי שְׁלֹמֹה בִּנְךָ״.
[9]בְּשָׁעָה שֶׁבָּנָה שְׁלֹמֹה אֶת בֵּית
הַמִּקְדָּשׁ בִּיקֵּשׁ לְהַכְנִיס אָרוֹן
לְבֵית קָדְשֵׁי הַקֳּדָשִׁים. דָּבְקוּ
שְׁעָרִים זֶה בָּזֶה. [10]אָמַר עֶשְׂרִים
וְאַרְבָּעָה רְנָנוֹת וְלֹא נַעֲנָה.
[11]אָמַר: ״ ׳שְׂאוּ שְׁעָרִים רָאשֵׁיכֶם

LITERAL TRANSLATION

as it is written: "Let those who fear You turn to me, etc." [1]Six months, from where do we [know this]? [2]As it is written: "And the days that David reigned over Israel were forty years; [107B] seven years he reigned in Hebron, and thirty-three years he reigned in Jerusalem." [3]And it is written: "In Hebron he reigned over Judah seven years and six months, etc." [4]And those six months — they do (lit., "it does") not count. [5]Infer from this [that] he was afflicted with leprosy.

[6]He said before Him: "Master of the universe, pardon me for that iniquity." "It is pardoned for you." [7]"Show me a sign for good, that they who hate me may see it, and be ashamed; because You, Lord, have helped me, and comforted me." [8]He said to him: "During your lifetime, I will not make it known, but I will make it known during the lifetime of your son Solomon." [9]When Solomon built the Temple, he wanted to bring the Ark into the Holy of Holies, [but] the gates stuck one to the other. [10]He recited twenty-four prayers, but was not answered. [11]He said: "'Lift up your heads, O you gates;

RASHI

בחברון מלך שבע שנים וששה חדשים — מדהכא חשיב להו ובאידך קרא לא חשיב להו — שמע מינה לא היה מלכותו שלימה, שנצטרע אותן ששה חדשים. הכי גרסינן — **אבל בחיי בנך אני מודיע**, ולא גרסינן לך. **עשרים וארבע רננות** — בין תפלה תחנה ורנה איכא עשרים וארבע.

NOTES

וְהָנֵי שִׁשָּׁה חֳדָשִׁים **And those six months.** The Rishonim ask: Surely, if David was afflicted with leprosy, it was while he reigned in Jerusalem (following his sin with Bathsheba). Why, then, does the verse in the Book of Kings deduct six months from his reign in Hebron? Some suggest that the six months were deducted from David's reign in Hebron to avoid detracting from the honor of Jerusalem (see *Jerusalem Talmud, Rosh Hashanah* 1:1). Others suggest that while in fact the six months should have been deducted from David's reign in Jerusalem, the verse deducts them from his reign in Hebron so that it will mention only whole years (see *Tosafot Yeshanim, Yoma* 22b).

עֶשְׂרִים וְאַרְבָּעָה רְנָנוֹת **Twenty-four prayers.** According to *Rashi*, this refers to the twenty-four expressions of "prayer," "supplication," and the like found in Solomon's prayer (I Kings 8). *Ramah* suggests that this refers to the twenty-four psalms which open with a term of "supplication" or "cry."

TRANSLATION AND COMMENTARY

O you gates; and be lifted up, you everlasting doors; and the King of Glory shall come in. Who is this King of Glory? The Lord strong and mighty, the Lord mighty in battle.' [1]**And it is stated** (Psalms 24:9): **'Lift up your heads, O you gates; and lift them up, you everlasting doors; that the King of Glory may come in.'"** [2]**But** Solomon **was still not answered.** [3]**When** Solomon **said** (II Chronicles 6:42): **"O Lord God, do not turn away the face of your anointed; remember the faithful love of David Your servant," he was immediately answered,** and the gates opened. [4]**At that time, the faces of David's enemies turned black** with disappointment **like the bottom of a cauldron, and all of Israel knew that the Holy One, blessed be He, had pardoned him for** his **iniquity,** for it was only for David's sake that Solomon was answered.

גֵּחֲזִי [5]Included among the ordinary people whom the Mishnah says do not have a portion in the World to Come is Elisha's attendant, **Gehazi.** [6]**For the verse states** (see II Kings 8:7): **"And Elisha went to Damascus."** [7]**Where did** Elisha **go,** and for what purpose? [8]**Rabbi Yoḥanan said:** Elisha **went to make Gehazi repent** of his evil ways, **but** Gehazi **did not repent.** [9]Elisha **said to him: "Repent."** [10]But Gehazi **answered him:** "It is **from you** yourself that I **learned:** [11]If **someone sins and** also **causes the community** at large **to sin, he is not permitted to do repentance."** [12]The Gemara asks: **What had** Gehazi **done** to cause other people to sin? [13]**There are those who say** that using a huge **magnetic stone,** Gehazi **suspended the** golden **calf** that had been erected **by Jeroboam,**

וְהִנָּשְׂאוּ פִּתְחֵי עוֹלָם וְיָבוֹא מֶלֶךְ הַכָּבוֹד מִי זֶה מֶלֶךְ הַכָּבוֹד ה׳ עִזּוּז וְגִבּוֹר ה׳ גִּבּוֹר מִלְחָמָה׳, [1]וְנֶאֱמַר: ׳שְׂאוּ שְׁעָרִים רָאשֵׁיכֶם וּשְׂאוּ פִּתְחֵי עוֹלָם וְיָבוֹא מֶלֶךְ הַכָּבוֹד וגו׳ ׳ ". [2]וְלֹא נַעֲנָה. [3]כֵּיוָן שֶׁאָמַר: "ה׳ אֱלֹהִים אַל תָּשֵׁב פְּנֵי מְשִׁיחֶךָ זָכְרָה לְחַסְדֵי דָּוִיד עַבְדֶּךָ", מִיָּד נַעֲנָה. [4]בְּאוֹתָהּ שָׁעָה נֶהֶפְכוּ פְּנֵי שׂוֹנְאֵי דָוִד כְּשׁוּלֵי קְדֵירָה, וְיָדְעוּ כָּל יִשְׂרָאֵל שֶׁמָּחַל לוֹ הַקָּדוֹשׁ בָּרוּךְ הוּא עַל אוֹתוֹ הֶעָוֹן.

[5]גֵּחֲזִי — [6]דִּכְתִיב: "וַיֵּלֶךְ אֱלִישָׁע דַּמֶּשֶׂק". [7]לְהֵיכָא אֲזַל? [8]אָמַר רַבִּי יוֹחָנָן: שֶׁהָלַךְ לְהַחֲזִיר גֵּחֲזִי בִּתְשׁוּבָה, וְלֹא חָזַר. [9]אָמַר לוֹ: "חֲזוֹר בְּךָ". [10]אָמַר לוֹ: "כָּךְ מְקוּבְּלַנִי מִמְּךָ: [11]הַחוֹטֵא וּמַחְטִיא אֶת הָרַבִּים — אֵין מַסְפִּיקִין בְּיָדוֹ לַעֲשׂוֹת תְּשׁוּבָה". [12]מַאי עֲבַד? [13]אִיכָּא דְּאָמְרִי: אֶבֶן שׁוֹאֶבֶת תָּלָה

LITERAL TRANSLATION

and be lifted up, you everlasting doors; and the King of Glory shall come in. Who is this King of Glory? The Lord strong and mighty, the Lord mighty in battle.' [1]And it is stated: 'Lift up your heads, O you gates; and lift them up, you everlasting doors; that the King of Glory may come in, etc.'" [2]But he was not answered. [3]When he said: "O Lord God, do not turn away the face of your anointed; remember the faithful love of David Your servant," immediately he was answered. [4]At that same time, the faces of David's enemies turned [black] like the bottom of a cauldron, and all of Israel knew that the Holy One, blessed be He, had pardoned him for that iniquity.

[5]Gehazi — [6]as it is written: "And Elisha went to Damascus." [7]Where did he go? [8]Rabbi Yoḥanan said: He went to make Gehazi repent, but he did not repent. [9]He said to him: "Repent." [10]He said to him: "Thus I have received from you: [11]Someone who sins and causes the community to sin — they do not permit him to do repentance." [12]What did he do? [13]There are those who say: He suspended a magnetic stone

RASHI

וילך אלישע דמשק — להיכא אזל. **שואבת** — מגבהת מתכת בלא נגיעה, כעין אותה שלועזין *קלאמניס"ה בלעז, ועל ידי אותה אבן העמיד עגלים של ירבעם באויר.

LANGUAGE (RASHI)

קלאמניס"ה* This apparently should be ק"ל איימנ"ט. *Kal* is the Provencal for "stone," and *aimant* is Old French for "magnet."

NOTES

וַיֵּלֶךְ אֱלִישָׁע דַּמֶּשֶׂק And Elisha went to Damascus. It has been noted that there is no such verse in the Bible. We do find, however (II Kings 8:7): "And Elisha came [וַיָּבוֹא] to Damascus." *Maharsha* explains that the Gemara's problem is in fact the absence of a verse stating that Elisha went to Damascus. The Gemara explains that the Bible does not state that Elisha went to Damascus, because he failed to accomplish the purpose of his journey. He went to make Gehazi repent, but failed to do so.

אֵין מַסְפִּיקִין בְּיָדוֹ לַעֲשׂוֹת תְּשׁוּבָה They do not give him the opportunity to repent. The Rishonim note that this does not mean that someone who sins and also causes the community to sin cannot repent, or that his repentance will never be accepted, for if indeed he did repent, nothing can prevent it from being accepted. Rather, this means that Heaven does not assist such a person to repent, unlike other sinners (see *Rambam, Meiri*).

HALAKHAH

וּמַחְטִיא אֶת הָרַבִּים Someone who causes the community to sin. "Someone who sins and also causes the community to sin is not given the opportunity to repent, for his transgression is very great." (*Rambam, Sefer Mada, Hilkhot Teshuvah* 4:1.)

TRANSLATION AND COMMENTARY

and caused it to stand between Heaven and Earth, thus reinforcing the beliefs of those who accepted the calf as a god. [1]**There are** others **who say** that Gehazi **engraved a Divine Name in** the calf's **mouth,** [2]so that the calf **would proclaim** the beginning of the Ten Commandments, **and say, "I** am the Lord, your God," **and "You shall have no** other gods beside me." [3]**And there are** still others **who say** that Gehazi **pushed** Elisha's **Rabbinic students away from him,** so that they would not learn from him, [4]**as the verse** following Gehazi's departure from Elisha **states** (II Kings 6:1): **"And the sons of the Prophets said to Elisha, Behold now, the place where we dwell with you is too small for us."** [5]**This implies that until now** Elisha's disciples **had not** felt that they were too **many,** for until now Gehazi had kept many of Elisha's students from entering his academy.

תָּנוּ רַבָּנַן [6]**Our Rabbis taught** the following Baraita: **"The left hand should always push away** a sinner, while at the same time **the right hand should draw** him **close.** [7]One should **not** act **like Elisha, who pushed Gehazi away with two hands,** causing him to lose his place in the World to Come, **nor** should one act **like Yehoshua ben Peraḥyah, who pushed Jesus the Nazarene away with two hands.** [8]What happened with **Gehazi? As the verse states** (II Kings 5:23): **'And Naaman said, Be pleased to take two talents.** [9]**And he urged him, and bound two talents of silver in two bags, with two changes of garments.'** [10]And the next verses state (II Kings 5:25-26): **'And Elisha said to him, Where from, Gehazi? And he said, Your servant went nowhere at all. And he said to him, Went not my heart with you, when the man turned back from his chariot to meet you? Is it a time to receive money, and to receive garments, and oliveyards, and vineyards, and sheep, and oxen, and menservants, and maidservants?'** — thus rejecting him completely."

לְחַטַּאת יָרָבְעָם, וְהֶעֱמִידָהּ בֵּין שָׁמַיִם לָאָרֶץ. [1]וְאִיכָּא דְּאָמְרִי: שֵׁם חָקַק בְּפִיהָ, [2]וְהָיְתָה מַכְרֶזֶת וְאוֹמֶרֶת: "אָנֹכִי", וְ"לֹא יִהְיֶה לְךָ". [3]וְאִיכָּא דְּאָמְרִי: רַבָּנַן דְּחָה מִקַּמֵּיהּ, [4]שֶׁנֶּאֱמַר: "וַיֹּאמְרוּ בְנֵי הַנְּבִיאִים אֶל אֱלִישָׁע, הִנֵּה [נָא] הַמָּקוֹם אֲשֶׁר אֲנַחְנוּ יֹשְׁבִים שָׁם לְפָנֶיךָ צַר מִמֶּנּוּ". [5]מִכְּלָל דְּעַד הַשְׁתָּא לָא הָווּ (פָּיְישֵׁי) [צַר].

[6]תָּנוּ רַבָּנַן: "לְעוֹלָם תְּהֵא שְׂמֹאל דּוֹחָה וְיָמִין מְקָרֶבֶת. [7]לֹא כֶּאֱלִישָׁע שֶׁדְּחָפוֹ לְגֵחֲזִי בִּשְׁתֵּי יָדַיִם, וְלֹא כִּיהוֹשֻׁעַ בֶּן פְּרַחְיָא שֶׁדְּחָפוֹ לְיֵשׁוּ הַנּוֹצְרִי בִּשְׁתֵּי יָדָיו. [8]גֵּחֲזִי — דִּכְתִיב: 'וַיֹּאמֶר נַעֲמָן הוֹאֵל וְקַח כִּכָּרָיִם. [9](וַיִּפְצַר) [וַיִּפְרָץ] בּוֹ וַיָּצַר כִּכְּרַיִם כֶּסֶף וגו'. [10]'וַיֹּאמֶר אֵלָיו אֱלִישָׁע מֵאַיִן גֵּחֲזִי? וַיֹּאמֶר לֹא הָלַךְ עַבְדְּךָ אָנֶה וָאָנָה. וַיֹּאמֶר אֵלָיו לֹא לִבִּי הָלַךְ כַּאֲשֶׁר הָפַךְ אִישׁ מֵעַל מֶרְכַּבְתּוֹ לִקְרָאתֶךָ? הַעֵת לָקַחַת אֶת הַכֶּסֶף וְלָקַחַת בְּגָדִים וְזֵיתִים וּכְרָמִים וְצֹאן וּבָקָר וַעֲבָדִים וּשְׁפָחוֹת' ".

LITERAL TRANSLATION

for the transgression of Jeroboam, and caused it to stand between Heaven and Earth. [1]And there are those who say: He engraved a [Divine] Name in its mouth, [2]and it would proclaim and say, "I," and "You shall not have." [3]And there are those who say: He pushed the Rabbis away from him, [4]as it is stated: "And the sons of the Prophets said to Elisha, Behold now, the place where we dwell with you is too small for us." [5]This implies that until now they were not many.

[6]Our Rabbis taught: "The left hand should always push away, and the right hand draw close. [7]Not like Elisha who pushed Gehazi away with two hands, and not like Yehoshua ben Peraḥyah who pushed Jesus the Nazarene away with two hands. [8]Gehazi, as it is written: 'And Naaman said, Be pleased to take two talents. [9]And he urged him, and bound [two] talents of silver [in two bags], etc.' [10]'And Elisha said to him, Where from, Gehazi? And he said, Your servant went nowhere at all. And he said to him, Went not my heart with you, when the man turned back from his chariot to meet you? Is it a time to receive money, and to receive garments, and oliveyards, and vineyards, and sheep, and oxen, and menservants, and maidservants?'"

RASHI

רבנן דחה מקמיה — התלמידים דחה מישיבתו של אלישע. צר ממנו — מכלל דעד האידנא לא הוה צר. הואל וקח — השבע שאלישע שלחך. ויפצר בו — גחזי. העת לקחת את הכסף והבגדים וגו' — שמנה דברים קא חשיב בהאי קרא.

NOTES

שְׂמֹאל דּוֹחָה וְיָמִין מְקָרֶבֶת **The left hand should push away, and the right hand draw close.** *Ramah* explains that a person should take care that the force drawing the sinner close be greater than the force pushing him away, just as the right hand is stronger than the left.

אֱלִישָׁע שֶׁדְּחָפוֹ לְגֵחֲזִי **Elisha who pushed Gehazi away with two hands.** It may be asked: Where do we find that Elisha pushed Gehazi away with two hands? The Gemara apparently refers here to the punishment of leprosy with which Gehazi was afflicted, for a leper is required to distance himself from other people, and while in isolation, it is difficult for him to do repentance (*Ri'af*).

TRANSLATION AND COMMENTARY

וּמִי שְׁקַל [1]The Gemara asks: **But did** Gehazi really **take** from Naaman **all** eight things mentioned by Elisha? [2]Surely he **took** only **money and garments!** [3]**Rabbi Yitzḥak said: At that time, Elisha was sitting and teaching** the laws **regarding the eight** unclean, **creeping creatures.** [4]**Naaman, the commander of the army of the King of Aram, was afflicted by leprosy.** [5]**A certain** Jewish **girl who had been taken captive from Eretz Israel said to him: "If you go to Elisha, he will cure you."** [6]**When** Naaman **came** to Elisha, Elisha **said to him: "Go, and immerse yourself in the Jordan** River, and you will be cured." [7]Naaman **said to him: "Are you making fun of me?"** [8]**Those** attendants **who were with** their master Naaman **said to him: "What do you** have to **lose from** Elisha's suggestion? **Go,** and **try** it." [9]Naaman **went and immersed himself in the Jordan** River, **and was** promptly **cured.** [10]Naaman then **went and brought** Elisha **all those things that he had** with him. [11]But Elisha **did not want to accept** anything **from him.** [12]Meanwhile, Elisha's attendant **Gehazi slipped away from before him,** and **went and took** from Naaman **what he took, and deposited** the gifts.

כִּי אֲתָא [13]**When** Gehazi **returned, Elisha saw that leprosy had broken out upon his face,** and immediately understood that Gehazi must have taken something from Naaman. Therefore he was punished with the leprosy that had afflicted Naaman. [14]Elisha **said to** Gehazi: **"Wicked man!** [15]**The time must have arrived** for you **to receive** your **reward for** studying the laws governing **the eight** unclean, **creeping creatures,** so you took enough money from Naaman to purchase the eight items mentioned above. [16]**'So let the leprosy of Naaman cling to you, and to your seed forever,' and he went from before him snow white with leprosy."** (II Kings 5:27.)

[1]וּמִי שְׁקַל כּוּלֵּי הַאי? [2]כֶּסֶף וּבְגָדִים הוּא דִּשְׁקַל! [3]אָמַר רַבִּי יִצְחָק: בְּאוֹתָהּ שָׁעָה הָיָה אֱלִישָׁע יוֹשֵׁב וְדוֹרֵשׁ בִּשְׁמוֹנָה שְׁרָצִים. [4]נַעֲמָן שַׂר צְבָא מֶלֶךְ אֲרָם הָיָה מְצוֹרָע. [5]אֲמַרָה לֵיהּ הַהִיא רְבִיתָא דְּאִישְׁתַּבַּאי מֵאַרְעָא יִשְׂרָאֵל: ״אִי אָזְלַתְּ לְגַבֵּי אֱלִישָׁע, מַסֵּי לָךְ״. [6]כִּי אֲתָא אֲמַר לֵיהּ: ״זִיל טְבוֹל בְּיַרְדֵּן״. [7]אֲמַר לֵיהּ: ״אַחוּכֵי קָא מְחַיְּיכַתְּ בִּי״? [8]אָמְרִי לֵיהּ הָנְהוּ דַּהֲווּ בַּהֲדֵיהּ: ״מַאי נָפְקָא לָךְ מִינָּהּ? זִיל, נַסֵּי״. [9]אֲזַל וּטְבַל בְּיַרְדְּנָא, וְאִיתַּסִּי. [10]אֲתָא אַיְיתִי לֵיהּ כָּל הָנֵי דְּנָקֵיט. [11]לָא צְבִי לְקַבּוּלֵי מִינֵּיהּ. [12]גֵּחֲזִי אִיפַּטַּר מִקַּמֵּיהּ אֱלִישָׁע, אֲזַל שְׁקַל מַאי דִּשְׁקַל, וְאַפְקִיד.

[13]כִּי אֲתָא, חַזְיֵיהּ אֱלִישָׁע לְצָרַעַת דַּהֲוָה פָּרְחָה עֲלָוֵיהּ רֵישֵׁיהּ. [14]אֲמַר לֵיהּ: ״רָשָׁע! [15]הִגִּיעַ עֵת לִיטּוֹל שְׂכַר שְׁמֹנָה שְׁרָצִים. [16]׳וְצָרַעַת נַעֲמָן תִּדְבַּק בְּךָ וּבְזַרְעֲךָ לְעוֹלָם׳. וַיֵּצֵא מִלְּפָנָיו מְצֹרָע כַּשָּׁלֶג״.

LITERAL TRANSLATION

[1]But did he take all that? [2]It was money and garments that he took! [3]Rabbi Yitzḥak said: At that time, Elisha was sitting and teaching about the eight creeping creatures. [4]Naaman, the commander of the army of the King of Aram, was a leper. [5]A certain girl who had been taken captive from Eretz Israel said to him: "If you go to Elisha, he will cure you." [6]When he came, he said to him: "Go, and immerse yourself in the Jordan." [7]He said to him: "Are you making fun of me?" [8]Those who were with him said to him: "What do you lose from it; go, try." [9]He went and immersed himself in the Jordan, and was cured. [10]He went and brought him all those things that he held. [11]He did not want to accept [them] from him. [12]Gehazi slipped away from before Elisha, went, [and] took what he took, and deposited [them].

[13]When he came, Elisha saw the leprosy that had broken out on his face. [14]He said to him: "Wicked man! [15]The time has come to receive reward for the eight creeping creatures. [16]'So let the leprosy of Naaman cling to you, and to your seed forever,' and he went from before him snow white with leprosy."

RASHI

וגחזי מי שקל כולי האי — מנעמן, כסף ובגדים הוא דשקל דכתיב ״ויצר ככרים וגו׳״. **אותה שעה** — היה אלישע עוסק בפרק שמונה שרצים, אמר לו: הגיע עת ליטול שכר פרק שמונה שרצים שעסקתי וכו׳, ולהכי כתב בהאי קרא שמנה דברים כנגד אותו פרק, כלומר, בכסף ובגדים שקבלת ממנו, מנעמן, סבור אתה לקנות דברים הללו להיותם לך שכר שמונה שרצים.

NOTES

לָא צְבִי לְקַבּוּלֵי **He did not want to accept them.** Elisha did not want to accept anything from Naaman, so that Naaman would understand that he was not healed by any medical procedure that would require payment. Rather, he was cured with God's help. That is why Elisha became angry when Gehazi took the gifts from Naaman, for by doing so he appeared to deny the miraculous nature of Naaman's recovery (see *Maharsha*).

TRANSLATION AND COMMENTARY

LITERAL TRANSLATION

LANGUAGE

טרוטות **Oval.** This word might derive from Greek δηρος, *diros*, meaning "long" or "too long." It might also derive from Latin *teres etis*, meaning "oval, elongated with rounded ends." In this context it appears to mean that the eyes are very narrow.

וְאַרְבָּעָה אֲנָשִׁים [1]The verse states (II Kings 7:3): **"And there were four men afflicted with leprosy at the entrance of the gate."** [2]**Rabbi Yoḥanan said:** These four men were **Gehazi and his three sons,** for Gehazi and his descendants were cursed with leprosy.

יְהוֹשֻׁעַ בֶּן פְּרַחְיָה [3]The Gemara asks: **What was** the incident involving **Yehoshua ben Peraḥyah?** [4]**When King Yannai killed the Sages, Yehoshua ben Peraḥyah and** his disciple **Jesus fled to Alexandria in Egypt.** [5]**When peace was restored** between Yannai and the Sages, **Shimon ben Shetaḥ** (Yannai's brother-in-law, who had not fled) **sent him** a message, saying: **"From me, the holy city of Jerusalem, to you, Alexandria in Egypt: O sister, my husband is found among you, and I sit desolate."** That is to say, a prominent Torah scholar dwells in a faraway country, and Jerusalem needs leadership. [6]Yehoshua ben Peraḥyah understood what was being asked of him. **He rose, and headed back** to Eretz Israel. He **happened upon a certain inn,** where he **was shown great honor.** [7]Rabbi Yehoshua ben Peraḥyah **said: "How lovely is this inn."** [8]His disciple Jesus **said to him: "Master,** this inn is not so lovely, for the innkeeper's wife's **eyes are oval** and unattractive." [9]Rabbi Yehoshua ben Peraḥyah **said to** Jesus: **"Wicked man!** [10]Do you **engage yourself in** looking at the eyes of a married woman?" [11]Rabbi Yehoshua ben Peraḥyah immediately **took out four hundred shofars, and placed a ban upon** his errant disciple. [12]Jesus **appeared before** his master **several times, and said to him: "Accept me** back, for I have repented," [13]but Rabbi Yehoshua ben Peraḥyah **paid no attention to him.** [14]**One day** Rabbi Yehoshua ben Peraḥyah **was reciting the** *Shema,* **and** Jesus **came before him** with his usual request. [15]This time Rabbi Yehoshua ben Peraḥyah **intended to accept him** back, [16]and **he signaled him with his hand** to wait until he finished his prayers. [17]But Jesus misinterpreted the signal, and **thought** that his master **was pushing him away** again. [18]So **he went and stood up a brick** to symbolize an idol, **and bowed down to it.** [19]Rabbi Yehoshua ben Peraḥyah **said to him: "Repent."** [20]Jesus **said to him: "But surely it is from you** yourself that **I learned:**

[1]**"And there were four men afflicted with leprosy at the entrance of the gate."** [2]Rabbi Yoḥanan said: Gehazi and his three sons.

[3]Yehoshua ben Peraḥyah — what is it? [4]When King Yannai killed the Sages, Yehoshua ben Peraḥyah and Jesus went to Alexandria in Egypt. [5]When there was peace, Shimon ben Shetaḥ sent him: "From me, Jerusalem the holy city, to you, Alexandria in Egypt: O sister, my husband is found among you, and I sit desolate." [6]He rose [and] came and happened upon a certain inn. They did him a great honor. [7]He said: "How lovely is this inn." [8]He said to him: "Master, her eyes are oval." [9]He said to him: "Wicked man! [10]In that you engage?" [11]He took out four hundred shofars, and placed a ban upon him. [12]He came before him several times, [and] said to him: "Accept me." [13]He did not pay attention to him. [14]One day he was reciting the *Shema,* [and] he came before him. [15]He thought to accept him. [16]He made a sign to him with his hand. [17]He thought: He is pushing me away. [18]He went and stood up a brick and bowed down to it. [19]He said: "Repent." [20]He said to him:

---

[1]"וְאַרְבָּעָה אֲנָשִׁים הָיוּ מְצֹרָעִים פֶּתַח הַשָּׁעַר". [2]אָמַר רַבִּי יוֹחָנָן: גֵּחֲזִי וּשְׁלֹשָׁה בָּנָיו.

[3]יְהוֹשֻׁעַ בֶּן פְּרַחְיָה — מַאי הִיא? [4]כִּדְקַטְלִינְהוּ יַנַּאי מַלְכָּא לְרַבָּנַן אֲזַל יְהוֹשֻׁעַ בֶּן פְּרַחְיָה וְיֵשׁוּ לַאֲלֶכְּסַנְדְּרִיָא שֶׁל מִצְרַיִם. [5]כִּי הֲוָה שְׁלָמָא שְׁלַח לֵיהּ שִׁמְעוֹן בֶּן שָׁטַח: "מִינִי יְרוּשָׁלַיִם עִיר הַקֹּדֶשׁ לִיכִי אֲלֶכְּסַנְדְּרִיָה שֶׁל מִצְרַיִם: אֲחוֹתִי, בַּעֲלִי שָׁרוּי בְּתוֹכֵךְ וְאָנֹכִי יוֹשֶׁבֶת שׁוֹמֵמָה". [6]קָם אֲתָא וְאִתְרְמִי לֵיהּ הַהוּא אוּשְׁפִּיזָא. עֲבַדוּ לֵיהּ יְקָרָא טוּבָא. [7]אָמַר: "כַּמָּה יָפָה אַכְסַנְיָא זוֹ". [8]אָמַר לֵיהּ: "רַבִּי, עֵינֶיהָ טְרוּטוֹת". [9]אָמַר לֵיהּ: "רָשָׁע! [10]בְּכָךְ אַתָּה עוֹסֵק"? [11]אַפִּיק אַרְבַּע מְאָה שִׁיפּוּרֵי וְשַׁמְּתֵיהּ. [12]אֲתָא לְקַמֵּיהּ כַּמָּה זִימְנִין, אָמַר לֵיהּ: "קַבְּלָן". [13]לָא הֲוֵי קָא מַשְׁגַּח בֵּיהּ. [14]יוֹמָא חַד הֲוָה קָא קָרֵי קְרִיאַת שְׁמַע, אֲתָא לְקַמֵּיהּ. [15]סָבַר לְקַבּוּלֵי. [16]אַחֲוֵי לֵיהּ בִּידֵיהּ. [17]הוּא סָבַר: מִידְחָא דָּחֵי לִי. [18]אֲזַל זָקַף לְבֵינְתָּא וְהִשְׁתַּחֲוָה לָהּ. [19]אָמַר לֵיהּ: "הֲדַר בָּךְ"! [20]אָמַר לֵיהּ:

RASHI

ינאי מלכא — כהן גדול הוה וקטל כולהו רבנן, במסכת קדושין. שמעון בן שטח — אחי אשתו של ינאי המלך, והוא לא ברח. טרוטות — עגולות. אחוי ליה — רבי יהושע בן פרחיה. בידיה — דלקבלוהי.

NOTES

עֵינֶיהָ טְרוּטוֹת **Her eyes are oval.** According to *Arukh,* the innkeeper's wife's eyes blinked excessively, and she squinted.

TRANSLATION AND COMMENTARY

[1]**Anyone who sins and** also **causes the community to sin is not permitted to do repentance."** [2]**And a Sage said: Jesus performed magic and incited the people of Israel and led them astray.** Had Rabbi Yehoshua ben Peraḥyah not rejected Jesus so categorically, he would not have gone so far astray that he was not even given the opportunity to do repentance.

תַּנְיָא [3]**It was taught** in a related Baraita: **"Rabbi Shimon ben Elazar said:** [4]Sexual **passion, a young child, and a woman —** [5]**let the left hand push** each of them **away,** while at the same time **the right hand should draw** each of them **close.** A person should not nurture his sexual passion too zealously, lest he come to sin, but he should also not suppress it completely, lest he come to total abstinence and not engage in procreation. Similarly, a man should not give a young child or a woman too much freedom, lest they fall into bad ways, but he should also not discipline them too severely, lest he drive them into total despair."

תָּנוּ רַבָּנַן [6]**Our Rabbis taught** the following Baraita: "At different times, **Elisha was sick with three illnesses.** [7]**One** illness was a punishment **for inciting the bears against the young children** who jeered at him (as is described in II Kings 2:23-25). [8]**And one** illness served as a punishment **for pushing Gehazi away with two hands.** [9]**And one** illness was the illness **from which he died.** [10]Elisha's three illnesses are alluded to by **the verse** that **states** (II Kings 13:14): **'Now Elisha was fallen sick of his sickness of which he was to die,'** implying that he had suffered illnesses before."

עַד אַבְרָהָם [11]Having mentioned Elisha's sicknesses and death, the Gemara notes: **Until Abraham there was no old age.** [12]**Whoever saw Abraham would say: "It is Isaac,"** [13]and **whoever saw Isaac would say: "It is Abraham,"** because Abraham did not look older than his son Isaac. [14]**Abraham prayed** to God **that he should** be marked by the external signs of **old age, as the verse states** regarding Abraham, but not regarding any earlier Biblical figure (Genesis 24:1): **"And Abraham was old, advanced in age."** [15]**Until Jacob,** physical **weakness did not** serve as a prelude to death. [16]Jacob **prayed** to God to become weak, so that he could prepare himself and his children for his death. His prayer was answered, **and he became weak,** [17]**as the verse states** for the first time and with respect to Jacob (Genesis 48:1): **"And someone told Joseph, Behold, your father is sick."**

[1]״כָּךְ מְקוּבְּלַנִי מִמְּךָ: כׇּל הַחוֹטֵא וּמַחֲטִיא אֶת הָרַבִּים אֵין מַסְפִּיקִין בְּיָדוֹ לַעֲשׂוֹת תְּשׁוּבָה״. [2]וְאָמַר מָר: יֵשׁוּ כִּישֵּׁף וְהֵסִית וְהִדִּיחַ אֶת יִשְׂרָאֵל.

[3]תַּנְיָא: ״אָמַר רַבִּי שִׁמְעוֹן בֶּן אֶלְעָזָר: [4]יֵצֶר, תִּינוֹק, וְאִשָּׁה — [5]תְּהֵא שְׂמֹאל דּוֹחָה, וְיָמִין מְקָרֶבֶת.

[6]תָּנוּ רַבָּנַן: ״שְׁלֹשָׁה חֳלָאִים חָלָה אֱלִישָׁע. [7]אֶחָד שֶׁגֵּירָה דּוּבִּים בְּתִינוֹקוֹת. [8]וְאֶחָד שֶׁדְּחָפוֹ לְגֵחֲזִי בִּשְׁתֵּי יָדַיִם. [9]וְאֶחָד שֶׁמֵּת בּוֹ, [[10]שֶׁנֶּאֱמַר: ״וֶאֱלִישָׁע חָלָה אֶת חׇלְיוֹ וגו׳״].

[11]עַד אַבְרָהָם לָא הֲוָה זִקְנָה. [12]כׇּל דְּחָזֵי לְאַבְרָהָם אָמַר: ״הַאי יִצְחָק״, [13]כׇּל דְּחָזֵי לְיִצְחָק אָמַר: ״הַאי אַבְרָהָם״. [14]בְּעָא אַבְרָהָם רַחֲמֵי דְּלֶיהֱוֵי לֵיהּ זִקְנָה, שֶׁנֶּאֱמַר: ״וְאַבְרָהָם זָקֵן בָּא בַּיָּמִים״. [15]עַד יַעֲקֹב לָא הֲוָה חוּלְשָׁא. [16]בְּעָא רַחֲמֵי וַהֲוָה חוּלְשָׁא, [17]שֶׁנֶּאֱמַר: ״וַיֹּאמֶר לְיוֹסֵף הִנֵּה אָבִיךָ

LITERAL TRANSLATION

"Thus I have received from you: [1]Anyone who sins and causes the community to sin — they do not permit him to do repentance." [2]And a Sage said: Jesus performed magic and incited [the people of] Israel and led them astray.

[3]It was taught: "Rabbi Shimon ben Elazar said: [4]Passion, a young child, and a woman — [5]let the left hand push away, and the right hand draw close."

[6]Our Rabbis taught: "Elisha was sick with three illnesses. [7]One for inciting the bears against the young children. [8]And one for pushing Gehazi away with two hands. [9]And one from which he died, [10]as it is stated: 'Now Elisha was fallen sick of his sickness of which he was to die.'"

[11]Until Abraham there was no old age. [12]Whoever saw Abraham said: "It is Isaac." [13]Whoever saw Isaac said: "It is Abraham." [14]Abraham begged for mercy to have old age, as it is stated: "And Abraham was old, advanced in age." [15]Until Jacob there was no weakness. [16]He prayed, and he became weak, [17]as it is stated: "And someone told Joseph, Behold, your father

RASHI

יצר – תאותו, אם מרחיקה ממנו לגמרי ממעט ישיבת עולם, ואם מקרבה לגמרי בא לידי איסור, שאינו יכול לכבוש יצרו מדבר עבירה. **תינוק ואשה** – דעתן קלה ואם תדחה אותם מטרדן מן העולם. **חלה** – חד, **חליו** – תרי, **אשר ימות בו** – תלת. **בעא רחמי דלהוי חולשא** – כדי שיהא פנאי לבניו לבא כל אחד ואחד ממקומו להיות עליו בשעת מיתה, שכיון שרואין שנפל למטה יודעין שימות ומתקבצין ובאין.

NOTES

בְּעָא רַחֲמֵי וַהֲוָה חוּלְשָׁא **He prayed, and he became weak.** The Midrash explains that Jacob argued that a person who dies without first taking ill cannot know when to expect death and prepare his children for his demise. Elisha argued that a sick person should be allowed to recover, to encourage him to repent while threatened with death.

חֹלֶה״. [1]עַד אֱלִישָׁע לָא הֲוָה אִינִישׁ חֲלִישׁ דְּמִיתְפַּח. [2]וַאֲתָא אֱלִישָׁע וּבְעָא רַחֲמֵי וְאִיתְפַּח, [3]שֶׁנֶּאֱמַר: ״וֶאֱלִישָׁע חָלָה אֶת חָלְיוֹ אֲשֶׁר יָמוּת בּוֹ״.

משנה [4]דּוֹר הַמַּבּוּל אֵין לָהֶם חֵלֶק לָעוֹלָם הַבָּא, וְאֵין עוֹמְדִין בַּדִּין, [5]שֶׁנֶּאֱמַר: ״לֹא יָדוֹן רוּחִי בָאָדָם לְעֹלָם״ — [6]לֹא דִּין וְלֹא רוּחַ.

[7]דּוֹר הַפַּלָּגָה אֵין לָהֶם חֵלֶק לָעוֹלָם הַבָּא, [8]שֶׁנֶּאֱמַר: ״וַיָּפֶץ ה׳ אֹתָם מִשָּׁם עַל פְּנֵי כָל הָאָרֶץ״. [9]וּכְתִיב: ״וּמִשָּׁם הֱפִיצָם״. [10]״וַיָּפֶץ ה׳ אֹתָם״ — בָּעוֹלָם הַזֶּה. [11]״וּמִשָּׁם הֱפִיצָם ה׳״ — לָעוֹלָם הַבָּא.

[12]אַנְשֵׁי סְדוֹם אֵין לָהֶם חֵלֶק לָעוֹלָם הַבָּא, [13]שֶׁנֶּאֱמַר: ״וְאַנְשֵׁי סְדֹם רָעִים וְחַטָּאִים לַה׳ מְאֹד״. [14]״רָעִים״ — בָּעוֹלָם הַזֶּה. [15]״וְחַטָּאִים״ — לָעוֹלָם הַבָּא. [16]אֲבָל עוֹמְדִין בַּדִּין.

[17]רַבִּי נְחֶמְיָה אוֹמֵר: אֵלּוּ וָאֵלּוּ אֵין עוֹמְדִין בַּדִּין, [18]שֶׁנֶּאֱמַר:

LITERAL TRANSLATION

is sick." [1]Until Elisha nobody who was sick recovered. [2]And Elisha came and prayed and he recovered, [3]as it is stated: "Now Elisha was fallen sick of his sickness of which he was to die."

MISHNAH [4]The generation of the flood do not have a portion in the World to Come, and they will not stand for judgment, [5]as it is stated: "My spirit shall not always strive for man" — [6]no judgment and no spirit.

[7]The generation of the dispersion do not have a portion in the World to Come, [8]as it is stated: "So the Lord scattered them abroad from there upon the face of the whole earth." [9]And it is written: "And from thence did the Lord scatter them." [10]"So the Lord scattered them" — in this world. [11]"And from thence did the Lord scatter them" — in the World to Come.

[12]The people of Sodom do not have a portion in the World to Come, [13]as it is stated: "And the men of Sodom were wicked and sinners before the Lord exceedingly." [14]"Wicked" — in this world. [15]"And sinners" — in the World to Come. [16]But they will stand for judgment.

[17]Rabbi Neḥemyah says: These and these will not stand for judgment, [18]as it is stated:

TRANSLATION AND COMMENTARY

[1]**Until Elisha no sick** person ever **recovered** from his illness. [2]**Elisha came and prayed** to recover from his illness, **and** indeed **he recovered,** [3]**as the verse states** for the first time and with respect to Elisha (II Kings 13:14): **"Now Elisha was fallen sick of his sickness of which he was to die,"** which implies that he had previously suffered non-fatal illnesses.

MISHNAH דּוֹר הַמַּבּוּל [4]**The generation of the flood** (the contemporaries of Noah; see Genesis 5:5-13) **do not have a share in the World to Come, nor will they stand for judgment** following the Resurrection of the Dead. [5]This is derived from **the verse** that **states** (Genesis 6:3): **"My spirit** [רוּחִי] **shall not always strive** [יָדוֹן] **on account of man"** — [6]they will **not** stand for **judgment** [דִּין], **nor** will they have a **spirit** [רוּחַ] in the World to Come.

דּוֹר הַפַּלָּגָה [7]**The generation of the dispersion** (the builders of the Tower of Babel; see Genesis 11:1-9) **do not have a portion in the World to Come,** [8]**as the verse states** (Genesis 11:8): **"So the Lord scattered them abroad from there upon the face of the earth."** [9]**And the** next **verse states** (Genesis 11:9): **"And from thence did the Lord scatter them** abroad upon the face of all the earth." [10]**"So the Lord scattered them"** — punishing them **in this world.** [11]**"And from thence did the Lord scatter them"** — barring them from entry into **the World to Come.**

אַנְשֵׁי סְדוֹם [12]**The people of Sodom do not have a portion in the World to Come,** [13]**as the verse states** (Genesis 13:3): **"And the men of Sodom were wicked and sinners before the Lord exceedingly."** [14]**"Wicked"** — so that they were punished **in this world.** [15]**"And sinners"** — so that they will have no share **in the World to Come.** [16]**But they will stand for judgment,** and be sentenced to eternal damnation.

רַבִּי נְחֶמְיָה אוֹמֵר [17]**Rabbi Neḥemyah says: Neither** the generation of the flood **nor** the people of Sodom **will stand for judgment** following the Resurrection of the Dead, [18]**as the verse states** (Psalms 1:5): **"Therefore the**

RASHI

מתפח — מתרפא.

משנה לא ידון רוחי לא דין ולא רוח — שאין עומדין בדין, ואין להם רוח להיות עם הצדיקים, שיש להם חלק. ויפץ [ה׳ אותם ומשם הפיצם — ויפץ] בעולם הזה, ומשם הפיצם — בעולם הבא. אלו ואלו — אנשי דור המבול, ואנשי סדום, ובהדא פליג רבי נחמיה.

NOTES

אֵין עוֹמְדִין בַּדִּין **They will not stand for judgment.** Some wicked people will stand for judgment following the Resurrection of the Dead. God will reunite their souls with their bodies and judge them. But those listed here will not stand for such judgment. Following their deaths, they will perish totally and forever (see *Meiri*).

TRANSLATION AND COMMENTARY

wicked shall not stand [108A] **in the judgment, nor sinners in the congregation of the righteous."** [1]**"Therefore the wicked shall not stand in the judgment" — this is** a reference to **the generation of the flood,** about whom the verse states (Genesis 6:5): "That the wickedness of man was great upon the earth." [2]**"Nor sinners in the congregation of the righteous" — this is** a reference to **the people of Sodom,** about whom the verse states (Genesis 13:3): "And the men of Sodom were wicked and sinners."

אָמְרוּ לוֹ [3]The Sages **said to** Rabbi Neḥemyah: The people of Sodom **will not stand** for judgment **in the congregation of the righteous,** [4]**but they will stand** for judgment **in the congregation of the wicked,** and be sentenced to eternal damnation.

מְרַגְּלִים [5]**The spies** whom Moses sent out to scout the Land of Israel **do not have a portion in the World to Come,** [6]**as the verse states** (Numbers 14:37): **"Now those men that brought up the evil report upon the land died by the plague before the Lord."** [7]**"They died" — in this world.** [8]**"By the plague** before the Lord" **— in the World to Come.**

דּוֹר הַמִּדְבָּר [9]**The generation of the wilderness do not have a portion in the World to Come, and they will not stand for judgment,** [10]**as the verse states** (Numbers 14:35): **"In this wilderness they shall be consumed, and there they shall die."** "And there they shall die" — there in the World to Come they shall remain dead, and not stand for judgment. [11]**This is the position of Rabbi Akiva.** [12]**Rabbi Eliezer** disagrees and **says: Regarding** the generation of the wilderness, the verse **states** (Psalms 50:5): [13]**"Gather My pious ones together to Me; those that have made a Covenant with Me by sacrifice."** The generation of the wilderness entered into a Covenant with God with a sacrifice (see Exodus 24:6, 8), and the verse testifies that their portion awaits them in the World to Come.

עֲדַת קֹרַח [14]**The company of Korah will not rise up in the future** from the underworld, [15]**as the verse states** (Numbers 16:33): "And the earth covered over them, and they perished from among the congregation." **"And the earth covered over them" — in this world.** [16]**"And they perished from among the congregation" — in the World to Come.** [17]**This is the position of Rabbi Akiva.** [18]**Rabbi Eliezer** disagrees and **says: Regarding** the company

"עַל כֵּן לֹא יָקֻמוּ [108A] רְשָׁעִים בַּמִּשְׁפָּט וְחַטָּאִים בַּעֲדַת צַדִּיקִים". [1]"עַל כֵּן לֹא יָקוּמוּ רְשָׁעִים בַּמִּשְׁפָּט" — זֶה דּוֹר הַמַּבּוּל. [2]"וְחַטָּאִים בַּעֲדַת צַדִּיקִים" — אֵלּוּ אַנְשֵׁי סְדוֹם. [3]אָמְרוּ לוֹ: אֵינָם עוֹמְדִין בַּעֲדַת צַדִּיקִים, [4]אֲבָל עוֹמְדִין בַּעֲדַת רְשָׁעִים.

[5]מְרַגְּלִים אֵין לָהֶם חֵלֶק לָעוֹלָם הַבָּא, [6]שֶׁנֶּאֱמַר: "וַיָּמֻתוּ הָאֲנָשִׁים מוֹצִאֵי דִבַּת הָאָרֶץ רָעָה בַּמַּגֵּפָה לִפְנֵי ה׳". [7]"וַיָּמֻתוּ" — בָּעוֹלָם הַזֶּה. [8]"בַּמַּגֵּפָה" — לָעוֹלָם הַבָּא. [9]דּוֹר הַמִּדְבָּר אֵין לָהֶם חֵלֶק לָעוֹלָם הַבָּא, וְאֵין עוֹמְדִין בַּדִּין, [10]שֶׁנֶּאֱמַר: "בַּמִּדְבָּר הַזֶּה יִתַּמּוּ וְשָׁם יָמֻתוּ". [11]דִּבְרֵי רַבִּי עֲקִיבָא. [12]רַבִּי אֱלִיעֶזֶר אוֹמֵר: עֲלֵיהֶם הוּא אוֹמֵר: [13]"אִסְפוּ לִי חֲסִידָי; כֹּרְתֵי בְרִיתִי עֲלֵי זָבַח". [14]עֲדַת קֹרַח אֵינָהּ עֲתִידָה לַעֲלוֹת, [15]שֶׁנֶּאֱמַר: "וַתְּכַס עֲלֵיהֶם הָאָרֶץ" — בָּעוֹלָם הַזֶּה, [16]"וַיֹּאבְדוּ מִתּוֹךְ הַקָּהָל" — לָעוֹלָם הַבָּא. [17]דִּבְרֵי רַבִּי עֲקִיבָא. [18]רַבִּי אֱלִיעֶזֶר אוֹמֵר:

LITERAL TRANSLATION

"Therefore the wicked shall not stand [108A] in the judgment, nor sinners in the congregation of the righteous." [1]"Therefore the wicked shall not stand in the judgment" — this is the generation of the flood. [2]"Nor sinners in the congregation of the righteous" — these are the people of Sodom. [3]They said to him: They shall not stand in the congregation of the righteous, [4]but they shall stand in the congregation of the wicked.

[5]The spies do not have a portion in the World to Come, [6]as it is stated: "Now those men that brought up the evil report about the land died by the plague before the Lord." [7]"They died" — in this world. [8]"By the plague" — in the World to Come.

[9]The generation of the wilderness do not have a portion in the World to Come, and they will not stand for judgment, [10]as it is stated: "In this wilderness they shall be consumed, and there they shall die." [11][These are] the words of Rabbi Akiva. [12]Rabbi Eliezer says: Regarding them, it says: [13]"Gather My pious ones together to Me; those that have made a Covenant with Me by sacrifice."

[14]The company of Korah will not rise up in the future, [15]as it is stated: "And the earth covered over them" — in this world. [16]"And they perished from among the congregation" — in the World to Come. [17][These are] the words of Rabbi Akiva. [18]Rabbi Eliezer says:

RASHI

רשעים דור המבול — דכתיב [בהו] "כי רבה רעת האדם" (בראשית ו): חטאים אנשי סדום — דכתיב בהו "רעים וחטאים" (שם יג). אבל עומדים הם כו׳ — שחיין ונדונים.

TRANSLATION AND COMMENTARY

of Korah, the verse **states** (I Samuel 2:6): [1]**"The Lord kills, and gives life; He brings down to the grave, and brings up,"** teaching us that they do indeed have a portion in the World to Come.

GEMARA תָּנוּ רַבָּנַן [2]**Our Rabbis taught** a related Baraita: **"The generation of the flood do not have a portion in the World to Come,** [3]**as the verse states** (Genesis 7:23): **'And He destroyed every living thing that was upon the face of the earth,** both man, and cattle, and creeping things, and the birds of the heaven; they were destroyed from the earth.' [4]**'And He destroyed every living thing'** — punishing them **in this world.** [5]**'They were destroyed from the earth'** — and barred from entering **the World to Come.** [6]**This is the position of Rabbi Akiva.** [7]**Rabbi Yehudah ben Betera says: They will not live** in the World to Come, **nor will they be judged,** [8]**as the verse states** (Genesis 6:3): **'My spirit** [רוּחִי] **shall not always strive** [יָדוֹן] **for man'** — they will **not** stand for **judgment** [דִּין], **nor** will they have a **spirit** [רוּחַ] in the World to Come. [9]**Another explanation** of this verse might also be offered: **'My spirit** [רוּחִי] **shall not strive** [יָדוֹן]**' — their souls** [נִשְׁמָתָן] **shall not return to their cases** [נִדְנָהּ], that is to say, their bodies. [10]**Rabbi Menaḥem the son of Rabbi Yosef says: Even** at the Resurrection of the Dead, **when the Holy One, blessed be He, returns souls to corpses, the souls** of the generation of the flood **will cause themselves suffering in Gehinom,** [11]**as the verse states** (Isaiah 33:11): **'You shall conceive chaff; you shall bring forth stubble; your breath** [רוּחֲכֶם] **is a fire that shall devour you.'** Your own breath ['soul,' רוּחֲכֶם] shall devour you."

תָּנוּ רַבָּנַן [12]**Our Rabbis taught** the following Baraita: **"The generation of the flood only became haughty** and began to sin **because of the** great **bounty that the Holy One, blessed be He, bestowed upon them.** [13]**And what is written about** that generation? The verse states (Job 21:9): **'Their houses are safe without fear, nor is the**

עֲלֵיהֶם הוּא אוֹמֵר: [1]"ה' מֵמִית וּמְחַיֶּה; מוֹרִיד שְׁאוֹל וַיָּעַל".

גמרא [2]תָּנוּ רַבָּנַן: "דּוֹר הַמַּבּוּל אֵין לָהֶם חֵלֶק לָעוֹלָם הַבָּא", [3]שֶׁנֶּאֱמַר: 'וַיִּמַח אֶת כָּל הַיְקוּם אֲשֶׁר עַל פְּנֵי הָאֲדָמָה'. [4]'וַיִּמַח אֶת כָּל הַיְקוּם' — בָּעוֹלָם הַזֶּה, [5]'וַיִּמָּחוּ מִן הָאָרֶץ' — לָעוֹלָם הַבָּא. [6]דִּבְרֵי רַבִּי עֲקִיבָא. [7]רַבִּי יְהוּדָה בֶּן בְּתֵירָא אוֹמֵר: לֹא חַיִּין וְלֹא נִדּוֹנִין, [8]שֶׁנֶּאֱמַר: 'לֹא יָדוֹן רוּחִי בָאָדָם לְעֹלָם' — לֹא דִּין וְלֹא רוּחַ. [9]דָּבָר אַחֵר: 'לֹא יָדוֹן רוּחִי' — שֶׁלֹּא תְּהֵא נִשְׁמָתָן חוֹזֶרֶת לְנִדְנָהּ. [10]רַבִּי מְנַחֵם בְּרַבִּי יוֹסֵף אוֹמֵר: אֲפִילּוּ בְּשָׁעָה שֶׁהַקָּדוֹשׁ בָּרוּךְ הוּא מַחֲזִיר נְשָׁמוֹת לִפְגָרִים מֵתִים, נִשְׁמָתָן קָשָׁה לָהֶם בְּגֵיהִנָּם, [11]שֶׁנֶּאֱמַר: 'תַּהֲרוּ חֲשַׁשׁ תֵּלְדוּ קַשׁ רוּחֲכֶם אֵשׁ תֹּאכַלְכֶם'".

[12]תָּנוּ רַבָּנַן: "דּוֹר הַמַּבּוּל לֹא נִתְגָּאוּ אֶלָּא בִּשְׁבִיל טוֹבָה שֶׁהִשְׁפִּיעַ לָהֶם הַקָּדוֹשׁ בָּרוּךְ הוּא. [13]וּמַה כְּתִיב בָּהֶם? 'בָּתֵּיהֶם שָׁלוֹם מִפָּחַד וְלֹא שֵׁבֶט

LITERAL TRANSLATION

Regarding them, it says: [1]"The Lord kills, and gives life; He brings down to the underworld, and brings up."

GEMARA [2]Our Rabbis taught: "The generation of the flood do not have a portion in the World to Come, [3]as it is stated: 'And He destroyed every living thing that was on the face of the earth.' [4]'And He destroyed every living thing' — in this world. [5]'And they were destroyed from the earth' — in the World to Come. [6][These are] the words of Rabbi Akiva. [7]Rabbi Yehudah ben Betera says: They will not live, and they will not be judged, [8]as it is stated: 'My spirit shall not always strive for man' — no judgment and no spirit. [9]Another explanation: 'My spirit shall not strive' — their souls shall not return to their cases. [10]Rabbi Menaḥem the son of Rabbi Yosef says: Even when the Holy One, blessed be He, returns souls to corpses, their souls will cause them suffering in Gehinom, [11]as it is stated: 'You shall conceive chaff; you shall bring forth stubble; your breath is a fire that shall devour you.'"

[12]Our Rabbis taught: "The generation of the flood only became haughty because of the bounty that the Holy One, blessed be He, bestowed upon them. [13]And what is written about them? 'Their houses are safe without fear, nor is the rod

RASHI

גמרא נשמתן קשה להם בגיהנם — נשמת עלמן שרפתן, דכתיב "רוחכם אש תאכלכם" (ישעיהו לג).

NOTES

נִשְׁמָתָן קָשָׁה לָהֶם **Their souls will cause them suffering.** The punishment meted out to the generation of the flood will be greater than the punishment meted out to others, for they themselves will bring about their own destruction. This is the meaning of the verse: "You shall conceive chaff; you shall bring forth stubble; your breath is a fire that shall devour you." The bodies of the generation of the flood will serve as fuel, like chaff and stubble, and their souls will take the place of fire and burn them (see *Maharsha*).

TRANSLATION AND COMMENTARY

rod of God upon them.' [1]And **the** next **verse states** (Job 21:10): **'Their bull genders, and does not fail; their cow calves, and does not cast her calf.'** [2]And **the** next **verse states** (Job 21:11): **'They send forth their little ones like a flock, and their children dance.'** [3]And **the** next **verse states** (Job 21:12): **'They take the timbrel and lyre, and rejoice at the sound of the pipe.'** [4]And elsewhere **the verse states** (Job 36:11): **'They shall spend their days in prosperity, and their years in pleasures.'** [5]And **the verse states** (Job 21:13): 'They spend their days in wealth, **and in a moment go down to She'ol.'** [6]And that success and prosperity **caused them to say** (Job 21:14-15): **'To God, Depart from us; for we desire not the knowledge of Your ways. What is the Almighty, that we should serve Him, and what profit should we have, if we pray to Him?'** [7]The generation of the flood **said: 'Do we need** God **for anything else but rain?** Surely **we have rivers and springs from which we are** well **supplied** with water, and so He has nothing to offer us.' [8]**The Holy One, blessed be He, said: 'They provoke me with the** great **bounty** — the abundant water — **that I have bestowed upon them, and** therefore **with** water **will I punish them,'** [9]**as the verse states** (Genesis 6:17): **'And, behold, I will bring the flood of waters.'** [10]**Rabbi Yose** disagrees and **says: The generation of the flood only became haughty** and began to sin **in consequence of the eyeball, which is similar to water,** for they lifted their eyes, and saw what did not belong to them, and took what was not theirs to take, [11]**as the verse states** (Genesis 6:2): 'And the distinguished men saw that the daughters of men were fair; **and they took them wives of all whom they chose.'** [12]Therefore God **punished them with water, which is similar to the eyeball, as the verse states** (Genesis 7:11): **'All the fountains** [מַעְיָנוֹת, which alludes to עַיִן, "eye"] **of the great deep were broken open, and the flues of Heaven were opened.'"**

אֱלוֹהַּ עֲלֵיהֶם׳. [1]וּכְתִיב: ׳שׁוֹרוֹ עִבַּר וְלֹא יַגְעִל; תְּפַלֵּט פָּרָתוֹ וְלֹא תְשַׁכֵּל׳. [2]וּכְתִיב: ׳יְשַׁלְּחוּ כַצֹּאן עֲוִילֵיהֶם וְיַלְדֵיהֶם יְרַקֵּדוּן׳. [3]וּכְתִיב: ׳יִשְׂאוּ בְּתֹף וְכִנּוֹר וְיִשְׂמְחוּ לְקוֹל עוּגָב׳. [4]וּכְתִיב: ׳יְכַלּוּ יְמֵיהֶם בַּטּוֹב וּשְׁנֵיהֶם בַּנְּעִימִים׳. [5]וּכְתִיב: ׳וּבְרֶגַע שְׁאוֹל יֵחָתּוּ׳. [6]וְהִיא גָּרְמָה, שֶׁאָמְרוּ לָאֵל: ׳סוּר מִמֶּנּוּ; וְדַעַת דְּרָכֶיךָ לֹא חָפָצְנוּ. מַה שַּׁדַּי, כִּי נַעַבְדֶנּוּ, וּמַה נּוֹעִיל כִּי נִפְגַּע בּוֹ?׳ [7]אָמְרוּ: ׳כְּלוּם צְרִיכִין אָנוּ לוֹ אֶלָּא לְטִיפָּה שֶׁל גְּשָׁמִים? יֵשׁ לָנוּ נְהָרוֹת וּמַעְיָנוֹת שֶׁאָנוּ מִסְתַּפְּקִין מֵהֶן׳. [8]אָמַר הַקָּדוֹשׁ בָּרוּךְ הוּא: ׳בַּטּוֹבָה שֶׁהִשְׁפַּעְתִּי לָהֶן בָּהּ מַכְעִיסִין אוֹתִי — וּבָהּ אֲנִי דָּן אוֹתָם׳, [9]שֶׁנֶּאֱמַר: ׳וַאֲנִי הִנְנִי מֵבִיא אֶת הַמַּבּוּל מַיִם׳. [10]רַבִּי יוֹסֵי אָמַר: ׳דּוֹר הַמַּבּוּל לֹא נִתְגָּאוּ אֶלָּא בִּשְׁבִיל גַּלְגַּל הָעַיִן, שֶׁדּוֹמֶה לַמַּיִם, [11][שֶׁנֶּאֱמַר: ׳וַיִּקְחוּ לָהֶם נָשִׁים מִכֹּל אֲשֶׁר בָּחָרוּ׳]. [12]לְפִיכָךְ דָּן אוֹתָן בַּמַּיִם, שֶׁדּוֹמֶה לְגַלְגַּל הָעַיִן, שֶׁנֶּאֱמַר: ׳נִבְקְעוּ כָּל מַעְיְנוֹת תְּהוֹם רַבָּה וַאֲרֻבֹּת הַשָּׁמַיִם נִפְתָּחוּ׳״.

LITERAL TRANSLATION

of God upon them.' [1]And it is written: 'Their bull genders, and does not fail; their cow calves, and does not cast her calf.' [2]And it is written: 'They send forth their little ones like a flock, and their children dance.' [3]And it is written: 'They take the timbrel and lyre, and rejoice at the sound of the pipe.' [4]And it is written: 'They shall spend their days in prosperity, and their years in pleasures.' [5]And it is written: 'And in a moment they go down to the underworld.' [6]And that caused [it], for they said: 'To God, Depart from us; for we desire not the knowledge of Your ways. What is the Almighty, that we should serve Him, and what profit should we have, if we pray to Him?' [7]They said: 'Do we need Him for anything beside a drop of rain? We have rivers and springs from which we are supplied.' [8]The Holy One, blessed be He, said: 'They provoke me with the bounty that I bestowed upon them — and with it I will punish them,' [9]as it is stated: 'And, behold, I will bring the flood of waters.' [10]Rabbi Yose says: The generation of the flood only became haughty because of the eyeball which is similar to water, [11]as it is stated: 'And they took them wives of all whom they chose.' [12]Therefore He punished them with water, which is similar to the eyeball, as it is stated: 'All the fountains of the great deep were broken open, and the flues of Heaven were opened.'"

BACKGROUND

מַעְיָנוֹת תְּהוֹם Fountains of the great deep. The three springs mentioned here are the major hot springs found in Eretz Israel. "Gader" refers to "Ḥamat Gader," where a hot spring is found to this day. The location of "Beiram" is unclear, though it is apparently in TransJordan, north of the Sea of Galilee.

RASHI

בשביל גלגל העין – שרואין טובתן שלימה, והיו גובהין עיניהם ומנאפין אחר עיניהם. **במים** – שדומה לגלגל העין, מעינות שנובעין ממקום קטן כמו עין.

NOTES

גַּלְגַּל הָעַיִן The eyeball. Some suggest that the generation of the flood began to sin in consequence of the eyeball, that is to say, because they beheld the great bounty that God had bestowed upon them (*Ramah*).

[1] אָמַר רַבִּי יוֹחָנָן: דּוֹר הַמַּבּוּל בְּ״רַבָּה״ קִלְקְלוּ, וּבְ״רַבָּה״ נִידּוֹנוּ. [2] בְּ״רַבָּה״ קִלְקְלוּ, שֶׁנֶּאֱמַר: ״וַיַּרְא ה׳ כִּי רַבָּה רָעַת הָאָדָם״. [3] וּבְ״רַבָּה״ נִידּוֹנוּ, שֶׁנֶּאֱמַר: ״כָּל מַעְיְנוֹת תְּהוֹם רַבָּה״.

[4] אָמַר רַבִּי יוֹחָנָן: שְׁלֹשָׁה נִשְׁתַּיְּירוּ מֵהֶם: [5] בְּלוּעָה דְּגָדֵר, וְחַמֵּי טִבֶּרְיָא, וְעֵינְיָא רַבָּתִי דְּבֵירָם.

[6] ״כִּי הִשְׁחִית כָּל בָּשָׂר אֶת דַּרְכּוֹ עַל הָאָרֶץ״. [7] אָמַר רַבִּי יוֹחָנָן: מְלַמֵּד שֶׁהִרְבִּיעוּ בְּהֵמָה עַל חַיָּה, וְחַיָּה עַל בְּהֵמָה, וְהַכֹּל עַל אָדָם, וְאָדָם עַל הַכֹּל. [8] אָמַר רַבִּי אַבָּא בַּר כָּהֲנָא: וְכוּלָּם חָזְרוּ, חוּץ מִתּוּשְׁלַמִי.

[9] ״וַיֹּאמֶר ה׳ לְנֹחַ קֵץ כָּל בָּשָׂר בָּא לְפָנַי״. [10] אָמַר רַבִּי יוֹחָנָן: בֹּא וּרְאֵה כַּמָּה גָּדוֹל כֹּחָהּ שֶׁל חָמָס, שֶׁהֲרֵי דּוֹר הַמַּבּוּל עָבְרוּ עַל הַכֹּל וְלֹא נֶחְתַּם עֲלֵיהֶם גְּזַר דִּינָם עַד שֶׁפָּשְׁטוּ יְדֵיהֶם בְּגָזֵל, [11] שֶׁנֶּאֱמַר: ״כִּי מָלְאָה הָאָרֶץ חָמָס מִפְּנֵיהֶם וְהִנְנִי מַשְׁחִיתָם אֶת הָאָרֶץ״. [12] וּכְתִיב: ״הֶחָמָס

LITERAL TRANSLATION

[1] Rabbi Yoḥanan said: The generation of the flood sinned greatly, and they were punished greatly. [2] They sinned greatly, as it is stated: "And the Lord saw that great was the wickedness of man." [3] And they were punished "greatly," as it is stated: "All the fountains of the great deep."

[4] Rabbi Yoḥanan said: Three of them remain: [5] The Gulf of Gader, the hot springs of Tiberias, and the great spring of Beiram.

[6] "For all flesh had corrupted its way upon the earth." [7] Rabbi Yoḥanan said: This teaches that they mated a [domestic] animal with a beast, and a beast with a [domestic] animal, and every creature with man, and man with every creature.

[8] Rabbi Abba bar Kahana said: And they all returned, except for the *tushlami*.

[9] "And God said to Noah, The end of all flesh is come before Me." [10] Rabbi Yoḥanan said: Come and see how great is the power of robbery, for the generation of the flood violated everything, but their judgment was not sealed until they sent out their hands with theft, [11] as it is stated: "For the earth is filled with robbery through them; and, behold, I will destroy them with the earth." [12] And it is written: "Robbery

TRANSLATION AND COMMENTARY

אָמַר רַבִּי יוֹחָנָן [1] **Rabbi Yoḥanan said: The generation of the flood sinned "greatly," and they were punished "greatly."** How so? [2] **They sinned "greatly," as the verse states** (Genesis 6:5): **"And the Lord saw that great was the wickedness of man."** [3] **And they were punished "greatly," as the verse states** (Genesis 7:11): **"All the fountains of the great deep** were broken open."

אָמַר רַבִּי יוֹחָנָן [4] **Rabbi Yoḥanan said: Three of** the hot fountains that were broken open during the flood **remain** to this day: [5] **The Gulf of Gader, the hot springs of Tiberias, and the great spring of Beiram.**

כִּי הִשְׁחִית כָּל בָּשָׂר [6] The verse states (Genesis 6:12): **"For all flesh had corrupted its way upon the earth."** [7] **Rabbi Yoḥanan said: This teaches that** the generation of the flood **mated a domestic animal with a** wild **beast, and a** wild **beast with a domestic animal, and every** type of **creature with man, and man with every** type of **creature,** so that all flesh had corrupted its way.

אָמַר רַבִּי אַבָּא בַּר כָּהֲנָא [8] **Rabbi Abba bar Kahana said:** After the flood, **all** creatures **went back** to mate only with their own kind, **except for the *tushlami*,** a type of bird that mates with other species of birds.

וַיֹּאמֶר ה׳ [9] The verse states (Genesis 6:13): **"And God said to Noah, The end of all flesh is come before Me;** for the earth is filled with robbery through them; and, behold, I will destroy them with the earth." [10] **Rabbi Yoḥanan said: Come and see how great is the punishment** imposed **for violent robbery, for the generation of the flood violated every** possible transgression, **but their judgment was not sealed until they used their hands** to engage in **violent** robbery, [11] **as the verse states** (Genesis 6:13): **"For the earth is filled with robbery through them; and, behold, I will destroy them with the earth."** [12] **And** elsewhere **the verse states** (Ezekiel

RASHI

שלשה נשתיירו – מאותן מעינות של דור המבול שהיו חמין, כדאמר לקמן: ברותחין קלקלו – ברותחין נדונו. **וכולן חזרו** – להזדווג עם מיניהם. **חוץ מתושלמי** – עוף הוא, שאותו עדיין תרבות רעה שמזדווג עם הכל, **תושלמי** – עוף אחד, ובמסכת חולין (סב ע״ב) גבי שמונה ספיקות איתא: והרנוגא תושלמי ומרדא, ודרכו של אותו עוף להרביע כל הבריות.

NOTES

כִּי הִשְׁחִית כָּל בָּשָׂר For all flesh corrupted its way. Even though the generation of the flood mated together animals of different species, the question raised below, "If man sinned, how did the cattle sin?" is still valid, for animals are not bound by the Torah's prohibition against crossbreeding, and furthermore, the different species of animals did not mate together on their own. Rather, they were forced to do so by the wicked people of Noah's generation (see *Maharsha, Rabbi Ya'akov Emden*).

הֶחָמָס קָם Violence is risen. Some understand this as a metaphor for the quality of justice: The quality of justice stood up erect like a stick before God, and argued before

TRANSLATION AND COMMENTARY

7:11): **"Robbery is risen up into a rod of wickedness: not from them, not from their multitude, not from their splendor, and no wailing for them."** [1] **Rabbi Elazar said: This teaches that** violence **stood** up **erect like a stick** ("violence is risen up into a rod"), **and stood before the Holy One, blessed be He, and said to Him:** [2] **'Master of the Universe, not from them, not from their multitude, not from their splendor; and no wailing for them.** No benefit shall be derived from any member of this generation, and not one of them is fit to live.' [3] **And the judgment was sealed even regarding Noah,** that he, too, was to die in the flood, [4] **as the verse states:** "And no wailing [נֹהַ] for them" — which may also be read as: **'And no Noah** [נֹחַ] **among them.'"**

תָּנָא [5] **A Tanna of the School of Rabbi Yishmael taught** a similar idea in a Baraita: **"The judgment was issued even regarding Noah,** for he, too, was sentenced to die along with the rest of his generation, **but he found favor in the eyes of the Lord,** and was spared through His mercy, [6] **as the verses state** (Genesis 6:7-8): **'For I repent that I have made them. And Noah found favor in the eyes of the Lord.'"** This Tanna joins the words "and Noah" to the first verse, so that the verses read: "For I repent that I have made them and Noah, but he found favor in the eyes of the Lord."

וַיִּנָּחֶם ה׳ [7] The verse states (Genesis 6:6): **"And the Lord repented that He had made man on the earth."** [8] **When Rav Dimi came** to Babylonia from Eretz Israel, **he said** that this verse should be understood as follows: **The Holy One, blessed be He, said: I did well that I prepared graves for them in the earth,** for just as they were created from the earth, so, too, they should be buried in the earth. [9] The Gemara asks: **How is this inferred** from the verse cited above? [10] The Gemara explains: **Here, the verse states: "And the Lord repented** [וַיִּנָּחֶם]. [11] **And elsewhere, the verse states** (Genesis 50:21): **"And he comforted them** [וַיְנַחֵם]**, and spoke to their heart."** Just as, there, the word נחם denotes satisfaction and contentment, so, too, here, the word נחם should be understood in that sense, and not in the sense of "repent" or "relent."

קָם לְמַטֵּה רֶשַׁע לֹא מֵהֶם וְלֹא מֵהֲמוֹנָם וְלֹא מֶהֱמֵיהֶם וְלֹא נֹהַ בָּהֶם״. [1] אָמַר רַבִּי אֶלְעָזָר: מְלַמֵּד שֶׁזָּקַף עַצְמוֹ כְּמַקֵּל, וְעָמַד לִפְנֵי הַקָּדוֹשׁ בָּרוּךְ הוּא, וְאָמַר לְפָנָיו: [2] ״רִבּוֹנוֹ שֶׁל עוֹלָם, לֹא מֵהֶם וְלֹא מֵהֲמוֹנָם וְלֹא מֶהֱמֵיהֶם וְלֹא נֹהַ בָּהֶם״. ([3] וְאַף עַל נֹחַ נֶחְתַּם גְּזַר דִּין, [4] שֶׁנֶּאֱמַר: ״וְלֹא נֹחַ בָּהֶם״).

[5] תָּנָא דְּבֵי רַבִּי יִשְׁמָעֵאל: ״אַף עַל נֹחַ נֶחְתַּךְ גְּזַר דִּין, אֶלָּא שֶׁמָּצָא חֵן בְּעֵינֵי ה׳, [6] שֶׁנֶּאֱמַר: ׳נִחַמְתִּי כִּי עֲשִׂיתִם. וְנֹחַ מָצָא חֵן בְּעֵינֵי ה׳׳״.

[7] ״וַיִּנָּחֶם ה׳ כִּי עָשָׂה אֶת הָאָדָם בָּאָרֶץ״. [8] כִּי אֲתָא רַב דִּימִי אָמַר: אָמַר הַקָּדוֹשׁ בָּרוּךְ הוּא: יָפֶה עָשִׂיתִי שֶׁתִּקַּנְתִּי לָהֶם קְבָרוֹת בָּאָרֶץ. [9] מַאי מַשְׁמַע? [10] כְּתִיב הָכָא: ״וַיִּנָּחֶם ה׳״. [11] וּכְתִיב הָתָם: ״וַיְנַחֵם אוֹתָם וַיְדַבֵּר עַל לִבָּם״.

LITERAL TRANSLATION

is risen up into a rod of wickedness: not from them, not from their multitude, not from their splendor, and no wailing for them." [1] Rabbi Elazar said: This teaches that it stood up erect like a stick, and stood before the Holy One, blessed be He, and said before Him: [2] "Master of the Universe, not from them, not from their multitude, not from their splendor, and no wailing for them." [3] And the judgment was sealed even regarding Noah, [4] as it is stated, "And no Noah among them."

[5] [A Tanna] of the School of Rabbi Yishmael taught: "The judgment was issued even regarding Noah, but he found favor in the eyes of the Lord, [6] as it is stated: 'For I repent that I have made them. And Noah found favor in the eyes of the Lord.'"

[7] "And the Lord repented that He had made man on the earth." [8] When Rav Dimi came, he said: The Holy One, blessed be He, said: I did well that I prepared graves for them in the earth. [9] What is the inference? [10] It is written here: "And the Lord repented." [11] And it is written there: "And he comforted them, and spoke to their heart."

RASHI

שזקף – החמס עצמו כמקל, והיינו החמס קם למטה רשע. לא מהם – אין תועלת לא בהם ולא בהמונם ולא במשאם. מהמהם – *אשטריא בלעז. כי נחמתי כי עשיתים ונח – סמוכין דרש. יפה עשיתי וכו׳ – שאיבדתי דרך רשעים כזה.

LANGUAGE (RASHI)

אשטריי״א* This should apparently be אישטרי״ט, from the Old French *estrit*, meaning "struggle," "great effort," "conflict."

NOTES

Him. Others suggest that the stolen property stood up before God and hurled accusations against the violent robbers (see *Ramah, Maharsha*).

אַף עַל נֹחַ נֶחְתַּם גְּזַר דִּין **The judgment was issued even regarding Noah.** Even though all agree that Noah was a worthy man, the judgment was sealed against him as well. Some maintain that he was not sufficiently righteous to be spared when a decree of destruction was issued against his entire generation. Others argue that by right Noah should have been punished for the sins of his generation, and that it was only because of God's special kindness that he was spared (see *Ramah, Iyyun Ya'akov*).

קְבָרוֹת בָּאָרֶץ **Graves in the earth.** *Ramah* explains: God said that He did well when man first sinned, and instead of

LANGUAGE

פְּלְיָיטוֹן ***Foliatum.*** This word apparently derives from the Latin *foliatum*, meaning an "oil or ointment made from the leaves of various aromatic plants."

TRANSLATION AND COMMENTARY

וְאִיכָּא דְּאָמְרִי [1]**Some say** that Rav Dimi said that the verse should be understood as follows: God said: **I did not do well that I prepared graves for them in the earth,** for they should never have been created only to be destroyed. How is this inferred from the verse? [2]**Here, the verse states: "And the Lord repented."** [3]**And elsewhere the verse states** (Exodus 32:14): **"And the Lord repented of the evil which He thought to do to His people."** Just as, there, the word נחם denotes relenting and repentance, so, too, here, the word נחם should be understood in the same sense.

אֵלֶּה תּוֹלְדוֹת [4]Regarding Noah, the verse states (Genesis 6:9): **"These are the generations of Noah: Noah was a just man, and perfect in his generations."** What is meant by the qualification "in his generations"? [5]**Rabbi Yoḥanan said: In his** wicked **generations,** Noah was considered a righteous man, **but in other generations,** he would **not** have been considered a righteous man. [6]**Resh Lakish** disagreed and **said:** Even **in his** wicked **generations,** Noah was a righteous man, **and all the more so** would he have been a righteous man **in other generations.**

אָמַר רַבִּי חֲנִינָא [7]**Rabbi Ḥanina said:** According to **Rabbi Yoḥanan, to what may** Noah **be compared?** To **a barrel of wine in a storeroom** filled **with vinegar.** [8]As long as it stays **in that place, its aroma goes forth,** for it is far better smelling than the vinegar. But when it is **no** longer **in that place, its aroma does not go forth.**

אָמַר רַבִּי אוֹשַׁעְיָא [9]**Rabbi Oshaya said:** According to **Resh Lakish, to what may** Noah **be compared?** [10]**To a flask of foliatum** — an aromatic oil prepared from the leaves of spikenard — **which is in a place of filth.** [11]While it is **in that place, its aroma goes forth** despite the foul smell of its surroundings; **all the more so,** then, does its aroma go forth when it is **in a place of spices.**

וַיִּמַח [12]The verse states (Genesis 7:23): **"And He destroyed every living thing that was on the face of the earth,** both man, and cattle, and creeping things, and the birds of the Heaven." [13]The Gemara asks: **If man sinned, how did the cattle sin?** [14]**A Tanna taught** a Baraita **in the name of Rabbi Yehoshua ben Korḥah: "This is like a person who erected a bridal canopy for his son, and prepared all kinds of food** with which

[1]וְאִיכָּא דְּאָמְרִי: לֹא יָפֶה עָשִׂיתִי שֶׁתִּקַּנְתִּי לָהֶם קְבָרוֹת בָּאָרֶץ. [2]כְּתִיב הָכָא: ״וַיִּנָּחֶם״. [3]וּכְתִיב הָתָם: ״וַיִּנָּחֶם ה׳ עַל הָרָעָה אֲשֶׁר דִּבֶּר לַעֲשׂוֹת לְעַמּוֹ״.

[4]״אֵלֶּה תּוֹלְדוֹת נֹחַ: [נֹחַ אִישׁ צַדִּיק תָּמִים הָיָה בְּדֹרֹתָיו״]. [5]אָמַר רַבִּי יוֹחָנָן: בְּדוֹרוֹתָיו, וְלֹא בְּדוֹרוֹת אֲחֵרִים. [6]וְרֵישׁ לָקִישׁ אָמַר: בְּדוֹרוֹתָיו, כָּל שֶׁכֵּן בְּדוֹרוֹת אֲחֵרִים.

[7]אָמַר רַבִּי חֲנִינָא: מָשָׁל דְּרַבִּי יוֹחָנָן לְמָה הַדָּבָר דּוֹמֶה — לְחָבִית שֶׁל יַיִן שֶׁהָיְתָה מוּנַּחַת בְּמַרְתֵּף שֶׁל חוֹמֶץ, [8]בִּמְקוֹמָהּ — רֵיחָהּ נוֹדֵף, שֶׁלֹּא בִּמְקוֹמָהּ — אֵין רֵיחָהּ נוֹדֵף.

[9]אָמַר רַבִּי אוֹשַׁעְיָא: מָשָׁל דְּרֵישׁ לָקִישׁ לְמָה הַדָּבָר דּוֹמֶה — לִצְלוֹחִית שֶׁל פְּלְיָיטוֹן שֶׁהָיְתָה מוּנַּחַת בִּמְקוֹם הַטִּנּוֹפֶת, [10]בִּמְקוֹמָהּ — רֵיחָהּ נוֹדֵף, [11]וְכָל שֶׁכֵּן בִּמְקוֹם הַבּוֹסֶם.

[12]״וַיִּמַח אֶת כָּל הַיְקוּם אֲשֶׁר עַל פְּנֵי הָאֲדָמָה״. [13]אִם אָדָם חָטָא, בְּהֵמָה מֶה חָטְאָה? [14]תָּנָא מִשּׁוּם רַבִּי יְהוֹשֻׁעַ בֶּן קָרְחָה: ״מָשָׁל לְאָדָם שֶׁעָשָׂה

LITERAL TRANSLATION

[1]And some say: I did not do well that I prepared graves for them in the earth. [2]It is written here: "And the Lord repented." [3]And it is written there: "And the Lord repented of the evil which He thought to do to His people."

[4]"These are the generations of Noah: Noah was a just man, and perfect in his generations." [5]Rabbi Yoḥanan said: In his generations, but not in other generations. [6]And Resh Lakish said: In his generations, [and] all the more so in other generations.

[7]Rabbi Ḥanina said: To what may that of Rabbi Yoḥanan be compared — to a barrel of wine which lay in a storeroom for vinegar. [8]In its place — its smell goes forth. Not in its place — its smell does not go forth.

[9]Rabbi Oshaya said: To what may that of Resh Lakish be compared — to a flask of foliatum which lay in a place of filth. [10]In its place — its smell goes forth. [11]And all the more so, in a place of spices.

[12]"And He destroyed every living thing that was on the face of the earth." [13]If man sinned, how did the cattle sin? [14][A Tanna] taught in the name of Rabbi Yehoshua ben Korḥah: "It is like a man who erected

RASHI

לא יפה עשיתי — דאפשר היו חוזרין. **כל שכן** — אילו הוה בדורות אחרים היה צדיק יותר. **פלייטון** — בושם שריחו נודף, ואינו אפרסמון.

NOTES

inundating the world immediately with a flood, He introduced death into the world, and prepared graves in the earth, allowing mankind to die off gradually. Thus a single man could emerge, survive the flood, and make a new beginning.

TRANSLATION AND COMMENTARY

to celebrate his wedding. [1]**A few days** before the wedding, however, **the son died, and** the father **stood up and overturned the bridal canopy,** [2]**saying: 'I did everything only for my son.** [3]**Now that he is dead, why do I need a bridal canopy?'** [4]**So, too, the Holy One, blessed be He, said: I created the cattle and the beasts only for man.** [5]**Now that man has sinned** and will therefore be destroyed, **why do I need cattle and beasts?'"**

מִכֹּל [6]The verse states (Genesis 7:22): **"Of all that was on the dry land, died."** Only the creatures on the dry land were destroyed, **but not the fish in the sea.**

דָּרַשׁ רַבִּי יוֹסֵי [7]**Rabbi Yose from Caesarea expounded: What is** meant by **the verse that states** (Job 24:18): [8]**"He was light upon the waters; their portion is cursed in the earth"?** [9]**This** verse **teaches that the righteous Noah rebuked** the people of his generation **and said to them: "Repent, for if not, the Holy One, blessed be He, will bring the flood upon you, and cause your corpses to float on the water like bottles** filled with air, [10]**as the verse states: 'He was light upon the waters.'"** [11]**And moreover, a curse will be taken from them to all who come into the world,** for people will curse each other, "May you be like the generation of the flood," [12]**as the verse states: "Their portion is cursed in the earth."** The verse cited above continues (Job 24:18): [13]**"No treader turns toward their vineyards."** [14]**This teaches that** the people of Noah's generation **used to clear paths in the vineyards,** meaning that they would walk along crooked paths like those found in vineyards. When Noah rebuked them, [15]**they said to him: "Who prevents** the flood from coming right now?" [16]Noah **said to them: "I have one pigeon** — Methuselah — **that must be removed from you** before the flood comes and inundates the world. Methuselah must first die a

חוּפָּה לִבְנוֹ, וְהִתְקִין מִכָּל מִינֵי סְעוּדָה. [1]לְיָמִים מֵת בְּנוֹ, עָמַד (וּבִלְבֵּל) [וּפִזֵּר] אֶת חוּפָּתוֹ. [2]אָמַר: ׳כְּלוּם עָשִׂיתִי אֶלָּא בִּשְׁבִיל בְּנִי. [3]עַכְשָׁיו שֶׁמֵּת, חוּפָּה לָמָּה לִי? [4]אַף הַקָּדוֹשׁ בָּרוּךְ הוּא אָמַר: ׳כְּלוּם בָּרָאתִי בְּהֵמָה וְחַיָּה אֶלָּא בִּשְׁבִיל אָדָם. [5]עַכְשָׁיו שֶׁאָדָם חוֹטֵא, בְּהֵמָה וְחַיָּה לָמָּה לִי׳ ״?

[6]״מִכֹּל אֲשֶׁר בֶּחָרָבָה מֵתוּ״ — וְלֹא דָּגִים שֶׁבַּיָּם.

[7]דָּרַשׁ רַבִּי יוֹסֵי דְּמִן קֵסָרִי: מַאי דִּכְתִיב: [8]״קַל הוּא עַל פְּנֵי מַיִם; תְּקֻלַּל חֶלְקָתָם בָּאָרֶץ״? [9]מְלַמֵּד שֶׁהָיָה נֹחַ הַצַּדִּיק מוֹכִיחַ בָּהֶם וְאוֹמֵר לָהֶם: ״עֲשׂוּ תְּשׁוּבָה, וְאִם לָאו הַקָּדוֹשׁ בָּרוּךְ הוּא מֵבִיא עֲלֵיכֶם אֶת הַמַּבּוּל, וּמַקְפֶּה נִבְלַתְכֶם עַל הַמַּיִם כְּזִיקִין, [10]שֶׁנֶּאֱמַר: ׳קַל הוּא עַל פְּנֵי מַיִם׳״. [11]וְלֹא עוֹד אֶלָּא שֶׁלּוֹקְחִין מֵהֶם קְלָלָה לְכָל בָּאֵי עוֹלָם, [12]שֶׁנֶּאֱמַר: ״תְּקֻלַּל חֶלְקָתָם בָּאָרֶץ״. [13]״לֹא יִפְנֶה דֶּרֶךְ כְּרָמִים״. [14]מְלַמֵּד שֶׁהָיוּ מְפַנִּים דֶּרֶךְ כְּרָמִים. [15]אָמְרוּ לוֹ: ״וּמִי מְעַכֵּב״? [16]אָמַר לָהֶם: ״פְּרֵידָה אַחַת יֵשׁ לִי לְהוֹצִיא

LITERAL TRANSLATION

a bridal canopy for his son, and prepared all kinds of food. [1]After a few days, his son died, [and] he stood up and overturned his bridal canopy. [2]He said: 'I did nothing except for my son. [3]Now that he has died, why do I need a bridal canopy?' [4]So, too, the Holy One, blessed be He, said: 'I did not create cattle and beasts, except for man. [5]Now that man has sinned, why do I need cattle and beasts?' "

[6]"Of all that was on the dry land, died" — but not the fish in the sea.

[7]Rabbi Yose from Caesarea expounded: What is that which is written: [8]"He was light upon the waters; their portion is cursed in the earth"? [9]This teaches that the righteous Noah rebuked them and said to them: "Repent, and if not, the Holy One, blessed be He, will bring the flood upon you, and cause your corpses to float on the water like bottles, [10]as it is stated: 'He was light upon the waters.'" [11]And moreover, they will take from them a curse to all who come into the world, [12]as it is stated: "Their portion is cursed in the earth." [13]"No treader turns toward their vineyards." [14]This teaches that they would clear paths in the vineyards. [15]They said to him: "Who prevents [it]?" [16]He said to them: "I have one pigeon to remove

RASHI

מקיפה — מציף, כמו ״ויצף הברזל״ דמתרגמינן וקפא (מלכים ב, ו). כזיקין — נודות. לא יפנה דרך כרמים אמרו לו ומי מעכב — [מיד], שאינו עושה אם יש בידו כח לעשות כך. [פרידה] אחת יש לי להוציא מכם — מתושלח הצדיק ימות קודם, ולא יהיה נדון עמכם.

NOTES

לֹא יִפְנֶה דֶּרֶךְ כְּרָמִים **We will not clear the path of the vineyards.** Some explain that the members of the generation of the flood used to trample through other people's vineyards, without showing any concern about the damage that they were causing (see *Rabbi Ya'akov Emden*). Most understand this as a metaphor. According to *Rashi*, the "path of the vineyards" is a corrupt thorn-filled path. According to *Ramah*, it is the correct path, from which the generation of the flood veered away. The Jerusalem Talmud appears to have understood this as a euphemism for the unnatural intercourse in which the generation of the flood engaged.

פְּרֵידָה אַחַת יֵשׁ לִי **I have one pigeon.** *Ramah* had a reading of the Gemara, according to which it was Methuselah who

TRANSLATION AND COMMENTARY

natural death, so that he will not perish in the flood along with the rest of the generation." [108B] [1]They said to him: **"If so, we will not abandon the paths of the vineyards,** but rather we will continue in our wicked ways."

דָּרַשׁ רָבָא [2]**Rava expounded: What is** meant by **the verse that states** (Job 12:5): **"Contempt** [בּוּז] **is ready in the thought of him that is at ease, for those that are ruined** [לַפִּיד], **that slip with their feet"?** [3]**This** verse **teaches that the righteous Noah rebuked** the wicked people of his generation, hoping to make them repent. He **said things to them that were as harsh as torches** [לַפִּידִים], **but they** just **sneered** [בּוֹזִים] **at him, saying: "Old man!** [4]**Why** are you building **this ark?"** [5]Noah **said to them: "The Holy One, blessed be He,** is going to **bring a flood upon you."** [6]His wicked contemporaries **said** to him: **"What** type **of flood** is God planning to bring upon us? [7]**If** He plans to bring upon us **a flood of fire,** we are not worried for **we have something called** *alita* which will protect us from the flames. [8]**And if He** plans to **bring** upon us **a flood of water,** we have nothing to fear, for **if** He is going to **bring** the floodwaters **from the ground, we have iron plates with which we can pave the ground.** [9]**And if He brings** the floodwaters down **from Heaven, we have something called** *ekev*, [10]**and some say it is called** *ekesh*, that will absorb the water." [11]Noah **said to them:** "If God so desires, **He can bring** floodwaters **from between the heels of your feet,** [12]**as the verse states: 'Ready for those that slip with their feet.'"**

תַּנְיָא [13]**It was taught** in a Baraita: **"The floodwaters** brought upon Noah's contemporaries **were as**

מִכֶּם״. [108B] [1]״אִם כֵּן לֹא נְפַנֶּה דֶּרֶךְ כְּרָמִים״.

[2]דָּרַשׁ רָבָא: מַאי דִּכְתִיב: ״לַפִּיד בּוּז לְעַשְׁתּוּת שַׁאֲנָן נָכוֹן לְמוֹעֲדֵי רָגֶל״? [3]מְלַמֵּד שֶׁהָיָה נֹחַ הַצַּדִּיק מוֹכִיחַ אוֹתָם, וְאָמַר לָהֶם דְּבָרִים שֶׁהֵם קָשִׁים כַּלַּפִּידִים, וְהָיוּ בּוֹזִים [מְבַזִּין] אוֹתוֹ, אָמְרוּ לוֹ: ״זָקֵן! [4]תֵּיבָה זוֹ — לָמָּה״? [5]אָמַר לָהֶם: ״הַקָּדוֹשׁ בָּרוּךְ הוּא מֵבִיא עֲלֵיכֶם אֶת הַמַּבּוּל״. [6]אָמְרוּ: ״מַבּוּל שֶׁל מָה? [7]אִם מַבּוּל שֶׁל אֵשׁ, יֵשׁ לָנוּ דָּבָר אַחֵר וַעֲלִיתָה שְׁמָהּ. [8]וְאִם שֶׁל מַיִם הוּא מֵבִיא — אִם מִן הָאָרֶץ הוּא מֵבִיא, יֵשׁ לָנוּ עֲשָׁשִׁיּוֹת שֶׁל בַּרְזֶל שֶׁאָנוּ מְחַפִּין בָּהֶם אֶת הָאָרֶץ, [9]וְאִם מִן הַשָּׁמַיִם הוּא מֵבִיא, יֵשׁ לָנוּ דָּבָר וְעֶקֶב שְׁמוֹ, [10]וְאָמְרִי לָהּ עֵקֶשׁ שְׁמוֹ״. [11]אָמַר לָהֶם: ״הוּא מֵבִיא מִבֵּין עִקְבֵי רַגְלֵיכֶם, [12]שֶׁנֶּאֱמַר: ׳נָכוֹן לְמוֹעֲדֵי רָגֶל׳״.

[13]תַּנְיָא: ״מֵימֵי הַמַּבּוּל קָשִׁים

LITERAL TRANSLATION

from you." [108B] [1]"If so, we will not clear the paths of the vineyards."

[2]Rava expounded: What is that which is written: "Contempt is ready in the thought of him that is at ease, for those that are ruined, that slip with their feet"? [3]This teaches that the righteous Noah rebuked them, and said things to them that were as harsh as torches, and they sneered at him, [and] said to him: "Old man! [4]This ark — why?" [5]He said to them: "The Holy One, blessed be He, will bring a flood upon you." [6]They said: "A flood of what? [7]If a flood of fire, we have something else, and it is called *alita*. [8]And if He will bring [a flood] of water — if He brings [it] from the ground, we have iron plates with which we can pave the ground, [9]and if He brings [it] from Heaven, we have something, and it is called *ekev*, [10]and some say it is called *ekesh*." [11]He said to them: "He will bring [it] from between the heels of your feet, [12]as it is stated: 'Ready for those that slip with their feet.'"

[13]It was taught: "The waters of the flood were as thick

RASHI

אם כן לא נפנה דרך כרמים – [כלומר לא נסור ולא נפנה את דרך הכרמים], אלא כל שעה נלך בהם, כלומר, אם כן לא נלך דרך כבושה ולא נחזור מסורינו אלא נלך ונקלקל השורה, דרכים משובשים בקוצים ודרקנים כעין שבילי כרמים. **לעשתות** – כמו עשתונות, שיושבין שאנן וחושבין מחשבות רעות. **עליתה שמה** – אין אש שולט בה. **מבין עקבי רגליכם** – בשכבת זרע שלכם יכול למחות אתכם, לישנא אחרינא: מבין עקבי רגליכם – מן הרגל יוצא ממש מים אם היה רוצה, ואי אפשר לכפות רגליכם בעששיות.

NOTES

delivered the rebuke. According to this, "I have one pigeon" refers to Noah. God was waiting for Noah to be born and complete all that had to be done before the flood.

לַפִּיד בּוּז Contempt is ready. The word לַפִּיד, whose meaning is obscure in the verse in Job, ordinarily means a torch. "Words that are as harsh as torches" are harsh reproaches indeed. The following words in the verse from Job, לְעַשְׁתּוּת שַׁאֲנָן, are understood here as referring to the "iron plates (עֲשָׁשִׁיּוֹת)" with which the "complacent" (שַׁאֲנָן) members of the generation wished to pave the ground, and thus prevent the floodwaters from washing them away (*Maharsha*).

עֲלִיתָה שְׁמָהּ It is called *alita*. Some identify the *alita* with the salamander. In ancient times, it was thought that someone who anointed himself with the blood of a salamander became fireproof (see *Arukh*).

עֶקֶב שְׁמוֹ It is called *ekev*. According to the Geonim, *ekev* is a kind of sponge.

[1]כִּשְׁכְבַת זֶרַע, שֶׁנֶּאֱמַר: ״נָכוֹן לְמוֹעֲדֵי רָגֶל״. [2]אָמַר רַב חִסְדָּא: בְּרוֹתְחִין קִלְקְלוּ בַּעֲבֵירָה, וּבְרוֹתְחִין נִידּוֹנוּ. [3]כְּתִיב הָכָא: ״וַיָּשֹׁכּוּ הַמָּיִם״, [4]וּכְתִיב הָתָם: ״וַחֲמַת הַמֶּלֶךְ שָׁכָכָה״. [5]״וַיְהִי לְשִׁבְעַת הַיָּמִים וּמֵי הַמַּבּוּל הָיוּ עַל הָאָרֶץ״, [6]מַה טִּיבָם שֶׁל שִׁבְעַת הַיָּמִים? [7]אָמַר רַב: אֵלּוּ יְמֵי אֲבֵילוּת שֶׁל מְתוּשֶׁלַח. [8]לְלַמֶּדְךָ שֶׁהֶסְפֵּדָן שֶׁל צַדִּיקִים מְעַכְּבִין אֶת הַפּוּרְעָנוּת לָבֹא. [9]דָּבָר אַחֵר: ״לְשִׁבְעַת״ — שֶׁשִּׁינָּה עֲלֵיהֶם הַקָּדוֹשׁ בָּרוּךְ הוּא סֵדֶר בְּרֵאשִׁית, [10]שֶׁהָיְתָה חַמָּה יוֹצֵאת מִמַּעֲרָב וְשׁוֹקַעַת בַּמִּזְרָח. [11]דָּבָר אַחֵר: שֶׁקָּבַע לָהֶם הַקָּדוֹשׁ בָּרוּךְ הוּא זְמַן גָּדוֹל, [12]וְאַחַר כָּךְ זְמַן קָטָן. [13]דָּבָר אַחֵר: ״לְשִׁבְעַת הַיָּמִים״ — שֶׁהִטְעִימָם מֵעֵין הָעוֹלָם הַבָּא, [14]כְּדֵי שֶׁיֵּדְעוּ מָה טּוֹבָה מָנְעוּ מֵהֶן. [15]״מִכֹּל הַבְּהֵמָה הַטְּהוֹרָה תִּקַּח לְךָ שִׁבְעָה שִׁבְעָה אִישׁ

LITERAL TRANSLATION

as semen, [1]as it is stated: "Ready for those that slip with their feet."

[2]Rav Ḥisda said: With heat they sinned, and with heat they were punished. [3]It is written here: "And the waters were assuaged." [4]And it is written there: "Then the king's wrath was assuaged."

[5]"And it came to pass after seven days, that the waters of the flood were upon the earth." [6]What is the nature of [these] seven days? [7]Rav said: These are the days of mourning for Methuselah. [8]This teaches you that eulogies for the righteous prevent tribulations from coming.

[9]Another explanation: "After seven" — the Holy One, blessed be He, changed the order of creation for them, [10]so that the sun rose in the West, and set in the East.

[11]Another explanation: The Holy One, blessed be He, set a long time for them, [12]and afterwards a short time.

[13]Another explanation: "After seven" — He gave them a taste like the World to Come, [14]so that they would know what good He withheld from them.

[15]"Of every clean beast you shall take to you by sevens, male

TRANSLATION AND COMMENTARY

thick as semen, [1]**as the verse states: "Ready for those that slip with their feet,"** the word "feet" serving here as a euphemism for the penis.

אָמַר רַב חִסְדָּא [2]**Rav Ḥisda said: With** the **heat** of passion **they sinned,** as the verse states (Genesis 6:12): "For all flesh had corrupted its way upon the earth," **and with hot** floodwaters **they were punished.** How do we know that the floodwaters were hot? [3]**Here, the verse states** (Genesis 8:1): **"And the waters were assuaged** [וַיָּשֹׁכּוּ]." [4]**And, elsewhere, the verse states** (Esther 7:10): **"Then the king's wrath** [חֲמַת] **was assuaged** [שָׁכָכָה]."

וַיְהִי לְשִׁבְעַת [5]The verse states (Genesis 7:10): **"And it came to pass after seven days, that the waters of the flood were upon the earth."** [6]**What is the nature of these seven** extra **days** between Noah's entry into the ark and the onset of the flood? [7]**Rav said: These are the** seven **days of mourning for** the righteous man **Methuselah.** [8]**This teaches you that eulogies for a righteous** person **prevent tribulations from coming** to the world.

דָּבָר אַחֵר [9]The Gemara suggests **another explanation: "After seven"** — during the period of the flood, **the Holy One, blessed be He, changed the natural order** that had been established during the seven days of creation, [10]**so that the sun rose in the West, and set in the East.**

דָּבָר אַחֵר [11]The Gemara offers yet **another explanation:** First **the Holy One, blessed be He, set a long** period of **time** for repentance **for** Noah's contemporaries — a hundred-and-twenty years (Genesis 6:3) — [12]**and afterwards** when He saw that they continued to sin, He gave them **a short time** extra — another week — hoping that they might still repent.

דָּבָר אַחֵר [13]The Gemara proposes **one** final **explanation: "After seven"** — God **gave** Noah's generation **a taste of the World to Come** — the "seventh day," following the "six days" of human history — [14]**so that they would know what good He withheld from them** on account of their sins.

מִכֹּל הַבְּהֵמָה [15]The verse states (Genesis 7:2): **"Of every clean beast you shall take to you by sevens, male**

RASHI

בשכבת זרע — רותחין ועבין, היו עבין לא גרסינן ופירוש הוא. **חמת המלך שככה** — נחה מרתחו, הכי נמי מים נחו מרותחן. **סדרי בראשית** — והיינו לשבעת הימים — סדר שבעת ימי בראשית שינה להם. **זמן קטן אחר זמן גדול** — בתחילה אמר להן והיו ימיו מאה ועשרים שנה, כשעבר זמן זה ולא שבו לטובה חזר וקבע להם זמן קטן.

NOTES

מַה טִּיבָם שֶׁל שִׁבְעַת הַיָּמִים? **What is the nature of these seven days?** *Midrash Tanḥuma* explains that these seven days are the seven days of mourning that God set aside for Himself in order to grieve over the world that He was about to destroy.

LANGUAGE

גּוּלָמִישׁ *Gulamish.* The source of this word is apparently the Persian *gulamus,* meaning "a type of willow" (*Salix balchica*).

TRANSLATION AND COMMENTARY

and female (literally, 'man and wife')." [1]The Gemara asks: **Does** the concept of **marriage** apply to **a beast?** [2]**Rabbi Shmuel bar Nahmani said in the name of Rabbi Yonatan:** By stressing that the beasts were to be taken in as couples, the verse teaches that Noah was only to bring in animals **that had not been used for the sin** of mating with beasts of other kinds.

מְנָא יָדַע [3]The Gemara asks: **How was** Noah **to know** which animals were fit? [4]**Rav Ḥisda said:** Noah **passed** the animals **before the ark.** [5]**Whichever animal the ark accepted, it was clear that it had not been used for sin.** [6]**And whichever** animal **the ark did not accept** inside, **it was clear that it had been used for sin.** [7]**Rabbi Abbahu said:** Noah only brought into the ark **those** animals **that came** to him **on their own.**

עֲשֵׂה לְךָ [8]The verse states (Genesis 6:14): **"Make you an ark of gopher wood."** [9]**What is "gopher wood"?** [10]**Rav Adda said: The Sages of the School of Rabbi Shela said:** [11]**This** refers to the tree otherwise known as ***mavligah.*** [12]**And some say:** This refers to the tree called ***gulamish.***

צֹהַר תַּעֲשֶׂה לַתֵּבָה [13]The verse states (Genesis 6:16): **"A window [צֹהַר] shall you make for the ark."** [14]**Rabbi Yoḥanan said:** The word צֹהַר, translated here as "window," may also be understood in the sense of "noon [צָהֳרַיִם]." **The Holy One, blessed be He,** [15]**said to Noah: "Place precious stones and jewels** that are luminescent **in** the ark, **so that they** will **give you light** that is as bright **as noon.**

וְאֶל אַמָּה [16]The same verse continues (Genesis 6:16): **"And to a cubit shall you finish it above."** [17]The ark should be broad at the bottom and narrow at the top, **for in that way it will stand** straight in the water.

תַּחְתִּיִּם שְׁנִיִּם [18]The same verse concludes (Genesis 6:16): **"With lower, second, and third stories shall you make it."** [19]**A Sage taught** a Baraita: [20]**"The lower story** was set aside **for dung, the middle story** was intended **for the beasts** that Noah took with him into the ark, and **the upper story** was designated **for man** — Noah and his family."

וְאִשְׁתּוֹ״. [1]אִישׁוּת לִבְהֵמָה מִי אִית לַהּ? [2]אָמַר רַבִּי שְׁמוּאֵל בַּר נַחְמָנִי אָמַר רַבִּי יוֹנָתָן: מֵאוֹתָם שֶׁלֹּא נֶעֶבְדָה בָּהֶם עֲבֵירָה.

[3]מְנָא יָדַע? [4]אָמַר רַב חִסְדָּא: שֶׁהֶעֱבִירָן לִפְנֵי הַתֵּיבָה. [5]כָּל שֶׁהַתֵּיבָה קוֹלַטְתּוֹ, בְּיָדוּעַ שֶׁלֹּא נֶעֶבְדָה בָּהֶם עֲבֵירָה. [6]וְכָל שֶׁאֵין הַתֵּיבָה קוֹלַטְתּוֹ — בְּיָדוּעַ שֶׁנֶּעֶבְדָה בָהּ עֲבֵירָה. [7]רַבִּי אַבָּהוּ אָמַר: מֵאוֹתָן הַבָּאִין מֵאֵילֵיהֶן.

[8]״עֲשֵׂה לְךָ תֵּבַת עֲצֵי גֹפֶר״. [9]מַאי גּוֹפֶר? [10]אָמַר רַב אַדָּא: אָמְרִי דְּבֵי רַבִּי שֵׁילָא: [11]זוֹ מַבְלִיגָה. [12]וְאָמְרִי לַהּ: גּוּלָמִישׁ. [13]״צֹהַר תַּעֲשֶׂה לַתֵּבָה״. [14]אָמַר רַבִּי יוֹחָנָן: [15]אָמַר לוֹ הַקָּדוֹשׁ בָּרוּךְ הוּא לְנֹחַ: ״קְבַע בָּהּ אֲבָנִים טוֹבוֹת וּמַרְגָּלִיּוֹת, כְּדֵי שֶׁיְּהִיוּ מְאִירוֹת לָכֶם כַּצָּהֳרַיִם״. [16]״וְאֶל אַמָּה תְּכַלֶּנָּה מִלְמַעְלָה״. [17]דִּבְהָכִי [הוּא] דְּקָיְימָא.

[18]״תַּחְתִּיִּם שְׁנִיִּם וּשְׁלִשִׁים תַּעֲשֶׂהָ״. [19]תָּנָא: [20]״תַּחְתִּיִּים לַזֶּבֶל, אֶמְצָעִיִּים לַבְּהֵמָה, עֶלְיוֹנִים לָאָדָם״.

LITERAL TRANSLATION

and female." [1]Does a beast have marriage? [2]Rabbi Shmuel bar Nahmani said in the name of Rabbi Yonatan: From those that had not been used for sin.

[3]How did he know? [4]Rav Ḥisda said: He passed them before the ark. [5]Whichever [animal] the ark accepted, it was clear that it had not been used for sin. [6]And whichever the ark did not accept, it was clear that it had been used for sin. [7]Rabbi Abbahu said: From those who came on their own.

[8]"Make you an ark of gopher wood." [9]What is gopher? [10]Rav Adda said: [The Sages] of the School of Rabbi Shela said: [11]This is *mavligah.* [12]And some say: *Gulamish.*

[13]"A window shall you make for the ark." [14]Rabbi Yoḥanan said: The Holy One, blessed be He, [15]said to Noah: "Place in it precious stones and jewels, so that they give you light [as bright] as noon."

[16]"And to a cubit shall you finish it above." [17]For in that way it will stand.

[18]"With lower, second, and third stories shall you make it." [19][A Sage] taught: [20]"The lower story for dung, the middle story for beasts, the upper story for man."

RASHI

אישות לבהמה מי אית ליה — נקבה אחת נשכבת לכמה זכרים ואין זו אישות. **שלא נעבדה בהן עבירה** — שלא נזקקו אלא לבן זוגם. **מבליגה** — עץ הוא.

NOTES

אֲבָנִים טוֹבוֹת Precious stones. The Jerusalem Talmud explains that Noah brought those precious stones into the ark in order to distinguish between day and night, for the stones would shine more brightly during the night.

TRANSLATION AND COMMENTARY

וַיְשַׁלַּח אֶת הָעֹרֵב [1]The verse states (Genesis 8:7): **"And he sent forth the raven,** which went forth to and fro, until the waters were dried up from the earth." [2]**Resh Lakish said: The raven gave Noah** what it considered to be **an irrefutable argument** why it should not be sent off in search of dry land. [3]The raven **said to** Noah: **"Your master,** God, **hates me, and you** also **hate me.** [4]**Your master hates me,** for He instructed you to take in **seven** of each **clean animal,** but only **two of** each **unclean** animal. [5]**And you** also **hate me, for you leave** alone those **species** from which you took in **seven** members, **and send off** in search of dry land **a species** from which you took in only **two** members. [6]Now, **if the Angel of Heat or the Angel of Cold** were to **meet me,** and cause me harm, **will not the world be lacking one creature?** [7]**Or perhaps you are interested in my mate,** the female raven, for yourself?" [8]Noah **said to** the raven: **"Wicked one!** [9]If my wife, who **is** ordinarily **permitted to me, was** nevertheless **forbidden to me** during our stay in the ark, then **all the more so** would beasts and birds be which **are** always **forbidden to me,** and are certainly forbidden to me in the ark!" [10]The Gemara asks: **From where do we know that** those who entered the ark **were forbidden** to engage in sexual intercourse during the period of the flood? [11]**For the verse** instructing Noah to enter into the ark **states** (Genesis 6:18): **"And you shall come into the ark, you, and your sons, and your wife, and your sons' wives with you,"** separating the men, Noah and his sons, from the women, Noah's wife and his sons' wives. [12]**And the verse** instructing Noah to leave the ark **states** (Genesis 8:16): **"Go out of the ark, you, and your wife, and your sons, and your sons' wives with you,"** joining the men with their wives. [13]**And Rabbi Yohanan said: From here** the Rabbis **inferred** that those who entered the ark **were forbidden to engage in sexual intercourse** during the flood.

תָּנוּ רַבָּנַן [14]**Our Rabbis taught** the following Baraita: "The following **three** violated the prohibition and **mated in the ark, and all of them were punished** for their transgression: **A dog, a raven, and Ham** the son

[1]״וַיְשַׁלַּח אֶת הָעֹרֵב״. [2]אָמַר רֵישׁ לָקִישׁ: תְּשׁוּבָה נִיצַּחַת הֱשִׁיבוֹ עוֹרֵב לְנֹחַ. [3]אָמַר לוֹ: ״רַבְּךָ שׂוֹנְאֵנִי וְאַתָּה שְׂנֵאתַנִי. [4]רַבְּךָ שׂוֹנְאֵנִי — מִן הַטְּהוֹרִין שִׁבְעָה, מִן הַטְּמֵאִים שְׁנַיִם. [5]וְאַתָּה שְׂנֵאתַנִי — שֶׁאַתָּה מַנִּיחַ מִמִּין שִׁבְעָה וְשׁוֹלֵחַ מִמִּין שְׁנַיִם. [6]אִם פּוֹגֵעַ בִּי שַׂר חַמָּה אוֹ שַׂר צִנָּה, לֹא נִמְצָא עוֹלָם חָסֵר בְּרִיָּה אַחַת? [7]אוֹ שֶׁמָּא לְאִשְׁתִּי אַתָּה צָרִיךְ״? [8]אָמַר לוֹ: ״רָשָׁע! [9]בַּמּוּתָּר לִי נֶאֱסַר לִי; בַּנֶּאֱסָר לִי לֹא כָּל שֶׁכֵּן״. [10]וּמְנָלַן דְּנֶאֱסְרוּ? [11]דִּכְתִיב: ״וּבָאתָ אֶל הַתֵּבָה אַתָּה וּבָנֶיךָ וְאִשְׁתְּךָ וּנְשֵׁי בָנֶיךָ אִתָּךְ״. [12]וּכְתִיב: ״צֵא מִן הַתֵּבָה אַתָּה וְאִשְׁתְּךָ וּבָנֶיךָ וּנְשֵׁי בָנֶיךָ אִתָּךְ״. [13]וְאָמַר רַבִּי יוֹחָנָן: מִיכָּן אָמְרוּ שֶׁנֶּאֶסְרוּ בְּתַשְׁמִישׁ הַמִּטָּה.

[14]תָּנוּ רַבָּנַן: ״שְׁלֹשָׁה שִׁמְּשׁוּ בַּתֵּיבָה, וְכוּלָּם לָקוּ: כֶּלֶב,

LITERAL TRANSLATION

[1]"And he sent forth the raven." [2]Resh Lakish said: The raven gave Noah an irrefutable argument. [3]It said to him: "Your master hates me, and you hate me. [4]Your master hates me — from the clean [animals] seven, from the unclean, two. [5]And you hate me — for you leave the species of seven, and send off from a species of two. [6]If the Angel of Heat or the Angel of Cold meets me, will not the world be lacking one creature? [7]Or perhaps you need my mate?" [8]He said to it: "Wicked one! [9]That which is permitted to me was forbidden to me; that which is forbidden to me, all the more so!" [10]And from where do we [know] that they were forbidden? [11]For it is written: "And you shall come into the ark, you, and your sons, and your wife, and your sons' wives with you." [12]And it is written: "Go out of the ark, you, and your wife, and your sons, and your sons' wives with you." [13]And Rabbi Yoḥanan said: From here they said that they were forbidden [to engage] in sexual intercourse.

[14]Our Rabbis taught: "Three mated in the ark, and all of them were punished: A dog,

RASHI

במותר לי — אפילו באשתי אני אסור, (בני נח — שם חם ויפת). **רק** — רוקק זרע מפיו לפיה של נקבה.

NOTES

בַּמּוּתָּר לִי נֶאֱסַר לִי That which is permitted to me was forbidden to me. *Maharam Yaffe* explains the passage in a slightly different manner: The male raven was concerned that Noah might mate a bird of another species with the female raven. Thus, Noah said to him: If that which is ordinarily permitted to him — mating animals of the same species — is now forbidden to him in the ark, then all the more so is that which is ordinarily forbidden to him — crossbreeding animals of different species — now forbidden.

TRANSLATION AND COMMENTARY

of Noah. [1]**The dog** was punished so that thereafter it **remained bound** to its mate during intercourse; **the raven** was punished so that thereafter it **spat** its seed into its mate's mouth; **and Ham was punished** with a change **in** the color of **his skin** [Ham was the father of Kush, the father of the black race]."

וַיְשַׁלַּח [2]The verse states (Genesis 8:8): **"And he sent forth the dove from him, to see if the waters were abated."** [3]**Rabbi Yirmeyah said: From here** we learn **that the dwelling place of clean birds is** in close proximity to that **of the righteous,** for Noah sent the dove "from him."

וְהִנֵּה עֲלֵה [4]The verse states (Genesis 8:11): **"And, lo, in her mouth was an olive leaf plucked off** [*taraf*]." [5]**Rabbi Elazar said:** The olive branch shows the dove's piety, for **the dove said to the Holy One, blessed be He: "Master of the Universe! Let my food be as bitter as an olive,** just as long as it is **placed in Your hand, rather than sweet as honey, and placed in the hand of flesh and blood.** I am ready to eat bitter food, provided that You are my source of sustenance, and not man." [6]The Gemara asks: **From where may we infer that** the term *taraf* **bears the sense of food?** [7]The Gemara explains: **For the verse states** (Proverbs 30:8): **"Feed me** [*hatrifeni*] **with my allotted portion."**

לְמִשְׁפְּחֹתֵיהֶם [8]The verse states (Genesis 8:19): **"After their kinds, they went out of the ark."** [9]**Rabbi Yoḥanan said:** In some cases, only **their kinds** went out of the ark, **but not** the animals **themselves,** for some of them died in the ark.

אָמַר רַב חָנָא בַּר בִּיזְנָא [10]**Rav Ḥana bar Bizna said:** Abraham's servant **Eliezer** once **said to Shem the elder,** the son of Noah: [11]**"The verse states** (Genesis 8:19): **'After their kinds, they went out of the ark.' Where were**

LITERAL TRANSLATION

a raven, and Ham. [1]The dog was bound, the raven spat, [and] Ham was punished in his skin."

[2]"And he sent forth the dove from him, to see if the waters were abated." [3]Rabbi Yirmeyah said: From here [we learn] that the dwelling place of clean birds is with the righteous.

[4]"And, lo, in her mouth was an olive leaf plucked off." [5]Rabbi Elazar said: The dove said before the Holy One, blessed be He: "Master of the Universe! Let my food be as bitter as an olive but placed in Your hand, and let it not be sweet as honey and placed in the hand of flesh and blood." [6]From where [may we] infer that [the word] *taraf* bears the sense of food? [7]As it is written: "Feed me with my allotted portion."

[8]"After their kinds, they went out of the ark." [9]Rabbi Yoḥanan said: Their kinds, but not them.

[10]Rav Ḥana bar Bizna said: Eliezer said to Shem the elder: [11]"It is written: 'After their kinds, they went out

וְעוֹרֵב, וְחָם. [1]כֶּלֶב נִקְשַׁר, עוֹרֵב רָק, חָם לָקָה בְּעוֹרוֹ״.

[2]״וַיְשַׁלַּח אֶת הַיּוֹנָה מֵאִתּוֹ לִרְאוֹת הֲקַלּוּ הַמַּיִם״. [3]אָמַר רַבִּי יִרְמְיָה: מִכָּאן שֶׁדִּירָתָן שֶׁל עוֹפוֹת טְהוֹרִים עִם הַצַּדִּיקִים.

[4]״וְהִנֵּה עֲלֵה זַיִת טָרָף בְּפִיהָ״. [5]אָמַר רַבִּי אֶלְעָזָר: אָמְרָה יוֹנָה לִפְנֵי הַקָּדוֹשׁ בָּרוּךְ הוּא: ״רִבּוֹנוֹ שֶׁל עוֹלָם! יִהְיוּ מְזוֹנוֹתַי מְרוּרִים כַּזַּיִת וּמְסוּרִים בְּיָדְךָ, וְאַל יִהְיוּ מְתוּקִים כַּדְּבַשׁ וּמְסוּרִים בְּיַד בָּשָׂר וָדָם״. [6]מַאי מַשְׁמַע דְּהַאי טָרָף לִישָּׁנָא דִמְזוֹנֵי הוּא? [7]דִּכְתִיב: ״הַטְרִיפֵנִי לֶחֶם חֻקִּי״.

[8]״לְמִשְׁפְּחֹתֵיהֶם יָצְאוּ מִן הַתֵּבָה״. [9]אָמַר רַבִּי יוֹחָנָן: לְמִשְׁפְּחוֹתָם, וְלֹא הֵם.

[10]אָמַר רַב חָנָא בַּר בִּיזְנָא: אָמַר לֵיהּ אֱלִיעֶזֶר לְשֵׁם רַבָּא: [11]״כְּתִיב: ׳לְמִשְׁפְּחֹתֵיהֶם יָצְאוּ

RASHI

לקה בעורו – שיצא ממנו כוש. מאתו – גבי עורב לא כתיב מאתו, מכאן שדירתם כו׳, כלומר, הנאה הוא שדרים אצלם, שמכירים בצדיקים, כדאמרינן בדוכתי אחריתא. זית טרף בפיה – בפיה היתה שואלת מזון טרף של זית. למשפחותיהם יצאו מן התיבה – אלמא כל חד וחד בפני עצמו היה ולא היו אוכלין כולם במקום אחד, אלא משפחות [משפחות] היו שרויין. אמר ליה אליעזר – [עבד אברהם]. לשם רבא – גדול, בנו של נח.

NOTES

כֶּלֶב נִקְשַׁר **The dog was bound.** *Ramah* explains that the dog's punishment was that thereafter it would be tied up with a chain so as not to cause others damage or injury.

יִהְיוּ מְזוֹנוֹתַי מְרוּרִים כַּזַּיִת **Let my food be as bitter as an olive.** Since Noah provided the dove with all of its food, the question arises: Why did the dove return to the ark with an olive leaf in its mouth? Rabbi Elazar explains that the dove meant to show that it preferred to eat food as bitter as an olive provided by God, rather than food as sweet as honey provided by man (*Ramah*).

לְמִשְׁפְּחוֹתָם, וְלֹא הֵם **Their kinds, but not them.** Some explain that Rabbi Yoḥanan is referring here to insects, which lack bones and live for less than a year. Their kinds went out of the ark, but not the same individual creatures (*Rabbi Ya'akov Emden, Ri Berlin*). Others suggest that Rabbi Yoḥanan means to say that the animals left the ark and were spared from the flood not by their own merits, but in order to preserve their kind (*Hokhmat Mano'aḥ*). *Ramah* explains that all of the animals went out of the ark not in the healthy condition they were in when they entered the ark, for the difficult conditions that prevailed in the ark weakened them greatly.

TRANSLATION AND COMMENTARY

you during your stay in the ark, and what did you do?" [1]Shem **said to him: "We had great trouble in the ark** tending to all the animals. Any **creature whose way it was to be fed during the day, we fed during the day,** and any creature **whose way it was to be fed at night, we fed at night.** [2]**As for the chameleon,** my **father** Noah **did not know what it eats.** [3]**One day he was sitting and peeling a pomegranate, and a worm fell from** the fruit, **and** the chameleon **ate it.** [4]**From that time on, he would knead bran** with water, **and when it became wormy,** he would feed it to the chameleon, and **it would eat it.** [5]**As for the lion, a fever** took hold of it and **sustained it.** [6]**For Rav said: Not less than six days, and not more than twelve** days, **does a fever sustain** a sick person, so that he can live off his body's reserves without taking in any additional food. [7]**As for the** bird called *avarshinah* [referred to in the Bible as the *hol*], my **father** Noah once **found it lying in the hold of the ark,** [8]**and said to it: 'Do you not want** any **food** to eat?' [9]The bird **answered: 'I saw that you were busy** feeding the other animals, and **so I said that I would not trouble you** by asking for food for myself.' [10]My father **said to** the self-sacrificing bird: **'May it be** God's **will that you never die,'** [11]**as the verse states** (Job 29:18): **'Then I said, I shall die in my nest, and I shall multiply my days like the** ***hol.***'"

אָמַר רַב חָנָה בַּר לְוָאֵי [12]**Rav Ḥana bar Liva'ei said:** Noah's son, **Shem the elder,** once **said to** Abraham's servant, **Eliezer: "When the kings of the East and the West** against whom your master Abraham went out in battle **came upon you, what did you do?"** [13]Eliezer

מִן הַתֵּבָה׳. אַתּוּן הֵיכָן הֲוֵיתוּן״? [1]אָמְרוּ לֵיהּ: ״צַעַר גָּדוֹל הָיָה לָנוּ בַּתֵּיבָה, בְּרִיָּה שֶׁדַּרְכָּהּ לְהַאֲכִילָהּ בַּיּוֹם, הֶאֱכַלְנוּהָ בַּיּוֹם, שֶׁדַּרְכָּהּ לְהַאֲכִילָהּ בַּלַּיְלָה, הֶאֱכַלְנוּהָ בַּלַּיְלָה. [2]הַאי זִקִיתָא, לָא הֲוָה יָדַע אַבָּא מָה אָכְלָה. [3]יוֹמָא חַד הֲוָה יָתֵיב וְקָא פָּאלֵי רִמּוֹנָא, נְפַל תּוֹלַעְתָּא מִינָּהּ, אָכְלָה. [4]מִיכָּן וְאֵילָךְ הֲוָה גַּבֵּיל לָהּ חִיזְרָא, כִּי מַתְלַע, אָכְלָה. [5]אַרְיָא אִישְׁתָּא זִינְתֵיהּ. [6]דַּאֲמַר רַב: לָא בְּצִיר מִשִּׁיתָּא, וְלָא טְפֵי מִתְּרֵיסָר, זָיְנָא אִישְׁתָּא. [7]אֲוַרְשִׁינָה, אַשְׁכְּחִינֵיהּ אַבָּא דְּגָנֵי בְּסִפְנָא דְּתֵיבוּתָא, [8]אֲמַר לֵיהּ: ״לָא בָּעֵית מְזוֹנֵי״? [9]אֲמַר לֵיהּ: חָזֵיתִיךְ דַּהֲוַת טְרִידָא, אָמִינָא לֹא אַצַעֲרָךְ״. [10]אֲמַר לֵיהּ: ״יְהֵא רַעֲוָא דְּלֹא תָּמוּת, [11]שֶׁנֶּאֱמַר: ׳וָאֹמַר עִם קִנִּי אֶגְוָע וְכַחוֹל אַרְבֶּה יָמִים׳ ״.

[12]אָמַר רַב חָנָה בַּר לְוָאֵי: אָמַר שֵׁם רַבָּא לֶאֱלִיעֶזֶר: ״כִּי אָתוּ עֲלַיְיכוּ מַלְכֵי מִזְרָח וּמַעֲרָב, אַתּוּן הֵיכִי עֲבִידִיתוּ״? [13]אֲמַר

LITERAL TRANSLATION

of the ark.' Where were you?" [1]They said to him: "We had great trouble in the ark. A creature whose way it was to be fed during the day, we fed during the day, [and a creature] whose way it was to be fed at night, we fed at night. [2][As for] the chameleon, Father did not know what it eats. [3]One day he was sitting and peeling a pomegranate, [and] a worm fell from it, [and] it ate it. [4]From then on he kneaded bran, [and] when it became wormy, it ate it. [5][As for] the lion, a fever sustained it. [6]For Rav said: Not less than six [days], and not more than twelve, does a fever sustain. [7][As for] *avarshinah*, Father found it lying in the hold of the ark, [8][and] said to it: "Do you not want food?" [9]It said to him: "I saw that you were busy, [so] I said that I would not trouble you." [10]He said to it: "May it be [His] will that you not die, [11]as it is stated: 'Then I said, I shall die in my nest, and I shall multiply my days like the *hol*.'" [12]Rav Ḥana bar Liva'ei said: Shem the elder said to Eliezer: "When the kings of the East and the West came upon you, what did you do?" [13]He said

RASHI

היכי הויתון — היאך הייתם יכולין להכין עינייכם בכך לעשות לכל בריה ובריה תפלה. **זקיתא** — שם בריה. **פאלי** — מחתך, כמו פלי פלויי במסכת נדה (כא,ב). **אישתא זינתיה** — חמה אחזתו וזנהו, ולא היה חושש לדרוס מאכל בהמות. **לא בציר משיתא ולא טפי מתריסר זיינא אישתא** — אין לך חמה קלה שלא תהא חמימותו יכולה לזונו ששת ימים שלא ימות בלא מאכל, ואין לך חמה שיכולה לזון יותר משנים עשר ימים בלי מאכל ומשתה כל שהוא, ואית דגרסי לא פחות משיתא ירחי, ולא טפי מתריסר זנתא אשתא, ואארי קאי, כלומר לא פחות מששה חדשים ולא יותר משנים עשר חדשים, ולא נהירא לי. **אורשינא** — עוף ושמו חול בלשון המקרא, ואינו מת לעולם. **בספנא** — בחדר ספון ומתוקן לו.

NOTES

זִקִיתָא Chameleon. According to the Geonim, the *zekita* is a small bird.

אֲוַרְשִׁינָה ***Avarshinah.*** When the Gemara says that the *avarshinah* never dies, it means that it lives a very long life (*Ramah*). According to the Midrashim on Job 29:18, the *avarshinah* (the *hol*, or phoenix) returns to its nest after a thousand years, is burned, and is then reborn. (The commentators to those Midrashim explain that the bird does not actually die, but rather reaches a state of total exhaustion.)

BACKGROUND

זִקִיתָא Chameleon.

Common chameleon

Chameleons are reptiles belonging to the order of lizards, of which many species are found in many countries in the world. They range in length from 20 to 30 cm., and their color changes according to the light, to their mood, and to the background against which they are found. Chameleons eat various insects which they catch by stretching out their extremely long tongues (up to 45 cm.) with great rapidity.

When they are captured, chameleons breathe out noisily, and perhaps this gave rise to their name in Aramaic (זיקא = air). Many legends are attached to chameleons, including the idea that they survive on air alone, which is why the Gemara emphasizes that Noah found that it ate insects. The chameleon symbolized the element of air.

אִישְׁתָּא זִינְתֵיהּ A fever sustained it. A person who is ill with a high fever generally does not eat, and sick animals live for a certain time while they are nourished from excess fat stored in their bodies.

LANGUAGE

אֲוַרְשִׁינָה ***Avarshina.*** In Persian this word is *varshana*, and it might be derived from the Assyrian *urs samnu*, meaning "a kind of wild dove," which is how the Geonim interpreted it.

LANGUAGE

דורון Gift. From the Greek δῶρον, *doron*, meaning "a gift."

TRANSLATION AND COMMENTARY

said to him: "The Holy One, blessed be He, brought Abraham, and sat him at His right side, **and we cast dust** at the enemy, **and it turned into swords,** and we cast **straw** at them, **and it turned into arrows."** [1]This is alluded to by **the verse** that **states** (Psalms 110:1): **"A Psalm of David. The Lord says to my master, Sit you at My right hand, until I make your enemies your footstool."** This psalm was recited by Eliezer, who said that God told his master Abraham to sit beside Him on His right. [2]**And** another **verse states** (Isaiah 41:2): **"Who raised up one from the East whom righteousness met wherever he set his foot, gave the nations before him, and made him rule over his kings; his sword makes them as dust, his bow as driven straw."** This verse alludes to Abraham, who came from Aram Naharayim, which is located in the East.

נחום איש גם זו [3]It was related that **Naḥum of Gamzo was accustomed to say regarding whatever happened to him: "This, too, [*gam zo*] is all for the good."** [4]**One day** the people of **Israel had to send a gift to the emperor.** [5]The people **asked** themselves: **"With whom** [109A] **shall we send** the gift? [6]**Let us send it with Naḥum of Gamzo, who is accustomed to miracles,** for many miracles have been performed for him in the past." Naḥum set off on his journey with the gift for the emperor in his bag. [7]**When he arrived at a certain inn, he asked** whether he could **spend the night** there. [8]His fellow lodgers **said to him: "What do you have with you** in your bag?" [9]Naḥum **said to them: "I bring tribute to the emperor."** [10]Taking advantage of Naḥum's guilelessness, the other lodgers **arose during** the middle of **the night, opened** Naḥum's **bag, and took** out **all that was in it, and** then **refilled** the bag **with earth.** [11]**When** Naḥum later **arrived** at the emperor's palace, and opened his bag in order to

לֵיהּ: ״אַיְיתֵי הַקָּדוֹשׁ בָּרוּךְ הוּא לְאַבְרָהָם, וְאוֹתְבֵיהּ מִימִינֵיהּ, וַהֲוָה שָׁדֵינַן עַפְרָא וְהָווּ חָרְבֵי, גִּילֵי וְהָוְיֵ גִּירֵי. [1]שֶׁנֶּאֱמַר: ״מִזְמוֹר לְדָוִד. נְאֻם ה׳ לַאדֹנִי שֵׁב לִימִינִי עַד אָשִׁית אֹיְבֶיךָ הֲדֹם לְרַגְלֶיךָ״. [2]וּכְתִיב: ״מִי הֵעִיר מִמִּזְרָח צֶדֶק יִקְרָאֵהוּ לְרַגְלוֹ יִתֵּן לְפָנָיו גּוֹיִם וּמְלָכִים יַרְדְּ יִתֵּן כֶּעָפָר חַרְבּוֹ כְּקַשׁ נִדָּף קַשְׁתּוֹ״.

[3]נַחוּם אִישׁ גַּם זוֹ הֲוָה רָגִיל דְּכָל דַּהֲוָה סָלְקָא לֵיהּ, אֲמַר: ״גַּם זוֹ לְטוֹבָה״. [4]יוֹמָא חַד בְּעוּ [יִשְׂרָאֵל] לְשַׁדּוּרֵי דּוֹרוֹן לְקֵיסָר. [5]אָמְרִי: ״בַּהֲדֵי [109A] מַאן נְשַׁדַּר? [6]נְשַׁדַּר בַּהֲדֵי נַחוּם אִישׁ גַּם זוֹ, דִּמְלוּמָּד בְּנִסִּים הוּא״. [7]כִּי מְטָא לְהַהוּא דִּיוּרָא בְּעָא לְמֵיבַת. [8]אָמְרִי לֵיהּ: ״מַאי אִיכָּא בַּהֲדָךְ״? [9]אָמַר לְהוּ: ״קָא מוֹבִילְנָא כַּרְגָּא לְקֵיסָר״. [10]קָמוּ בְּלֵילְיָא, שָׁרֵינְהוּ לְסִיפְטֵיהּ, וּשְׁקַלוּ כָּל דַּהֲוָה גַּבֵּיהּ, וּמְלָנְהוּ עַפְרָא. [11]כִּי מְטָא לְהָתָם

LITERAL TRANSLATION

to him: "The Holy One, blessed be He, brought Abraham, and sat him at His right, and we cast dust and it became swords, [and we cast] straw, and it became arrows." [1]As it is stated: "A Psalm of David. The Lord says to my master, Sit you at My right hand, until I make your enemies your footstool." [2]And it is written: "Who raised up one from the East whom righteousness met wherever he set his foot, gave the nations before him, and made him rule over his kings; his sword makes them as dust, his bow as driven straw."

[3]Naḥum of Gamzo was accustomed that whatever happened to him, he said: "This, too, is for the good." [4]One day Israel had to send a gift to the emperor. [5]They said: "With whom [109A] shall we send [it]? [6]Let us send it with Naḥum of Gamzo, who is accustomed to miracles." [7]When he arrived at a certain inn, he asked to spend the night. [8]They said to him: "What do you have with you?" [9]He said to them: "I bring tribute to the emperor." [10]They arose during the night, opened his bag, and took all that was in it, and filled it with earth. [11]When he arrived there,

RASHI

[נאום ה' כו'] אליעזר אמר פסוק זה — ״נאם ה' לאדני״ אמר הקב״ה לאברהם: שב לימיני אדני וכו'. ממזרח זה אברהם — שבא מארם נהרים, שהוא במזרח, דכתיב (במדבר כג) ״מן ארם ינחני בלק מלך מואב וגו'״. כל דהוה סלקא ליה — כל דבר המאורע ליה. בהדי מאן — ביד מי נשלח. כי מטא לההוא דיירא — כשהגיע לאותו מלון. למיבת — ללון. שרינהו לסיטפיה — התירו הארגזים והמרצופין ופתחום, ונטלו כל מה שבתוכו.

NOTES

שְׁקַלוּ...וּמְלָנְהוּ עַפְרָא They took...and filled it with earth. This passage has also been explained as follows: Naḥum of Gamzo knew that the lodgers had stolen the tribute that he meant to give to the emperor. But he decided to proceed on his mission, because the most important aspect of the tribute was not its monetary value, but rather its symbolic value. He explained to the emperor that the dirt was a symbol of submission, and that it was of the earth of Abraham. That is to say, Abraham, who emerged victorious in many battles and who was regarded as a "prince of God," accomplished what he did through gentle speech and personal submission. Such behavior is as effective as swords and arrows. The emperor tried out the new policy of soft speech on a district that he had previously been unable to conquer, and when it succeeded, he bestowed great honor upon Naḥum (*Sefer HaḤayyim*).

TRANSLATION AND COMMENTARY

present the emperor with the gift, **it was found** that the bag was filled with **earth.** [1]The emperor **said: "The Jews are making fun of me."** [2]And so his men **took** Naḥum **out to be executed.** [3]Even in this desperate situation, Naḥum **declared: "This, too, is all for the good."** [4]Immediately, the Prophet **Elijah came, and appeared to the** executioners **like one of their** own kind. [5]Elijah **said to them: "Perhaps,** there is more to the Jews' gift than meets the eye, for **the earth** which they sent **might be of the earth of Abraham our forefather, who cast earth** at his enemies **which turned into swords,** and **straw which turned into arrows."** [6]The emperor's men **examined** the earth, **and** indeed the earth **was found** to have those miraculous powers. [7]**There was a** certain **district that they had been** previously **unable to capture.** [8]**They cast** some of **the earth** that Naḥum had given them **toward that** district, **and** this time they were able to **capture it.** [9]As a token of their gratitude, **they brought** Naḥum **into the** imperial **treasure house, and said: "Take whatever pleases you."** [10]Naḥum **filled his bag with gold,** and started on his homeward journey. [11]**When he came back** to the same inn, **those lodgers** who had filled his bag with earth **said to him: "What did you bring to the king's palace?"** [12]Naḥum **said to them: "That which I took from here, I brought there."** [13]The lodgers **took** more of their earth, **and brought** it **to** the emperor. When it proved to be ordinary dirt, the emperor **had the lodgers put to death.**

דּוֹר הַפַּלָּגָה [14]We have learned in our Mishnah: **"The generation of the dispersion** — those who built the Tower of Babel — **do not have a portion in the World to Come."** [15]The Gemara asks: **What did they do?** [16]**The Sages of the School of Rabbi Shela said:** The builders of the tower sinned when they said: **"Let us build a tower, and go up to Heaven, and strike it with axes, so that its waters flow."**

מְחַכוּ [17]When the Sages **in Eretz Israel** heard this explanation, **they laughed** and said: **They should have built** the tower **on a mountain,** and **not** in a valley, as is stated in the Torah!

אִישְׁתַּכַּח עַפְרָא. [1]אָמַר: ״אַחוּכֵי קָא מְחַיְּיכִי בִּי יְהוּדָאֵי״! [2]אַפְּקוּהוּ לְמִקְטְלֵיהּ. [3]אָמַר: ״גַּם זוֹ לְטוֹבָה״. [4]אֲתָא אֵלִיָּהוּ, וְאִידַּמֵּי לְהוּ כְּחַד מִינַּיְיהוּ, [5]אָמַר לְהוּ: ״דִּילְמָא הַאי עַפְרָא מֵעַפְרָא דְּאַבְרָהָם אָבִינוּ הוּא, דַּהֲוָה שָׁדֵי עַפְרָא הָווּ חָרְבֵי, גִּילֵי הָווּ גִּירֵי״. [6]בַּדּוּק וְאַשְׁכְּחוּ הָכִי. [7]הֲוָה מְחוֹזָא דְּלָא הָווּ קָא יַכְלִי לֵיהּ לְמִיכְבְּשֵׁיהּ, [8]שְׁדוּ מֵהַהוּא עַפְרָא עֲלֵיהּ — וּכְבָשׁוּהּ. [9]עַיְילוּהוּ לְבֵי גְּנָזָא, אָמְרִי: ״שְׁקוֹל דְּנִיחָא לָךְ״. [10]מַלְיֵיהּ לְסִיפְטָא דְּהַבָא. [11]כִּי הֲדַר אֲתָא אֲמַרוּ לֵיהּ הָנָךְ דִּיוּרֵי: ״מַאי אַמְטֵית לְבֵי מַלְכָּא״? [12]אָמַר לְהוּ: מַאי דְּשָׁקְלִי מֵהָכָא — אַמְטַאי לְהָתָם. [13]שָׁקְלִי אִינְהוּ, אַמְטוּ לְהָתָם. קַטְלִינְהוּ לְהָנָךְ דִּיוּרֵי.

[14]״דּוֹר הַפַּלָּגָה אֵין לָהֶם חֵלֶק לָעוֹלָם הַבָּא וכו׳״. [15]מַאי עֲבוּד? [16]אָמְרִי דְּבֵי רַבִּי שֵׁילָא: ״נִבְנֶה מִגְדָּל וְנַעֲלֶה לָרָקִיעַ, וְנַכֶּה אוֹתוֹ בְּקַרְדּוּמוֹת, כְּדֵי שֶׁיָּזוּבוּ מֵימָיו״.

[17]מְחַכוּ עֲלָהּ בְּמַעַרְבָא: אִם כֵּן לִיבְנוּ אֶחָד בְּטוּרָא!

LITERAL TRANSLATION

it was found to be earth. [1]He said: "The Jews are making fun of me." [2]They took him out to kill him. [3]He said: "This, too, is for the good." [4]Elijah came, and appeared to them like one of them. [5]He said to them: "Perhaps that earth is of the earth of Abraham our forefather, who cast earth and it became swords, [who cast] straw, and it became arrows." [6]They examined [the earth], and it was found thus. [7]There was a district that they had not been able to capture. [8]They cast some of that earth upon it, and captured it. [9]They brought him into the treasure house, [and] said: "Take what pleases you." [10]He filled his bag with gold. [11]When he returned and came, those lodgers said to him: "What did you bring to the king's palace?" [12]He said to them: "What I took from here, I brought there." [13]They took, [and] brought there. They killed those lodgers.

[14]"The generation of the dispersion do not have a portion in the World to Come, etc." [15]What did they do? [16][The Sages] of the School of Rabbi Shela said: "Let us build a tower, and go up to Heaven, and strike it with axes, so that its waters flow."

[17]They laughed at this in the West: If so, they should have built one on a mountain!

RASHI

אחוכי – מצחקי. הנך דיורי – אותן בני הכפרים. אם כן ליבנו אחד בטורא – אם כן שבנו כדי לעלות לרקיע, למה בנו אותו בבקעה, היה להם לבנות על אחד ההרים.

NOTES

שֶׁיָּזוּבוּ מֵימָיו **So that its waters flow.** Some explain that the builders of the tower wished to strike Heaven with axes, so that its waters would flow and God would be unable to bring another flood (*Maharsha*). Others suggest that they wanted to strike Heaven so that its waters would flow and there would always be rain (*Ramah*).

TRANSLATION AND COMMENTARY

אֶלָּא [1]**Rather, Rabbi Yirmeyah bar Elazar said:** Those who built the Tower of Babel **were divided into three groups.** [2]**One** group **said: "Let us go up and live there."** [3]**And one** group **said: "Let us go up and worship idols** there." [4]**And one** group **said: "Let us go up and wage war** from there." [5]**Those who said: "Let us go up and live there," God scattered** across the world. [6]**Those who said: "Let us go up and wage war** from there" — [7]God turned them into **apes, and spirits, and demons, and night-demons.** [8]**And those who said: "Let us go up and worship idols"** — [9]God fulfilled in them the verse (Genesis 11:9): **"Because there the Lord did confound the language of all the earth."**

תַּנְיָא [10]**It was taught** in a related Baraita: **"Rabbi Natan says: All** those who were involved in the building of the Tower of Babel **had idol worship in mind.** [11]**Here the verse states** (Genesis 11:4): **"And let us make us a name,"** [12]**and elsewhere the verse states** (Exodus 23:13): **"And make no mention of the name of other gods."** [13]**Just as there,** we are dealing with **idol worship, so, too, here** we are dealing with **idol worship.**

אָמַר רַבִּי יוֹחָנָן [14]**Rabbi Yoḥanan said: The Tower** of Babel — the upper **third was burnt,** the lower **third sunk** into the ground, **and** the middle **third** still **stands.**

אָמַר רַב [15]**Rav said: The air** surrounding **the** remains of the **tower causes** a person **to forget** what he has learned, just as it caused the people of Babel to forget their mother tongue.

[1](אֶלָּא) אָמַר רַבִּי יִרְמְיָה בַּר אֶלְעָזָר: נֶחְלְקוּ לְשָׁלֹשׁ כִּיתּוֹת. [2]אַחַת אוֹמֶרֶת: "נַעֲלֶה וְנֵשֵׁב שָׁם". [3]וְאַחַת אוֹמֶרֶת: "נַעֲלֶה וְנַעֲבוֹד עֲבוֹדָה זָרָה". [4]וְאַחַת אוֹמֶרֶת: "נַעֲלֶה וְנַעֲשֶׂה מִלְחָמָה". [5]זוֹ שֶׁאוֹמֶרֶת: "נַעֲלֶה וְנֵשֵׁב שָׁם", הֱפִיצָם ה׳. [6]וְזוֹ שֶׁאוֹמֶרֶת: "נַעֲלֶה וְנַעֲשֶׂה מִלְחָמָה" — [7]נַעֲשׂוּ קוֹפִים וְרוּחוֹת וְשֵׁידִים וְלִילִין. [8]וְזוֹ שֶׁאוֹמֶרֶת: "נַעֲלֶה וְנַעֲבוֹד עֲבוֹדָה זָרָה" — [9]"כִּי שָׁם בָּלַל ה׳ שְׂפַת כָּל הָאָרֶץ".

[10]תַּנְיָא: "רַבִּי נָתָן אוֹמֵר: כּוּלָּם לְשֵׁם עֲבוֹדָה זָרָה נִתְכַּוְּונוּ. [11]כְּתִיב הָכָא: "נַעֲשֶׂה לָנוּ שֵׁם". [12]וּכְתִיב הָתָם: "וְשֵׁם אֱלֹהִים אֲחֵרִים לֹא תַזְכִּירוּ". [13]מַה לְּהַלָּן, עֲבוֹדָה זָרָה, אַף כָּאן עֲבוֹדָה זָרָה.

[14]אָמַר רַבִּי יוֹחָנָן: מִגְדָּל — שְׁלִישׁ נִשְׂרַף, שְׁלִישׁ נִבְלַע, שְׁלִישׁ קַיָּים.

[15]אָמַר רַב: אֲוִיר מִגְדָּל מְשַׁכֵּחַ.

LITERAL TRANSLATION

[1]Rather, Rabbi Yirmeyah bar Elazar said: They were divided into three groups. [2]One said: "Let us go up and live there." [3]And one said: "Let us go up and worship idols." [4]And one said: "Let us go up and wage war." [5]Those who (lit.,"that which") said: "Let us go up and live there," God scattered. [6]And those who (lit.,"that which") said: "Let us go up and wage war" — [7]they became apes, and spirits, and demons, and night-demons. [8]And those who (lit.,"that which") said: "Let us go up and worship idols" — [9]"Because there the Lord did confound the language of all the earth."

[10]It was taught: "Rabbi Natan says: All of them had idol worship in mind. [11]It is written here: "And let us make us a name." [12]And it is written there: "And make no mention of the name of other gods." [13]Just as below, idol worship, so, too, here, idol worship.

[14]Rabbi Yoḥanan said: The tower — a third was burnt, a third was swallowed up, and a third stands.

[15]Rav said: The air of the tower causes forgetfulness (lit., "to forget").

RASHI

הפיצם ה׳ — פיזרם בכל העולם. **שדים** — יש להם צורת אדם ואוכלין ושותין כבני אדם. **רוחין** — בלי גוף וצורה. **לילין** — צורת אדם — אלא שיש להם כנפים, במסכת נדה (כד,ב). **זו שאומרה נעבוד עבודה זרה כי שם בלל ה׳** — בלבל לשונם כדי שלא יהא אחד מכוון לדעת חבירו לעבוד עבודה זרה. **שליש [נבלע]** — נבלעו יסודותיה משוקעת היא בקרקע עד שליש, ושליש של מעלה נשרף, ושליש אמצעי קיים בקרקע, ולא שיהא עומד באויר. **אויר מגדל** — מראש המגדל (כלומר) [כמו אוירה של עיר], מי שעומד סביב למגדל ורואה אוירה ומראה גובה שלו. **משכח** — שכן נגזר על אותו מקום שישכח ולכך הם עצמם שכחו את לשונם.

NOTES

נַעֲלֶה וְנֵשֵׁב...נַעֲלֶה וְנַעֲשֶׂה מִלְחָמָה **Let us go up and live there...let us go up and wage war.** Some explain (following most versions of the Midrash): "Let us go up and live there" — in Heaven. "Let us go up and wage war" — against God (see *Binyan Shlomo*). But the wording found in our Gemara implies that the first group said: "Let us go up and live there" — in the tower. Their sin was that they did not want to settle and develop the land (see *Or HaḤayyim* on the Torah). The second group said: "Let us go up and wage war" — against our enemies, for from the height of the tower we can more easily defeat our enemies (*Ramah*).

שְׁלִישׁ קַיָּים **A third stands.** Part of the tower was left standing to serve as a reminder and a warning to the later generations (*Binyan Shlomo, Rabbi Ya'akov Emden*).

אֲוִיר מִגְדָּל מְשַׁכֵּחַ **The air of the tower causes to forget.** It was decreed that the air surrounding the remains of the tower should cause a person to forget what he learned, so that people will not return at some later point and try to rebuild the tower (*Ramah*).

TRANSLATION AND COMMENTARY

אָמַר רַב יוֹסֵף [1]Rav Yosef said: Babylon and the neighboring city of Bursif are a bad sign for Torah. Their proximity to the Tower of Babel causes a person to forget what he has learned.

מַאי בּוּרְסִיף [2]The Gemara asks: What is the meaning of the name Bursif? [3]Rabbi Assi said: An empty pit (*bor shafi*). The city of Bursif causes a person to become empty of Torah knowledge.

אַנְשֵׁי סְדוֹם [4]We have learned in our Mishnah: **"The people of Sodom do not have a portion in the World to Come."** [5]**Our Rabbis taught** the following Baraita: **"The people of Sodom do not have a portion in the World to Come,** [6]**as the verse states** (Genesis 13:13): **'But the men of Sodom were wicked and sinners before the Lord exceedingly.'** [7]**'Wicked'** — so that they were punished **in this world. 'And sinners'** — so that they will have no share **in the World to Come."**

אָמַר רַב יְהוּדָה [8]**Rav Yehudah said** that the redundancy in the verse may be understood differently: The word **"wicked"** implies that the people of Sodom sinned **with their bodies.** [9]The words **"and sinners"** teach that the people of Sodom also sinned **with their money,** dealing cruelly with their less fortunate neighbors. [10]The word **"wicked"** alludes to sins relating to **their bodies, as the verse** reporting Joseph's response to Potifar's wife's overtures **states** (Genesis 39:9): **"How, then, can I do this great wickedness, and sin against God."** [11]And the words **"and sinners"** allude to sins relating to **their money, as the verse states** (Deuteronomy 15:9): "And your eye is evil against your poor brother, and you give him nothing...**for it shall be reckoned to you as a sin."** [12]The words **"before the Lord"** imply that the people of Sodom were guilty of **blasphemy.** [13]The word **"exceedingly"** teaches that the people of Sodom **sinned intentionally.**

בְּמַתְנִיתָא תָּנָא [14]**A Tanna taught a Baraita** which interprets the verse in a slightly different manner: "The word **'wicked'** implies that the people of Sodom sinned **with their money.** [15]The words **'and sinners'** teach that the people of Sodom also sinned **with their bodies.** [16]The word **'wicked** [רָעִים]' alludes to sins relating to **their money, as the verse states** (Deuteronomy 15:9): **'And your eye be evil** [וְרָעָה] **against your poor brother,**

[1]אָמַר רַב יוֹסֵף: בָּבֶל וּבוּרְסִיף סִימָן רַע לַתּוֹרָה.
[2]מַאי בּוּרְסִיף? [3]אָמַר רַבִּי אַסִי: בּוֹר שָׁאפִי.
[4]"אַנְשֵׁי סְדוֹם אֵין לָהֶם חֵלֶק לָעוֹלָם הַבָּא וכו'". [5]תָּנוּ רַבָּנַן: "אַנְשֵׁי סְדוֹם אֵין לָהֶן חֵלֶק לָעוֹלָם הַבָּא, [6]שֶׁנֶּאֱמַר: 'וְאַנְשֵׁי סְדֹם רָעִים וְחַטָּאִים לַה' מְאֹד'. [7]'רָעִים' — בָּעוֹלָם הַזֶּה. 'וְחַטָּאִים' — לָעוֹלָם הַבָּא".
[8]אָמַר רַב יְהוּדָה: "רָעִים" — בְּגוּפָן. [9]"וְחַטָּאִים" — בְּמָמוֹנָם. [10]"רָעִים" בְּגוּפָן, דִּכְתִיב: "וְאֵיךְ אֶעֱשֶׂה הָרָעָה הַגְּדֹלָה הַזֹּאת וְחָטָאתִי לֵאלֹהִים"? [11]"וְחַטָּאִים" בְּמָמוֹנָם, דִּכְתִיב: "וְהָיָה בְךָ חֵטְא". [12]"לַה'" — זוֹ בִּרְכַּת הַשֵּׁם. [13]"מְאֹד" — שֶׁמִּתְכַּוְּונִים וְחוֹטְאִים.
[14]בְּמַתְנִיתָא תָּנָא: "'רָעִים' — בְּמָמוֹנָם. [15]'וְחַטָּאִים' — בְּגוּפָן. [16]'רָעִים' בְּמָמוֹנָם, דִּכְתִיב: 'וְרָעָה עֵינְךָ בְּאָחִיךָ הָאֶבְיוֹן'.

LITERAL TRANSLATION

[1]Rav Yosef said: Babylon and Bursif are a bad sign for Torah.

[2]What is Bursif? [3]Rabbi Assi said: An empty pit.

[4]"The people of Sodom do not have a portion in the World to Come, etc." [5]Our Rabbis taught: "The people of Sodom do not have a portion in the World to Come, [6]as it is stated: 'But the men of Sodom were wicked and sinners before the Lord exceedingly.' [7]'Wicked' — in this world. 'And sinners' — in the World to Come."

[8]Rav Yehudah said: "Wicked" — with their bodies. [9]"And sinners" — with their money. [10]"Wicked" with their bodies, as it is written: "How, then, can I do this great wickedness, and sin against God?" [11]"And sinners" with their money, as it is written: "For it shall be reckoned to you as a sin." [12]"Before the Lord" — this is blasphemy (lit., "the blessing of God"). [13]"Exceedingly" — who sin intentionally.

[14][A Tanna] taught in a Baraita: "'Wicked' — with their money. [15]'And sinners' — with their bodies. [16]'Wicked' with their money, as it is written: 'And your eye is evil against your poor brother.'

RASHI

בבל ובורסיף – סימן רע לתורה – שמשכחין התלמוד מפני שעומדים באויר המגדל. למה נקרא שמה בורסיף בור שאפי – בור שנתרוקן מימיו, כלומר משכח האדם כל מה שלומד. שאפי – כמו (בבא מציעא ס,א): השופה את היין, לשון (ירמיהו מח) "הורק מכלי אל כלי" ומפני מה שמה בבל – [שמשכחת] אמר רב יוסף: "כי שם בלל", לפי שבלבל הקדוש ברוך הוא את לשונם לשם לכך היא משכחת. סימן רע – כלומר שמם סימן שכחה היא. רעים בגופן – שטופים בזימה. השמר לך פן יהיה עם לבבך בליעל וגו' והיה בך חטא – והיינו ממון.

NOTES

בּוּרְסִיף **Bursif.** It has been suggested that Bursif means *bur min hasefer,* "void of the book," for the place causes a person to become empty of Torah knowledge (*Arukh*).

TRANSLATION AND COMMENTARY

and you give him nothing.' [1]And the words **'and sinners'** allude to sins relating to **their bodies, as the verse states** (Genesis 39:9): 'How can I do this great wickedness, **and sin against God.'** [2]The words **'before the Lord'** imply that the people of Sodom were guilty of **blasphemy.** [3]The word **'exceedingly** [מְאֹד]' teaches that the people of Sodom were also guilty of **bloodshed, as the verse states** (II Kings 21:16): **'Moreover Manasseh shed very [מְאֹד] much innocent blood in Jerusalem.'"**

תָּנוּ רַבָּנַן [4]**Our Rabbis taught** the following Baraita: **"The people of Sodom became haughty** and were then led to sin **only in consequence of the** abundant **bounty that the Holy One, blessed be He, bestowed upon them.** [5]**And which verses apply to them?** The verses that state (Job 28:5-8): [6]**'The earth, from which comes bread; and under it is turned up as it were fire. The stones of it are the place of sapphires; and it has dust of gold. There is a path which no bird of prey knows, and which the falcon's eye has not seen. The lion's whelps have not trodden it, nor the fierce lion passed by it.'** That passage refers to Sodom, for the very next verse states (Job 28:9): 'He puts forth His hand upon the rock; He overturns the mountains by the roots.' [7]The people of Sodom **said: 'Since** we have an abundance of bounty — **earth from which comes bread, and which has the dust of gold — why do we need wayfarers?** Surely **they come to** stay by **us only in order to deplete our money. Come, let us cause the law** for the protection **of travelers to be forgotten in our land,** so that wayfarers will no longer come to our doors,' [8]**as the verse states** (Job 28:4): **'He breaks open a watercourse in a place far from inhabitants, forgotten by foot travelers, they are dried up, they have moved away from men.'"**

דָּרַשׁ רָבָא [9]**Rava expounded: What is** meant by **the verse that states** (Psalms 62:4): **"How long will you seek to overwhelm a man? You will all be murdered like a leaning wall, or a tottering fence"?** [10]**This teaches that** the people of Sodom would **set their eyes on a person**

[1]'וְחַטָּאִים' בְּגוּפָן, דִּכְתִיב: 'וְחָטָאתִי לֵאלֹהִים'. [2]'לַה'' — זוֹ בִּרְכַּת הַשֵּׁם. [3]'מְאֹד' — זוֹ שְׁפִיכוּת דָּמִים, שֶׁנֶּאֱמַר: 'וְגַם דָּם נָקִי שָׁפַךְ מְנַשֶּׁה בִּירוּשָׁלַיִם הַרְבֵּה מְאֹד [וגו']'".

[4]תָּנוּ רַבָּנַן: "אַנְשֵׁי סְדוֹם לֹא נִתְגָּאוּ אֶלָּא בִּשְׁבִיל טוֹבָה שֶׁהִשְׁפִּיעַ לָהֶם הַקָּדוֹשׁ בָּרוּךְ הוּא. [5]וּמַה כְּתִיב בָּהֶם? [6]'אֶרֶץ מִמֶּנָּה יֵצֵא לָחֶם, וְתַחְתֶּיהָ נֶהְפַּךְ כְּמוֹ אֵשׁ. מְקוֹם סַפִּיר אֲבָנֶיהָ וְעַפְרֹת זָהָב לוֹ. נָתִיב לֹא יְדָעוֹ עָיִט וְלֹא שְׁזָפַתּוּ עֵין אַיָּה. לֹא הִדְרִיכוּהוּ בְנֵי שָׁחַץ לֹא עָדָה עָלָיו שָׁחַל'. [7]אָמְרוּ: 'וְכִי מֵאַחַר שֶׁאֶרֶץ מִמֶּנָּה יֵצֵא לָחֶם וְעַפְרֹת זָהָב לוֹ, לָמָּה לָנוּ עוֹבְרֵי דְרָכִים? שֶׁאֵין בָּאִים אֵלֵינוּ אֶלָּא לְחַסְּרֵינוּ [מִמָּמוֹנֵנוּ], בּוֹאוּ וּנְשַׁכַּח תּוֹרַת רֶגֶל מֵאַרְצֵנוּ', [8]שֶׁנֶּאֱמַר: 'פָּרַץ נַחַל מֵעִם גָּר הַנִּשְׁכָּחִים מִנִּי רָגֶל דַּלּוּ מֵאֱנוֹשׁ נָעוּ'".

[9]דָּרַשׁ רָבָא: מַאי דִּכְתִיב: "עַד אָנָה תְּהוֹתְתוּ עַל אִישׁ תְּרָצְּחוּ כֻלְּכֶם כְּקִיר נָטוּי גָּדֵר הַדְּחוּיָה"? [10]מְלַמֵּד שֶׁהָיוּ נוֹתְנִין עֵינֵיהֶן בְּבַעֲלֵי מָמוֹן, וּמוֹשִׁיבִין אוֹתוֹ

LITERAL TRANSLATION

[1]'And sinners' with their bodies, as it is written: 'And sin against God.' [2]'Before the Lord' — this is blasphemy. [3]'Exceedingly' — this is bloodshed, as it is stated: 'Manasseh also shed very much innocent blood in Jerusalem.'"

[4]Our Rabbis taught: "The people of Sodom became haughty only in consequence of the bounty that the Holy One, blessed be He, bestowed upon them. [5]And what is written regarding them? [6]'The earth, from which comes bread; and under it is turned up as it were fire. The stones of it are the place of sapphires; and it has dust of gold. There is a path which no bird of prey knows, and which the falcon's eye has not seen. The lion's whelps have not trodden it, nor the fierce lion passed by it.' [7]They said: 'Since it is earth from which comes bread, and it has dust of gold, why do we have wayfarers? They come to us only to deplete our money. Come, let us cause the law of travelers (lit., "the foot") to be forgotten in our land,' [8]as it is stated: 'He breaks open a watercourse in a place [far] from inhabitants, forgotten by foot travelers, they are dried up, they have moved away from men.'"

[9]Rava expounded: What is that which is written: "How long will you seek to overwhelm a man? You will all be murdered like a leaning wall, or a tottering fence"? [10]This teaches that they set their eyes on people with money, and sat him

RASHI

ארץ ממנה יצא לחם — ארץ שבעה וטובה היא. ותחתיה נהפך כמו אש — ואחר כן נהפכה. וכי מאחר שארץ ממנה יצא לחם — שיש לנו שיפוע לחם למה לנו עוברי דרכים. ונשכח — שלא יעברו עוברי דרכים בארצנו. פרץ — הקב"ה נחל גפרית ואש. מעם גר — ממקום הליכתו שהיה הולך למעלה והשליכו עליהם הנשכחים מני רגל, — ונתדלדלו (מאדם) [מארצם] ונעו לדראון. גר — *קורנט"ל בלעז, כמו (שמואל ב, יד) "מים הנגרים". תהותתו — תבקשו תרמיות ותואנות. תרצחו כולכם — על ידי קיר נטוי וגדר הדחויה.

LANGUAGE (RASHI)

קורנט"ל* This should be קורנ"ט, Old French *courant*, meaning "current," or "a powerful stream of water."

אֵצֶל קִיר נָטוּי, וְדוֹחִין אוֹתוֹ עָלָיו, וּבָאִים וְנוֹטְלִין אֶת מָמוֹנוֹ. [1]דָּרַשׁ רָבָא: מַאי דִּכְתִיב: ״חָתַר בַּחֹשֶׁךְ בָּתִּים יוֹמָם חִתְּמוּ לָמוֹ לֹא יָדְעוּ אוֹר״? [2]מְלַמֵּד שֶׁהָיוּ נוֹתְנִים עֵינֵיהֶם בְּבַעֲלֵי מָמוֹן, וּמַפְקִידִים אֶצְלוֹ אֲפַרְסְמוֹן, וּמַנִּיחִים אוֹתוֹ בְּבֵית גִּנְזֵיהֶם. [3]לָעֶרֶב בָּאִים וּמְרִיחִין אוֹתוֹ כַּכֶּלֶב, שֶׁנֶּאֱמַר: ״יָשׁוּבוּ לָעֶרֶב יֶהֱמוּ כַכָּלֶב וִיסוֹבְבוּ עִיר״. [4]וּבָאִים וְחוֹתְרִים שָׁם וְנוֹטְלִין אוֹתוֹ מָמוֹן.

[5]״עָרוֹם יָלִינוּ מִבְּלִי לְבוּשׁ וְאֵין כְּסוּת בַּקָּרָה... [6]חֲמוֹר יְתוֹמִים יִנְהָגוּ יַחְבְּלוּ שׁוֹר אַלְמָנָה... [7]גְּבֻלוֹת יַשִּׂיגוּ, עֵדֶר גָּזְלוּ וַיִּרְעוּ... [8]וְהוּא לִקְבָרוֹת יוּבָל וְעַל גָּדִישׁ יִשְׁקוֹד״. [9]דָּרַשׁ רַבִּי יוֹסֵי בְּצִיפּוֹרִי: [10]אִחַתְּרִין הַהִיא לֵילְיָא תְּלָת מְאָה מַחְתַּרְתָּא בְּצִיפּוֹרִי. [11]אֲתוּ וְקָא מְצַעֲרִי לֵיהּ, אֲמַרוּ לֵיהּ: ״יְהָבִית אוֹרְחֵיהּ לְגַנָּבֵי״. [12]אֲמַר לְהוּ: ״מִי הֲוָה יָדַעְנָא דְּאָתוּ גַּנָּבֵי״? [13]כִּי קָא נָח נַפְשֵׁיהּ דְּרַבִּי יוֹסֵי שָׁפְעִי מַרְזְבֵי דְּצִיפּוֹרִי דְּמָא.

LITERAL TRANSLATION

next to a leaning wall, and they pushed it on him, and came and took his money.

[1]Rava expounded: What is that which is written: "In the dark they dig through houses; by day they shut themselves up; they know not the light"? [2]This teaches that they set their eyes on people with money, and deposited balsam with him, and they would place it in their treasure houses. [3]At night they came and smelled it like a dog, as it is stated: "They return at evening; they howl like a dog, and go round about the city." [4]And they burrowed there and took that money.

[5]"They lie all night naked without clothing, and they have no covering in the cold....[6]They drive away the ass of the fatherless; they take the widow's ox for a pledge....[7]Some remove the landmarks; they violently steal flocks, and feed them....[8]For he is brought to the grave, and watch is kept over his tomb." [9]Rabbi Yose of Sepphoris expounded: [10]That night three hundred burrows were burrowed in Sepphoris. [11]They came and troubled him, [and] said to him: "You showed the way to the thieves." [12]He said to them: "Did I know that thieves would come?" [13]When Rabbi Yose died the spouts of Sepphoris flowed with blood.

TRANSLATION AND COMMENTARY

with money, sit him down **next to a leaning wall, push** the wall **upon him** and kill him, **and** then **come and take his money.**

דָּרַשׁ רָבָא [1]**Rava expounded: What is** meant by **the verse that states** (Job 24:16): **"In the dark they dig through houses; by day they shut themselves up; they know not the light"?** [2]**This teaches that** the people of Sodom would **set their eyes on a person with money, and deposit** strong-smelling **balsam with him, and** the moneyed person **would place** the balsam together with his own valuables **in his treasure house.** [3]Later **that night** the depositors would **come** back **and follow the scent** of the balsam **like a dog, as the verse states** (Psalms 59:7): **"They return at evening; they howl like a dog, and go round about the city."** [4]Led by the scent of the balsam, **they would burrow** into the rich man's house, **and take his money.**

עָרוֹם יָלִינוּ [5]The verses state (Job 24:7): **"They lie all night naked without clothing, and they have no covering in the cold"**; (Job 24:3): [6]**"They drive away the ass of the fatherless;** [7]**they take the widow's ox for a pledge"**; (Job 24:2): **"Some remove the landmarks;** [8]**they violently steal flocks, and feed them"**; and (Job 21:32): **"For he is brought to the grave, and watch is kept over his tomb."** [9]**Rabbi Yose of Sepphoris expounded** these verses, and in the course of the discussion, he explained how the people of Sodom practiced their thievery. [10]**That night** thieves **broke into three hundred houses in Sepphoris,** making use of the devices mentioned by Rabbi Yose in his lecture. [11]The people of Sepphoris **went** to Rabbi Yose, **and troubled him** about the matter, **and said to him:** "It was you who **showed the thieves the way** to steal." [12]Rabbi Yose **said to** the angry residents: **"Was I to know that,** in the wake of my lecture, **thieves would come** and rob you?" [13]**When Rabbi Yose died, the spouts of Sepphoris flowed with blood** in mourning over that city's great Sage.

RASHI

יומם חתמו למו — היום סותמים וסוגרין כאילו לא ידעו אור, כלומר סותמין וחותמין. **אפרסמון** — שלהם להפקידו ביד בעלי ממון, כדי שיהו מניחין פקדון שלהם בבית גנזיהם, ובלילה מריחין האפרסמון וחותרין שם, מנהגו של מפקיד לצרר וחותם. **דרש רבי יוסי** — בי מדרשא חתר בחשך בתים. **איחתרו תלת מאה מחתרתא** — על ידי ריח אפרסמון, שהיו מריחין ויודעין היכן מניחין ממונם. **מי הוה ידענא דאתו גנבי** — לישנא אחרינא: מי הוה ידענא דגנבי אתון. **שפעי מרזבי דציפורי דמא** — דאדם גדול הוה, ואיידי דאמר לעיל איחתרו מחתרתי בציפורי — דאתרא דר׳ יוסי התם, הוה נקיט נמי הא מילתא, דכי נח נפשיה כו׳ לאשמועינן דמציפורי הוה.

NOTES

שָׁפְעֵי מַרְזְבֵי דְּצִיפּוֹרִי דְּמָא **The spouts of Sepphoris flowed with blood.** Some explain that this detail shows Rabbi Yose's greatness and righteousness, so that the people of Sepphoris would know that there was nothing wrong with

BACKGROUND

אֲפַרְסְמוֹן **Balsam.**

A branch of balsam and its fruit.

The plant referred to here is probably *Comniphora opobalsamum*, of the Burseraceae family. Balsam is a bush or low tree (3-5 meters). Its branches are very thin, and its compound leaves are composed of very many small leaves. It appears that the balsam referred to here is the צֳרִי, one of the ingredients of the incense in the Temple. The finest scent is gathered from what drips in droplets from the ends of the stalks (נטף מעצי הקטף), but in general it is produced by boiling the branches. The perfume is used to produce incense and aromatic oil.

During Second Temple times Eretz Israel was an important center for the cultivation of balsam, especially near Jericho.

[1]אָמְרִי: ״דְּאִית לֵיהּ חַד תּוֹרָא מַרְעֵי חַד יוֹמָא, [2]דְּלֵית לֵיהּ לִירְעֵי תְּרֵי יוֹמֵי״. [3]הַהוּא יַתְמָא בַּר אַרְמַלְתָּא הֲבוּ לֵיהּ תּוֹרֵי לְמִרְעֵיהּ, [4]אֲזַל שְׁקַלִינְהוּ וּקְטַלִינְהוּ. [5]אֲמַר לְהוּ: [109B] [6]״דְּאִית לֵיהּ תּוֹרָא נִשְׁקוֹל חַד מַשְׁכָּא. [7]דְּלֵית לֵיהּ תּוֹרָא נִשְׁקוֹל תְּרֵי מַשְׁכֵּי״. [8]אֲמַרוּ לֵיהּ: ״מַאי הַאי״? [9]אֲמַר לְהוּ: ״סוֹף דִּינָא כִּתְחִילַּת דִּינָא. [10]מַה תְּחִילַּת דִּינָא, דְּאִית לֵיהּ תּוֹרָא מַרְעֵי חַד יוֹמָא, דְּלֵית לֵיהּ תּוֹרֵי מַרְעֵי תְּרֵי יוֹמֵי, [11]אַף סוֹף דִּינָא: דְּאִית לֵיהּ חַד תּוֹרָא לִשְׁקוֹל חַד, דְּלֵית לֵיהּ תּוֹרָא לִשְׁקוֹל תְּרֵי״.

[12]דַּעֲבַר בְּמַבָּרָא נֵיתֵיב חַד זוּזָא. [13]דְּלָא עֲבַר בְּמַבָּרָא נֵיתֵיב תְּרֵי. [14]דַּהֲוָה לֵיהּ תּוֹרָא [דָּרָא] דִּלְבְנֵי — אָתֵי כָּל חַד וְחַד שָׁקֵיל חֲדָא, [15]אָמַר לֵיהּ: ״אֲנָא חֲדָא דִּשְׁקַלִי״. [16]דַּהֲוָה שָׁדֵי תּוּמֵי אוֹ שַׁמְכֵּי — אָתוּ כָּל חַד וְחַד שָׁקֵיל חֲדָא, [17]אָמַר לֵיהּ: ״אֲנָא חֲדָא דִּשְׁקַלִי״.

[18]אַרְבַּע דַּיָּינֵי הָיוּ בִּסְדוֹם:

TRANSLATION AND COMMENTARY

אָמְרִי [1]The Gemara now describes some more of the wicked practices of the people of Sodom. They **said: "Someone who has one ox must graze** the city's flocks for **one day.** [2]**Someone who does not have** any oxen **must graze** the city's animals for **two days."** [3]It was related that **a certain orphan, the son of a widow, was** once **given** the city's **oxen to graze.** [4]**He went and took them and killed them.** [5]He then **said to** the owners of the oxen: [109B] [6]**"Anyone who had one ox may take one hide.** [7]**Anyone who did not have** any **oxen may take two hides."** [8]The owners of the oxen protested and **said to him: "What is** the meaning of **this?"** [9]The orphan **said to them: "The logic at the end is like the logic at the beginning.** [10]**Just like the logic at the beginning — someone who has one ox must graze** the city's oxen for **one day, while he who does not have** any **oxen must graze** those animals for **two days** — [11]**so,** too, **the logic at the end — anyone who had one ox may take one** hide, **and anyone who did not have** any **oxen may take two** hides."

דַּעֲבַר בְּמַבָּרָא [12]Another law was passed in Sodom: **Someone who crosses** a river **by ferry must pay one** *zuz.* [13]**Someone who** fords the river and **does not cross by ferry, must pay two** *zuz.* [14]Another wicked practice prevailed in Sodom: If **someone had a row of bricks, everyone would come and take one** brick, [15]**and** each person would **say to** the owner of the bricks: **"I** only **took one** brick," but all of the bricks would be taken. [16]And similarly, if **someone spread out garlic or onions** to dry, **everyone would come and take one** garlic or an onion, [17]**and** would **say to** the owner: **"I** only **took one,"** but all the garlic or onions would be taken.

אַרְבַּע דַּיָּינֵי [18]It was related that **there were four judges in Sodom,** whose names reflected their judicial conduct:

LITERAL TRANSLATION

[1]They said: "He who has one ox must graze one day. [2]He who does not have must graze two days." [3]To a certain orphan, the son of a widow, they gave oxen to graze. [4]He went and took them and killed them. [5]He said to them: [109B] [6]"He who has an ox may take one hide. [7]He who does not have an ox may take two hides." [8]They said to him: "What is this?" [9]He said to them: "The end of the judgment is like the beginning of the judgment. [10]Just as at the beginning of the judgment, he who has [one] ox must graze one day, [while] he who does not have oxen must graze two days, [11]so the end of the judgment: He who has one ox may take one, [and] he who does not have an ox may take two."

[12]He who crosses by ferry must pay one *zuz.* [13]He who does not cross by ferry must pay two. [14]He who has a row of bricks — everyone comes [and] takes one, [15][and] says to him: "I took one." [16]He who spread out garlic or onions — everyone comes [and] takes one, [17][and] says to him: "I took one."

[18]There were four judges in Sodom:

RASHI

דאית ליה תורא — כך היה מנהגם של אנשי סדום, מי שהיה לו שור אחד רועה כל בהמות העיר יום אחד, ומי שאין לו בהמה מגלגלין עליו לרעות שני ימים. **אמר להו** — יתמי למרי דתורא: דאית ליה חד תורא כו׳. **דעבר במברא** — שהמעברות שלהם מימיו עזין והיו דנין כך. **דלא עבר במברא** — אלא בא דרך אחר. **דהוה ליה דרא דלבני** — מי שהיו לו שורת לבנים ומגבל ועושה אותן, היה בא כל חד וחד ונוטל אחת. **שדי תומי או שמכי** — מי שהיה מפזר ושוטח לפניו שומים או בצלים ליבשן כל אחד ואחד היה נוטל אחת. **אומר לו** — לנגזל: מה חסרתי לך לא לקחתי ממך אלא שום אחד, ונמצא קרח מכאן ומכאן.

NOTES

what he had said in his lecture, even though it had caused them financial loss (see *Binyan Shlomo, Ramah*). According to an alternative reading, when Rabbi Yose died, the people of Sepphoris did not want to involve themselves in his burial at first. The spouts of the city flowed with blood in order to convince the residents to prepare for Rabbi Yose's funeral and show him proper respect.

מִנְהֲגֵי סְדוֹם **The practices of Sodom.** Most of the Sodomite practices mentioned here are alluded to by the verses in Job 24 cited above: "They lie all night naked without

שַׁקְרָאִי, וְשַׁקְרוּרָאִי, זַיְיפַי, וּמַצְלֵי דִּינָא. [1]דְּמָחֵי לֵיהּ לְאִיתְּתָא דְּחַבְרֵיהּ וּמַפְלָא לֵיהּ — [2]אָמְרִי לֵיהּ: "יְהַבָהּ נִיהֲלֵיהּ דְּנִיעַבְּרָהּ נִיהֲלִיךְ". [3]דְּפָסֵיק לֵיהּ לְאוּדְנָא דַּחֲמָרָא דְּחַבְרֵיהּ, [4]אֲמַרוּ לֵיהּ: "הַבָה נִיהֲלֵיהּ עַד דְּקָדְחָא". [5]דְּפַדַע לֵיהּ לְחַבְרֵיהּ — אָמְרִי לֵיהּ: "הַב לֵיהּ אַגְרָא דִּשְׁקַל לָךְ דְּמָא". [6]דַּעֲבַר בְּמַבָּרָא יָהֵיב אַרְבָּעָה זוּזֵי. [7]דַּעֲבַר בְּמַיָּא יָהֵיב תְּמָנֵי זוּזֵי. [8]זִימְנָא חֲדָא אֲתָא הַהוּא כּוֹבֵס, אִיקְלַע לְהָתָם. [9]אֲמַרוּ לֵיהּ: הַב אַרְבַּע זוּזֵי. [10]אָמַר לְהוּ: "אֲנָא בְּמַיָּא עֲבַרִי". [11]אֲמַרוּ לֵיהּ: "אִם כֵּן הַב תְּמַנְיָא, דַּעֲבַרְתְּ בְּמַיָּא". [12]לָא יָהֵיב, פַּדְיוּהוּ. [13]אֲתָא לְקַמֵּיהּ דְּדַיָּינָא, אָמַר לֵיהּ: "הַב לֵיהּ אַגְרָא דְּשָׁקֵיל לָךְ דְּמָא, וּתְמַנְיָא זוּזֵי דַּעֲבַרְתְּ בְּמַיָּא". [14]אֱלִיעֶזֶר עֶבֶד אַבְרָהָם אִיתְרַמִּי הָתָם, פַּדְיוּהִי. [15]אֲתָא לְקַמֵּיהּ דַּיָּינָא, אָמַר לֵיהּ: "הַב לֵיהּ אַגְרָא דִּשְׁקַל לָךְ דְּמָא". [16]שְׁקַל

LITERAL TRANSLATION

Shakrai, Shakrurai, Zaifai, and Matzlei Dina: [1]Someone who strikes his fellow's wife and causes her to miscarry — [2]they say to him: "Give her to him so that he can impregnate her for you." [3]Someone who cuts off the ear of his fellow's ass — [4]they say to him: "Give it to him until it is grown in." [5]Someone who injured his fellow — they say to him: "Pay him a fee for he bled you." [6]Someone who crosses by ferry must pay four *zuz*. [7]Someone who crosses in the water must pay eight *zuz*. [8]One time a certain washerman happened to come there. [9]They said to him: "Pay four *zuz*." [10]He said to them: "I crossed in the water." [11]They said to him: "If so, pay eight, for you crossed in the water." [12]He did not pay, [and] they injured him. [13]He came before a judge, who said to him: Pay him a fee for he bled you, and eight *zuz* for you crossed in the water." [14]Eliezer the servant of Abraham happened to come there, [and] they injured him. [15]He came before a judge, who said to him: "Pay him a fee, for he bled you." [16]He took

TRANSLATION AND COMMENTARY

Shakrai ("Liar"), **Shakrurai** ("Prevaricator"), **Zaifai** ("Forger"), **and Matzlei Dina** ("Perverter of Justice"). The edicts that they issued included the following: [1]If **someone strikes a man's wife and causes her to miscarry,** [2]**they say to** the woman's husband: **"Hand** your wife **over to** the assailant, **so that he can impregnate her for you."** [3]If **someone cuts off the ear of another person's ass,** [4]**they say to** the ass's owner: **"Hand** the ass **over** to the one who caused the damage **until** the ear **grows in** again." [5]If **someone injured another person, they say** to the victim: **"Pay** your assailant **a fee, for he bled you,** and deserves to be paid for his services." [6]If **someone crosses** a river **by ferry, he must pay four** *zuz*. [7]If **he crosses in the water, he must pay eight** *zuz*.

זִימְנָא חֲדָא [8]**Once a certain washerman happened to come** to Sodom, [9]and **they said to him: "Pay** us **four** *zuz* for crossing the river by ferry." [10]**He said to them:** "But **I crossed** the river **in the water."** [11]**They said to him: "If so,** then you must **pay** us **eight** *zuz* **for crossing** the river **in the water."** [12]The washerman **refused to pay, and** so **they** struck and **injured him.** [13]**He came before a judge** demanding compensation, but the judge **said to him:** "Pay your assailant **a fee, for he bled you,** and deserves to be paid for his services, **and** pay another **eight** *zuz* **for crossing** the river **in the water."** [14]It was related that **Eliezer, the servant of Abraham,** once **happened to come there, and** one of the local residents struck and **injured him.** [15]**He came before a judge** demanding compensation, but the judge **said to him: "Pay** your assailant **a fee, for he bled you."** [16]Eliezer then **took a stone,**

LANGUAGE (RASHI)

כפרדור״א* This apparently should be **נפרדור״א**, from the Old French *nafredure*, meaning "an injury."

RASHI

זייפא — ומצלי דין. **יהבה ניהליה** — וישכב עמה עד שתהיה מעוברת. **עד דקדחא** — עד שתצמח אזנו. **דפדע** — עשה לו פצע, כמו פדעת במסכת עבודה זרה (כח,א) = *כפרדור״א בלעז. **דעבר במיא** — עובר ברגליו במים.

NOTES

clothing" alludes to the enactment passed in Sodom to strip a person of his cloak if he invites a guest for a meal. "They drive away the ass of the fatherless" alludes to their ruling regarding someone who cut off the ear of another person's ass. "They take the widow's ox for a pledge" alludes to their rules regarding grazing the city's oxen. The orphan and the widow mentioned in these verses allude to the story about the orphan, the son of a widow, who grazed the city's oxen (*Maharsha*). The various practices are cited here to show that not only did the people of Sodom sin in the most evil manner as individuals, but they also enacted wicked laws as a community in order to oppress the weakest members of society.

דְּעָבַר בְּמַיָּא Who crosses in the water. The commentators explained the devious reasoning behind these perverse laws. The people of Sodom argued that those who cross a river in the water must pay double, for they reduce the amount of water in the river (*Ramah*). Alternatively, they imposed a double fine, because they suspected those who crossed a river in the water of smuggling in order to avoid paying customs (*Margoliyot HaYam*). Or else, they argued that they enacted the fine in order to discourage people from crossing the river in the water, which would put their lives in danger (*Yad Yosef*).

גְּלָלָא, פַּדְיוּהִי אִיהוּ לְדַיָּינָא. [1]אֲמַר: "מַאי הַאי"? [2]אֲמַר לֵיהּ: "אַגְרָא דִּנְפַק לִי מִינָּךְ — הַב נִיהֲלֵיהּ לְהַאי, [3]וְזוּזֵי דִּידִי כִּדְקָיְימִי קָיְימִי".

[4]הָוְיָא לְהוּ פּוּרְיָיתָא דְּהָווּ מַגְנֵי עֲלָהּ אוֹרְחִין. [5]כִּי מַאֲרִיךְ, גָּיְיזִי לֵיהּ. [6]כִּי גּוּץ, מַתְחִין לֵיהּ. [7]אֱלִיעֶזֶר עֶבֶד אַבְרָהָם אִקְלַע לְהָתָם, אֲמַרוּ לֵיהּ: "קוּם גְּנֵי אַפּוּרְיָא". [8]אֲמַר לְהוֹן: "נִדְרָא נְדָרִי, מִן יוֹמָא דְּמִיתַת אִמָּא לָא גְּנֵינָא אַפּוּרְיָא".

[9]כִּי הֲוָה מִתְרַמֵּי לְהוּ עַנְיָא יָהֲבוּ לֵיהּ כָּל חַד וְחַד דִּינָרָא, וּכְתִיב שְׁמֵיהּ עֲלֵיהּ, [10]וְרִיפְתָּא לָא הָווּ מַמְטֵי לֵיהּ. [11]כִּי הֲוָה מָיֵית, אָתֵי כָּל חַד וְחַד שָׁקֵיל דִּידֵיהּ. [12]הָכִי אַתְנוּ בֵּינַיְיהוּ: כָּל מַאן דְּמַזְמִין גַּבְרָא לְבֵי הִילּוּלָא — לִשְׁלַח גְּלִימָא. [13]הֲוֵי הַאי הִילּוּלָא, אִקְלַע אֱלִיעֶזֶר לְהָתָם, וְלָא יָהֲבוּ לֵיהּ נַהֲמָא. [14]כִּי בָּעֵי לְמִסְעַד, אֲתָא אֱלִיעֶזֶר וִיתֵיב לְסֵיפָא דְּכוּלְּהוּ. [15]אֲמַרוּ לֵיהּ: "מַאן אַזְמְנָךְ לְהָכָא"? [16]אֲמַר לֵיהּ לְהַהוּא [דִּיתֵיב]: "אַתָּה זִמַּנְתָּן". [[17]אֲמַר: "דִּילְמָא שָׁמְעִי

LITERAL TRANSLATION

a stone, and he himself wounded the judge. [1]He said: "What is this?" [2]He said to him: "The fee that is due me from you — pay it to that one, [3]and my money will remain where it is."

[4]They had a bed upon which they made guests lie down. [5]If he was [too] long, they would cut him. [6]If he was [too] short, they would stretch him. [7]Eliezer the servant of Abraham happened to come there, [and] they said to him: "Come, lie down on the bed." [8]He said to them: "I took a vow from the day that my mother died not to lie down on a bed."

[9]When a poor person happened to come to them, everyone would give him a dinar, and his name was written on it, [10]and they would not give him bread. [11]When he died, everyone would come and take his [dinar]. [12]Thus they agreed among themselves: Whoever invites someone to a wedding — they will remove his cloak. [13]There was a certain wedding, [and] Eliezer happened to come there, and they did not give him bread. [14]When he wanted to eat, Eliezer came and sat at the end of all of them. [15]They said to him: "Who invited you here?" [16]He said to the one who was sitting: "You invited me." [17]He said: "Perhaps they will hear

TRANSLATION AND COMMENTARY

and struck and **wounded the judge.** [1]The judge **asked: "What is** the meaning of **this?"** [2]Eliezer **said to** the judge: **"The fee that you** now **owe me** for bleeding you, you **pay it** on my behalf **to the one** who bled me, [3]**and my money will remain** by me **where it is."**

הָוְיָא לְהוּ פּוּרְיָיתָא [4]It was further related that the people of Sodom **had a bed upon which they would make guests** passing through the city **lie down.** [5]**If** the guest **was too long** for the bed, **they would cut** his limbs to make him fit, [6]and **if he was too short, they would stretch him.** [7]**Eliezer, the servant of Abraham,** once **happened to come** to Sodom, **and** the local residents **said to him: "Come, lie down on** this **bed."** [8]Eliezer outsmarted **them and said: "I took a vow on the day that my mother died never to lie down** again **on a bed."**

כִּי הֲוָה [9]**Whenever a poor person happened to come to** Sodom, **everyone would give him a dinar, and** each of the donors **would write his name on** the coin that he gave. [10]But after they provided the pauper with money, **nobody would give him** any **bread** for it, and the poor person would starve to death. [11]**After** the pauper **died, everyone would come and take** back **his dinar.** [12]The people of Sodom also **agreed among themselves** as follows: **Whoever invites a stranger to a wedding will** be publicly humiliated and **have his cloak removed.** [13]There once **was a certain wedding, and Eliezer,** the servant of Abraham, **happened to attend, but he was not given any bread** to eat. [14]**When he wanted to eat, Eliezer went and sat** down **at the end of** the crowd. [15]The other guests **said to him: "Who invited you here?"** [16]Eliezer **said to the** person **who was sitting** next to him: "Was it not **you** who **invited me** to the wedding?" [17]The person sitting next to Eliezer **said** to himself: **"Perhaps** the others **will hear** rumors **about me, that**

RASHI

גללא — מקל, לישנא אחרינא: אבן. **אמר ליה** — דיינא לאליעזר: מאי האי: אמר ליה אליעזר: אגרא דמחייבת לי דשקלי לך דמא, הב ליה לההוא גברא דשקל לי דמא, וזוזי דידי כדקיימי קיימי, לישנא אחרינא הכי גרסינן: ולואי כדקאי קאי, כך אמר ליה דיין: מי יתן שהייתי כבתחילה. **הכי אתנו בהדייהו כל מאן דמזמן** — אכסניא לבי הלולא. **לשלחו לגלימיה** — יפשיטו את בגדי אותו האיש שהזמינו. **ואתא אליעזר** — עבד אברהם. **ויתיב אסיפא דכולהו** — הלך וישב בסוף כולם. **אמרו ליה** — **מאן אזמנך להכא. אמר להם** — אליעזר למאן דיתיב גביה: את זמנתני להכא. **שקל גלימיה** — דיתיב לגביה ורהט לברא, שהיה מתיירא שלא ישמעו אנשי המקום שאליעזר אמר שהוא זימנו ולישלחו למאניה, הלך וישב לו אצל השני ואמר כמו כן, וכן לכל אחד ואחד עד דאזלי כולהו ואכל אליעזר כל הסעודה. **כי אריך גייצו ליה** — כשהאורח ארוך יותר מן המטה מקצרין אותו בסכין, גייצי לשון גוץ, כן שמעתי, ואית דגרסי: גיידי ליה. **ומתחין ליה** — עד דמתפרקי אבריו. **וכתיב שמיה עילויה** — כדי שיכיר כל אחד ואחד דינר שלו ויחזור ויטלנו. **ורפתא לא ממטו ליה** — התנו ביניהם שלא יתנו לו פת כדי שימות ברעב, וכשמת — אזיל כל חד וחד ושקיל לדינרא דידיה.

TRANSLATION AND COMMENTARY

I invited Eliezer as my guest, **and they will** come and **have my cloak removed** from me in public." [1]To avoid this, **the** person **who sat next to** Eliezer **took his cloak, and ran outside.** [2]Eliezer **did the same thing to all** the people at the table **until all** the people **left** the wedding hall, **and he ate the** entire **meal** by himself.

הֲוָיָא הַהִיא רְבִיתָא [3]It was further related that once **there was a certain girl** in Sodom **who carried bread out to a poor person in a pitcher,** so that nobody would see her charitable act, [4]but **the matter** nevertheless **became known.** [5]The people of Sodom decided to punish her, and so **they smeared her with honey and placed her on the top of the** city's **wall.** [6]**Wasps came and stung her** until she died. [7]**And this is** the meaning of **the verse that states** (Genesis 18:20): **"And the Lord said, Because the cry of Sodom and Gomorra is great."** [8]**And Rav Yehudah said in the name of Rav:** The word "great [רַבָּה]" intimates that God decreed the destruction of the cities of Sodom and Gomorra [9]because of **the matter of the girl** [רִיבָה] who was put to death on account of an act of lovingkindness that she had performed.

מְרַגְּלִים [10]We have learned in our Mishnah: **"The spies** whom Moses sent out to scout the Land of Israel **do not have a portion in the World to Come,** [11]**as the verse states** (Numbers 14:37): **'Now those men who brought the evil report about the land died of the plague before the Lord.'** [12]**'They died' — in this world.** [13]**'By the plague** before the Lord' — **in the World to Come.** [14]**The company of Korah do not have a portion in the World to Come, as the verse states** (Numbers 16:33): 'And the earth closed upon them, and they perished from among the congregation.' [15]**'And the earth closed upon them' — in this world.** [16]**'And they perished from among the congregation' — in the World to Come.** [17]**This is the position of Rabbi Akiva.**

בֵּי דַּאֲנָא אַזְמִינְתֵּיהּ וּמְשַׁלְחִי לֵיהּ מָאנֵיהּ דְּהַאי גַּבְרָא״].
[1]שְׁקַל גְּלִימֵיהּ הַהוּא דְּיָתֵיב גַּבֵּיהּ, וּרְהַט לְבָרָא. [2]וְכֵן עֲבַד לְכוּלְּהוּ עַד דְּנָפְקִי כּוּלְּהוּ וְאָכְלָא אִיהוּ לִסְעוּדְתָא.
[3]הֲוָיָא הַהִיא רְבִיתָא דַּהֲוַת קָא מַפְּקָא רִיפְתָּא לְעַנְיָא בְּחַצְבָּא. [4]אִיגְלַאי מִלְּתָא. [5]שַׁפְיוּהָ דּוּבְשָׁא וְאוֹקְמוּהָ עַל אִיגַּר שׁוּרָא. [6]אֲתָא זִיבּוּרֵי וַאֲכַלוּהָ. [7]וְהַיְינוּ דִּכְתִיב: ״וַיֹּאמֶר ה׳ זַעֲקַת סְדֹם וַעֲמֹרָה כִּי רָבָּה״. [8]וְאָמַר רַב יְהוּדָה אָמַר רַב: [9]עַל עִיסְקֵי רִיבָה.
[10]״מְרַגְּלִים אֵין לָהֶם חֵלֶק לָעוֹלָם הַבָּא, [11]שֶׁנֶּאֱמַר: ׳וַיָּמֻתוּ הָאֲנָשִׁים מוֹצִאֵי דִבַּת הָאָרֶץ רָעָה בַּמַּגֵּפָה׳. [12]׳וַיָּמֻתוּ׳ — בָּעוֹלָם הַזֶּה. [13]׳בַּמַּגֵּפָה׳ — לָעוֹלָם הַבָּא״. [14]״עֲדַת קֹרַח אֵין לָהֶם חֵלֶק לָעוֹלָם הַבָּא, שֶׁנֶּאֱמַר: [15]׳וַתְּכַס עֲלֵיהֶם הָאָרֶץ׳ — בָּעוֹלָם הַזֶּה. [16]׳וַיֹּאבְדוּ מִתּוֹךְ הַקָּהָל׳ — לָעוֹלָם הַבָּא. [17]דִּבְרֵי רַבִּי

LITERAL TRANSLATION

about me that I invited him and they will remove the garment of that man." [1]The one who sat next to him took his cloak, and ran outside. [2]And he did the same thing to all of them until they all went out, and he ate the meal.

[3]There was a certain girl who carried bread to a poor person in a pitcher. [4]The matter became known. [5]They smeared her with honey and placed her on the roof of the wall. [6]Wasps came and ate her. [7]And this is what is written: "And the Lord said, Because the cry of Sodom and Gomorra is great." [8]And Rav Yehudah said in the name of Rav: [9]About the matter of a girl.

[10]"The spies do not have a portion in the World to Come, [11]as it is stated: 'Now those men who brought the evil report about the land died of the plague.' [12]'They died' — in this world. [13]'Of the plague' — in the World to Come." [14]"The company of Korah do not have a portion in the World to Come, as it is stated: [15]'And the earth closed upon them' — in this world. [16]'And they perished from among the congregation' — in the World to Come. [17][These are] the words of Rabbi

RASHI

רביתא — נערה. בחצבא — בתוך כד שלה כשיוצאת לשאוב מים. שפיוה — סכו אותה. איגר שורא — על גג החומה. כי רבה — על עסקי ריבה.

NOTES

דַּהֲוַת קָא מַפְּקָא רִיפְתָּא **Who carried bread to a poor person.** According to the Midrash, the girl who served the poor person bread was one of the daughters of Lot. The Midrash adds that it was regarding this girl that God said (Genesis 18:21): "I will go down now, and see whether they have done altogether according to her cry, which is come to me."

׳בַּמַּגֵּפָה׳ — לָעוֹלָם הַבָּא **'By the plague' — in the World to Come.** It may be asked: How does the word "plague" imply punishment in the World to Come? It has been argued that the spies' punishment in the World to Come is derived from the expression: "By the plague before the Lord," which implies that the spies were smitten before the Lord, so they would no longer exist before Him (*Hayyim Shenayim Yeshalem*).

TRANSLATION AND COMMENTARY

[1]**Rabbi Eliezer** disagrees and **says: Regarding** the company of Korah, the verse **states** (I Samuel 2:6): [2]**'The Lord kills, and gives life; He brings down to the grave, and brings up,'** teaching us that that they do indeed have a portion in the World to Come."

תָּנוּ רַבָּנַן [3]**Our Rabbis taught** a related Baraita: **"The company of Korah do not have a portion in the World to Come,** [4]**as the verse states** (Numbers 16:33): **'And the earth closed upon them' — in this world.** [5]**'And they perished** [וַיֹּאבְדוּ] **from among the congregation' — in the World to Come.** [6]**This is the position of Rabbi Akiva.** [7]**Rabbi Yehudah ben Betera** disagrees and **says:** Even though the verse testifies about the company of Korah, that they were lost [וַיֹּאבְדוּ], **they are like a lost object that is** still **being sought** and will in the end be found, [8]**as the verse states** (Psalms 119:176): **'I have gone astray like a lost sheep; seek out Your servant, for I do not forget Your commandments.'"**

וַיִּקַּח [קֹרַח] [9]The Gemara now expounds the verse dealing with Korah which states (Numbers 16:1): "Now Korah, the son of Yitzhar, the son of Kehat, the son of Levi...took men." **"Now Korah *took*."** [10]**Resh Lakish said:** Korah *took* **a bad bargain for himself,** for through his wicked deeds, he forfeited his portion in the World to Come. [11]The name **"Korah"** intimates, that through Korah's actions, **a bald spot** [*korhah*] **was created in Israel,** for he and his company were swallowed up by the earth. [12]The words **"the son of Yitzhar"** intimate that Korah was **a son who caused the entire world to boil** with anger **against him like noon** [*tzaharayim*]. [13]The words, **"the son of Kehat,"** intimate that Korah was **a son who blunted** [*hikhah*] **the teeth of his parents,** bringing them grief on account of his misdeeds. [14]The words **"the son of Levi"** intimate that Korah was **a son who became an escort** [*levayah*] **in Gehinom.**

וְלִיחֲשׁוֹב [15]The Gemara asks: If the names of Korah's forebears were meant to be interpreted in a manner that is disparaging to Korah, then the verse **should also have mentioned** that Korah was **"the son of Jacob,"** [16]and we would have interpreted those words as intimating that Korah was **a son who bent himself** [*akav*] **towards Gehinom!**

אָמַר [17]**Rav Shmuel bar Rav Yitzḥak said: Jacob prayed** not be mentioned among Korah's ancestors,

עֲקִיבָא. [1]רַבִּי אֱלִיעֶזֶר אוֹמֵר: עֲלֵיהֶם אָמַר הַכָּתוּב: [2]'ה' מֵמִית וּמְחַיֶּה מוֹרִיד שְׁאוֹל וַיָּעַל'".

[3]תָּנוּ רַבָּנַן: "עֲדַת קֹרַח אֵין לָהֶם חֵלֶק לָעוֹלָם הַבָּא, [4]שֶׁנֶּאֱמַר: 'וַתְּכַס עֲלֵיהֶם הָאָרֶץ' — בָּעוֹלָם הַזֶּה. [5]'וַיֹּאבְדוּ מִתּוֹךְ הַקָּהָל' — לָעוֹלָם הַבָּא. [6]דִּבְרֵי רַבִּי עֲקִיבָא. [7]רַבִּי יְהוּדָה בֶּן בְּתֵירָא אוֹמֵר: הֲרֵי הֵן כַּאֲבֵידָה הַמִּתְבַּקֶּשֶׁת, [8]שֶׁנֶּאֱמַר: 'תָּעִיתִי כְּשֶׂה אֹבֵד בַּקֵּשׁ עַבְדֶּךָ כִּי מִצְוֹתֶיךָ לֹא שָׁכָחְתִּי'".

[9]"וַיִּקַּח [קֹרַח]". [10]אָמַר רֵישׁ לָקִישׁ: שֶׁלָּקַח מִקָּח רַע לְעַצְמוֹ. [11]"קֹרַח" — שֶׁנַּעֲשָׂה קָרְחָה בְּיִשְׂרָאֵל. [12]"בֶּן יִצְהָר" — בֵּן שֶׁהִרְתִּיחַ עָלָיו אֶת כָּל הָעוֹלָם כַּצָּהֳרַיִם. [13]"בֶּן קְהָת" — בֵּן שֶׁהִקְהָה שִׁינֵּי מוֹלִידָיו. [14]"בֶּן לֵוִי" — בֵּן שֶׁנַּעֲשָׂה לְוָיָה בְּגֵיהִנָּם.

[15]וְלִיחֲשׁוֹב נַמִי בֶּן יַעֲקֹב — [16]בֵּן שֶׁעָקַב עַצְמוֹ לְגֵיהִנָּם!

[17]אָמַר רַב שְׁמוּאֵל בַּר רַב יִצְחָק: יַעֲקֹב בִּיקֵּשׁ רַחֲמִים עַל

LITERAL TRANSLATION

Akiva. [1]Rabbi Eliezer says: Regarding them, the verse says: [2]'The Lord kills, and gives life; He brings down to the grave, and brings up.'"

[3]Our Rabbis taught: "The company of Korah do not have a portion in the World to Come, [4]as it is stated: 'And the earth closed upon them' — in this world. [5]'And they perished from among the congregation' — in the World to Come. [6][These are] the words of Rabbi Akiva. [7]Rabbi Yehudah ben Betera says: They are like a lost object that is being sought, [8]as it is stated: 'I have gone astray like a lost sheep; seek out Your servant, for I do not forget Your commandments.'"

[9]"Now Korah took." [10]Resh Lakish said: He took a bad bargain for himself. [11]"Korah" — a bald spot was made in Israel. [12]"The son of Yitzhar" — a son who caused the entire world to boil against him like noon. [13]"The son of Kehat" — a son who blunted the teeth of his parents. [14]"The son of Levi" — a son who became an escort in Gehinom.

[15]And let them count also the son of Jacob — [16]a son who bent himself toward Gehinom!

[17]Rav Shmuel bar Rav Yitzḥak said: Jacob asked for mercy for

RASHI

רבי יהודה בן בתירא אומר ויאבדו הרי הן כאבידה המתבקשת — ובאין לעולם הבא, שכך אמר דוד על בני קרח "תעיתי כשה אובד בקש עבדך", הם תעו כשה אובד, ואתה ברחמיך הרבים בקש עבדך ותביאם לעולם הבא. **מצותיך לא שכחתי** — שקיימו כל מצותיך, כדכתיב (במדבר טז) "כי כל העדה כולם קדושים". **מקח רע** — התחיל בקטטה. **שעשה קרחה בישראל** — שנבלעו. **שהרתיח** — שהכעים. **הקהה שיני מולידיו** — שנתביישו אבותיו במעשיו הרעים. **בקש רחמים על עצמו** — שלא יהא נמנה עמהם.

NOTES

יַעֲקֹב בִּיקֵּשׁ רַחֲמִים עַל עַצְמוֹ **Jacob asked for mercy upon himself.** Jacob prayed for his name not to be mentioned together

TRANSLATION AND COMMENTARY

[1]**as the verse states** (Genesis 49:6): **"Let my soul not come into their council; to their assembly let my honor not be united."** [2]**"Let my soul not come into their council" — this** refers to **the spies** sent by Moses to scout the Land of Israel. [3]**"To their assembly let my honor not be united" — this** refers to **the company of Korah.** Jacob prayed not to be associated with the spies, nor with the company of Korah.

דָּתָן [4]The Gemara now interprets the names of the other leaders who joined Korah's uprising, as the verse continues (Numbers 16:1): "And Datan and Abiram, the sons of Eliab, and On, the son of Peleth, of the sons of Reuben." **"Datan"** was called by that name because he **violated the law** [*dat*] **of God.** [5]**"Abiram"** was called by that name because he **hardened** [*iber*] **himself not to do repentance.** [6]**"On"** was called by that name because he removed himself from the band of rebels, repented, and **sat** as if **in mourning** [*aninut*] over the sin that he had committed. [7]He was called "the son of **Peleth,"** because **wonders were performed** for him which allowed him to be saved. [8]He was **"the son of Reuben" — a son who saw** [*ra'ah*] **and understood** [*heivin*] the severity of his offense, and repented in time to be saved.

אָמַר רַב [9]**Rav said: On the son of Peleth** did not repent on his own, but rather it was **his wife** who **saved him.** [10]**She said to him: "What will come of** all this **for you?** [11]If Moses emerges victorious and **remains the master, you will be his disciple.** [12]**And** even **if** Korah wins and **becomes the master, you will** still only be **his disciple!"** [13]On **said to** his wife: **"What shall I do? I was in on the plan** from the beginning, **and I swore to them** that I would join them." [14]His wife **said to him: "I know that the entire congregation is holy,** [15]**as the verse states** (Numbers 16:3): **'For all the congregation are holy,'** [16]and no one will enter our tent if I am not fully attired. **Sit** down, **for I will save you."** [17]On's wife **gave him wine to drink, and made him drunk, and lay him down inside** their tent. [18]**She** then **sat in the entrance** of the tent,

עַצְמוֹ, [1]שֶׁנֶּאֱמַר: ״בְּסֹדָם אַל תָּבֹא נַפְשִׁי בִּקְהָלָם אַל תֵּחַד כְּבֹדִי״. [2]״בְּסֹדָם אַל תָּבֹא נַפְשִׁי״ — אֵלּוּ מְרַגְּלִים. [3]״בִּקְהָלָם אַל תֵּחַד כְּבֹדִי״ — זֶה עֲדַת קֹרַח. [4]״דָּתָן״ — שֶׁעָבַר עַל דַּת אֵל, [5]״אֲבִירָם״ — שֶׁאִיבֵּר עַצְמוֹ מֵעֲשׂוֹת תְּשׁוּבָה, [6]״וְאוֹן״ — שֶׁיָּשַׁב בַּאֲנִינוּת, [7]״פֶּלֶת״ — שֶׁנַּעֲשׂוּ לוֹ פְּלָאוֹת, [8]״בֶּן רְאוּבֵן״ — בֵּן שֶׁרָאָה וְהֵבִין.

[9]אָמַר רַב: אוֹן בֶּן פֶּלֶת אִשְׁתּוֹ הִצִּילַתּוּ. [10]אֲמַרָה לֵיהּ: ״מַאי נָפְקָא לָךְ מִינָּהּ״? [11]אִי מַר רַבָּה, אַנְתְּ תַּלְמִידָא. [12]וְאִי מַר רַבָּה, אַנְתְּ תַּלְמִידָא״. [13]אֲמַר לָהּ: ״מַאי אַעֲבֵיד? הֲוַאי בְּעֵצָה, וְאִשְׁתַּבַּעִי לִי בַּהֲדַיְיהוּ״. [14]אֲמַרָה לֵיהּ: ״יָדַעְנָא דְּכוּלָּהּ כְּנִישְׁתָּא קַדִּישְׁתָּא נִינְהוּ, [15]דִּכְתִיב: ׳כִּי כָל הָעֵדָה כֻּלָּם קְדֹשִׁים׳״. [16]אֲמַרָה לֵיהּ: ״תּוּב, דַּאֲנָא מַצִּילְנָא לָךְ״. [17]אַשְׁקִיתֵיהּ חַמְרָא, וְאַרְוִיתֵיהּ, וְאַגְנִיתֵיהּ גַּוָּאֵי. [18]אוֹתְבָה עַל בָּבָא,

LITERAL TRANSLATION

himself, [1]as it is stated: "Let my soul not come into their council; to their assembly let my honor not be united." [2]"Let my soul not come into their council" — these are the spies. [3]"To their assembly let my honor not be united" — this refers to the company of Korah. [4]"Datan" — who violated the law of God. [5]"Abiram" — who hardened himself against doing repentance. [6]"And On" — who sat in mourning. [7]"Peleth" — for whom wonders were performed. [8]"The son of Reuben" — a son who saw and understood.

[9]Rav said: On the son of Peleth, his wife saved him. [10]She said to him: "What will come of it for you? [11]If the one is the master, you are the disciple. [12]And if the one is the master, you are the disciple." [13]He said to her: "What shall I do? I was in on the plan, and I swore with them." [14]She said to him: "I know that the entire congregation is holy, [15]as it is written: 'For the whole congregation are all holy.' [16]She said to him: Sit, for I will save you." [17]She gave him wine to drink, and made him drunk, and lay him down inside. [18]She sat in the entrance,

RASHI

אלו מרגלים — דלא כתיב בהן פלוני בן יעקב. **שאיבר לבבו** — חזק לבו כמו (ישעיהו מו) ״אבירי לב״. **שישב באנינות** — שעשה תשובה על שהיה עמהם תחילה בעצה. **נעשו לו פלאות** — (שפירש) [שניצל] מהם. **ראה והבין** — שאין מנהגן כשורה ופירש מהם. **אי מר רבה** — אם ינצח משה — מכל מקום אתה תלמיד, ואם קרח מנצח — אתה תלמיד, מה לך בשררה זו. **הואי בעצה** — אני הייתי עמהן בעצה, ונשבעתי להם שאם יקראוני אלך עמהם. **דכולה כנישתא קדישין** — כולם צנועים וקדושים, ולא יכנסו אלי אם אני פרועה.

NOTES

with the names of the descendants of his sons Simeon and Levi when they stumbled. Thus, Jacob's name was not mentioned in connection with the incident involving Zimri (of the tribe of Simeon), nor in connection with the company of Korah (of the tribe of Levi). But when the verse records the genealogy of the sons of Korah who served in the Temple, their genealogy is traced back all the way to Jacob.

TRANSLATION AND COMMENTARY

[110A] **and untied her hair**, as if she were undressing to bathe. [1]**Anyone who came** near the tent to call upon On to join the revolt **saw her, and went back,** [2]**and meanwhile** Korah and his company **were swallowed up** in the earth, and On the son of Peleth was saved.

אִיתְּתֵיהּ דְּקֹרַח [3]While On's wife saved him from disaster, Korah's wife encouraged him to rebel. **Korah's wife said to him: "See what** that **Moses is doing.** [4]He made himself the **king; his brother** Aaron **he made the High Priest; his brother's sons he made deputy priests.** [5]**If** someone **comes with terumah, he says** to him: 'The terumah **must be** given **to a priest.'** [6]And **if** someone **comes with the** first **tithe, which you** as a Levite are entitled to **take, he says:** 'You must **give one tenth** of what you received **to a priest** as tithe-terumah.' [7]**And furthermore, he** had you **shave off** all **your hair,** as the verse states (Numbers 8:7): 'And let them shave all your flesh,' **and he rolls you around like excrement,** as if **he** had **set** his **eye on your hair.** He resented your good looks." [8]Korah **said to** his wife: "But **surely** Moses **also** removed his hair like all the other Levites!" [9]**She said to him: "When** he saw that **everyone** else shaved off his hair **because** he had instructed them to do so, and they recognized **his greatness,** [10]**he also said: 'Let me die with the Philistines** — I will pacify them by shaving off my hair, too.' [11]**And furthermore,** Moses **told you to place a thread of blue** upon the fringe of each corner of your garment (Numbers 15:38). [12]Now, **if you think that a thread of blue** on the fringes of a garment **is considered a commandment,** [13]then why not **take out cloaks** that are entirely **blue, and dress all** the members **of your school** in them? Moses simply made up that

[110A] וּסְתַרְתָּהּ לְמַזְיָהּ. [1]כָּל דַּאֲתָא חַזְיָהּ, הֲדַר, [2]אַדְּהָכִי וְהָכִי אִבְלְעוּ לְהוּ.

[3]אִיתְּתֵיהּ דְּקֹרַח אֲמַרָה לֵיהּ: "חֲזֵי מַאי קָעָבֵיד מֹשֶׁה. [4]אִיהוּ הֲוָה מַלְכָּא; לַאֲחוּהּ שַׁוְויֵהּ כָּהֲנָא רַבָּא; לִבְנֵי אֲחוּהִי שַׁוְינְהוּ סְגַנֵּי דְּכָהֲנָא. [5]אִי אַתְיָא תְּרוּמָה, אֲמַר: 'תֶּיהֱוֵי לַכֹּהֵן'. [6]אִי אָתוּ מַעֲשֵׂר דְּשָׁקִילְתוּ אַתּוּן, אֲמַר: 'הֲבוּ חַד מֵעֲשָׂרָה לַכֹּהֵן'. [7]וְעוֹד, דְּגָיֵיז לֵיהּ לְמַזְיַיכוּ, וּמִיטְלַל לְכוּ כִּי כּוּפְתָא. עֵינָא יְהַב בְּמַזְיַיכוּ". [8]אֲמַר לָהּ: "הָא אִיהוּ נַמִי קָא עָבֵיד"! [9]אֲמַרָה לֵיהּ: "כֵּיוָן דְּכוּלְּהוּ רְבוּתָא דִּידֵיהּ, [10]אָמַר אִיהוּ נַמִי: 'תָּמֹת נַפְשִׁי עִם פְּלִשְׁתִּים'. [11]וְעוֹד: דְּקָאֲמַר לְכוּ עָבְדִיתוּ תְּכֶלְתָּא. [12]אִי סָלְקָא דַּעֲתָךְ תְּכֶלְתָּא חֲשִׁיבָא [מִצְוָה], [13]אַפֵּיק גְּלִימֵי דִּתְכֶלְתָּא וְכַסִּינְהוּ לְכוּלְּהוּ מְתִיבְתָּךְ".

LITERAL TRANSLATION

[110A] and untied her hair. [1]Whoever came saw her, and went back, [2]and meanwhile they were swallowed up.

[3]Korah's wife said to him: "See what Moses is doing. [4]He is king; his brother he made High Priest; his brother's sons he made deputy priests. [5]If terumah comes, he says: 'It should be for a priest.' [6]If tithes come which you take, he says: 'Give one of ten to a priest.' [7]And furthermore, he shaved your hair, 'and rolls you around like excrement. He set an eye on your hair.' " [8]He said to her: "Surely he also did it!" [9]She said to him: "Since all of them for his greatness, [10]he also said: 'Let me die with the Philistines.' [11]And furthermore, he told you to make a [thread of] blue. [12]If it enters your mind that a [thread of] blue is considered a commandment, [13]take out cloaks of blue and cover all of them of your school."

RASHI

סתרה למזיה – שערה, וישבה על פתח הבית, כל מי שהיה בא לקרוא – רואה ראשה פרוע וחוזר. מעשר – ראשון דשקליתו אתון, אמר: הבו חד מעשרה לכהן. דגייז למזייכו – דכתיב (במדבר ח) "והעבירו תער על [כל] בשרם" ומשחק בכם כאילו אתם שוטים. בכופתא – רעי, כמו בטולא דכופתא דאמרן לעיל (לח,ב) כגלל הזה אתם חשובים בעיניו. עינא יהב – עין נתן בשעריכם כדי שלא יהא בכם נויה כמותו. אמר לה – קרח: איהו נמי, משה עצמו גלח כל שערו. כיון דכולא רבותא דידיה הוא – אינו חושש אם גילח עצמו, דקאמר לנפשיה "תמות נפשי עם פלשתים" אגזוז שערי כמותם ומה לי בכך, שהם מקיימין אפילו מה שאני מלוה לשחוק – אגזוז עכשיו כמותם כדי להפיס דעתם. ועוד דקאמר לכו – עשו פתיל תכלת בארבע כנפות הבגד, ואי סלקא דעתך תכלת חשוב – מפני מה לא יאמר לעשות כל הבגד כולו תכלת. אפיק גלימא דתכלתא – קח לך בגדים של תכלת וכסינהו לכולהו מתיבתך וכסה בהן בבית המדרש אתה וחבורתך.

NOTES

דְּכוּלְּהוּ רְבוּתָא דִּידֵיהּ **Since all of them for his greatness.** On's wife meant: Moses enjoys great authority and distinction, and so he suffered little shame and disgrace when he shaved off his hair. But you, Korah, do not enjoy a distinguished position, and so you were greatly disgraced by Moses' order to remove all your hair (*Maharsha*).

דְּקָאֲמַר לְכוּ עָבְדִיתוּ תְּכֶלְתָּא **He told you to make a thread of blue.** The Midrash expands on this story, and relates how Korah challenged Moses and asked him whether a garment that is entirely blue requires a blue fringe, and similarly, whether a house filled with sacred scrolls requires a mezuzah. Korah is connected to the commandment to put fringes on the corners of one's garment because the passage directly preceding the story of Korah's rebellion relates to that commandment, suggesting that Korah challenged Moses about it.

[1]הַיְינוּ דִּכְתִיב: ״חַכְמוֹת נָשִׁים בָּנְתָה בֵיתָהּ״ — [2]זוֹ אִשְׁתּוֹ שֶׁל אוֹן בֶּן פֶּלֶת. [3]״וְאִוֶּלֶת בְּיָדֶהָ תֶהֶרְסֶנָּה״ — [4]זוֹ אִשְׁתּוֹ שֶׁל קֹרַח.

[5]״וַיָּקֻמוּ לִפְנֵי מֹשֶׁה וַאֲנָשִׁים מִבְּנֵי יִשְׂרָאֵל חֲמִשִּׁים וּמָאתָיִם״ — [6]מְיוּחָדִים שֶׁבָּעֵדָה. [7]״קְרִאֵי מוֹעֵד״ — שֶׁהָיוּ יוֹדְעִים לְעַבֵּר שָׁנִים וְלִקְבּוֹעַ חֳדָשִׁים. [8]״אַנְשֵׁי שֵׁם״ — שֶׁהָיָה לָהֶם שֵׁם בְּכָל הָעוֹלָם.

[9]״וַיִּשְׁמַע מֹשֶׁה וַיִּפֹּל עַל פָּנָיו״. [10]מַה שְּׁמוּעָה שָׁמַע? [11]אָמַר רַבִּי שְׁמוּאֵל בַּר נַחֲמָנִי אָמַר רַבִּי יוֹנָתָן: שֶׁחֲשָׁדוּהוּ מֵאֵשֶׁת אִישׁ, [12]שֶׁנֶּאֱמַר: ״וַיְקַנְאוּ לְמֹשֶׁה בַּמַּחֲנֶה״.

[13]אָמַר רַבִּי שְׁמוּאֵל בַּר יִצְחָק: מְלַמֵּד שֶׁכָּל אֶחָד וְאֶחָד קִנֵּא אֶת אִשְׁתּוֹ מִמֹּשֶׁה, [14]שֶׁנֶּאֱמַר: ״וּמֹשֶׁה יִקַּח אֶת הָאֹהֶל וְנָטָה לוֹ מִחוּץ לַמַּחֲנֶה״.

LITERAL TRANSLATION

[1]This is what is written: "The wisdom of women builds her house" — [2]this is the wife of On the son of Peleth. [3]"Folly plucks it down with her hands" — [4]this is the wife of Korah.

[5]"And they rose up before Moses, with certain of the children of Israel, two hundred and fifty" — [6]the distinguished among the assembly. [7]"Regularly summoned to the congregation" — they knew how to intercalate the years and fix the months. [8]"Men of renown" — they had a name throughout the world.

[9]"And Moses heard, and fell on his face." [10]What report did he hear? [11]Rabbi Shmuel bar Naḥmani said in the name of Rabbi Yonatan: That they suspected him regarding a married woman, [12]as it is stated: "And they envied Moses in the camp."

[13]Rabbi Shmuel bar Yitzḥak said: This teaches that everyone warned his wife regarding Moses, [14]as it is stated: "And Moses would take the tent, and pitch it outside the camp."

TRANSLATION AND COMMENTARY

commandment regarding a blue thread." [1]**The following is** the meaning of **the verse** that **states** (Proverbs 14:1): **"The wisdom of women builds her house"** — [2]**this** refers to **the wife of On the son of Peleth** who saved her husband's life. [3]**"Folly plucks it down with her hands"** — [4]**this** refers to **the wife of Korah,** who encouraged her husband to rebel and brought him to his death.

וַיָּקֻמוּ לִפְנֵי מֹשֶׁה [5]The verse states (Numbers 16:2): **"And they rose up before Moses, with certain of the children of Israel, two-hundred-and-fifty** princes of the assembly." Who were these people? [6]**The** most **distinguished** people **among the assembly.** [7]**"Regularly summoned to the congregation** [קְרִאֵי מוֹעֵד]" — people **who knew how to intercalate the years and fix the months,** and thus were fit to fix the Festivals [מוֹעֲדִים]. [8]**"Men of renown** [שֵׁם]" — people **who had a name** [שֵׁם] **throughout the world.**

וַיִּשְׁמַע מֹשֶׁה [9]The verse states (Numbers 16:4): **"And Moses heard, and fell on his face."** [10]The Gemara asks: **What report did** Moses **hear?** [11]**Rabbi Shmuel bar Naḥmani said in the name of Rabbi Yonatan:** Moses heard **that** the people **suspected him** of having an affair **with a married woman,** [12]**as the verse states** (Psalms 106:16): **"And they envied** [וַיְקַנְאוּ] **Moses in the camp,"** the word וַיְקַנְאוּ intimating that every man warned [קִנֵּא] his wife not to seclude herself with Moses.

אָמַר [13]**Rabbi Shmuel bar Yitzḥak said: This teaches that every man warned his wife** not to seclude herself **with Moses,** [14]**as the verse states** (Exodus 33:7): **"And Moses would take the tent, and pitch it outside the camp."** Moses removed himself entirely, so that people would no longer suspect him of impropriety.

RASHI

קנא לאשתו – אל (הסתר) [תסתרי] עם משה, קנוי היינו התראה. ונטה לו מחוץ למחנה – יצא מחוץ למחנה שלא יחשדוהו עוד.

NOTES

שֶׁחֲשָׁדוּהוּ מֵאֵשֶׁת אִישׁ **They suspected him regarding a married woman.** The Rishonim ask: What brought the Rabbis to interpret the Biblical story in this manner? It has been suggested that this interpretation is connected to what the Rabbis said about the verse (Proverbs 6:32): "He who commits adultery with a woman lacks understanding," that whoever rules over the community not for the sake of Heaven is regarded as an adulterer. Thus, when the Gemara says that the people suspected him of adultery, it means that they accused him of usurping authority by illegitimate means (*Rabbi Ḥiyya Rofe*). It might be added, according to the plain sense of the text, that the Torah itself testifies that Moses pitched his tent outside the camp, and he dwelled there alone without his wife. The women of Israel continued to come to him with their questions, and their husbands may have suspected him of improper conduct. To counter this claim, the Torah itself states that Moses's attendant Joshua never left his tent, and thus Moses could never have secluded himself with any of the women who came before him (*Ri'af*). Others point out that the verse, which teaches that Moses pitched his tent outside the camp, follows the story regarding the golden calf. According to Rabbinical tradition, the women of Israel refused to contribute their jewelry for the construction of the calf, and this may have led the men of Israel to object that their wives obeyed Moses more than they did their own husbands (*Margoliyot HaYam*).

LITERAL TRANSLATION

[1] "And Moses rose and went to Datan and Abiram." [2] Resh Lakish said: From here [we learn] that we may not maintain dissension. [3] For Rav said: Whoever maintains dissension violates a negative precept, [4] as it is stated: "That he will not be like Korah and his company."

[5] Rav Ashi said: He deserves to be afflicted with leprosy. [6] It is written here: "To him by the hand of Moses." [7] And it is written there: "And the Lord said furthermore to him, Put now your hand into your bosom."

[8] Rabbi Yose said: Whoever challenges the kingdom of the House of David deserves to have a snake bite him. [9] It is written here: "And Adoniah slaughtered sheep and oxen and fat cattle by the stone of Zocheleth." [10] And it is written there: "With the poison of crawling things of the dust."

[11] Rav Ḥisda said: Whoever disagrees with his master is like someone who disagrees with the Divine Presence, [12] as it is stated: "When they strove against the Lord."

[1] ״וַיָּקָם מֹשֶׁה וַיֵּלֶךְ אֶל דָּתָן וַאֲבִירָם״. [2] אָמַר רֵישׁ לָקִישׁ: מִכָּאן שֶׁאֵין מַחֲזִיקִין בְּמַחֲלוֹקֶת. [3] דְּאָמַר רַב: כָּל הַמַּחֲזִיק בְּמַחֲלוֹקֶת עוֹבֵר בְּלָאו, [4] שֶׁנֶּאֱמַר: ״וְלֹא יִהְיֶה כְקֹרַח וְכַעֲדָתוֹ״.

[5] רַב אַשִׁי אָמַר: רָאוּי לִיצְטָרֵעַ. [6] כְּתִיב הָכָא: ״בְּיַד מֹשֶׁה לוֹ״. [7] וּכְתִיב הָתָם: ״וַיֹּאמֶר ה׳ לוֹ עוֹד הָבֵא נָא יָדְךָ בְּחֵיקֶךָ״.

[8] אָמַר רַבִּי יוֹסֵי: כָּל הַחוֹלֵק עַל מַלְכוּת בֵּית דָּוִד רָאוּי לְהַכִּישׁוֹ נָחָשׁ. [9] כְּתִיב הָכָא: ״וַיִּזְבַּח אֲדֹנִיָּהוּ צֹאן וּבָקָר וּמְרִיא עִם אֶבֶן הַזֹּחֶלֶת״. [10] וּכְתִיב הָתָם: ״עִם חֲמַת זֹחֲלֵי עָפָר״.

[11] אָמַר רַב חִסְדָּא: כָּל הַחוֹלֵק עַל רַבּוֹ כְּחוֹלֵק עַל הַשְּׁכִינָה, [12] שֶׁנֶּאֱמַר: ״בְּהַצֹּתָם עַל ה׳ ״.

RASHI

מכאן שאין מחזיקין במחלוקת — שמחל על כבודו והוא עצמו הלך לבטל מחלוקת. חולק על רבו — חולק על ישיבתו. אשר הצו על משה ועל אהרן בעדת קרח בהצותם על ה׳ — מעלה עליהם הכתוב כאלו היו חולקים כלפי שכינה.

TRANSLATION AND COMMENTARY

וַיָּקָם מֹשֶׁה [1] The verse states (Numbers 16:25): **"And Moses rose and went to Datan and Abiram."** [2] **Resh Lakish said: From here** we learn **that a person may not maintain dissension,** even if he feels that he is in the right. Datan and Abiram should have gone to Moses to appease him, but Moses waived his honor and went to make peace with them and put an end to the dissension. [3] And similarly, **Rav said: Whoever maintains dissension violates a negative precept,** [4] **as the verse states** (Numbers 17:5): **"That he will not be like Korah and his company;** as the Lord said to him by the hand of Moses," teaching that one may not exacerbate an existing controversy as did Korah, but rather one must make every effort to bring the controversy to a close.

רַב אַשִׁי אָמַר [5] **Rav Ashi said:** Someone who nurtures dissension like Korah **deserves to be afflicted with leprosy.** [6] **Here, the verse states** (Numbers 17:5): "That he will not be like Korah and his company; as the Lord said **to him by the hand of Moses."** [7] **And elsewhere, the verse states** (Exodus 4:6): **"And the Lord said furthermore to him, Put now your hand into your bosom**...behold, his hand was diseased, as white as snow." Just as, there, Moses' hand was afflicted with leprosy, so, too, here, someone who conducts himself like Korah, and not as the Lord said by the hand of Moses, deserves to be afflicted with leprosy.

אָמַר רַבִּי יוֹסֵי [8] **Rabbi Yose said: Whoever challenges the kingdom of the House of David deserves to be bitten by a snake.** [9] **Here, the verse states** (I Kings 1:9): **"And Adoniah slaughtered sheep and oxen and fat cattle by the stone of Zocheleth** [הַזֹּחֶלֶת]." [10] **And elsewhere, the verse states** (Deuteronomy 32:24): **"With the poison of crawling things** [זֹחֲלֵי] **of the dust."** This teaches that Adoniah, who challenged the kingdom of the House of David at the stone of Zocheleth, deserved to be bitten by a crawling thing (*zochalei*) of the dust, a snake.

אָמַר רַב חִסְדָּא [11] **Rav Ḥisda said: Whoever disagrees with his master is like someone who disagrees with the Divine Presence,** [12] **as the verse states** (Numbers 26:9): "Who strove against Moses and against Aaron in the company of Korah, **when they strove against the Lord,"** thus teaching that the challenge to Moses was regarded as a challenge to God.

HALAKHAH

כָּל הַמַּחֲזִיק בְּמַחֲלוֹקֶת **Whoever maintains dissension.** "One is forbidden to maintain dissension, even if justice is on one's side, but rather one must make all efforts to appease his opponent and make peace with him." *Ramban* counts this among the six-hundred-and-thirteen Torah commandments, but *Rambam* does not. (*She'iltot, Parashat Korah; Rif, Rosh.*)

כָּל הַחוֹלֵק עַל רַבּוֹ **Whoever disagress with his master.** "Whoever disagrees with his master, or quarrels with him, or complains against him, or speaks evil of him, is regarded as if he had challenged, quarreled with, complained against, or spoken evil of the Divine Presence." (*Shulḥan Arukh, Yoreh De'ah* 242:2.)

TRANSLATION AND COMMENTARY

אָמַר רַבִּי חָמָא [1]Rabbi Ḥama the son of Rabbi Ḥanina said: Whoever quarrels with his master is regarded like someone who quarrels with the Divine Presence, [2]as the verse states (Exodus 20:13): "This is the water of Merivah; because the children of Israel strove with the Lord," even though it was with Moses that the children of Israel strove and quarreled.

אָמַר רַבִּי חֲנִינָא בַּר פַּפָּא [3]Rabbi Ḥanina bar Pappa said: Whoever complains against his master, claiming that he has been treated unfairly, is regarded as if he had complained against the Divine Presence, [4]as the verse states (Exodus 16:8): "Your murmurings are not against us, but against the Lord." Even though the children of Israel had in fact complained against Moses and Aaron, Moses regarded their complaints as directed at God.

אָמַר רַבִּי אַבָּהוּ [5]Rabbi Abbahu said: Whoever speaks ill of his master, saying that he had erred about a certain matter or committed a sin, is regarded as if he had spoken ill of the Divine Presence, [6]as the verse states (Numbers 21:5): "And the people spoke against God, and against Moses," thus equating speaking against Moses to speaking against God.

עֹשֶׁר שָׁמוּר [7]The verse states (Ecclesiastes 5:12): "Riches are kept for their owner to his hurt." [8]Resh Lakish said: This refers to the riches of Korah. From where do we know that Korah was a wealthy man? This is derived from the verse that states (Deuteronomy 11:6): "And what He did to Datan and Abiram, the sons of Eliab, the son of Reuben; how the earth opened its mouth, and swallowed them up, and their households, and their tents, [9]and every living thing that followed them [בְּרַגְלֵיהֶם]." [10]And Rabbi Elazar said: These last words refer to a person's money that stands him up on his feet [רַגְלָיו]. [11]And Rabbi Levi said: Just the keys to Korah's treasure house were a load of three hundred white mules, [12]and all of Korah's keys and locks were made of leather, so they were light. From here we may surmise how great were Korah's treasures themselves.

[1]אָמַר רַבִּי חָמָא בְּרַבִּי חֲנִינָא: כָּל הָעוֹשֶׂה מְרִיבָה עִם רַבּוֹ כְּעוֹשֶׂה עִם שְׁכִינָה, [2]שֶׁנֶּאֱמַר: "הֵמָּה מֵי מְרִיבָה; אֲשֶׁר רָבוּ בְנֵי יִשְׂרָאֵל אֶת ה׳".

[3]אָמַר רַבִּי חֲנִינָא בַּר פַּפָּא: כָּל הַמִּתְרַעֵם עַל רַבּוֹ כְּאִילּוּ מִתְרַעֵם עַל הַשְּׁכִינָה, [4]שֶׁנֶּאֱמַר: "לֹא עָלֵינוּ תְלֻנֹּתֵיכֶם כִּי אִם עַל ה׳".

[5]אָמַר רַבִּי אַבָּהוּ: כָּל הַמְהַרְהֵר אַחַר רַבּוֹ כְּאִילּוּ מְהַרְהֵר אַחַר שְׁכִינָה, [6]שֶׁנֶּאֱמַר: "וַיְדַבֵּר הָעָם בֵּאלֹהִים וּבְמֹשֶׁה".

[7]"עֹשֶׁר שָׁמוּר לִבְעָלָיו לְרָעָתוֹ". [8]אָמַר רֵישׁ לָקִישׁ: זֶה עוֹשְׁרוֹ שֶׁל קֹרַח. [9]"וְאֵת כָּל הַיְקוּם אֲשֶׁר בְּרַגְלֵיהֶם". [10]אָמַר רַבִּי אֶלְעָזָר: זֶה מָמוֹנוֹ שֶׁל אָדָם, שֶׁמַּעֲמִידוֹ עַל רַגְלָיו. [11]וְאָמַר רַבִּי לֵוִי: מַשּׂוֹי שְׁלֹשׁ מֵאוֹת פְּרָדוֹת לְבָנוֹת הָיוּ מַפְתְּחוֹת שֶׁל בֵּית גְּנָזָיו שֶׁל קֹרַח, [12]וְכוּלְּהוּ אַקְלִידֵי וְקִילְפֵי דְּגִילְדָא.

LITERAL TRANSLATION

[1]Rabbi Ḥama the son of Rabbi Ḥanina said: Whoever quarrels with his master is like someone who quarrels with the Divine Presence, [2]as it is stated: "This is the water of Merivah; because the children of Israel strove with the Lord."

[3]Rabbi Ḥanina bar Pappa said: Whoever complains against his master is [regarded] as if he complained against the Divine Presence, [4]as it is stated: "Your murmurings are not against us, but against the Lord."

[5]Rabbi Abbahu said: Whoever speaks ill of his master is [regarded] as if he had spoken ill of the Divine Presence, [6]as it is stated: "And the people spoke against God, and against Moses."

[7]"Riches are kept for their owner to his hurt." [8]Resh Lakish said: This refers to (lit., "is") the riches of Korah. [9]"And every living thing that followed them." [10]Rabbi Elazar said: This is the money of a person that stands him up on his feet. [11]And Rabbi Levi said: The keys to Korah's treasure house were a load of three hundred white mules, [12]and all the keys and locks were of leather.

RASHI

מריבה — תגר וקטטה לפטפט נגדו בדברים. מתרעם — אומר על רבו שנוהג לו מדה כבושה ומדת אכזרית. מהרהר — מחפה עליו דברים. אקלידי = מפתחות. וקולפי = מנעולים. דגילדי — כולם, המפתחות והמנעולים של עור היו, ואף על פי כן היו שלש מאות פרדות טעונות, לישנא אחרינא: דגלדא — לצורך שקים והמרצופין וכיסין של עור היו.

LANGUAGE

אַקְלִידֵי **Key.** This derives from the Greek κλεις, *kleis*, meaning "a key," or from κλειδιον, *kleidion*, "a small key."

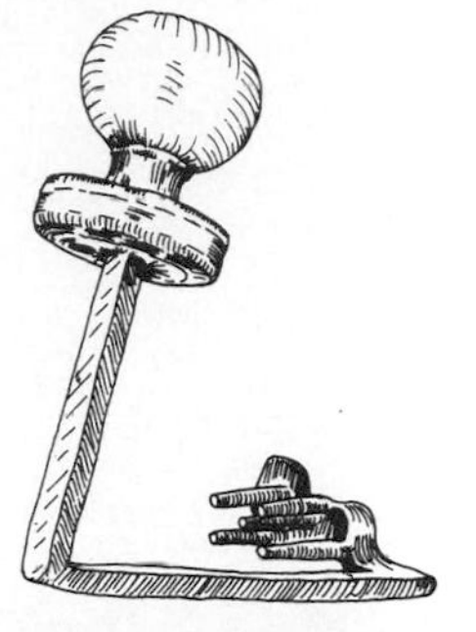

A key from the Mishnaic period.

NOTES

וַיְדַבֵּר הָעָם בֵּאלֹהִים וּבְמֹשֶׁה **And the people spoke against God, and against Moses.** Some have explained this proof as follows: The verse mentions not only that the people spoke against God, but also that they spoke against Moses, implying that the two offenses are equal. Otherwise, it should only have mentioned the more serious offense (*Rabbenu Yehonatan*). Alternatively, since the people could not possibly have spoken against God, it must be that speaking against Moses was treated as speaking against God. The argument could also be as follows: If the people did not believe in God, then why did they still speak out against Moses, who merely served as His representative? Rather, although they only spoke against Moses, the verse views such behavior as speaking against God Himself (*Ramah*).

TRANSLATION AND COMMENTARY

אָמַר רַבִּי חָמָא [1]**Rabbi Ḥama the son of Rabbi Ḥanina said: Joseph buried three treasures in Egypt** from the money he collected when he sold grain to the hungry Egyptians: [2]**One** of the treasures **was** later **revealed to Korah, one was revealed to Antoninus the son of Asverus,** King of Rome, **and** [3]**one** remains **hidden away for the righteous** and is to be enjoyed by them **in the future** in the days of the Messiah.

וְאָמַר רַבִּי יוֹחָנָן [4]**Rabbi Yoḥanan said: Korah** himself **was neither among those who were swallowed** up by the earth, **nor among those who were burnt,** but rather among those who died in the plague. [5]Korah was **not among those who were swallowed** up by the earth, **for the verse states** (Numbers 16:32): "And the earth opened her mouth, and swallowed...[6]**and all the men who were with Korah,"** implying that the men who were with Korah were swallowed up, [7]**but not Korah** himself. [8]**Neither** was Korah **among those who were burnt, for the verse states** (Numbers 26:10): **"When the fire devoured two-hundred-and-fifty men,"** implying that the two-hundred-and-fifty men were devoured by the fire, [9]**but not Korah** himself.

בְּמַתְנִיתָא תָּנָא [10]**A Sage taught** differently **in** the following **Baraita: "Korah was among those who were burnt,** and he **was among those who were swallowed** up by the earth. [11]Korah was **among those who were swallowed** up by the earth, **for the verse states** (Numbers 16:32): 'And the earth opened her mouth, **and swallowed them up together with Korah.'** [12]And Korah was also **among those who were burnt, for the verse states** (Numbers 16:35): **'And there came out a fire from the Lord, and consumed the two-hundred-and-fifty men** that offered the incense,' [13]**and Korah** himself **was among** the two-hundred-and-fifty men that offered the incense."

[1]אָמַר רַבִּי חָמָא בְּרַבִּי חֲנִינָא: שָׁלֹשׁ מַטְמוֹנִיּוֹת הִטְמִין יוֹסֵף בְּמִצְרַיִם: [2]אַחַת נִתְגַּלְּתָה לְקֹרַח, וְאַחַת נִתְגַּלְּתָה לְאַנְטוֹנִינוּס בֶּן אַסְוֵירוּס, [3]וְאַחַת גְּנוּזָה לַצַּדִּיקִים לֶעָתִיד לָבוֹא.

[4]וְאָמַר רַבִּי יוֹחָנָן: קֹרַח לֹא מִן הַבְּלוּעִים וְלֹא מִן הַשְּׂרוּפִין. [5]לֹא מִן הַבְּלוּעִין, דִּכְתִיב: [6]"וְאֵת כָּל הָאָדָם אֲשֶׁר לְקֹרַח", [7]וְלֹא קֹרַח. [8]וְלֹא מִן הַשְּׂרוּפִים, דִּכְתִיב: "בַּאֲכֹל הָאֵשׁ אֵת חֲמִשִּׁים וּמָאתַיִם אִישׁ", [9]וְלֹא קֹרַח.

[10]בְּמַתְנִיתָא תָּנָא: "קֹרַח מִן הַשְּׂרוּפִין, וּמִן הַבְּלוּעִין. [11]מִן הַבְּלוּעִים, דִּכְתִיב: 'וַתִּבְלַע אֹתָם וְאֶת קֹרַח'. [12]מִן הַשְּׂרוּפִין, דִּכְתִיב: 'וַתֵּצֵא אֵשׁ מִלִּפְנֵי ה' [וְאֵשׁ יָצְאָה מֵאֵת ה'], וַתֹּאכַל אֵת הַחֲמִשִּׁים וּמָאתַיִם אִישׁ', [13]וְקֹרַח בַּהֲדַיְיהוּ".

LITERAL TRANSLATION

[1]Rabbi Ḥama the son of Rabbi Ḥanina said: Joseph buried three treasures in Egypt: [2]One was revealed to Korah, and one was revealed to Antoninus the son of Asverus, [3]and one is hidden away for the righteous in the future.

[4]And Rabbi Yoḥanan said: Korah was not among those who were swallowed, nor among those who were burnt. [5]Not among those who were swallowed, for it is written: [6]"And all the men who were with Korah," [7]but not Korah. [8]Nor among those who were burnt, for it is written: "When the fire devoured two-hundred-and-fifty men," [9]and not Korah.

[10][A Sage] taught in a Baraita: "Korah was among those who were burnt, and among those who were swallowed. [11]Among those who were swallowed, for it is written: 'And it swallowed them up together with Korah.' [12]Among those who were burnt, for it is written: 'And there came out a fire from the Lord, and consumed the two-hundred-and-fifty men,' [13]and Korah was among them."

RASHI

לא מן הבלועין ולא מן השרופין — אלא במגפה מת. **ולא קרח** — מאתים וחמשים היו לבד קרח, דכתיב "חמשים ומאתים מחתות ואתה ואהרן איש מחתתו". **מן הבלועים ומן השרופין היה** — שנשרפה נשמתו וגוף קיים, ואחר כך נתגלגל עד מקום הבלועין ונבלע, דכתיב בפרשת פנחס "ותבלע אותם ואת קרח" עמהם, ור' יוחנן דאמר לא מן הבלועין ולא מן השרופין דריש ליה להאי "ואת קרח" לאחריו, ואת קרח במות העדה במגפה. **וקרח בהדייהו** — מדכתיב ותאכל את החמשים ומאתים איש מקריבי הקטרת וקרח ממקריבי הקטרת היה, דכתיב "חמשים ומאתים מחתות ואתה ואהרן איש מחתתו", אי נמי: "ואת" — לרבות קרח עמהם.

PEOPLE

אַנְטוֹנִינוּס בֶּן אַסְוֵירוּס Antoninus the son of Asverus. It cannot be known exactly which Roman emperor the Sages refer to here. However, it may be that it was Antoninus the son of Septimus Severus, known more commonly as Caracala, who reigned from 212 to 217. He is famous for having granted Roman citizenship to all inhabitants of the empire. He is also famous for wasting enormous sums on gifts to the soldiers and for constructing magnificent edifices.

NOTES

לֹא מִן הַבְּלוּעִים Not among those who were swallowed. *Maharsha* explains that Korah himself was not punished as severely as some of the other members of his company because his crime was not as grave. He had good reason to think he was fit for a position of authority over the people (see *Rashi* on the Torah). Alternatively, Korah's punishment was less severe by virtue of the credit to be earned by his descendants, some of whom became important leaders of the people, including the Temple singers descended from Korah, and the Prophet Samuel.

מִן הַשְּׂרוּפִין, וּמִן הַבְּלוּעִין Among those who were burnt, and among those who were swallowed. The Midrash explains that Korah was burned, so that the other members of Korah's company who suffered that punishment would not complain that Korah caused them to rebel but was not punished like them. He was swallowed up by the earth, so

TRANSLATION AND COMMENTARY

אָמַר רָבָא [1]**Rava said: What is** meant by **the verse that states** (Habakkuk 3:11): **"The sun and moon stand still in their habitation** [זְבֻלָה], **at the light of Your arrows as they speed"?** [2]**This teaches that the sun and the moon went up to the Fourth Heaven** [זְבוּל], the seat of the heavenly Temple, **and said before** God: **"Master of the Universe!** [3]**If You perform a judgment for** Moses **the son of Amram,** and find him righteous and Korah You find guilty, **we will go out** and illuminate the world. **But if not, we will not go out."** The sun and the moon continued in their protest, [4]**until** God **shot arrows at them,** and **said to them: "Regarding My honor you never objected.** Every day you see people bowing down to yourselves, yet you never said anything. [5]**But regarding the honor of flesh and blood** — the honor of Moses — **you** now **raise an objection."** [6]The Gemara adds: **And now** the sun and the moon **do not go out** to illuminate the world **until they are beaten** and forced to do so, for they do not wish to insult God's honor by pleasing idol-worshipers.

דָּרַשׁ רָבָא [7]**Rava expounded: What is** the meaning of **the verse that states** (Numbers 16:30): [8]**"But if the Lord creates a new thing, and the earth opens her mouth"?** [9]**Moses said before the Holy One, blessed be He: "If Gehinom has** already been **created, fine.** [10]**And if not, let God create it** now." [11]The Gemara asks: **For what,** precisely, did Moses pray? [12]**If you say** that Moses asked God **to create** Gehinom, **literally,** that is to say, that Gehinom did not yet exist, and now it should exist — there is a difficulty, **for surely** the verse states (Ecclesiastes 1:9): **"There is nothing new under the sun."** [13]**Rather,** Moses asked God **to bring the entrance** to Gehinom **closer** so that Korah and his company could be swallowed up by the earth.

וּבְנֵי קֹרַח לֹא מֵתוּ [14]The verse states (Numbers 26:11) **"But the children of Korah did not die." A Sage taught** a Baraita: **"They said in the name of our master:** [15]**A place was fortified** and set aside **for** Korah's children high up **in Gehinom, and** so they did not descend

[1]אָמַר רָבָא: מַאי דִּכְתִיב: "שֶׁמֶשׁ יָרֵחַ עָמַד זְבֻלָה לְאוֹר חִצֶּיךָ יְהַלֵּכוּ"? [2]מְלַמֵּד שֶׁעָלוּ שֶׁמֶשׁ וְיָרֵחַ לִזְבוּל, אָמְרוּ לְפָנָיו: "רִבּוֹנוֹ שֶׁל עוֹלָם! [3]אִם אַתָּה עוֹשֶׂה דִּין לְבֶן עַמְרָם, נֵצֵא. וְאִם לָאו, לֹא נֵצֵא". [4]עַד שֶׁזָּרַק בָּהֶם חִיצִּים. [5]אָמַר לָהֶן: "בִּכְבוֹדִי לֹא מְחִיתֶם, בִּכְבוֹד בָּשָׂר וָדָם מְחִיתֶם"! [6]וְהָאִידָּנָא לָא נָפְקִי עַד דְּמָחוּ לְהוּ.

[7]דָּרַשׁ רָבָא: מַאי דִּכְתִיב: [8]"וְאִם בְּרִיאָה יִבְרָא ה' וּפָצְתָה הָאֲדָמָה אֶת פִּיהָ"? [9]אָמַר מֹשֶׁה לִפְנֵי הַקָּדוֹשׁ בָּרוּךְ הוּא: "אִם בְּרִיאָה גֵּיהִנָּם, מוּטָב. [10]וְאִם לָאו, יִבְרָא ה'". [11]לְמַאי? [12]אִילֵימָא לְמִבְרְיֵיהּ מַמָּשׁ — וְהָא "אֵין כָּל חָדָשׁ תַּחַת הַשָּׁמֶשׁ". [13]אֶלָּא, לְקָרוֹבֵי פִּיתְחָא.

[14]"וּבְנֵי קֹרַח לֹא מֵתוּ". תָּנָא: "מִשּׁוּם רַבֵּינוּ אָמְרוּ: [15]מָקוֹם

LITERAL TRANSLATION

[1]Rava said: What is that which is written: "The sun and moon stand still in their habitation, at the light of Your arrows as they speed"? [2]This teaches that the sun and the moon went up to the Fourth Heaven, and said before Him: "Master of the Universe! [3]If You perform a judgment for the son of Amram, we will go out. But if not, we will not go out." [4]Until He cast arrows at them. [5]He said to them: "Regarding My honor you did not object, but regarding the honor of flesh and blood you object." [6]And now they do not go out until they hit them.

[7]Rava expounded: What is that which is written: [8]"But if the Lord creates a new thing, and the earth opens her mouth"? [9]Moses said before the Holy One, blessed be He: "If Gehinom was created, fine. [10]And if not, let God create [it]." [11]For what? [12]If you say to actually create it — but surely "There is nothing new under the sun." [13]Rather, to bring the entrance closer.

[14]"But the children of Korah did not die." [A Sage] taught: "They said in the name of our master: [15]A place

RASHI

שמש ירח עמד זבולה – לעיל מיניה כתיב ותבקע ארץ, בשעת בקיעת הארץ שנבלעו בקרקע שמש וירח עלו לאותו רקיע ששמו זבול ואמרו להקב"ה: אם אי אתה עושה דין לבן עמרם מקרח ועדתו. **לא נצא** – ונאיר לעולם. **בכבודי לא מחיתם** – שהרי בכל יום מלכי מזרח ומערב בשעה שמניחין כתריהן בראשם משתחוים לחמה. **והאידנא לא נפקי עד דמחו להו** – שכך גזר עליהם המקום, כן שמעתי, לישנא אחרינא: והאידנא לא נפקי – מאחר שראו שהקפיד הקב"ה על שלא מיחה לכבודו – עד דמחו להו לא נפקי, שחסו לכבוד המקום על בני אדם שמשתחוים לשמש וירח. **אין כל חדש תחת השמש** – ואי גיהנם לא אברי עד ההוא שעתא הוה ליה חדש. **לקרובי פתחא** – שיקרב פתחה של גיהנם ותפתח הארץ במקום שהן.

NOTES

that those who received that punishment would not present a similar complaint. The Midrash also explains that the fire burned Korah among the men who offered the incense, and his body rolled until it reached the opening in the earth, where he was swallowed up.

TRANSLATION AND COMMENTARY

to the depths of that place [they 'died not'], [1]but rather **they sat** in their designated area **and recited songs."**

אָמַר [2]**Rabbah bar Bar Ḥannah said: Once I was walking along the road, and a certain Arab** came over and **said to me:** [3]**"Come** and **I will show you** the place where the company of **Korah were swallowed up."** [4]**I went** with him, **and saw two cracks** in the ground **from which steam was rising.** [5]My Arab guide **took a ball of wool, soaked it in water, placed it on the point of his spear, and passed it** over the cracks, **and** the ball of wool **became singed,** thus indicating how hot the fire down below had to be. [6]The Arab **said to me: "Listen** closely **to what you hear."** [7]**And I heard them saying** as follows: **"Moses and his Torah are true, and we** ourselves **are liars."** [110B] [8]The Arab **said to** Rabbah bar Ḥannah: **"Every thirty days Gehinom returns them** to this place **like meat** that is turned **in a pot** to cook it well. [9]**And they say** as follows: **'Moses and his Torah are true, and we** ourselves **are liars.'"**

דּוֹר הַמִּדְבָּר [10]We learned in our Mishnah: **"The generation of the wilderness do not have a portion in the World to Come."** [11]**Our Rabbis taught** a related Baraita: **"The generation of the wilderness do not have a portion in the World to Come, as the verse states** (Numbers 14:35): **'In this wilderness they shall be consumed, and there they shall die.'** [12]**'They shall be consumed' — in this world.** [13]**'And there they shall die'** — they shall remain dead **in the World to Come.** [14]**And** regarding the generation of the wilderness, the verse **says** (Psalms 95:11): **'Whereupon I swore in My anger that they should not enter into My rest'** — they shall not enjoy eternal rest. [15]**This is the position of Rabbi Akiva.** [16]**Rabbi Eliezer** disagrees and **says:** The generation of the wilderness **will go** in the end **to the World to Come,** [17]**for the verse states** (Psalms 50:5): **'Gather My pious ones together to Me;** those

נִתְבַּצֵּר לָהֶם בְּגֵיהִנָּם. [1]וְיָשְׁבוּ עָלָיו וְאָמְרוּ שִׁירָה״.
[2]אָמַר רַבָּה בַּר בַּר חָנָה: זִימְנָא חֲדָא הֲוָה קָאָזְלִינָא בְּאוֹרְחָא, אָמַר לִי הַהוּא טַיָּיעָא: [3]״תָּא, וְאַחֲוֵי לָךְ בְּלוּעֵי דְּקֹרַח״. [4]אֲזֵיל, חֲזָא תְּרֵי בִּזְעֵי דַּהֲוָה קָא נָפַק קִיטְרָא מִנַּיְיהוּ. [5]שְׁקַל גְּבָבָא דְּעַמְרָא, אַמְשְׁיֵּיהּ מַיָּא, וְאוֹתְבֵיהּ בְּרֵישׁ רוּמְחֵיהּ, וְאַחַלְפֵיהּ הָתָם, אִיחֲרַךְ. [6]אָמַר לִי: ״אַצֵּית מַה שָׁמְעַתְּ״. [7]וּשְׁמָעִית דְּהָווּ קָאָמְרִי הָכִי: ״מֹשֶׁה וְתוֹרָתוֹ אֱמֶת, וְהֵן בַּדָּאִים״. [110B] [8]אָמַר לֵיהּ: ״כָּל תְּלָתִין יוֹמִין מְהַדְּרָא לְהוּ גֵּיהִנָּם כְּבָשָׂר בְּתוֹךְ קַלַּחַת, [9]וְאָמְרִי הָכִי: ׳מֹשֶׁה וְתוֹרָתוֹ אֱמֶת וְהֵן בַּדָּאִים׳ ״.
[10]״דּוֹר הַמִּדְבָּר אֵין לָהֶם חֵלֶק לָעוֹלָם הַבָּא וכו׳ ״. [11]תָּנוּ רַבָּנַן: ״דּוֹר הַמִּדְבָּר אֵין לָהֶם חֵלֶק לָעוֹלָם הַבָּא, שֶׁנֶּאֱמַר: ׳בַּמִּדְבָּר הַזֶּה יִתַּמּוּ וְשָׁם יָמֻתוּ׳. [12]׳יִתַּמּוּ׳ — בָּעוֹלָם הַזֶּה. [13]׳וְשָׁם יָמֻתוּ׳ — בָּעוֹלָם הַבָּא. [14]וְאָמַר: ׳אֲשֶׁר נִשְׁבַּעְתִּי בְאַפִּי אִם יְבֹאוּן אֶל מְנוּחָתִי׳. [15]דִּבְרֵי רַבִּי עֲקִיבָא. [16]רַבִּי אֱלִיעֶזֶר אוֹמֵר: הֵן בָּאִין לָעוֹלָם הַבָּא, [17]שֶׁנֶּאֱמַר: ׳אִסְפוּ לִי חֲסִידָי;

LITERAL TRANSLATION

was fortified for them in Gehinom, [1]and they sat upon it and recited songs."

[2]Rabbah bar Bar Ḥannah said: Once I was walking along the road, [and] a certain Arab said to me: [3]"Come, I will show you those swallowed up with Korah." [4]He went, and saw two cracks from which steam came out. [5]He took a ball of wool, soaked it in water, and placed it on the point of his spear, and passed it there, [and] it was singed. [6]He said to me: "Listen to what you hear." [7]And I heard them saying thus: "Moses and his Torah are true, and they are liars." [110B] [8]He said to him: "Every thirty days Gehinom returns them like meat in a pot, [9]and they say thus: 'Moses and his Torah are true, and they are liars.'"

[10]"The generation of the wilderness do not have a portion in the World to Come, etc." [11]Our Rabbis taught: "The generation of the wilderness do not have a portion in the World to Come, as it is stated: 'In this wilderness they shall be consumed, and there they shall die.' [12]'They shall be consumed' — in this world. [13]'And there they shall die' — in the World to Come. [14]And it says: 'Whereupon I swore in My anger that they should not enter into My rest.' [15][These are] the words of Rabbi Akiva. [16]Rabbi Eliezer says: They will come to the World to Come, [17]for it is stated: 'Gather My pious ones together to Me;

RASHI

נתבצר — מלשון (ישעיהו כז) עיר בצורה, התקין להון הקב״ה מקום גבוה, שלא העמיקו כל כך בגיהנם, ולא מתו. טייעא = סוחר ישמעאל. בלועי — מקום שנתבלעו שם עדת קרח. בזעא — רואה נקב שממנו יוצא עשן. גבבא — גיזה. אמשיה — שרה אותה במים, לשון (ברכות יד,ב) משי ידיה. (וכל שלשים יום — חוזר לגיהנם ועולה שם). אמר ליה — ההוא טייעא. כל תלתין יומין מהדר להו גיהנם — הכא. ואמרי הכי משה ותורתו אמת — שנשה כמה פעמים ורואה שכל שלשים יום עשן יוצא משם ושומע שאומרין: משה ותורתו אמת וכו׳. באפי — לא גרסינן. שנאמר — לעיל מיניה קרא ״ארבעים שנה אקוט בדור״ — דהיינו דור המדבר.

TRANSLATION AND COMMENTARY

that have made a covenant with Me by sacrifice.' The generation of the wilderness made a Covenant with God with a sacrifice, and the verse testifies that they will be gathered to God. [1]**But how,** then, **do I explain** the verse: **'Whereupon I swore in My anger** that they should not enter into My rest'? [2]God said: **In My anger I swore** that they shall not have a portion in the World to Come, **but** later **I relented.** [3]**Rabbi Yehoshua ben Korḥah says: This verse** does not refer to the generation of the wilderness, but rather it **refers to the later generations.** [4]**'Gather My pious ones together to Me' — this is** a reference to **the righteous people of every generation;** [5]**'those that have made a covenant with Me by sacrifice' —** [6]**this is** a reference to **Ḥananiah, Mishael, and Azariah, who surrendered themselves into a fiery furnace** in order to keep God's Covenant. [7]**'By sacrifice' — this is** a reference to **Rabbi Akiva and his colleagues, who surrendered themselves to slaughter in order to keep the words of Torah.** [8]**Rabbi Shimon ben Menasya says:** The generation of the wilderness **will** indeed **go** in the end **to the World to Come,** [9]**for the verse states** (Isaiah 35:10): **'And the ransomed of the Lord shall return, and come to Zion with songs.'** The generation of the wilderness, whom God ransomed from Egypt, will come again to Zion with songs."

אָמַר רַבָּה בַּר בַּר חָנָה [10]**Rabbah bar Bar Ḥannah said in the name of Rabbi Yoḥanan: Rabbi Akiva abandoned his** usual **kindness** when he said that the generation of the wilderness will not have a portion in the World to Come. [11]**For the verse states** about them (Jeremiah 2:2): **"Go and cry in the ears of**

LITERAL TRANSLATION

those who made a covenant with Me by sacrifice.' [1]But how do I explain, 'Whereupon I swore in My anger'? [2]In My anger I swore, but I relented. [3]Rabbi Yehoshua ben Korḥah says: This verse was only stated regarding the coming generations. [4]'Gather My pious ones together to Me' — these are the righteous people of every generation; [5]'Those who made a covenant with Me by sacrifice' — [6]these are Ḥananiah, Mishael, and Azariah, who surrendered themselves into a fiery furnace. [7]'By sacrifice' — these are Rabbi Akiva and his colleagues, who surrendered themselves to slaughter for the words of Torah. [8]Rabbi Shimon ben Menasya says: They will come to the World to Come, [9]for it is stated: 'And the ransomed of the Lord shall return, and come to Zion with songs.'"

[10]Rabbah bar Bar Ḥannah said in the name of Rabbi Yoḥanan: Rabbi Akiva abandoned his kindness. [11]For it is stated: "Go and cry in the ears of Jerusalem,

כֹּרְתֵי בְרִיתִי עֲלֵי זָבַח׳. [1]אֶלָּא מָה אֲנִי מְקַיֵּים, ׳אֲשֶׁר נִשְׁבַּעְתִּי בְאַפִּי׳? [2]בְּאַפִּי נִשְׁבַּעְתִּי, וְחוֹזְרַנִי בִּי. [3]רַבִּי יְהוֹשֻׁעַ בֶּן קָרְחָה אוֹמֵר: לֹא נֶאֱמַר פָּסוּק זֶה אֶלָּא כְּנֶגֶד דּוֹרוֹת הַבָּאִים. [4]׳אִסְפוּ לִי חֲסִידָי׳ — אֵלּוּ צַדִּיקִים שֶׁבְּכָל דּוֹר וָדוֹר; [5]׳כֹּרְתֵי בְרִיתִי עֲלֵי זָבַח׳ — [6]אֵלּוּ חֲנַנְיָה מִישָׁאֵל וַעֲזַרְיָה שֶׁמָּסְרוּ עַצְמָן לְתוֹךְ כֶּבֶשׁ הָאֵשׁ. [7]׳עֲלֵי זָבַח׳ — [אֵלּוּ] רַבִּי עֲקִיבָא וַחֲבֵירָיו שֶׁמָּסְרוּ עַצְמָן לִשְׁחִיטָה עַל דִּבְרֵי תוֹרָה. [8]רַבִּי שִׁמְעוֹן בֶּן מְנַסְיָא אוֹמֵר: בָּאִים הֵן לָעוֹלָם הַבָּא, [9]שֶׁנֶּאֱמַר: ׳וּפְדוּיֵי ה׳ יְשֻׁבוּן וּבָאוּ צִיּוֹן בְּרִנָּה׳״.

[10]אָמַר רַבָּה בַּר בַּר חָנָה אָמַר רַבִּי יוֹחָנָן: שְׁבַקָהּ רַבִּי עֲקִיבָא לַחֲסִידוּתֵיהּ. [11]שֶׁנֶּאֱמַר: ״הָלֹךְ וְקָרָאתָ בְאָזְנֵי יְרוּשָׁלַיִם

RASHI

כורתי בריתי עלי זבח — והיינו דור המדבר שכרתו ברית של מקום על זבחים ושלמים דכתיב (שמות כד) "ויזבחו זבחים שלמים", וכתיב (שם) "ויזרוק על העם ויאמר הנה דם הברית אשר כרת ה' עמכם". **נשבעתי וחוזרני בי** — והיינו "אשר נשבעתי באפי" — מפני כעסי נשבעתי ומתחרט אני. **אלו חנניה מישאל ועזריה** — שמסרו עצמן למיתה בשביל בריתו של מקום. **ופדויי ה'** — אלו דור המדבר שנפדו ממצרים. **שבקיה רבי עקיבא לחסידותיה** — שרגיל לזכות את ישראל והשתא מחייב להו, דאמר לעיל (קח,א): דור המדבר אין להם חלק לעולם הבא, ולקמן מפרש מאי חסידותיה. **שנאמר הלוך וקראת** — כלומר שהרי היה יכול לדרוש שיש להם חלק [לעולם הבא] דכתיב "הלוך וקראת וגו'".

NOTES

בְּאַפִּי נִשְׁבַּעְתִּי **In My anger I swore.** The Jerusalem Talmud concludes from here that an oath may be nullified if the person who took it claims that he swore in anger, and without giving due consideration to its content.

וּפְדוּיֵי ה׳ יְשֻׁבוּן **And the ransomed of the Lord shall return.** *Maharsha* explains that this verse must be referring to the generation of the wilderness, for it speaks of those who are "the ransomed of the Lord" even before they return to Zion with songs. Who were ransomed by God? The generation of the wilderness whom God took out of Egypt.

שְׁבַקָהּ רַבִּי עֲקִיבָא לַחֲסִידוּתֵיהּ **Rabbi Akiva abandoned his kindness.** The term *ḥasidut* is used here in the sense of acting leniently and demonstrating kindness, qualities generally attributed to Rabbi Akiva. Rabbi Yoḥanan expressed his astonishment that Rabbi Akiva acted out of character, harshly criticizing the generation of the wilderness (see *Margoliyot HaYam*).

לֵאמֹר...זָכַרְתִּי לָךְ חֶסֶד נְעוּרַיִךְ אַהֲבַת כְּלוּלֹתָיִךְ לֶכְתֵּךְ אַחֲרַי בַּמִּדְבָּר בְּאֶרֶץ לֹא זְרוּעָה״. [1]וּמָה אֲחֵרִים בָּאִים בִּזְכוּתָם, הֵם עַצְמָן לֹא כָּל שֶׁכֵּן?!

מִשְׁנָה [2]עֲשֶׂרֶת הַשְּׁבָטִים אֵינָן עֲתִידִין לַחֲזוֹר, [3]שֶׁנֶּאֱמַר: ״וַיַּשְׁלִכֵם אֶל אֶרֶץ אַחֶרֶת כַּיּוֹם הַזֶּה״. [4]מָה הַיּוֹם הוֹלֵךְ וְאֵינוֹ חוֹזֵר, אַף הֵם הוֹלְכִים וְאֵינָן חוֹזְרִים. [5]דִּבְרֵי רַבִּי עֲקִיבָא. [6]רַבִּי אֱלִיעֶזֶר אוֹמֵר: ״כַּיּוֹם הַזֶּה״. [7]מָה יוֹם מַאֲפִיל וּמֵאִיר, [8]אַף עֲשֶׂרֶת הַשְּׁבָטִים שֶׁאֲפֵילָה לָהֶן, כָּךְ עֲתִידָה לְהָאִיר לָהֶם.

גְּמָרָא [9]תָּנוּ רַבָּנַן: ״עֲשֶׂרֶת הַשְּׁבָטִים אֵין לָהֶם חֵלֶק לָעוֹלָם הַבָּא, [10]שֶׁנֶּאֱמַר: ׳וַיִּתְּשֵׁם ה׳ מֵעַל אַדְמָתָם בְּאַף וּבְחֵמָה וּבְקֶצֶף גָּדוֹל׳. [11]׳וַיִּתְּשֵׁם ה׳ מֵעַל

LITERAL TRANSLATION

saying... I remember in your favor, the devotion of your youth, your love as a bride, when you did go after Me in the wilderness, in a land that was not sown." [1]Now, if others come by their merits, they themselves all the more so!

MISHNAH [2]The ten tribes will not return, [3]for it is stated: "And He cast them into another land, as it is this day." [4]Just as the day goes and does not return, so, too, they go and do not return. [5][These are] the words of Rabbi Akiva. [6]Rabbi Eliezer says: "As it is this day." [7]Just as the day grows dark and becomes light, [8]so, too, the ten tribes for whom it is dark, in the future it will be light for them.

GEMARA [9]Our Rabbis taught: "The ten tribes do not have a portion in the World to Come, [10]as it is stated: 'And the Lord rooted them out of their land in anger, and in wrath, and in great indignation.' [11]'And the Lord rooted them out of

TRANSLATION AND COMMENTARY

Jerusalem, saying...I remember in your favor, the devotion of your youth, your love as a bride, when you did go after Me in the wilderness, in a land that was not sown." [1]**Now, if others will go** to the World to Come **through the merits** of the generation who left Egypt and followed God into the wilderness, then **all the more so** will the members of the generation of the wilderness **themselves** surely go to the World to Come!

MISHNAH עֲשֶׂרֶת הַשְּׁבָטִים [2]**The ten tribes** that were sent into exile by Sennacherib, King of Assyria (II Kings 17:6), **will not return** again to Eretz Israel **in the future,** not even in the days of the Messiah, [3]**for the verse states** (Deuteronomy 29:27): **"And He cast them into another land, as it is this day."** [4]**Just as the day goes** by **and does not return** again, **so, too,** did the ten tribes **go** out of Eretz Israel **never to return again.** [5]**This is the position of Rabbi Akiva.** [6]**Rabbi Eliezer** disagrees and **says:** The ten tribes will indeed return to Eretz Israel, for the verse states: "And He cast them into another land, **as it is this day."** [7]**Just as the day grows dark** at night **and** then **becomes light** again the next morning, [8]**so, too,** will it be for **the ten tribes for whom** today **it is dark — in the future it will be light for them** when they return to Eretz Israel.

GEMARA תָּנוּ רַבָּנַן [9]**Our Rabbis taught** a related Baraita: **"The ten tribes** that were sent into exile **do not have a portion in the World to Come,** [10]**as the verse states** (Deuteronomy 29:27): **'And the Lord rooted them out of their land in anger, and in wrath, and in great indignation;** and He cast them into another land, as it is this day.' [11]The words **'and the Lord rooted them out of their land'** refer to their

RASHI

משנה עשרת השבטים – שהגלה סנחריב שנאמר (מלכים ב יח) "וינחם בחלח ובחבור נהר גוזן וערי מדי". אין עתידים לחזור – ממקום שגלו, והא דאמרינן בגמרא דירמיה החזירן – לא שהחזירן כולן – אלא מקצתם החזיר. שנאמר וישליכם אל ארץ אחרת כיום הזה – שכך גזר להם הקב״ה – שכיון שעוזבין את תורתו הוא מגלה אותן. כיום הזה מה היום מאפיל – בבקר אפל ובצהרים מאיר, אי נמי: בערב אפל והולך, ולמחרתו מאיר, אף עשרת השבטים (אין) עתידין לחזור להיות להם חלק לעולם הבא, לא בבניהם ובני בניהם קאמר, אלא אותן שגלו עצמן אין להם חלק שרשעים גמורין הם, אבל בניהם ודורות הבאים זוכין ומזכין, מפי רבי. וישליכם – משמע שיהו כולם גולין במקום אחד אל ארץ אחרת, והיינו עשרת השבטים שהגלם סנחריב והושיבם במקום אחד כדאמרינן (לעיל לד,א) שהוליכם למדינת אפריקי, אבל שני השבטים לא גלו למקום אחד אלא נתפזרו בכל הארצות, ועליהם הוא אומר "אשרקה להם ואקבצם" (זכריה י). הכי גרסינן מתניתין – עשרת השבטים אין עתידין לחזור.

גמרא תנו רבנן עשרת השבטים אין להם חלק לעולם הבא שנאמר ויתשם ה׳ מעל אדמתם וגו׳ – ואית דמפרשי עשרת השבטים אין להם חלק לעולם הבא – היינו לימות המשיח, שלא יקבלם משיח עם שאר גליות לפי שספרו בגנות ארץ ישראל כדאמרן לעיל (שם), כי מטו שוש וכו׳, ובדבר הזה נענשו מרגלים.

NOTES

עֲשֶׂרֶת הַשְּׁבָטִים **The ten tribes.** Some Rishonim note that when the Mishnah speaks here of the ten tribes, it refers to the first generation of exiles, who do not have a portion in the World to Come because of their wickedness. But their descendants will in fact return to Eretz Israel, and enjoy their share in the future world (*Rabbi David Bonfil*). Moreover, some members of the ten tribes remained in Eretz Israel, and joined with the tribes of Judah and Benjamin, as is stated in the Book of Chronicles, and they will certainly have a share in the World to Come (see *Be'er Sheva*).

אַדְמָתָם׳ — בָּעוֹלָם הַזֶּה; [1]׳וַיַּשְׁלִכֵם אֶל אֶרֶץ אַחֶרֶת׳ — לָעוֹלָם הַבָּא. [2]דִּבְרֵי רַבִּי עֲקִיבָא. [3]רַבִּי שִׁמְעוֹן בֶּן יְהוּדָה אִישׁ כְּפַר עַכּוֹ אוֹמֵר מִשּׁוּם רַבִּי שִׁמְעוֹן: אִם מַעֲשֵׂיהֶם כַּיּוֹם הַזֶּה, אֵינָן חוֹזְרִין. [4]וְאִם לָאו, חוֹזְרִין. [5]רַבִּי אוֹמֵר: בָּאִים הֵם לָעוֹלָם הַבָּא, [6]שֶׁנֶּאֱמַר: ׳בַּיּוֹם הַהוּא יִתָּקַע בְּשׁוֹפָר גָּדוֹל וגו׳ ׳ ״.

[7]אָמַר רַבָּה בַּר בַּר חָנָה אָמַר רַבִּי יוֹחָנָן: שְׁבָקָהּ רַבִּי עֲקִיבָא לַחֲסִידוּתֵיהּ. [8]שֶׁנֶּאֱמַר: ״הָלֹךְ וְקָרָאתָ אֶת הַדְּבָרִים הָאֵלֶּה צָפוֹנָה וְאָמַרְתָּ שׁוּבָה מְשֻׁבָה יִשְׂרָאֵל נְאֻם ה׳ לוֹא אַפִּיל פָּנַי בָּכֶם כִּי חָסִיד אֲנִי נְאֻם ה׳ לֹא אֶטּוֹר לְעוֹלָם״.

[9]מַאי חֲסִידוּתֵיהּ? [10]דְּתַנְיָא: ״קְטַנֵּי בְנֵי רִשְׁעֵי יִשְׂרָאֵל אֵין בָּאִין לָעוֹלָם הַבָּא, [11]שֶׁנֶּאֱמַר: ׳כִּי הִנֵּה הַיּוֹם בָּא בֹּעֵר כַּתַּנּוּר וְהָיוּ כָל זֵדִים וְכָל עֹשֵׂה רִשְׁעָה קַשׁ וְלִהַט אֹתָם הַיּוֹם הַבָּא אָמַר ה׳ צְבָאוֹת אֲשֶׁר לֹא יַעֲזֹב

LITERAL TRANSLATION

their land' — in this world; [1]'And cast them into another land' — in the World to Come. [2][These are] the words of Rabbi Akiva. [3]Rabbi Shimon ben Yehudah of Kefar Akko says in the name of Rabbi Shimon: If their deeds are like this day, they will not return. [4]And if not, they will return. [5]Rabbi says: They will come to the World to Come, [6]for it is stated: 'And it shall come to pass on that day, that a great shofar shall be blown, etc.'"

[7]Rabbah bar Bar Ḥannah said in the name of Rabbi Yoḥanan: Rabbi Akiva abandoned his kindness. [8]For it is stated: "Go, and proclaim these words toward the north, and say, Return you faithless Israel, says the Lord; and I will not frown upon you; for I am merciful, says the Lord, and I will not bear a grudge for ever."

[9]What is his kindness? [10]As it was taught: "Minors who are the children of the wicked of Israel do not come to the World to Come, [11]for it is stated: 'For, behold, that day is coming; it burns like a furnace; and all the arrogant, and all who do wickedly, shall be stubble; and the day that is coming shall burn them up, says the Lord of hosts, so that it will leave them neither

TRANSLATION AND COMMENTARY

punishment **in this world;** [1]the words **'and cast them into another land'** refer to their punishment **in the World to Come.** [2]**This is the position of Rabbi Akiva.** [3]**Rabbi Shimon ben Yehudah of Kefar Akko said in the name of Rabbi Shimon:** The words 'as it is this day' teach us as follows: **If their deeds** continue to be as wicked **as** they are on **this day, they will not return** to Eretz Israel. [4]**But if** their deeds do **not** remain the same, but rather they repent of their evil ways, **they will** indeed **return** to Eretz Israel. [5]**Rabbi** Yehudah HaNasi **says:** The ten tribes **will go** in the end **to the World to Come,** [6]**for the verse states** (Isaiah 27:13): **'And it shall come to pass on that day, that a great shofar shall be blown,** and they shall come who were lost in the land of Assyria, and the outcasts in the land of Egypt, and shall worship the Lord in the holy mountain at Jerusalem.' The words 'who were lost in the land of Assyria' refer to the ten tribes, and the words 'the outcasts in the land of Egypt' refer to the generation of the wilderness, both of which will have a portion in the World to Come."

אָמַר [7]**Rabbah bar Bar Ḥannah said in the name of Rabbi Yoḥanan: Rabbi Akiva abandoned his** usual **kindness** when he said that the ten tribes do not have a portion in the World to Come. Surely Rabbi Akiva treated the ten tribes harshly, [8]**for the verse states** (Jeremiah 3:12): **"Go, and proclaim these words toward the north, and say, Return you faithless Israel, says the Lord; and I will not frown upon you; for I am merciful, says the Lord, and I will not bear a grudge for ever,"** implying that the ten tribes will indeed return to Eretz Israel.

מַאי חֲסִידוּתֵיהּ [9]The Gemara asks: **What** did Rabbah bar Bar Ḥannah mean when he referred to Rabbi Akiva's **kindness?** [10]The Gemara explains: **As it was taught** in the Baraita: **"Children of the wicked of Israel** who died while they were still **minors,** thus having neither merit of their own nor ancestral merit, **do come to the World to Come,** [11]**for the verse states** (Malachi 3:19): **'For, behold, that day is coming; it burns like a furnace; and all the arrogant, and all who do wickedly, shall be stubble; and the day that is coming shall**

RASHI

רבי שמעון אומר — מאי כהיום הזה — לומר לך: אם מעשיהם כהיום הזה לא יהא להם חלק לעולם הבא. **ואם [לאו]** — שיחזרו בתשובה, יחזרו גם הם מגלות ויש להם חלק לעולם הבא. **האובדים בארץ אשור** — אלו עשרת השבטים, והנדחים בארץ מצרים — אלו דור המדבר, וכן לשון התוספתא ולא שמעתי עוד. **שובה משובה** — שכל ישראל עתידין לחזור. **קטני בני רשעי ישראל** — רשעי ישראל עצמן פשיטא דאין להם חלק לעולם הבא, כדאמרינן בפרק בתרא דכתובות (קיא,ב) רפאים בל יקומו — מי שמרפה עצמו מדברי תורה, אבל בנים שלהם קטנים ולא חטאו, פליגי בהו.

NOTES

קְטַנֵּי בְנֵי רִשְׁעֵי יִשְׂרָאֵל **Minors who are the children of the wicked of Israel.** Most of the commentators understand that when the Baraita says that the children of wicked Jews who die young will not come to the World to Come, it does not refer to the world of disembodied souls, but rather to the Resurrection of the Dead. The issue under discussion is

LANGUAGE

פַּתְיָא Child. In Arabic فتي, is a young man, which is appropriate to the version of the Midrash, that in Arabia a child is called gullible (פתי). *Arukh* had the reading פנטי here, from the Italian *fante*, meaning "infant."

TRANSLATION AND COMMENTARY

burn them up, says the Lord of hosts, so that it will leave them neither root nor branch.' The words 'root' and 'branch' both refer to children. [1]The word **'root'** teaches that the children of the wicked will die young **in this world;** [2]and the word **'branch'** teaches that they will not have a portion **in the World to Come.** [3]**This is the position of Rabban Gamliel.** [4]**Rabbi Akiva** disagrees and **says:** The young children of the wicked **will go** in the end **to the World to Come,** [5]**for the verse states** (Psalms 116:6): **'The Lord preserves the simple** [*peta'im*],**' and in the sea towns a child is called** *patya.* Thus, the verse teaches that God preserves even the children of the wicked. [6]**And** another verse **states** (Daniel 4:20): **'Hew down the tree, and destroy it; yet leave the stump of its roots in the earth.'** Even if the wicked fathers are punished, the stumps of their roots, their children, will still live on after them. [7]**But how,** then, **do I explain** the verse: **'So that it will leave them neither root nor branch'?** [8]God **will not leave** the wicked **a mitzvah, nor** even **the remnant of a mitzvah,** for which they must receive reward in the World to Come. Whatever reward they receive will be in this world. [9]**Another explanation:** The word **'root'** refers to **the soul,** and the word [10]**'branch'** refers to **the body.** The wicked will be destroyed both in body and in soul. Rabban Gamliel and Rabbi Akiva disagree only about the children of the wicked of Israel who died as minors. [11]**But** regarding **the children of the wicked of the nations of the world** who died while they were still **minors, all agree that they will not go to the World to Come."** [12]**And Rabban Gamliel derives this from** the verse that states (Isaiah 26:14): **"And You have made all their memory to perish."** Thus, we see that Rabbi Akiva is characterized by kindness, for he grants the minor children of the wicked of Israel a portion in the World to Come.

אִתְּמַר [13]**It was asked:** Regarding **a minor** who died, **from what age does he have** a portion in **the World to Come?** [14]**Rabbi Ḥiyya and Rabbi Shimon the**

LITERAL TRANSLATION

root nor branch.' [1]'Root' — in this world; [2]'branch'— in the World to Come. [3][These are] the words of Rabban Gamliel. [4]Rabbi Akiva says: They will come to the World to Come, [5]for it is stated: 'The Lord preserves the simple,' for in the sea towns they call a child *patya.* [6]And it says: 'Hew down the tree, and destroy it; yet leave the stump of its roots in the earth.' [7]But how do I explain: 'So that it will leave them neither root nor branch'? [8]He will not leave them a mitzvah nor the remnant of a mitzvah. [9]Another explanation: 'Root' — this is the soul. [10]'Branch' — this is the body. [11]But minors who are the children of the wicked of the nations of the world — all agree that they will not come to the World to Come." [12]And Rabban Gamliel derives this from: "And You have made all their memory to perish."

[13]It was stated: A minor, from when does he come to the World to Come? [14]Rabbi Ḥiyya and Rabbi

לָהֶם שֹׁרֶשׁ וְעָנָף׳. [1]׳שֹׁרֶשׁ׳ — בָּעוֹלָם הַזֶּה; [2]׳וְעָנָף׳ — לָעוֹלָם הַבָּא. [3]דִּבְרֵי רַבָּן גַּמְלִיאֵל. [4]רַבִּי עֲקִיבָא אוֹמֵר: בָּאִים הֵם לָעוֹלָם הַבָּא, [5]שֶׁנֶּאֱמַר: ׳שֹׁמֵר פְּתָאִים ה׳׳, שֶׁכֵּן קוֹרִין בִּכְרַכֵּי הַיָּם לִינוּקָא פַּתְיָא. [6]וְאוֹמֵר: ׳גֹּדּוּ אִילָנָא וְחַבְּלוּהִי בְּרַם עִקַּר שָׁרְשׁוֹהִי בְּאַרְעָא שְׁבֻקוּ׳. [7]וְאֶלָּא מָה אֲנִי מְקַיֵּים, ׳לֹא יַעֲזֹב לָהֶם שֹׁרֶשׁ וְעָנָף׳? [8]שֶׁלֹּא יַנִּיחַ לָהֶם לֹא מִצְוָה וְלֹא שִׁיּוּרֵי מִצְוָה. [9]דָּבָר אַחֵר: ׳שֹׁרֶשׁ׳ — זוֹ נְשָׁמָה. [10]׳וְעָנָף׳ — זֶה הַגּוּף. [11]אֲבָל קְטַנֵּי בְנֵי רִשְׁעֵי אוּמּוֹת הָעוֹלָם — דִּבְרֵי הַכֹּל אֵין בָּאִין לָעוֹלָם הַבָּא״. [12]וְרַבָּן גַּמְלִיאֵל נָפְקָא לֵיהּ מִ״וַתְּאַבֵּד כָּל זֵכֶר לָמוֹ״.

[13]אִתְּמַר: קָטָן, מֵאֵימָתַי בָּא לָעוֹלָם הַבָּא? [14]רַבִּי חִיָּיא וְרַבִּי

RASHI

שורש וענף — אלו בנים קטנים שלהם. **שורש בעולם הזה** — שימותו נפלים. **וענף לעולם הבא** — שאף על פי שאבותיהם היו רשעים — הם לא חטאו. **עיקר שרשוהי בארעא שבוקו** — אלו הבנים הקטנים שאף על פי שאבות אין להם חלק, תקנה יש להם. **שלא יניח** — להם הקב״ה. **לא מצוה ולא שיורי מצוה** — לא מצוה חמורה ולא מצוה קלה, הכל יהא מעביר ומשלם שכרם לאלתר כדי לטרדן מן העולם. **זו נשמה** — שמעמדת הגוף כשרש שמעמיד האילן. **אבל קטני בני רשעי אומות העולם** — דוקא קאמר רשעי, דאילו חסידי אומות העולם פליגי בה, ואיכא למאן דאמר הן עצמן באין, ואיכא למאן דאמר אינן באין, כדאמרן (קה) ישובו רשעים לשאולה כל גוים שכחי אלהים״ — מכאן שאין להם חלק, אמר לו ר׳ יהושע: וכי נאמר בכל גוים והלא לא נאמר אלא ״כל גוים שכחי אלהים״ — הא אין שכחי אלהים — יש להן חלק [לעולם הבא]. **הכי גרסינן** — אבל קטני רשעי אומות העולם דברי הכל אינן באין. **מותאבד כל זכר למו נפקא ליה** — כלומר לתנא דברייתא, והאי דנפקא ליה דברי הכל היא, דהא שורש וענף מיבעיא ליה למר כדאית ליה, ומר כדאית ליה.

NOTES

whether such children will be restored to life at the time of the resurrection (*Rabbi David Bonfil*). Regarding certain Halakhic matters (such as eulogies), young children are not treated as independent beings. The Baraita refers only to the young children of wicked Jews, for their parents will certainly enjoy a share in the future world, for all of Israel have a portion in the World to Come (*Be'er Sheva*; but see also *Rashi*), and the young children of righteous Jews will also have a share in that world through the merit of their parents.

שִׁמְעוֹן בַּר רַבִּי. [1]חַד אָמַר: מִשָּׁעָה שֶׁנּוֹלַד. [2]וְחַד אָמַר: מִשָּׁעָה שֶׁסִּיפֵּר. [3]מַאן דַּאֲמַר מִשָּׁעָה שֶׁנּוֹלַד, [4]שֶׁנֶּאֱמַר: ״יָבֹאוּ וְיַגִּידוּ צִדְקָתוֹ לְעַם נוֹלָד כִּי עָשָׂה״. [5]וּמַאן דַּאֲמַר מִשָּׁעָה שֶׁסִּיפֵּר, [6]דִּכְתִיב: ״זֶרַע יַעַבְדֶנּוּ יְסֻפַּר לַה׳ לַדּוֹר״.

[7]אִתְּמַר: רָבִינָא אָמַר: מִשָּׁעָה שֶׁנִּזְרַע, [8]דִּכְתִיב: ״זֶרַע יַעַבְדֶנּוּ״. [9]רַבִּי נַחְמָן בַּר יִצְחָק אָמַר: מִשָּׁעָה שֶׁנִּימּוֹל, [10]דִּכְתִיב: ״עָנִי אֲנִי וְגֹוֵעַ מִנֹּעַר; נָשָׂאתִי אֵמֶיךָ, אָפוּנָה״.

[11]תָּנָא מִשּׁוּם רַבִּי מֵאִיר: ״מִשָּׁעָה שֶׁיֹּאמַר אָמֵן, [12]שֶׁנֶּאֱמַר: ׳פִּתְחוּ שְׁעָרִים וְיָבֹא גוֹי צַדִּיק שֹׁמֵר אֱמֻנִים׳. [13]אַל תִּקְרֵי ׳שֹׁמֵר אֱמֻנִים׳, [14]אֶלָּא ׳שֶׁאוֹמֵר אָמֵן׳״.

LITERAL TRANSLATION

Shimon the son of Rabbi [disagreed]. [1]One said: From the time that he is born. [2]And one said: From the time that he talks. [3]The one who said from the time that he is born, [4][said so] because it is stated: "They shall come, and shall declare His righteousness to a people that shall be born, that He has done this." [5]And the one who said from the time that he talks, [6][said so] because it is written: "Their seed shall serve Him; it shall be told of the Lord to the coming generation."

[7]It was stated: Ravina said: From the time that he is conceived, [8]for it is written: "Their seed shall serve Him." [9]Rabbi Naḥman bar Yitzḥak said: From the time that he is circumcised, [10]for it is written: "I am poor and close to death from youth; I suffer Your terrors, I am numb."

[11][A Sage] taught in the name of Rabbi Meir: "From the time that he says Amen, [12]for it is stated: 'Open the gates, so that the righteous nation that keeps faithfulness may enter.' [13]Do not read 'that keeps faithfulness,' [14]but rather 'who says Amen.'"

TRANSLATION AND COMMENTARY

son of Rabbi Yehuda HaNasi **disagreed** about the matter. [1]**One** of the Amoraim **said:** A baby has a portion in the World to Come **from the time that he is born.** [2]**And the other** Amora **said:** The child only has a portion in the World to Come **from the time that he talks.** [3]The authority **who said, "from the time that he is born,"** supports his position with [4]**the verse that states** (Psalms 22:32): **"They shall come, and shall declare His righteousness to a people that shall be born, that He has done this."** [5]**And the** authority **who said, "from the time that he talks,"** supports his view with [6]**the verse that states** (Psalms 22:31): **"Their seed shall serve Him; it shall be told of the Lord to the coming generation."** The child is "of the Lord" only from the time that it speaks.

אִתְּמַר [7]**It was stated** that there are other opinions regarding this matter: **Ravina said:** A baby already has a portion in the World to Come **from the time that it is conceived,** even before it is born, [8]**as the verse states** (Psalms 22:31): **"Their seed shall serve Him,"** the word "seed" alluding to the time of conception. [9]**Rabbi Naḥman bar Yitzḥak said:** A child only has a portion in the World to Come **from the time that he is circumcised,** [10]**for the verse states** (Psalms 88:16): **"I am poor and close to death from youth; I suffer Your terrors** [נָשָׂאתִי אֵמֶיךָ], **I am numb** [אָפוּנָה]." This verse can also be interpreted Midrashically: From the time that I bear Your fear [נָשָׂאתִי אֵמֶיךָ] and carry the sign of circumcision, I turn to You [אָפוּנָה] and belong to You.

תָּנָא [11]**A Sage taught** a related Baraita **in the name of Rabbi Meir:** "A child only has a portion in the World to Come **from the time that he answers Amen,** [12]**for the verse states** (Isaiah 26:2): **'Open the gates, so that the righteous nation that keeps faithfulness may enter.'** [13]**Do not read** the verse as it is written: שֹׁמֵר אֱמֻנִים, **'that keeps faithfulness.'** [14]**But rather** read it as: ׳שֶׁאוֹמֵר אָמֵן׳, **'who says Amen.'** From the time that a child can answer Amen, the gates to the World to Come are open before him."

RASHI

זרע יעבדנו יסופר לה׳ לדור – זרע המסופר יעבדנו לה׳ לדור ודור שיחזור לו ויחיה. משעה שנזרע – משעה שנקלט הזרע במעי אשה אפילו הפילה אמו ונמחה – יש לו חלק לעתיד דכתיב ״זרע יעבדנו״ והכי אמר בכתובות בפרק בתרא (קיא,א) ״נבלתי יקומון״ – לרבות נפלים. עני אני וגוע מנוער – אף על פי שאני עני גויעתי חשובה גויעה וראוי לומר עלי ויגוע ויאסף כלומר שזוכה אני לעתיד לבא כלדיקים שנאמר בהן גויעה, ומאימתי – משעה שאני נושא אמיך ופחדך – אפונה – מתגלגלת ושכונה עלי, והיינו מילה שבבשרו שאנו משמרים מאימתו של הקב״ה. אפונה – לשון אופן.

NOTES

מִשָּׁעָה שֶׁנִּימּוֹל **From the time that he is circumcised.** *Ramah* understands the proof-text as follows: "I am poor and close to death from my youth" means I am afflicted from the days of my youth when I underwent circumcision. Since David speaks about that milestone with pride, it must carry as a reward a portion in the World to Come.

מִנֹּעַר; נָשָׂאתִי... **From youth; I suffer...** Some suggest that this passage is the source of the custom to circumcise children who died before they were eight days old (*Geonim*).

אַל תִּקְרֵי ׳שֹׁמֵר אֱמֻנִים׳ **Do not read 'that keeps faithfulness.'** Some argue that it is appropriate to describe a person with the expressions אִישׁ אֱמֻנִים and בַּעַל אֱמֻנִים, "a man of faith," but the expression שֹׁמֵר אֱמֻנִים, "keeper of faith," is an odd designation, and so the Baraita interprets it homiletically as "one who says Amen" (*Riaf*). This does not contradict the plain sense of the verse, for as the Gemara explains, the word Amen is an expression of faith and faithfulness, and so a person who says Amen is someone "who keeps faithfulness."

מַאי "אָמֵן"? [2] אָמַר רַבִּי [1] [111A]
חֲנִינָא: אֵל מֶלֶךְ נֶאֱמָן.
[3] "לָכֵן הִרְחִיבָה שְׁאוֹל נַפְשָׁהּ
וּפָעֲרָה פִיהָ לִבְלִי חֹק". [4] אָמַר
רֵישׁ לָקִישׁ: לְמִי שֶׁמְּשַׁיֵּיר
אֲפִילּוּ חוֹק אֶחָד.
[5] אָמַר רַבִּי יוֹחָנָן: לָא נִיחָא
לְמָרַיְיהוּ דְּאָמְרַתְּ לְהוּ הָכִי.
[6] אֶלָּא: אֲפִילּוּ לֹא לָמַד אֶלָּא
חוֹק אֶחָד.
[7] שֶׁנֶּאֱמַר "וְהָיָה בְכָל הָאָרֶץ
נְאֻם ה׳ פִּי שְׁנַיִם בָּהּ יִכָּרְתוּ
יִגְוָעוּ וְהַשְּׁלִשִׁית יִוָּתֶר בָּהּ".
[8] אָמַר רֵישׁ לָקִישׁ: שְׁלִישִׁי שֶׁל
שֵׁם.
[9] אָמַר לֵיהּ רַבִּי יוֹחָנָן: לָא נִיחָא
לְמָרַיְיהוּ דְּאָמְרַתְּ לְהוּ הָכִי.
[10] אֶלָּא: אֲפִילּוּ שְׁלִישִׁי שֶׁל נֹחַ.
[11] "כִּי אָנֹכִי בָּעַלְתִּי בָכֶם
וְלָקַחְתִּי אֶתְכֶם אֶחָד מֵעִיר
וּשְׁנַיִם מִמִּשְׁפָּחָה". [12] אָמַר רֵישׁ
לָקִישׁ: דְּבָרִים כִּכְתָבָן.

LITERAL TRANSLATION

[111A] [1] What is "Amen"? [2] Rabbi Ḥanina said: God, faithful king.

[3] "Therefore the underworld has enlarged itself, and opened its mouth without measure." [4] Resh Lakish said: To him who leaves out even one law.

[5] Rabbi Yoḥanan said: It is not pleasing to their master that you say that to them. [6] Rather, even if he learned only one law.

[7] It is stated: "And it shall come to pass, that in all the land, says the Lord, two parts in it shall be cut off and die, but the third shall be left in it." [8] Resh Lakish said: A third of Shem.

[9] Rabbi Yoḥanan said to him: It is not pleasing to their master that you say that to them. [10] Rather, even a third of Noah.

[11] "For I have taken you to Myself; and I will take out one of a city, and two of a family."

[12] Resh Lakish said: The words as they are written.

TRANSLATION AND COMMENTARY

[111A] "מַאי "אָמֵן [1] The Gemara asks: **What is** the special significance of the term, **"Amen"?** [2] **Rabbi Ḥanina said:** The term "Amen," אָמֵן, is an acrostic for the words אֵל מֶלֶךְ נֶאֱמָן, **"God, faithful king."**

לָכֵן הִרְחִיבָה שְׁאוֹל [3] The verse states (Isaiah 5:14): **"Therefore She'ol has enlarged itself, and opened its mouth without measure** [לִבְלִי חֹק]." [4] **Resh Lakish said:** It has enlarged itself and opened its mouth to receive **him who leaves out even one law** [חוֹק אֶחָד], and fails to observe it.

אָמַר רַבִּי יוֹחָנָן [5] **Rabbi Yoḥanan said** to Resh Lakish: **It is not pleasing to** Israel's **master** (God), **that you say that about them.** According to you, most of the people of Israel are destined for the underworld. [6] **Rather, even if** a person **learned only one law,** he has a portion in the World to Come. And the verse should be understood as follows: The underworld has enlarged itself and opened its mouth to receive him who is entirely without laws [לִבְלִי חֹק].

שֶׁנֶּאֱמַר [7] **The verse states** (Zechariah 13:8): **"And it shall come to pass, that in all the land, says the Lord, two parts in it shall be cut off and die, but the third shall be left in it."** [8] **Resh Lakish said: A third of** the descendants of **Shem,** the son of Noah, will survive, and the other two-thirds will perish. Then the surviving third will be put through the fire and be further refined, as it is stated in the next verse (Zechariah 13:9): "And I will bring the third part through the fire, and will refine them as silver is refined, and will try them as gold is tried."

אָמַר לֵיהּ [9] **Rabbi Yoḥanan said to** Resh Lakish: **It is not pleasing to** Israel's **master,** to God, **that you say that about them,** condemning Israel to such small numbers. [10] **Rather,** the verse means to say that **a third of** the descendants of **Noah** will survive, and all the rest will perish. Even after the surviving third is further refined, Israel will still be left in significant numbers.

כִּי אָנֹכִי בָּעַלְתִּי בָכֶם [11] The verse states (Jeremiah 3:14): **"For I have taken you to Myself; and I will take out one of a city, and two of a family."** [12] **Resh Lakish said: These words** should be understood **as they were written:** Only a small number of people — "one of a city, and two of a family" — will enjoy redemption, and all the rest will perish.

RASHI

מאי אמן — כשעונין על כל ברכה וברכה אמן, היאך משמע קבלת יראת שמים. אל מלך נאמן — בנוטריקון, שמאמין עליו הקב״ה. למי שמשייר אפילו חק אחד — מלשמרו — נידון בגיהנם. לא ניחא ליה למרייהו — אין הקב״ה רוצה שתהא דן את ישראל כל כך לכף חובה. פי שנים בה יכרתו — ויגועו והשלישית יותר בה. אמר ריש לקיש שלישי של שם — שמשני חלקים של כל העולם יהיו נכרתים, וחלק שלישי יותר בה, ואיזה חלק שלישי — כל שלישיות שיש לשלש אנו משלשין, שמנח נפרדו כל העולם ושלש בנים היו לו הרי שליש בניו — שם, ושלישי של שם הוא ארפכשד, כדכתיב בני שם עילם ואשור וארפכשד ולוד וארם, ומסתמא בזרעו של ארפכשד יהיה שארית, הואיל וישראל יוצאים ממנו, ושלישי של ארפכשד — שהוא שלישי של שם, שהוא שלישי של נח — יוותר וכל העולם יכרת, ולדברי ריש לקיש נמצאו ישראל מתמעטין ביותר, שמארפכשד יצאו ישראל כדכתיב בפרשת נח ארפכשד הוליד את שלח ושלח הוליד את עבר ועבר הוליד את פלג — עד אברהם, וכשאתה מחלק לשלשה חלקים זרעו של ארפכשד כגון בני ישראל וישמעאל שהן בני אברהם, ובני לוט ובני הרן, וכן שאר האומות שיצאו ממנו לשלשה חלקים, שמא ישראל יהיו מרובין וקרובין להיות כנגד כולם ולא יגיעו כל זרע ארפכשד להיות פי שנים אלא אם כן ישראל משלימין רובן או חציין — ונמצאו ישראל מתמעטין בתוך פי שנים.

TRANSLATION AND COMMENTARY

אֲמַר לֵיהּ [1]**Rabbi Yoḥanan said to** Resh Lakish: **It is not pleasing to** Israel's **master,** God, **that you said that about them,** condemning most Jews to destruction. [2]**Rather,** the verse should be understood as follows: **One** righteous person **in a city will exonerate the entire city, and two** righteous people **in a family will exonerate the entire family.**

יָתֵיב רַב כָּהֲנָא [3]Similarly, it was related that **Rav Kahana** once **sat before Rav, and said** that **the words** of the verse cited above, "I will take out one of a city, and two of a family,' [4]should be understood **as they were written,** that only a very small number of people will be redeemed. **Rav said to** Rav Kahana: **It is not pleasing to** Israel's **master,** God, **that you said that about them.** [5]**Rather, one** righteous person **in a city will exonerate the entire city, and two** righteous people **in a family will exonerate the entire family.**

חַזְיֵיהּ [6]It was further related that Rav once **saw** Rav Kahana **wash his hair** and pamper himself when he should have been engaged in Torah study, **and** only afterwards did **he go in and sit down before Rav** in the lecture hall. [7]Rav **said to** Rav Kahana, citing the verse (Job 28:13): **"Nor is it found in the land of the living** [הַחַיִּים]." Rav Kahana thought that Rav meant to intimate to him that he would not have a portion in the World to Come, [8]and so **he asked him: "Do you** mean to **curse me?"** [9]Rav **said to him: "I** was merely **citing a verse** in order to remind you that **Torah shall not be found in him who pampers** [מְחַיֶּה] **himself** while he should be studying, but only in him who studies Torah even in difficult circumstances."

תַּנְיָא [10]**It was taught** in a Baraita: **"Rabbi Sima'i says: The verse states** (Exodus 6:7): **'And I will take you to Me for a people.'** [11]**And the** next **verse states**

[1]אֲמַר לֵיהּ רַבִּי יוֹחָנָן: לָא נִיחָא לֵיהּ לְמָרֵייהוּ דְּאָמְרַתְּ לְהוּ הָכִי. [2]אֶלָּא, אֶחָד מֵעִיר מְזַכֶּה כָּל הָעִיר כּוּלָּהּ, וּשְׁנַיִם מִמִּשְׁפָּחָה מְזַכִּין כָּל הַמִּשְׁפָּחָה כּוּלָּהּ.

[3]יָתֵיב רַב כָּהֲנָא קַמֵּיהּ דְּרַב, וְיָתֵיב וְקָאָמַר: [4]״דְּבָרִים כִּכְתָבָן״. אֲמַר לֵיהּ רַב: לָא נִיחָא לֵיהּ לְמָרֵייהוּ דְּאָמְרַתְּ לְהוּ הָכִי. [5]אֶלָּא: אֶחָד מֵעִיר מְזַכֶּה כָּל הָעִיר, וּשְׁנַיִם מִמִּשְׁפָּחָה מְזַכִּין כָּל הַמִּשְׁפָּחָה.

[6]חַזְיֵיהּ דַּהֲוָה קָא חָיֵיף רֵישֵׁיהּ, וְסָלֵיק וְיָתֵיב קַמֵּיהּ דְּרַב. [7]אֲמַר לֵיהּ: ״וְלֹא תִמָּצֵא בְּאֶרֶץ הַחַיִּים״. [8]אֲמַר לֵיהּ: ״מֵילַט קָא לָיְיטַתְּ לִי״? [9]אֲמַר לֵיהּ: ״קְרָא קָאָמֵינָא. לֹא תִמָּצֵא תּוֹרָה בְּמִי שֶׁמְּחַיֶּה עַצְמוֹ עָלֶיהָ״.

[10]תַּנְיָא: ״רַב סִימַאי אוֹמֵר: נֶאֱמַר: ׳וְלָקַחְתִּי אֶתְכֶם לִי לְעָם׳. [11]וְנֶאֱמַר: ׳וְהֵבֵאתִי

LITERAL TRANSLATION

[1]Rabbi Yoḥanan said to him: It is not pleasing to their master that you said that to them. [2]Rather, one of a city exonerates the entire city, and two of a family exonerate the entire family.

[3]Rav Kahana sat before Rav, and sat, and said: [4]The words as they are written. Rav said to him: It is not pleasing to their master that you said that to them. [5]Rather, one of a city exonerates the entire city, and two of a family exonerate the entire family.

[6]He saw him wash his hair, and go up and sit before Rav. [7]He said to him: "Nor is it found in the land of the living." [8]He said to him: "Do you curse me?" [9]He said to him: "I cited a verse. Torah shall not be found in him who pampers himself for it."

[10]It was taught: "Rabbi Sima'i says: It is stated: 'And I will take you to Me for a people.' [11]And it is stated: 'And I will bring

RASHI

לא ניחא ליה למרייהו — להקב״ה, שאתה ממעט אותן כל כך, אלא אפילו שלישי של נח, כלומר מכל בני נח דהיינו מכל העולם כולו יותר השלים, ומסתמא אותו חלק השלישי שישראל בו, יהיה שארית ואם אין ישראל מרובין כל כך להיות אחד משלש שבעולם יהיו הגרים וחסידי אומות העולם להשלים לשלים, ואם הם מרובין להיות יותר מחלק השלישית יתמעטו קצת, ומכל מקום לרבי יוחנן אין ישראל מתמעטין כל כך כמו לדברי רבי שמעון בן לקיש, מפי רבי, לישנא אחרינא: שלישי של שם, והשלישית משמע שני שלים, לכך נאמר שלישית, שלישית של שלישי לשם, וכתיב ״ובני שם עילם ואשור וארפכשד״, וישראל מארפכשד הוו, ושלישית מארפכשד שהוא שלישי לשם — יותר, היינו שלישית מישראל, אלא שלישי שלישי של נח כלומר כולו — ארפכשד יותר בה, שהוא שלישי שלישי של נח, דשם היה בן שלישי של נח דכתיב (בראשית י) ״ובני נח שם חם ויפת״ וארפכשד שלישי לשם — ועיקר. **דברים ככתבן** — שלא ימלטו אלא אחד מעיר ושנים ממשפחה. **ולקחתי אחד מעיר** — בשביל חסיד אחד שבעיר, אקח את כל העיר כולה. **חזייה** — רב לרב כהנא. **דקא חייף רישיה** — חופף ראשו ומעדן בעצמו, בשעה שהיה לו ללמוד תורה. **לא תמצא בארץ החיים** — משמע שמקללו, לא תבוא לעולם הבא. **נאמר** — בפרשת וארא ״ולקחתי אתכם לי לעם״ וכתיב בתריה ״והבאתי אתכם אל הארץ״.

HALAKHAH

לֹא תִמָּצֵא תּוֹרָה בְּמִי שֶׁמְּחַיֶּה עַצְמוֹ עָלֶיהָ Torah shall not be found in him who pampers himself for it. "The words of the Torah shall not be found among those who study while indulging themselves in food and drink, but rather among those who study in privation and with little sleep." (*Shulḥan Arukh, Yoreh De'ah* 246:21.)

אֶתְכֶם׳. [1]מַקִּישׁ יְצִיאָתָן מִמִּצְרַיִם לְבִיאָתָן לָאָרֶץ. [2]מָה בִּיאָתָן לָאָרֶץ — שְׁנַיִם מִשִּׁשִּׁים רִיבּוֹא, [3]אַף יְצִיאָתָן מִמִּצְרַיִם — שְׁנַיִם מִשִּׁשִּׁים רִיבּוֹא״.

[4]אָמַר רָבָא: וְכֵן לִימוֹת הַמָּשִׁיחַ, [5]שֶׁנֶּאֱמַר: ״וְעָנְתָה שָׁמָּה כִּימֵי נְעוּרֶיהָ וּכְיוֹם עֲלוֹתָהּ מֵאֶרֶץ מִצְרָיִם״.

[6]תַּנְיָא: אָמַר רַבִּי אֶלְעָזָר בְּרַבִּי יוֹסֵי: פַּעַם אַחַת נִכְנַסְתִּי לַאֲלֶכְּסַנְדְּרִיָא שֶׁל מִצְרַיִם. [7]מָצָאתִי זָקֵן אֶחָד, וְאָמַר לִי: ״בֹּא וְאַרְאֲךָ מֶה עָשׂוּ אֲבוֹתַי לַאֲבוֹתֶיךָ. [8]מֵהֶם טִבְּעוּ בַּיָּם, מֵהֶם הָרְגוּ בַּחֶרֶב, מֵהֶם מִעֲכוּ בַּבִּנְיָן״. [9]וְעַל דָּבָר זֶה נֶעֱנַשׁ מֹשֶׁה רַבֵּינוּ, [10]שֶׁנֶּאֱמַר: ״וּמֵאָז בָּאתִי אֶל פַּרְעֹה לְדַבֵּר בִּשְׁמֶךָ הֵרַע לָעָם הַזֶּה״. [11]אָמַר לוֹ הַקָּדוֹשׁ בָּרוּךְ הוּא: ״חֲבָל עַל דְּאָבְדִין וְלָא מִשְׁתַּכְּחִין. [12]הֲרֵי

LITERAL TRANSLATION

you.' [1]It compares their Exodus from Egypt to their entry into the land. [2]Just as their entry into the land — two of six hundred thousand, [3]so, too, their Exodus from Egypt — two of six hundred thousand."

[4]Rava said: And similarly in the days of the Messiah, [5]for it is stated: "And she shall respond there, as in the days of her youth, and as in the day when she came up out of the land of Egypt."

[6]It was taught: Rabbi Elazar the son of Rabbi Yose said: Once I entered Alexandria of Egypt. [7]I found an old man, who said to me: "Come and I will show you what my fathers did to your fathers. [8]Some they drowned in the sea, some they slayed with the sword, some they crushed while building." [9]And for this matter, Moses our master was punished, [10]as it is stated: "For since I came to Pharaoh to speak in Your name, he has done evil to this people." [11]The Holy One, blessed be He, said to him: "Woe, for those who are gone and are not found. [12]Many

TRANSLATION AND COMMENTARY

(Exodus 6:8): **'And I will bring you into the land.'** [1]Thus, the passage **compares** the people of Israel's **Exodus from Egypt to their entry into the Land** of Israel. How so? [2]**Just as,** regarding **their entry into the Land** of Israel, only **two of** the **six hundred thousand** people who left Egypt entered the land, for, except for Joshua and Caleb, the entire generation died in the wilderness, [3]**so, too,** regarding **their Exodus from Egypt,** only **two of** every **six hundred thousand** Israelites participated in the Exodus, for the rest died in Egypt."

אָמַר רָבָא [4]**Rava said: And similarly,** regarding **the days of the Messiah,** only two of every six hundred thousand will enjoy redemption, [5]**as the verse** alluding to that period **states** (Hosea 2:17): **"And she shall respond there, as in the days of her youth, and as in the day when she came up out of the land of Egypt."**

תַּנְיָא [6]**It was taught** in a Baraita: **Rabbi Elazar the son of Rabbi Yose said: Once I entered Alexandria of Egypt,** [7]and **I found an old** Egyptian **man, who said to me: "Come, and I will show you what my** Egyptian **ancestors did to your** Jewish **forebears.** [8]**Some they drowned in the sea, some they slayed with the sword,** and **some they crushed while building,** using their bodies instead of bricks." [9]**And for this matter,** for the complaints and the criticism that **Moses our master** directed at God regarding the afflictions suffered by Israel in Egypt, he **was** later **punished.** When Pharaoh intensified the decrees against Israel, Moses complained to God, [10]**as the verse states** (Exodus 5:23): **"For since I came to Pharaoh to speak in Your name, he has done evil to this people;** neither have You delivered Your people at all." [11]**The Holy One, blessed be He, said to him: "Oh,** for the three Patriarchs **who are gone and have not been replaced,** for you are not at all like them. [12]**Many times I revealed Myself to**

RASHI

מה ביאתם לארץ שנים מששים רבוא — שלא נשתיירו מששים רבוא שיצאו ממצרים אלא שני אנשים, יהושע וכלב, כדאמרינן בבבא בתרא בפרק ״יש נוחלין״ (קכא, א): לא נגזרה גזרה לא בפחות מעשרים ולא ביותר מששים שנה, בהנך נמי, ששים רבוא שנמנו במדבר לא אחשוב לא פחות מבן עשרים שנה ויותר מששים. **אף יציאתן ממצרים שנים מששים רבוא** — שמכל ששים רבוא שהיו במצרים לא נשתייר מהם אלא שנים בלבד, ואותם שנים של ששים רבוא עלו [לששים רבואות שיצאו אחד מששים רבוא שהיו בהם] והשאר מתו כולם בשלשת ימי אפילה, שלא יהיו מצרים רואין במפלתן של ישראל. **וכן לימות המשיח** — שלא ישארו מכל ששים רבוא אלא שנים. **וענתה שמה כימי נעוריה וכיום עלותה מארץ מצרים** — עניים ושפלים יהיו כימי עלותה מארץ מצרים. **מעבו בבנין** — היו בונין אותם במקום לבנים. **ועל דבר זה נענש משה רבינו** — שכשראה שנעשה לישראל כך התחיל להתרעם ולהרהר לפני הקב״ה, אמר משה לפני הקב״ה ״ומאז באתי״. **אמר ליה חבל על דאבדין ולא משתכחין** — הפסד גדול יש על גדולים שאבדו ואיני יכול למצוא חסידים אחרים כמותם שאין אתה כאברהם ויצחק ויעקב שלא הרהרו אחרי מדותי.

NOTES

שְׁנַיִם מִשִּׁשִּׁים רִיבּוֹא Two of six hundred thousand. *Rabbi Ya'akov Emden* explains that for every six hundred thousand Israelites who ever lived in Egypt during all the years of Israel's servitude, two entered the Land of Israel. Thus, the percentage of those who entered the Land of Israel out of those who left Egypt is slightly larger. The same also applies regarding the Messianic period.

TRANSLATION AND COMMENTARY

Abraham, Isaac, and Jacob by the name of God Almighty (see Genesis 17:1, Genesis 35:11, Exodus 6:3), [1]**and never did they criticize My ways, nor did they ask me, 'What is Your name,'** the way that you did. [2]**I said to Abraham** (Genesis 13:17): **'Arise, walk through the land in the length of it and in the breadth of it; for I will give it to you.'** [3]And in the end **he sought a place to bury Sarah, but did not find one, until he purchased** the Machpelah Cave **for four hundred silver shekels, but** still **he did not criticize My ways,** or argue that I did not fulfill my promise. [4]Similarly, **I said to Isaac** (Genesis 26:3): **'Sojourn in this land, and I will be with you, and will bless you.'** [5]But when **his servants sought water to drink, they did not find any until they had a quarrel** with the herdsmen of Gerar, [6]**as the verse states** (Genesis 26:20): **'And the herdsmen of Gerar quarreled with Isaac's herdsmen, saying, The water is ours.'** [7]But nevertheless Isaac **did not criticize My ways,** or complain. Similarly, **I said to Jacob** (Genesis 28:13): **'The land on which you lie, to you will I give it.'** [8]But when **he sought a place to pitch his tent, he did not find one, until he purchased** property **for a hundred kasitah.** [9]**But** still **he did not criticize My ways.** [10]**And none** of the Patriarchs **asked me: 'What is Your name?'** [11]**But you,** on the other hand, **asked me at the** very **beginning** (see Exodus 3:13): **'What is Your name?'** [12]**And now you** complain and **say to Me** (Exodus 5:23): **'Neither have You delivered Your people at all.'** My answer to you is (Exodus 6:1): [13]**'Now shall you see what I will do to Pharaoh.'** [14]Now **you will see the war** that I will wage **against Pharaoh, but you will not see the war** that I will wage **against the thirty-one** Canaanite **kings,** for, because of your criticisms, you will not enter into the Land of Israel."

כַּמָּה פְּעָמִים נִגְלֵיתִי עַל אַבְרָהָם יִצְחָק וְיַעֲקֹב בְּאֵל שַׁדַּי, [1]וְלֹא הִרְהֲרוּ עַל מִדּוֹתַי, וְלֹא אָמְרוּ לִי, ׳מַה שְּׁמְךָ׳. [2]אָמַרְתִּי לְאַבְרָהָם: ׳קוּם, הִתְהַלֵּךְ בָּאָרֶץ לְאָרְכָּהּ וּלְרָחְבָּהּ כִּי לְךָ אֶתְּנֶנָּה׳. [3]בִּקֵּשׁ מָקוֹם לִקְבּוֹר אֶת שָׂרָה, וְלֹא מָצָא, עַד שֶׁקָּנָה בְּאַרְבַּע מֵאוֹת שֶׁקֶל כֶּסֶף, וְלֹא הִרְהֵר עַל מִדּוֹתַי. [4]אָמַרְתִּי לְיִצְחָק: ׳גּוּר בָּאָרֶץ הַזֹּאת וְאֶהְיֶה עִמְּךָ וַאֲבָרְכֶךָּ׳. [5]בִּקְשׁוּ עֲבָדָיו מַיִם לִשְׁתּוֹת וְלֹא מָצְאוּ עַד שֶׁעָשׂוּ מְרִיבָה, [6]שֶׁנֶּאֱמַר: ״וַיָּרִיבוּ רֹעֵי גְרָר עִם רֹעֵי יִצְחָק לֵאמֹר לָנוּ הַמָּיִם׳. [7]וְלֹא הִרְהֵר אַחַר מִדּוֹתַי. אָמַרְתִּי לְיַעֲקֹב: ׳הָאָרֶץ אֲשֶׁר אַתָּה שֹׁכֵב עָלֶיהָ לְךָ אֶתְּנֶנָּה׳. [8]בִּיקֵּשׁ מָקוֹם לִנְטוֹעַ אָהֳלוֹ וְלֹא מָצָא, עַד שֶׁקָּנָה בְּמֵאָה קְשִׂיטָה. [9]וְלֹא הִרְהֵר אַחַר מִדּוֹתַי. [10]וְלֹא אָמְרוּ לִי, ׳מַה שְּׁמְךָ׳? [11]וְאַתָּה אָמַרְתָּ לִי ׳מַה שְּׁמְךָ׳ בַּתְּחִלָּה? [12]וְעַכְשָׁיו אַתָּה אוֹמֵר לִי: ׳וְהַצֵּל לֹא הִצַּלְתָּ אֶת עַמֶּךָ׳. [13]׳עַתָּה תִרְאֶה אֵת אֲשֶׁר אֶעֱשֶׂה לְפַרְעֹה׳. [14]בְּמִלְחֶמֶת פַּרְעֹה אַתָּה רוֹאֶה, וְאִי אַתָּה רוֹאֶה בְּמִלְחֶמֶת שְׁלֹשִׁים וְאֶחָד מְלָכִים״.

LITERAL TRANSLATION

times I revealed Myself to Abraham, Isaac, and Jacob by [the name of] God Almighty, [1]and they did not criticize My ways, nor did they say to me, 'What is Your name.' [2]I said to Abraham: 'Arise, walk through the land in the length of it and in the breadth of it; for I will give it to you.' [3]He sought a place to bury Sarah, but did not find [one], until he purchased [one] for four hundred silver shekels, but he did not criticize My ways. [4]I said to Isaac: 'Sojourn in this land, and I will be with you, and will bless you.' [5]His servants sought water to drink, but did not find [any] until they had a quarrel, [6]as it is stated: 'And the herdsmen of Gerar quarreled with Isaac's herdsmen, saying, The water is ours.' [7]But he did not criticize My ways. I said to Jacob: 'The land on which you lie, to you will I give it.' [8]He sought a place to pitch his tent, but did not find [one], until he purchased [one] for a hundred kasitah. [9]But he did not criticize My ways. [10]And they did not say to Me: 'What is Your name?' [11]And you said to me at the start: 'What is Your name?' [12]And now you say to Me: 'Neither have You delivered Your people.' [13]'Now shall you see what I will do to Pharaoh.' [14]You will see the war with Pharaoh, but you will not see the war with the thirty-one kings."

RASHI

אל שדי — שאמרתי לו אני אל שדי פרה ורבה וגו׳ (בראשית לה), ״אני אל שדי התהלך לפני והיה תמים״ (שם יז), והייתי מבטיחו שכל ארץ ישראל לו ולבניו ולא אמרו מה שמך כמו שעשית אתה. **בתחלה אמרת לי מה שמך** — ועכשיו הרהרת על מדותי ואמרת ״הצל לא הצלת את עמך״. **לנטוע אהלו** — כמו [״ויטע] אהלי אפדנו״ (דניאל יא), ולשון נטיעה שייך באהל. **עתה תראה** — הפעם תראה נפלאות שאני עושה להם, מה ראה על איזה מדה (אחת) של שלש עשרה [מדות] ראה והשתחוה.

NOTES

אִי אַתָּה רוֹאֶה בְּמִלְחֶמֶת שְׁלֹשִׁים וְאֶחָד מְלָכִים But you will not see the war with the thirty-one kings. It would appear from this passage that Moses was not barred from entering the Land of Israel because of his sin at Mei Merivah, but that it had been decreed long before then that he would not lead his people into the Promised Land. It has been suggested that it was originally decreed that Moses would not witness the wars waged against the

TRANSLATION AND COMMENTARY

וַיְמַהֵר מֹשֶׁה [1]The verses state (Exodus 34:6-8): "And the Lord passed by before him, and proclaimed, The Lord, the Lord, mighty, merciful and gracious, long-suffering, and abundant in love and truth, keeping truth to thousands.... **And Moses made haste, and bowed his head toward the earth, and prostrated himself."** [2]**What did Moses see** in these divine attributes that caused him to quickly bow his head and prostrate himself? [3]**Rabbi Ḥanina ben Gamla said:** Moses **saw** the divine attribute of **"long-suffering,"** and quickly bowed down before God. [4]**The Rabbis** disagree and **say:** Moses quickly bowed down when **he saw** the divine attribute of **"truth."**

תַּנְיָא כְּמַאן דַּאֲמַר [5]A Baraita **was taught in accordance with the** Tanna **who said** that Moses bowed down when **he saw** the divine attribute of **"long-suffering,"** [6]**for it was taught: "When Moses went up on high** and ascended Mount Sinai, **he saw the Holy One, blessed be He, sitting and writing** the word **'long-suffering'** among His attributes, [7]and **he said to Him: 'Master of the Universe,** surely You mean that You are **long-suffering** only **for the righteous.'** [8]God **said to him:** 'No, I am long-suffering **even for the wicked.'** [9]Moses **said to** God: 'But surely **the wicked should perish!'** [10]God **said to him: 'Now you will see what you will need.'** [11]**When Israel sinned** with the spies who were sent out to scout the Land of Israel and Moses prayed to God on their behalf, God **said to him:** [12]**'Did you not** once **say to Me** that I should be **long-suffering** only **for the righteous?** According to you, they do not deserve My pardon.' [111B] [13]Moses **said to** God: **'Master of the Universe, did You not say to me** that You are long-suffering **even for the wicked?'** [14]**And this is** the meaning of **the verse that states** (Numbers 14:17): **'And now, I pray You, let**

[1]״וַיְמַהֵר מֹשֶׁה וַיִּקֹּד אַרְצָה וַיִּשְׁתָּחוּ״. [2]מָה רָאָה מֹשֶׁה? [3]רַבִּי חֲנִינָא בֶּן גַּמְלָא אָמַר: ״אֶרֶךְ אַפַּיִם״ רָאָה. [4]וְרַבָּנַן אָמְרִי: ״אֱמֶת״ רָאָה.

[5]תַּנְיָא כְּמַאן דַּאֲמַר: ״אֶרֶךְ אַפַּיִם״ רָאָה, [6]דְּתַנְיָא: ״כְּשֶׁעָלָה מֹשֶׁה לַמָּרוֹם מְצָאוֹ לְהַקָּדוֹשׁ בָּרוּךְ הוּא שֶׁיּוֹשֵׁב וְכוֹתֵב ׳אֶרֶךְ אַפַּיִם׳. [7]אָמַר לְפָנָיו: ׳רִבּוֹנוֹ שֶׁל עוֹלָם׳, אֶרֶךְ אַפַּיִם לַצַּדִּיקִים? [8]אָמַר לוֹ: ׳אַף לָרְשָׁעִים׳. [9]אָמַר לוֹ: ׳רְשָׁעִים יֹאבְדוּ׳. [10]אֲמַר לֵיהּ: ׳הָשְׁתָּא חָזֵית מַאי דְּמִבָּעֵי לָךְ׳. [11]כְּשֶׁחָטְאוּ יִשְׂרָאֵל, אָמַר לוֹ: [12]׳לֹא כָּךְ אָמַרְתָּ לִי, אֶרֶךְ אַפַּיִם לַצַּדִּיקִים׳? [111B] [13]אָמַר לְפָנָיו: ׳רִבּוֹנוֹ שֶׁל עוֹלָם, וְלֹא כָּךְ אָמַרְתָּ לִי אַף לָרְשָׁעִים׳? [14]וְהַיְינוּ דִּכְתִיב: ׳וְעַתָּה יִגְדַּל נָא

LITERAL TRANSLATION

[1]"And Moses made haste, and bowed his head toward the earth, and prostrated himself." [2]What did Moses see? [3]Rabbi Ḥanina ben Gamla said: He saw "long-suffering." [4]And the Rabbis said: He saw "truth."

[5]It was taught in accordance with the one who said: He saw "long-suffering," [6]for it was taught: "When Moses went up on high, he saw the Holy One, blessed be He, sitting and writing 'long-suffering.' [7]He said before Him: 'Master of the Universe, long-suffering for the righteous?' [8]He said to him: 'Even for the wicked.' [9]He said to Him: 'Let the wicked perish.' [10]He said to him: 'Now you will see what you will need.' [11]When Israel sinned, He said to him: [12]'Did you not say to Me, long-suffering for the righteous?' [111B] [13]He said before Him: 'Master of the Universe, did You not say to me, even for the wicked?' [14]And this is what is written: 'And now, I pray You, let

RASHI

אמת ראה — במדותיו שנקרא אמת, ונתיירא אם נתחייבו כלייה אם הוא דן אותן בדין גמור, ומיהר והתפלל עליהם שלא יהא דן אותן לפי מעשיהם. הכי גרסינן — **תניא כמאן דאמר ארך אפים ראה, דתניא כשעלה משה למרום וכו׳ אמר לו: רשעים יאבדו ולא יהיה לך ארך אפים עליהם. אמר לו** — הקב״ה, לא כך אמרת, ארך אפים לצדיקים ולא לרשעים. **אמר לפניו וכו׳** — והשתא [מסתברא] כמאן דאמר ארך אפים ראה, שכיון שראה [מדה זו] בהקדוש ברוך הוא שהוא ארך אפים אף לרשעים, שמח.

NOTES

Canaanite kings and the final conquest of the land, but he would nevertheless enter the country, and then later it was decreed that he would not even enter the land (see *Iyyun Ya'akov, Ri'af*). The Midrash implies that Moses was not punished for a single offense, but rather for a combination of offenses.

מָה רָאָה מֹשֶׁה **What did Moses see?** The discussion found here is based on the verse: "And Moses made haste, and bowed his head toward the earth, and prostrated himself," which implies that Moses bowed down even before God finished reciting the list of the thirteen attributes of divine mercy. Thus, the Gemara asks: What did Moses see that drove him to bow down and prostrate himself? According to the Rabbis, Moses bowed down when he saw the divine attribute of "truth." When he understood that God was truthful, and that His promises to the people of Israel would surely be fulfilled, he bowed down before God in joy. Alternatively, when he understood that God judged the world according to the standard of truth, he was afraid that the people of Israel would be condemned to destruction, so he bowed down before God in prayer so that the people of Israel would not be judged according to their deeds (*Ramah*).

TRANSLATION AND COMMENTARY

the power of my Lord be great, as You have spoken, saying,' which implies that Moses reminded God of His earlier promise." It stands to reason, according to this Baraita, that when Moses saw the divine attribute of "long-suffering" he bowed down in joy before God, knowing that He will be long-suffering even when the people of Israel sin.

רַבִּי חַגָּא [1]It was related that **Rabbi Ḥagga was** once **going up the stairs of the house of Rabbah bar Shela,** [2]when **he heard a child reciting** the verse (Psalms 93:5): **"Your testimonies are very sure; holiness becomes Your house, O Lord, for length of days."** The words "length of days" allude to God's quality of "long-suffering," and regarding that quality, Moses said: "Your testimonies are very sure," meaning that he had seen it at Sinai. We know that these words were recited by Moses, [3]for **near this verse** we find (Psalms 90:1): **"A prayer of Moses."** When Rabbi Hagga heard the child reciting that verse, [4]**he said: Infer from this that** it was when Moses **saw** the quality of **"long-suffering"** that he bowed down before God.

אָמַר רַבִּי אֶלְעָזָר [5]**Rabbi Elazar said in the name of Rabbi Ḥanina: In the future, the Holy One, blessed be He, will be,** as it were, **a crown on the head of each and every righteous man,** [6]**as the verse states** (Isaiah 28:5): **"In that day shall the Lord of hosts be for a crown of glory, and for a diadem of beauty, to the remnant of His people."** [7]**What is** meant by the words **"for a crown of glory** [צְבִי], **and for a diadem** [צְפִירַת] **of beauty"**? [8]God will be a crown **for those who do His will** (in Aramaic, the word צְבִי bears the sense of "will") **and await** [מְצַפִּים] **His salvation.** [9]**You might have thought** that God will be a crown **for anyone** who does His will, even if he is proud and haughty. [10]**Therefore the verse continues: "To the remnant** [לִשְׁאָר] **of His people"** — [11]God will only be a crown **for him who** is modest and **considers himself like a** mere **remainder** [שְׁיָרִים].

וּלְרוּחַ מִשְׁפָּט [12]The next verse continues (Isaiah 28:6): **"And for a spirit of judgment to him that sits in judgment, and for strength to them that turn back the battle to the gate."** [13]**"And for a spirit of judgment**

כֹּחַ ה׳ כַּאֲשֶׁר דִּבַּרְתָּ לֵאמֹר׳״.
[1]רַבִּי חַגָּא הֲוָה סָלֵיק וְאָזֵיל
בְּדַרְגָּא דְּבֵי רַבָּה בַּר שֵׁילָא.
[2]שַׁמְעֵיהּ לְהַהוּא יְנוּקָא דַּאֲמַר:
״עֵדֹתֶיךָ נֶאֶמְנוּ מְאֹד לְבֵיתְךָ
נַאֲוָה קֹדֶשׁ ה׳ לְאֹרֶךְ יָמִים״.
[3]וּסְמִיךְ לֵיהּ: ״תְּפִלָּה לְמֹשֶׁה
וגו׳ ״. [4]אָמַר: שְׁמַע מִינָּהּ ״אֶרֶךְ
אַפַּיִם״ רָאָה.
[5]אָמַר רַבִּי אֶלְעָזָר אָמַר רַבִּי
חֲנִינָא: עָתִיד הַקָּדוֹשׁ בָּרוּךְ הוּא
לִהְיוֹת עֲטָרָה בְּרֹאשׁ כָּל צַדִּיק
וְצַדִּיק, [6]שֶׁנֶּאֱמַר: ״בַּיּוֹם הַהוּא
יִהְיֶה ה׳ צְבָאוֹת לַעֲטֶרֶת צְבִי
וְלִצְפִירַת תִּפְאָרָה לִשְׁאָר עַמּוֹ
וגו׳ ״. [7]מַאי ״לַעֲטֶרֶת צְבִי
וְלִצְפִירַת תִּפְאָרָה״? [8]לָעוֹשִׂים
רְצוֹנוֹ וּמְצַפִּים לִישׁוּעָתוֹ. [9]יָכוֹל
לַכֹּל. [10]תַּלְמוּד לוֹמַר: ״לִשְׁאָר
עַמּוֹ״ — [11]לְמִי שֶׁמֵּשִׂים עַצְמוֹ
כְּשִׁירַיִם.
[12]״וּלְרוּחַ מִשְׁפָּט לַיּוֹשֵׁב עַל
הַמִּשְׁפָּט וְלִגְבוּרָה מְשִׁיבֵי
מִלְחָמָה שָׁעְרָה״. [13]״וּלְרוּחַ

LITERAL TRANSLATION

the power of my Lord be great, as You have spoken, saying.'"

[1]Rabbi Ḥagga was going up the stairs of the house of Rabbah bar Shela. [2]He heard a child saying: "Your testimonies are very sure; holiness becomes Your house, O Lord, for length of days." [3]And close to it: "A prayer of Moses." [4]He said: Infer from this [that] he saw "long-suffering."

[5]Rabbi Elazar said in the name of Rabbi Ḥanina: The Holy One, blessed be He, will in the future be a crown on the head of each and every righteous man, [6]for it is stated: "In that day shall the Lord of hosts be for a crown of glory, and for a diadem of beauty, to the remnant of His people, etc." [7]What is "for a crown of glory, and for a diadem of beauty"? [8]To those who do His will and await His salvation. [9]You might think for all. [10][Therefore] the verse states: "To the remnant of His people" — [11]to him who makes himself like a remainder.

[12]"And for a spirit of judgment to him that sits in judgment, and for strength to them that turn back the battle to the gate." [13]"And for a spirit of

RASHI

עדותיך וגו׳ ה׳ לאורך ימים — היינו מדת ארך אפים, ועליה אמר משה ״עדותיך נאמנו מאד״ שראה אותו בחורב, ופסוק זה משה רבינו עליו השלום אמרו דכתיב לעיל מיניה ״תפלה למשה איש האלהים וגו׳ ״. **יכול לכל** — למי שעושין רצונו אף על פי שמתגאה. **כשירים** — שיריים שאין נחשבין, כך אינו חשוב בעיניו ואינו מתגאה. **ולרוח משפט** — שופט את רוחו.

NOTES

עֵדֹתֶיךָ נֶאֶמְנוּ מְאֹד **Your testimonies are very sure.** It is not clear from this passage how Rabbi Ḥagga inferred from the child's words that Moses saw the attribute of "long-suffering." But if we compare this version of the story to that found in the Midrash, we may say as follows: Rabbi Ḥagga heard the child recite the last verse in Psalms 93: "Your testimonies are very sure; holiness becomes Your house, O Lord, for length of days," and then the first verse in Psalms 94: "O Lord, God, to whom vengeance belongs; O God, to whom vengeance belongs." Taking the two verses together, he understood that God waits a long time ("length of days") before he takes vengeance on the wicked. The words in Psalms 90, "A prayer of Moses," teach us that the collection of Psalms 90-99 are all psalms of Moses (as is stated explicitly in the Midrash).

מִשְׁפָּט״ — זֶה הָרוֹדֶה אֶת יִצְרוֹ. 1״וְלַיּוֹשֵׁב עַל הַמִּשְׁפָּט״ — זֶה הַדָּן דִּין אֱמֶת לַאֲמִיתּוֹ. 2״וְלִגְבוּרָה״ — זֶה הַמִּתְגַּבֵּר בְּיִצְרוֹ. 3״מְשִׁיבֵי מִלְחָמָה״ — זֶה שֶׁנּוֹשֵׂא וְנוֹתֵן בְּמִלְחַמְתָּהּ שֶׁל תּוֹרָה. 4״שָׁעְרָה״ — אֵלּוּ שֶׁמַּשְׁכִּימִין וּמַעֲרִיבִין בְּבָתֵּי כְנֵסִיּוֹת וּבָתֵּי מִדְרָשׁוֹת. 5אָמְרָה מִדַּת הַדִּין לִפְנֵי הַקָּדוֹשׁ בָּרוּךְ הוּא: ״רִבּוֹנוֹ שֶׁל עוֹלָם, מַה נִּשְׁתַּנּוּ אֵלּוּ מֵאֵלּוּ? 6אָמַר לָהּ: ״וְגַם אֵלֶּה בַּיַּיִן שָׁגוּ וּבַשֵּׁכָר תָּעוּ [וגו׳] פָּקוּ פְּלִילִיָּה״. 7וְאֵין פּוּקָה אֶלָּא גֵּיהִנָּם, שֶׁנֶּאֱמַר: ״לֹא תִהְיֶה זֹאת לְךָ לְפוּקָה״. 8וְאֵין פְּלִילָה אֶלָּא דַּיָּינִין, שֶׁנֶּאֱמַר: ״וְנָתַן בִּפְלִלִים״.

משנה 9אַנְשֵׁי עִיר הַנִּדַּחַת אֵין לָהֶם חֵלֶק לָעוֹלָם הַבָּא, 10שֶׁנֶּאֱמַר: ״יָצְאוּ אֲנָשִׁים בְּנֵי

LITERAL TRANSLATION

judgment" — this is someone who subjugates his [evil] inclination. 1"To him that sits in judgment" — this is someone who judges an absolutely true judgment. 2"And for strength" — this is someone who overcomes his [evil] inclination. 3"To them that turn back the battle" — this is someone who negotiates the war of Torah. 4"To the gate" — these are the ones who come early and late to the synagogues and study halls. 5The attribute of justice said before the Holy One, blessed be He: "Master of the Universe, how are these different from those?" 6He said to it: "But they also reel with wine, and stagger with strong drink...they stumble [*paku*] in judgment [*peliliyah*]." 7And *pukah* is only Gehinom, as it is stated: "That this shall not be a cause of stumbling [*pukah*] to you." 8And *pelilah* is only judges, as it is stated: "And he shall pay as the judges [*biflelim*] determine."

MISHNAH 9The inhabitants of a subverted city do not have a portion in the World to Come, 10for it is stated: "Certain men,

TRANSLATION AND COMMENTARY

[וּלְרוּחַ מִשְׁפָּט]" — **this** refers to **someone who subjugates his evil inclination** [הָרוֹדֶה אֶת יִצְרוֹ]. 1**"To him that sits in judgment" — this** refers to **someone who judges an absolutely true judgment.** 2**"And for strength** [וְלִגְבוּרָה]" — **this** refers to **someone who overcomes** [הַמִּתְגַּבֵּר] **his evil inclination,** and forces himself to follow his inclination to do good. 3**"To them that turn back the battle" — this** refers to **someone who negotiates the war of Torah.** 4**"To the gate"** — **this** refers to **those who come early** in the day **and** stay **late** in the evening to open and close the gates **of the synagogues and study halls.** 5**The attribute of justice said before the Holy One, blessed be He: "Master of the Universe, how are these** people with all these fine qualities **different from** the rest of the people who do God's will and await His salvation? Surely they are all righteous people!" 6God **answered** (Isaiah 28:7): **"But they also reel with wine, and stagger with strong drink...they stumble** [*paku*] **in judgment** [*peliliyah*]." 7Their misdeeds will be punished **for** the word *pukah* in this context **refers to Gehinom, as the verse states** (I Samuel 25:31): **"That this shall not be a cause of stumbling** [*pukah*] **to you."** 8**And** the word *pelilah* in this context **refers to judges, as the verse states** (Exodus 21:22): **"And he shall pay as the judges** [*biflelim*] **determine."**

MISHNAH אַנְשֵׁי עִיר הַנִּדַּחַת 9Earlier in the tractate (76b), we learned that the inhabitants of a city, most of whose inhabitants have become idolaters (see Deuteronomy 13:13-19), are liable to death by the sword (decapitation). Our Mishnah adds that **the inhabitants of a subverted city do not have a portion in the World to Come,** 10**as the verse states** (Deuteronomy 13:14): **"Certain men, wicked persons, are gone out from**

RASHI

שרודה ביצרו — שבועט ביצרו וחוזר בתשובה מן העבירה שעבר. **ומתגבר ביצרו** — מרגיז יצר טוב על יצר הרע, אם היצר הרע אמר לו: עשה עבירה זו — לא דיו שנמנע מן העבירה, אלא הולך ועושה מצוה ומתגבר עדיף מרודה. **שערה** — אלו בתי כנסיות. **מה נשתנו אלו מאלו** — שיש בהם מדות הללו מן השאר — אמר הקדוש ברוך הוא: **ביין שגו. אין פלילה אלא דיינין.**

משנה יצאו אנשים בני בליעל מקרבך — שאין להם חלק לעולם הבא.

NOTES

הָרוֹדֶה אֶת יִצְרוֹ...הַמִּתְגַּבֵּר בְּיִצְרוֹ Someone who subjugates his evil inclination...someone who overcomes his evil inclination. Someone who subjugates his evil inclination does not allow himself to follow its wicked path, whereas someone who overcomes his evil inclination makes use of his good inclination and forces himself to do good (*Ramah*). *Rashash* suggests that subjugating one's evil inclination means punishing it with afflictions that correspond to the enjoyment that one received from one's sins.

אַנְשֵׁי עִיר הַנִּדַּחַת אֵין לָהֶם חֵלֶק לָעוֹלָם הַבָּא The inhabitants of an idolatrous city do not have a portion in the World to Come. The Rishonim ask: Why is this so? Surely we learned earlier in this chapter that even the wicked have a portion in the future world! Some suggest that this statement refers to citizens of an idolatrous city who were not executed. Since they did not atone for their sin, they are still regarded as heretics who deny God (see *Tosafot, Tosafot Yom Tov, Rabbi Ya'akov Emden*). Some Rishonim did not have the reading: "The inhabitants of an idolatrous city do not have a portion in the World to Come," and argue that such a reading is untenable (*Ramah, Rabbi David Bonfil;* see *Melekhet Shlomo*).

בְלִיַּעַל מִקִּרְבֶּךָ וַיַּדִּיחוּ אֶת יֹשְׁבֵי עִירָם לֵאמֹר״.

[1]וְאֵינָן נֶהֱרָגִים עַד שֶׁיִּהְיוּ מַדִּיחֶיהָ מֵאוֹתָהּ הָעִיר, [2]וּמֵאוֹתוֹ הַשֵּׁבֶט, [3]וְעַד שֶׁיּוּדַּח רוּבָּהּ, [4]וְעַד שֶׁיַּדִּיחוּהָ אֲנָשִׁים. [5]הִדִּיחוּהָ נָשִׁים וּקְטַנִּים, אוֹ שֶׁהוּדַּח מִיעוּטָהּ, [6]אוֹ שֶׁהָיָה מַדִּיחֶיהָ חוּצָה לָהּ — הֲרֵי אֵלּוּ כַּיְּחִידִים.

[7]וּצְרִיכִין שְׁנֵי עֵדִים וְהַתְרָאָה לְכָל אֶחָד וְאֶחָד. [8]זֶה חוֹמֶר בַּיְּחִידִים מִבַּמְרוּבִּים: [9]שֶׁהַיְּחִידִים בִּסְקִילָה; [10]לְפִיכָךְ

LITERAL TRANSLATION

wicked persons, are gone out from among you, and have subverted the inhabitants of their city, saying." [1]And they are not slain unless their subverters are from the same city, [2]and from the same tribe, [3]and unless the majority are subverted, [4]and unless men subverted it. [5][If] women or children subverted it, or if a minority were subverted, [6]or if the subverters were from outside of it — they are like individuals.

[7]And they need two witnesses and a warning for each and every one. [8]This is a stringency regarding individuals over many: [9]Individuals are [liable to] stoning; [10]therefore

TRANSLATION AND COMMENTARY

among you, and have subverted the inhabitants of their city, saying." The subverters "are gone out from among you," that is to say, they are gone out from the congregation of Israel and have lost their portion in the World to Come. The idolatrous inhabitants of the city are treated like the subverters, and they have also forfeited their place in the World to Come.

וְאֵינָן נֶהֱרָגִים [1]The inhabitants of a subverted city **are not slain** by the sword **unless the subverters** who led them astray after false gods **came from that city,** as the verse states: "Certain men...have subverted the inhabitants of their city," not those of another city. [2]Similarly, the inhabitants of an idolatrous city are not slain by the sword unless their subverters came **from the same tribe** as the people of the subverted city, as the verse states: "From among you." [3]They are also not slain **unless the majority** of the inhabitants of the city **were subverted** to commit idolatry, for the word מִקִּרְבֶּךָ, "from among you," may also be understood as if it read מֵרוּבְּךָ, "from your majority." [4]Nor are they slain **unless men subverted** them, as the verse states: "Certain men are gone out." [5]But **if women or children subverted** the inhabitants of the city, **or if** only **a minority** of the inhabitants **were subverted,** [6]**or if the subverters came from outside** the city, the inhabitants of the subverted city **are** treated **like individuals** who committed idolatry, and are therefore liable to be punished by stoning, and not decapitation.

וּצְרִיכִין [7]Whether only a minority of the city worshiped idols or a majority of the inhabitants were led astray, **two witnesses** to the offense **and a warning** given prior to the commission of the crime **are needed for each and every** offender. [8]In **this** respect the law applying to **individuals** who practice idolatry **is more stringent than** the law applying to **a community.** [9]**Individuals** who commit idolatry **are liable to** the more stringent mode of execution, death by **stoning.** [10]**Therefore** the Torah was more lenient regarding **their money**

RASHI

וידיחו את (אנשי) [יושבי] עירם — הא אין נהרגים עד שיהיו מדיחיה מאותה העיר ואותה השבט עצמה דכתיב "מקרבך" — מקרב אותו שבט עצמו. **עד שיודח רובה** — דכתיב "ויושבי העיר" משמע ישובה של עיר — היינו רובה, לישנא אחרינא: עד שיודח רובה, דכתיב "מקרבך" קרי ביה מרובך. הכי גרסינן — **עד שיודח רובה עד שידיחוה אנשים. או שהיו מדיחיה חוצה לה** — שלא היו מאותה העיר. **הרי אלו ביחידים** — שהן בסקילה וממונן פלט. **וצריכים שני עדים והתראה לכל אחד** — כדיליף בגמרא, יחידים בסקילה — לפיכך ממונן פלט ומתוך שהחמרת עליו במיתתו הקלת עליו בממונו.

NOTES

מֵאוֹתוֹ הַשֵּׁבֶט From the same tribe. Our commentary follows *Rashi,* who derives this law from the word מִקִּרְבֶּךָ, "from among you." Some point out that the word מִקִּרְבֶּךָ is used below to exclude a border city from the law of an idolatrous city. *Rosh* explains that the word מִקִּרְבֶּךָ is found twice in the passage relating to a subverted city, and each instance of the word serves as the source of a different law.

HALAKHAH

אֵינָן נֶהֱרָגִים עַד שֶׁיִּהְיוּ מַדִּיחֶיהָ מֵאוֹתָהּ הָעִיר They are not slain unless their inciters are from the same city. "A city does not become an idolatrous city unless the subverters who led the people astray came from that city, and from the same tribe as the citizens of that city, and unless there were at least two male inciters, and unless a majority of the inhabitants of the city were subverted. But if the subverters were women, or minors, or from a different city, or if only a minority of the citizens were subverted, the city is not an idolatrous city, and the offenders are judged as individual idolaters." (*Rambam, Sefer Mada, Hilkhot Avodah Zarah* 4:2.)

צְרִיכִין שְׁנֵי עֵדִים וְהַתְרָאָה They need two witnesses and a warning. "Two witnesses to the offense and a warning given prior to the commission of the crime are needed for each and every citizen of the idolatrous city who committed idolatry." (*Rambam, Sefer Mada, Hilkhot Avodah Zarah* 4:5.)

יְחִידִים מִבַּמְרוּבִּים Individuals and the many. "The inhabitants of an idolatrous city who committed idolatry are subject to death by decapitation, and their property is destroyed. Individuals who worship an idol are subject to death by stoning, and their property is spared and passes to their heirs." (*Rambam, Sefer Mada, Hilkhot Avodah Zarah* 4:2,6.)

TRANSLATION AND COMMENTARY

and property; which **are spared,** and pass to their heirs. [1]But if **a community** practices idolatry, its members **are liable to** the more lenient mode of execution, death by **the sword.** [2]**Therefore** the Torah was more stringent with **their money** and property, ordering that all their possessions **be destroyed,** as the verse states (Deuteronomy 13:16): "Destroy it utterly, and all that is in it, and its cattle with the edge of the sword."

הַכֵּה תַכֶּה [3]Regarding an idolatrous city, the verse states (Deuteronomy 13:16): **"You shall surely smite the inhabitants of that city with the edge of the sword."** From here we learn that if most of the inhabitants of a city succumbed to idolatry, [4]and **a company of ass-drivers or a company of camel-drivers who were passing from place to place** camped in the city for thirty days, and were not subverted to idolatry, **they** join the residents of the city who resisted idolatry to form a majority, and thus **they save** the city from being declared an idolatrous city. Those who committed idolatry are treated like individuals who worshiped idols; they are executed by stoning, and their property passes to their heirs. Conversely, if only a minority of the residents of a city were subverted to idolatry, and a company of ass-drivers or camel-drivers camped there for thirty days, and they became idolaters, they are counted with the minority of residents. If they form a majority, they cause the city to be condemned as an idolatrous city. The guilty parties are slain by the sword, and their property is utterly destroyed.

שֶׁנֶּאֱמַר [5]**The verse states** (Deuteronomy 13:16): **"Destroying it utterly, and all that is in it, and its cattle with the edge of the sword."** [6]**From here** the Sages **said** that **the property of the righteous** citizens that is found **within** the city itself **is destroyed,** as the verse states: [7]"All that is in it," but that which is found **outside of** the city **is spared,** as the verse states: "Destroying it utterly" — "it," and not the property of the righteous that is found outside the city. [8]The property **of the wicked, both** that which is **inside** the city, **and** that which is **outside it, is destroyed,** as the verse states (Deuteronomy 13:17): "And you shall gather *all* of its spoil."

שֶׁנֶּאֱמַר [9]**The verse states** (Deuteronomy 13:17): **"And you shall gather all of its spoil into the midst of the open place of the city."** [10]If the idolatrous city **does not have an open place** in which the entire community

LITERAL TRANSLATION

their money is spared. [1]The many are [liable to] the sword; [2]therefore their money is lost.

[3]"You shall surely smite the inhabitants of that city with the edge of the sword." [4]A company of ass-drivers or a company of camel-drivers who were passing from place to place — they save it.

[5]It is stated: "Destroy it utterly, and all that is in it, and its cattle with the edge of the sword." [6]From here they said: The property of the righteous within it is lost; [7]outside of it is spared. [8]And that of the wicked, both inside it and outside of it, is lost.

[9]It is stated: "And you shall gather all of its spoil into the the open place, etc." [10]If it does not have an open place, they make

מָמוֹנָם פָּלֵט. [1]וְהַמְרוּבִּין בְּסַיִף; [2]לְפִיכָךְ מָמוֹנָם אָבֵד.

[3]"הַכֵּה תַכֶּה אֶת יֹשְׁבֵי הָעִיר הַזֹּאת לְפִי חָרֶב". [4]הַחַמֶּרֶת וְהַגַּמֶּלֶת הָעוֹבֶרֶת מִמָּקוֹם לְמָקוֹם — הֲרֵי אֵלּוּ מַצִּילִין אוֹתָהּ.

[5]שֶׁנֶּאֱמַר: "הַחֲרֵם אֹתָהּ וְאֶת כָּל אֲשֶׁר בָּהּ וְאֶת בְּהֶמְתָּהּ לְפִי חָרֶב". [6]מִכָּאן אָמְרוּ: נִכְסֵי צַדִּיקִים שֶׁבְּתוֹכָהּ אוֹבְדִין; [7]שֶׁבְּחוּצָה לָהּ פְּלֵיטִין. [8]וְשֶׁל רְשָׁעִים, בֵּין שֶׁבְּתוֹכָהּ בֵּין שֶׁבְּחוּצָה לָהּ, הֲרֵי אֵלּוּ אוֹבְדִין.

[9]שֶׁנֶּאֱמַר: "וְאֶת כָּל שְׁלָלָהּ תִּקְבֹּץ אֶל תּוֹךְ רְחֹבָהּ וגו׳". [10]אִם אֵין לָהּ רְחוֹב, עוֹשִׂין לָהּ

RASHI

הכה תכה את יושבי העיר ההיא לפי חרב החמרת והגמלת העוברת ממקום למקום מצילין — מדכתיב "יושבי" מכלל דשיירה של חמרים וגמלים שנשתהו בעיר שלשים יום, כדמפרש בגמרא דהוו להו יושבי העיר — הרי אלו מצילין אם רוב אנשי העיר הודחו, וחמרים וגמלים משלימין המיעוט ועושה אותם רוב — מצילין עליהם שאין ממונם אבד, אלא נדונים כיחידים, וגורמין נמי לעשות אותה עיר הנדחת אם משלימים לעיר הנדחת לעשות רוב, אלא הא פסיקא טפי, דחמרת וגמלת אין דעתם מעורבת עם בני העיר להיות נדונין עמהן. הכי גרסינן — החרם אותה וכל אשר בה מכאן אמרו צדיקים וכו׳ ושל רשעים בין מתוכה בין מחוצה לה אבודים, בגמרא מפרש לה מדכתיב "כל". **ואת כל שללה תקבוץ אל תוך רחובה אין לה רחוב עושין לה רחוב** — ורחובה דהשתא נמי משמע.

HALAKHAH

נִכְסֵי צַדִּיקִים שֶׁבְּתוֹכָהּ The property of the righteous within it. "The property of the righteous members of an idolatrous city that is found within the city itself is burned together with the rest of the property of the city. But any of their property that is found outside the city is not destroyed." (*Rambam, Sefer Mada, Hilkhot Avodah Zarah* 4:7.)

נִכְסֵי רְשָׁעִים The property of the wicked. "The property of the wicked members of an idolatrous city that was found outside the city and was gathered into the city is burned along with the rest of the property of the city. But if it was not gathered into the city, it is spared and passes to their heirs." (*Rambam, Sefer Mada, Hilkhot Avodah Zarah* 4:10.)

אִם אֵין לָהּ רְחוֹב If it does not have an open place. "If the idolatrous city does not have an open place, an open

TRANSLATION AND COMMENTARY

is accustomed to assemble, **an open place is made for it** now, in order to fulfill the requirement set by this verse. [1]If the city's **open space is outside** the city wall, **it is brought inside** the city by constructing a new wall that includes the plaza.

שֶׁנֶּאֱמַר [2]**The verse continues** (Deuteronomy 13:17): **"And You shall burn with fire both the city and all its spoil, entirely, for the Lord your God."** [3]The words **"its spoil"** teach that only the spoil of the city is burned, **but not the spoil of Heaven.** [4]**From here** the Sages **said: Property that was consecrated** to the Temple, and is now found **inside** a subverted city, **is redeemed;** [5]**terumah** — the portion of produce that is set aside and given to a priest — must **be allowed to rot; the second tithe** produce **and sacred scrolls** must **be buried** in the ground.

כָּלִיל לַה׳ אֱלֹהֶיךָ [6]The verse reads (Deuteronomy 13:17): **"Entirely [כָּלִיל], for the Lord your God."** [7]**Rabbi Shimon said: The Holy One, blessed be He, said: "If you execute judgment against a subverted city** as I have commanded, burning the city and all its spoil to the ground — [8]I will **regard you as having offered before Me a whole [כָּלִיל] burnt-offering."**

וְהָיְתָה תֵּל עוֹלָם [9]The verse continues (Deuteronomy 13:17): **"And it shall be a heap for ever."** [10]This means that the area **may not** even **be made into** a place of **gardens and orchards.** [11]**This is the position of Rabbi Yose the Galilean.** [12]**Rabbi Akiva** disagrees and **says:** The words that follow, **"It shall not be built again,"** teach that the [13]idolatrous city **may not be rebuilt the way it had been** with houses and buildings, **but** the area **may be made into** a place of **gardens and orchards.**

רְחוֹב. [1]הָיְתָה רְחָבָהּ חוּצָה לָהּ, כּוֹנְסִין אוֹתָהּ לְתוֹכָהּ.
[2]שֶׁנֶּאֱמַר: "וְשָׂרַפְתָּ בָאֵשׁ אֶת הָעִיר וְאֶת כָּל שְׁלָלָהּ כָּלִיל לַה׳ אֱלֹהֶיךָ". [3]"שְׁלָלָהּ" — וְלֹא שְׁלַל שָׁמַיִם. [4]מִכָּאן אָמְרוּ: הַהֶקְדֵּשׁוֹת שֶׁבָּהּ יִפָּדוּ, [5]וּתְרוּמוֹת יֵרָקְבוּ, מַעֲשֵׂר שֵׁנִי וְכִתְבֵי הַקֹּדֶשׁ יִגָּנְזוּ.
[6]"כָּלִיל לַה׳ אֱלֹהֶיךָ". [7]אָמַר רַבִּי שִׁמְעוֹן: אָמַר הַקָּדוֹשׁ בָּרוּךְ הוּא: "אִם אַתֶּם עוֹשִׂין דִּין בְּעִיר הַנִּדַּחַת — [8]מַעֲלֶה אֲנִי עֲלֵיכֶם כְּאִילּוּ אַתֶּם מַעֲלִים עוֹלָה כָּלִיל לְפָנַי".
[9]"וְהָיְתָה תֵּל עוֹלָם" — [10]לֹא תֵּעָשֶׂה גַּנּוֹת וּפַרְדֵּסִים. [11]דִּבְרֵי רַבִּי יוֹסֵי הַגְּלִילִי. [12]רַבִּי עֲקִיבָא אוֹמֵר: "לֹא תִבָּנֶה עוֹד" — [13]לִכְמוֹת שֶׁהָיְתָה אֵינָהּ נִבְנֵית, אֲבָל נַעֲשֵׂית הִיא גַּנּוֹת וּפַרְדֵּסִים.

LITERAL TRANSLATION

an open place for it. [1][If] its open space was outside of it, they bring it inside.

[2]It is stated: "And You shall burn with fire both the city and all its spoil, entirely, for the Lord your God." [3]"Its spoil" — and not the spoil of Heaven. [4]From here they said: The consecrated property in it is redeemed, [5]and terumah is allowed to rot, the second tithe and sacred scrolls are buried.

[6]"Entirely, for the Lord your God." [7]Rabbi Shimon said: The Holy One, blessed be He, said: "If you execute judgment against a subverted city — [8]I regard you as having offered a whole burnt-offering before Me."

[9]"And it shall be a heap for ever" — [10]it shall not be made into gardens and orchards. [11][These are] the words of Rabbi Yose the Galilean. [12]Rabbi Akiva says: "It shall not be built again" — [13]as it was it shall not be built, but it may be made into gardens and orchards.

RASHI

היה רחובה חוצה לה — שמקום קבוץ בני העיר היה חוץ לעיר — כונסין אותה לעיר שצריך לעשות לה רחוב בתוכה, רחוב — פלטיא גדולה. את העיר ואת כל שללה ולא שלל שמים — דשלל שמים הוא. מכאן אמרו הקדשות שבתוכה יפדו — כלומר אין נשרפין אלא הרי הם כשאר הקדש שצריך פדייה כדי שוויו דשלל שמים הם. ותרומות ירקבו — ובגמרא מוקמי לה בתרומה ביד כהן דממון כהן הוא וחל עליה איסור דעיר הנדחת, דנהי דבשריפה לא הויא עם שאר שללה, דקדש אקרי, ולא מזלזלינן ביה כולי האי. מעשר שני — אף על פי שהוא נאכל לישראל הואיל וקדש איקרי לא אמרינן ישרף אלא יגנזו, וכן כתבי הקדש — יגנזו. הכי גרסינן — "כליל לה׳ אלהיך" אמר ר׳ שמעון: אמר הקדוש ברוך הוא וכו׳, כאילו אתה מעלה עולה שהוא כליל לפני. לא תעשה גנות ופרדסין וכו׳ — בגמרא מפרש במאי פליגי. לכמו שהיתה — ביישוב בתים.

HALAKHAH

place is built for it. If the open place was outside the city wall, a new wall is built in order to include the open place within the city." (*Rambam, Sefer Mada, Hilkhot Avodah Zarah* 4:6.)

וְשָׂרַפְתָּ בָאֵשׁ And you shall burn with fire. "The burning of an idolatrous city is a positive Torah commandment." (*Rambam, Sefer Mada, Hilkhot Avodah Zarah* 4:6,16.)

וְלֹא שְׁלַל שָׁמַיִם And not the spoil of Heaven. "If there is consecrated property in the idolatrous city, animals that have been consecrated to be offered on the altar are confined in an enclosure without food and left to die, and those animals that have been consecrated for their value to be used for maintaining the Temple are redeemed and then burned. According to *Raavad*, they are not burned. If there is second tithe or second-tithe money or sacred scrolls in the idolatrous city, they are buried in the ground." (*Rambam, Sefer Mada, Hilkhot Avodah Zarah* 4:13,15.)

TRANSLATION AND COMMENTARY

וְלֹא יִדְבַּק בְּיָדְךָ [1]The next verse states (Deuteronomy 13:18): **"And nothing of what was devoted to destruction shall remain in your hand,** that the Lord may turn from His burning wrath, and show you mercy." [2]**As long as the wicked are in the world,** God's **burning wrath is in the world.** [3]**When the wicked perish from the world,** His **burning wrath is removed from the world.**

GEMARA תָּנוּ רַבָּנַן [4]**Our Rabbis taught** the following Baraita: "The verse states (Deuteronomy 13:14): 'Certain men, wicked persons, are gone out from among you, and have subverted the inhabitants of their city, saying.' The words **'are gone out'** teach that the city is only declared an idolatrous city if the subverters **themselves** went out and led their townsmen astray, [5]**but not** if they subverted them with **their agents.** [6]**'Men'** — the plural term **'men'** denotes **not fewer than two** people, teaching that if the city was led astray by a single man, it is not declared an idolatrous city. [7]According to **another explanation,** the word **'men'** teaches that the city is only treated as an idolatrous city if the subverters were men, but **not** if they were **women or children.** [8]The expression, **'wicked persons** [בְּנֵי בְלִיַּעַל],' intimates that the subverters are **sons** [בָּנִים] **who cast the yoke** [עוֹל] **of Heaven from their necks.** [9]The words **'from among you'** teach that only a city in the middle of the country can be declared a subverted city, [10]**but not** a city situated **on the border** of Eretz Israel. If a city was subverted by **'inhabitants of their city,'** it may be declared an idolatrous city, **but not** if it was subverted by **inhabitants of another city.** [11]The word **'saying'** intimates that two **witnesses and a warning** ("saying" that idolatry is forbidden) **are required for each and every** offender."

[1]״וְלֹא יִדְבַּק בְּיָדְךָ מְאוּמָה מִן הַחֵרֶם״. [2]שֶׁכָּל זְמַן שֶׁהָרְשָׁעִים בָּעוֹלָם חֲרוֹן אַף בָּעוֹלָם. [3]אָבְדוּ רְשָׁעִים מִן הָעוֹלָם — נִסְתַּלֵּק חֲרוֹן אַף מִן הָעוֹלָם.

גמרא [4]תָּנוּ רַבָּנַן: ״׳יָצְאוּ׳ — הֵן, [5]וְלֹא שְׁלוּחִין. [6]׳אֲנָשִׁים׳ — אֵין אֲנָשִׁים פָּחוֹת מִשְּׁנַיִם. [7]דָּבָר אַחֵר: ׳אֲנָשִׁים׳, וְלֹא נָשִׁים; ׳אֲנָשִׁים׳ — וְלֹא קְטַנִּים. [8]׳בְּנֵי בְלִיַּעַל׳ — בָּנִים שֶׁפָּרְקוּ עוֹל שָׁמַיִם מִצַּוְּארֵיהֶם. [9]׳מִקִּרְבֶּךָ׳ — וְלֹא מִן הַסְּפָר. [10]׳יוֹשְׁבֵי עִירָם׳ — וְלֹא יוֹשְׁבֵי עִיר אַחֶרֶת. [11]׳לֵאמֹר׳ — שֶׁצְּרִיכִין עֵדִים וְהַתְרָאָה לְכָל אֶחָד וְאֶחָד״.

LITERAL TRANSLATION

[1]"And nothing of what was devoted to destruction shall remain in your hand." [2]All the time that the wicked are in the world, burning wrath is in the world. [3][When] the wicked perish from the world, burning wrath is removed from the world.

GEMARA [4]Our Rabbis taught: "'Are gone out' — they, [5]and not their agents. [6]'Men' — 'men' is not less than two. [7]Another explanation: 'Men,' and not women; 'men,' and not children. [8]'Wicked persons' — sons who cast the yoke of Heaven from their necks. [9]'From among you' — and not from the border. [10]'The inhabitants of their city' — and not the inhabitants of a another city. [11]'Saying' — they require witnesses and a warning for each and every person."

RASHI

גמרא **יצאו הם ולא שלוחם** — אם המדיחין עצמן יצאו והדיחן והרי הם מרובים ודינן בסייף, אבל אם הדיחו על ידי שליח — כיחידים, הם בסקילה וממונם פלט. **אין אנשים פחות משתים** — דעל ידי מדיח אחד אין נעשית עיר הנדחת. **בקרבך** — משמע באמצע ולא מן הספר, שאם היתה עיר של ספר בין מחוז נכרים למחוז ישראל אינה נעשית עיר הנדחת דגזירת הכתוב היא שלא תעשה עיר הנדחת. **יושבי העיר ולא יושבי עיר אחרת** — דהיינו מדיחיה מחוצה לה. **לאמר נלכה ונעבדה** — משמע שצריכים להיות לפנינו, שכך אומרים "נלכה ונעבדה", ואין אמירה אלא בעדים, אלמא צריך עדים לכל אחד ואחד שיעידו עליהם מה שאמרו, והכא נמי צריך התראה לכל אחד ואחד מהם.

NOTES

הֵן, וְלֹא שְׁלוּחִין **They, and not their agents.** The Rishonim ask: Why not treat the agents as subverters, and the city as an idolatrous city for the rule is that there is no agency for transgression, and so the agents should be regarded as acting on their own. Some answer that they were possibly from a different city, so that the city cannot be declared an idolatrous city on the basis of their incitement (*Ramah, Rosh, Meiri,* and others). Others propose that the agents say that they are inciting to idolatry in the name of others, and so they are regarded as if they were minors (*Rosh*). Alternatively, there may only be one agent acting on behalf of two inciters (*Kedushat Yom Tov, Rashash*).

HALAKHAH

וְלֹא יִדְבַּק בְּיָדְךָ מְאוּמָה **And nothing shall remain in your hand.** "Anyone who derives any benefit whatsoever from the property found in an idolatrous city is subject to lashes, for the verse states: And nothing of that which was devoted to destruction shall remain in your hand." (*Rambam, Sefer Mada, Hilkhot Avodah Zarah* 4:7.)

לֹא מִן הַסְּפָר **Not from the border.** "A city situated on the border of Eretz Israel cannot be declared an idolatrous city, and so its idolaters are judged as individuals." (*Rambam, Sefer Mada, Hilkhot Avodah Zarah* 5:4.)

LITERAL TRANSLATION

[1] It was stated: Rabbi Yoḥanan said: We divide one city between two tribes. [2] And Resh Lakish said: We do not divide one city between two tribes.

[3] Rabbi Yoḥanan raised an objection against Resh Lakish: [4] "Unless the subverters are from the same city, and from the same tribe." [5] Is it not that even if its subverters are from the same city — [6] if they are from the same tribe, yes, [7] [and] if not, no? [8] Infer from this: We divide one city between two tribes!

[9] No, when it fell to him as an inheritance. [10] Or else, when it was given to him as a gift.

[11] He objected: "'Nine cities out of those two tribes." [12] Is it not four-and-a-half from this one, and four-and-a-half from that one. [13] And infer from this: We divide one city between two tribes.

[14] No, four from this one, and five from this one.

[1] אִיתְּמַר: רַבִּי יוֹחָנָן אָמַר: חוֹלְקִין עִיר אַחַת לִשְׁנֵי שְׁבָטִים. [2] וְרֵישׁ לָקִישׁ אָמַר: אֵין חוֹלְקִין עִיר אַחַת לִשְׁנֵי שְׁבָטִים.

[3] אֵיתִיבֵיהּ רַבִּי יוֹחָנָן לְרֵישׁ לָקִישׁ: [4] "עַד שֶׁיִּהוּ מַדִּיחֶיהָ מֵאוֹתָהּ הָעִיר, וּמֵאוֹתוֹ שֵׁבֶט". [5] מַאי לָאו אַף עַל גַּב דְּמַדִּיחֶיהָ מֵאוֹתָהּ הָעִיר — [6] אִי אִיכָּא מֵאוֹתוֹ שֵׁבֶט, אִין; [7] אִי לָא, לָא? [8] שְׁמַע מִינָּהּ: חוֹלְקִין עִיר אַחַת לִשְׁנֵי שְׁבָטִים!

[9] לָא, דְּנָפְלָה לֵיהּ בִּירוּשָּׁה. [10] אִי נַמִי, דִּיהֲבוּהָ נִיהֲלֵיהּ בְּמַתָּנָה.

[11] אֵיתִיבֵיהּ: "עָרִים תֵּשַׁע מֵאֵת שְׁנֵי הַשְּׁבָטִים הָאֵלֶּה". [12] מַאי לָאו אַרְבַּע וּפַלְגָּא מֵהַאי, וְאַרְבַּע וּפַלְגָּא מֵהַאי. [13] וּשְׁמַע מִינָּהּ: חוֹלְקִין עִיר אַחַת לִשְׁנֵי שְׁבָטִים!

[14] לָא, אַרְבָּעָה מֵהַאי וְחָמֵשׁ מֵהַאי.

TRANSLATION AND COMMENTARY

אִיתְּמַר [1] **It was stated** that the Amoraim disagree about the following matter: **Rabbi Yoḥanan said:** When Eretz Israel is divided among the twelve tribes, **one city may be divided between two tribes.** [2] **Resh Lakish** disagreed and **said: One city may not be divided between two tribes.**

אֵיתִיבֵיהּ [3] **Rabbi Yoḥanan raised an objection against Resh Lakish:** We learned in the Mishnah: [4] "The inhabitants of an idolatrous city are not slain by the sword **unless the subverters** who led them astray **came from that city, and from the same tribe** as the people of the city." [5] **Does this not** mean **that even if the subverters came from that city,** there is an additional requirement? [6] **If** the subverters came **from the same tribe** as the people of the city, it may **indeed** be declared an idolatrous city, [7] **but if not,** it may **not** be so declared, and the offenders are liable to be punished by stoning and not decapitation. [8] **Infer from this** that **one city may** in fact **be divided between two tribes.**

לָא [9] The Gemara rejects this argument: **No,** one city may not be divided between two tribes, but someone from a different tribe can own property in the city, as **when** he **acquired** it **by inheritance** from his mother. Thus, he lives in the city belonging to his mother's tribe, while he himself is a member of his father's tribe. [10] **Or else,** the property **was given to him as a gift** by a member of a different tribe.

אֵיתִיבֵיהּ [11] Rabbi Yoḥanan **raised** another **objection** against Resh Lakish: The verse recording the allocation of cities to the tribe of Levi states (Joshua 21:16): **"Nine cities out of those two tribes,"** that is to say, the Levites received nine cities from the tribes of Judah and Simeon. [12] **Does this not** mean that they received **four-and-a-half** cities **from this** tribe, Judah, **and four-and-a-half** tribes **from that** tribe, Simeon? [13] We may therefore **infer from this** that **one city may** in fact **be divided between two tribes.**

לָא [14] The Gemara answers: **No,** the verse means that the Levites received **four** cities **from the one** tribe, **and five** cities **from the** other.

RASHI

חולקין עיר אחת — בתחלה כשחלקו ישראל את הארץ היו רשאין ליתן ולחלוק עיר אחת לשני שבטים, כגון אם אירע להם עיר בתחום ומקצת מושכת לתחום אחר, שבט אחד נוטל חלק באותו קצת הארץ, על פי הגורל נחלקה הארץ, אם נפתלי עולה תחום גינוסר עולה עמו, דהכי אמרינן בבבא בתרא בפרק "יש נוחלין ומנחילין" (קכב,א). אין חולקין — אלא כולה של אותו השבט שרובה בתחומיה. מאי לאו אף על גב דמדיחיה מאותה עיר — אם יהיו מאותו שבט נעשית עיר הנדחת, ואי לא — לא, שאם אינו מאותו שבט שהודחו אלא משבט אחר שבעיר אינו בסייף אלא בסקילה, אלמא אפשר שיהו מן אותה העיר ולא מאותו שבט, והיכי דמי? כגון שחלקו עיר אחת לשני שבטים. לא — לעולם אימא לך דאין חולקין; והיכי משכחת לה מאותה עיר ולא מאותו שבט — כגון דנפלה למדיחיה בירושה מקצת העיר על ידי בת יורשת נחלה. ערים תשע מאת שני השבטים האלה — ממטה יהודה וממטה שמעון נטלו תשע ערים ונתנום ללוים. מאי לאו דשקל מהאי ארבע ופלגא — שהיתה עיר אחת של יהודה ושמעון ונטלו מהם — אלמא חולקין עיר אחת לשני שבטים, הכי גרסינן: לא ארבע מהאי וחמש מהאי.

NOTES

חוֹלְקִין עִיר אַחַת לִשְׁנֵי שְׁבָטִים We divide one city between two tribes. According to *Ramah*, the Amoraim disagree about whether or not it will be possible to divide up one city between two tribes in the Messianic period. The Gemara does not bring support for Rabbi Yoḥanan from Jerusalem, which was divided between the tribes of Judah and Benjamin, for Jerusalem was an exceptional case, divided between the two tribes by divine instruction (*Tosafot Yeshanim, Yoma*).

TRANSLATION AND COMMENTARY

אִי הָכִי [1]The Gemara asks: **If so, let** the verse **state explicitly** which tribe gave the extra city!

[112A] **קַשְׁיָא** [2]The Gemara concludes: Indeed, the wording of the verse **is difficult** according to Resh Lakish, who said that one city may not be divided between two tribes.

אִיבַּעְיָא לְהוּ [3]**The following question arose** among the scholars: **If** the residents of a city **incited themselves** to idolatry, **what is the law?** [4]Do we say that, since **the Torah states** (Deuteronomy 13:14): "Certain men, wicked persons, are gone out from among you, **and have subverted** the residents of their city," the law of an idolatrous city applies only if the residents of the city were led astray by inciters, **and not if they subverted themselves?** [5]**Or perhaps** we say that the law applies **even if they subverted themselves.**

תָּא שְׁמַע [6]The Gemara answers: **Come and hear** what we have learned in our Mishnah: **"If women or children subverted** the residents of the city, they are treated like individuals who committed idolatry, and are therefore liable to be executed by stoning, and not decapitation." If the law of an idolatrous city applies even if the residents of the city subverted themselves, [7]then **why** does the law not apply if they were subverted by women or children? [8]**Let** them **be** considered **as if they subverted themselves!**

הָנָךְ [9]The Gemara rejects this argument. The two cases are not comparable. People who subverted themselves **follow their own** inclinations and therefore can be expected to cling to their idolatrous beliefs and practices. But in the case of the Mishnah, **they follow** the subversive arguments of **women or children,** and therefore they might abandon idolatry as quickly and easily as they accepted it. Thus, the law of an idolatrous city might not apply when the people were subverted by women or children, but it does apply if they subverted themselves.

עַד שֶׁיּוּדַּח רוּבָּהּ [10]We have learned in the Mishnah: "The law of an idolatrous city does not apply **unless the majority** of the residents of the city **were incited** to commit idolatry." [11]**How should** the court **act** if it

[1]אִי הָכִי לִפְרוֹשׁ פָּרוֹשֵׁי!

[112A] [2]קַשְׁיָא.

[3]אִיבַּעְיָא לְהוּ: הוּדְּחוּ מֵאֲלֵיהֶן מַהוּ? [4]"וַיַּדִּיחוּ" אָמַר רַחֲמָנָא, וְלֹא שֶׁהוּדְּחוּ מֵאֲלֵיהֶן. [5]אוֹ דִילְמָא, אֲפִילּוּ הוּדְּחוּ מֵאֲלֵיהֶן?

[6]תָּא שְׁמַע: "הִדִּיחוּהָ נָשִׁים וּקְטַנִּים". [7]אַמַּאי? [8]לֶיהֱוֵי כְּהוּדְּחוּ מֵאֲלֵיהֶן!

[9]הָנָךְ בָּתַר נַפְשַׁיְיהוּ גְּרִידֵי; הָנֵי בָּתַר נָשִׁים וּקְטַנִּים גְּרִידֵי.

[10]"עַד שֶׁיּוּדַּח רוּבָּהּ". [11]הֵיכִי

LITERAL TRANSLATION

[1]If so, let it state explicitly!

[112A] [2]It is difficult.

[3]It was asked of them: [If] they subverted themselves, what [is the law]? [4]The Torah (lit., "the Merciful") said "and they have subverted," and not that they subverted themselves. [5]Or perhaps, even if they subverted themselves.

[6]Come [and] hear: "[If] women or children subverted it." [7]Why? [8]Let them be as if they were subverted by themselves!

[9]They follow themselves; they follow women and children.

[10]"Unless the majority are subverted." [11]How

RASHI

אי הכי לפרוש פרושי — הי ניניהו שבט דשקיל מיניה חמש, והי ניניהו דשקיל מיניה ארבע, ואמאי כתיב "ערים תשע מאת שני השבטים"? משמע דבשוה שקל. **קשיא** — לשון הפסוק קשה לתרץ למאן דאמר חולקין אבל לא תיובתא. **גרידי** — בדל"ת = נמשכין, וכן גרים רבי בכוליה התלמוד: מגריד גריד, ונראה לי שהוא לשון גרידא, דמפרשינן יחיד על שם שהוא יחיד משוך ומופרש הוא מן הכל ואין לאחרים סביביו, ולשון ארמי הוא, ואין דומה לו בפסוק (ודומה לו) אבל גורדו ומעמידו על גלדו (ראש השנה כז,ב) הוא לשון עברי ודומה לו בפסוק (איוב ב) "ויקח לו חרש להתגרד בו" בדל"ת, ופירוש: לשון חטיטה, שמחטט וגורד בסכין או בכל דבר, וגורר ברי"ש לשון עברי הוא כמו (שבת כב,א): גורר אדם מטה כסא ושלחן, וכן (בבא בתרא פו,א): היה מגרר ויוצא מגרר ויוצא. **בתר נפשייהו גרידי** — ומעשיהם מעשה, ואדוקים ביותר, הואיל ומעצמם הם נדחין ודין הוא שיעשה עיר הנדחת. **אבל הנך דהודחו בתר נשים וקטנים גרידי** — שאין אדוקים כל כך. **היכי עבדינן** — היאך נעשין

NOTES

קַשְׁיָא It is difficult. The Gemara does not use the expression, תְּיוּבְתָּא, which indicates a conclusive refutation, for it might be argued that here we are dealing with the tribes of Judah and Simeon. The territory of Simeon was surrounded by that of Judah, so the two territories may be considered as one. Thus, the verse speaks of "nine cities out of those two tribes," without specifying how many cities belong to each tribe (*Rabbi David Bonfil, Ran*).

HALAKHAH

הוּדְּחוּ מֵאֲלֵיהֶן If they subverted themselves. "If the residents of a city subverted themselves to idolatry, without any inciters, they are judged as individuals who practiced idolatry." (Even though the Gemara left this matter undecided, in capital cases we follow the lenient position; see *Leḥem Mishneh*. Or else this ruling follows from the law regarding inciters who are women or minors; see *Mishneh LeMelekh*.) (*Rambam, Sefer Mada, Hilkhot Avodah Zarah* 4:2.)

הֵיכִי עָבְדִינַן? How do we act? "When the Great Sanhedrin hears that a city has been incited to idolatry, it sends two Torah scholars to warn the city's inhabitants against continuing the practice. If the citizens do not forsake their

עָבְדִינַן? [1]אָמַר רַב יְהוּדָה: דָּנִין וְחוֹבְשִׁין, דָּנִין וְחוֹבְשִׁין.
[2]אָמַר לֵיהּ עוּלָּא: נִמְצָא אַתָּה מְעַנֶּה אֶת דִּינָן שֶׁל אֵלּוּ!
[3]אֶלָּא, אָמַר עוּלָּא: דָּנִין וְסוֹקְלִין, [4]דָּנִין וְסוֹקְלִין.
[5]אִיתְּמַר: רַבִּי יוֹחָנָן אָמַר: [6]דָּנִין וְסוֹקְלִין, דָּנִין וְסוֹקְלִין. [7]וְרֵישׁ לָקִישׁ אָמַר: מַרְבִּין לָהֶן בָּתֵּי דִינִין.
[8]אִינִי? [9]וְהָאָמַר רַבִּי חָמָא בַּר יוֹסֵי אָמַר רַבִּי אוֹשַׁעְיָא: ״וְהוֹצֵאתָ אֶת הָאִישׁ הַהוּא אוֹ אֶת הָאִשָּׁה הַהִיא״. [10]אִישׁ וְאִשָּׁה אַתָּה מוֹצִיא לִשְׁעָרֶיךָ וְאִי אַתָּה מוֹצִיא כָּל הָעִיר כּוּלָּהּ לִשְׁעָרֶיךָ!

LITERAL TRANSLATION

do we act? [1]Rav Yehudah said: We judge and incarcerate, we judge and incarcerate.
[2]Ulla said to him: Thus you delay the punishment of those!
[3]Rather, Ulla said: We judge and stone, [4]we judge and stone.
[5]It was stated: Rabbi Yoḥanan said: [6]We judge and stone, we judge and stone. [7]And Resh Lakish said: We set up many courts for them.
[8]Is it so? [9]But surely Rabbi Ḥama bar Yose said in the name of Rabbi Oshaya: "Then shall you bring out that man or that woman." [10]A man or a woman you bring out to your gates, but you do not bring out the entire city to your gates!

TRANSLATION AND COMMENTARY

suspects that a majority of the city's inhabitants have committed idolatry, but this has not yet been established as fact? [1]**Rav Yehudah said:** The court **judges** one of the suspected idolaters, **and incarcerates** him if he is found guilty, and then it **judges** the next suspected idolater, **and incarcerates** him if he is found guilty, until a majority of the citizens are found guilty of idolatry. Then all the convicted idolaters are executed by decapitation. If only a minority of the citizens are found guilty, the guilty individuals are executed by stoning.

אֲמַר לֵיהּ [2]**Ulla said to** Rav Yehudah: If so, **the execution of the** convicted idolaters **will be postponed** until it is established whether or not a majority of the citizens have been led astray to idolatry. This outcome violates the law that capital punishment may not be postponed even to the next day!

אֶלָּא [3]**Rather, Ulla said:** The court **judges** the first suspected idolater **and executes** him **by stoning** if he is found guilty, [4]**and** then it **judges** the next suspected idolater, **and executes** him **by stoning** if he, too, is found guilty, until a majority of the inhabitants are found guilty of idolatry. From then on the convicted idolaters are executed by decapitation.

אִיתְּמַר [5]**It was stated** that the Amoraim disagreed about the matter: **Rabbi Yoḥanan said:** [6]The court **judges** the first suspected idolater **and executes** him **by stoning** if he is found guilty, **and** then **it judges** the next suspected idolater, **and executes** him **by stoning** if he, too, is found guilty, until a majority of the citizens are found guilty of idolatry. [7]**Resh Lakish** disagreed and **said: Many** different **courts are set up** so that all the suspected idolaters can be judged on the same day. If a majority of the city's residents are convicted of idolatry, they are all executed by decapitation. And if only a minority are found guilty, they are all executed by stoning.

אִינִי [8]The Gemara asks: **Is this really so?** [9]**But surely Rabbi Ḥama bar Yose said in the name of Rabbi Oshaya:** The verse relating to an individual idolater states (Deuteronomy 17:5): **"Then shall you bring that man or that woman…**out **to your gates."** [10]**An** individual **man or woman you bring out to your gates,** that is to say, the gates of a minor Sanhedrin, a local court of twenty-three judges. **But you do not bring an entire city out to your gates.** They must be brought to the Great Sanhedrin, the high court of seventy-one judges sitting in Jerusalem!

RASHI

רובא נדחים הואיל דצריכין עדים והתראה לכל אחד ואחד. **דנין וחובשין** — כשרואין שתים או שלשה מהם עובדים עבודה זרה לא יסקלו אותן ומניחין כל האחרים מלסקול, אלא דנין אותם לסקילה וחובשין אותם בבית הסוהר, וכן עושין עד שרואין אם מצטרפין לרובא, וחוזרין ודנין אותם דין אחר להריגה ומאבדין את ממונם. **ומענה את דינם** — שלאחר שנגמר דינם אתה משהה אותם ומענה את דינם. **דנין וסוקלין** — עד אליין, דמחזקינן להו כיחידים ודנין וסוקלין, ומאליין ואילך נתברר הדבר למפרע שהודחו רובא — והוו בסייף וממונם אבד, ומאליין ואילך אי אתה רשאי למשכן למיתה חמורה. **וריש לקיש אמר מרבין להם בתי דינין** — לאו משום דאין דנין שנים ביום אחד, דהא אמרת בפרק ״נגמר הדין״ (סנהדרין מו,א) דבמיתה אחת דנין, אלא משום דנפישי עדים לכל אחד ואחד, ואין פנאי לחקור כל אחד ואחד ביום אחד — מרבים להם בתי דינים כדי שתתקבל עדותן ביום אחד, ויגמור דין כולם ביום אחד. **לשעריך** — לבית דין שבשעריך, דהיינו סנהדרי קטנה. **ואי אתה מוציא** — אלא בסנהדרי גדולה.

HALAKHAH

idolatrous ways, the city is placed under siege and captured. A large number of courts are then established. Anyone against whom stands the testimony of two witnesses that he worshiped an idol after having received a proper warning, is set aside. If the majority of the inhabitants of the city succumbed to idolatry, the offenders are brought before the Great Sanhedrin, where their verdict is issued, and they are executed by decapitation." (*Rambam, Sefer Mada, Hilkhot Avodah Zarah* 4:6.)

TRANSLATION AND COMMENTARY

אֶלָּא [1]The Gemara answers: **Rather,** the procedure of judging the inhabitants of an idolatrous city is as follows: **Many** different **courts** of twenty-three judges **are set up** so that all the suspected idolaters can be brought before a court on the same day. The various courts **study their cases,** and if they conclude that a majority of the city's inhabitants have committed idolatry, they do not issue a judgment. [2]Rather, they **send them up to the Great Sanhedrin** in Jerusalem, **and** that High Court **concludes their judgment,** issues death sentences, **and executes them** by decapitation.

הַכֵּה תַכֶּה [3]The verse states (Deuteronomy 13:19): **"You shall surely strike the residents of that city** with the edge of the sword." [4]**Our Rabbis taught** a Baraita: "If the majority of the residents of a city were incited to idolatry, and **a company of ass-drivers or a company of camel-drivers who were passing from place to place slept inside** the city **and were subverted** along **with it,** the following distinction applies: [5]**If** the ass-drivers or camel-drivers **remained** in the city **for** at least **thirty days,** they are regarded as residents of the subverted city. [6]**They are executed by the sword, and their money** and property **are destroyed.** [7]But if they remained in the city for **less** time **than that,** they are treated as individual idolaters. [8]**They are executed by stoning, and their money** and property **are spared** and passed to their heirs."

וּרְמִינְהִי [9]The Gemara **points out a contradiction** between this Baraita and a Mishnah (*Bava Batra* 8a) which states: [10]**"How long must** a person **live in a city before he is considered** a resident **of the city** and therefore required to pay city taxes? [11]**Twelve months."** Why, regarding an idolatrous city, is a person regarded as a resident of the city after thirty days, but when it comes to paying municipal taxes, he is only considered a resident after twelve months?

אָמַר רָבָא [12]**Rava said: There is** really **no difficulty.** Only citizens are required to share in the city's expenses, [13]and in order **to be considered a citizen,** a person must live there for twelve months. [14]But the law of an idolatrous city applies to all residents of the city, and in order **to be considered a resident of the city,** thirty days suffice.

[1]אֶלָּא: מַרְבִּין לָהֶן בָּתֵּי דִינִין, וּמְעַיְּינִין בְּדִינֵיהֶן, [2]וּמַסְּקִינַן לְהוּ לְבֵית דִּין הַגָּדוֹל, וְגָמְרִי לְהוּ לְדִינַיְיהוּ, וְקָטְלִי לְהוּ.

[3]״הַכֵּה תַכֶּה אֶת יֹשְׁבֵי הָעִיר וכו׳״. [4]תָּנוּ רַבָּנַן: ״הַחַמֶּרֶת וְהַגַּמֶּלֶת הָעוֹבֶרֶת מִמָּקוֹם לְמָקוֹם — לָנוּ בְּתוֹכָהּ וְהוּדְּחוּ עִמָּהּ, [5]אִם נִשְׁתַּהוּ שָׁם שְׁלֹשִׁים יוֹם, [6]הֵן בְּסַיִיף, וּמָמוֹנָן אָבֵד. [7]פָּחוֹת מִיכָּן, [8]הֵן בִּסְקִילָה, וּמָמוֹנָן פָּלֵט״.

[9]וּרְמִינְהִי: [10]״כַּמָּה יְהֵא בָּעִיר וִיהֵא כְּאַנְשֵׁי הָעִיר? [11]שְׁנֵים עָשָׂר חֹדֶשׁ״!

[12]אָמַר רָבָא: לָא קַשְׁיָא. [13]הָא, לְמֶיהֱוֵי מִבְּנֵי מָתָא. [14]הָא לְמֶיהֱוֵי מִיָּתְבֵי מָתָא.

LITERAL TRANSLATION

[1]Rather, we set up many courts for them, and study their cases, [2]and bring them up to the High Court, and they conclude their judgments, and execute them.

[3]"You shall surely smite the inhabitants of that city, etc." [4]Our Rabbis taught: "A company of ass-drivers or a company of camel-drivers who were passing from place to place — if they slept inside it and were subverted with it, [5][and] if they remained there for thirty days, [6]they are [executed] by the sword, and their money is destroyed. [7]Less than that, [8]they are [executed] by stoning, and their money is spared."

[9]And cast them together: [10]"How long must one be in the city so that one is like the people of the city? [11]Twelve months."

[12]Rava said: It is not difficult. [13]This, to be like the people of the city. [14]This to be a resident of the city.

RASHI

אלא מרבין להם בתי דינין ומעייני בדיניהם — אם הוו מרובים ואם הודחו רובם — מעלים את כולן לבית דין הגדול. **כמה יהא בעיר** — משנה בהשותפין. **ויהא כאנשי העיר** — ליתן בצורכי העיר. **למיהוי כבני מתא** — שיהא נקרא כבני העיר — אין נקרא בפחות משנים עשר חדש, אבל להקרות מיושבי העיר — כיון ששהה שלשים יום נקרא מאנשי העיר וקרינן בהו ״את יושבי העיר ההוא״.

HALAKHAH

הַחַמֶּרֶת וְהַגַּמֶּלֶת **A company of ass-drivers and a company of camel-drivers.** "If a company of ass-drivers or camel-drivers passed through a city and were incited to idolatry along with the inhabitants of that city, and they remained in the city for at least thirty days, they are executed by decapitation and their property is destroyed. If they were in the city for less than thirty days, they are sentenced to death by stoning, and their property is spared and passes to their heirs." (*Rambam, Sefer Mada, Hilkhot Avodah Zarah* 4:9.)

TRANSLATION AND COMMENTARY

וְהָתַנְיָא [1]**And** similarly **it was taught** in the following Baraita: [2]"If **someone was forbidden by a vow to derive** any **benefit from the people of a** particular **city,** the following distinction applies: [3]**If a person dwelled** in that city for at least **twelve months,** the person who took the vow **is forbidden to derive benefit from him.** [4]But if he dwelled in that city for **less** time **than that,** the person who took the vow **is permitted to derive benefit from him.** [5]If someone was forbidden by a vow to derive benefit **from the residents of a** particular **city,** the law is different. [6]**If** a person **dwelled** in that city for at least **thirty days,** the person who took the vow **is forbidden to derive benefit from him.** [7]But if he dwelled in that city for **less** time **than that,** the person who took the vow **is permitted to derive benefit from him.**"

הַחֲרֵם [8]The verse states (Deuteronomy 13:16): **"Destroying it, and all that is in it."** [9]**Our Rabbis taught** a Baraita: "The verse states: **'Destroying it, and all that is in it.'** [10]The words 'that is in it' **exclude the property of the righteous that is** found **outside** the city. [11]The words **'and *all* that is in it' include the property of the righteous that is** found **inside** the city. The next verse states (Deuteronomy 13:17): 'And you shall gather all of its spoil into the open place of the city.' [12]The words **'its spoil'** teach that only the spoil of the city is burned, **but not the spoil of Heaven.** [13]The words **'and *all* its spoil' include the property of the wicked that is** found **outside** the city. [14]**Rabbi Shimon said: Why did the Torah say that the property of the righteous that is** found **inside** the city **is destroyed?** [15]Rabbi Shimon explained: **What caused** the righteous **to live in** that city? **Their money** and property prevented them from moving away. [16]**Therefore their money** and property **are destroyed** together with the money and property of the wicked."

אָמַר מָר [17]**It was stated** above, in the Baraita: "The words **'And you shall gather *all* its spoil' include the**

[1]וְהָתַנְיָא: [2]"הַמּוּדָּר הֲנָאָה מִבְּנֵי הָעִיר — [3]אִם יֵשׁ אָדָם שֶׁנִּשְׁתַּהָא שָׁם שְׁנֵים עָשָׂר חֹדֶשׁ, אָסוּר לֵיהָנוֹת מִמֶּנּוּ. [4]פָּחוֹת מִיכָּן, מוּתָּר לֵיהָנוֹת מִמֶּנּוּ. [5]בְּיוֹשְׁבֵי הָעִיר — [6]אִם נִשְׁתַּהָא שְׁלֹשִׁים יוֹם, אָסוּר לֵיהָנוֹת מִמֶּנּוּ. [7]פָּחוֹת מִיכָּן, מוּתָּר לֵיהָנוֹת מִמֶּנּוּ".

[8]"הַחֲרֵם אֹתָהּ וְאֶת כׇּל אֲשֶׁר בָּהּ כו'". [9]תָּנוּ רַבָּנַן: "'הַחֲרֵם אוֹתָהּ וְאֶת כׇּל אֲשֶׁר בָּהּ' — [10]פְּרָט לְנִכְסֵי צַדִּיקִים שֶׁבְּחוּצָה לָהּ. [11]'וְאֶת כׇּל אֲשֶׁר בָּהּ' — לְרַבּוֹת נִכְסֵי צַדִּיקִים שֶׁבְּתוֹכָהּ. [12]'שְׁלָלָהּ' — וְלֹא שֶׁל שָׁמַיִם. [13]'וְאֶת כׇּל שְׁלָלָהּ' — לְרַבּוֹת נִכְסֵי רְשָׁעִים שֶׁחוּצָה לָהּ. [14]אָמַר רַבִּי שִׁמְעוֹן: מִפְּנֵי מָה אָמְרָה תּוֹרָה נִכְסֵי צַדִּיקִים שֶׁבְּתוֹכָהּ יֹאבְדוּ? [15]מִי גָּרַם לָהֶם שֶׁיָּדוּרוּ בְּתוֹכָהּ? — מָמוֹנָם. [16]לְפִיכָךְ מָמוֹנָם אָבֵד". [17]אָמַר מָר: "'וְאֶת כׇּל שְׁלָלָהּ תִּקְבֹּץ' — לְרַבּוֹת נִכְסֵי רְשָׁעִים

LITERAL TRANSLATION

[1]And it was taught: [2]"Someone who was forbidden by a vow [to derive] benefit from the people of the city — [3]if there is a person who dwelled there for twelve months, he is forbidden to derive benefit from him. [4]Less than that, he is permitted to derive benefit from him. [5]From the residents of the city — [6]if he dwelled there thirty days, he is forbidden to derive benefit from him. [7]Less than that, he is permitted to derive benefit from him."

[8]"Destroying it, and all that is in it, etc." [9]Our Rabbis taught: "'Destroying it, and all that is in it' — [10]except the property of the righteous that is outside it. [11]'And all that is in it' — including the property of the righteous that is inside it. [12]'Its spoil' — and not the spoil of Heaven. [13]'And all its spoil' — including the property of the wicked that is outside it. [14]Rabbi Shimon said: Why did the Torah say that the property of the righteous that is inside it shall be lost? [15]What caused them to live in it? — their money. [16]Therefore their money is lost."

[17]Master said: "'And you shall gather all its spoil' — including the property of the wicked

RASHI

והתניא — בניחותא. **המודר הנאה** — שאומר הרי עלי קונם אם אהנה. **החרם אותה פרט לנכסי צדיקים שבחוצה לה** — שאם היו צדיקים דרים בתוכה והוי להו נכסים מופקדים במקום אחר ביד אחרים אין מחרימין אותן, אבל נכסים שיש להם באותה העיר מחרימין אותן, וטעמא מפורש לקמן. **אמר רבי שמעון מפני מה וכו'** — בכל דוכתי דרש רבי שמעון טעמא דקרא. **הכי גרסינן** — אמר מר ואת כל (שללה) אשר בה לרבות נכסי רשעים שבחוצה לה.

HALAKHAH

בְּנֵי הָעִיר **The people of the city.** "A person is only considered a citizen for the purpose of paying municipal taxes after he has lived in that city for twelve months." (*Shulḥan Arukh, Ḥoshen Mishpat* 163:2.)

בְּנֵי הָעִיר וְיוֹשְׁבֵי הָעִיר **The people of the city and the residents of the city.** "If someone was forbidden by a vow to derive any benefit from the residents of a particular city, he is forbidden to derive benefit from anyone who dwelled in the city for as little as thirty days. If he was forbidden by a vow to derive any benefit from the people of the city, he is only forbidden to derive benefit from people who dwelled in that city for at least twelve months." (*Shulḥan Arukh, Yoreh De'ah* 217:32.)

TRANSLATION AND COMMENTARY

property of the wicked that is found **outside** the city." [1]**Rav Ḥisda said:** The verse refers to the property of the wicked **that can be gathered into** the city on that same day. That property must be gathered into the open place of the city and burned. But property which cannot reach the city on that same day is not destroyed.

אָמַר רַב חִסְדָּא [2]**Rav Ḥisda said: The deposits of the residents of an idolatrous city are permitted** for benefit (as will be explained below).

הֵיכִי דָּמֵי [3]The Gemara asks: **How do you visualize the case?** [4]**If you say** that Rav Ḥisda refers to deposits belonging to people **of another city, and** those deposits **are** now **in** the idolatrous city, [5]**it is obvious that they are permitted** for benefit, [6]for **they are not** included in **"its spoil"**! [7]**Rather,** Rav Ḥisda must be referring to **their** own deposits, i.e., deposits belonging to the inhabitants of the idolatrous city, **and** those deposits **are** now **in another city**. But if so, there is a difficulty: [8]**If** those deposits **can be gathered into** the city on that same day, **why are they permitted** for benefit? [9]**And if they cannot be gathered into** the city on that same day, **surely** Rav Ḥisda himself already **said once** that only property which can be gathered into the subverted city on that same day is destroyed!

לָא [10]The Gemara answers: **No,** Rav Ḥisda is **in fact** referring to deposits belonging to people **of another city that were deposited in** the idolatrous city. [11]**What we are dealing with here is** similar to when a resident of the idolatrous city **accepted responsibility for** the property. [12]**You might have said** that **since** that, person

שֶׁבְּחוּצָה לָהּ״. [1]אָמַר רַב חִסְדָּא: וּבַנִּקְבָּצִים לְתוֹכָהּ.
[2]אָמַר רַב חִסְדָּא: פִּקְדוֹנוֹת שֶׁל אַנְשֵׁי עִיר הַנִּדַּחַת מוּתָּרִין.
[3]הֵיכִי דָּמֵי? [4]אִי לֵימָא דְּעִיר אַחֶרֶת, וְאִיתְנְהוּ בְּגַוַּהּ, [5]פְּשִׁיטָא דְּמוּתָּרִין. [6]לָאו ״שְׁלָלָהּ״ הוּא! [7]וְאֶלָּא דִּידְהוּ, וְאִיתְנְהוּ בְּעִיר אַחֶרֶת. [8]אִי דְּנִקְבָּצִין לְתוֹכָהּ, אַמַּאי מוּתָּרִין? [9]וְאִי אֵין נִקְבָּצִין לְתוֹכָהּ, הָא אֲמַרָהּ חֲדָא זִימְנָא!
[10]לָא, לְעוֹלָם דְּעִיר אַחֶרֶת דְּמִפַּקְדִי בְּתוֹכָהּ. [11]וְהָכָא בְּמַאי עָסְקִינַן כְּגוֹן דְּקַבִּיל עֲלֵיהּ אַחֲרָיוּת. [12]מַהוּ דְּתֵימָא: כֵּיוָן

LITERAL TRANSLATION

that is outside it." [1]Rav Ḥisda said: That which can be gathered into it.

[2]Rav Ḥisda said: The deposits of the inhabitants of a subverted city are permitted.

[3]How do you visualize the case? [4]If you say of another city, and they are in it, [5]it is obvious that they are permitted. [6]It is not "its spoil"! [7]Rather, theirs, and they are in another city. [8]If they can be gathered into it, why are they permitted? [9]And if they cannot be gathered into it, surely he said one time!

[10]No, in fact [the deposits of people] of another city that were deposited in it. [11]What we are dealing with here is when he accepted responsibility for it. [12]You might have said: Since

RASHI

אמר רב חסדא ובנקבצין לתוכה — נכסי רשעים הקרובין לעיר שיכולים לקבצם לתוך העיר באותו יום עצמו שכונסין שלל העיר לרחוב לשורפן הן אבודים עמה, אבל רחוקים דאין מגיעין לעיר — אינן אבודים, ודוקא שכבר היו לתוכה אלא שמעכשיו היו מופקדים ביד אחרים, אבל לא היו מעולם בתוכה כגון דנפלה להם בירושה לא קרינא ביה "שללה" ואין הממון אבד. **אלא דידהו** — דבני עיר הנדחת ומופקדים הם בעיר אחרת. **הא אמרה** — רב חסדא ובנקבצין לתוכה, והא אין נקבצין. **דקבל עליו אחריות** — בני

NOTES

בַּנִּקְבָּצִים לְתוֹכָהּ That which can be gathered into it. This expression has been understood in various ways. Our commentary follows *Rashi,* who explains that the Gemara refers here to property belonging to the wicked which is found nearby and can be gathered into the city on the same day that the property found inside the city is collected and burned. According to *Meiri,* the Gemara refers here to animals that graze outside the city and are gathered into the city every evening. Some suggest that the Gemara refers here to property that is sometimes brought into the city, excluding property that was never brought into the city (*Ramah*). *Rambam* seems to understand that the Gemara is referring here to the property of the wicked that was found inside the city at the time that that city's spoil was sent up in flames.

כְּגוֹן דְּקַבִּיל עֲלֵיהּ אַחֲרָיוּת As when he accepted responsibility for it. The Gemara concludes that property belonging to people of another city that was deposited in the idolatrous city is not destroyed, even if a resident of the subverted city had accepted responsibility for the property. The difficulty has been raised based on the laws of Pesaḥ. Regarding the prohibition against having leavened bread in one's

HALAKHAH

בַּנִּקְבָּצִים לְתוֹכָהּ That which can be gathered into it. "If the wicked members of an idolatrous city had property deposited with people living outside the idolatrous city, that which is gathered into the city is burned together with the rest of the property of the idolatrous city, but any property that was not gathered into the city is spared and passes to their heirs," following Rav Ḥisda. (*Rambam, Sefer Mada, Hilkhot Avodah Zarah* 4:10.)

פִּקְדוֹנוֹת שֶׁל אַנְשֵׁי עִיר הַנִּדַּחַת The deposits of the inhabitants of an idolatrous city. "Property belonging to people of another city that was deposited in an idolatrous city is not burned along with the rest of the property of the idolatrous city, even if a resident of the city had accepted responsibility for the property." (*Rambam, Sefer Mada, Hilkhot Avodah Zarah* 4:10.)

דְּקַבִּיל עֲלֵיהּ אַחֲרָיוּת, כְּדִידֵיהּ דָּמֵי. [1]קָא מַשְׁמַע לָן.

[2]אָמַר רַב חִסְדָּא: בְּהֵמָה, חֶצְיָהּ שֶׁל עִיר הַנִּדַּחַת, וְחֶצְיָהּ שֶׁל עִיר אַחֶרֶת, אֲסוּרָה. [3]עִיסָּה, חֶצְיָהּ שֶׁל עִיר הַנִּדַּחַת וְחֶצְיָהּ שֶׁל עִיר אַחֶרֶת, מוּתֶּרֶת. [4]מַאי טַעְמָא? [5]בְּהֵמָה כְּמַאן דְּלָא פְּלִיגָא דָּמְיָא. [6]עִיסָּה כְּמַאן דִּפְלִיגָא דָּמְיָא.

[7]בָּעֵי רַב חִסְדָּא: בֶּהֱמַת עִיר הַנִּדַּחַת — [8]מַהוּ דְּתִיתְהַנֵּי בָּהּ שְׁחִיטָה לְטַהֲרָהּ מִידֵי נְבֵילָה? [9]״לְפִי חָרֶב״ אָמַר רַחֲמָנָא, [10]לָא שְׁנָא שְׁחָטָהּ מִשְׁחַט לָא שְׁנָא

LITERAL TRANSLATION

he accepted responsibility for it, it is like his. [1][Therefore,] he teaches us.

[2]Rav Ḥisda said: An animal, half of which is of a subverted city, and half of which is of another city, is forbidden. [3]Dough, half of which is of a subverted city, and half of which is of another city, is permitted. [4]What is the reason? [5]An animal is regarded as if it were not divided. [6]Dough is regarded as if it were divided.

[7]Rav Ḥisda asked: The animal of a subverted city — [8]is ritual slaughter effective on it to purify it from [the impurity] of a carcass? [9]The Torah said: "With the edge of the sword," [10]making no distinction between whether he slaughtered it and whether

TRANSLATION AND COMMENTARY

accepted responsibility for the property, **it is** considered **as if** it were **his,** and so it must be destroyed. [1]**Therefore,** Rav Ḥisda **teaches us** that it is not so, but rather such deposits are permitted for benefit.

אָמַר רַב חִסְדָּא [2]**Rav Ḥisda said: An animal, half of which** belongs to a resident **of an idolatrous city, and** the other **half of which** belongs to someone from another **city, is** entirely **forbidden.** [3]But **dough, half of which** belongs to a resident **of an idolatrous city, and** the other **half of which** belongs to someone from another **city** — the part belonging to the inhabitant of the other city **is permitted.** [4]**What is the reason** for the distinction? [5]**An animal is regarded as if it were not divided.** As long as the animal is alive, none of it can be eaten. So when half of the animal becomes forbidden, the entire animal becomes forbidden. [6]But **dough is regarded as if it were** already **divided,** since it can always be divided. When half of the dough becomes forbidden, the other half remains permitted.

בָּעֵי רַב חִסְדָּא [7]**Rav Ḥisda asked: Regarding an animal** belonging to a resident **of an idolatrous city,** [8]**does ritual slaughter help** to prevent **it from** contracting **the ritual impurity of a carcass?** A dead animal, unless ritually slaughtered, is a primary source of ritual impurity. Rav Ḥisda is asking whether this source of impurity can be avoided by slaughtering the animals of an idolatrous city in the ritual manner. The Gemara explains the two sides of the question: [9]Do we say that, since **the Torah said** (Deuteronomy 13:16): "You shall surely strike the inhabitants of that city **with the edge of the sword,"** [10]**making no distinction between whether he slaughtered**

RASHI

עיר הנדחת. כמאן דלא פליגא — אי אפשר לכזית בשר בלא שחיטה, ואפילו שחטה משחט אין בשחיטתו כלום דלא לשחיטה קיימא אלא למיתה, ושחיטתה זו היא מיתת הבהמה, ואין היתר אפילו החצי — שאין של עיר הנדחת, דכי שחט לסימן דעיר הנדחת אינו שוחט אלא ממית, ולא מהניא ביה שחיטה. עיסה — כל אימת דבעי פליג לה, ואין חלק של עיר הנדחת מעורב בו. לא שנא שחטה משחט לא שנא קטלא מקטיל — דבין בשחיטה ובין בהריגה קרינא ביה "לפי חרב" דאפילו שחטה מיתה בעלמא היא ולא מהני מידי, או דילמא לפי חרב — היינו שלא כדרך שחיטה, אבל דרך שחיטה מהניא לה לטהרה מידי נבילה, דנהי דלאכילה

NOTES

possession on Pesaḥ, a deposit for which the trustee has accepted responsibility is regarded as his, so that the trustee violates the prohibition. *Rosh* explains that the verse that states that no leavened bread shall be seen or found on one's property extends the prohibition to include leavened bread belonging to someone else for which one accepted responsibility.

בְּהֵמָה וְעִיסָּה **An animal and dough.** *Ran* and others appear to have had a different reading of the Gemara: "An animal, half of which is of an idolatrous city, and half of which is of another city, is forbidden, because meat the size of an olive is not permitted without ritual slaughter." Ritual slaughter requires the cutting of two organs, the windpipe and the esophagus. But regarding a jointly-owned animal, one of the organs belongs to a resident of the idolatrous city, and is therefore forbidden for benefit. Therefore the ritual slaughter of the animal is ineffective, and it is forbidden to eat the animal.

HALAKHAH

בְּהֵמָה, חֶצְיָהּ שֶׁל עִיר הַנִּדַּחַת **An animal, half of which is of an idolatrous city.** "If an animal was found in an idolatrous city, and it was owned jointly by an inhabitant of the city and an outsider, it is forbidden. But if dough was found in the city, and it was owned jointly by an inhabitant of the city and an outsider, the outsider's portion is permitted, and the part belonging to the subverted city is burned." (*Rambam, Sefer Mada, Hilkhot Avodah Zarah* 4:11.)

מַהוּ דְּתִיתְהַנֵּי בָּהּ שְׁחִיטָה? **Is ritual slaughter effective?** "If an animal belonging to an inhabitant of an idolatrous city was slaughtered, it is forbidden for benefit." (*Rambam, Sefer Mada, Hilkhot Avodah Zarah* 4:12.)

TRANSLATION AND COMMENTARY

the animal **and whether he killed it** without ritual slaughter, so that even if the animal was ritually slaughtered, it contracts the ritual impurity of a carcass? [1]**Or perhaps** we say that, **since** the animal **was slaughtered, ritual slaughter does** indeed **help** to prevent it from contracting the ritual impurity of a carcass. [2]**What is the law?**

תֵּיקוּ [3]The Gemara does not find an answer to Rav Ḥisda's question, and so it concludes: The question raised in the previous passage **remains unresolved.**

בָּעֵי רַב יוֹסֵף [4]**Rav Yosef asked: What is the law** regarding **the hair of the righteous women** living in an idolatrous city? Must it be burned along with the rest of the property of the righteous that is found within the city itself, or not?

אָמַר רָבָא [5]**Rava said:** Is it clear to you that the hair **of the wicked women** living in a subverted city **is forbidden?** [6]But surely **the verse states** (Deuteronomy 13:17): "And **you shall gather** all of its spoil...**and burn** with fire." [7]This law applies to **that which lacks only gathering and burning,** [8]**excluding that which lacks detaching, gathering, and burning.** Hair lacks detaching, for before it can be gathered and burned, it must first be removed from the women's heads!

אֶלָּא [9]**Rather, Rava said:** The question arises **regarding a wig** belonging to a righteous woman living in an idolatrous city, whether or not it must be burned along with the rest of the property of the righteous that is found within the city.

הֵיכִי דָּמֵי [10]The Gemara asks: **How** precisely **do you visualize the case?** [11]If the wig **is** securely **attached to** the woman's **body,** as when it is plaited into her hair, [12]**it** should be treated **like her body.** Just as the clothing worn by the righteous woman is not burned, so, too, should her wig not be burned!

לָא [13]The Gemara answers: **No, it is necessary** to raise the question if the wig **hangs** now **on a peg.** The Gemara explains the two sides of the question: [14]Do we say that the wig **is** treated **like** all **the** other **property**

LITERAL TRANSLATION

he killed it. [1]Or perhaps, since he slaughtered it, ritual slaughter is effective. [2]What [is the law]?

[3]Let it stand.

[4]Rav Yosef asked: The hair of righteous women — what [is the law]?

[5]Rava said: That of the wicked women — is it forbidden? [6]It is written: "You shall gather...and burn." [7]That which lacks only gathering and burning. [8]To the exclusion of that which lacks detaching, gathering, and burning.

[9]Rather, Rava said: Regarding a wig.

[10]How do you visualize the case? [11]If it is attached to her body, [12]it is like her body.

[13]No, it is necessary where it hangs on a peg. [14]It is like the property of the righteous that is in it,

קְטָלָא מִקְטַל? [1]אוֹ דִּלְמָא, כֵּיוָן דִּשְׁחָטָהּ, מְהַנְיָא לָהּ שְׁחִיטָה.

[2]מַאי?

[3]תֵּיקוּ.

[4]בָּעֵי רַב יוֹסֵף: שֵׂיעַר נָשִׁים צִדְקָנִיּוֹת — מַהוּ?

[5]אָמַר רָבָא: הָא דִּרְשָׁעִיּוֹת — אָסוּר? [6]״תִּקְבֹּץ...וְשָׂרַפְתָּ״ כְּתִיב. [7]מִי שֶׁאֵינוֹ מְחוּסָּר אֶלָּא קְבִיצָה וּשְׂרֵיפָה. [8]יָצָא זֶה שֶׁמְּחוּסָּר תְּלִישָׁה וּקְבִיצָה וּשְׂרֵיפָה.

[9]אֶלָּא, אָמַר רָבָא: בְּפֵיאָה נָכְרִית.

[10]הֵיכִי דָּמֵי? [11]אִי דִּמְחוּבָּר בְּגוּפָהּ, [12]כְּגוּפָהּ דָּמְיָא.

[13]לָא, צְרִיכָא דְּתָלֵי בְּסִיבְטָא.

[14]כְּנִכְסֵי צַדִּיקִים שֶׁבְּתוֹכָהּ דָּמֵי,

RASHI

איתסרה ואיסור הנאה הוא, אבל תיהני לטהרה מידי נבלה. **שיער נשים צדקניות** — שבעיר הנדחת מהו אי הוו בכלל ואת כל שללה תשרף — או לא. **רשעניות** — פשיטא לן דישרף עם שלל העיר. **תלישה** — שצריך לגלחה. **פיאה נכרית** — גדיל של שערות דעלמא שעושין לנוי, קא מבעי ליה לרב יוסף אם של צדקניות הוי. **מחובר בגופה** — שנקשר בה. **בגופה דמי** — וכשם שאין שורפין מלבושין שעליהן שהרי צדקניות הן — כך אין שורפין אותו גדיל. **דתלי בסבטא** — תלה אותו גדיל ביתד ואין קשורין בה עכשיו.

NOTES

דְּתָלֵי בְּסִיבְטָא **As when it hangs on a peg.** Some understand that, when the Gemara speaks of a wig that is attached to a woman's body, it refers to a woman who attaches the wig to her head with wax or another adhesive. When it speaks of a wig that hangs on a peg, it refers to a wig attached to a pin that a woman keeps behind her ear (*Ramah*).

HALAKHAH

שֵׂיעַר נָשִׁים צִדְקָנִיּוֹת **The hair of righteous women.** "The hair of the inhabitants of an idolatrous city, both that of men and that of women, is permitted for benefit." (*Rambam, Sefer Mada, Hilkhot Avodah Zarah* 4:12.)

פֵּיאָה נָכְרִית **A wig.** "A wig belonging to an inhabitant of an idolatrous city is forbidden for benefit." (*Rambam, Sefer Mada, Hilkhot Avodah Zarah* 4:12.)

TRANSLATION AND COMMENTARY

of the righteous that is found **in** the idolatrous city, **and** therefore **it is destroyed?** [1]**Or perhaps** we say that, **since** the woman **goes in and out** all the time wearing her wig, **it is** treated **like a garment** even when it is not on her head, and so it is not destroyed.

תֵּיקוּ [2]The Gemara does not find an answer to Rav Yosef's question, and so it concludes: The question raised in the previous passage **remains unresolved.**

וְאֶת כָּל שְׁלָלָהּ תִּקְבֹּץ [3]The verse states (Deuteronomy 13:17): **"And you shall gather all the spoil of it in the open place of the city."** [4]**Our Rabbis taught** a Baraita: **"If** the idolatrous city **does not have an open place** in which the entire community is accustomed to assemble, **it cannot become an idolatrous city.** [5]**This is the position of Rabbi Yishmael.** [6]**Rabbi Akiva** disagrees and **says:** If the city **does not have an open place, an open place is made for it** now, in order to fulfill the requirement set by the verse." [7]The Gemara asks: **Regarding what** point **do** Rabbi Yishmael and Rabbi Akiva **disagree?** [8]The Gemara explains: **The one** Tanna — Rabbi Yishmael — **maintains:** [9]The words **"its open place" imply** that the law of an idolatrous city applies only if the city had an open place **from the outset.** [10]**And the other** Tanna — Rabbi Akiva — **maintains:** [11]The words **"its open place" imply** that the law of an idolatrous city applies **even** if an open place is made for it **now.**

[112B] וְהַהֶקְדֵּשׁוֹת שֶׁבָּהּ יִפָּדוּ [12]We learned in the Mishnah: **"Property that was consecrated** to the Temple, and is now found inside the idolatrous city, **is redeemed."** [13]**Our Rabbis taught** a related Baraita: **"If in** the idolatrous city **there were sacrifices,** those animals **which were consecrated** to be offered **on the altar are** confined in an enclosure without food and **left to die,** [14]and those animals **which were consecrated** for their value to be used **for maintaining the Temple are redeemed;**

וְאָבַד. [1]אוֹ דִּלְמָא, כֵּיוָן דְּעָיְילָא וְנָפְקָא, כִּלְבוּשָׁהּ דָּמֵי.

[2]תֵּיקוּ.

[3]"וְאֶת כָּל שְׁלָלָהּ תִּקְבֹּץ אֶל תּוֹךְ רְחֹבָהּ וכו׳". [4]תָּנוּ רַבָּנַן: "אֵין לָהּ רְחוֹב, אֵינָהּ נַעֲשֵׂית עִיר הַנִּדַּחַת. [5]דִּבְרֵי רַבִּי יִשְׁמָעֵאל. [6]רַבִּי עֲקִיבָא אוֹמֵר: אֵין לָהּ רְחוֹב, עוֹשִׂין לָהּ רְחוֹב". [7]בְּמַאי קָמִיפַּלְגִי? [8]מָר סָבַר: [9]"רְחוֹבָהּ" — מֵעִיקָּרָא מַשְׁמַע. [10]וּמָר סָבַר: [11]"רְחוֹבָהּ" — הָשְׁתָּא נַמִי מַשְׁמַע.

[112B] [12]"וְהַהֶקְדֵּשׁוֹת שֶׁבָּהּ יִפָּדוּ כו׳". [13]תָּנוּ רַבָּנַן: "הָיוּ בָּהּ קָדְשֵׁי קָדָשִׁים, קָדְשֵׁי מִזְבֵּחַ יָמוּתוּ; [14]קָדְשֵׁי בֶּדֶק הַבַּיִת יִפָּדוּ;

LITERAL TRANSLATION

and it is lost. [1]Or perhaps, since she goes in and she goes out, it is like her garment.

[2]Let it stand.

[3]"And you shall gather all the spoil of it into the open place of the city, etc." [4]Our Rabbis taught: "[If] it does not have an open place, it cannot become a subverted city. [5][These are] the words of Rabbi Yishmael. [6]Rabbi Akiva says: [If] it does not have an open place, they make for it an open place." [7]Regarding what do they disagree? [8]The one maintains: [9]"Its open place" — implies from the outset. [10]And the one maintains: [11]"Its open place" — implies also now.

[112B] [12]"And the consecrated property in it is redeemed, etc." [13]Our Rabbis taught: "If there were in it the holiest sacrifices, that which is consecrated for the altar, they are left to die; [14]that which is consecrated for maintaining the Temple is redeemed;

RASHI

כיון דעיילא ונפקא — רגילה לקושרה תדיר אף על פי שלא קשרתו עכשיו כל מקום שיהא שם נדון כמלבוש שעליה, דכל שעתא דעתה עליה וכשאר מלבושין דמי. רחובה מעיקרא משמע — רחובה שהיה לה מתחלה, ולא שעושין לה רחוב עכשיו. היו בה קדשי מזבח — כגון עולות ואשמות של רשעים בתוכה, נהי דלא קרינן בהו "את כל בהמתה לפי חרב" דהא לא בהמתה היא אלא בהמת שמים, אלא מאיסותא הוא להקריב קרבנות של רשעים הללו שהודחו — הלכך ימותו, כונסין אותן לכיפה ומאכילין אותן שעורין עד שכריסן נבקעת, דאפילו דמיהם אסור כדלקמן. שנאמר כליל לה׳ אלהיך — לא גרסינן.

NOTES

רְחוֹבָהּ" — מֵעִיקָּרָא מַשְׁמַע" **"Its open place" — implies from the outset.** Some explain this ruling as follows: Rabbi Yishmael interprets the words "its open place" as referring to the place where the people of the city are accustomed to assemble. If the city does not have an open space, an open place cannot be made for it now, for it never would have been used as the city's central gathering-place. Rabbi Akiva argues that, since the newly constructed open place could now be used in that manner, it fulfills the requirement that the city must have "its open place" (*Rabbi David Bonfil*).

קָדְשֵׁי מִזְבֵּחַ יָמוּתוּ **Those which are consecrated for the altar, they are left to die.** Injuring a consecrated animal and causing it a blemish is forbidden. Thus the consecrated animals found in an idolatrous city are confined in an enclosure without food and left to die.

HALAKHAH

קָדְשֵׁי מִזְבֵּחַ יָמוּתוּ **That which is consecrated for the altar.** "If in the idolatrous city there were animals which had been consecrated to be offered on the altar, they are confined in an enclosure without food and left to die," following Rabbi Yoḥanan against Resh Lakish (*Kesef Mishneh; Ra'avad* disagrees with this ruling). (*Rambam, Sefer Mada, Hilkhot Avodah Zarah* 4:13.)

TRANSLATION AND COMMENTARY

[1] if there is **terumah,** it **is left to rot; and** if there is **the second tithe or sacred scrolls,** they **are buried.** [2] **Rabbi Shimon says:** The words **'its cattle'** teach that the law of an idolatrous city does **not** apply to **an animal that is a firstborn or a tithe-animal;** the words [3] **'its spoil' exclude consecrated money and** second-**tithe money."**

אָמַר מָר [4] The Gemara now explains the Baraita: **It was taught,** above: **"If in** the idolatrous city **there were sacrifices,** those animals **which were consecrated** to be offered **on the altar are** confined in an enclosure without food and **left to die."** [5] The Gemara asks: **Why are** such animals **left to die?** [6] **Let** the animals **graze until they** receive blemishes that **render them unfit** to be offered on the altar. [7] Once disqualified, the animals **should** then **be sold, and the money** received **should be used** to purchase **free-will offerings!**

רַבִּי יוֹחָנָן אָמַר [8] **Rabbi Yoḥanan said:** Even though these sacrifices are not regarded as spoil of the idolatrous city, but rather spoil of Heaven, they must all be left to die, because the verse states (Proverbs 21:27): **"The sacrifice of the wicked is an abomination."**

רֵישׁ לָקִישׁ אָמַר [9] **Resh Lakish said:** These sacrifices **are** regarded **as belonging to their owners,** and are therefore treated like the rest of the animals in the idolatrous city, to which we apply the verse (Deuteronomy 13:16): "Destroying it, and all that is in it, and its cattle, with the edge of the sword." Why are the sacrifices regarded as spoil of the idolatrous city, and not spoil of Heaven? [10] Because **we are dealing here with sacrifices for which** a person **is responsible.** The animals were consecrated in such a manner that, if they are lost or harmed, their owners must bring other animals in their place. [11] **And** the Baraita follows the position of **Rabbi Shimon, who said** elsewhere that sacrifices for which a person is responsible are regarded as **belonging to their owners.**

הָא מִדְּסֵיפָא [12] The Gemara objects: But **surely since the last clause** of the Baraita **is** explicitly the view of **Rabbi Shimon,** [13] **the first clause** of the Baraita **cannot** also **follow** the view of **Rabbi Shimon!**

בְּקָדָשִׁים קַלִּים [14] The Gemara corrects itself: Rather, the Baraita is dealing with **sacrifices of lesser holiness,**

[1] וּתְרוּמוֹת יֵרָקְבוּ, וּמַעֲשֵׂר שֵׁנִי וְכִתְבֵי הַקֹּדֶשׁ יִגָּנְזוּ. [2] רַבִּי שִׁמְעוֹן אוֹמֵר: ׳בְּהֶמְתָּהּ׳ — וְלֹא בֶּהֱמַת בְּכוֹר וּמַעֲשֵׂר; [3] ׳שְׁלָלָהּ׳ — פְּרָט לְכֶסֶף הֶקְדֵּשׁ וְכֶסֶף מַעֲשֵׂר׳״.
[4] אָמַר מָר: ״הָיוּ בָּהּ קָדְשֵׁי קָדָשִׁים, קָדְשֵׁי מִזְבֵּחַ יָמוּתוּ״. [5] וְאַמַּאי יָמוּתוּ? [6] יִרְעוּ עַד שֶׁיִּסְתָּאֲבוּ, [7] וְיִמָּכְרוּ, וְיִפְּלוּ דְּמֵיהֶן לִנְדָבָה!
[8] רַבִּי יוֹחָנָן אָמַר: ״זֶבַח רְשָׁעִים תּוֹעֵבָה״.
[9] רֵישׁ לָקִישׁ אָמַר: מָמוֹן בְּעָלִים הוּא, [10] וְהָכָא בְּקָדָשִׁים שֶׁחַיָּיב בְּאַחֲרָיוּתָן, [11] וְרַבִּי שִׁמְעוֹן הִיא, דְּאָמַר: מָמוֹן בְּעָלִים הוּא.
[12] הָא מִדְּסֵיפָא רַבִּי שִׁמְעוֹן הִיא, [13] רֵישָׁא לָאו רַבִּי שִׁמְעוֹן! [14] בְּקָדָשִׁים קַלִּים, וְאַלִּיבָּא דְּרַבִּי

LITERAL TRANSLATION

[1] and terumah is left to rot; and the second tithe and sacred scrolls are buried. [2] Rabbi Shimon says: 'Its cattle' — and not an animal that is a firstborn or a tithe-animal; [3] 'its spoil' — except for consecrated money and tithe money."

[4] The Master said: "If there were in it the holiest sacrifices, that which is consecrated for the altar, they are left to die." [5] Why are they left to die? [6] Let them graze until they become unfit, [7] and let them be sold, and their money fall for a free-will offering!

[8] Rabbi Yoḥanan said: "The sacrifice of the wicked is an abomination."

[9] Resh Lakish said: It is the money of their owners, [10] and here [we are dealing] with sacrifices for which he is responsible, [11] and it is Rabbi Shimon, who said: It is the money of their owners.

[12] Surely since the last clause is Rabbi Shimon, [13] the first clause is not Rabbi Shimon!

[14] Sacrifices of lesser holiness, and according to Rabbi

RASHI

רבי שמעון אומר וכו׳ — לקמן מפרש טעמא. **זבח רשעים תועבה** — ואפילו דמיהן אסורין. **ורבי שמעון הוא דאמר** — ב״הזהב״ (בבא מציעא נו,ב): קדשים שחייב באחריותן ממון בעלים הוא, ויש בהם אונאה, הלכך לענין עיר הנדחת נמי ממון בעלים הוא ודיינינהו לפי חרב כשאר בהמות שבתוכה, והלכך אסורין דמיהן בהנאה, והאי דקאמר ימותו, ולא אמר שיחרימו אותה עמהם — משום כבוד שמים.

NOTES

קָדָשִׁים קַלִּים **Sacrifices of lesser holiness.** "The holiest sacrifices" include burnt-offerings, sin-offerings, guilt-offerings,

HALAKHAH

וְלֹא בֶּהֱמַת בְּכוֹר וּמַעֲשֵׂר **And not an animal that is a firstborn or a tithe-animal.** "A blemished firstborn or tithe-animal found in an idolatrous city is included in "its cattle," and therefore slain by the sword." (According to *Rambam*, Rabbi Shimon disagrees with the anonymous first Tanna on this matter, and the law follows the anonymous first Tanna. According to *Ra'avad*, Rabbi Shimon explains the position of the anonymous first Tanna. Thus the law is in accordance with his position that a firstborn and a tithe-animal are considered "the spoil of Heaven," and therefore not subject to the law of an idolatrous city.) (*Rambam, Sefer Mada, Hilkhot Avodah Zarah* 4:14.)

יוֹסֵי הַגְּלִילִי, דְּאָמַר: [1]קָדָשִׁים קַלִּים מָמוֹן בְּעָלִים.
[2]אֲבָל קָדְשֵׁי קֳדָשִׁים, מַאי? [3]יִפָּדוּ. [4]אַדִּתְנֵי סֵיפָא: [5]"קָדְשֵׁי בֶדֶק הַבַּיִת יִפָּדוּ", [6]לִיפְלוֹג וְלִיתְנֵי בְּדִידָהּ: [7]בַּמֶּה דְּבָרִים אֲמוּרִים? [8]בְּקָדָשִׁים קַלִּים. [9]אֲבָל קָדְשֵׁי קֳדָשִׁים יִפָּדוּ!
[10]כֵּיוָן דְּאִיכָּא חַטָּאת שֶׁמֵּתוּ בְּעָלֶיהָ דִּלְמִיתָה אָזְלָא, [11]לָא פְּסִיקָא לֵיהּ.
[12]בִּשְׁלָמָא רַבִּי יוֹחָנָן לֹא אָמַר כְּרֵישׁ לָקִישׁ, דִּכְתִיב: "זֶבַח רְשָׁעִים תּוֹעֵבָה". [13]אֶלָּא רֵישׁ לָקִישׁ מַאי טַעְמָא לֹא אָמַר כְּרַבִּי יוֹחָנָן?
[14]אָמַר לָךְ: כִּי אָמְרִינַן "זֶבַח רְשָׁעִים תּוֹעֵבָה" — הָנֵי מִילֵּי הֵיכָא דְּאִיתְנְהוּ בְּעֵינַיְיהוּ?

LITERAL TRANSLATION

Yose the Galilean, who said: [1]Sacrifices of lesser holiness are the money of their owners.
[2]But [regarding] the holiest sacrifices, what [is the law]? [3]They are redeemed. [4]Rather than teaching the last clause: [5]"That which is consecrated for maintaining the Temple is redeemed," [6]let it distinguish and teach regarding this itself: [7]About what are these things said? [8]Regarding sacrifices of lesser holiness. [9]But the holiest sacrifices are redeemed!
[10]Since there is a sin-offering whose owner died which goes to death, [11]he could not state it categorically.
[12]Granted that Rabbi Yoḥanan did not say like Resh Lakish, for it is written: "The sacrifice of the wicked is an abomination." [13]But what is the reason that Resh Lakish did not say like Rabbi Yoḥanan?
[14]He can say to you: When do we say that the sacrifice of the wicked is an abomination — those words [apply] in their original state.

TRANSLATION AND COMMENTARY

such as individual peace-offerings and thank-offerings, **and it follows** the position of **Rabbi Yose the Galilean, who said:** [1]**Sacrifices of lesser holiness are** regarded **as belonging to their owners,** and are therefore treated like the rest of the animals in the idolatrous city.

אֲבָל [2]The Gemara asks: **But** according to this, **what is the law regarding sacrifices of the highest sanctity,** such as burnt-offerings and guilt-offerings? They are grazed until they receive blemishes that render them unfit to be offered on the altar. [3]Then **they are redeemed,** and the money with which they were redeemed is used to purchase other sacrifices. [4]But if so, **rather than teaching in the next clause** of the Baraita: [5]"If in the idolatrous city there were animals **which were consecrated** for their value to be used **for maintaining the Temple,** they **are redeemed,**" [6]the Baraita **should have made a distinction and taught regarding this** law **itself** as follows: [7]**In what cases does this law,** that the animals are left to die, **apply?** [8]Only **regarding sacrifices of lesser holiness.** [9]**But sacrifices of the highest sanctity are** grazed until they receive blemishes and then they are **redeemed!**

כֵּיוָן דְּאִיכָּא [10]The Gemara explains: **Since** among the sacrifices of the highest grade **there are** also sin-offerings, and the law is that **a sin-offering whose owner died is** confined in an enclosure and **left to die,** [11]the Tanna of the Baraita **could not have stated categorically** that sacrifices of the highest grade are allowed to graze until they receive blemishes and then redeemed. Therefore, he formulated the law with respect to animals that were consecrated for their value to be used in maintaining the Temple, for in all cases they are redeemed.

בִּשְׁלָמָא [12]The Gemara notes: **Granted that Rabbi Yoḥanan did not say the same as Resh Lakish, for** he relies on **the verse that states: "The sacrifice of the wicked is an abomination."** [13]**But** the question may be raised: **Why did Resh Lakish not say the same as Rabbi Yoḥanan?**

אָמַר לָךְ [14]The Gemara explains: Resh Lakish **can say to you: When do we say that the sacrifice of the wicked is an abomination? That is** only **when** the animals **themselves** which were designated by the wicked for

RASHI

ואליבא דרבי יוסי הגלילי דאמר — בפרק קמא דבבא קמא (יב,ב): ומעלה מעל בה' — לרבות קדשים קלים שהם ממונו, והואיל וממונו הם אסורים בהנאה, דאפילו דמיהן בהמתם מיקרו אבל קדשי קדשים אמאי ירעו — דהא ודאי הם עצמם אינם קרבים ד"זבח רשעים תועבה", אלא ירעו עד שיסתאבו וימכרו ויפלו דמיהם לנדבה. **אי הכי מדתני סיפא וכו'** — דקא מפליג בין קדשי מזבח לקדשי בדק הבית. **ליפלוג וליתני בדידה** — בקדשי מזבח עצמן בין קדשים קלים לקדשי קדשים. **דלמיתה אזלא** — כדאמרינן (תמורה טז,א): חמש חטאות מתות. **לא פסיקא ליה** — למיתני קדשי קדשים דעיר הנדחת ירעו, דכיון דמתו להם אותם רשעים אי איכא חטאות שהפרישו בחייהם אזלי למיתה, דכל חטאות שמתו בעליהם — מתות, במסכת הוריות (ו,א) מפרש טעמא, אבל שאר קדשי קדשים כגון אשמות שמתו בעליהם — ירעו. **דאיתנהו בעינייהו** — דהן עצמן ודאי אינן קרבים משום זבח רשעים תועבה.

NOTES

and communal peace-offerings. They are regarded as sacred property from the time of their consecration, and only after they are slaughtered do the priests acquire the right to derive certain benefit from them. "Sacrifices of lesser holiness" include individual peace-offerings, thank-offerings, firstborn animals, animal tithes, and others. Only after they are slaughtered and their blood is sprinkled on the altar do they attain their full sanctity. The Sages disagree about the degree of sanctity with which sacrifices of lesser holiness are endowed prior to their slaughter.

TRANSLATION AND COMMENTARY

sacrifice are offered on the altar. [1] **But here, since** the situation **has changed,** and the animals are redeemed, the ruling **has changed,** and the sacrifices purchased with the redemption money are not an abomination.

רַבִּי שִׁמְעוֹן אוֹמֵר [2] It was taught in the Baraita: **"Rabbi Shimon says:** The words **'its cattle'** [3] teach that the law of an idolatrous city does **not** apply to **an animal that is a firstborn or a tithe-animal."** [4] The Gemara asks: **What are we dealing with** here? [5] **If you say** that Rabbi Shimon refers to **unblemished animals** that are otherwise fit for the altar, **they are** surely in the category of **"the spoil of Heaven,"** and so they should be excluded from destruction by the words "its spoil." [6] **Rather,** Rabbi Shimon must be referring to **blemished animals** that are no longer fit for the altar, and therefore may be eaten by their owners. [7] But such animals **should** indeed **be** included in the category of **"its spoil,"** like all the other animals found in a subverted city!

אָמַר רָבִינָא [8] **Ravina said: In fact,** Rabbi Shimon refers to **blemished animals,** but they are not destroyed together with the rest of the animals in the city, because the words "its cattle" teach that the law of an idolatrous city applies only to an animal which **is eaten as "its cattle,"** that is to say, as an ordinary animal belonging to a resident of the city. [9] **This excludes** an animal **which is not eaten as "its cattle,"** [10] **but** rather as an animal qualified by some other epithet, such **as a firstborn or a tithe-animal,** and **which is** therefore regarded as **the spoil of Heaven.**

וּפְלִיגָא [11] The Gemara notes that Ravina's explanation of the Baraita **disagrees with** that of **Shmuel, for** regarding that Baraita **Shmuel said: All are sacrificed, and all are redeemed.** [12] The Gemara asks: **What did Shmuel mean** by this, for at first glance his words make no sense? [13] The Gemara explains: Shmuel meant to **say as follows: Any** animal **which is** fit to

[1] אֲבָל הָכָא, כֵּיוָן דְּאִישְׁתַּנֵּי, אִישְׁתַּנֵּי.

[2] ״רַבִּי שִׁמְעוֹן אוֹמֵר: ׳בְּהֶמְתְּךָ׳ — [3] וְלֹא בֶּהֱמַת בְּכוֹר וּמַעֲשֵׂר״. [4] בְּמַאי עָסְקִינַן? [5] אִילֵימָא בִּתְמִימִין — שְׁלַל שָׁמַיִם הוּא! [6] אֶלָּא, בְּבַעֲלֵי מוּמִין. [7] ׳שְׁלָלָהּ׳ נִינְהוּ!

[8] אָמַר רָבִינָא: לְעוֹלָם בְּבַעֲלֵי מוּמִין, וּמִי שֶׁנֶּאֱכָל בְּתוֹרַת ״בְּהֶמְתְּךָ״. [9] יָצְאוּ אֵלּוּ שֶׁאֵין נֶאֱכָלִין בְּתוֹרַת ״בְּהֶמְתְּךָ״, [10] אֶלָּא בְּתוֹרַת בְּכוֹר וּמַעֲשֵׂר, דִּשְׁלַל שָׁמַיִם נִינְהוּ.

[11] וּפְלִיגָא דִּשְׁמוּאֵל, דְּאָמַר שְׁמוּאֵל: הַכֹּל קָרֵב, וְהַכֹּל נִפְדֶּה. [12] מַאי קָאָמַר? [13] הָכִי

LITERAL TRANSLATION

[1] But here, since they were changed, they were changed.

[2] "Rabbi Shimon says: 'Your cattle' — [3] and not an animal that is a firstborn or a tithe-animal." [4] What are we dealing with? [5] If you say with unblemished animals — it is the spoil of Heaven. [6] Rather, with blemished animals. [7] It is "its spoil"!

[8] Ravina said: In fact, with blemished animals, and that which is eaten as "your cattle." [9] This excludes that which is not eaten as "your cattle," [10] but as a firstborn or a tithe-animal, which is the spoil of Heaven.

[11] And this is in disagreement with Shmuel, for Shmuel said: All are sacrificed, and all are redeemed. [12] What did he say? [13] Thus

RASHI

אבל הכא — דאיכא למימר ירעו ויפלו דמיהם לנדבה. **כיון דאישתני** — ליכא הכא ״זבח רשעים תועבה״. **ולא בהמת בכור ומעשר** — שאם היו בה בכורות או מעשר בהמה שהוא של ישראל וחלבו ודמו קרב, אין מחרימין אותו עמה, דלא מיקרי ״בהמתה״. **שלל שמים הוא** — ומשללה נפקא. **אלא בבעלי מומים** — שאין בהם חלק לגבוה אלא נאכלין לבעלים — שללה נינהו, אמאי אין מחרימין אותן עמה. **לעולם בבעלי מומין** — ואפילו הכי אין נשרפין עמה, דדרשינן לקרא הכי: ״בהמתה״ — למי שנאכל לבעלים בתורת בהמתם, יצאו אלו שיש להם שם לווי שאין נאכלים בתורת בהמתם, שאין אומרין: בהמת עיר הנדחת, אלא בהמת בכור ומעשר של עיר הנדחת. **ופליגא** — הא דרבינא אדשמואל, דאמר שמואל עלה דהא מילתא דרבי שמעון כי הוה קשיא לן במאי עסקינן, הוי מתרץ הכי: הכל קרב והכל נפדה. **מאי קאמר הכי קאמר** — כל שהוא קרב לגבוה כשהוא תם, וכשהוא בעל מום צריך פדייה, כגון שאר קדשים קלים חוץ ממעשר בהמה ובכור, הנהו מ״שללה״ נפקא דאין מחרימין אותם עמה, דהואיל וצריכי פדייה במומן — שלל שמים קרינן ביה, ופליג עליה דתנא קמא דאמר: קדשים קלים ממון בעלים הוא.

NOTES

שֶׁאֵין נֶאֱכָלִין בְּתוֹרַת ״בְּהֶמְתְּךָ״ That which is not eaten as "your cattle." Our commentary follows *Rashi*, who explains that firstborn and tithe-animals are not included in the category of "its cattle," because they bear an added designation, that is to say, even after they are blemished, they continue to be called "firstborns" or "tithe-animals." Others explain that even after firstborn and tithe-animals acquire blemishes, so that they may be eaten like other unconsecrated kosher animals, they are still governed by special laws that distinguish them from ordinary animals. For example, they may not be sold or weighed like other animals. Thus, they also do not fall under the category of "its cattle" regarding an idolatrous city.

TRANSLATION AND COMMENTARY

be **sacrificed** on the altar **when it is unblemished, and** which is **redeemed when it is blemished** (any sacrifice of lesser holiness other than a firstborn and a tithe-animal) [1]**is excluded** from the law pertaining to an idolatrous city **by** the words "its **spoil**" — "its spoil," and not the spoil of Heaven. [2]**And any** animal **which is** fit to be **sacrificed** on the altar **when it is unblemished, but** which is **not redeemed when it is blemished,** but rather is eaten by its owners even without redemption, [3]**like a firstborn or a tithe-animal, is excluded** from the law pertaining to an idolatrous city **by** the words "its **cattle.**" This exclusion only applies while the animal is unblemished, and the animal is fit for the altar. But if the animal is blemished, it is indeed regarded as "its cattle," and therefore destroyed with the rest of the animals of the city.

תְּרוּמוֹת יֵרָקְבוּ [4]We have learned in our Mishnah: "If **terumah** is found in an idolatrous city, it must **be left to rot.**" [5]**Rav Ḥisda said: This law applies only to terumah** that has not yet been given to a priest, and is still **in the hands of an ordinary Jew.** Such terumah is not burned, for it does not belong to the ordinary Jew, and he might still have given it to a righteous priest living in another city. The terumah may also not be eaten, for the ordinary Jew might also have given it to a wicked priest living in the idolatrous city and so it is left to rot. [6]**But** as for **terumah** that is already **in the hands of a priest** living in the idolatrous city, **since it belongs to him, it is burned** together with the rest of the property found in the city.

מְתִיב רַב יוֹסֵף [7]**Rav Yosef raised an objection:** Our Mishnah continues: **"Second-tithe** produce **and sacred scrolls** must **be buried."** [8]**But surely the second tithe in the hands of an ordinary Jew is like terumah in the hands of a priest.** Just as terumah belongs to the priest, so, too, does the second tithe belong to the ordinary Jew and is his to eat in Jerusalem, [9]**and** nevertheless the Mishnah **states:** "Second-tithe produce must **be buried,"** and it does not say that it must be burned!

קָאָמַר: כָּל שֶׁקָּרֵב כְּשֶׁהוּא תָּם, וְנִפְדֶּה כְּשֶׁהוּא בַּעַל מוּם, [1]מִ״שְּׁלַל״ אִימְעִיט. [2]וְכָל שֶׁקָּרֵב כְּשֶׁהוּא תָּם, וְאֵינוֹ נִפְדֶּה כְּשֶׁהוּא בַּעַל מוּם, [3]כְּגוֹן בְּכוֹר וּמַעֲשֵׂר, מִ״בְּהֶמְתָּה״ נָפְקָא.

[4]״תְּרוּמוֹת יֵרָקְבוּ״. [5]אָמַר רַב חִסְדָּא: לֹא שָׁנוּ אֶלָּא תְּרוּמָה בְּיַד יִשְׂרָאֵל. [6]אֲבָל תְּרוּמָה בְּיַד כֹּהֵן, כֵּיוָן דְּמָמוֹנֵיהּ הוּא, תִּשָּׂרֵף.

[7]מְתִיב רַב יוֹסֵף: ״מַעֲשֵׂר שֵׁנִי וְכִתְבֵי הַקֹּדֶשׁ יִגָּנְזוּ״. [8]וְהָא מַעֲשֵׂר שֵׁנִי בְּיַד יִשְׂרָאֵל כִּתְרוּמָה בְּיַד כֹּהֵן דָּמֵי, [9]וְקָתָנֵי: ״יִגָּנְזוּ״!

LITERAL TRANSLATION

he said: Anything which is sacrificed when it is unblemished, and redeemed when it is blemished, [1]is excluded by "spoil." [2]And anything which is sacrificed when it is unblemished, but not redeemed when it is blemished, [3]like a firstborn and a tithe-animal, goes out because of "cattle."

[4]"Terumah is left to rot." [5]Rav Ḥisda said: They only taught [this] regarding terumah in the hand[s] of an ordinary Jew. [6]But terumah in the hand[s] of a priest, since it is his money, it is burned.

[7]Rav Yosef objected: "The second tithe and the sacred scrolls are buried." [8]But surely the second tithe in the hand[s] of an ordinary Jew is like terumah in the hand[s] of a priest, [9]and it states: "They are buried"!

RASHI

וכל שקרב כשהוא תם, ואינו נפדה כשהוא בעל מום — אלא נאכל לבעלים כגון בכור ומעשר, ההוא לאו שלל שמים מקרו, ואפילו בתמותן, ולא מצי למפרך: והא בתמותן שלל שמים הוא — שהרי נאכל במומו, והלכך אצטריך "בהמתה" למעוטי בכור ומעשר תמימים דמ"שללה" ליכא למעוטינהו, והיינו פליגא דאיהו מוקי לה אפילו בתמימים, דקסבר בכור ומעשר בעלי מומין "בהמתה" קרינן ביה — ובסייף. **תרומה ביד ישראל** — שעדיין לא נתנה לכהן, דאפילו אותו ישראל רשע הוא תרומה שבידו אינה נשרפת עם שאר שללה, דהא לאו דידיה הוא — דשמא היה נתנה לכהן צדיק שבחוצה לה, הלכך אינה נשרפת, דהיינו כפקדון דעיר אחרת ואתנהו בגוה דאמר לעיל דמותרין, ונהי דבאכילה לא שרינא לה דשמא היה נתנה לכהן רשע שבתוכה — הלכך ירקבו, אבל תרומה ביד כהן דממוניה הוא — תשרף. **וקתני יגנזו** — אף על גב דממוניה הוא — לא אמר תשרף.

NOTES

מַעֲשֵׂר שֵׁנִי **The second tithe.** Second tithe is the tithe set aside after the priestly dues (terumah) are given to the priests, and the first tithe is given to the Levites. The second tithe is given during the first, second, fourth, and fifth years of the Sabbatical cycle. After the second tithe is set aside, it is brought to Jerusalem to be eaten there by its owner. If the journey to Jerusalem is too long, so that it is difficult to carry all the second tithe there, or if the produce becomes ritually impure, it can be redeemed for an equivalent sum of money. This redemption money is brought to Jerusalem, where it is spent on food. One may not eat the second tithe while in a state of ritual impurity, nor while in mourning. Rabbi Meir and the Rabbis disagree about the essence of the second tithe. According to the

HALAKHAH

תְּרוּמוֹת יֵרָקְבוּ **Terumah is left to rot.** "The terumah found in an idolatrous city that has been given to a priest must be left to rot. The terumah that is still in the possession of an ordinary Jew is given to a priest living in another city." (*Rambam, Sefer Mada, Hilkhot Avodah Zarah* 4:14.)

TRANSLATION AND COMMENTARY

אֶלָּא [1]**Rather, if** something **was said** about the matter, **it was said as follows:** [2]**Rav Ḥisda said: This law applies only to terumah** that is already **in the hands of a priest** living in the idolatrous city. Even though the terumah belongs to the priest, since it is sacred, it is not burned. Rather, it is left to rot. [3]**But terumah** that was not yet given to a priest, and is still **in the hands of an ordinary Jew, is given to a** righteous **priest** living **in another city,** for it does not belong to the ordinary Jew, and is therefore not governed by the law pertaining to an idolatrous city.

תְּנַן הָתָם [4]Regarding the question of who owns second-tithe produce, **we have learned elsewhere** in a Baraita: **"Dough** made **from second-tithe** grain **is exempt from *ḥallah,*** the portion of the dough that must be set aside and given to a priest. [5]**This is the view of Rabbi Meir.** [6]**But the Sages** disagree and **say** that **there is an obligation** to set aside *ḥallah* even from such dough."

אָמַר רַב חִסְדָּא [7]**Rav Ḥisda said: The disagreement** between Rabbi Meir and the Sages **relates to the second tithe** that has been brought **to Jerusalem,** where it may now be eaten by its owner. [8]**Rabbi Meir maintains** that **the second tithe is** considered **sacred property** which its owner may eat in Jerusalem. Since it is sacred property, the priestly gift of *ḥallah* need not be set aside from it. [9]**And the Rabbis maintain** that the second tithe **is** considered a person's ordinary **secular property,** and so it is subject to the obligation of *ḥallah.* [10]**But in the outlying areas** outside Jerusalem, where the second tithe may not be eaten without first being redeemed, **all** — both Rabbi Meir and the Sages — **agree** that dough made from second-tithe grain **is exempt** from ḥallah, for there it is certainly regarded as sacred property.

מֵתִיב רַב יוֹסֵף [11]**Rav Yosef raised an objection** from our Mishnah which states: "If **second-tithe** produce **or sacred scrolls** were found in an idolatrous city, they must **be buried** in the ground." [12]**What are we dealing with** here? [13]**If you say** that the Mishnah is referring to second-tithe produce belonging to an inhabitant of **Jerusalem,**

[1]אֶלָּא, אִי אִתְּמַר הָכִי אִתְּמַר: [2]אָמַר רַב חִסְדָּא: לֹא שָׁנוּ אֶלָּא תְּרוּמָה בְּיַד כֹּהֵן. [3]אֲבָל תְּרוּמָה בְּיַד יִשְׂרָאֵל — תִּנָּתֵן לַכֹּהֵן שֶׁבְּעִיר אַחֶרֶת.

[4]תְּנַן הָתָם: "עִיסָּה שֶׁל מַעֲשֵׂר שֵׁנִי פְּטוּרָה מִן הַחַלָּה. [5]דִּבְרֵי רַבִּי מֵאִיר. [6]וַחֲכָמִים מְחַיְּיבִין". [7]אָמַר רַב חִסְדָּא: מַחֲלוֹקֶת בְּמַעֲשֵׂר שֵׁנִי בִּירוּשָׁלַיִם, [8]דְּרַבִּי מֵאִיר סָבַר: מַעֲשֵׂר שֵׁנִי מָמוֹן גָּבוֹהַּ הוּא. [9]וְרַבָּנַן סָבְרִי: מָמוֹן הֶדְיוֹט הוּא. [10]אֲבָל בַּגְּבוּלִין — דִּבְרֵי הַכֹּל פָּטוּר.

[11]מְתִיב רַב יוֹסֵף: "מַעֲשֵׂר שֵׁנִי וְכִתְבֵי הַקֹּדֶשׁ יִגָּנְזוּ". [12]בְּמַאי עָסְקִינַן? [13]אִילֵימָא בִּירוּשָׁלַיִם, מִי הָוְיָא עִיר הַנִּדַּחַת?

LITERAL TRANSLATION

[1]Rather, if it was stated, it was stated thus: [2]Rav Ḥisda said: They only taught [this] regarding terumah in the hand[s] of a priest. [3]But terumah in the hand[s] of an ordinary Jew — is given to a priest in another city.

[4]We have learned there: "The dough of the second tithe is exempt from *ḥallah.* [5][These are] the words of Rabbi Meir. [6]But the Sages say there is an obligation."

[7]Rav Ḥisda said: The disagreement is about the second tithe in Jerusalem, [8]for Rabbi Meir maintains: The second tithe is sacred property. [9]And the Rabbis maintain: It is private property. [10]But in the outlying areas — all agree that it is exempt.

[11]Rav Yosef objected: "The second tithe and the sacred scrolls are buried." [12]What are we dealing with? [13]If you say of Jerusalem, does it become a subverted city?

RASHI

אלא תרומה ביד כהן — דממוניה הוא ולא מזלזלין בה כולי האי, הואיל וקדש הוא. **לכהן שבעיר אחרת** — כלומר לכהן שלא הודח עמהן. **אבל בגבולין** — שאין לה היתר אכילה אלא בפדייה — **דברי הכל פטורה מן החלה,** דממון גבוה הוא, לישנא אחרינא: אבל בגבולין דאין לה היתר אכילה בשעת חיוב חלה, דהיינו בשעת גלגול העיסה, לא קרינא ביה "ראשית עריסותיכם" (במדבר טו), ואפילו פדאה לאחר מיכן — פטור מן החלה.

NOTES

Rabbis, the second tithe is considered a person's ordinary secular property, except that the Torah imposed an obligation to use that property in a specific manner: eating it in Jerusalem in a state of ritual purity. According to the Rabbis, the second tithe is considered sacred property, except that the Torah granted the owner permission to eat it in Jerusalem.

HALAKHAH

עִיסָּה שֶׁל מַעֲשֵׂר שֵׁנִי **The dough of the second tithe.** "The dough made from second-tithe grain that has already been brought into Jerusalem is liable to be used for *ḥallah*. But dough made from second-tithe grain in the outlying areas is exempt from *ḥallah*," following Rav Ḥisda. (*Rambam, Sefer Zera'im, Hilkhot Bikkurim* 6:4.)

[1] וְהָתַנְיָא: ״עֲשָׂרָה דְּבָרִים נֶאֶמְרוּ בִּירוּשָׁלַיִם, וְזוֹ אַחַת מֵהֶן: אֵינָהּ נַעֲשֵׂית עִיר הַנִּדַּחַת״. [2] וְאֶלָּא בְּעִיר אַחֶרֶת, וְאַסְקוּהוּ לְגַוַּהּ. [3] הָא קְלָטוּהוּ מְחִיצוֹת! [4] אֶלָּא לָאו בַּגְּבוּלִין? וְקָתָנֵי: ״יִגָּנְזוּ״!
[5] לֹא, לְעוֹלָם דְּעִיר אַחֶרֶת, וְאַסְקוּהוּ לְגַוַּהּ. [6] וְהָכָא בְּמַאי עָסְקִינַן שֶׁנִּטְמָא.
[7] וְלִפְרְקֵיהּ, דְּאָמַר רַבִּי אֶלְעָזָר: מִנַּיִן לְמַעֲשֵׂר שֵׁנִי שֶׁנִּטְמָא שֶׁפּוֹדִין אוֹתוֹ אֲפִילּוּ בִּירוּשָׁלַיִם? [8] תַּלְמוּד לוֹמַר: ״לֹא תוּכַל שְׂאֵתוֹ״. [9] וְאֵין

LITERAL TRANSLATION

[1] But surely it was taught: "Ten things were said about Jerusalem, and this is one of them: It does not become a subverted city." [2] Rather, of another city, and they brought it inside it. [3] Surely, the partitions absorbed it. [4] Rather, is it not in the outlying areas? And it states: "They are buried"!
[5] No, in fact of another city, and they brought it inside it. [6] And here we are dealing with when it becomes ritually impure.
[7] Then let him redeem it, for Rabbi Elazar said: From where [do we know] that second tithe that has become ritually impure may be redeemed even in Jerusalem? [8] The verse states: "So that you cannot carry it." [9] And

TRANSLATION AND COMMENTARY

there is a difficulty, for **can** Jerusalem **become an idolatrous city?** [1] **But surely it was taught** otherwise in a Baraita: **"Ten things were said about Jerusalem, and this is one of them:** Jerusalem **cannot become an idolatrous city."** [2] **Rather,** the Mishnah must be referring to second tithe that belongs to an inhabitant of **another city,** which **was brought** to Jerusalem before that other city was declared an idolatrous city. [3] But **surely** that, too, is difficult, for when the second tithe was brought into Jerusalem, its **partitions** — the walls of Jerusalem — **"absorbed" it,** so that it could no longer be taken out of the city to be redeemed. That being the case, the second tithe should not be regarded as belonging to the idolatrous city, and therefore it should be permitted to be eaten. [4] **Rather,** is not the Mishnah referring to second tithe that is still **in the outlying areas** outside of Jerusalem? **And it states:** "The second tithe **must be buried** in the ground"! Now, if all agree that second tithe outside Jerusalem is exempt from *ḥallah* because it is regarded as sacred property, why should the second-tithe produce found in the idolatrous city be buried? If it is sacred property, it should be brought to Jerusalem and eaten!

לֹא [5] The Gemara answers: **No, in fact** the Mishnah is referring to second tithe belonging to an inhabitant **of another city** which **had** already **been brought** to Jerusalem before that city was declared an idolatrous city. [6] **And here we are dealing with** second tithe that **had become ritually impure,** and therefore can no longer be eaten even in Jerusalem, and so it must be buried.

וְלִפְרְקֵיהּ [7] The Gemara asks: Why bury the second tithe? **Let it be redeemed, for Rabbi Elazar said: From where do we know that second-tithe** produce **that has become ritually impure may be redeemed even in Jerusalem,** where ritually pure tithe cannot be redeemed? [8] **For the verse** describing the circumstances under which second-tithe produce may be redeemed **states** (Deuteronomy 14:24-25): "And if the way is too long for you **so that you are not able to carry it** [שְׂאֵתוֹ]...then you shall turn it into money." [9] **And** there the word

RASHI

עשרה דברים נאמרו בירושלים — בפרק "מרובה" (בבא קמא פב,ב) חשיב להו. **אלא בעיר אחרת ואסקו לגוה** — שהיה אותו מעשר שני של אחד מבני עיר הנדחת והעלו אותו לירושלים קודם שהודחה, ואחר כך הודחו, אם כן אמאי יגנזו, — לשתרו נמי באכילה, דהא קלטינהו מחילות דהיינו חומה. **אלא לאו בגבולין** — ולא מטו ליה, וקתני: יגנזו, ואינו יוצא לישרף בתמיה. **ואם איתא** — דבגבולין, לדברי הכל ממון גבוה הוא — לשתרי נמי באכילה, אלא לאו ממון הדיוט הוא, ונהי דבשריפה לא משום זילותא. **לעולם דעיר הנדחת ואסקיה לגוה** — ודקאמרת לשתרו נמי באכילה — דהא קלטוהו מחילות. **הכא במאי עסקינן בשנטמא** — דלאו בר אכולי בטומאה הוא דכתיב (דברים כו) "לא בערתי ממנו בטמא". ולקמן פריך: מאי איריא עיר הנדחת, אפילו בחולה לה. **ואפילו בירושלים** — לאחר שנכנס, ואף על גב דדרשינן (שם יד) "כי ירחק ממך המקום...וצרת הכסף בידך" — ברחוק מקום אתה פודה וכו', ולא בקרוב מקום.

NOTES

עֲשָׂרָה דְּבָרִים נֶאֶמְרוּ בִּירוּשָׁלַיִם Ten things were said about Jerusalem. The ten things that were said about Jerusalem, the ten laws that are unique to Jerusalem, are in part Rabbinic enactments that were intended to prevent ritual impurity or filth from entering the city. Some of the laws stem from the unique status of Jerusalem which does not belong to any one tribe, but rather to all of Israel. For that reason certain laws, including that of an idolatrous city, do not apply to Jerusalem.

HALAKHAH

אֵינָהּ נַעֲשֵׂית עִיר הַנִּדַּחַת It does not become an idolatrous city. "Jerusalem cannot become an idolatrous city, even if the majority of its inhabitants practice idolatry." (*Rambam, Sefer Avodah, Hilkhot Bet HaBeḥirah* 7:14; *Sefer Mada, Hilkhot Avodah Zarah* 4:4.)

מַעֲשֵׂר שֵׁנִי שֶׁנִּטְמָא שֶׁפּוֹדִין אוֹתוֹ Second tithe that has become ritually impure may be redeemed. "Second-tithe produce that has become ritually impure may be redeemed even in Jerusalem," following Rabbi Elazar. (*Rambam, Sefer Zera'im, Hilkhot Ma'aser Sheni* 2:8.)

TRANSLATION AND COMMENTARY

"carry" (*se'eto*) **refers to eating,** a use of the word *se'eto* found elsewhere, [1]**as the verse states** (Genesis 43:34): **"And he** [Joseph] **took portions** [*mas'ot* — derived from the same root as *se'eto*] to them **from before him,"** where the word "portions" refers to portions of food. Rabbi Elazar interprets the verses in Deuteronomy about the laws of tithe-redemption as follows: If you are too far away from Jerusalem to bring the second tithe to consume it in the city, you may redeem it; and if you have brought the second tithe to Jerusalem but cannot eat it because it is ritually impure, you may redeem it even in Jerusalem.

הָכָא [2]The Gemara argues that Rabbi Elazar's ruling does not apply. **Here, we are dealing** not with the original second-tithe produce, but **with** foodstuffs **bought with second-tithe money** to be eaten in Jerusalem, and which subsequently became ritually impure. Only the actual second-tithe produce can be redeemed in Jerusalem, but not the produce purchased with second-tithe money.

[113A] וְלִיפְרְקֵיהּ [3]The Gemara now challenges this last assumption: Why assume that we cannot redeem produce which was purchased with second-tithe money and which subsequently became ritually impure? **Let** the food that was bought with second-tithe money **be redeemed,** [4]**as we have learned** elsewhere in the Mishnah (*Ma'aser Sheni* 3:10): "Food which was **bought with second-tithe money and which became ritually impure may be redeemed."** If it can be redeemed, why does our Mishnah say that it must be buried?

כְּרַבִּי יְהוּדָה [5]The Gemara answers: Our Mishnah's ruling, which implies that it may not be redeemed, **is in accordance with** the viewpoint of **Rabbi Yehudah, who said** in that same Mishnah in *Ma'aser Sheni*: [6]"Food which was bought with second-tithe money and which became ritually impure **must be buried,** and cannot be redeemed."

אִי הָכִי [7]The Gemara is still not satisfied with this explanation: **If** it is **so,** that the Mishnah deals with foodstuffs bought with second-tithe money, and is in accordance with the viewpoint of Rabbi Yehudah, **why does it speak** of a case of the second tithe **of an idolatrous city?** [8]The same law should apply **even** if the second tithe came from **an ordinary city!**

אֶלָּא [9]The Gemara responds by rejecting the previous interpretations of the Mishnah and suggesting a new one: **Rather,** the Mishnah is referring to **ritually pure second tithe** which was brought to Jerusalem, **and** to a similar situation **when the partitions** (the walls of Jerusalem) **fell.** The Mishnah is referring to a particular instance when the walls of Jerusalem fell after the second-tithe produce had entered the city. Now, the law is that, once second tithe has entered the walls of Jerusalem, it may no longer be redeemed, since it is "absorbed," as it were, by the walls, and must therefore be eaten in Jerusalem. However, if the walls of Jerusalem fall, the second tithe may no longer be eaten, since it must be eaten within the walls of Jerusalem. [10]**And** the Mishnah was taught

"שְׂאֵת" אֶלָּא אֲכִילָה, [1]שֶׁנֶּאֱמַר: "וַיִּשָּׂא מַשְׂאֹת מֵאֵת פָּנָיו".
[2]הָכָא בְּמַאי עָסְקִינַן בְּלָקוּחַ.
[113A] [3]וְלִיפְרְקֵיהּ, [4]דִּתְנַן: "הַלָּקוּחַ בְּכֶסֶף מַעֲשֵׂר שֶׁנִּטְמָא יִפָּדֶה"!
[5]כְּרַבִּי יְהוּדָה, דְּאָמַר: [6]"יִקָּבֵר".
[7]אִי הָכִי, מַאי אִירְיָא עִיר הַנִּדַּחַת? [8]אֲפִילּוּ דְּעָלְמָא נַמִי!
[9]אֶלָּא, לְעוֹלָם בְּטָהוֹר, וּכְגוֹן דִּנְפוּל מְחִיצוֹת, [10]וְכִדְרָבָא,

LITERAL TRANSLATION

"carry" only [means] eating, [1]as it is stated: "And he took portions from before him."

[2]Here, we are dealing with what was bought [with second-tithe money].

[113A] [3]Let him redeem it, [4]for we have learned: "That which was bought with second-tithe money that became ritually impure may be redeemed."

[5][It is] according to Rabbi Yehudah, who said: [6]"It must be buried."

[7]If so, why does it specify a subverted city? [8]Even an ordinary [city] also!

[9]Rather, [the Mishnah is referring] to ritually pure [second tithe], and [to a similar situation] (lit., "like") when the partitions fell; [10]and [the Mishnah was taught]

RASHI

ואין שאת אלא אכילה — והכי קאמר קרא: "כי ירחק ממך המקום", או כי לא תוכל לאוכלו שנטמא, "וצרת הכסף בידך". בלקוח — שכבר הוציאה בהוצאה לכסף מעשר ונתנוהו ביין ושכר ובשר ונטמא אותו לקוח, דההוא לית ליה פדייה, וכי קאמר רבי אלעזר במעשר שני גופיה שהעלה פירות מעשר שני לירושלים ונטמאו. וליפרקיה לכוליה — ומשני כר' יוחנן, דאמר לא אלים למתפס פדיונו בההיא משנה גופא, במסכת מעשר שני (פרק ג' משנה י') והיינו נמי מעשר שני דקאמר: יגנז בקבורה. אלא לעולם — במעשר שני דעיר הנדחת טהור, ואסקוה לגוה, ודקאמר ליתסרי באכילה דהא קלטוהו מחיצות אחר שנכנס לחומת ירושלים.

HALAKHAH

הַלָּקוּחַ בְּכֶסֶף מַעֲשֵׂר שֶׁנִּטְמָא **That which was bought with second-tithe money.** "Food bought with second-tithe money which became ritually impure through contact with a 'father of ritual impurity' may be redeemed," following the anonymous Tanna of the Mishnah. (*Rambam, Sefer Zera'im, Hilkhot Ma'aser Sheni* 7:1,2.)

TRANSLATION AND COMMENTARY

in accordance with the viewpoint of **Rava, for Rava said:** The rule about **partitions for eating** — that second tithe may only be eaten within the walls of Jerusalem — **applies by Torah law,** [1]but the rule about partitions **for absorption** — that second tithe may no longer be redeemed after it has entered the city — **applies by Rabbinic law.** Torah law requires that second tithe be eaten only within the walls of Jerusalem, for the verse states (Deuteronomy 12:18): "But you must eat them before the Lord your God," and this is understood as a reference to the city of Jerusalem. But the rule that second tithe that has entered Jerusalem is "absorbed," as it were, by the walls and hence may no longer be redeemed even after it has left the city applies only by Rabbinic decree. [2]And it stands to reason that **the Rabbis** only **decreed** that the walls of Jerusalem should "absorb" second tithe brought into the city **while the walls are** still **standing.** [3]But **if** the walls of the city **are no** longer **standing, the Rabbis** presumably **would not** issue such a **decree.** Just as second tithe that has entered Jerusalem is "absorbed" by the walls, so that it may no longer be taken out of the city to be redeemed, so, too, is it "absorbed" by the walls so that second tithe coming from an idolatrous city is no longer regarded as belonging to that city. But if the walls of Jerusalem are no longer standing, the second tithe is once again regarded as belonging to the idolatrous city. Therefore the second-tithe produce must be buried.

כִּתְבֵי הַקֹּדֶשׁ יִגָּנְזוּ [4]We have learned in our Mishnah: "If **sacred scrolls** are found in a subverted city, they **must be buried."** [5]**Our Mishnah was not** taught **in accordance with** the viewpoint of **Rabbi Eliezer, for it was taught** in a Baraita: [6]**"Rabbi Eliezer says: Any city that has in it at least one mezuzah cannot become an idolatrous city, for the verse states** (Deuteronomy 13:17): **'And you shall burn with fire both the city and all its spoil, entirely.'** [7]**And where there is a mezuzah, it is not possible** to burn the city with all its spoil, [8]**for the verse** regarding idols **states** (Deuteronomy 12:3): 'And you shall destroy the name of them out of that place,' and the next verse continues (Deuteronomy 12:4): **'This you shall not do to the Lord your God.'** One is forbidden to destroy anything containing the Divine Name, and the name of God is included in the text of the mezuzah."

דְּאָמַר רָבָא: מְחִיצָּה לֶאֱכוֹל דְּאוֹרַיְיתָא; [1]לִקְלוֹט, דְּרַבָּנַן. [2]וְכִי גְּזוּר רַבָּנַן, כִּי אִתְנְהוּ לִמְחִיצָּה; [3]כִּי לֵיתְנְהוּ לִמְחִיצָּה, לָא.

[4]"כִּתְבֵי הַקֹּדֶשׁ יִגָּנְזוּ". [5]מַתְנִיתִין דְּלָא כְּרַבִּי אֱלִיעֶזֶר, דְּתַנְיָא: [6]"רַבִּי אֱלִיעֶזֶר אוֹמֵר: כָּל עִיר שֶׁיֵּשׁ בָּהּ אֲפִילּוּ מְזוּזָה אַחַת אֵינָהּ נַעֲשֵׂית עִיר הַנִּדַּחַת, שֶׁנֶּאֱמַר: 'וְשָׂרַפְתָּ בָאֵשׁ אֶת הָעִיר וְאֶת כָּל שְׁלָלָהּ כָּלִיל'. [7]וְהֵיכָא דְּאִיכָּא מְזוּזָה, לָא אֶפְשָׁר, [8]דִּכְתִיב: "לֹא תַעֲשׂוּן כֵּן לַה׳ אֱלֹהֵיכֶם".

LITERAL TRANSLATION

according to Rava, for Rava said: Partitions for eating [apply] by Torah law; [1]for absorption, by Rabbinic law. [2]And when the Rabbis decreed, [it was for a time] when the partitions exist; [3][but] when the partitions do not exist, not.

[4]"Sacred scrolls are buried." [5]Our Mishnah is not in accordance with Rabbi Eliezer, for it was taught: [6]"Rabbi Eliezer says: Any city that has in it at least one mezuzah cannot become a subverted city, for it is stated: 'And you shall burn with fire both the city and all its spoil, entirely.' [7]And where there is a mezuzah, it is not possible, [8]for it is written: 'This you shall not do to the Lord your God.'"

RASHI

דאמר רבא — בשחיטת חולין פרק "בהמה המקשה" (סח). מחיצות לאכול דאורייתא — מן התורה מצוה לאכול לפנים מן החומה. אבל מחיצות לקלוט — שיהיו מחיצות קולטות בין לענין פדייה בין לכל ענין — מדרבנן הוא, וכי גזור רבנן דתיהני קליטת מחיצות למעשר דשוב אינו יכול לפדותו, ולענין עיר הנדחת נמי שלא יהא בשריפה היכא דאיתנהו מחיצות. דכתיב — "ואבדתם את שמם מן המקום ההוא וגו'" וסמיך ליה "לא תעשון כן לה' אלהיכם", ובמזוזה הואיל וכתיב בה אזכרות אי אפשר לשריפה משום

NOTES

מְחִיצָּה לֶאֱכוֹל וְלִקְלוֹט **Partitions for eating and for absorption.** *Ra'avad* does not have the reading: "And where the partitions had fallen." He understands that the distinction between partitions for eating and partitions for absorption suffices to explain our Mishnah. Since the rule about partitions for absorption applies only by Rabbinic law, second-tithe produce of an idolatrous city which is brought to Jerusalem does not receive the sanctity of Jerusalem, and the prohibition against removing it from Jerusalem is only due to the Rabbinic ruling that "partitions absorb." That Rabbinic ruling cannot cancel the Biblical law forbidding the second tithe of an idolatrous city from being eaten, and so the produce must be buried (see *Rabbi David Bonfil*).

HALAKHAH

מְחִיצָּה לֶאֱכוֹל **Partitions for eating.** "If someone eats second tithe outside the walls of Jerusalem, he is liable to lashes, for he violated the prohibition, 'You may not eat within your gates the tithe of your corn, or of your wine, or of your oil.'" (*Rambam, Sefer Zera'im, Hilkhot Ma'aser Sheni* 2:5.)

מְחִיצָּה לִקְלוֹט **Partitions for absorption.** "If second-tithe produce was brought into Jerusalem (even second tithe of *demai*; see *Kesef Mishneh*), it may not be taken out again, for it was 'absorbed' by the walls of the city. The rule that the walls of Jerusalem absorb second tithe applies by Rabbinic law," following our Gemara. (*Rambam, Sefer Zera'im, Hilkhot Ma'aser Sheni* 2:9.)

1"רַבִּי שִׁמְעוֹן אוֹמֵר: אָמַר הַקָּדוֹשׁ בָּרוּךְ הוּא וכו׳". 2לֵימָא בִּדְרַבִּי אָבִין אָמַר רַבִּי אִילְעָא קָמִיפַּלְגִי? 3דְּאָמַר רַבִּי אָבִין אָמַר רַבִּי אִילְעָא: 4"כָּל מָקוֹם שֶׁאַתָּה מוֹצֵא כְּלָל בַּעֲשֵׂה וּפְרָט בְּלֹא תַעֲשֶׂה, 5אֵין דָּנִין אוֹתוֹ בִּכְלָל וּפְרָט, 6דְּמָר אִית לֵיהּ דְּרַבִּי אָבִין, 7וּמָר לֵית לֵיהּ דְּרַבִּי אָבִין?

8לָא, דְּכוּלֵּי עָלְמָא אִית לְהוּ

TRANSLATION AND COMMENTARY

רַבִּי שִׁמְעוֹן אוֹמֵר [1]We have learned in our Mishnah: **"Rabbi Shimon said: The Holy One, blessed be He,** said: 'If you execute judgment against an idolatrous city as I have commanded, burning the city and all its spoil to the ground — I will regard you as having offered before Me a whole burnt-offering.'" And the Mishnah continues with the dispute between Rabbi Yose the Galilean and Rabbi Akiva as to whether gardens and orchards may be planted on the ruins of an idolatrous city. [2]The Gemara asks: **Shall we say that** Rabbi Yose the Galilean and Rabbi Akiva **disagree about what Rabbi Avin said in the name of Rabbi Il'a?** [3]**For Rabbi Avin said in the name of Rabbi Il'a:** When a generalization in the Torah is followed by a detail, we assume that the generalization refers only to what was specified in the detail. [4]But **wherever the generalization** is stated regarding **a positive commandment, and the detail** is stated regarding the corresponding **negative commandment,** [5]**we do not interpret** the verse **according to the rule of generalization and detail.** [6]May it be suggested that **one Sage,** Rabbi Yose the Galilean, **agrees with Rabbi Avin,** [7]**and the other Sage,** Rabbi Akiva, **does not agree with Rabbi Avin?** How so? The verse regarding an idolatrous city states (Deuteronomy 13:17): "And it shall be a heap for ever; it shall not be built again." The first half, "and it shall be a heap for ever," is a generalization formulated as a positive commandment, implying that nothing may be planted on the ruins of an idolatrous city. The second half, "it shall not be built again," is a detail formulated as a negative commandment, implying that buildings may not be constructed, but gardens and orchards may be planted. Rabbi Akiva appears to disagree with Rabbi Avin, for he interprets the verse according to the rule of generalization and detail. He restricts the generalization in accordance with the detail, teaching that the idolatrous city may not be rebuilt as it was with houses and buildings, but that it may be planted with gardens and orchards. And Rabbi Yose the Galilean appears to agree with Rabbi Avin, for he does not invoke the rule of generalization and detail. According to him, the general ruling, which is worded as a positive commandment, forbids even the establishment of gardens and orchards, and the detailed ruling formulated as a negative commandment forbids the construction of buildings.

לָא [8]The Gemara rejects this argument: **No, all** the Tannaim, both Rabbi Yose the Galilean and Rabbi

LITERAL TRANSLATION

[1]"Rabbi Shimon said: The Holy One, blessed be He, said, etc." [2]Shall we say that they disagree about what Rabbi Avin said in the name of Rabbi Il'a? [3]For Rabbi Avin said in the name of Rabbi Il'a: [4]Wherever you find a generalization in a positive commandment, and a detail in a negative commandment, [5]we do not interpret it according to [the rule of] generalization and detail, [6]for the one Sage agrees with Rabbi Avin, [7]and the other Sage does not agree with Rabbi Avin?

[8]No, all (lit., "the whole world") agree

RASHI

קרא דלא תעשון כן ואנן בעינן שללה וליכא — דהאי שלל שמים הוא. בכלל בעשה ופרט בלא תעשה — כגון "והיתה תל עולם" — כלל, דאפילו גנות ופרדסים לא תעשה אלא תהיה תל עולם שהוא עשה, "לא תבנה עוד" — בנין בתים, והוא לא תעשה, אין דנין אותו בכלל ופרט לומר אין בכלל אלא מה שבפרט, דלא תעשה פירוש הוא, כלומר: "והיתה תל עולם" לבנין קאמר, אבל לגנות ופרדסים — שרי, אלא תרי מילי קאמר קרא, דלא אמרינן פירושי קמפרש, אלא מילי מילי קאמר, "והיתה תל עולם" — לגנות ופרדסים, "לא תבנה עוד" — כל בנינין שבעולם ואפילו לגנות ופרדסים "לא תבנה עוד", ודרשינן ליה לדבר שהיה בכלל, ויצא מן הכלל ללמד, לא ללמד על עצמו יצא אלא ללמד על הכלל כולו יצא, ולומר בנין בכלל היה, ולמה יצא — להקיש לך מה בנין מיוחד שהוא ישוב בני אדם אף כל בנין כגון גנות ופרדסים. (לישנא אחרינא) ורבי יוסי הגלילי סבר אין דנין כר׳ אבין, ודריש הכי: והיתה תל עולם — מכל מילי, שלא יעשה בה שום דבר "ולא תבנה עוד" — דמשמע בנין בתים, אשמועינן לאו בבנין בתים, וגנות ופרדסים — איסור עשה הוא דאיכא, כך שמעתי. רבי עקיבא סבר דנין — דלא כרבי אבין. דכולי עלמא אית להו דרבי אבין — ואפילו רבי עקיבא, והא דקאמר דעיר הנדחת נעשית גנות ופרדסים — לאו משום דבעלמא לית ליה דרבי אבין, דודאי מלתא קא מפרשי והיתה תל עולם — במאי — בבנין

NOTES

דְּכוּלֵּי עָלְמָא אִית לְהוּ דְּרַבִּי אָבִין **All agree with Rabbi Avin.** *Ra'avad* emended the reading to: "All disagree with Rabbi Avin," for according to the standard reading there is a difficulty: If we do not evoke the role of generalization and detail, then it is clear why Rabbi Yose the Galilean says that even gardens and orchards may not be planted on the ruins of a subverted city, and there is no need to base his position on the word "again." Moreover, if we do not invoke the rule of generalization and detail, how can Rabbi Akiva permit the planting of gardens and orchards on the ruins of the subverted city? This should be forbidden by the verse: "And it shall be a heap forever." But most Rishonim accept

TRANSLATION AND COMMENTARY

Akiva, would **agree with Rabbi Avin** in other places, [1]**and here they disagree about** the following matter: [2]**One Sage,** Rabbi Yose the Galilean, **maintains** that the word עוֹד, **"again"** ("it shall not be built *again*"), **implies** that the ruins of the idolatrous city may not be rebuilt **at all.** [3]**And the other Sage,** Rabbi Akiva, **maintains** that the word **"again"** teaches that the subverted city **may not be rebuilt the way it was,** with houses and buildings, [4]**but** it **may be made into** a place of **gardens and orchards.**

תָּנוּ רַבָּנַן [5]**Our Rabbis taught** the following Baraita: **"If there were trees in** the idolatrous city that were **detached** from the ground, **they are forbidden** as spoil of a subverted city. [6]But trees that are still **attached** to the ground **are permitted,** for the verse states (Deuteronomy 13:17): 'And you shall gather all of its spoil...and burn with fire,' teaching that the law applies to that which lacks only gathering and burning, excluding that which lacks detaching, gathering, and burning. [7]But the trees **of another city, whether they were detached** from the ground or are still **attached** in place, **are** all **forbidden** [as will be explained below]."

מַאי ״עִיר אַחֶרֶת״ [8]The Gemara asks: **What is** the Baraita referring to when it speaks of **"another city"**?

אָמַר רַב חִסְדָּא [9]**Rav Ḥisda said:** The Baraita refers to the city of **Jericho, as the verse states** (Joshua 6:17, 26): [10]**"And the city shall be devoted,** it, and all that is in it**...to the Lord....And Joshua charged them at that time by oath, saying, Cursed be the man before the Lord, that rises up to build this city Jericho; he shall lay its foundation with his firstborn, and with his youngest son shall he set up the gates of it."** The words "it, and all that is in it" teach that even trees that were still attached to the ground were included in the ban.

[1] דְּרַבִּי אָבִין, וְהָכָא בְּהָא קָמִיפַּלְגִי: [2] מָר סָבַר: ״עוֹד״ לְגַמְרֵי מַשְׁמַע. [3] וּמָר סָבַר: ״עוֹד״ — לִכְמָה שֶׁהָיְתָה אֵינָהּ נִבְנֵית, [4] אֲבָל נַעֲשֵׂית הִיא גַּנּוֹת וּפַרְדֵּסִים.

[5] תָּנוּ רַבָּנַן: ״הָיוּ בָּהּ אִילָנוֹת תְּלוּשִׁין אֲסוּרִין; [6] מְחוּבָּרִין, מוּתָּרִין. [7] שֶׁל עִיר אַחֶרֶת, בֵּין תְּלוּשִׁין בֵּין מְחוּבָּרִין, אָסוּר״.

[8] מַאי ״עִיר אַחֶרֶת״?

[9] אָמַר רַב חִסְדָּא: יְרִיחוֹ, דִּכְתִיב: [10] ״וְהָיְתָה הָעִיר חֵרֶם...לַה׳...וַיַּשְׁבַּע יְהוֹשֻׁעַ בָּעֵת הַהִיא, לֵאמֹר, אָרוּר הָאִישׁ לִפְנֵי ה׳ אֲשֶׁר יָקוּם וּבָנָה אֶת הָעִיר הַזֹּאת אֶת יְרִיחוֹ; בִּבְכֹרוֹ יְיַסְּדֶנָּה, וּבִצְעִירוֹ יַצִּיב דְּלָתֶיהָ״.

LITERAL TRANSLATION

with Rabbi Avin, [1]and here they disagree about this: [2]One Sage maintains: "Again" means [not] at all. [3]And the other Sage maintains: "Again" — the way it was, it shall not be [re]built, [4]but it may be made into gardens and orchards.

[5]Our Rabbis taught: "If detached trees were in it, they are forbidden; [6]attached [trees], they are permitted. [7]Of another city, whether detached or attached, they are forbidden."

[8]What is "another city"?

[9]Rav Ḥisda said: Jericho, as it is written: [10]"And the city shall be devoted...to the Lord....And Joshua charged them at that time by oath, saying, Cursed be the man before the Lord, that rises up to build this city Jericho; He shall lay its foundation with his firstborn, and with his youngest son shall he set up the gates of it."

RASHI

בתים, דלא תבנה עוד לא משמע ליה בכל בניין, דקסבר עוד — לכמו שהיתה משמע, כלומר לא תחזור ולא תבנה עוד, משמע כגון שהיתה מתחלה לא תבנה עוד, אבל נעשה גנות ופרדסים. ומר סבר עוד לגמרי משמע — כגון דאמר לעולם ועד ועוד לשון ועד הוא, שלא תבנה לעולם לשום דבר — לא לבנין בתים ולא לגנות ופרדסים לא תבנה עוד. מחוברין מותרין — ד״תקבוץ ושרפת״ אמרה רחמנא, מי שאינו מחוסר אלא קביצה ושריפה, יצא זה שמחוסר תלישה וקביצה ושריפה. וכל אשר בה — אפילו אילנות מחוברין אשר בה נאסרין. הכי גרסינן: וישבע יהושע לאמר ארור האיש וגו׳ — וקרא קדרים ואזיל ״בבכורו ייסדנה ובצעירו יציב דלתיה״ — וכשיעמיד דלתיה ימות בנו הקטן.

NOTES

the standard reading, for it is difficult to say that the position of the Amoraim Rabbi Avin and Rabbi Il'a was rejected by all the Tannaim. Rather, according to Rabbi Akiva, the word "again" appears to be extraneous, and so it teaches that even the words "and it shall be a heap for ever" mean only that the city may not be rebuilt as it was with houses and buildings. And Rabbi Yose the Galilean puts forward an alternative explanation of the word "again" in order to counter Rabbi Akiva's argument (see *Rabbi David Bonfil, Ran*).

״עוֹד״ לְגַמְרֵי מַשְׁמַע **"Again" means at all.** In the Torah we find examples of both senses of the word עוֹד. The word is used in the sense of "not at all" in the verse (Deuteronomy 4:39): "That the Lord He is God in Heaven above, and upon the Earth beneath; there is no other [עוֹד]," that is to say, there is no other at all. And the word is used in the sense of "in the same way" in the verse (Deuteronomy 3:26): "Speak no more [עוֹד] to Me of this matter," that is to say, speak not again about the same matter (*Ramah*).

HALAKHAH

הָיוּ בָּהּ אִילָנוֹת **If there were trees in it.** "The fruit of an idolatrous city that has already been detached from the trees is forbidden for benefit, but that which is still attached to the trees is permitted," following the Baraita. (*Rambam, Sefer Mada, Hilkhot Avodah Zarah* 4:13.)

TRANSLATION AND COMMENTARY

תַּנְיָא [1]It was taught in a Baraita: "Jericho may not be rebuilt and given the name of another city, nor may another city be built and given the name of Jericho. [2]For the verse states (I Kings 16:34): 'Ḥi'el the Beth-eli built Jericho; with Abiram his firstborn he laid its foundation, and with his youngest son Seguv set up its gates,' and according to tradition, Ḥi'el did not rebuild Jericho. Rather, he built another city and named it Jericho. Nevertheless he was subject to the curse that was pronounced by Joshua."

תַּנְיָא [3]It was taught in another Baraita: "With the death of his firstborn, Abiram, who was a wicked man, Ḥi'el should not necessarily have understood that the curse pronounced by Joshua applied to him. For Abiram might have died because of his wickedness. [4]But with the death of his youngest son, Seguv, who was not a wicked man, Ḥi'el should finally have understood that his sons died on account of the curse."

אֲבִירָם וּשְׂגוּב [5]The Gemara asks: What did Abiram and Seguv do, so that one should be regarded a wicked man, and the other not? [6]What does the Baraita mean to say here?

הָכִי קָאָמַר [7]The Gemara answers: The Baraita means to say the following: With the death of his firstborn, Abiram, that wicked man Ḥi'el should already have understood that his youngest son Seguv would also die if he — Ḥi'el — continued to build Jericho.

מִמַּשְׁמַע שֶׁנֶּאֱמַר [8]The Baraita continues: "From the statement in the verse, 'With Abiram his firstborn,' would I not know that Seguv is his youngest son? [9]Why, then, does the verse state: 'His youngest son, Seguv'? [10]The verse teaches that, while building Jericho, Ḥi'el buried all his sons, from his firstborn, Abiram, to his youngest son, Seguv."

אַחְאָב [11]King Ahab was Ḥi'el's friend. [12]He and the Prophet Elijah went to inquire about Ḥi'el's welfare

[1]תַּנְיָא: ״לֹא יְרִיחוֹ עַל שֵׁם עִיר אַחֶרֶת, וְלֹא עִיר אַחֶרֶת עַל שֵׁם יְרִיחוֹ, [2]דִּכְתִיב: ׳בָּנָה חִיאֵל בֵּית הָאֱלִי אֶת יְרִיחֹה; בַּאֲבִירָם בְּכֹרוֹ יִסְּדָהּ, וּבִשְׂגוּב צְעִירוֹ הִצִּיב דְּלָתֶיהָ׳״.

[3]תַּנְיָא: ״בַּאֲבִירָם בְּכוֹרוֹ — רָשָׁע, לֹא הָיָה לוֹ לִלְמוֹד. [4]בִּשְׂגוּב צְעִירוֹ — הָיָה לוֹ לִלְמוֹד״.

[5]אֲבִירָם וּשְׂגוּב, מַאי עֲבוּד? [6]מַאי קָאָמַר?

[7]הָכִי קָאָמַר: בַּאֲבִירָם בְּכוֹרוֹ הָיָה לוֹ לִלְמוֹד לְאוֹתוֹ רָשָׁע בִּשְׂגוּב צְעִירוֹ.

[8]״מִמַּשְׁמַע שֶׁנֶּאֱמַר, ׳בַּאֲבִירָם בְּכוֹרוֹ׳, אֵינִי יוֹדֵעַ שֶׁשְּׂגוּב צְעִירוֹ? [9]מַה תַּלְמוּד לוֹמַר: ׳שְׂגוּב צְעִירוֹ׳? [10]מְלַמֵּד שֶׁהָיָה מְקַבֵּר וְהוֹלֵךְ מֵאֲבִירָם עַד שְׂגוּב״.

[11]אַחְאָב שׁוֹשְׁבִינֵיהּ הֲוָה. [12]אֲתָא אִיהוּ וְאֵלִיָּהוּ לְמִשְׁאַל

LITERAL TRANSLATION

[1]It was taught: "Not Jericho by the name of another city, and not another city by the name of Jericho, [2]for it is written: 'Ḥi'el the Beth-eli built Jericho; with Abiram his firstborn he laid its foundation, and with his youngest son Seguv set up its gates.'"

[3]It was taught: "With Abiram his firstborn — a wicked man, he should not have learned. [4]With his youngest son Seguv — he should have learned."

[5]Abiram and Seguv, what did they do? [6]What did he say?

[7]He said thus: With Abiram his firstborn that wicked man should have learned about his youngest son Seguv.

[8]"By deduction from what is stated, 'With Abiram his firstborn,' would I not know that Seguv is his youngest son? [9]Why does the verse state: 'His youngest son Seguv'? [10]It teaches that he continued to bury from Abiram to Seguv."

[11]Ahab was his friend. [12]He and Elijah went to inquire

RASHI

לא יריחו על שם עיר אחרת — שלא יבנה יריחו ויסב שמה על שם עיר אחרת, ולא עיר אחרת על שם יריחו — שאפילו בנה עיר אחרת וקראה יריחו אסור לבנותה, שאפילו שם יריחו ימחה לעולם, וכתיב ״בימיו בנה חיאל בית האלי את יריחו״ — בימיו — של אחאב, ועל שעבר על האלה קרי ליה ״בית האלי״. **את יריחו** — ולא יריחו עצמו בנה אלא עיר אחרת על שם יריחו, שקראה לה יריחו ולא אתפרש הא מנלן. **באבירם בכורו יסדה** — אבירם רשע, כשמת אבירם הרשע לא היה לו לחיאל ללמוד שלא לבנות את יריחו. **אבירם ושגוב מאי עבוד** — דקרי להו רשעים. **איני יודע ששגוב צעירו** — מילתא באנפי נפשיה הוא, ולמדרשא, ממשמע שנאמר ״באבירם בכורו״ — איני יודע ששגוב צעירו — אלא מה תלמוד לומר ״שגוב צעירו״ — שהיה קובר והולך מאבירם ועד שגוב שהוא צעיר מכלם. **אחאב שושבינו** — אוהבו של חיאל היה אחאב.

NOTES

אַחְאָב שׁוֹשְׁבִינֵיהּ הֲוָה **Ahab was his friend.** This account is based on the placement of the story of Ḥi'el the Beth-eli at the end of I Kings 17, between the description of the wicked deeds of Ahab and Elijah's oath barring the rain. Surely Elijah took his oath on account of Ahab's wicked deeds. Why, then, does the story of Ḥi'el separate them? The Gemara explains that Elijah's oath was occasioned by Ahab's remarks to Ḥi'el when he came to comfort him after the death of his children (*Maharsha*).

TRANSLATION AND COMMENTARY

while he was **in the house of mourning**, grieving for the death of his sons. [1]Ḥi'el **sat** before his two visitors **and said: "Perhaps when Joshua pronounced** his **curse, he cursed as follows:** [2]**Jericho** may **not** be rebuilt and given **the name of another city, nor** may **another city** be built and given **the name of Jericho.** And my sons died because I violated that prohibition!" [3]**Elijah said to** Ḥi'el: **"Yes,** that was the curse, and this appears to be your punishment." [4]Ahab turned to Elijah and **said to him: "Now, if the curse** pronounced **by Moses was not fulfilled** — [5]**for the verses state** (Deuteronomy 11: 16-17): **'And you turn aside, and serve** other gods.... [6]**And then the Lord's anger be inflamed against you, and He shut up the heaven,'** [7]**and that man,** myself, **set up an idol by each and every furrow** throughout the land, **and** nevertheless **the rain** came down in such abundance, **not** even **allowing** me **to go out and serve** the idols — [8]is it then possible that **the curse** pronounced by **his disciple Joshua was fulfilled?"** [9]**Immediately** (I Kings 17:1 — the verse following the description of Ḥi'el's building of the city of Jericho and the death of his sons): **"And Elijah the Tishbite, who was of the inhabitants of Gilead, said** to Ahab, **As the Lord God of Israel lives,** before whom I stand, **there shall not be dew or rain** these years, but according to my word." [10]Elijah **prayed and was given the key to the rain, and** then **he rose up, and went** off.

וַיְהִי דְּבַר ה׳ [11]The verses state (I Kings 17:2,3,6): **"And the word of the Lord came to him, saying, Go from here, and turn eastward, and hide yourself by Wadi Kerit....And the ravens brought him bread and**

בִּשְׁלָמָא בֵּי טַמְיָא. [1]יָתֵיב וְקָאָמַר: "דִּילְמָא כִּי מֵילַט יְהוֹשֻׁעַ, הָכִי לָט: [2]לֹא יְרִיחוֹ עַל שֵׁם עִיר אַחֶרֶת, וְלֹא עִיר אַחֶרֶת עַל שֵׁם יְרִיחוֹ". [3]אֲמַר לֵיהּ אֵלִיָּהוּ: "אִין". [4]אֲמַר לֵיהּ: "הָשְׁתָּא לְוָוטְתָא דְּמֹשֶׁה לָא קָא מִקַּיְּימָא — [5]דִּכְתִיב: 'וְסַרְתֶּם וַעֲבַדְתֶּם וגו׳'; [6]וּכְתִיב: 'וְחָרָה אַף ה׳ בָּכֶם וְעָצַר אֶת הַשָּׁמַיִם וגו׳'; [7]וְהַהוּא גַּבְרָא אוֹקֵים לֵיהּ עֲבוֹדָה זָרָה עַל כָּל תֶּלֶם וָתֶלֶם, וְלָא שָׁבֵיק לֵיהּ מִיטְרָא דְּמֵיזַל מִיסְגַּד לֵיהּ — [8]לְוָוטָתָא דִּיהוֹשֻׁעַ תַּלְמִידֵיהּ מִקַּיְּימָא"? [9]מִיָּד: "וַיֹּאמֶר אֵלִיָּהוּ הַתִּשְׁבִּי מִתֹּשָׁבֵי גִּלְעָד חַי ה׳ אֱלֹהֵי יִשְׂרָאֵל...אִם יִהְיֶה...טַל וּמָטָר וגו׳". [10]בָּעֵי רַחֲמֵי וְהָבוּ לֵיהּ אַקְלִידָא דְּמִטְרָא, וְקָם וַאֲזַל. [11]"וַיְהִי דְּבַר ה׳ אֵלָיו לֵאמֹר לֵךְ מִזֶּה וּפָנִיתָ לְּךָ קֵדְמָה וְנִסְתַּרְתָּ בְּנַחַל כְּרִית וְהָעֹרְבִים מְבִיאִים

LITERAL TRANSLATION

about his welfare in the house of mourning. [1]He sat and said: "Perhaps when Joshua cursed, he cursed as follows: [2]Not Jericho by the name of another city, and not another city by the name of Jericho." [3]Elijah said to him: "Yes." [4]He said to him: "Now if the curse of Moses was not fulfilled — [5]for it is written: 'And you turn aside, and serve, etc.'; [6]and it is written: 'And then the Lord's anger will be inflamed against you, and He will shut up the heaven, etc.'; [7]and that man set up an idol by each and every furrow, and the rain did not allow him to go and serve it — [8][is it possible that] the curse of Joshua his disciple was fulfilled?" [9]Immediately: "And Elijah the Tishbite, who was of the inhabitants of Gilead said....As the Lord God of Israel lives...there shall not be dew or rain, etc." [10]He asked for mercy and they gave him the key to the rain, and he rose up, and went.

[11]"And the word of the Lord came to him, saying, Go from here, and turn eastward, and hide yourself in Wadi Kerit....And the ravens brought

RASHI

בי טמיא — ויש אומרים בי טעמא, בית האבל שמטעימים אותו בדברים לנחמו, ובכמה דוכתין כתיב בבראשית רבה טמיא בלא עיי"ן לשון אבל. **על כל תלם ותלם** — שורה וערוגה, ומקום גבוה הוא. **ולא שביק מיטרא מיזל ומסגד** — שהיה הלכלוך הולך וגדל מרוב הגשמים הבאין לעולם שאין מניחין לילך להשתחוות לעבודה זרה מתוך דרכים מלוכלכות בטיט. **מיד ויאמר אליהו חי ה׳ אם יהיה השנים האלה מטר וגו׳** — האי קרא סמוך לקרא ד"חיאל בית האלי". **אקלידא דמטרא** — מפתח של מטר.

NOTES

לְמִשְׁאַל בִּשְׁלָמָא בֵּי טַמְיָא **To inquire about his welfare in the house of mourning.** Many Rishonim have the reading: לְמִשְׁאַל טַעֲמָא. *Ramah* suggests that Ahab and Elijah came to ask Ḥi'el what was the reason [טַעֲמָא] that all of his sons died.

וְלֹא עִיר אַחֶרֶת עַל שֵׁם יְרִיחוֹ **And not another city by the name of Jericho.** The Gemara assumes here that Ḥi'el did not rebuild the city of Jericho, but rather that he built another city, and called it Jericho. The Jerusalem Talmud explains the basis of this assumption. Ḥi'el was not of the tribe of Benjamin, and so he could not have rebuilt Jericho, which is situated on Benjaminite territory. Moreover, it is unlikely that Ḥi'el, who came from the Kingdom of Israel, would rebuild the city of Jericho which was found in the territory of the Kingdom of Judah.

וְהָעֹרְבִים מְבִיאִים **And the ravens brought.** *Maharsha* explains that the matter of the ravens is mentioned here in order to explain why the Prophet Elijah was not sensitive to the distress caused by the drought. Since the ravens supplied Elijah with food from Ahab's slaughterhouse, he

TRANSLATION AND COMMENTARY

meat in the morning." [1]**From where did** the ravens bring the bread and meat?

אָמַר רַב יְהוּדָה [2]**Rav Yehudah said in the name of Rav:** They brought the food **from Ahab's slaughter-house.**

וַיְהִי מִקֵּץ יָמִים [3]The verse states (I Kings 17:7): **"And it came to pass after some days, that the wadi dried up, because there was no rain in the land." When** God **saw that there was** great **distress in the world** because of the extended drought, and that Elijah did not notice the suffering that he was causing by not allowing the rain to fall, He made Elijah return the key to the rain. [4]**For the verses state** (I Kings 17:8-9): **"And the word of the Lord came to him, saying, Arise, go to Tzarafat";** [5]**and** a later **verse states** (I Kings 17:17): **"And it came to pass after these things, that the son of the woman, the mistress of the house, fell sick."** [6]Elijah **prayed so that he would be given the key to the Resurrection of the Dead** to revive the boy. [7]**He was told** from Heaven: "The keys to most of God's treasures were given out to various agents, who were placed in charge of each of those treasures. However, **three keys were not** ordinarily **given out to an agent,** but were kept by God Himself: [8]The key **of a woman in childbirth,** the key **to rain, and** the key **to the Resurrection of the Dead.** You, Elijah, have already been given the key to rain. If you receive the key to the Resurrection of the Dead, [9]people **will say: Two** keys **are** now **in the hand of the disciple, and** only **one** key is left **in the hand of the master.** [10]**Bring** back the key to the rain, **and** then you may **take** the key to the Resurrection of the Dead," **as the verse states** (I Kings 18:1): **'Go, appear before Ahab; and I will give rain.'"**

דָּרַשׁ הַהוּא [11]**A certain Galilean expounded before Rav Ḥisda: What is that** incident involving **Elijah like?** [12]It is **like someone who locked his door and** then **lost the key.** Similarly, Elijah locked the gate to rain but then lost the key, that is to say, he was forced to surrender control over the rain.

לוֹ לֶחֶם וּבָשָׂר בַּבֹּקֶר וגו׳ ״.
[1]מֵהֵיכָא?
[2]אָמַר רַב יְהוּדָה אָמַר רַב: מִבֵּי טַבָּחֵי דְּאַחְאָב.
[3]״וַיְהִי מִקֵּץ יָמִים וַיִּיבַשׁ הַנָּחַל כִּי לֹא הָיָה גֶשֶׁם בָּאָרֶץ״. [4]כֵּיוָן דַּחֲזָא דְּאִיכָּא צַעֲרָא בְּעָלְמָא, כְּתִיב: ״וַיְהִי דְבַר ה׳ אֵלָיו לֵאמֹר, קוּם, לֵךְ צָרְפָתָה״; [5]וּכְתִיב: ״וַיְהִי אַחַר הַדְּבָרִים הָאֵלֶּה, חָלָה בֶּן הָאִשָּׁה בַּעֲלַת הַבָּיִת״, [6]בְּעָא רַחֲמֵי לְמֵיתַן לֵיהּ אַקְלִידָא דִּתְחִיַּית הַמֵּתִים. [7]אָמְרִי לֵיהּ: ״שָׁלֹשׁ מַפְתְּחוֹת לֹא נִמְסְרוּ לְשָׁלִיחַ: [8]שֶׁל חַיָּה, וְשֶׁל גְּשָׁמִים, וְשֶׁל תְּחִיַּית הַמֵּתִים. [9]יֹאמְרוּ: שְׁתַּיִם בְּיַד תַּלְמִיד וְאַחַת בְּיַד הָרַב! [10]אַיְיתֵי הָא, וְשָׁקֵיל הַאי, דִּכְתִיב: ׳לֵךְ, הֵרָאֵה אֶל אַחְאָב; וְאֶתְּנָה מָטָר׳ ״.
[11]דָּרַשׁ הַהוּא גְּלִילָאָה קַמֵּיהּ דְּרַב חִסְדָּא: מָשָׁל דְּאֵלִיָּהוּ לְמָה הַדָּבָר דּוֹמֶה? [12]לְגַבְרָא דְּטַרְקֵיהּ לְגַלֵּיהּ וְאַבְדֵיהּ לְמַפְתְּחֵיהּ.

LITERAL TRANSLATION

him bread and meat in the morning." [1]From where? [2]Rav Yehudah said in the name of Rav: From the slaughterhouse of Ahab.

[3]"And it came to pass after some days, that the wadi dried up, because there was no rain in the land." [4]When He saw that there was distress in the world, as it is written: "And the word of the Lord came to him, saying, Arise, go to Tzarafat"; [5]and it is written: "And it came to pass after these things, that the son of the woman, the mistress of the house, fell sick," [6]he asked for mercy, that He might give him the key to the Resurrection of the Dead. [7]They said to him: "Three keys were not given to an agent: [8]That of a woman in childbirth, that of rain, and that of the Resurrection of the Dead. [9]They will say: Two are in the hand of the disciple, and one is in the hand of the master. [10]Bring this one, and take that one, as it is written: 'Go, appear before Ahab; and I will give rain.'"

[11]A certain Galilean expounded before Rav Ḥisda: That of Elijah, what is it like? [12]Like someone who locked his door and lost the key.

RASHI

כיון דחזא — הקדוש ברוך הוא דאיכא צערא בעלמא, אמר ליה הקדוש ברוך הוא לאליהו: לך לצרפתה, לגלגל הדבר שיחזיר לו מפתח של מטר כדקא מפרש ואזיל. **שלש מפתחות לא נמסרו ביד שליח** — על אוצרו של הקדוש ברוך הוא יש מפתחות, ומסרם ליד שלוחים הממונים, אבל שלש מפתחות יש לו בידו, שלא מינה שליח עליהם, וקאמר הקדוש ברוך הוא לאליהו: אותם שלש מפתחות עכבתי בידי מבראשית ולא מניתי שליח עליהם אלא אותך שעשיתי ממונה על אחת מהם, ועתה תשאל מפתח שני — יאמרו: שנים ביד תלמיד ואחד ביד הרב. **דטרקיה לגליה** — שסתם שער שלו ואבדיה למפתחיה, כך עשה אליהו נעל לשערי מטר ולבסוף אבד המפתח של גשמים, שלא נפתח השער של מטר על ידו. **דכתב לך הראה אל אחאב ואתנה מטר** — ולא כתיב ותן מטר.

NOTES

did not realize how grave the situation had become, for surely the king had more abundant supplies of bread and meat than ordinary people.

לֹא נִמְסְרוּ לְשָׁלִיחַ **They were not given to an agent.** *Ramah* explains that all three keys were never given to the same agent. Others suggest that the three keys were never given to an agent permanently to do with them as he pleased (*Tosafot, Ta'anit*).

TRANSLATION AND COMMENTARY

דָּרַשׁ רַבִּי יוֹסֵי [1] **Rabbi Yose expounded in Sepphoris: The distinguished** Prophet **Elijah** [113B] **was hot tempered,** and therefore he cursed Ahab, saying (I Kings 17:1): "As the Lord God of Israel lives, before whom I stand, there shall not be dew or rain these years, but according to my word." [2] Elijah **was accustomed to come** every day and visit Rabbi Yose. [3] But now **he stayed away from him for three days, and did not come.** [4] **When** Elijah finally **came** after his three-day absence, Rabbi Yose **said to him: "Why did the Master not come** the last few days?" [5] Elijah **said to him:** "I did not come because **you called me hot tempered!"** [6] Rabbi Yose **said to him: "Surely** your response **proves that Master is hot tempered."**

וְלֹא יִדְבַּק בְּיָדְךָ [7] We learned in the Mishnah: "The verse states (Deuteronomy 13:18): **'And nothing of that which was devoted to destruction shall remain in your hand,** that the Lord may turn from His burning wrath, and show you mercy.' [8] **As long as the wicked are in the world,** God's **burning wrath is in the world.** When the wicked perish from the world, His burning wrath is removed from the world." [9] The Gemara asks: **Who are the wicked** discussed here? [10] **Rav Yosef said:** The Mishnah refers here to **thieves.**

תָּנוּ רַבָּנַן [11] **Our Rabbis taught** a related Baraita: **"When a wicked man comes into the world,** God's **wrath comes into the world** along with him, [12] **as the verse states** (Proverbs 18:3): **'When the wicked comes into the world, then contempt also comes, and with ignominy reproach.'** [13] **When a wicked man perishes from the world, good comes into the world,**

[1] דָּרַשׁ רַבִּי יוֹסֵי בְּצִיפּוֹרִי: אַבָּא אֵלִיָּהוּ [113B] קַפְּדָן. [2] הֲוָה רָגִיל לְמֵיתֵי גַּבֵּיהּ. [3] אִיכְסֵיהּ מִינֵּיהּ תְּלָתָא יוֹמֵי וְלָא אֲתָא. [4] כִּי אֲתָא אֲמַר לֵיהּ: "אַמַּאי לָא אֲתָא מָר"? [5] אֲמַר לֵיהּ: "קַפְּדָן קָרֵית לִי"! [6] אֲמַר לֵיהּ: "הָא דְּקַמָּן, דְּקָא קָפֵיד מָר".

[7] "'וְלֹא יִדְבַּק בְּיָדְךָ מְאוּמָה מִן הַחֵרֶם'. [8] כָּל זְמַן שֶׁרְשָׁעִים בָּעוֹלָם חֲרוֹן אַף בָּעוֹלָם וכו׳'". [9] מַאן רְשָׁעִים? [10] אֲמַר רַב יוֹסֵף: גַּנָּבֵי.

[11] תָּנוּ רַבָּנַן: "רָשָׁע בָּא לָעוֹלָם, חָרוֹן בָּא לָעוֹלָם, [12] שֶׁנֶּאֱמַר: 'בְּבוֹא רָשָׁע בָּא גַּם בּוּז וְעִם קָלוֹן חֶרְפָּה'. [13] רָשָׁע אָבַד מִן הָעוֹלָם, טוֹבָה בָּאָה לָעוֹלָם,

LITERAL TRANSLATION

[1] Rabbi Yose expounded in Sepphoris: Father Elijah [113B] was hot tempered. [2] He was accustomed to come to him. [3] He hid from him for three days, and did not come. [4] When he came, he said to him: "Why did the Master not come?" [5] He said to him: "You called me hot tempered!" [6] He said to him: "Surely this before us [proves] that the Master is hot tempered."

[7] "'And nothing of that which was devoted to destruction shall remain in your hand.' [8] All the time that the wicked are in the world, burning wrath is in the world, etc." [9] Who are the wicked? [10] Rav Yosef said: Thieves.

[11] Our Rabbis taught: "[When] a wicked man comes into the world, wrath comes into the world, [12] as it is stated: 'When the wicked comes, then contempt also comes, and with ignominy reproach.' [13] [When] a wicked man perishes from the world, good comes into the world,

RASHI

אבא אליהו — חביבי וגדולי. היה קפדן — שכעס על אחאב, ואמר חי ה׳ אם יהיה השנים האלה טל ומטר. איכסיה מיניה — שהיה רגיל למיתי לבי מדרשו כל יומא, ולא אתא בתלתא יומא. אמר ליה — רבי יוסי. הא דקמא דקא קפיד מר — הרי על דבר זה שאמרתי עליך קפיד, שלא באת אלי שלושה ימים מקפדנות שקצפת עלי.

NOTES

הָא דְּקַמָּן, דְּקָא קָפֵיד מָר **Surely this before us proves that the Master is hot tempered.** *Ramah* has the reading: מַאי דְּקַמָּא דְּקָא קָפֵיד מָר. If you are not ordinarily a hot-tempered person, then why are you angry and resentful now? It may be asked: Why didn't Rabbi Yose prove to Elijah that he was hot tempered from the oath he took relating to Ahab? *Torat Ḥayyim* explains that Elijah could have countered that he was acting zealously on behalf of the Torah, so Rabbi Yose had to show him that he was hot tempered by nature.

מַאן רְשָׁעִים? — גַּנָּבֵי **Who are the wicked? — thieves.** The Rishonim and Aharonim explain this enigmatic passage in various ways. *Ramah* explains that anyone who takes property which was placed under a ban is called a thief, as we find regarding Achan (Joshua 7). Alternatively, the Gemara is referring here to those who steal property belonging to an idolatrous city, and thus bring God's wrath upon the world (*Ri'af, Melekhet Shlomo*). Others suggest that we are dealing here with ordinary thieves, who violate the ban proclaimed by the courts upon all those who steal and do not return the stolen property (*Maharsha*). *Rabbi Tzvi Hayyot* explains that those who steal from the non-Jewish authorities are regarded as if they had violated the most severe prohibitions and taken property which was forbidden by a ban, for their actions endanger the entire Jewish community.

בָּא גַּם בּוּז וְעִם קָלוֹן חֶרְפָּה **Then comes also contempt, and with ignominy reproach.** It has been suggested that the word קָלוֹן alludes to fire (the root קלה means "burn"), and thus it is similar to the word חָרוֹן ("wrath"), which is derived from the root חרה, denoting "burning." Thus, it follows from the verse that when a wicked man comes into the world, wrath also comes into the world (*Rashash*).

TRANSLATION AND COMMENTARY

[1]**as the verse states** (Proverbs 11:10): **'But when the wicked perish, there is jubilation.'** The exact opposite may be said about the righteous: [2]**When a righteous man passes from the world, evil comes into the world,** [3]**as the verse states** (Isaiah 57:1): **'The righteous** man **perishes, and no man lays it to heart; and merciful men are taken, none understand that because of the evil the righteous is taken.'** The righteous man is spared evil by being removed from the world before the evil comes. Thus, when a righteous man dies, one should expect evil. [4]**When a righteous man comes into the world,** evil ceases and **good comes into the world** along with him, [5]**as the verse** regarding Noah **states** (Genesis 5:29): **'This one shall comfort us for our work and the toil of our hands.'"**

[1]שֶׁנֶּאֱמַר: 'וּבַאֲבֹד רְשָׁעִים רִנָּה'. [2]צַדִּיק נִפְטָר מִן הָעוֹלָם, רָעָה בָּאָה לָעוֹלָם, [3]שֶׁנֶּאֱמַר: 'הַצַּדִּיק אָבָד וְאֵין אִישׁ שָׂם עַל לֵב וְאַנְשֵׁי חֶסֶד נֶאֱסָפִים בְּאֵין מֵבִין כִּי מִפְּנֵי הָרָעָה נֶאֱסַף הַצַּדִּיק'. [4]צַדִּיק בָּא לָעוֹלָם, טוֹבָה בָּאָה לָעוֹלָם, [5]שֶׁנֶּאֱמַר: 'זֶה יְנַחֲמֵנוּ מִמַּעֲשֵׂנוּ וּמֵעִצְּבוֹן יָדֵינוּ'".

הדרן עלך כל ישראל יש להם חלק וסליקא לה מסכת סנהדרין

LITERAL TRANSLATION

[1]as it is stated: 'But when the wicked perish, there is jubilation.' [2]When a righteous man passes from the world, evil comes into the world, [3]as it is stated: 'The righteous perishes, and no man lays it to heart; and merciful men are taken, none understanding that because of the evil the righteous is taken.' [4]When a righteous man comes into the world, good comes to the world, [5]as it is stated: 'This one shall comfort us for our work and the toil of our hands.'"

RASHI

מפני הרעה — קודם שתבא הרעה הצדיק נאסף מכלל דכיון שמת — הרעה באה, אבל צדיק בא לעולם פסקה הרעה, שנאמר זה ינחמנו.

הדרן עלך כל ישראל וסליקא לה מסכת סנהדרין

NOTES

צַדִּיק בָּא לָעוֹלָם When a righteous man comes into the world. The words, "This one shall comfort us," were pronounced at the time of Noah's birth, explaining why he was given that name. Thus, it follows that as soon as a righteous person comes into the world, good and comfort come into the world as well.

Conclusion to Chapter Eleven

This chapter fulfills and concludes tractate *Sanhedrin*. It fills in the picture of Jewish existence with respect to inner matters of faith, adding to the first chapters that deal mainly with matters that are to be corrected in the social realm.

The chapter does not clarify the tenets of Jewish faith systematically. It deals mainly with certain fundamentals that require reinforcing and clarification against heretical beliefs, especially belief in the Resurrection of the Dead and the coming of the Messiah. Indeed, these matters complement the image of the Jewish commonwealth beyond the bounds of time and place and reality as it encompasses an ideal reality of Messianic days, and, beyond them, of the Resurrection of the Dead and life in the World to Come. These matters round out the picture to the highest level of human and national reality. In general, the chapter does not deal with descriptions of the Messianic age or of the End of Days itself. Rather, it emphasizes the factors that connect the Jewish religion and the national past to these heights. Finding the connection between verses from the Torah and the Resurrection of the Dead and also the descriptions of the birth pangs of the Messianic age and the end of redemption provide an additional connection between existing reality and future reality.

From this basic point one must also understand the extensive place accorded by this chapter to historical evaluation, both of individuals (the five kings and the four ordinary men who have no part in the World to Come) and also of entire periods (the generation of the flood, the generation of the division, the Israelites who left Egypt, the sect of Korah, and others). These evaluations offer an opportunity not only for understanding the past of the Jewish people but also for a fuller evaluation of highly influential individuals and whole communities, present in every generation. The figures described lived in the past, but in various forms they are eternal types, and they offer a warning for the future.

The laws governing an idolatrous city must be seen in the same light. True, the Sages said that an idolatrous city has never existed and will never exist, but the laws governing an idolatrous city constitute a constant warning on how far one must go to preserve the spiritual health of the Jewish commonwealth, and it shows the rigor with which one must act to prevent degeneration and descent to the low level of entire generations which lost both this world and the World to Come.

Therefore, this chapter complements the picture of the Jewish commonwealth, going beyond matters of individual law and order and becoming an expression of all of Judaism.

List of Sources

Aḥaronim, lit., "the last," meaning Rabbinic authorities from the time of the publication of Rabbi Yosef Caro's code of Halakhah, *Shulḥan Arukh* (1555).

Arba'ah Turim, code of Halakhah by Rabbi Ya'akov ben Asher, b. Germany, active in Spain (c. 1270-1343).

Arukh, Talmudic dictionary, by Rabbi Natan of Rome, 11th century.

Arukh LeNer, novellae on the Talmud by Rabbi Ben Tzion Ya'akov Etlinger, Germany (1798-1871).

Baḥ (Bayit Ḥadash), commentary on *Arba'ah Turim,* by Rabbi Yoel Sirkes, Poland (1561-1640).

Be'er HaGolah, commentary on unusual Aggadic passages in the Talmud by Rabbi Yehudah Loew ben Betzalel of Prague (1525-1609).

Bereshit Rabbah, Midrash on the Book of Genesis.

Bertinoro, Ovadyah, 15th century commentator on the Mishnah.

Bet Yosef, Halakhic commentary on *Arba'ah Turim* by Rabbi Yosef Caro (1488-1575), which is the basis of his authoritative Halakhic code, *Shulḥan Arukh.*

Birkei Yosef, novellae on *Shulḥan Arukh* by Rabbi Ḥayyim Yosef David Azulai, Israel and Italy (1724-1807).

Darkhei Moshe, commentary on *Tur* by Rabbi Moshe ben Isserles, Poland (1525-1572).

Ein Ya'akov, collection of Aggadot from the Babylonian Talmud by Rabbi Ya'akov ben Shlomo Ḥabib, Spain and Salonika (c. 1445-1515).

Even HaEzer, section of *Shulḥan Arukh* dealing with marriage, divorce, and related topics.

Geonim, heads of the academies of Sura and Pumbedita in Babylonia from the late 6th century to the mid-11th century.

Hagahot Maimoniyot, commentary on *Mishneh Torah,* by Rabbi Meir HaKohen, Germany, 14th century.

Hagahot Ram Arak, novellae on the Talmud by Rabbi Meir Arak, Poland, early 20th century.

Hagahot Ri Pik Berlin, Rabbi Yeshayahu Pik Berlin, Talmudic scholar, Breslau (1725-1799).

Halakhot Gedolot, a code of Halakhic decisions written in the Geonic period. This work has been ascribed to Sherira Gaon, Rav Hai Gaon, Rav Yehudah Gaon and Rabbi Shimon Kayyara.

Ḥamra Veḥaye, novellae on tractate *Sanhedrin,* by Rabbi Ḥayyim Benevisti, Turkey, 17th century.

Hayyim Shenayim Yeshalem, novellae on *Sanhedrin,* by Rabbi Shmuel Vital.

Ḥokhmat Manoaḥ, commentary on the Talmud by Rabbi Manoaḥ ben Shemaryah, Poland, 16th century.

Ḥoshen Mishpat, section of *Shulḥan Arukh* dealing with civil and criminal law.

Imrei Tzvi, novellae of the Talmud by Rabbi Tzvi Kohen, Vilna, 19th century.

Iyyun Ya'akov, commentary on *Ein Ya'akov,* by Rabbi Ya'akov bar Yosef Riesher, Prague, Poland, and France (d. 1733).

Keli Yakar, commentary on the Torah by Rabbi Shlomo Efrayim of Luntshitz, Poland (d. 1619)

Keneset HaGedolah (see *Shayarei Keneset HaGedolah*).

Kesef Mishneh, commentary on *Mishneh Torah,* by Rabbi Yosef Caro, author of *Shulḥan Arukh.*

Keset HaSofer, laws regarding the writing of Torah scrolls and mezuzahs, by Rabbi Shlomo Ganzfried, Hungary (19th century).

Ketzot HaḤoshen, novellae on *Shulḥan Arukh, Ḥoshen Mishpat,* by Rabbi Aryeh Leib Heller, Galicia (1754?-183).

Kos Yeshuot, novellae on the Talmud by Rabbi Shmuel HaKohen Shatin, Germany (d. 1719).

Leḥem Mishneh, commentary on the *Mishneh Torah,* by Rabbi Avraham di Boton, Salonica (1560-1609).

Lekaḥ Tov, Midrashim and commentary on the Torah by Rabbi Tuvyah the son of Rabbi Eliezer, Bulgaria (11th century).

Levush, abbreviation of *Levush Mordekhai,* Halakhic code by Rabbi Mordekhai Yaffe, Poland (1530-1612).

Magen Avraham, commentary on *Shulḥan Arukh, Oraḥ Hayyim,* by Rabbi Avraham HaLevi Gombiner, Poland (d. 1683).

Maggid Mishneh, commentary on *Mishneh Torah,* by Rabbi Vidal de Tolosa, Spain, 14th century.

Maharal, Rabbi Yehudah Loew ben Betzalel of Prague (1525-1631). Novellae on the Talmud.

Maharam Schiff, novellae on the Talmud by Rabbi Meir ben Ya'akov HaKohen Schiff (1605-1641), Frankfurt, Germany.

Maharik, Rabbi Yosef Kolon, France and Italy (c. 1420-1480). Responsa literature.

Maharsha, Rabbi Shmuel Eliezer ben Yehudah HaLevi Edels, Poland (1555-1631). Novellae on the Talmud.

Maharshal, Rabbi Shlomo ben Yeḥiel Luria, Poland (1510-1573). Novellae on the Talmud.

Maharshashakh, Rabbi Shmuel Shotten, Germany (17th century). Novellae on the Talmud.

Margoliyot HaYam, novellae on tractate *Sanhedrin* by Rabbi Reuben Margoliyot, Poland, 20th century.

Megaleh Amukot, Kabbalistic commentary on the Torah by Rabbi Natan Shapiro, Poland (1585-1633).

Meir Einei Soferim, laws regarding the writing of Torah scrolls, mezuzahs, and bills of divorce, by Rabbi David Krosik.

Meiri, commentary on the Talmud (called *Bet HaBeḥirah*), by Rabbi Menaḥem ben Shlomo, Provence (1249-1316).

Mekhilta, Halakhic Midrash on the Book of Exodus.

Melekhet Shlomo, commentary on the Mishnah by Rabbi Shlomo Adeni, Yemen and Israel (1567-1626).

Melo HaRo'im, commentary on the Talmud by Rabbi Ya'akov Tzvi Yolles, Poland (c. 1778-1825).

Menorat HaMa'or, Anthology of Midrashim, by Rabbi Yitzḥak Abohav (15th century).

Midrash Shir HaShirim Rabbah, Midrash on the Song of Songs.

Midrash Tanḥuma, see *Tanḥuma.*

Mishneh LeMelekh, commentary on *Mishneh Torah* by Rabbi Yehudah ben Shmuel Rosanes, Turkey (1657-1727).

Mishnah Berurah, commentary on *Shulḥan Arukh, Oraḥ Ḥayyim,* by Rabbi Yisrael Meir HaKohen, Poland (1837-1933).

Mitzpeh Eitan, glosses on the Talmud by Rabbi Avraham Maskileison, Byelorussia (1788-1848).

Nimmukei Yosef, commentary on *Hilkhot HaRif,* by Rabbi Yosef Ḥaviva, Spain, early 15th century.

Oraḥ Ḥayyim, section of *Shulḥan Arukh* dealing with daily religious observances, prayers, and the laws of the Sabbath and Festivals.

Pirkei DeRabbi Eliezer, Aggadic Midrash on the Torah.

Pitḥei Teshuvah, compilation of responsa literature on *Shulḥan Arukh* by Rabbi Avraham Tzvi Eisenstadt, Russia (1812-1868).

Ra'avad, Rabbi Avraham ben David, commentator and Halakhic authority. Wrote comments on *Mishneh Torah.* Provence (c. 1125-1198?).

Rabbenu Ḥananel (ben Ḥushiel), commentator on the Talmud, North Africa (990-1055).

Rabbenu Meshulam, French Tosafist, 12th century.

Rabbenu Sa'adya Gaon, scholar and author, Egypt and Sura, Babylonia (882-942).

Rabbenu Shimshon of Sens, Tosafist, France and Eretz Israel (late 12th-early 13th century).

Rabbenu Tam, commentator on the Talmud, Tosafist, France (1100-1171).

Rabbenu Yehonatan of Lunel, Yehonatan ben David HaKohen of Lunel, Provence, Talmudic scholar (c.1135-after 1210).

Rabbenu Yonah, see *Talmidei Rabbenu Yonah.*

Rabbenu Zeraḥyah HaLevi, author of *HaMa'or,* commentary on *Hilkhot HaRif.* Spain, 12th century.

Rabbi David Bonfil (Bonfied), commentary on tractate *Sanhedrin* by Rabbi David Bonfil (Bonfied), France, 11th century.

Rabbi David Pardo, novellae on the Talmud, Italy, 18th century.

Rabbi E. M. Horowitz, Rabbi Elazar Moshe Horowitz, novellae on the Talmud, Pinsk (19th century).

Rabbi Issac Ḥaver, novellae on the Talmud by Rabbi Issac Ḥaver, Poland, 18th century.

Rabbi Tzvi Ḥayyot (Chajes), Galician Rabbi, 19th century.

Rabbi Ya'akov Emden, Talmudist and Halakhic authority, Germany (1697-1776).

Rabbi Yehudah Almandri, author of commentary on *Rif,* tractate *Sanhedrin,* Syria, 13th century.

Rabbi Yeshayahu Pik Berlin, Talmudic scholar, Breslau (1725-1799).

Rabbi Yitzḥak Ibn Giyyat, Halakhist, Bible commentator and liturgical poet, Spain (1038-1089).

Rabbi Yosef of Jerusalem, French Tosafist of the twelfth and thirteenth centuries, France and Eretz Israel.

Rabbi Yoshiyah Pinto, Eretz Israel and Syria (1565-1648). Commentary on *Ein Ya'akov.*

Rabbi Zeraḥyah ben Yitzḥak HaLevi, Spain, 12th century. Author of *HaMa'or,* Halakhic commentary on *Hilkhot HaRif.*

Radak, Rabbi David Kimḥi, grammarian and Bible commentator, Narbonne, Provence (1160?-1235?).

Radbaz, Rabbi David ben Shlomo Avi Zimra, Spain, Egypt, Eretz Israel, and North Africa (1479-1574). Commentary on *Mishneh Torah.*

Raḥ, Rabbenu Ḥananel (ben Ḥushiel), commentator on the Talmud, North Africa (990-1055).

Ramah, novellae on the Talmud by Rabbi Meir ben Todros HaLevi Abulafiya, Spain (c. 1170-1244). See *Yad Ramah.*

Rambam, Rabbi Moshe ben Maimon, Rabbi and philosopher, known also as Maimonides. Author of *Mishneh Torah,* Spain and Egypt (1135-1204).

Ramban, Rabbi Moshe ben Naḥman, commentator on Bible and Talmud, known also as Naḥmanides, Spain and Eretz Israel (1194-1270).

Ran, Rabbi Nissim ben Reuven Gerondi, Spanish Talmudist (1310?-1375?).

Rash, Rabbi Shimshon ben Avraham, Tosafist, commentator on the Mishnah, Sens (late 12th- early 13th century).

Rashash, Rabbi Shmuel ben Yosef Shtrashun, Lithuanian Talmud scholar (1794-1872).

Rashba, Rabbi Shlomo ben Avraham Adret, Spanish Rabbi famous for his commentaries on the Talmud and his responsa (c. 1235-c.1314).

Rashbam, Rabbi Shmuel ben Meir, commentator on the Talmud, France (1085-1158).

Rashi, Rabbi Shlomo ben Yitzḥak, the paramount commentator on the Bible and the Talmud, France (1040-1105).

Rav Aha of Sabha, author of *She'iltot,* Babylonia, 8th century.

Rav Hai Gaon, Babylonian Rabbi, head of Pumbedita Yeshivah, 10th century.

Rav Natronai Gaon, of the Sura Yeshivah, 9th century.

Rav Sherira Gaon, of the Pumbedita Yeshivah, 10th century.

Rav Tzemaḥ Gaon, Tzemaḥ ben Ḥayyim, Gaon of Sura (889-895).

Rema, Rabbi Moshe ben Yisrael Isserles, Halakhic authority, Poland (1525-1572).

Responsa of Ḥatam Sofer, responsa literature by Rabbi Moshe Sofer (Schreiber), Pressburg (1763-1839).

Ri, Rabbi Yitzḥak ben Shmuel of Dampierre, Tosafist, France (died c. 1185).

Ri Almandri, Rabbi Yehudah Almandri. Author of commentary on *Rif,* tractate *Sanhedrin,* Syria, 13th century.

Ri Migash, Rabbi Yosef Ibn Migash, commentator on the Talmud, Spain (1077-1141).

Ri Yolles, Rabbi Ya'akov Tzvi Yolles, Talmudic scholar, Poland (c. 1778-1825).

Rif, Rabbi Yitzḥak Alfasi, Halakhist, author of *Hilkhot HaRif,* North Africa (1013-1103).

Rishonim, lit., "the first," meaning Rabbinic authorities active between the end of the Geonic period (mid-11th century) and the publication of *Shulḥan Arukh* (1555).

Ritva, novellae and commentary on the Talmud by Rabbi Yom Tov ben Avraham Ishbili, Spain (c. 1250-1330).

Riva, Rabbenu Yitzḥak ben Asher, Tosafist, novellae on tractate *Sanhedrin.*

Rosh, Rabbi Asher ben Yeḥiel, also known as Asheri, commentator and Halakhist, German and Spain (c. 1250-1327).

Sanhedrei Ketanah, novellae on tractate *Sanhedrin* by Rabbi Avraham Yehoshua Bornstein, Russia, 19th century.

Sefer Meir Einayim, see *Sma.*

Shakh (Siftei Kohen), commentary on the *Shulḥan Arukh* by Rabbi Shabbetai ben Meir HaKohen, Lithuania (1621-1662).

Shayarei Keneset HaGedolah, a Halakhic work by Rabbi Ḥayyim Benevisti, Turkey, 17th century.

Shelah (Shenei Luḥot HaBrit), an extensive work on Halakhah, ethics and Kabbalah by Rabbi Yeshayahu ben Avraham HaLevi Horowitz. Prague, Poland and Eretz Israel (c. 1565-1630).

She'eilot U'Teshuvot HaMibit, Responsa literature of Rabbi Moshe of Tirani, Sefad (1500-1580).

Shemot Rabbah, Midrash on the Book of Exodus.

Shulḥan Arukh, code of Halakhah by Rabbi Yosef Caro, b. Spain, active in Eretz Israel (1488-1575).

Sifrei, Halakhic Midrash on the Books of Numbers and Deuteronomy.

Sma, (Sefer Meirat Einaim), commentary on *Shulḥan Arukh, Ḥoshen Mishpat,* by Rabbi Yehoshua Falk Katz, Poland (c.1550-1614).

Smag, (Sefer Mitzvot Gedolot), an extensive work on the positive and negative commandments by Rabbi Moshe ben Ya'akov of Coucy, 13th century.

Talmid Rabbenu Peretz, commentary on the Talmud by the school of Rabbi Peretz of Corbiel, France (13th century)

Talmidei Rabbenu Yonah, commentary on *Hilkhot HaRif* by the school of Rabbi Yonah of Gerondi, Spain (1190-1263).

Tanḥuma, Midrash on the Five Books of Moses.

Tashbatz, Respona literature of Rabbi Shimon ben Tzemaḥ Duran, Spain and Algeria (1361-1444).

Taz, abbreviation for *Turei Zahav.* See *Turei Zahav.*

Tiferet Yisrael, commentary on the Mishnah, by Rabbi Yisrael Lipshitz, Germany (1782-1860).

Torat Ḥayyim, novellae on the Talmud by Rabbi Avraham Ḥayyim Shor, Galicia (d.1632).

Tosafot, collection of commentaries and novellae on the Talmud, expanding on Rashi's commentary, by the French-German Tosafists (12th and 13th centuries).

Tosafot Ḥadashim, commentary on the Mishnah by Rabbi Shimshon Bloch, Hamburg, Germany (d. 1737).

Tosefot Hokhmei Angli'a, collection of novellae on the Talmud by English Tosafists (13th century).

Tosefot Rabbenu Peretz, Tosefot of the school of Rabbi Peretz ben Eliyahu of Corbeil (d. 1295).

Tosefot Rosh, an edition based on *Tosefot Sens* by the *Rosh,* Rabbi Asher ben Yeḥiel, Germany and Spain (c. 1250-1327).

Tosefot Yom Tov, commentary on the Mishnah by Rabbi Yom Tov Lipman HaLevi Heller, Prague and Poland (1579-1654).

Tur, abbreviation of *Arba'ah Turim,* Halakhic code by Rabbi Ya'akov ben Asher, b. Germany, active in Spain (c. 1270-1343).

Tzofnat Pa'ane'aḥ, novellae and commentaries by Rabbi Yosef Rozin, Lithuania (1858-1936).

Yad Malakhi, a work on Talmudic and Halakhic methodology, by Rabbi Malakhi ben Ya'akov HaKohen, Italy (died c. 1785).

Yafeh Mar'eh, commentary on the Midrash by Rabbi Shmuel Yaffe, Turkey, 16th century.

Yalkut (see *Yalkut Shimoni*).

Yalkut Shimoni, Aggadic Midrash on the Bible.

Yefeh Enayim, cross-references and notes to the Jerusalem Talmud, by Rabbi Yeshayahu Pik Berlin, Breslau (1725-1799).

Yoreh De'ah, section of *Shulḥan Arukh* dealing mainly with dietary laws, interest, ritual purity, and mourning.

About the Type

This book was set in Leawood, a contemporary typeface designed by Leslie Usherwood. His staff completed the design upon Usherwood's death in 1984. It is a friendly, inviting face that goes particularly well with sans serif type.